"A THIRD REICH, AS I SEE IT"

"A THIRD REICH, AS I SEE IT"

Politics, Society, and Private Life in the Diaries of Nazi Germany, 1933–1939

Janosch Steuwer

translated by
Bernard Heise

INDIANA UNIVERSITY PRESS

This book is a publication of

Indiana University Press
Office of Scholarly Publishing
Herman B Wells Library 350
1320 East 10th Street
Bloomington, Indiana 47405 USA

iupress.org

© Wallstein Verlag, Göttingen 2017
© 2023 by Indiana University Press
Cover photo, titled "Das Tagebuch (The Diary)," is taken from the official publication of the 1934 Nuremberg rallies.

The translation of this work was funded by Geisteswissenschaften International—Translation Funding for Work in the Humanities and Social Sciences from Germany, a joint initiative of the Fritz Thyssen Foundation, the German Federal Foreign Office, the collecting society VG WORT, and the Borsenverein des Deutschen Buchhandels (German Publishers & Booksellers Association).

All rights reserved
No part of this book may be reproduced or utilized in any form or by any means, electronic or mechanical, including photocopying and recording, or by any information storage and retrieval system, without permission in writing from the publisher. The paper used in this publication meets the minimum requirements of the American National Standard for Information Sciences—Permanence of Paper for Printed Library Materials, ANSI Z39.48-1992.

Manufactured in the United States of America

First printing 2023

Library of Congress Cataloging-in-Publication Data

Names: Steuwer, Janosch, author. | Heise, Bernard, translator.
Title: "A Third Reich, as i see it" : politics, society, and private life in the diaries of Nazi Germany, 1933-1939 / Janosch Steuwer ; translated by Bernard Heise.
Other titles: Drittes Reich, wie ich es auffasse. English
Description: Bloomington, Indiana : Indiana University Press, 2023. | Originally published: "Ein Drittes Reich, wie ich es auffasse" : Politik, Gesellschaft und privates Leben in Tagebüchern 1933-1939. Göttingen : Wallstein Verlag, 2017. | Includes bibliographical references and index.
Identifiers: LCCN 2022042984 (print) | LCCN 2022042985 (ebook) | ISBN 9780253065322 (hardback) | ISBN 9780253065339 (paperback) | ISBN 9780253065346 (ebook)
Subjects: LCSH: Germany—Politics and government—1933-1945. | Germany—Social policy—20th century. | Germany—Social conditions—1933-1945. | German diaries. | National socialism—Public opinion. | Germans—Attitudes.
Classification: LCC DD256.5 .S76613 2023 (print) | LCC DD256.5 (ebook) | DDC 943.086—dc23/eng/20220920
LC record available at https://lccn.loc.gov/2022042984
LC ebook record available at https://lccn.loc.gov/2022042985

CONTENTS

Acknowledgments   vii

Abbreviations   ix

Introduction   1

Part One   33

1 The Social Dynamics of the "Seizure of Power"   39

2 The Search for a Personal Stance toward the Nazi Regime   72

3 Establishing a Personal Stance toward the Regime while under Social Observation   122

Part Two   167

4 The National Socialist Education Project   173

5 Political Self-Formation in the Nazi Education Project   224

Part Three   329

6 A New Political Culture in a New Political System   337

7 The Government and Its Volk   372

8 The Private and the Limits of the National Socialist Political System   463

Conclusion   517

Notes   535

Bibliography   601

Index of Persons   645

Index of Subjects   647

ACKNOWLEDGMENTS

This book would not have been possible without the suggestions, criticism, and encouragement I owe to numerous friends and colleagues.

Constantin Goschler was an indispensable pillar of support in the long process of preparing this book. During our discussions, I especially benefited from his ability to fortify my thoughts and ideas, which has given them a clarity that I would never have achieved on my own. I am grateful that he served as my primary adviser on the doctoral thesis that was the genesis for this book. As secondary adviser, Svenja Goltermann too supported the study right from the start with extraordinary commitment and interest, providing many important pointers and critical suggestions. From both I learned how to independently pursue my thoughts and repeatedly reexamine my own findings. Their encouragement and confidence in the project were very important to me, particularly in the initial stage when financing was difficult and the project's realization could not yet be foreseen. I thank the German Research Foundation for making it possible for me finally to write the study free of material concerns.

At Ruhr-University Bochum, I was pleased to write this study in an extraordinary climate of intellectual freedom and collegial argument, from which I benefited greatly. Here in our many discussions and with his insightful objections, Rüdiger Graf in particular opened up new avenues of thought for me and was an invaluable discussion partner when I was dealing with all the questions raised during the course of doctoral studies. Eva Balz, Henning Borggräfe, and Hanne Leßau read the entire manuscript, often understanding my arguments better than I did myself. They helped ensure that I did not lose the thread. I am grateful to Walter Sperling for the many conversations about our research and the pitfalls of academic writing; I learned a lot from him.

Bernd Weisbrod and Michael Wildt have benevolently supervised this study from the start. I am grateful to them for their many valuable suggestions, just as I am to the participants of the various colloquia and workshops with whom I was able to discuss my work.

My copyeditor Tanja Ruzicska played an important role in the completion of the book. Her precise interventions made the text a little shorter and above all better. I am grateful to Mark Roseman for bringing my book to the attention of Indiana University Press and to Dee Mortensen and Gary Dunham for including it in the publishing program. I have Bernard Heise to thank for the fact that the book can now appear in English. He dedicated himself to the translation not only with great patience but also with a precise eye for my argumentation and language. I am grateful to the Börsenverein des Deutschen Buchhandels for awarding the book the *Geisteswissenschaften International* translation funding prize, which made this English edition possible.

I am especially thankful to the diarists or their relatives who donated to the archives the documents investigated here—and especially to Gerd Büntzley, who gave me access to the diaries of his father specifically for this project. Throughout the entire study, I was very much aware that for them this meant an extraordinary disclosure of personal matters.

Finally, without Hanne Leßau I would not have been able to write this book. Her wisdom, precise observations, and persistent inquiries enriched the entire manuscript in all of its drafts. Only in our mutual reflections on our respective books did I manage to find my perspective on the history told by this one.

Cologne, August 2022

ABBREVIATIONS

AdK	Akademie der Künste
AdsD	Archiv der sozialen Demokratie
ADW	Allgemeiner Deutscher Waffenring (General German Weapons Ring, umbrella organization for fighting fraternities)
Bann	Hitler Youth unit
Block	Smallest unit of the NSDAP party organization, which includes a number of residential blocks
Blockleiter	Block warden, low-ranking NSDAP party official
BArch-MA	Bundesarchiv-Militärarchiv
BayHStA	Bayerisches Hauptstaatsarchiv
BdM	Bund Deutscher Mädel (League of German Girls, part of the Hitler Youth)
DAF	Deutsche Arbeitsfront (German Labor Front, organization of employees and employers, which replaced the independent trade unions)
DHM	Deutsches Historisches Museum
DNVP	Deutschnationale Volkspartei (German National People's Party, national conservative party, 1918–1933)
DTA	Deutsches Tagebucharchiv
DVP	Deutsche Volkspartei (German People's Party, national liberal party, 1918–1933)
FAD	Freiwilliger Arbeitsdienst (Voluntary Labor Service, replaced by the Reich Labor Service in 1935)
Fähnlein	Hitler Youth unit
FHI	Fritz-Hüser-Institut für Literatur und Kultur der Arbeitswelt
FZH	Forschungsstelle für Zeitgeschichte in Hamburg
Gleichschaltung	Synchronization of Germany's political, economic, and social institutions under National Socialism
HJ	Hitlerjugend (Hitler Youth)

IfZ	Institut für Zeitgeschichte
ISGV	Institut für sächsische Geschichte und Volkskunde
KdF	Kraft durch Freude (Strength through Joy, travel and leisure organization of the German Labor Front)
Kempowski-Bio	Kempowski-Biografienarchiv
KPD	Kommunistische Partei Deutschlands (Communist Party of Germany, 1919–1933)
Kreisleiter	District leader of the NSDAP party organization
Kreisleitung	District office of the NSDAP party organization
LA	Landesarchiv
LBI	Leo Baeck Institut
LgA	Lebensgeschichtliches Archiv
LHA	Landeshauptarchiv
LWL	Landschaftsverband Westfalen-Lippe
LZ	Luftschiff Zeppelin (Airship Zeppelin)
MLHA	Mecklenburgisches Landeshauptarchiv
NS	Nationalsozialismus (National Socialism)
NSDAP	Nationalsozialistische Deutsche Arbeiterpartei (National Socialist German Workers' Party)
NSKK	Nationalsozialistisches Kraftfahrkorps (National Socialist Motor Corps)
NSKOV	Nationalsozialistische Kriegsopferversorgung (National Socialist War Victim's Care)
Ortsgruppe	Local chapter of the NSDAP party organization
RAD	Reichsarbeitsdienst (Reich Labor Service)
SA	Sturmabteilung (Storm Detachment, paramilitary organization of the NSDAP)
SächsHStA	Sächsisches Hauptstaatsarchiv
SdP	Sudetendeutsche Partei (Sudeten German Party, Party of the German Minority in Czechoslovakia, 1933–1938)
SOPADE	Exile organization of the Social Democratic Party of Germany, 1933–1940
SPD	Sozialdemokratische Partei Deutschlands (Social Democratic Party of Germany, 1890–1933)

SS	Schutzstaffel (Protection Squadron, paramilitary organization of the NSDAP)
StA	Staatsarchiv
StdA	Stadtarchiv
USPD	Unabhängige Sozialdemokratische Partei Deutschlands (Independent Social Democratic Party of Germany, socialist party, 1917–1931)
ZfA	Zentrum für Antisemitismusforschung

"A THIRD REICH, AS I SEE IT"

INTRODUCTION

In late 1938, just a few months after immigrating to England, Raimund Pretzel began working on his autobiography. Born in 1907 in Berlin and also raised there, the lawyer had most recently worked in the capital as a journalist before leaving for the United Kingdom, officially for reporting purposes. From the outset, the journalistic assignment in England was just a way for him to circumvent the Nazi regime's strict emigration regulations and start a new life in exile. Pretzel followed his pregnant girlfriend, who was deemed Jewish in National Socialist Germany and had already emigrated a few weeks earlier. The couple married immediately after Pretzel's arrival and managed to rent a small house in Cambridge thanks to some seed money they had brought along. But even though their initial circumstances compared favorably to those of other émigrés, restarting a professional career proved difficult. Raimund Pretzel's hopes of finding a position as a trained lawyer at the university fell through, as did efforts to find work as a press photographer or journalist. He lacked the connections and had not yet achieved the popularity he would gain during and after the Second World War under the pseudonym he assumed in English exile: Sebastian Haffner.

The writing work that kept him busy during the first months of his emigration was part of an effort to earn his own living, for "émigrés with literary aims could, of course, consider as a potential source of income their knowledge about the Third Reich, which back then in late 1938 already had all of Europe on tenterhooks."[1] In spring 1939, Haffner finally managed win over a publisher for his book project, for which he received a small weekly advance.[2] The book emerged as the result of material necessities and, accordingly, closely targeted a British audience and their interest in political developments in Germany. Thus, for Haffner, taking an autobiographical approach was not necessarily an obvious choice. That he nonetheless did so can be read as evidence that he viewed his emigration as a major turning point in his life, since the autobiographical form also gave him the chance for self-reflection on a phase of life that was obviously over. But a different aspect is far more important: the subjective perspective of an autobiography allowed Haffner to foreground what he deemed a central feature of the

National Socialist dictatorship and wanted to make intelligible to his British audience. Thus he did not structure the book according to the chronology of his own life but instead shifted the focus to his personal experiences under National Socialism. He presented those experiences as the story of a duel: a confrontation between "an exceedingly powerful, formidable, and ruthless state" (the Nazi regime) "and an insignificant, unknown private individual" (Haffner himself). His memories of the period before 1933, on the other hand, only form the "prologue," recounted as the "journey" to the dueling ground: "We have arrived.... We enter the lists." In the unfinished manuscript, this section occupied less than half of the space taken up by the period from January to fall 1933.[3]

Haffner justified this imbalanced structure early with a very basic rationale: "Clearly, historical events have varying degrees of intensity. Some may almost fail to impinge on true reality, that is, on the central, most personal part of a person's life. Others can wreak such havoc there that nothing is left standing." He illustrated this idea by comparing two events: "'1890: Wilhelm II dismisses Bismarck.' Certainly a key event in German history, but scarcely an event at all in the biography of any German outside its small circle of protagonists. Life went on as before. No family was torn apart, no friendship broke up, no one fled their country. Not even a rendezvous was missed or an opera performance cancelled.... Now compare that with '1933: Hindenburg sends for Hitler.' An earthquake shatters 66 million lives."[4]

Looking back from 1939, Haffner saw Hitler's appointment as Reich chancellor on January 30, 1933, as a decisive break. He reported in detail how, in the wake of the seizure of power, his career plans were smashed, his long-term friendships fell apart, and his everyday life increasingly changed. But the break was indeed much deeper, for it fundamentally changed his and everyone's position with regard to historical events. "There is ... an important difference between what happened before 1933 and what came afterward," because earlier historical events had admittedly been observed and discussed but one's "innermost being remained untouched." Previous events "we watched ... unfold. They occupied us and excited us, sometimes they even killed one or another of us or ruined him; but they did not confront us with ultimate decisions of conscience.... We gained experience, acquired convictions, but remained basically the same people. However, no one who has, willingly or reluctantly, been caught up in the machine of the Third Reich can honestly say that of himself."[5] According to Haffner, "official, academic history" was blind to the "differences in intensity of historical occurrences" because it focused too closely on political events.⁶ It overlooked the "simple truth . . . [that] the decisive historical events take place among us, the anonymous masses. The most powerful dictators, ministers, and generals are powerless against the simultaneous mass decisions taken individually and almost unconsciously by the population at large. It is a characteristic of these decisions that they do not manifest themselves as mass movements or demonstrations. Mass assemblies are quite incapable of independent action. Decisions that influence the course of history arise out of the individual experiences of thousands or millions of individuals."⁷ Those who want to address this dimension of history—and thus the specific character of the 1933 National Socialist seizure of power—need to "read biographies, not those of statesmen but the all-too-rare ones of unknown individuals."⁸

Haffner left the manuscript unfinished in fall 1939, but the relevance of his deliberations even now, more than eighty years after being recorded, is shown by the work's ongoing popular success since its posthumous publication under the title *Defying Hitler*. Countless positive reviews and large print runs testify to the extraordinary and broad respect for a text that brought Haffner "more fame and recognition" after his death "than most of his many books published after the war."⁹ *Defying Hitler* became a key text in the public confrontation with National Socialism during the first decades of the twenty-first century.

The book's success was also facilitated by Haffner's focus on a dimension of the establishment of National Socialism about which historical scholarship had hardly anything to say.¹⁰ To be sure, academic history in the twenty-first century no longer by any means (still) conforms to Haffner's thumbnail portrait of a scholarly endeavor focused solely on political events at the state level. But with regard to the extensive historiographical literature about 1933 and the start of Nazi rule, this portrait is still quite accurate. Early contemporary history in the 1960s and 1970s had focused on the National Socialist seizure of power as a central topic through which the discipline established itself as a "science for democracy."¹¹ "Understanding the failure of democracy in Germany and thereby contributing to democracy's current preservation" had become a central concern of the new discipline, which firmly restricted itself to the political history of the seizure of power, particularly in the face of the memories of contemporaries who were still alive.¹² As a result of this constellation, the transition from the Weimar Republic to the National Socialist dictatorship became one of the undoubtedly most researched yet also "most strongly canonized segment[s] of the history of the Third Reich," whose interpretation paid no attention to the experiences of Germans.[13] Nor did anything change in this regard when scholars began focusing on the history of everyday life, so popular in the 1980s. Countless studies reconstructed the processes of the assumption and consolidation of National Socialist power in cities and municipalities throughout Germany, but they did not pay much attention to the experiences and perceptions of contemporaries.[14] As late as the seventy-fifth anniversary of the seizure of power, Andreas Wirsching noted that "even though it might seem as if we know . . . almost everything about the year 1933," there were still major gaps of knowledge "with regard to the social history of the year 1933, the experiential history of those living at the time—and, namely, those living at the time who belonged to neither the political players nor prominent victims. And this means that at issue here is nothing other than the experiential history of the vast majority of the German people."[15]

This is precisely what Haffner repeatedly tried to talk about in his autobiography. He stressed again and again that his story was "the private story of just one, not particularly important or interesting, young person in the Germany of 1933" fighting his "private duel with the Third Reich," much like the "thousands, maybe hundreds of thousands of such duels . . . [that] have been fought in Germany during the last six years."[16] His case was "typical" and for this very reason could be used to "easily judge the chances for mankind in Germany today."[17] Naturally, we are reading a narrative understatement here; Haffner was anything but an average case, both with respect to his social origins and with regard to his relationship to National Socialism. The fact that historians have nonetheless repeatedly referred to his text along those lines and invoked episodes from his autobiography in place of historical knowledge about contemporary reactions to the political developments serves as evidence for the insufficient state of research in this regard.[18] While no doubt an impressive work of German literature in exile, *Defying Hitler* is by no means a documentary account about the months of 1933. For purposes of historical scholarship, it does less to provide answers than to raise questions about the experiential and social history of the establishment of National Socialism. Taking Haffner's autobiography seriously means inquiring into the specific "intensity" of the start of the Nazi dictatorship. It calls for us to pursue the significance of the Nazi seizure of power for contemporaries and to observe their reactions and perceptions as part of a history of the establishment of National Socialism by turning our attention to the "unknown private individual." That is the aim of this book.

The Individual Challenge of National Socialism

Sebastian Haffner's insistence in his autobiography that "the Nazi revolution had abolished the old distinction between politics and private life," which is why "it was quite impossible to treat it merely as a 'political event,'"[19] was directly related to the fact that, even during the Weimar Republic, the National Socialist leadership strove to do much more than just restructure the political system. Because of its specific understanding of politics, the National Socialist German Workers' Party (NSDAP) differed radically from the democratic parties of the Weimar Republic. It was not interested in realizing specific political projects but rather directed its political activities according to the idea of a fundamentally different future that it meant to bring about. What this future should look like remained vague, but even as blurred vision it guided the "pragmatic revolutionism" that governed National Socialist policy before 1933.[20] "Pragmatic revolutionism" combined the striving for an imprecisely characterized "fundamental revolutionary upheaval with a concrete strategy for activity."[21] Hence, daily political work, "comradely association" within Nazi organizations, and the violent marches and demonstrations were always already understood as anticipating the future they were trying to create. This wholly different future was to be realized not only by the attainment of political power but also through the daily behavior of National Socialists.

For the Nazi leadership, therefore, the interventions in the political system in spring 1933 were not simply linked to the aspiration of securing its own new position of power. Rather, right from the outset, the regime clearly indicated its ambition to radically reshape German society. After his appointment on January 30, 1933, the new Reich chancellor, Adolf Hitler, declined to present a government program, coming out two days later via radio with nothing but a "Call of the Reich government to the German Volk." In the weeks that followed, he also refused to respond to related questions from the other parties: "A program with a few very concrete points would presumably have been possible for a government at any time. But after your management, after your activities, after your degradations, the German Volk must be rebuilt from the ground up, just as you have destroyed it down to the ground! That is our program!"[22] Instead of specific policy measures, in their speeches of February 1933 Hitler and his leading Nazi politicians repeatedly presented the narrative of a country run into the ground by the parties of the Weimar Republic, which they countered with the promise of comprehensive change. National Socialism was primarily a societal project. This was reflected from the beginning in the language of the statements of the new regime and its representatives, which turned on Germany's "political and economic resurrection," on "national renewal" and "national uprising," and on the "reestablishment of our Volk" and the "creation of the Volksgemeinschaft."[23]

The aspiration for fundamental and comprehensive transformation was characteristically embodied above all in the concept of the "Volksgemeinschaft" (people's community), even though one should not overlook that it could be and was formulated with other concepts as well.[24] Volksgemeinschaft, however, played a prominent role, and the intensive use of the term long after 1933 also preserved the aspiration for change even beyond the Nazi dictatorship's initial phase. When one looks at National Socialism as a societal project, the question about its establishment seems broader than the way it is understood in scholarship focused narrowly on the political seizure of power. After Hitler's appointment as Reich chancellor at the end of January 1933, the democratic institutions of the Weimar Republic were dismantled at an incredible pace, and by summer 1933 they were largely eliminated, with the final vestiges disappearing one year later. But this certainly did not mean that the National Socialist social project had now been realized—and this is precisely what set the Nazi dictatorship apart from the preceding Weimar democracy: for its entire existence, the dictatorship was geared not to preserving but to transforming the social order.[25]

The concept of the Volksgemeinschaft so aptly captured the Nazi regime's overarching aspiration for fundamental change because it contained a specific temporal structure.[26] It drew its significance primarily from the twofold experience of the beginning and end of the First World War, which inscribed the concept in equal measure with the retrospectively formed idea of a unified nation in August 1914 and the experience of social fragmentation resulting from the German Revolution of 1918. Ever since then, *Volksgemeinschaft* was not a category that grasped the present state of society but rather a concept aimed at a society of the future. It described the fiction of a unified society that had once been reached at the start of the war but then was lost again; and now, as an objective, it was supposed to guide political action.[27] Already during the Weimar Republic, there was anything but consensus on what this future society should look like, and nothing about this changed after the National Socialist movement seized power.[28] The concept's various modes of use were held together by its function: it was always used to discuss or attempt to advance social and political change. *Volksgemeinschaft* always served to measure the present against a utopian future and to determine what had already been accomplished and what still needed to be achieved. Thus, even after political power had been secured, establishing National Socialism remained one of the core concerns of the Nazi regime and provided the rationale for the social dynamics of the following years.

Combined with the programmatic aspiration for change was an understanding of social transformation that relied on changes from below, even after extensive authority had been achieved for the assertion of state power. The term *Volksgemeinschaft* aimed less at structural changes than at the broad social integration and massive personal involvement of Germans in the processes of transformation.[29] It was not by chance that the first time Hitler spoke out publicly as Reich chancellor was with the previously mentioned "call," which he used to announce new elections for the purpose of enlisting the German people: "In light of the inability of the current Reichstag... we assign to the German Volk itself that task which we support."[30] The "resurrection of our Volk," Hitler declared repeatedly in February 1933, will not come about "on its own." The government wants "to work, but the Volk must help. It should never believe that liberty, happiness, and life are suddenly gifted by heaven. Everything is rooted only in one's own will, in one's own work."[31] Since the aspiration for change by no means involved only the political system, the demand that individuals actively do their part referred to much more than their voting behavior in the Reichstag election slated for early March 1933. The societal project of the Nazi regime reached far beyond the previous limits of the political sphere and claimed that many modes of behavior and attitudes previously held to be apolitical were now politically relevant. As a result, precisely in areas previously thought to be within the private realm, Germans were called on to behave in accordance with the new circumstances. This was the experience underlying Haffner's comment that the "division between politics and private life" had basically been abolished and that the start of National Socialist rule formed a fundamental challenge to the modes of thought and behavior of people living in Germany.[32]

Germans' reactions to the challenge of National Socialism, the changes in their ideas about who they were, the time in which they lived, and their relationship to these times constitute one of the subjects of this book. At the same time, the book shows the extent to which and how Germans' various forms of perception and reaction shaped the Nazi regime and its policymaking options. Since the regime leadership intended to implement its sociopolitical ideas by harnessing broad levels of society, the realization of key aspects of Nazi policy was and remained dependent on the massive change of individual conduct. The book looks at this individual challenge of National Socialism in this twofold sense: the challenge constituted by the Nazi regime to the thoughts and actions of individual Germans, and the challenge posed by their mass reactions to the policymaking of the regime.

The political demands on the people were extremely complex. Sebastian Haffner only managed to grasp the Nazi state's all-encompassing "assault" on everyday life with a list: the state demanded from the "insignificant, unknown private individual," as Haffner stylized himself, that he "give up his friends, abandon his lovers, renounce his beliefs and assume new, prescribed ones. He must use a new form of greeting, eat and drink in ways he does not fancy, employ his leisure in occupations he abhors, make himself available for activities he despises, and deny his past and individuality."[33] While seemingly unsystematic, the list nonetheless mirrors the three central dimensions of the individual challenge of National Socialism arising from the aspiration for fundamental transformation contained in the concept of the Volksgemeinschaft: the focus was equally on the transformation of (1) society, (2) its individual members, and (3) the political system that joined the individual and the collective.

New Rules of Social Belonging

First, as we have seen, *Volksgemeinschaft* was shorthand for the social order already sought by the National Socialist movement during the Weimar Republic, yet both before and after 1933 it concealed a "broad, indeed extremely disparate spectrum of social objectives."[34] It was generally used to describe the hope for the liberation of society from social tensions and unrest, although this goal was to be achieved not by striving for social equality but by "driving conflicts based on social inequality out of the political sphere."[35]

The vision of harmonious coexistence was founded on imagining the Volksgemeinschaft as a society liberated from internal "enemies." Instead of linking to state efforts to eliminate social inequality, the term *Volksgemeinschaft* as a societal-political category was associated above all with practices of exclusion and inclusion aimed at changing the rules of social belonging. The exclusion of supposed "enemies" and "Volksfremde" (elements alien to the ethnic nation) formed the core of the Nazi social project, which was directed primarily against population groups seen as "racially inferior"—first and foremost German Jews—and identified "opponents" by means of their ideological differences with National Socialism.

Group designations such as *Volksgenossen* (Volk comrades) and *Gemeinschaftsfremde* (persons alien to the community) were used to assert new social differences according to which Germans were henceforth to align their routine behavior, above all by breaking off contact with parts of the population defined as *gemeinschaftsfremd*. In this sense, Haffner spoke of the demand to give up his friends and abandon his lovers. But the reorganization of social belonging did not refer only to dissociation from supposed "opponents" and "enemies." Rather, an individual's belonging basically came to depend on his personal commitment to the new society and new regime. Together, the demands for distancing and commitment constituted specific challenges, especially to people's everyday social relationships, in which one's own position as well as those of others were now supposed to depend on the person's respective proximity to the Nazi regime. How contemporaries defined their own relationship to the new regime and appropriated the new ideologically justified delineations as their own, thereby changing their own position and the positions of others in the social fabric of everyday life, is investigated in the first part of this book.

New Forms of Lifestyle and Self-Contemplation

Second, directed toward the future and transformation, the concept of the Volksgemeinschaft was also used to discuss changes to individual lifestyles and self-perception. The rise of the term *Volksgemeinschaft* in the early twentieth century occurred in close connection with the emergence of various social currents and reform movements that strove for the "improvement" and "education of man." Accordingly, during the Weimar Republic, within the National Socialist movement the "awareness of the future and temporal transition" was "reflected not only in the ideas of a 'new time' and 'new world,' but rather also of a 'new man' or 'new race.'"[36] After 1933, along with the plans for new rules of social belonging, these ideas too were supposed to be realized.

The intention was to create the "National Socialist man," who, according to aspirations, was distinguished not only by his altered lifestyles but also by his altered self-understanding. Both were meant to be achieved by disseminating new models for individual lifestyles and self-observation that called on individuals to adjust their understanding of themselves and their everyday lives. As with the Volksgemeinschaft as a vision of societal-political order, associated with these utopian ideas in the 1930s were specific practices intended to help educate Germans to new self-images and lifestyles. The process addressed the entire spectrum of an individual's lifestyle, such that after 1933 individuals found themselves confronted, for example, by requirements to live "socially," comprehend their bodies with new racial categories, and understand themselves as the result of their own ancestral line. The challenge of National Socialism therefore called the individual's personal lifestyle and self-conceptions into question, which gave rise to Haffner's comment about the individual having to deny "his past and his individuality." The ways in which contemporaries began to question existing lifestyles and self-perceptions and to transform them with new political categories is investigated in the second section of the book.

New Forms of Political Behavior and Evaluation

Third, the use of the concept of the Volksgemeinschaft in the 1930s raised questions about the legitimation of political rule. This was a legacy of the First World War. The "invention of the Volksgemeinschaft" between 1914 and 1918 was closely linked to intellectual debates about the future of Germany's political order, in which the "August experience"—that is, the supposed jubilation in Germany at the outbreak of World War I—"stylized as an experience shared by the entire Volk," was elevated "to the basis for an organizational idea," one that replaced monarchical legitimation of political rule after the war.[37]

At the same time, the entire society's involvement in the "total war" led to the enduring politicization of the masses, who also increasingly viewed themselves "as the subject and not just the object of German politics."[38] The First World War fundamentally changed the relationship between society and the political system and awakened wide-ranging expectations with regard to political participation; the concept of the Volksgemeinschaft picked up these expectations and continuously formulated them, even during the National Socialist dictatorship.[39] The Nazi regime often reaffirmed the intention of creating greater proximity between the Volkswille (will of people) and politics than had been managed by the Weimar Republic. Accordingly, already during the first months of its rule, the regime not only tried to change the political decision-making mechanisms but also sought to establish new structures and practices intended to ensure society's involvement with the political system.

Haffner alluded to the pressure exercised by the Nazi regime with these new forms of political involvement and the enormous amount of time the regime demanded from individuals when he pointed out that the individual was now supposed to "employ his leisure time in occupations he abhors." In this case, the individual challenge of National Socialism appeared in the questions of how to act appropriately within the new political system and how to appropriately evaluate the political activity of state leadership. The third section of the book investigates how contemporaries reacted to this problem and were forced to develop new forms of political behavior and evaluation, which led to lasting effects not only on the relationship between the society and the political system but also on private life.

The multilayered individual challenges of National Socialism essentially manifested themselves in three dimensions: affiliations and dissociations in everyday social relationships; one's private lifestyle and self-perception; and one's own political activities and judgments. These are post hoc analytical distinctions, which were not made by the Nazi regime, for whom the individual's commitment and new personal lifestyle were the expression of a transformed "personality" that simultaneously ensured the complete alignment between the state leadership and citizens. Germans were often confronted with all three dimensions of the individual challenge of National Socialism at the same time. Even so, the book examines them separately because it focuses less on the detailed description of the reactions of individual persons than on systematic findings on how contemporaries reacted to the individual challenge of National Socialism after 1933 and how their reactions influenced the Nazi regime and its policymaking.[40] In this respect, the three sections of the book can be read independently. At the same time, they are organized according to an internal logic, each concentrating on a different time period and thereby as a whole following the social changes over the 1930s. In the conclusion, the findings from the different parts of the book are brought together to consider the question of how German society and the Germans had changed by the beginning of the Second World War.

Diaries and How They Should Be Read

Entirely in keeping with Sebastian Haffner, in my book I look at the "biographies of unknown private individuals" and base my analysis on an assessment of contemporary personal testimonies, thus on texts written by and on the initiative of contemporaries themselves. The focus here is on diaries produced in Germany between 1930 and 1939.

Such sources are very popular with the public and within the academic field of history. The published diaries of Victor Klemperer and Anne Frank, for example, encounter great public interest, and many recent studies on Nazi history cite diary entries on aspects of widely diverse themes.[41] Yet surprisingly, this pretty much sums up the way these historical sources are currently used. On the one hand, a few individual diaries, usually by authors deemed both ordinary and especially astute, are left to more or less speak for themselves. On the other hand, historians like to use diaries in their studies to illustrate and adorn their arguments, which, however, are based on other sources.[42] Both approaches are valid, but they exploit the epistemic value of diaries in a rudimentary way, for these texts can also be used to acquire systematic insights into National Socialist rule that cannot be gained from other sources.

If diaries are used not as supplementary but rather as main sources, it is important to comprehend them as a form of contemporary personal testimony and thereby clearly distinguish them from retrospective personal testimonies like autobiographies, memoirs, and oral history interviews. This distinction stands to reason but is by no means generally honored within the field of historical scholarship.[43] Studies in experiential history still do not clearly differentiate between contemporary diaries and letters, on the one hand, and memoirs written at a later date, on the other.[44] But retrospections on earlier events are always decisively influenced by what happened after these events occurred. When the 1930s were remembered after the war, for example, this process always happened in the shadow of the violence and mass criminality precipitated by developments that began in 1933. However, this obvious fact is not the most important reason for distinguishing between retrospective and contemporary personal testimonies. Mainly, texts written under Nazi rule do not concur with today's reader expectations about which aspects of National Socialism are worth remembering and recounting. In contrast to reports written by contemporary witnesses after 1945, who together with historians as members of the same present tend to share the same opinions about which questions should be directed toward the National Socialist past, diaries are basically not written to serve our (later) interest in this period. Even though we evaluate them for the purpose of our questions, they naturally set their own substantive themes. This difference is precisely what provides for decisive insights into how people handled the individual challenge of National Socialism.

There is an entire range of reasons why researchers of the Nazi period have thus far used diaries chiefly as supplementary sources to illustrate general arguments. The most important is perhaps the frequent assumption that general findings cannot be drawn from these subjective sources. "Diaries, letters, or autobiographies that allow for statements about the former attitudes of citizens toward the Nazi regime are few, often stored in a scattered fashion (and privately), and moreover limited to a small—nonrepresentative—group of the population."[45] To be sure, descriptions from individual diaries cannot be meaningfully extrapolated so as to apply to the society. They constitute the commentary of specific persons who are not subsumed by the social characteristics of the author's biography. Nonetheless, one can also gain fundamental and generally applicable findings from diaries. But this requires that they be dealt with in a methodologically reflective manner that takes seriously the specifics of the genre.

To begin with, this means recognizing that diaries are not what they are still usually read as being—namely, unfiltered reports about the writers and their everyday lives. The textual character of diaries has been intensely investigated by Philippe Lejeune, known particularly for his reflections on autobiographies. As opposed to what has long been common practice in literary scholarship, however, he does not grasp the diary as a subgenre of the autobiography but rather as an independent textual form that follows its own textual logic.[46] According to Lejeune, diaries differ fundamentally from other texts because their authors do not fully know the material and do not have it completely under autonomous command. Diarists occupy a different authorial position than writers of autobiographies. The latter can adapt the narrated past to the requirements set by the present and by the literary genre and thereby form a coherent (life) history. "The same cannot be said of the future. Diarists never have control over what comes next in their texts. They write with no way of knowing what will happen next in the plot, much less how it will end. The past is wonderfully malleable. . . . The future is pitiless and unforeseeable."[47] This special starting point of writing has far-reaching textual ramifications. Diaries do not contain a text conceptualized as a completed whole; rather, they are fragmental and characterized mainly by repetitions and variations. They are not held together by an overarching narrative but rather follow their subject over the course of time and explicitly mark the independence of the various entries by way of the dating process.

As a textual form, diaries make of their authors only two formal demands: that they date their notations and that they write about themselves—their own everyday life and own feelings and thoughts.[48] Consequently, the diary possesses a large spectrum of diverse characteristics. Therefore, according to Lejeune, it can be only poorly understood using the traditional tools of textual analysis. Diaries should not be viewed as literary products but must be read as the expression of a process, a specific social practice.[49] Diaries are "records of a life process rather than finished narratives about a life, and as such they are only part of the practice of narrating and understanding what a life means."[50] Therefore, diary writing is largely a performative practice that only through execution creates what it talks about. Diarists do not record existing thoughts and emotions but rather first produce them in a writing process whose unique characteristic lies precisely in the arrangement of concrete experiences—retrospectively and prospectively—within one's own life context.

In this sense, Lejeune turns against the widespread talk of the diary as a "mirror" and points out that, on the contrary, the diary constitutes a "filter" through which the author perceives his or her own world—and this always only selectively within context of the subject thematized in the diary. Writing a diary involves "separating the real, digesting it, rejecting most of it, and making sense of the rest." While this everyday work of interpretation does not occur only in diaries, the diary "takes it to the extreme by laying down the results and building these results into a series."[51] Diaries must therefore be defined and analyzed as a "series of dated traces" (série de traces datées) of this interpretive process, which is used for self-reflection about oneself and one's relationship with the environment over the course of time.[52]

Thus, diaries are not a direct translation of their author's lives into text, even though academic historians often still read them that way:[53] they do not "mirror . . . the strong mood fluctuations of their authors" in an unadulterated way; they do not provide an undistorted "view of their authors' inner lives" and "emotional ambivalences"[54]; they also by no means allow for an "insight into the direct experience of historical events."[55] Diaries assist their authors to first literally make the thoughts that are written down in them. Even as totalities, they do not reveal a portrait of the author but rather a more or less continually administered process of self-understanding.

Precisely because they do not reflect "the feelings and forms of conduct of the diarist in a comprehensive manner," they do not possess any "cross-sectional character" but rather are extremely selective and fragmented.[56] Diaries do not reveal the personalities of their authors, not their feelings, thoughts, and behaviors; instead, they document the search performed in this medium for interpretations found through writing. Diary writing constitutes a central technique in the modern era for processing experience, and diaries can be used to reconstruct not so much the real experiences of individual persons but rather the process of experience itself.

These deliberations illustrate the immense value of diaries as sources for dealing with the questions posed in this book—namely, how contemporaries reacted to the start of National Socialist rule and how their reactions shaped the Nazi regime's options for policymaking. And indeed, in the 1930s many contemporaries used their diaries to reflect on the various changes both in their everyday lives and in politics. One such person was Hans Maschmann, a Volksschule teacher born in 1887. In spring 1933, after a prolonged hiatus, Maschmann began keeping a diary again, purposely using his regular and detailed entries to deal with and establish his relationship to the new political developments. Until well into the war, his diary infrequently addressed any subject apart from politics, which Maschmann grappled with intensely. We will later examine his notations in detail, but also worth mentioning at this point are the surviving love letters that the married man wrote to a female acquaintance with whom he began an affair that same year. Politics have no part in these letters, whose author seems buoyant, sensitive, and unaffected by political occurrences, whereas the diarist seems obsessed with and depressed by the political developments. The persons emerging from the diary and the love letters are quite different, and neither is identical with the real person of the writer. At most, each shows a specific segment of this person.[57] In this sense, Hans Maschmann's diary hardly allows for any conclusions about the degree to which the political changes after 1933 also influenced his emotions and thoughts beyond the writing of his diary. Yet his diary is an ideal source to indicate that after 1933 he was intensely preoccupied with the changes that accompanied the establishment of National Socialism.

Naturally, Germans did not react to the challenge of National Socialism only through the medium of the diary, and the everyday behaviors of Germans are especially important for questions about the extent to which individual forms of reaction in turn influenced the Nazi regime's policymaking options. This change, too, can be observed using diaries. Even if diarists do not simply record existing thoughts and feelings but rather first generate them while writing, they refer to actual experiences, which they reflect on and document by using the diary. Diary writing is therefore not merely performative but also at the same time descriptive, for it is literally an autobiographical activity: diary authors write about their lives. This too constitutes a central and unique aspect of diaries, which Philippe Lejeune highlights by not assigning diaries to the established category of nonfiction but instead suggesting for them a new concept based on the author's specific position as a writer. The fact that diarists do not know what will happen in the future and what subjects they will write about limits the options for fiction. For deliberate inventions would not only need to be plausibly integrated into the description of present life but in later entries also repeatedly harmonized with life's further developments—a task that would be "impossible, at least very difficult." Autobiographies are in many respects shaped by fictional elements, for indeed the past "does not contradict you." The future, on the other hand, does not permit flouncing around at whim: the "diary is 'anti-fictional.'"[58] This does not mean that one can simply view statements contained in diaries as true. They too must be reviewed with respect to their plausibility, enhancements, stylization, and omissions. Rather, with the concept of anti-fiction, Lejeune highlights the high degree to which this textual genre relates to the reality that is addressed within but that is external to the text. Diaries therefore also enable the (however partial) observation of everyday behavior, and thus they can be used to investigate not only the changes to interpretations of the world and of selves but also the transformation of specific modes of behavior after the start of National Socialist rule.

These deliberations about the textual character of the diary illustrate why this source can also be used to gain valid findings at the general level. To be sure, individual diaries show only those thoughts recorded by specific persons, and these remain unique even in comparison with other diaries.[59] Yet although the respective written records are unique, the authors in their deliberations nonetheless had to draw on shared ideas, terms, and assumptions. The way in which persons lent meaning to experiences; the categories, concepts, and models of thought that they applied in the process; and what they judged important and unimportant are temporally specific, and in this respect they can be historicized. Insofar as diaries do not document fully formed assessments but the assessment process, they allow us to identify the temporally specific foundations of the individual reactions to the start of the Nazi dictatorship and to formulate generalizable answers to the questions posed here. The diaries used here are therefore also queried comparatively with respect to commonalities regarding logic, concepts, and unquestioned fundamental assumptions. Admittedly, this process does not provide any information as to the typicality or frequency of certain reactions found in individual diaries to the individual challenge of National Socialism. But it enables an understanding of the fundamental ways in which Germans reacted to the start of National Socialist rule. And it has the advantage of taking the specificity of individual diaries seriously and can investigate the concrete reactions to the individual challenge of National Socialism case by case without having to forgo generalizable results. Because we are searching for commonalities in how these reactions functioned, individual diaries do not need to take a back seat to general statements. Instead, through their singularity they can illustrate the reactions that in individual cases led from contemporary modes of reaction.

Sources

This book is based on the assessment of approximately 140 diaries—largely unpublished—from the period 1930 to 1939. The supposition voiced frequently even in more recent studies—namely, that contemporary personal testimonies are "rare for the prewar years"—is not one I can confirm.[60] Given the more than sixty million Germans confronted by the individual challenge of National Socialism, 140 diaries may seem like a small number. But as previously emphasized, the point here is not about the statistically representative nature of concrete experiences; rather, it is to search widely diverse diaries for the foundational conditions of individual experience.[61] For this purpose, the 140 diaries make it possible to take into consideration a large number of contemporary perspectives, which, however, assumes a heterogeneous sample of sources: the more heterogeneous it is, the greater the number of different perspectives and positions that can be considered and the more one can ensure that the modes of reaction found in the comparison do not apply only to a certain group of persons. Those elements that were not specific to individual persons but rather set the overall parameters according to which contemporaries dealt with the individual challenge of National Socialism are revealed at precisely those points where one can identify commonalities among different and even contradictory reactions.[62]

But how heterogeneous can a source sample from diaries be when only a portion of contemporaries kept diaries and this sample documents merely a segment of the thoughts, actions, and feelings of its writers? This question must be posed in three respects: with regard to the social profile of the diarist and the consideration of whether these sources exclude certain social groups right from the outset; with a view to the form of the diary and the assessment of the extent to which the segmental character of diary writing conceals relevant content; and with a view to the relationship between National Socialism and diary writing, and also a reflection on the extent to which diarists may have generally shared a certain—perhaps predominantly critical—attitude toward National Socialism. These questions cannot be resolved by deliberating on the textual character of the diary but can be addressed by considering the historical development of diary writing in early twentieth-century Germany.[63]

Until the end of the nineteenth century, the development of the diary was closely tied to the formation of the bourgeoisie, which as a social configuration was defined by virtue of a certain "bourgeois" lifestyle.[64] Reading and writing practices took on a major role in this regard, as the bourgeoisie used them to set itself apart from the nobility, which was more oriented toward ceremony, as well as from the illiterate sub-bourgeois classes; the bourgeoisie thereby enacted its own self-identity.[65] To lend expression to the bourgeois self, diary writing was characterized by strong formalization, which within the genre's narrow conventions demanded that authors primarily deal with their own interiority in a so-called *journal intime*. The nineteenth-century diary was therefore socially exclusive and formally canonized. This radically changed at the turn of the twentieth century. The growth of general literacy, the creation of modern mass consumer culture, and political and social changes led to a massive increase and social broadening of diary writing between 1880 and 1930. At the start of the twentieth century, diaries were being kept by an unprecedented number of authors with the most widely diverse social origins.[66]

Notwithstanding the lack of reliable information on the social distribution of diary writing, it is clear that by the 1930s diary writing was no longer limited to a specific social group, even though this writing practice was distributed unevenly across the different social classes. The sources brought together here show that diarists appeared in all social classes, and therefore it has been possible to take authors with very different social origins into consideration. To be sure, diaries by lawyers, doctors, students, teachers, and other authors with educated middle-class backgrounds or academic occupations make up two-fifths of the source samples. But the remaining three-fifths come from authors who were wage and salary employees, self-employed, or unemployed: for example, the diary of Claus Behr, wine dealer and barkeep from the Black Forest, or the diary of Franz Wallner, a delivery driver and laborer from Munich. Fritz Schlösser worked as a porter at the central train station in Essen, and Walter Lohs ran a farm in a village north of Chemnitz. As also shown by these examples, the source selection contains diaries coming from various regions of the German Reich and written by authors from both urban and rural areas. Likewise, it includes various age groups, although most of the diaries come from gainfully employed adults. Diaries by men and women are more or less equally represented.

The social expansion of diary writing in the first decades of the twentieth century was also accompanied by the pluralization of writing practices and relaxation of the diary's formal strictures. The origins of this development can already be seen in the late nineteenth century as bourgeois diarists increasingly rebelled against the rigid genre boundaries of the diary.[67] Above all, however, new writers from other social classes broadened diary writing to include writing purposes previously unknown to the medium.[68] The focus in many diaries now turned to social and political topics, as well as to the author's relationship with the surrounding environment, which by no means displaced the established bourgeois diary. In contrast to the canonization of the diary format in the eighteenth and nineteenth centuries, the twentieth century was marked by the "coexistence or . . . competition of the various functions of the popular diary."[69]

In this respect, too, one cannot identify within my source material any overarching similarity or common style among the diaries. Some diary authors, such as the artist Luise Klempt, still used their entries mainly to deal with their inner lives. In contrast, others chronicled their observations about their everyday life or events in their social environs. In the case of the city archivist Stephan Weidenbach, this went so far that in his private diary he reported almost exclusively on developments in his hometown Andernach and largely refrained from commenting on his personal life. Meanwhile others, such as the aforementioned Hans Maschmann, kept diaries to orient themselves with respect to political developments, whereas some authors kept diaries very much in the traditional manner for religious soul-searching. Thus diary writing in the 1930s could be reflective or used for reporting, it could concentrate on the author's social surroundings or on the inner world, or it could generally refer to a broad spectrum of various topics. Basically, it did not exclude any topics or spheres of life.

Nonetheless, diaries of the 1930s have a blind spot. It lies in the fact that, as the authors' written confrontation with their own life, they leave open the question about the extent to which ideas, deliberations, and assessments expressed in the diary were also the subject of communications with third parties. It has always been seen as an advantage of this type of source that, "in a time in which public opinion was monopolized and the published word censored," the diary could be used to "counter the prepackaged propaganda image with self-lived experiences."[70] But this credible assumption only raises the questions of precisely where public communication differed from the diary entry and to what extent the thoughts recorded therein were restricted to the transcriptions. To a limited degree, diaries themselves provide answers by frequently reporting on conversations with third parties. However, the study also draws on letters as supplemental sources, which, when compared to diaries, allow for more precise determinations on the degree to which ideas expressed in diaries were confined to that medium.

However, the notion that researchers of National Socialism can use the diary as a source for uncensored thought also raises the question about the degree to which there was a general conflict between National Socialism, with its collectivist propaganda, and the diary, which seemingly presumes individuality. Can this source really be used to obtain a differentiated understanding of the individual challenge of National Socialism, or does it mainly reproduce the voices of opponents and victims of the Nazi regime? Especially older studies have repeatedly grasped the diary per se in this sense as a document that shows "how people try to obstruct the constantly threatening, indeed 'totalitarian' encroachment of depraved politics on private life."[71] Such clear-cut characterizations are rarely found in more recent historical research. But here too, the strong concentration on the diaries of victims, their use for describing the "linguistic counter-discourses to totalitarian languages," and, for example, the assessment that it is "extremely dangerous to keep a diary in a dictatorship" show how strongly the diary continues to be associated mainly with anti–National Socialist attitudes.[72] And yet the diaries of Joseph Goebbels and Alfred Rosenberg are not alone in suggesting that there was no basic contradiction between keeping a diary and National Socialism. All told, National Socialist policy and ideology were by no means as anti-individualist as alleged by the cited estimations. During the Weimar Republic, the NSDAP already had repeatedly referred to the diary format in its propaganda texts to disseminate its own political ideas. This continued after 1933, and especially in the camps of the Hitler Youth, League of German Girls, and Reich Labor Service, as well as on Strength through Joy tours, various agents of the regime tried to encourage participants to keep diaries and pushed for the acceptance of new forms of diary writing.[73]

In this respect, the diaries consulted here document a wide range of different positions toward National Socialism. Among them are diaries whose authors were members of the NSDAP or worked in an honorary or full-time capacity for the Nazi regime. The bookbinder Helmut Böhme, for example, was an NSDAP member since 1923 and worked as a Kreisleiter in Freiberg in Saxony since 1929. On the other hand, Franz Buesgen, a savings bank employee in Herne, only joined the Sturmabteilung (SA) and NSDAP in 1936 but reported in similar detail about his activities there. The study also looks at diaries written by people who situated themselves at a remove from the Nazi regime and often criticized its policies in writing. The Communist Erwin Oehl wrote his diary while in protective custody in spring 1933. The school director Georg Witzmann had sat in the Thüringen Landtag for the liberal German People's Party until being dismissed from the parliament in 1933, after which he followed political developments in his diary. And Daniel Lotter, a Franconian gingerbread baker, who began keeping a diary on the first anniversary of the seizure of power, had been the chairman of a Freemason lodge in his hometown of Fürth since 1931. The diary authors examined in this study also include German Jews who came into conflict with the Nazi regime not because of their political views but because of their supposed racial inferiority.

Reading Diaries

Diaries thus offer a broad view into the contemporary reactions of Germans to the individual challenge of National Socialism. But how should they be read so that they can answer the questions raised here? First of all, I feel it is important to recall once more that these texts were not written for today's readers. What emerged as a major advantage of these sources compared to retrospective personal testimonies creates lasting complications for how diaries are handled. This is already reflected by the fact that diaries are often written in handwriting that is substantially more difficult to read than surviving letters by the same author. For this reason, they also frequently contain words or sentence fragments that remain illegible even after intensive efforts.[74] Even just their external appearance highlights the fact that they are not addressed to us, not even in those places where diarists purposely address future generations, because their addressees are not us but persons of the future imagined by the writers.

The external illegibility also percolates into the content of entries, which is largely filled with allusions and assumptions. Because they are not written for strangers, diary entries are based on implicit knowledge that authors rarely explain. This starts already with the mention of people. The self-evident manner in which for the writer a name refers to a specific social relationship does not apply to outside readers. Often it is difficult even just to determine whether a person mentioned was an author's work colleague, friend, or relative.[75] Therefore diaries are not readily accessible at first glance. Making them even more difficult to understand, they do not proceed along an overarching narrative but rather follow each subject as it comes into view over an unforeseeable course of time. It is no more possible to quickly find one's bearings in diaries than it is to skim them fleetingly in search of specific key words. Instead, diaries very much demand an in-depth reading that does not concentrate exclusively on those entries that seemingly respond directly to one's questions. A methodologically appropriate treatment of these historical sources is enabled by precisely this look at the supposedly irrelevant, which also reveals meanings that might remain incomprehensible at first.

When reading, I pay special attention to the process of diary writing. How the diary was written; what themes, subjects, and questions were dealt with; and how this changed over time hold decisive insights into how individuals dealt with the challenges of National Socialism. It is by no means inevitable that an individual subject—such as one's relationship to the Nazi regime—will be addressed in a diary at a specific time. Rather, the large degree to which answers to the questions posed here can be found in diaries is itself perhaps the strongest evidence for the sustained impact of the start of National Socialist rule on the thoughts and actions of contemporaries. In particular, the appearance of new subjects and ways of writing testifies to the changes undergone by the authors that were prompted by the Nazi regime, as does their disappearance. Because diaries could be kept in a variety of forms and because general writing conventions were lacking, one must work out the specific context of use for each diary—that is, the writer's intentions for keeping the diary and the choice of which subjects to raise and questions to ask as determined by those intentions. Only against this background can we identify and interpret changes in how the diaries were written. In this respect, this book also tells a story about diary writing in the 1930s.

But identifying a diary's context of use is also critically important because its entries can only be properly interpreted within this context. As banal as it sounds, it is important to ask specific diaries only those questions they can answer. In many examples in the literature, this is very much in doubt. Mary Fulbrook, for example, notes in her study *Dissonant Lives* that "one of the oddest aspects" emerging from the investigation of social perceptions of the 1938 anti-Jewish pogroms was that "some adults seem to have failed even to register what was going on." She demonstrates this by quoting from a "relatively typical" diary entry of a female physician, who on November 28, 1938, complains about her unhappiness and loneliness but, as in previous days, makes no comment about the massive anti-Jewish violence.[76] But to me the diary does not seem to support Fulbrook's interpretation. Viewed as whole, the diary shows that its author—a woman around thirty years old—wrote it primarily to deal with her emotional world and the everyday influences on that world. Her diary illustrates that the nineteenth-century bourgeois practice of diary writing, which pertained to one's own interiority, had by no means vanished in the 1930s. The author used her diary in this sense mainly to reflect on her emotions, particularly those provoked by what she felt were problematic social relationships with work colleagues, friends, and especially her former lover. Politics, on the other hand, had no place in her diary, at least not until the beginning of the war; the young woman so completely ignored politics that, had her entries not been dated, only the one-time mention of the "Labor Front" in a list of employment formalities that needed to be resolved would situate the diary in the National Socialist period.[77] Given this background, the entry cited by Fulbrook seems less surprising and outrageous than suggested by her juxtaposition of the entry with the pogrom. On the contrary, within its context of use, the entry is thoroughly consistent. In this respect, one cannot conclude from the entry whether the diarist was interested in political events or did not even register them. We simply know nothing about her perception and assessment of Nazi politics in the 1930s; instead, we only know what is noted in the diary. And at least during this period, the diary deals with part of her life where politics did not belong. In their own segmented nature, diaries speak about their author's ideas and lived reality, and only within those limits can we properly interpret individual statements and entries.

Within this thematic framework, individual diary entries must be read in the first instance as performative texts. Therefore, in all three parts of this book I ask about the significance of diary writing per se for how people handled the individual challenge of National Socialism. The analysis of individual ways of writing thereby provides insight into the individual authors' thoughts about National Socialism, their self-perception, and their political observations of the world. That analysis is supplemented by a look at social conceptions of the diary and its integration into the practice of National Socialist rule, which likewise clarifies the connection between diary writing and the political and social developments of the 1930s.

In a second step, the entries are investigated with regard to everyday forms of behavior and their author's lived reality outside of the text. This makes it possible to gain insights into how individual contemporaries, outside the diary, reacted to claims made on them by power. Naturally, the representation of reality external to the diary text is permanently marked by its performative quality, which is why entries cannot simply be read as "thick descriptions."[78] Here too the diary is only discussing a specific segment that is dependent on the respective writing purpose. In this thematic segment, however, diaries do indeed contain references to their protagonists' everyday behavior—references that can also be identified within the analysis of the respective writing practices.

In practice, this means understanding all interpretations as well as expressed emotions and perceptions as elements that in diary writing could help organize experiences and behaviors in the author's own life contexts. When writers report on discussions in their diaries, for example, these entries are naturally not word-for-word renditions of conversations, even if interlocutors are directly quoted. Here it is always important to ask about the function performed by the rendering of the discussion in the diary for the self-image created by the author. But such entries can also be read as a source to identify people the author spoke to and the subjects they discussed. Asking only about their performative quality would miss the fact that diary writing interprets real experiences and behaviors. The same applies, for example, to reports about mass Nazi rallies that people witnessed firsthand or over the radio. Here too one must ask how the process of diary writing influenced the description of the experience. Yet these diary entries testify quite well about the ways and extent to which specific diarists participated in the mass festivals of the Nazi regime. At the same time, observable behaviors cannot be seen necessarily as the consequence of reflection processes in the diary, which were sometimes intense. Above all, diaries show the post facto self-understanding of performed behaviors and not so much their underlying motives. However, in light of the rapid and fundamental changes that began in 1933, these retrospective interpretations of new behaviors and the reconciliation of these behaviors with one's previous life context were critically important. It was through them that contemporaries fell in line with and simultaneously advanced the changes in society.

Current State of Research

The beginning of social historical research into National Socialism was marked by the so-called Bavaria Project, whose end was in turn marked by the "Herausforderung des Einzelnen"—the "challenge of the individual."[79] Such was the title of the sixth volume in the series brought out by the Institut für Zeitgeschichte, which in 1983 rounded out the institute's publication of results from its Bavaria during the Nazi Period research project, launched ten years before. The studies emerging from the project described for the first time the "functional history of the Nazi regime 'from below,' from the social base."[80] Hence, in the late 1970s they established a new historiographical perspective on National Socialism focused on the relationship between the Nazi regime and society, formulating many of the theses and questions that continue to dominate research to this very day. The last volume of the Bavaria Project was not among the formative studies that still guide research in part because of the significance assigned to this final volume from within the project itself: in the foreword, Martin Broszat pointed out that the focus on the "challenge of the individual" was meant to complement the analytical investigations of the previous volumes. In the conclusion of the research project, the findings developed in the other studies were supposed to be brought home to the public in a "poignant narrative form," "also biographically and in story form." He noted that the "stories of individual resistance" selected for the volume were "humanly touching" and revealed what lay "behind the keywords of 'resistance and persecution.'"[81] The "challenge of the individual" was about conveying historical knowledge, not acquiring it.

As a central formulation in my book, the "individual challenge of National Socialism" refers to this early shift of attention toward individual people of the 1930s and 1940s, but with its twofold meaning, it also contends that individual cases can be used not only to illustrate but also to investigate historical events. The following evaluation of diaries is therefore not meant to explain life trajectories, individual experiences, or biographical developments. Rather, the knowledge being sought is more about the entanglement of individual lifestyles and perceptions with historical circumstances, whose significance must be grasped from the perspective of contemporaries. The view "from within"—quasi from within history itself—provides for insights into historical contexts that cannot be gained solely through historiographical retrospection.[82] In this respect, I am firmly convinced that the restricted perspectives of those contemporaries who did not influence political and social processes from powerful institutions and positions are important for more than merely conveying historiographical knowledge. Rather, they can also provide explanations for historical events.

Informed by this interest, my book falls in line with the new social history of National Socialism emerging in recent years from the intense discussions around the key word *Volksgemeinschaft*.[83] Although extensive debates have done little to clarify more precisely the meaning of the concept, and even though the concept's historiographical role remains controversial, the dispute about the Volksgemeinschaft has established a perspective on the social history of National Socialism that differs fundamentally from earlier approaches.[84] Compared to the social-historical perspectives that dominated well into the 1990s, the new research is based on a modified concept of society. It no longer asks about structures and long-term developmental trends but rather, using predominantly cultural-historical approaches, grasps the society of National Socialism as a specific societal configuration whose function and dynamics must be revealed through the detailed analysis of social practice.[85] This has brought to the fore the Nazi regime's aspirations for change and its efforts to transform German society, the effects of which are now being investigated in changes to the rules of social belonging and modes of interaction, instead of in underlying social structures.[86] My book is aligned with this branch of research insofar as it similarly emphasizes the Nazi regime's aspiration for fundamental social change and asks about its consequences. At the same time, however, it also broadens this view because it not only considers the conduct of contemporaries within specific practices of rule but also analyzes their reflections on it and their underlying interpretations and perceptions in this regard.

In doing so, I am following up on a demand that has been made repeatedly in recent scholarly discussions. Because Volksgemeinschaft was a concept used in Nazi propaganda, some have criticized its use as a historiographical category. It is precisely this criticism, which has sometimes been quite severe, that has heightened the awareness of the need for a more precise outline of the social relevance of ideological categories.[87] This has pushed established perspectives of a history of ideas into the background. Recent studies no longer attempt to clarify the meaning of diffuse ideological categories such as Volksgemeinschaft.[88] In light of the "ambiguity of the concept 'Volksgemeinschaft' and the incongruence of usage contexts," this study looks at the specific usage and understanding of ideological concepts during the National Socialist era.[89] Diaries provide a good foundation for such an endeavor. By examining the reflections of their authors, here too I am picking up on impulses from recent research, although I do not restrict myself to the term *Volksgemeinschaft* but instead basically inquire about whether and how ideological categories were subsumed into contemporaries' interpretations of themselves and the world.

However much my book thus joins the current scholarly discussions, it also advances into terrain that still remains largely unexplored, whose contours have been recently outlined by Moritz Föllmer. Föllmer criticized the recent scholarly discussion for only skirting the edges of the "interplay between the ideological and institutional context of the Third Reich and the level of Germans' self-understandings, motivations, and actions."[90] But it is precisely by looking at the "subjective dimension of Nazism" that we can help overcome "the particularly marked specialization of the historiography on the Third Reich" and create "connections between differently focused studies."[91] The development of Nazi rule obviously did not only possess "a subjective dimension but was dependent on it to become widely acceptable, translate ideology into practice, and produce extremely violent outcomes."[92] In this respect, it is time "for Third Reich specialists to problematize subjectivity more explicitly."[93]

So far there are only a small number of preliminary studies on this matter. To be sure, as early as 1986 the philosopher Wolfgang Fritz Haug called for more attention to be paid to "ideological subjection," the absorption of National Socialist ideologemes into individual ways of life and self-images.[94] But at the same time, he noted that hardly any sources were available for investigating them. He was not alone in therefore limiting his investigation to the analysis of ideological texts and guidebooks. Other studies, too, failed to follow up on his suggestions. In recent research, it has chiefly been Moritz Föllmer himself who has performed important groundwork for investigating the subjective dimension of National Socialism. In his study on "individuality and modernity in Berlin," he argues that National Socialist rule was not simply characterized by the striving for collectivism but also fell in line with a longer search "for an acceptable form of individuality."[95] Föllmer sees the "core message" of the Nazi regime not in collectivism but in the fact "that individuality and community were compatible and even mutually reinforcing."[96] In this respect, researchers needed to ask about how the Nazi regime transformed and politically shaped individuality, as well as deal with the "historicisation of semantics and practices of individuality before, during and after the Reich."[97]

Just how illuminating diaries can be for such a project is shown by the intensive research into Soviet subjectivity, set in motion above all by Jochen Hellbeck's study on diary writing under Stalinism.[98] Much as Föllmer does for Germany, Hellbeck too notes that "the primary effect on individuals' sense of self of the Revolution of 1917 and of Soviet revolutionary practice was not repressive, but productive."[99] He demonstrates this through an extensive analysis of diaries used by their authors in the 1930s as "active tools" to accommodate themselves to the changed conditions after the revolution and to advance social development by working on their own selves.[100] Hellbeck's study led to an intense discussion about diaries and the conditions of Soviet subjectivity, which has profoundly expanded the understanding of Stalinism.[101]

Research into National Socialism is still a long way from having this kind of discussion. Despite the vast number of historical studies that quote from individual diaries of the 1930s and 1940s, there has been hardly any systematic interest in the diaries of National Socialism. Research into experiential history has done much with the evaluation of oral history interviews and field post letters.[102] For this reason too, the experiential history of National Socialism has been inscribed with a stronger focus on the war years, a feature also shared by the few systematic studies of diaries under National Socialism. Published in the early 1990s, Susanne zur Nieden's study of women's diaries from the second half of the war likewise concentrates on the 1940s, as do more recent studies by Alexandra Garbarini, Benjamin Möckel, and Nick Stargardt.[103] In contrast, only sporadic references have been made to the importance of diaries for researching the 1930s, primarily in connection with the perception of political events in 1933.[104] Most arguments with respect to the experiential history of National Socialism during the years of peace are based either on self-testimonies created after 1945 or on moral reports by exile groups and Nazi security agencies, which only very loosely document the perceptions of Germans.[105]

While diaries have generally received only minimal attention, and mostly with regard to the war years of the Nazi dictatorship, the studies of diaries done thus far have contributed little to the understanding of the subjective dimension of National Socialism because they simply do not ask about it. This is especially the case for investigations that focus their analysis on individual diaries.[106] Overall, interest in dairies from the National Socialist period has previously concentrated mainly on the tension between governance and society and hence on the various forms of suffering, resistance, and collaboration of their respective authors. Thus the question regarding the transformation of the individual and one's self-accommodation to the new political conditions—posed very productively with respect to the Soviet Union—does not come into view. So far diaries have been used to refer to the subjective dimension of National Socialism only in connection with concentration camps, whereby diary writing has been interpreted as an effort by authors to "internally free themselves through writing from the hell in which they had to live."[107] Beyond these "places of terror," however, the connection between National Socialist rule and individual conceptions and practices of the self still remain largely unresolved.

Only Peter Fritzsche has pursued this problem more deeply in his work. As early as the 1990s, he pointed out the Nazi regime's abilities "to manufacture an alternative public sphere in which Germans identified themselves increasingly as *Volksgenossen*."[108] He advanced this idea in two more recent studies. On the basis above all of edited diaries of the 1930s and 1940s, in his book, *Life and Death in the Third Reich*, he noted that "the National Socialist revolution intensified self-scrutiny." For this reason, according to Fritzsche, self-testimonies from this period provide for deep insights "into the effort Germans made to come to terms with National Socialism." Fritzsche uses them to illustrate, in different contexts, how individual contemporaries "fitted National Socialist words and concepts into everyday life."[109] In his succinct account, covering the entire period of National Socialist rule, he is thereby able to point out the spectrum across which individual self-images and modes of life in the 1930s and 1940s were shaped and altered by National Socialist politics, even though there is often little space for a detailed and comprehensive analysis of how this actually happened. Nonetheless, *Life and Death in the Third Reich* develops the first important theses in this regard.

In addition, in a study about the writings left behind by Franz Göll, a white-collar worker from Berlin, Fritzsche dealt more closely with a diary; using this individual case, he also impressively demonstrated in methodological terms just how much the documents enable "genuine insight in the social psychology of Germany's extraordinarily violent twentieth-century history."[110] Here too, Fritzsche pays special attention to the confrontation with National Socialism. He shows how Göll, after his initial approval, became increasingly critical of the Nazi regime. Nonetheless, his self-conception was shaped by National Socialist politics—for example, he started reconstructing his genealogy in his diary within the context of Nazi racial policy. Fritzsche thus shows that, for an understanding of the subjective dimension of National Socialism, it is not enough to ask only about political attitudes. Political assessments and changes to individual self-conceptions did not have to go hand in hand under National Socialist rule. It is also against this background that I chose a systematic organization for my book that picks up on various lines of argument set out by Peter Fritzsche and further elaborates them on the basis of a broad foundation of sources.

Even though by and large there are only a few previous works dedicated to diaries and the subjective dimension of National Socialism, this book would nonetheless not have been possible without the extensive literature on many diverse aspects of social life in the 1930s. Inasmuch as the book engages with the perspectives of contemporaries, a very broad spectrum of diverse topics that the historical literature usually deals with in isolation comes up for discussion: the political history of the seizure of power, the destruction of the workers' parties, practices of social exclusion, state control and public reception of the media, and the functional principles of the National Socialist public sphere. The list can be seamlessly expanded—also coming up for discussion are education plans of the Nazi state and Nazi camp pedagogy, Nazi history of the body, racist social policy, the literary policy of the Nazi regime, anti-Jewish violence and the Aryanization of Jewish property, political manifestos and the staging of Hitler in the media, elections and plebiscites, the political popularity of the Nazi regime, and the actions of local NSDAP organizations and their functionaries. The diaries of the 1930s do not adhere to the internal divisions of academic research literature. Only because of the broadly diversified and extensive state of knowledge achieved by research into National Socialism over the past decades do we have the contextual knowledge required for interpreting individual diaries and comprehending their entries as part of historical developments.

PART ONE

On the evening of January 30, 1933, thousands of members of the Sturmabteilung (SA), Schutzstaffel (SS), and Stahlhelm moved through the heart of Berlin in a giant torchlight procession. The march led through the Brandenburg Gate, moved along Unter den Linden, and then veered right into the Wilhelmstraße, where in front of the Reich Chancellery it was reviewed by Reich President Paul von Hindenburg and the new Reich chancellor, Adolf Hitler, who had just been appointed that morning. Watched and cheered by the new Reich leadership and passersby, the torchlight procession included some twenty thousand participants. Not only in the capital but in many other cities as well, National Socialist and national conservative associations celebrated Hitler's appointment as the chancellor of a government made up of members of the NSDAP and German National People's Party (DNVP), as well as other national conservative politicians.[1]

Torchlight processions and marches provided the public image for the start of National Socialist rule in the following weeks as well. The election campaign for the new Reichstag election in early March, called by the new Reich chancellor immediately after his appointment, created numerous opportunities for such events, as did the electoral victory achieved in the shadow of the Reichstag fire and the first meeting of the new Reichstag, celebrated as the Day of Potsdam and staged as the founding act of the new National Socialist state. The climax of the marches of spring 1933 occurred on May 1, proclaimed by the regime as the Day of National Labor and featuring the participation of millions of Germans in mass processions organized in every German city and municipality.

The marches held on January 30 and during the next election campaign had still been informed by the proven concept of the National Socialist "propaganda marches" of the Weimar period.[2] But especially with the celebrations of May 1, 1933, their character changed decisively. As the NSDAP moved from an opposition party to become the bearer of the new state, the processions no longer sought to intimidate political opponents and win over new adherents by demonstrating strength and solidarity. Instead, the processions of May 1 were supposed to create a "visible symbol . . . for the dawn of a new German Volksgemeinschaft" and draw in large sections of the populace beyond the party's own base.[3] It was no coincidence that the choice fell on the traditional labor day of the workers' movement, for the Nazi regime was primarily offering workers a chance to find their place within the new state. Taking up an old demand of the workers' parties and unions, the Nazi regime used one of its first laws to declare this day a state holiday.[4]

Yet since this offer for integration expressly consisted of including workers in a national community that promised equality with other social strata, the purpose of May 1 was actually to mobilize the entire populace. Thus in 1934, the Day of National Labor holiday was accordingly rebranded as the National Holiday of the German Volk, and even in 1933, the newly appointed Reich minister of public enlightenment and propaganda, Joseph Goebbels, deliberately directed his appeal "to the entire German Volk": "Men and women! We appeal to you in cities and the countryside! . . . The First of May is supposed to see the Volk united and consolidated and be a signal to the entire world that Germany has awakened and is looking for and finding the path to freedom and bread." The Reich minister's appeal let Germans know how they were supposed to participate. "On this day let work rest! Garland your houses and the streets of the cities and villages with fresh greenery and with the flags of the Reich! . . . Germans of all estates, tribes, and occupations, reach out your hands to each other! United we march into the new era!"[5] Flanking the main appeal was a "veritable press campaign." Starting in mid-April, "hardly a day went by without the [publication] of appeals by national, civic, and religious associations, societies, or groups for participation on May 1."[6] Unions, trade guilds, and business associations exhorted people to participate, as did low-level party organizations, which often repeated Goebbels's invitations "much more sharply—in the form of an order and as an undisguised threat."[7] Intense pressure and numerous appeals equally did their part to ensure that on May 1, 1933, millions of participants throughout Germany actually marched through decorated streets in broad demonstrative processions made up of numerous delegations from "commercial and unionist, athletic and ecclesiastic, national and National Socialist organizations."[8]

By direction of the Reich Ministry for Public Enlightenment and Propaganda, the local May Day celebrations throughout the territory of the Reich were "mandatorily aligned according to the timetable and content requirements" of the central rally in Berlin.[9] All across the country, the demonstrative processions were followed by rallies, which in the evening culminated with Adolf Hitler's speech from the Tempelhof Field in Berlin, broadcast by radio. The new Reich chancellor used his speech to call for the joining and mutual understanding of the various social strata, which was also meant to ensure the due recognition of workers. At the same time, he stressed that the extensive mobilization of the population for May 1 was not supposed to be a onetime event and that the population's collaboration would be required and expected in the future as well. The government wanted "to work, and we will work!" Hitler promised. "Only, ultimately everything depends on the German Volk itself, on you, in the trust that you place in us; it depends on the strength with which you commit yourself to the national state. Only if all of you yourselves become one in the will to save Germany can the German man also find his salvation in Germany.... The German Volk has revived. It will no longer tolerate within itself men who are not for Germany!"[10] Hitler outlined here the core of National Socialism's sociopolitical program: on one side, the Volk—the people—united in thought and action and thus supporting the Nazi regime; on the other side, its enemies. This was the model used by the National Socialist regime in its effort to reorganize German society: henceforth, social belonging would depend on the individual's willingness to commit to the Nazi regime. Everyone would soon need to decide on which side they would stand—except, of course, those whom the regime deemed "alien" and "opponents" from the very outset.

When they printed the speech the next day, the newspapers left out the speech's final, openly threatening remarks. Even so, the message had reached people by radio. Carl Dürkefälden, a retired industrial worker born in 1867 who supplemented his pension with a little agricultural work in a village near Peine, had also heard the speech on the radio and remembered in particular Hitler's final words. In spring 1933, Dürkefälden was worried about his youngest son, Karl, born in 1902, who like him had worked in a steel mill. But Karl had lost his job in 1931 and thus moved back in with his parents, and in spring 1933 altercations repeatedly arose between the son and his parents, which Karl related in detail in his diary. As Karl noted, the conflicts occurred because in spring 1933 his parents had become "fanatical followers of Hitler," just like his two siblings.[11] He himself was skeptical about the National Socialist movement. His father frequently tried to convince him to abandon his aloofness and join the NSDAP. As Karl Dürkefälden noted in his diary, this also happened on May 2, when "while plowing under potatoes Father started again: he said he really did not want to start on politics with me again. 'But did you hear Hitler's radio speech yesterday? No! He said whoever does not want to at all, for him there is no room in Germany. I just wanted to tell you that so you know the score. . . . Here they are all in it now, what more do you then want?'" The father repeatedly cajoled his son. On the previous day, as well, he had "come out to us to work me over again. When I said to him again, I do not at all oppose the matter, but I want to stay neutral, he said: 'That is precisely it: nobody should stay neutral.'"[12]

The first part of this book pursues the question of how contemporaries dealt with the Nazi regime's far-reaching demand for affiliation and the associated efforts to fundamentally change the everyday social relationships of Germans. In the first chapter, I look at the reactions of contemporaries to the start of National Socialist rule and the social dynamics generated by the seizure of power through the demand for individual commitment. This chapter looks first at those Germans immediately impacted by the mass violence that formed the foundation for establishing the Nazi dictatorship (1). Next, however, it asks mainly about how extensively and in what manner those people not considered by the regime to be "enemies" and "opponents" were affected by the start of the Nazi dictatorship and the demand for commitment (2 and 3).

The second chapter analyzes how individuals established their own positions toward the new regime. To do so, first I show why in 1933–1934 diaries in particular formed an important medium in which people reflected on their relationship to National Socialism (1). On the basis of a precise evaluation of diary entries, I then investigate how even those who held other political convictions prior to 1933 could now find positions that, as demanded, also demonstrated commitment to the new regime (2 and 3). Here I am interested in understanding the internal logic and problems that determined the search for an individual's own relationship to National Socialism. The last subsection moves on from the early years of the Nazi dictatorship to elucidate how positions found in 1933–1934 developed in the years that followed (4).

The third chapter finally focuses on the way people established their position toward the Nazi regime as a social process. The search for one's personal stance at the start of the Nazi dictatorship occurred not just through written monologues but also always took place under the attentive observation of friends, acquaintances, coworkers, and relatives. This deeply influenced the behavior of contemporaries and their interpersonal social relationships (1 and 2). Above all, the reciprocal observations among Germans produced effects that by the mid-1930s increasingly forced those people declared to be "enemies" and "opponents" into social isolation (3), even if they escaped the violence of the Nazi regime.

1

THE SOCIAL DYNAMICS OF THE "SEIZURE OF POWER"

1. In "Our Streets": State Violence and Social Marginalization in 1933

In January 1938, just a few months before Sebastian Haffner left Berlin, immigrated to Cambridge, and started working on his autobiography, a book by another Berliner was published in Great Britain. Its author, Hans Schwalm, had a lot in common with Sebastian Haffner. Like Haffner, Schwalm had been forced to leave Germany and seek refuge in England, except he had done so three years earlier. He too had grown up in the capital and sharply repudiated National Socialism, and he was around Haffner's age. But instead of being a civil servant in the Prussian Ministry of Culture, Schwalm's father had been a bricklayer. Schwalm himself had worked in Berlin as a toolmaker, lathe operator, and businessman before entering long-term unemployment in the early 1930s. He owed his literary interests not to his parental upbringing but rather to the Communist Workers Youth, where he played an active role as early as the 1920s.

In 1930, he became a member of the Communist Party of Germany (KPD), and the next year, he got involved with the League of Proletarian-Revolutionary Authors, which was affiliated with the party. He soon became the organization leader of the local Berlin chapter, although his own efforts as a writer remained largely unsuccessful. A few isolated articles appeared in the *Rote Fahne*. Yet whereas Johannes R. Becher, Georg Lukács, Alfred Döblin, Walter Mehring, and other members of the Weimar period's leftist literary elite argued about the poetological and political alignment of contemporary literature, Schwalm presented his texts in agitprop theater groups and as a lecturer in the rear courtyards of tenements in Berlin.[1] The publication less than ten years later of an English version of an almost three-hundred-page novel by Schwalm owed less to his talent as a writer than to the historical circumstances of the book's origin. In spring 1933, the terror unleashed after Hitler's appointment as Reich chancellor shattered the workers' movement, including the League of Proletarian-Revolutionary Authors, in just a few short weeks. Many of the league's prominent members—including Bertolt Brecht, Johannes R. Becher, Anna Seghers, and Franz Carl Weiskopf—fled abroad as early as February 1933. Egon Erwin Kisch and other lesser-known members were arrested. Some did not survive their imprisonment and torture. In May 1933 when the books of newly banned authors were burned, they included the works of many members of the League of Proletarian-Revolutionary Authors.

Hans Schwalm had escaped the terror of the SA despite his activities as a Communist functionary, and starting in May 1933, he and a few other members who stayed in Berlin tried to resume the association's activities in the underground. The group wrote and distributed illegal pamphlets and, via Schwalm, maintained contact with the party's federal leadership, which had fled to Prague and been given information and articles for publication abroad.[2] Even before working for the resistance, Schwalm had started to keep a diary about political developments and the effects of the seizure of power on his everyday life. Schwalm kept up his daily records even though their discovery would pose a risk not just to him but also to the illegal operation. Then while still in Germany, he reworked them into a novel manuscript, which he boldly smuggled over the German-Czechoslovakian border. Schwalm had not started his diary with authorial ambitions, and its reworking followed less from literary aspirations than from the illegal nature of the work: to avoid endangering comrades still living in Germany, he changed the names, appearances, and family relationships of his protagonists. To disguise himself, Schwalm took on a pseudonym, under which he became famous after the book's international publication. Ultimately, as with Haffner, the pseudonym became his legal name: Jan Petersen.

In other respects, the author tried to dispel any impression that the revision was a fictional text. He described the book in the subtitle as "a chronicle written in the heart of fascist Germany" and preserved the writing's immediacy by telling the story from the perspective of a protagonist named Jan (the eponym was no coincidence) in approximately eighty sections, some of them dated. Like a diary, the text is not held together by an "integrative principle that continuously shapes the narrated material"[3] but rather by chronologically described daily events and by a theme that Petersen specifically highlighted during the revision process and that ultimately gave the novel its title: *Our Street*.[4]

This street is Wallstraße in Berlin-Charlottenburg (today Zillestraße), part of a working-class neighborhood where the young communist Jan and his comrades live, as the author did before emigrating. The novel begins on January 21, 1933, with the narrator and his friends Richard Hütting and Franz Zander taking a walk, during which they observe the preparations underway for the next day's NSDAP demonstration in front of the Karl Liebknecht House. In the novel, the author primarily tells the story of these three young communists to the summer of 1934. By way of the narrator's detailed observations and the recorded reports of friends and acquaintances, the book unfolds into a striking panorama of the rapid and profound changes to the narrator's immediate surroundings that accompany the start of National Socialist rule.

The topography of Wallstraße deeply changes in spring 1933: the workers' taverns where the protagonists still socialize in the last days of January are shut down. The SA occupies the Social Democratic "People's Centre" at the end of the street, now used to imprison many of the street's residents, who are often tortured and sometimes killed.[5] The building and its adjoining section of the street also become dangerous for Jan and his comrades, who avoid it for fear of checkpoints. Time and again, the narrator talks about arrests, raids, and the brutal violence of the SA with which the new rulers intervene in the space of the street, where the young men had felt protected before 1933. The Communist flags and wall-sized slogans that once dominated the street scene disappear. Showing up increasingly instead are swastika flags and brown uniforms. In summer 1933, the Wallstraße is renamed Maikowski Straße, after the SA leader Hans Maikowski, who died there on the night of January 30, 1933, in clashes between the SA and street residents. Despite the unclear circumstances surrounding his death, Nazi propaganda throughout Germany stylized Maikowski as a "blood sacrifice and martyr."[6] A memorial plaque is mounted at the place he died. Business owners add pictures of the Führer to their display windows and begin to identify their establishments as "German stores."

But the changes are not limited to the topographical environment. In the novel, the changes to the street also symbolize the pervasive effects of the new political circumstances on the protagonists' daily lives. Although Jan and his friends are determined to continue advancing the idea of Communism, the new political situation compels them to adopt conspiratorial behavior and reinforces their distrust of neighbors and acquaintances. To protect the illegal infrastructure of their operation, the friends no longer greet one another in the street. Comrades sought by the SA are forced to hide in other parts of the city, where large sections of the political work are also transferred. Dissemblance and distrust dominate their behavior toward neighbors and comrades whose political positions are no longer precisely known. The protagonists lose "the connection to the world in which they move: to their family members, their living space, to the fellow residents of their building and surroundings: to the 'street.'" A "process of gradual, constantly accruing individual and collective isolation" turns them into strangers in an environment previously very familiar to them, and in the course of the novel, all attempts to adapt to the new conditions do nothing to stop more and more people from getting arrested and murdered—as are Franz Zanger and Richard Hütting in the end.[7]

The English translation of the novel met with great interest in Great Britain when it appeared in January 1938.[8] The reviews printed in Communist and union-affiliated newspapers were just as extensive as those in the liberal *Economist* and the conservative *Daily Telegraph*, and in terms of their assessments, the reviews hardly differed. The novel was generally seen—as expressed in the *Times*—as a "remarkable and moving book" that, as a firsthand factual account, stood out among the scores of books about Nazi Germany.[9] As such, it was also widely read, which owed much to its inclusion in the program of the Left Book Club. The openly antifascist book club, with around fifty thousand subscribers in 1938, introduced the book to a mass public audience and played a major role in its success, which began with its initial publication as a serial story in a Swiss daily newspaper and in Russian translation in 1936.[10] Thirty years later, translations into eight more languages and especially the publication of the book in Germany (where it became a classic of antifascist literature in the young German Democratic Republic [GDR]) brought the novel international fame and made it a widely read book with a total of eight hundred thousand published copies.[11]

Its first readers in the 1930s included exiled writers who had already fled in early 1933; they had no personal impressions about daily life in Nazi Germany and used *Our Street* as a source for their own work. Anna Seghers resorted to the book for her novel *The Seventh Cross*, as did Bertolt Brecht for his drama *Fear and Misery of the Third Reich* and the directors of the movie *Professor Mamlock*, which was filmed in the Soviet Union in 1938.

The movie, like the works by Seghers and Brecht, reached an international audience of millions.[12] In this way, too, Petersen's novel contributed substantially to how contemporaries abroad pictured the effects of the National Socialist seizure of power on the everyday life of Germans. Even to this day, literary works like Petersen's *Our Street* still shape our image of the everyday ramifications of the advent of Nazi rule.[13]

With their focus on violence and terror, the works of exile literature that reported their authors' personal experiences brought one (if not the central) aspect of the establishment of National Socialism to center stage. Violence played a key role in implementing the Nazi dictatorship and remained a constitutive factor for National Socialist rule and politics.[14] In spring 1933, it helped nip any potential political resistance in the bud, enabled National Socialism's own followers to actively take part in the seizure of power, and, because it was widely visible, made it clear to those well beyond the circle of its immediate victims that political power relationships had changed.[15]

Although violence had fundamentally shaped the National Socialist movement's awareness of itself and politics from the very beginning,[16] the start of National Socialist rule signified a crucial turning point. While state agencies during the Weimar Republic still kept the violence of the Nazi movement within bounds, the executive power of the state's monopoly on violence merged with the street terror of the SA to produce an unprecedented brutality, especially after the Reichstag fire in late February 1933.[17] In many cities, local SA divisions, in particular, dragged thousands of people to detainment and torture centers set up in empty factories, barracks, or basements, where they tormented them. The number of these facilities is unknown but was probably "in the hundreds."[18] In March and April 1933, such facilities were used to imprison more than forty-five thousand people throughout Germany, with eighty thousand people imprisoned during the year as a whole.[19] Although local party agencies or authorities established these prisons, in summer 1933 the Nazi regime began bringing them under centralized control, using these "early camps" as the starting point for the creation of the concentration camp system, which early on came to embody National Socialist terror.[20]

But the terrorizing violence of the seizure of power was by no means restricted to these "places of terror."[21] In rural regions, roaming SA detachments tortured political opponents openly in the streets.[22] In big cities, the arenas for violence were above all streets in working-class districts. Between March and July 1933 in Hamburg alone, the police carried out around 850 raids in working-class neighborhoods.[23] To pass the time, local SA troopers also engaged in unorganized violence. In spring 1933, the Berlin doctor Walter Lindemann was trying to join the SA and reported in his diary how he thus frequented the local "Sturmlokal"—that is, the pub serving as the local SA hangout—even before his official acceptance. His entries discuss the heavy consumption of alcohol and ubiquitous violence. One evening Lindemann finally became part of the action when "the SA people . . . simply took my car" and carried out "raids against communists." "Among other things, we also took a Jew and a very nice-looking Jewess (18–20 years) along. This poor girl sat next to me in the back of the car. . . . They first properly beat up the poor girl and then Schulz and Schmidt violated her indecently!!"[24]

Tens of thousands of people fled abroad in 1933 to escape this violence.[25] The overall number of those affected remains unknown. There is no information that could provide an overview of the scope of adverse health effects that accompanied the mass imprisonment and torture. We have not even been able to reliably reconstruct the number of fatalities incurred during the seizure of power. The early-1960s estimate of five hundred to six hundred people murdered by October 1933 should probably be considered a minimum.[26] Flight, imprisonment, torture, and death are the most obvious and existential ways in which people experienced the start of National Socialist rule.

The street terror in the months after January 30, 1933, affected many groups but especially German Jews and the functionaries and members of the workers' movement, first and foremost Communists.[27] The terror was driven both by SA Sturm units' desire for revenge on those they had already battled during the Weimar Republic and by the new government's anxieties about possible resistance. The dynamics resulting from the violent efforts "from below" and "from above" led to an "undifferentiated demolition straight through the workers' movement" carried out jointly by the SA and police agencies in the spring and summer of 1933 and vividly reported by Petersen's novel.[28] At the same time—and the novel refers to this explicitly—the changes to the traditional ways of life of urban industrial workers that accompanied the terror decisively facilitated the persecution of resistance attempts. Whereas the workers' parties—especially the KPD—had gained their political strength during the Weimar Republic by mobilizing neighborly relationships in workers' districts, now life in such close quarters became a source of danger.[29] The more people sided with the new regime after January 30, 1933, the greater the risk that neighborly proximity and mutual knowledge about one another's political beliefs would be used for denunciations, which thus made illegal work ever more difficult. In just a few weeks, even in workers' districts previously dominated by Communism, this led to a situation where "the few steadfast opponents of the Nazis had to live largely in social isolation and denounced and maligned by neighbors."[30]

This is a key reason why hardly any diary records have survived from the early workers' resistance of 1933. Petersen's narrator repeatedly reflects on the dangers of writing, with even just the clatter of his own typewriter, audible in the neighboring apartments, already sparking anxieties about denunciation. The author himself took on a detailed cover story, joining the Reich Literature Chamber in 1933 and publishing an apolitical short story to justify ownership of a typewriter. Nonetheless, fear of discovery led him to hide his manuscript for *Our Street* outside his home.[31] And in illegal circulars, the KPD, too, repeatedly pointed out to its members the need for conspiratorial conduct and stressed the importance of avoiding any written notes because, if discovered, they could be used as incriminating material.[32]

The diary of Wilhelm Scheidler shows just how justified such fears were.[33] Born in 1912 as the son of a bricklayer in Odenwald, Scheidler had completed an apprenticeship in the mayoral office of his home village in the 1930s. At that time he also joined the Social Democratic Party of Germany (SPD) and held offices for the party. In fall 1932, he had started a diary, which he kept on loose-leaf paper on a daily basis. In spring 1933 after the Reichstag fire, when the terror against the workers' movement reached his local area as well, Scheidler and his father collected "all Social Democratic writings, . . . stowed them in boxes," and hid them in storage. Stuff that seemed even more dangerous to him ("my party-political books and important documents") he packed into a "small wooden box," which his "father walled . . . up in a dry and protected, extremely secure place." Scheidler also put all "109 sheets of my diary" that he had written thus far into the box.[34] We learn about this from sheet number 110, on which Scheidler continued his diary that very same day. However, faced with the risk of searches and confiscations, he undertook not to "describe everything openly" in his diary. He did not know "whether someday the police will search my place and I don't want to let any material fall into their hands through my diary."[35] His efforts were in vain. In September, the police conducted searches against local political opponents and turned up the diary. Scheidler was arrested and brought to the Osthofen concentration camp, which had been set up in a former gunpowder factory. His diary was confiscated; the document, which had been written in shorthand, was transcribed; and on the basis of the entries, Scheidler was charged before the special court with making "treacherous statements." His diary remained with the court files, where it survives to this day.[36]

The broad lack of records from the proletarian resistance of 1933 heavily underscores the importance of *Our Street* as a novel composed at that time. To be sure, the book can hardly be read as a reliable source for the factual history of the Wallstraße in Berlin. But precisely because it was still 1933–1934 when Petersen deliberately rendered his records in literary form, *Our Street* can lend expression to an experience of the seizure of power for which hardly any contemporary sources survive. For the social history of the establishment of National Socialism, the novel documents a fundamentally important—even if very specific—perspective on the Nazi seizure of power. The book makes its readers highly aware of this. While taking a walk, the narrator, Jan, notices the large swastika flags on the Charlottenburg town hall. As he runs past the town hall, the "street pavements are crowded with the busy everyday life. No one looks up at the flags. We are the only ones who always blaze with rage at the sight. Do the others just accept things as they are? Has it already become part of their lives, something that seems unchangeable?"[37] The narrator repeatedly occupies himself with attitudes and thoughts of people outside his own communist circle, but, because of the narrative's pronounced subjectivity, they remain just as unfathomable to the reader as to the young communists themselves. One can appreciate this as the author's insight into the restricted nature of one's personal perspective but also recognize it as a political decision to give a voice precisely to the victims of the seizure of power—which opens up an illuminating perspective: no other point of view so lucidly renders the consequences of the onset of National Socialist rule for everyday life in Germany than that of the fled, arrested, tortured, and slain victims of the seizure of power. Yet Petersen's meticulous description of the changes in the social environment of his protagonists—changes that decisively facilitated the terror of the state and forced into social isolation those unwilling or unable to adapt to the new requirements—is precisely what points to the need to also ask about other perspectives. Only by surveying different points of view can we understand why contemporaries like Jan Petersen, with lives previously so well integrated in "their streets," lost their connection to their surrounding world within just a few short weeks.

2. A "National Uprising": The Start of Nazi Rule as a Suprapartisan Event

Otmar Krämer* did not write in his diary every day. Born in 1879 as the son of a district judge, he started studying for a law degree at age nineteen but soon had to give up his studies because of illness, whereupon he completed an apprenticeship in agronomy. From 1908 to the late 1920s, he worked as a domain counselor on various manors until the economic crisis in the agricultural sector left him unemployed. In the early 1930s, without regular employment, he lived with his wife and four children in Weimar. He prefaced his diary, which he had been keeping since 1916, with a quote emphasizing that when writing a diary one must "drop any aspiration for orderliness and regularity," and indeed his entries, which covered occupational, family, and political developments alike, had no regular rhythm.[38]

The fourth volume of his diary, which he started in 1932, contains three entries for that year: April 24 and 27, and a final entry for September 21. In earlier periods too, his entries were often months apart, with retrospective summaries reporting on the intervening periods. So the fact that he might make a new entry in early February 1933 did not simply follow as a matter of course, and indeed, the author clearly noted that the timing was not an accident. This time he prefaced his usual summary with a preamble: "Before I continue my chronicle today on February 3, 1933, I must mention the event which is the first in twenty years to have filled the vast majority of the German Volk with national passion and enthusiasm again, after the 30th of July 1914, the 30th of January 1933, the day on which Adolf Hitler became the Volk's chancellor of the German Reich!" Krämer knew he was witnessing a historical turning point—and that awareness made him fetch his diary at this particular moment in early February 1933. He and other diarists felt that this political event could only be properly grasped through historical comparisons. When he came to speak about it in his thematically organized entry, he noted, "We stand at the beginning of a new time. The period when the nationalist German man was a second-rate man, the time when the National Socialist was seen as a nationalist hothead, is over. He is in power and he has the will to keep and extend this position of power, despite all—and I mean all—opposition."[39]

Otmar Krämer's enthusiasm about Hitler's appointment as Reich chancellor is not surprising, for in his diary he had previously spoken out in support of Hitler and the NSDAP. His sons, members of the Hitler Youth, went to school in "brown shirts" with his approval, even 1932 when the Hitler Youth was banned. And like Krämer, on or shortly after January 30, 1933, other NSDAP supporters and members rejoiced in their diaries over Hitler's appointment as Reich chancellor. "At noon we listened to the radio, for starters: *Hitler Reich chancellor!* We are completely over the moon!" noted Karoline Buttmann in her diary on January 30, 1933; she was the wife of Rudolf Buttmann, who with the reestablishment of the NSDAP in 1925 was accepted under membership number 4.[40] Max Dingler, a zoologist who had actually already joined the NSDAP in 1922 and participated in the 1923 Hitler putsch, outlined the date of January 30, 1933, in his pocket calendar with a decorative frame embellished with a swastika. The words "Hitler Reich chancellor" disclosed his reasons for making this date stand out so prominently; then his notes (which were always brief) went on to express his disappointment at having "watched out in vain for an SA march."[41] And Helmut Böhme, a bookbinder who had been an NSDAP member since 1923 and a Kreisleiter in Freiberg (Saxony) since 1929, noted, "The first decisive victory has now been achieved. On January 30 our highest leader was appointed Reich chancellor. On the evening of this historical day, hundreds of thousands of SA and Stahlhelm comrades proceeded past the palace of the Reich chancellor. Boisterous shouts of Heil were brought forth for Hitler and Hindenburg again and again. An entire Volk breathes a sigh of relief. The rising of the nation begins!"[42] In his next entry, written after the Reichstag election in early March, it was clear to Böhme that "the victory has been fought for and won! On March 5, 288 National Socialists were elected to the German Reichstag. This means that the disgrace of November 1918 has been expunged from German history. . . . Germany has awakened!"[43]

On January 30, 1933, members and supporters of the NSDAP not only celebrated a victory but also spoke about a historical day. This had less to do with their particular clairvoyance about future developments than with the expectations that the National Socialist movement had already stoked among its supporters during the Weimar Republic. Although the statements made in National Socialist brochures, texts, and speeches during the Weimar Republic were remarkably scattered, they very much shared a "certain attitude toward the future," a "form of appropriating the future . . . which assumed a fundamental upheaval that was to be brought about through the movement's own actions."[44] Nazi propaganda repeatedly fueled "expectations of an epochal change," which would start with the attainment of power. Thus it had already declared in advance that the date of the accession to power would be a historical event.[45] Typified, for example, by the proclamation "Germany has awakened!" found in many diaries, these expectations shaped the way NSDAP supporters and members reacted to January 30, 1933. "Germany awaken!" had been one of the NSDAP's key slogans in its political conflicts during the Weimar Republic, especially for the SA. "Through the metaphor of sleeping and wakefulness, respectively, night and day," the slogan was supposed to elucidate the "contrast between the present and future after the turning point," which needed to be created through a successful struggle for political power.[46] With Hitler's appointment as Reich chancellor, this oft-invoked future now seemed to have become the present; Germany seemed to have actually "woken up," and the realization of the movement's ideological objectives appeared within reach. This was how the new regime, with its pronouncements in spring 1933, repeatedly ascribed historical significance to itself.

Against this background, the diary entries of NSDAP members and supporters for January 30, 1933, should be understood primarily as evidence for the ideological character of their authors' perceptions; they cannot be read straightforwardly as a description of the society's reaction to the start of National Socialist rule. By no means was the "entire Volk" gripped by "nationalist passion and enthusiasm" in a way that compared to the mythical August Experience (that is, the Spirit of 1914), as claimed by Otmar Krämer and Helmut Böhme. Even just a glance at the fled, arrested, tortured, and slain victims of spring 1933 makes this clear. Accordingly, on January 30, 1933, many diarists described themselves not as enthusiastic but, in the words of the union functionary Theodor Thomas, for example, as "completely stunned" by Hitler's appointment.[47] A comment by Stephan Weidenbach, a teacher and town archivist in Andernach, no doubt better captured the spectrum of the immediate reactions of German society to the appointment of the new Reich chancellor: "Today at noon it became known that Adolf Hitler has been appointed Reich chancellor. For this reason disappointed but also joyous faces. Individual houses with flags."[48]

Nevertheless, in their diaries in spring 1933, NSDAP supporters and members drew on the interpretive figure of a "rising of the nation" to make note of the actual start of National Socialist rule. They deemed these concepts, configured in advance, appropriate for describing their own experience of the seizure of power. Despite its ideological content, this slogan was quite well suited for describing much of the social reaction outside the National Socialist movement as well. By January 30, 1933, enthusiasm about the accession of Hitler's government already reached far beyond long-term members and supporters of the NSDAP. Walter Lindemann, for example, the medical doctor born in 1906 who in spring 1933 participated in "raids on communists" while seeking to join the SA, noted on January 30, 1933, in block letters (in a diary otherwise written in Sütterlin script), *"Adolf Hitler Reich chancellor!"* and "Herr Reich President von Hindenburg appointed Adolf Hitler as Reich chancellor this morning. Vice chancellor: *Franz v. Papen,* Interior: *Frick,* Exterior: as before v. Neurath, *Economy: Privy Councillor Hugenberg, Labor: Seldte.*—Today I witnessed a *world historical day.* In the evening I went to the Wilhelmstraße and there were tens of thousands of people who cheered Hindenburg and Hitler. . . . It was an uplifting sight, all of Berlin on its feet and all of the people, whether workers, white-collar employees, students, all gripped by the one national fire: fatherland. Let us pray to God that there now is a turn in the fate of Germany."[49] Luise Solmitz likewise celebrated the new government. Born in 1889, she graduated from teachers' college in 1910 but only worked as a teacher until 1919, and in the early 1930s, she lived as a housewife with her husband and daughter in Hamburg. On January 30, 1933, she wrote, "*Hitler* is *Reich chancellor!* And what a cabinet! . . . Hitler, Hugenberg, Seldte, Papen!!! On each of them hangs a large part of my German hope. National Socialist élan, German Nationalist reason, the apolitical Stahlhelm, and Papen, whom we have not forgotten. . . . Huge torchlight procession in front of Hindenburg and Hitler by National Socialists and Stahlhelm, who are finally, finally, going together again. This is a memorable 30th of January."[50]

In the final years of the Weimar Republic, both Walter Lindemann and Luise Solmitz had repeatedly discussed the NSDAP in their diaries, frequently expressing their sympathy but also their displeasure. For their part, they aligned themselves with other parties on the conservative right. In the Reichstag election of 1932, Lindemann had voted for the DNVP, and Solmitz had supported the left-liberal German Democratic Party before she too turned more strongly to the DNVP. Correspondingly, in their diaries on January 30, 1933, they not only celebrated the victory of the National Socialist movement but also rejoiced over the cabinet, which consisted of leading politicians from the conservative right. Pressured by right-wing conservative politicians, Reich President Hindenburg had finally declared his willingness to appoint Hitler as Reich chancellor, but only under the precondition that the majority of ministers in the coalition government would not be NSDAP members. This tactic of boxing in Hitler and the NSDAP within a broad coalition of national conservative politicians from various organizations and "taming" them in accordance with conservative interests had been deliberately pursued primarily by Franz von Papen, who belonged to the cabinet as the Reich chancellor's deputy, and Alfred Hugenberg, the chairman of the DNVP, who as Reich minister of economics, agriculture, and food now held one of the cabinet's most important posts. To be sure, this attempt at conservative "taming" had already failed by spring 1933 because Hitler dominated the government's work from the outset. However, the setup, which in principle provided for a coalition government, was critically important to Germans' perceptions of the new regime.[51]

Walter Lindemann and Luise Solmitz saw the start of National Socialist rule as an event reaching far beyond the National Socialist movement, and they wanted to take part. Luise Solmitz and her husband wanted to publicly express their sympathy with the new government already on January 31, 1933. But unlike their neighbors, they did not hang a swastika flag from their window. Instead they chose the old black-white-red flag of Imperial Germany, the hallmark of right-wing conservatives during the Weimar Republic.[52] Their public show of sympathy was primarily meant for the national conservative part of the new government. In her diary less than one week later, Solmitz justified her enthusiasm not by citing the appeal of National Socialism but with the words, "My ideal was, remains Germany; where I see that championed is where I go."[53] Time and again she emphasized in her diary how her approval in spring 1933 hinged precisely on this collaboration between conservatives and the extreme right. On February 28, she praised the "unique division of labor" of the new government's different "pillars," which allowed von Papen "to contend for the people that Hitler does not get" and win them over for the government.[54] Looking ahead to the elections of early March, Solmitz was hoping for a "majority... with list 1 and 5."[55] Situated on list 1, the NSDAP, with 43.9 percent, actually failed to win its own majority in the election. Thus Hitler remained dependent on a coalition with the electoral alliance Battle Front Black-White-Red, which had been formed specifically for this election (list 5, 8 percent) and which mainly comprised his governing partners, the DNVP and Stahlhelm. Despite large gains for the NSDAP, the election results were rather disappointing for the party's leadership, which was striving for sole power. Yet these results were what allowed contemporaries like Luise Solmitz to celebrate the outcome of the election in the first place. On election day, the family supplemented its black-white-red flag with a swastika pennant, and in her diary Luise Solmitz noted enthusiastically, "A wonderful, an unimagined and intoxicating victory! Majority! Finally. A victory that we all, the fatherland-minded, have won for Hitler."[56]

Walter Lindemann was also hoping in February 1933 that "the Battle Front Black-White-Red (Hugenberg, v. Papen, Seldte) and the National Socialists" would achieve "the absolute majority" and celebrated the electoral outcome because the "German Volk . . . has committed itself with more than 51% to a national government."[57] Other diarists, as well, frequently described the political events of spring 1933 as a "national triumphal march,"[58] "national uprising of the Volk,"[59] or "national revolution."[60] They did not greet all of the political developments with the same enthusiasm as Solmitz and Lindemann, but by using such phrases, they too described the onset of the National Socialist dictatorship admittedly not as a nonpartisan but certainly as a suprapartisan event.

The concept of "national" contained two dimensions of meaning: First, it designated the political orientation of the new government, which was made up of political forces that had already successfully appropriated this concept and made it a defining feature of their programs.[61] Second, however, it also contained the claim that the government's policies were being made for the entire nation and therefore also needed to be supported by all Germans—a claim meant to work both ways. On March 21, 1933, Luise Solmitz wrote in her diary about the tears of joy that she and "all those we spoke to" ("the shopkeeper's wife, the cobbler's wife, the fine-foods dealer") had cried on the Day of Potsdam. In her description, she justified those tears with words attributed to a friend: "Anyone who did not cry at this has no heart in his breast and is not a German."[62] Consistently described by the new Reich chancellor in his initial pronouncements as a collection of "men of national parties and associations," the new government also called itself a "national government" in this double sense: programmatically as a government fundamentally different from the previous governments of the "November parties," which had declared the Weimar Republic and created its constitution; and as a government that transcended parties, borne by the entire nation and working for its weal.[63]

Spread equally by government propaganda from above and through the massive enthusiasm of NSDAP members, Nazi-movement sympathizers, and other supporters of the new government, this interpretation of the appointment of the Hitler government was responsible for the sweeping social dynamics that marked the beginning of National Socialist rule. For as a "national" event, the accession of the new government affected the entire nation and challenged every one of its members to take a stance. In the interplay between the official demands and the social pressure created by supporters' open display of enthusiasm, the interpretation of the beginning of the National Socialist dictatorship as a "national uprising of the entire Volk" generated a dynamic within which all contemporaries were ultimately confronted by the question of how they personally stood toward the new regime, not necessarily as early as spring 1933 but in the course of 1933–1934.

The Dynamics and Scope of the Demand for Commitment

While they seem unremarkable at first glance, the traces left behind by the seizure of power in apolitical diaries particularly testify to these dynamics inherent to the start of National Socialist rule. Franz Wallner, for example, was born in 1892 and was basically unemployed; in Munich in the early 1930s, he tried to stay afloat with various odd jobs: as an installer, security guard, warehouse worker, and delivery driver. He had kept a diary since 1910, using it chiefly to keep track of his private income and expenses. For this purpose, Wallner used large-format accounting books, but he entitled them "Memorial," indicating his concern with recording daily events to remember them later on. He registered the stages of the day with extremely brief notes. For January 31, 1933, for example, he noted, "Midday on foot to get stamped [for unemployment benefits], after that to the town hall. Given abatement for citizen tax of 18 M, after that to the revenue office. Turned in tax card for 1932, after that to the Möllner family, with them visited the Göppel family, then back to Möllner, later Herr Göppel came." On this particular day, however, he added an unusual annotation: "At three in the afternoon Adolf Hitler became Reich Chancellor."[64] Politics and political events had actually never played a role in Wallner's diary writing before. To be sure, entries made during the Weimar Republic sometimes noted the Reichstag and presidential elections, but this happened for fewer than half of the election days, and the act of voting also made these political events part of Wallner's day. However, his diary had never mentioned the accession to power of a new Reich chancellor. The appointment of Adolf Hitler was the first such event that Wallner deemed important enough to record in his "Memorial"—albeit most likely after the fact, as suggested by the date, which is one day off.

But this annotation was not the end of it. In spring 1933, the diary also noted the attendance of a "Hitler rally" on February 24; the Reichstag election on March 5, in which Wallner voted for the Bavarian People's Party; the electoral victory of the NSDAP; the first "meeting of the Reichstag in Potsdam"; Adolf Hitler's forty-fourth birthday; the "Day of National Labor"; and an excursion to the Dachau concentration camp, which Wallner visited as part of a bicycle trip on Easter Sunday.[65] Wallner always recorded these political events with extremely brief remarks and without any personal commentary, and the scattered notes tell us nothing about what he thought of them. But read as a whole and in contrast to his earlier entries, they show that Wallner continuously kept tabs on political events related to the start of National Socialist rule and found them sufficiently worth remembering that he recorded them in his diary. No other political event in the truly eventful developments since the 1920s had ever managed to enter his largely apolitical diary in any comparable fashion.

The same applied to numerous diaries from 1933. In spring 1933 and the following months, many authors confronted political developments with much greater intensity than during the final years of the Weimar Republic. In the course of 1933, even diaries formally meant for other purposes were frequently used to reflect on political developments. Thus, for example, Curt Weber*, a businessman from Freiburg born in 1880, and Wolf Busse*, a bank employee in Berlin seven years his junior, both prefaced their travel diaries for the summer holidays of 1933 with a paragraph related to political events in Germany.[66] The political developments of 1933 also insinuated themselves into parental diaries for small or unborn children.[67] In the case of the diary of Ludwig Bröcking*, they even made their way into a project that had long since been completed. To celebrate special wedding anniversaries in the family, the Düsseldorf lawyer had prepared a typewritten transcription of his war and postwar diary, which he had professionally printed in a small run and bound as books. Undoubtedly costing a pretty penny, the work was finished in December 1932, but in March 1933, Bröcking decided to append an afterword on the current state of affairs because "particularly in these times, we again seem to be standing at the turning point in the fate and history of the German fatherland."[68]

The diaries clearly show time and again that this increased attentiveness was not just due to the rapid events themselves. Another major factor was the demand that individuals personally commit to the new regime, which brought political events directly to bear on contemporaries. The introductory paragraph in the travel diary of the Freiburg businessman Weber, for example, began deliberately with the comment that "Germany's national uprising under Hitler has naturally brought much conflict and commotion for all non-indifferent persons because of the internal realignment it caused." Evidently the author also saw himself as part of this group, for instead of just going on to review the political events since January 1933, Weber also briefly summarized the changes to his own personal attitude toward the new government.[69] In much the same way, in his afterword the Düsseldorf lawyer Bröcking first surveyed the political development of the National Socialist movement up to the electoral victory in the Reichstag election of March 5, 1933, but after that he explained in detail his own stance regarding the new regime.[70]

Even diarists writing in the bourgeois tradition—that is, dealing only with the world of internal emotions and deliberately excluding any social and political events—felt pressured to use their writing to clarify their relationship to the new government. Luise Klempt, a Munich fresco painter born in 1889, diligently kept a diary since youth. Her estate includes 176 diaries, which the author used primarily and above all in times of crisis to sort out her emotional world, which was substantially influenced by her love affairs. Klempt had interrupted her diary writing in summer 1931 and then picked it up again in early July 1933. As the painter pointed out in her first entry after the hiatus, during these "two happy years (basically three!)" with her life partner she "no longer had the need to release herself from inner tensions by writing feverishly." She had her "joyful tranquility," and "everything was so even and calm." But the mood was gone now that her partner stood "under the spell of other women again," which this time broke up the relationship.[71] In summer 1933, Klempt wrote of intense struggles with the sorrow and pain caused by the relationship conflict, as she had often done years before.

But against the backdrop of political events, Klempt now doubted whether she should be allowed simply to continue her type of diary writing. "The turbulent world, the 'awakening' of an entire Volk somehow rushes past me. I am ashamed of how much personal heartache fills me up, and yet am much too anchored with my roots in an individualistic age to be able to participate in this collectivism,"[72] she noted in her second entry after resuming her diary.

Then four months later she rationalized her writing style with these words: "So little of the huge upheaval has come through in these pages—I am almost ashamed that the female experience preoccupies me more than all of the external events. Never have political events shaken and agitated me so much that I needed to grapple with them in writing in order to gain clarity of mind. Yes, I am ashamed of myself and before others that this was so, but I cannot undo it and it probably won't be much different in future. Earlier I sometimes tried to describe certain things that lie beyond my personal experience—but I always found this to be a deviation from the essential and ultimately dropped it entirely."[73]

In truth, political events rarely made their way into her diary in the years that followed either, but even just the fact that Luise Klempt felt challenged to justify herself strongly testifies to the pressure arising from the demand that individuals commit themselves to the Nazi regime.

Significantly younger and born in 1905, Artur Streiter reacted in a similar way. As a youth, Streiter had started apprenticing as a tradesman, but he then came into contact with the anarchist movement and in the 1920s lived in various independently organized communes. Here he tried rather unsuccessfully to establish himself as a writer and painter. While Luise Klempt was able to make a living from her fresco painting, Streiter, who unlike Klempt had no artistic training, was primarily dependent on his wife's earnings and state benefits. Although he managed to get a few essays and especially reviews printed in anarchist and other left-wing journals in the 1920s, he was still far from being able to survive on the honorariums. In any case, his more extensive writings—for example, a study on the poems and person of Friedrich Hölderlin, whom he greatly admired—went unpublished. Even so, Streiter insisted on being an artist. "To write a book, be read, respected, earn money"—such were the goals he noted in 1930 in his diary, which was strongly defined by his self-conception as an artist.[74] Rejected texts had come to mean setbacks to his life's ambitions, and he repeatedly wrestled with this in his diary. Yet he also constantly expressed the hope that "at some point the hour will come when I must sit myself down to write, when I need to write about everything that moves me today already." But until this moment "I must report about me, about my life and experience; every hour of the path must be recorded, the path I took toward the work."[75] This was precisely what his diary was for.

Only this self-conception as an artist can explain how the diary of an anarchist like Artur Streiter failed to mention the political events related to the establishment of the National Socialist dictatorship. Instead of discussing the terroristic menace of the seizure of power, the prohibition of the very journals that had previously printed his texts, or the destruction of the anarchist movement, the diary primarily talks about an intense confrontation with literature and art, everyday errands, and financial worries. Emulating the ideal of the reclusive, unworldly poet, Streiter tried to sustain his self-conception beyond the spring of 1933 as well. But the social dynamics of the start of National Socialist rule made this increasingly difficult. In October 1934, he finally acknowledged resignedly in his diary that "in our time there is no possibility of life for those of a Hölderlin nature. It does not allow unworldly lyrical sentimentality. It does not even allow you to have your human emotions. It allows only one-sided 'political decisions.' It demands a completely different 'life ethos'—it demands! What is there left for the poet in this time?—A completely different ardency of emotion, fervor of suffering, of a suffering from this time that has turned away from this time. But then in this time there is no time for him as a poet—no effectiveness—for in the motor noise and noise of military marches there is no room for peacefulness, contemplativeness, meditation, which the poet of course needs."[76]

Hitler's appointment as Reich chancellor on January 30, 1933, led to various different reactions within German society. Some contemporaries rejoiced, others were appalled, and still others hardly felt personally affected at first. In general, however, many Germans paid significantly more attention to the political events of spring 1933 than to the changes of government and other important political events of recent years. However, even those personally uninterested in dealing with Hitler's appointment as Reich chancellor did not remain unaffected by the political developments that it set in motion. On January 30, 1933, the new regime and its enthusiastic supporters saw that the historical event they had longed for had finally arrived, fulfilling their hopes for a fundamental turning point in Germany's development. Accordingly, they understood the start of the National Socialist dictatorship as a "national rising." And for these reasons, they made demands for support and commitment, which they directed to all Germans. In a diary entry just four days after Hitler's appointment, Otmar Krämer formulated this all-embracing claim as follows: "Today everyone in Germany, whether friend, enemy, or neutral party, is forced to take a position on National Socialism."[77] As a result of this demand, the start of Nazi rule developed dynamics that ultimately challenged all contemporaries to determine their relationship to the new regime. At some point even people who, like Artur Streiter, resolutely tried to avoid contending with the new political circumstances were confronted by the question of their stance toward the new regime. Conditioned by expectations bred before 1933, the interpretation of the seizure of power as a "national uprising" that would lay hold of the entire Volk was self-affirming, decisively helping ensure that the start of the Nazi dictatorship actually affected the entire people. In late December 1934, just a few weeks after Artur Streiter had acknowledged his loss of hope in his diary, Christoph Ahrens*, born in Hamburg in 1878, looked back on the year as it drew to a close. Ahrens had been a seaman until the early 1920s, when health reasons forced him to stop, and now he was trying his hand at painting and writing. He too wrote about his efforts to take his first steps as an artist but discussed political events more directly than Streiter. "*Politically* the year was marked by the expansion and consolidation of the authority of the Third Reich. Important successes were achieved in foreign policy," Ahrens noted in his review. In conclusion, he declared, "One is affected today by all of these processes. Today everyone is in one form or another pulled into the vortex of events, and if he wants to go on living he must swim to survive."[78]

3. In the "Vortex of Events": Positioning as a Political and Biographical Problem

In the late Weimar Republic, the National Socialist movement had been just one—albeit important—political force among others that many people frequently dealt with in their diaries. During these years, taking a position toward National Socialism (if one did not want to come out as a supporter of the movement) meant expressing a political opinion from a distance guaranteed by the Weimar constitutional state. Freedom of opinion, freedom of religion and conscience, and the inviolability of the home were written into the 1919 Weimar Constitution as fundamental principles. Together with other legal regulations, these principles ensured that a person's political orientation remained a private matter: an individual could decide whether and how to express oneself on political phenomena such as the National Socialist movement. Accordingly, statements about the NSDAP made before 1933 mainly show up in diaries whose authors generally used them to deal with political events. A typical example is the diary of Friedhelm Müller*: under the heading "My Position on National Socialism," it assessed the programs and policies of the NSDAP in eight enumerated sections. Born in 1875 and working as the rector of a secondary school in a small town in Saxony since 1925, Müller wrote this appraisal in summer 1932 because "a few people who are close to me . . . have joined National Socialism" and he therefore felt the "need" to "justify my basic rejection."[79] Until 1933, this was the kind of response prompted by the question about one's personal position toward National Socialism: a political statement, a personal political assessment of the NSDAP and its leading politicians made from a distance. Admittedly, most Germans never formulated their response in such an explicit and categorical way but instead expressed it as commentary occasioned by specific events.

But this changed sharply in the first half of 1933 because political developments gave the question about one's personal "position on National Socialism" a fundamentally different form. Since all other political organizations were either banned or made to fall in line, the NSDAP, as the previous representative of National Socialism, moved into a relatively unclarified liminal position: it was "institutionally separate from the state administration and personnel-wise merged with the state through various personal unions at the leadership level."[80] Thus when people contemplated their position on National Socialism, they also faced the question of what precisely they were meant to take a position on. Was the new government a representative of National Socialism and thus a particular political actor? Or did it represent the state and nation as a whole? Even after the early phase of the Nazi dictatorship, the Reich government acted equally as a National Socialist regime that pursued a specific political program and also as the representative of the entire nation. This was publicly underlined, for example, by the fact that (until 1937) many ministries continued to be led by ministers who were not members of the NSDAP. At issue was one's commitment to the new government, but whether one viewed this government as the representative of National Socialism or of the nation made an important difference and therefore strongly shaped the associated political deliberations.[81]

The appointment of Hitler as Reich chancellor, however, did not only change the entity to which people were supposed to determine their relationship. Even more decisive, since spring 1933, one's own position was no longer merely a question of political assessment but rather one of personal commitment. Until 1933, one's relationship to National Socialism was considered an individual political opinion. But the new government demanded that Germans make a "commitment" to the government. To be sure, political arguments and assessments continued to play an important role, but the question of one's relationship to National Socialism was raised in much wider terms, ultimately affecting the entire person. As diaries from 1933–1934 frequently make clear, aligning oneself with the government meant much more than having a good, approving opinion about it.

In mid-July, for example, Karl Möhring*, born in 1905, began a diary entry with these emblematic words: "A new page in the book of history has opened up, both for the history of Germany and for my own history."[82] This was not the first entry that dealt with the author's personal relationship to National Socialism. Möhring was a pastor's son who in the early 1930s studied various subjects in the humanities in Göttingen. In his diary, which he started in 1928, he had already discussed political developments and frequently recorded his assessments of the National Socialist movement before 1933. Even though he also held firm right-wing conservative and authoritarian positions, Möhring criticized the movement clearly and at length. In light of these discussions, when the Nazis first took power he was initially uncertain about his personal position on National Socialism. As late as the end of April 1933, he still predicted that in the future he would "essentially not arrive at a different stance on National Socialism and Hitler."[83]

But less than three months later, in the entry that began with the comment about the opening of a new page in the "book of history," he confessed that "in the wake of the events of the last weeks" he needed to "revise his judgment" and that "in the course of May" he had declared himself to be an "advocate of National Socialism." The entry clearly shows that Möhring had found this very difficult. He explicitly took up the contradiction between his new position and what he had said earlier in his diary about the NSDAP, emphasizing that his current "position on National Socialism . . . seems to stand in stark contrast to my earlier statements, but it is not."[84] To counter this impression, he wrote a wide-ranging argument showing that his problem was not due to any change of his political opinion. Indeed, it was relatively easy to reconcile many of the political assessments he had made before 1933 with the new government. What bothered Möhring was the question of whether, given his change of stance, he could still trust his own political judgment.

In the following weeks, he frequently returned to this point. When he drew up his annual review in early 1934, it strongly voiced the uncertainty that taking a position on National Socialism had triggered in him. "One leaves the year 1933 smarter than when one entered, and hopefully many have entered the new year with this realization. Because everyone is capable of learning much that is new, regardless whether he is a National Socialist or not," Möhring wrote as he began his review. The detailed paragraph dedicated to his "purely personal position on the political events of the year 1933" reveals that this assessment was largely about himself. The political events "naturally had to make a strong impression on me as well, since the laws of nature seemed to have suddenly reversed themselves. In the beginning it seemed to me almost as when mosquitoes fly into a burning candle. Should I have so fundamentally deceived myself with my judgment?"[85] This fear was precisely what fed Möhring's self-doubt. His problem with his commitment to the Nazi regime did not arise because he was unable to bridge his political differences with National Socialism. What bothered Möhring was what such a commitment to the Nazi regime meant for his previous life.

To align themselves with the new regime, many people had to revise their former political judgments and evaluate National Socialism more positively than before. But a modified, affirmative political statement was not enough. Instead, commitment to the Nazi regime was combined with questions that, before 1933, had never mattered when determining one's personal relationship to National Socialism. Above all, it raised the problem of how a new affirmation of National Socialism fit within one's own life. Many people, when taking a position on the new regime, began to renegotiate their views about previous and future biographical developments against the background of current political events: How would a potential commitment to the Nazi regime relate to one's previous political attitudes and opinions? And what significance would this have for one's personal future? Many people experienced the start of National Socialist rule not only as a political change but also as a personal turning point, an event that opened "a new page in the book of the history . . . for the history of Germany and for my own."[86]

Much like Karl Möhring, in the context of establishing their position on the Nazi regime in 1933–1934, other diarists not only thought about the new regime but also reflected on themselves and their previous political opinions. In November 1934, Walter Lindemann, the Berlin doctor who on January 30, 1933, had been among the spectators of the torchlight procession in the Wilhelmstraße, recorded his "joyful satisfaction and . . . true pride" in having taken "the straight völkisch path since 1922 . . . strictly nationalist, völkisch, and antisemitic, illuminated by a reverence for God, without which there is nothing."

As evidence for this, he copied three of his own diary entries from fall 1931, in which he commented on the suicide of a figure in the Berlin Sklarek scandal:[87] "This is how the Lord our God punishes the scoundrels who have enriched themselves at the expense of the poorest of the poor, the Barmats, Sklareks, and whatever all of them are called. Verily, the powder is too dear for them. One should erect a proper pedestal for them and string them all up on it. Thus each morning a couple of the Lewis, Cohns, Oppenheimers, Moldenhauers, and whatever all of them are called. . . . One should best hang them up in all of the busy places in Berlin and let them hang until they have rotted, and underneath it should read: This is how the fatherland punishes its traitors."

Commenting in 1934, Lindemann wrote, "When I read these lines, I believe that I probably did not need to adjust myself in the new Reich, the way thousands, indeed hundreds of thousands, indeed almost millions of Germans had to do, those who were enthusiastic supporters of the Center Party, the German People's Party, Social Democrats and Communists. Where are they now?"[88] In his diary Lindemann had in fact repeatedly commented on developments in the Weimar Republic from a nationalistic, right-wing conservative point of view, but back then he had not been a member of the NSDAP and had voted for the DNVP in elections. Looking back from 1934, Lindemann nonetheless perceived a continuity in his political convictions that linked his past political opinions to his present approval of the new regime, which he also adhered to on an organizational level by having joined the SA in summer 1933.

A similar claim of biographical continuity appeared in the comment "My idea was, is, remains Germany," written by Luise Solmitz in her diary in spring 1933. Her statement did not just describe the distinctive nature of the government's political orientation. Rather, Solmitz built on it by adding that "today it no longer seems conceivable" to her that she once associated this ideal with the German Democratic Party "as the largest bourgeois party."[89] In this way Solmitz, too, expressly emphasized that her current enthusiasm was consistent with her earlier attitudes, even though it might seem otherwise. Her mother, on the other hand, whose letters Luise Solmitz copied into her diary, had voted for the DNVP during the elections of the Weimar Republic, and her earlier political opinions complicated matters for her when she took a position on the new regime. Admittedly, the "gigantic upheaval" and "revolution from the right" made a big impression on her. "One can only be amazed," she wrote in early March 1933, "by how bloodlessly everything took place and how one knew how to render the Communists harmless. They walked all over the earlier governments and became increasingly impudent."[90] Nonetheless, in spring 1933 she still could not make a commitment. In the elections on March 5, 1933, she "did not vote for Hitler. I cannot change my convictions that fast, like a dress."[91]

Other people assessed the new regime in largely positive terms yet held political convictions that kept them from committing to National Socialism. For example, this clearly applied to Ludwig Bröcking, the Düsseldorf lawyer who had his diaries of 1914 to 1923 transcribed and printed. As he wrote in his belatedly added afterword, during the Reichstag election in early March 1933, he himself had "again voted for the Center Party with my entire family. Why?" In his detailed reply to his own question, he began by stressing that his "records on all of the preceding pages"—referring to the diary of 1914 to 1923—clearly show that he had "always with hot fervor been aligned with and fought for the program items that are now being highlighted by the National Socialist Hitler Party." Accordingly, in 1933 he had "every reason now to follow the National Socialist movement or join the . . . Battle Front 'Black-White-Red.'" He justified his failure to do so by first pointing out isolated differences with the new regime's domestic policies. "Mainly I remained with the Center Party because in all of the undulations of the daily struggle I am still too metaphysically inclined. I could not and cannot leave the party in the lurch that *by itself* defended the rights of Catholics and my religion ('Kulturkampf') throughout the past, especially now when it is being so furiously stormed." While clearly noting the political conflict between the new regime and the Center Party, Bröcking did not use it to justify the way he voted. After all, he strongly stressed his political proximity to the Nazi regime. He was prevented from "following the National Socialist movement" by a personal obligation stemming from his earlier relationship to the Center Party.[92]

Biographical Reflections: Looking to the Past and Future

When searching for their position, many people were more deeply concerned with what they envisioned for the future than with how they could reconcile an affirmation of the Nazi regime with their previous life trajectory. Sometimes the future became apparent when they looked back. Bröcking, for example, finalized his argument with the general conclusion that "whoever, as a Catholic, loves his Church and religion, today he cannot yet vote for any party other than the Center Party."[93] He thus left himself open to the possibility of a different position in the future. So did the mother of Luise Solmitz, who wrote in her letter, "I voted German National [Deutschnationale Volkspartei] again, could not decide for Hitler. That will probably still come."[94] People perceived the start of National Socialist rule as a time of fundamental change—as a moment when, in the words of Bröcking, "we . . . stand once more at the turning point of the fate and history of the German fatherland"[95]—and related that to their own lives as well; they could only understand their stance toward the regime as a snapshot in time, as a transitory phenomenon.

A large number of people expected major future changes in their private spheres as well, and many tied this expectation to concrete hopes for betterment and the realization of their own life plans. Such was the case with Erich Rahmacher*, a postal employee from southern Germany born in 1890, who at Christmas in 1933 started keeping a diary again. "Some might naturally laugh about it, hearing that an 'old' boy of 43 years is starting to write a diary again. . . . I don't mind, I am writing anyway," Rahmacher wrote to begin his first entry. He went on: "He whose heart is full, his mouth runneth over! I have found a connection again, connection to my beloved paddling and to the Punch and Judy show—and all that goes with it. And a connection to the big Hitler thing! That is probably the most exhilarating." Rahmacher had already been an enthusiastic puppeteer and water sports enthusiast in the 1920s, and he saw the "connection to the big Hitler thing" primarily as an opportunity to pursue these hobbies again as a Hitler Youth supervisor. Rahmacher admittedly pointed out that he did not want to "personally obtain any sort of advantages." But he wanted to "work [again] in my areas with youth and for youth" and thus expected that for "the next 10 or 20 years [I] would likely be allowed . . . to live the best days of my life. I am on cloud nine and I have probably never enjoyed being alive as much as I do now. I have plans! I have a passion for work—I would never have believed that I would ever be able to go at something again with such enthusiasm."[96]

Rahmacher linked very specific life plans to the start of National Socialist rule, and he fulfilled them in the years that followed by touring local Hitler Youth chapters throughout Germany with puppet shows and by serving as a water-sports instructor for the Hitler Youth. In contrast, the hopes that Gisela Brandt* attached to the new regime in 1933 were admittedly rather vague, but this made them no less intense. In the early 1930s, Brandt, born in 1895, lived with her husband and children in Dortmund in what were financially difficult circumstances for the family. In early 1932, the Brandt family renewed their attempts to get on their feet economically. With financial assistance from Gisela's mother, they opened a store, which was supposed to secure their livelihood. But business was bad. Time and again, Gisela Brandt complained in her diary about low turnover and money worries. "If we would just be able to see over the hill," she noted with resignation that summer. "We are so fed up with it. One must give up everything; one has to do without everything." The growing anxieties ate away at Brandt, who increasingly lost hope and confidence and repeatedly wrote that she and her husband had "firmly resolved to depart this life."[97] At the end of the year, they finally had to give up on the store, which left the family without an income. "Today we spent the last of our money," Gisela noted in mid-January 1933. "Now we just have mother's alms. This thought makes us both crazy."[98]

When the new government was appointed a few days later, she drew from it reassurance for herself and her family. "Hitler has been Reich Chancellor for 14 days. I now have a little more hope for a better future. For now we have let go a little of the suicidal thoughts," she noted in her diary in mid-February.[99] Not that her financial distress eased over the next few weeks or months—she still spoke about it at length in her diary. Yet she associated the start of National Socialist rule with hopes that her own circumstances would improve. These hopes found their way into her writing: "I am no longer living for myself, just for the children now, and for some time have rid myself of all suicidal thoughts, if I do not want to leave the children alone in the world and because I have the hope that it will one day be better for our children. Adolf Hitler is working diligently on Germany's renewal and I place all my hopes on him. Of course, we ourselves will no longer get much from this, but the children."[100]

Like Erich Rahmacher and Gisela Brandt, many people in 1933 hoped that the start of the Nazi dictatorship would lead to private betterment. The extent to which they particularly tied hopes of economic improvement to the start of National Socialist rule has frequently been emphasized by scholars, especially in relation to the massive wave of people joining the NSDAP between February and April 1933. In spring 1933, the NSDAP accepted approximately 1.6 million new members before the party stopped admitting newcomers in early May in an effort to control the "massive rush."[101]

Economic motives and attempts to benefit professionally from NSDAP membership undisputedly played a major role here; correspondingly, the masses of so-called Märzgefallene (Victims of March) have usually been seen as evidence for the "degree of the opportunism" that gripped German society in spring 1933.[102] Arguments against such an interpretation have variously insisted that one cannot simply "impute to all applicants the motive of pure opportunism, that is, the unhesitating exploitation of a trend to further one's own interests," and that, "naturally, convinced National Socialists, who for whatever motives had not yet affiliated themselves with the party, also joined."[103]

In light of diaries such as those of Erich Rahmacher and Gisela Brandt, however, I feel that questions about the degree to which economic or political motives determined decisions to join the NSDAP in spring 1933 should be reconsidered, because it is a false opposition. Of course there were contemporaries who joined the NSDAP for careerist reasons or otherwise publicly declared their support for National Socialism while concealing their actual political opinions. But the diary entries suggest that linking private life plans to the development of the Nazi regime by no means precluded the decision to join for political considerations.

In much the same way that diarists reconciled their previous political opinions with their new stance toward the Nazi regime in their accounts, so too was the view of their personal future closely related to how they positioned themselves politically. Rahmacher and Brandt committed themselves to the Nazi regime primarily because of private motives, but in both cases this commitment also included a political stance—and this stance was much stronger than what was needed for realizing private life plans within the space for opportunism created by the Nazi regime. Rahmacher did not merely become a member of the Hitler Youth and assume leadership functions there. He spoke firmly about having found a "connection to the big Hitler thing" and expressed support for the new regime in his private diary. Gisela Brandt, whose diary before 1933 had not dealt with politics at all but only with her everyday economic distress and anxieties about the future, acted similarly. In her diary too, the private hopes that she tied to the new regime included a political stance in favor of that regime. In late March, for example, she wrote with enthusiastic approval about the "uplifting celebration" of the "Day of Potsdam": "Parades after parades. And one has a wonderful view of it all from our apartment. The entire city a sea of flags. One is duly celebrating Germany's uprising."[104]

Brandt's political consent was very much motivated by private anxieties and longings, as shown in this entry a few lines later when she related her experience of the Day of Potsdam to her own situation: "There are days that I find fairly joyful because I no longer have the consuming worries. But then old worries come again like the wheel: whether everything will still turn out for the good?"[105] Standing up politically for the new regime was very closely combined with private hopes, which in turn very much depended on the Nazi regime's political success. "It actually all turned out even better than I expected. A summer of work lies behind me, like never before. Success after success," Rahmacher wrote in October 1934, summarizing his involvement thus far with the Hitler Youth. He added emphatically: "I actually have only one worry: the less than favorable overall situation. Politically, economically, internally and externally. If Hitler falls, I will tumble too. I would not be able to start all over again. I am bound to the Hitler Youth in life and death, for better and worse."[106] Diaries like those of Erich Rahmacher and Gisela Brandt suggest that their positions toward the Nazi regime after 1933 should not be viewed simply in terms of the opposition of private and economic motives versus political motives; they should not be casually dismissed as apolitical opportunism or private careerism. Instead, they show how much a person's commitment to the Nazi regime essentially had a dualistic character that called for a statement of political approval and an explanation of how this statement fit within the person's previous and future trajectory.

Hence, the challenge intrinsic to the demand for commitment presented itself to different people with varying degrees of intensity. Whereas Luise Solmitz and Walter Lindemann could respond to this challenge with a few brief comments, someone like Karl Möhring needed to engage in more detailed reflection. How the demand for commitment presented itself to specific individuals and what answers they needed to find depended fundamentally on their biography. On one hand, those who had been members of the NSDAP before 1933 found it easier to align themselves with the Nazi regime in 1933; they needed less discussion because the new regime matched their own political views and the start of the regime could be interpreted as the fulfillment of their life's journey up to that point. On the other hand, people who had taken a distant or negative stance toward the NSDAP before 1933 faced much tougher questions that required greater reflection and more decisions. Thus their diaries, more so than those of others, clearly reveal the profound degree to which these two dimensions determined the position one took toward the new regime. They also allow us to identify the relevance of any differences that depended on whether a person's biographical perspective primarily looked forward or backward. For the decision forced by the demand for commitment was also multidimensional in terms of its biographical element: with this decision, individuals made a determination about what future opportunities they would have in a radically changing society and also about how they viewed their own life.

Erwin Oehl was an artist and author born in Munich in 1907. While establishing a stance toward the new regime in spring 1933, Oehl dealt above all with his personal political past. He had become a Communist in the late 1920s and actively participated in the Communist movement. Thus in spring 1933 he was taken into protective custody. During his time in the Landsberg prison, Oehl adopted a calculated program to cope with solitary confinement, only very gradually allowing himself any small tangible improvements to his prison routine. He did not partake of "*fruit* as a supplement to improve mood and digestion" until two weeks after his arrest; during the first four weeks, he deliberately avoided newspapers; in this context, only "after three weeks" did he begin "with the escalation: the *notebook*. I can now write and at the same time excerpt scientific and technical books."[107] But Oehl chiefly used his notebook to confront the "newly posed [by his imprisonment] *balance sheet* question ... which of course also requires a [?] political section, which I can (may) not do here." Even though he wanted to avoid incriminating himself with the diary, he used it as "a platform ... to critically review *my current relationship to man*."[108] Over the following days, Oehl returned time and again to his previous life and above all scrutinized his political development. Recorded in brief notes, his lengthy retrospective analysis always led to a single point: he finally "recognized that the yoke that compels the individual is put in place primarily by the development of the society; that you don't help everyone—when one helps the individual—but instead the individual when one helps everyone through the foundations of a new higher form of society." Looking back at his previous life, Oehl saw a "granite path of logic" that led from a "parental home" characterized by an "asocial—itself ingeniously embodied—individualism" to "social duty," which for him was actualized in the Communist idea. "A conscientious analysis of the struggles within the society, etc., etc., etc.: and the place has been determined.... I *know* where I belong and have recognized and *decided* this."[109]

Oehl too determined his relationship to the Nazi regime by means of both political and biographical deliberations. From his perspective, his previous development disallowed any position apart from opposition to the new regime—even though he was aware that this decision would have long-lasting consequences for his life plans. The same applied to Fritz Schössel*, a tailor born in 1871 who worked as a porter at the Essen central train station during the Weimar Republic. He had first joined the SPD and later the Communist Party. And he too wound up in protective custody in spring 1933. Schössel did not keep a diary during this period, but when "behind barred windows," he wrote "the beginning of a life sketch," which he filled out sometime after being released from prison.[110] Unlike Oehl, he did not explicitly deal with his stance toward political events, but this was nonetheless accomplished by his retrospective account of his life. Along with recounting his professional career, the life story Schössel told described his journey to the workers' movement. In this way, like Oehl, Schössel confirmed his oppositional political stance. In 1933 he too wanted to hang on to his previous political convictions.

By contrast, Henry Marx, born in 1911, was thoroughly prepared in 1933 to scrutinize his previous life and align his future life plans in accordance with the new regime. Marx, who in the early 1930s was a student in Berlin and was trying his hand at smaller journalistic ventures, worked intensely to break out of the social isolation that had enveloped him since the start of National Socialist rule because of his left-wing political views and Jewish origins. "The era is shaken to its inner core. We ourselves are standing right in thick of it—at the moment as its victims! . . . Private life takes a long step back again; after all, it is coupled to the life of the state, and one lives in a state that only recognizes you as a second-class state citizen, which now also is seen as an honor," Marx wrote in late 1933, describing how the appointment of the new government directly affected him.[111]

He had studied law until spring 1933 but then abandoned his studies in March because of the new regime's massive operation against socialist and Jewish lawyers. In his diary, he expressed frustration because "this decision was forced on me from outside," but with respect to the actual termination of his studies, he commented, "I do not regret it; I might also perhaps have done so of my own accord."[112] Marx tried again and again to find something positive about the consequences political events were having for his life, trying to grasp them as a personal challenge that he wanted to meet. "One can perceive an event, an entire era as pain or an affront, whereby they could become unbearable and probably usually do. But one can also perceive them more as an obstacle, sort of like sports, where you neither let them drive you into a corner nor fill you with rage," he noted soberly in summer 1933.[113]

In this sense, his annual review in early 1934 seemed almost joyful: "Whereas in the previous year I was steering toward an undetermined goal," he noted with regard to his legal studies, "new prospects have now suddenly opened up for me almost overnight. On January 15 [1934] I start working as a trainee in the bank of the Arnhold Brothers." The training period was not going to be easy, Marx wrote. "For the first time I am stepping into the hostile environment. But I have the resolute determination, particularly in these times, to set an example of how, in this land to which one happens to be tied simply by fate, one does not allow oneself to succumb. To me that seems to be the main thing."[114] Marx tried hard to come to terms with the new circumstances; he was willing to extensively change his life plans, and at the same time this changed his political views as well. Still, in May 1933 he had noted in his diary that, because of his leftist convictions, things were easier for him than for the "nationalist Jew," who "will now lose all support if he is expelled from the Volk, which was *his*."[115] But his entries over the following months clearly show that nationalist considerations grew ever more important as the year wore on. "The most severe endurance test," Marx wrote as he concluded his annual review in early 1934, "was imposed on us with regard to our relationship to Germany: for myself I can say that I have taken it on, that in this decisive hour the value of the German fatherland has been revealed to me. Here lies the actual positive aspect of all the events: the nation as a unity is henceforth a fact that all must take into account."[116]

Taking a position toward the new regime was both a political and a biographical decision. And each dimension conditioned the other: in the same way that Karl Möhring's revised political views after 1933 changed how he saw his own past and future, people's existing views about their own past, as in the case of Erwin Oehl, influenced the way they politically positioned themselves toward the Nazi regime. The same applied to plans for one's own future, as set down by Henry Marx. Precisely because these two dimensions inevitably referred to each other, the massive number of personal commitments to the Nazi regime should not be prematurely viewed as private opportunism or apolitical pandering to the new rulers. Insofar as the Nazi regime, together with open displays of enthusiasm by its supporters and sympathizers, pressed hard for people to definitively align themselves and also made it clear that their decision would largely determine their future opportunities in life, the question about their personal relationship to the new regime was critically different from the question about their opinion regarding National Socialism before 1933. Those wanting to escape social isolation or to avoid altering their life plans needed to work on harmonizing their political views about the new regime with their ideas about their previous and future journey through life. At the same time, there was no certainty that everyone who tried to bring them together would succeed. Despite his great efforts, Henry Marx failed in summer 1934 when he was denounced because of a political discussion at work. "If I had thought about the possibility of committing a subversive act even for a moment, I would certainly not have done it, considering the utter fruitlessness," he noted, writing about the incident in hindsight. Nonetheless, he was imprisoned in the Oranienburg concentration camp for two months, which shook his "life to its foundations."[117] There was no guarantee that people's efforts to make a personal commitment—politically and biographically—to the Nazi regime would actually be accepted by the latter. Yet if they did not do so, they would most certainly be choosing social isolation and persecution by the state.

2

THE SEARCH FOR A PERSONAL STANCE TOWARD THE NAZI REGIME

1. "I Am Withdrawing to My Diary Again": Using Diaries to Establish a Position toward the Regime

Diaries of the 1930s document in many different ways the social dynamics that the seizure of power developed from the demand for individual commitment. But often they did not just report on the respective author's challenge to determine a stance toward the new government. Rather, in the 1930s they were themselves an important tool for establishing one's position toward National Socialism. Diaries like that of Hans Maschmann illustrate this especially well. Born in 1887 in Hamburg, Maschmann started his diary in 1905 at the age of eighteen. For him it was part of his adolescent emancipation from his parental home and his intense effort to use education to escape from the proletarian milieu of his upbringing. In contrast to his parents, who first came from rural Schleswig-Holstein to the cosmopolitan city at the end of the nineteenth century because of economic distress, Maschmann was fascinated by intellectual and cultural matters. The diary created a space in which the young man, setting himself apart from his social origins, could test and fashion himself as a budding intellectual.

Having promised to later pay his parents back for two-thirds of his education costs, after grade school and military service he was able to attend a teachers' college and become a Volksschule teacher, which allowed him to pursue his interests in education and culture outside of the diary as well, making the diary less important. Maschmann ceased keeping his diary after completing his teacher training, but he picked it up again for a few months during his war service in 1916. He began writing more regularly again starting in 1922 after completing a short study program and doctorate, made possible by a fully paid leave of absence provided by the city of Hamburg in the interest of upgrading its Volksschule teachers. In 1926 the entries stop again, except for two brief entries added in July 1928, the final ones written during the Weimar Republic. It was only the start of the National Socialist dictatorship that led Maschmann to reach for his diary again in spring 1933.

The fact that this political event moved Maschmann to start writing again was closely related to the political dimension of his alienation from his parental home. In the same year that Maschmann began writing his diary as an eighteen-year-old, he refused for the first time to accompany his parents to church for communion—an event that even thirty years later seemed to him an important step in leaving his religiously dominated and conservative parental home.[1]

In turning away from his parents, Maschmann became a socialist, and in 1918 he participated in the November Revolution as a member of a workers' and soldiers' council; even at the end of the Weimar Republic, he still considered himself to be part of the Social Democratic and Socialist movement, although his direct political involvement had been limited to 1918–1919. Hence Maschmann was not immediately threatened by the massive violence that accompanied the start of National Socialist rule. But he was particularly challenged by the new regime's demand for commitment. In fact, Maschmann struggled intensely with his personal relationship to the Nazi regime. During this time, his diary did not merely mention the determination of his position; rather it was through and with diary writing itself that he struggled to determine where he stood. On March 31, 1933, after a four-year hiatus from writing, the very first sentence he wrote in his diary stated programmatically, "I am withdrawing to my diary again." He continued: "The things as they are happening in recent months, with pomp and bombastic intrusiveness, are not part of the best German minds. But they command the hour, perhaps for years; certainly for as long as the German soul is ordered to be silent."[2]

In his entries over the days that followed, Maschmann also strongly pointed out the massive monitoring of public communications. "The party inquisition is at work everywhere: in the taverns, streetcars, stores, and offices. Everyone takes care not to say a word of criticism for fear of spies. It is advisable to keep silent even with the best of friends."[3] And thus he reached for his diary, where the teacher and self-styled intellectual did anything but keep silent. Though his last lines had been written years before, on March 31, 1933, he began jotting down entries on a daily basis with an almost single-minded purpose: observing political occurrences and determining his own relationship to them. Even though Maschmann would later fall out of the daily rhythm of writing, he continued writing several times a week to grapple with the policies of the regime until long after the war began in 1939. The volume of these entries exceeded his previous diary many times over. Whereas his entries between 1916 and 1928 were frequently interrupted and filled half a notebook, the second half of that notebook only contained the entries for the months from March 1933 to July 1934. Along with this and a second thick volume for the years 1934 and 1935, by the start of the war his closely written notes had filled an additional eleven school notebooks. By the end of the war, the diary had grown by many further volumes, which as a whole document an intense confrontation with political events and the search for his position toward the Nazi regime.

It is not just that Hans Maschmann's diary reflects the start of National Socialist rule in an especially drastic way. Unlike the diaries of the anarchist Artur Streiter, the fresco painter Luise Klempt, or the unemployed Franz Wallner from Munich, which during the first two years of the Nazi dictatorship eventually came to talk about it because of the breakneck pace of political events, in Maschmann's case the start of Nazi rule, with its demand for commitment, did not force its way into a preexisting practice of diary writing. Instead, in spring 1933 Maschmann reacted to the now extant challenge to define one's relationship to the new regime by restarting his writing practice. Against the background of the profound political changes, which made Maschmann feel that it was impossible to go on speaking about politics with others, diary writing became the main instrument with which he sought his own position in the changing political environment.

Hans Maschmann was not alone in this regard. Indeed, many diarists tried to find their relationship to the Nazi regime through their writing, especially during the first years of the National Socialist dictatorship. Fritz Koch, for example, a lawyer born in 1896 who had been a member of the German Democratic Party during the Weimar Republic, began recording his thoughts on the political situation on unbound pieces of paper in spring 1934. "It is now May, 1934. For over a year already, the life of Germans has been under the sign of the swastika and much has changed. Improved?— Deteriorated? Oh, I cannot impartially judge! My feelings say no, no, so loudly that I find it difficult to properly understand the other voices within me and the voices of the environment."⁴ For precisely this reason, Koch struggled for clarity and orientation through the medium of writing, using written discussions to search for not just an emotional but also a rational position toward the new regime. Daniel Lotter, born in 1873 into a Fürth family of gingerbread bakers, started his diary on January 30, 1934, with a similar goal. He had taken over his parents' bakery in the late nineteenth century and still actively worked as a gingerbread baker in the 1930s. He also did not select the date for starting his diary at random. Rather, in his first sentences, Lotter referred directly to the first anniversary of Hitler's appointment as Reich chancellor, taking this occasion to write a commentary on political developments. After that he updated his diary on a regular basis and in further entries repeatedly talked about political events and his own position on matters.⁵

A longtime member of a Freemason lodge, Daniel Lotter was skeptical, much like Hans Maschmann and Fritz Koch. His written analysis of his personal position toward the Nazi regime generally turned on indecisiveness, skepticism, and criticism. Like Hans Maschmann, other authors felt they had been thrown back to their diaries because of the widespread monitoring of public communications and the persecution of both publicly and privately expressed criticism. In fact, right from the outset, the measures of the new regime and the arbitrary and often violent actions of the SA and other local Nazi organizations were not just directed toward combating organized political opponents. They also targeted individual expressions of discontent or critical commentaries. On March 21, 1933, in the shadow of the Day of Potsdam celebrations, the Nazi regime created the statutory and juridical basis for using state power to take action against "untrue or grossly distorted assertions" that "severely harm the reputation of the Reich government or a state government or the parties or associations standing behind these governments" by passing an ordinance "for the defense against treacherous attacks against the government of the national uprising" and setting up "special courts."⁶

In the practice of Nazi rule, these ordinances, later evolving into the so-called Treachery Act, could be used as an "all-purpose weapon against critical statements in everyday life and ... to suppress the exchange of information and opinion."⁷ But existing legal regulations, such as the criminal offense of "gross mischief," were also often used to criminally prosecute everyday expressions of deviating opinion. All told, by 1939 tens of thousands of undesirable expressions had been criminally prosecuted and punished this way.⁸ Yet beyond the threat of imprisonment and fines, the broad demand that people support and commit themselves to the Nazi regime deeply contributed to changing everyday communications on political subjects or driving them into nonpublic spaces. For example, Hans Maschmann in his first entries already referred to the countless dismissals in the civil service and commercial sector. As a result, he noted, "everyone is worried about his job and therefore keeps silent so as not to lose his bread."⁹ In this situation, diaries actually offered a protected space where people could formulate thoughts about the political situation that might have resulted in consequences if expressed publicly.

After 1945, when publishing their (revised) diaries from the National Socialist period, many German authors and politicians emphasized this reason for writing. As reported by forewords and publication announcements, their records were created, as one author put it, "in opposition to my hostile environment, which threatened to swallow me up at any moment." He explained, "I wrote it out of an intellectual survival instinct."¹⁰ According to interpretations circulating especially within literati discussions related to the publication of Ernst Jünger's wartime diary *Strahlungen* in 1949, "in the totalitarian state," the diary represented the "only possible conversation."¹¹ Regardless of its content, the diary documented its author's retreat into so-called inner emigration. It therefore had to be seen, in the words of yet another author, "as protection and self-defense of the individual, who in these times is tortured and abused in a way that even the darkest pessimists could not have imagined half a century ago."¹² It is almost impossible to overlook that this interpretation had a strong "practical function" for the postwar period. It enabled even those who could not show that they had experienced persecution to use their diaries as an "entry pass into the political life of occupied Germany" because "even just the form seemed exonerating."¹³ But the interpretation also found its way into literary and historical scholarship, and to some extent it still dominates the treatment of Nazi-period diaries today. It is no coincidence that what we value today about the diaries of Victor Klemperer, Willy Cohn, and Friedrich Kellner is that they feature an individual who stood up against the pressures of the times, who with the special "courage of the chronicler" wrote like "no one," so "openly without restraint ... about the terror in Germany as seen from the inside."¹⁴

But in 1933, the use of the diary as a means of determining one's stance was by no means limited to diarists who were hostile or critical toward the regime. Karl Möhring, the aforementioned student from Göttingen who in

1933 finally declared himself to be an "advocate of National Socialism," also determined his position by way of detailed written discussions.[15] Henry Marx, the young Jewish Socialist who was unwilling to accept that he was being driven into social isolation, also searched for a way to connect with mainstream society by engaging in intense discussions in his diary; he did not use the diary simply to document his obstacles.[16] Another example is Walter Lindemann, the Berlin doctor who on January 30, 1933, as a DNVP supporter celebrated the torchlight procession on the Wilhelmstraße and in his diary reassured himself about the continuity of his personal history: he accompanied his effort to be accepted by the SA and NSDAP with abundant reflection.[17]

In this respect, researchers should not simply accept the contemporary interpretation of the diary as a refuge for thoughts that can no longer be spoken in public, something that Hans Maschmann and other diarists had already outlined as early as 1933. To be sure, this interpretation referenced actual far-reaching changes in everyday communications wrought by the Nazi regime.[18] But during Nazi rule, in the diaries themselves, this interpretation was already part of how authors conceptualized themselves and defined their position. In the case of Maschmann, for example, his characterization of the relationship between the diary and the public sphere fell directly in line with his self-description as an intellectual, which he still cultivated in his diary in the 1930s. His entries frequently referenced literary works and assessed political events according to aesthetic and philosophical categories. As Maschmann noted in mid-April 1933, for example, "the artist" (as Maschmann viewed himself in his diary) had been "attached to the deepest German soul, German spirit" in the years before the Nazi dictatorship. But now he had been forced to "fall silent in isolation," his voice fading away "in the laughter of those focused on the day [Tagesgewandten], who had nothing but derision and mockery for the holy pathos of the sublime." His entries were deeply marked by this division between Maschmann himself, the intellectual who safeguarded spiritual and cultural values in his diary, and the materialistic masses, who determined the events of the day.[19] Maschmann's differences with the new regime were largely based on the fact that the regime was "not part of the best German minds," that it reckoned with the "lowest instincts in men" and was ruining "the character of the ... Volk" with its type of politics, as Maschmann had also already noted in his first two entries.[20] Intrinsic to this interpretation was his description of the diary as a safe haven and of himself as a lonely and rejected writer who, because he was an intellectual with a view toward spiritual and cultural development, really understood what is going on. "The diary only fulfills its purpose in these times if the author assesses the daily events against the highest spiritual and ethical values," Maschmann noted as a general claim in early July 1933; but he was primarily describing what the diary meant to him and how he dealt with the regime's demand for commitment.[21]

Especially in the first two years of National Socialist rule, many people used diaries for establishing their political position, and not solely because of the political monitoring of the public sphere and everyday communications. Another reason was the specific way the question about one's relationship to National Socialism was posed in 1933–1934 after Hitler's appointment as Reich chancellor. Diaries were especially well suited for this purpose precisely because, as we have seen, determining one's position basically required two different things: a political statement and an explanation of how this fit into one's life trajectory. Diaries were not just alternative places for entertaining potentially dangerous ideas. In 1933, the determination of one's position was personal. People needed to reflect on their life, earlier political opinions, and prospects for future developments, and discussing the questions this raised had traditionally been a subject of diary writing. Insofar as many people in 1933–1934 recorded political deliberations about their relationship to the Nazi regime in their diaries, some of which had been kept for many years, they were reacting to the twofold dimensions involved in establishing a position: first by using the entries to reflect on their own life context and second by integrating their political statement on the new regime in a fully material sense into their personal life context—the diary itself. The concurrence of the political monitoring of everyday communications and the specific form assumed by the challenge to define one's own relationship to the Nazi regime made the diary a predestined instrument for searching for one's personal stance. The diary also created a space in which one could record skepticism and make observations that could not readily be expressed in public. At the same time, it embodied per se a central place for reflecting on personal developments and therefore was an obvious place for thinking about how one's current political assessment of the Nazi regime related to one's previous and future life trajectory.

Naturally, the search for one's own position at the start of Nazi rule did not occur exclusively in the medium of the diary, nor did all diarists who addressed the problem of establishing a position also use their entries for that purpose. "The new ideas of the revolution are starting to intrude upon me and also want from me their right to debate with me. But I do not yet know how I should behave," noted Werner Stock*, for example, in summer 1933. Born in 1902, in the early 1930s Stock sold fuel to filling stations and calibrated fuel pumps as an employee of the Hanover branch of Kohle AG.[22] Even though Stock clearly spoke about the challenge to align himself, we know nothing about whether or how he dealt with it. To be sure, in later entries he frequently came to talk about political events, above all those from his everyday life, but he did not express in writing any thoughts about their classification and assessment. Therefore, the question of how Stock dealt with his own relationship to the Nazi regime must remain unanswered. In any event, for Stock the diary was not an instrument for defining his position.

At first this was also the case for Wolfgang Söller*. Born in 1882, Söller worked in the publishing trade before taking over the management of the Krupp Book Hall in 1910 and later also the firm's educational society in Essen. He was keeping his diary on a regular basis long before 1933, but never with more than a few entries per year. On January 7, 1933, he made a brief entry on the death of a neighbor and then did not reach for his diary again until September that same year. There had frequently been similarly long intervals between entries in earlier years as well; nonetheless, Söller began this entry in fall 1933 with these words: "After a long pause, the first in more than 20 years, an entry again. Politically the period was more than eventful, but in the case of such happenings does my commentary or criticism matter?"[23] It is not so much the actual length of the interval between the entries but rather Söller's interpretation—the first long pause in years—that indicates that the political events of spring 1933, while often leading to an intensification of diary writing, could also make diarists fall silent. The uncertainties and ambiguities that went hand in hand with the start of the Nazi dictatorship created problems for other diarists as well, such as the young Henry Marx, who in March 1933 noted that "there is truly no lack of material for diary entries, but missing is the tranquility, the inner equilibrium that is needed for these written sketches."[24] But while Marx nonetheless regularly made long entries in search of the proper assessment of the political situation, Söller determined his relationship to the political events during summer 1933 outside the diary. Not until September would he write an entry that inserted the position he found in his diary, namely, in the form of a detailed summary report with a number of methodically organized paragraphs.[25]

The diaries of Werner Stock, Wolfgang Söller, and Henry Marx outline the parameters for the way diaries were used to establish a position in 1933–1934. Their use varied in scope and took on different forms of expression. As in the case of Hans Maschmann, it could be the main purpose of diary writing, or the subject could be dealt with separately in existing diaries, often in comparatively detailed sections that were sometimes specifically identified with headings such as "Thoughts on National Socialism" or "The 'National' Revolution."[26] Some diarists spoke about this subject repeatedly, whereas others noted their position in a single entry. How individual contemporaries used the diary in connection with defining their own position depended chiefly on how familiar they were with written reflections and on the extent to which the rest of their diary writing was characterized by discussive or reportive elements and the debating of political developments. This meant that academically educated authors tended more toward recording recurrent, detailed discussions, but such discussions were certainly not limited to this group.[27] Although the search for one's position occurred in various forms and led to different positions, when read comparatively the corresponding diary entries allow us to work out the fundamental mechanisms people generally used in reaction to the regime's demand for commitment.

2. "Therefore I Advocate the Fourth Standpoint": Affirming Commitment While Avoiding the Demand for Unconditional Assent

In the summer and fall of 1933, Karl Möhring, the Göttingen student who in July 1933 saw the beginning of a new chapter in the book of history for both Germany and himself, filled his diary with detailed deliberations on his own stance toward the new regime. Even though Möhring had already declared himself an "advocate of National Socialism" in July, the question about his new political position continued to preoccupy him in the following weeks and months. He repeatedly came to talk about it in his diary, refining his position in detailed and slightly varying argumentation. Within this context, in mid-September 1933 Möhring prepared an enumerated summary of what he felt were the possible political opinions "in the present moment": "1. One is an unconditional, noncritical supporter of the NSDAP.... 2. One remains completely neutral.... 3. One is an unconditional opponent of the NSDAP."[28]

Möhring's analysis accurately described the formal combinatorics that informed the Nazi regime's efforts to reorganize social belonging and characterized its demand for commitment: on the one side, supporters truly loyal to the Nazi regime; on the other side, racially defined "enemies" and political "opponents"; and in between, the still undecided, who soon had to choose one of the two sides. Social belonging and participation in National Socialism were supposed to be determined according to these categorically envisioned alternatives. This model underlay Adolf Hitler's overt threat in his speech on May 1, 1933, that "people who are not for Germany" would no longer be tolerated.[29] And even Carl Schmitt, the so-called new crown jurist of the young Nazi dictatorship, celebrated "the perfect right of the German revolution" to ensure that no "alien type [could] meddle" in the nascent "process of growth.... We are learning once more to distinguish. We are learning above all to distinguish properly between friend and foe."[30] First formulated as early as 1927 in the article "The Concept of the Political," Schmitt's ideas could be used in the new political environment to theoretically legitimate, "if necessary, the relentless separating out of . . . identified adversaries from the great national Volksgemeinschaft."[31]

This clear tripartite division, however, did not shape only the regime's perspective. Sebastian Haffner, the protagonists in Jan Petersen's novel, and the resistance groups that fled into exile also structured their political environment according to the distinctions between themselves, their political opponents, and the masses of undecided. To this day, scholars and the public usually measure the spectrum of possible positions toward the Nazi regime according to this tripartite division, which ever since Raul Hilberg and the focus on the violent crimes of National Socialism has often been rendered in criminological terms as the triad of perpetrators, victims, and bystanders.[32]

In September 1933, however, Karl Möhring could not identify as belonging to any these three groups. If he was an "uncritical supporter of the NSDAP," he would "rightly be considered a dimwit and simpleton by all reasonable people," maintaining neutrality was just an expression of a "lack of interest or political aptitude," and opposition to the NSDAP was "under the circumstances of the moment . . . a fruitless opposition," the sort of thing he had always rejected earlier. "Therefore," Möhring continued, "I advocate the fourth standpoint. I declare myself an advocate of National Socialism, but retain my own opinion and independent criticism."[33] Möhring had already presented this line of thought in earlier discussions about his political standpoint. As he noted in early August 1933, it is "wrong and attests to an individualistic standpoint if one accepts a large part of the actions but finds fault with details and therefore stands aloof." But it was also wrong, in his estimation, "to unconditionally say yes and amen to everything."[34] In his written deliberations on his personal stance, Möhring repeatedly protested against the categorical division between criticism and belonging used by the regime and other political actors to evaluate the proximity and distance of individual persons—divisions that Möhring, too, principally viewed as options for political positions. His own "fourth standpoint," however, was based on a dissenting logic, which Möhring used to claim belonging despite his critical attitude toward the regime on many points.

Möhring considered this a special stance that left him sitting on the fence. As he determined in spring 1933, it was "definitely not [putting him] in a good position, even though it is better than standpoint no. 3." "Among 100% National Socialists," one might "possibly fall under suspicion of not being one, and among opponents, the suspicion of being an opportunist."[35] But Karl Möhring was wrong in thinking that his position was so unusual. When determining his stance toward the Nazi regime in 1933, Möhring was not alone in avoiding the demand for unconditional assent that was conjoined with demand for commitment. In fact, when establishing their position in 1933–1934, many people actually combined their commitment with criticism of National Socialism or the Nazi regime. This was also true of diarists who, unlike Karl Möhring, did not regularly speak about their relationship to the Nazi regime and use writing to search for their own position. The concurrence of commitment and criticism did not just influence the search for one's own relationship to the new regime; for many contemporaries, it was also a main feature of the position they ultimately established.

This is especially evident in diaries of people who did not make determining their position the main focus of their writing but instead summarized their stance toward the new regime in special entries. Take, for example, Wolfgang Söller, the librarian of the Krupp Book Hall, who in September 1933—after a supposedly "long" pause in writing—recorded his stance toward the Nazi regime in his diary. After asking with regard to current events, "Does my commentary or criticism matter?" he immediately responded by pointing out that, "basically, self-reflection on strength, purity, and desire can actually only be enthusiastically welcomed." Also "the person of the Führer, speech, writing, general attitude has a captivating effect." But "in the details," he wrote further, one could see "that one is perhaps getting older and does not share some of the exuberance." Above all, Söller noted, one had to be "superficial and heartless, if one did not think of the many victims that such a political process entails, the 'defamed,' those who have lost their position, etc."[36]

Another example is Karl Friedrich Eicher, the agriculturalist who reviewed and commented on the political developments of 1933 in his annually updated family chronicle. Although making different arguments and assessments, Eicher too claimed to belong without going along with everything. Born in 1864, Eichler had worked on his parents' farm ever since school, taking it over at the end of the nineteenth century and managing it until the 1940s. He had already sympathized with the nationalist right during the Weimar Republic and thus had strongly welcomed the political developments of the past year. He considered 1933 to be "probably the most significant year for our German fatherland in many centuries." Eichler extensively described the political events, which had laid the "cornerstone for a new Germany." Already that year "amazing things were accomplished" by way of the "Enabling Act for the new regime," which ensured that it "no longer needs the Reichstag to create new laws." Eichler likewise greatly approved of the suppression of the political left. "Peace and order prevail in our fatherland again, the whole of morality is becoming visible again, . . . two million unemployed have work again." Even "religion is reviving among the Volk," and all those who balked at these developments were "taken to institutions intended for this and must do all kinds of work under police supervision. . . . There is such a camp in neighboring Sachsenburg."[37]

At the start of the long section about political developments that opened Eichler's annual report, he emphasized that the seizure of power on January 30 had led to lasting changes "not only in the Reich and the German states but also in many subdistricts, cities, villages, corporations, and unions." He dedicated a second, similarly detailed section of his report to these changes within his own locality. Eichler had been a council member for the small village north of Chemnitz in which his farm was located, and in this section he described the "major changes" in his municipality. "Because throughout the Reich all Marxist and Communist representatives had to immediately vacate their offices in the manner described above, . . . completely new people"—exclusively NSDAP members—"entered the parliament in our locality as well, even though many of them did not have the confidence of the residents," as Eichler pointed out with obvious annoyance. He was "not happy about this composition," but the municipal administration and village residents could "do nothing to prevent it." Therefore, as Eichler noted somewhat ponderously, "on June 17, 1933, the writer of these lines resigned his office as mayor." He went on to detail his frustration with how the succession had been arranged, which ultimately put a man in office whom he considered wholly unsuitable. Despite his enthusiasm about the way the political changes of 1933 were "refloating the rather submerged ship of state," as a longtime local politician Eichler wanted nothing to do with them in his municipality.[38]

As with Wolfgang Söller, Karl Friedrich Eichler's personal stance on the political developments combined basic approval and his own commitment to the social "rising" in 1933 with criticism of certain dimensions of the start of Nazi rule. In contrast to Möhring, in Eichler's case commitment and criticism occurred abruptly side by side. His frustration with the Gleichschaltung of local political structures did nothing to change his delight with the political developments in general. Wolfgang Söller's empathy for the victims of the seizure of power likewise did not influence his assessment that, "basically," key aspects of this event "can actually only be enthusiastically welcomed." Even without abstract reflection, both refused the demand for unqualified adherence that accompanied the demand that they commit to a side. They did not level a categorical critique, nor did their critical evaluation of certain aspects of the start of Nazi rule lead them to abandon their fundamentally positive evaluation and commitment.

What the summarizing reviews show so clearly in their compact form is also evident in diaries that routinely commented on the day's political events. Here too, where one finds a basically positive reception of the start of Nazi rule, one can frequently also observe the coexistence of approval and criticism. This applies to Charlotte Bücker*, for example. Born in 1873, she came from relatively affluent circumstances, but she fell into poverty in the early 1930s and became dependent on the white-collar earnings of her daughter, with whom she lived in Berlin. On January 31, 1933, in her diary Bücker welcomed the fact that "Hitler—finally!—has become Reich chancellor, if not Reich president," and in the following weeks she seemed enthusiastic about the actions and propagandistic performances of the new regime.[39] She commented with satisfaction on the prohibition and Gleichschaltung of the democratic parties and unions, and as an astrology enthusiast, she repeatedly asked the stars about the fortune of the new regime. Then in mid-May 1933, together with her daughter, she attended an exhibit at the Research Institute for Intellectual Prehistory, a private organization of the Dutch humanities scholar Hermann Wirth, who later took part in the formation of the SS Research Community for Ancestral Heritage.[40] "We had the pleasure," noted Bücker, "of entering at the beginning of a tour through the exhibition guided personally by Professor Wirth." In her diary, she later seemed impressed by the collection, which "leads our thoughts in a completely different direction; for these people reject astrology." But Bücker did not discuss the reasons for their rejection, instead only noting that these people "are swastika-ists" [Hakenkreuzler] and that "Adolf Hitler, as well, does not want to hear anything about his horoscope but instead trusts in his own strength." "Everything that we saw and heard" was "very interesting," concluded Bücker, summarizing her visit and making it clear: "One always comes back to the old saying: 'to each his own.' . . . Ergo: we are sticking with noble astrology."[41]

Wolfgang Scharenberg, a lawyer and notary from Ribnitz in Mecklenburg born in 1883, was so excited by the start of Nazi rule that he not only expressed his approval in his diary but also made a strong dedicated effort to become actively involved. Scharenberg had already actively participated in the Lebensreform movement during the Weimar Republic. He tried to shape his life according to its principles but also took part in many associations and organizations whose efforts at fundamental renewal, according to Scharenberg, received major support after January 30, 1933. Against this background, he substantially increased his involvement again in 1933. He became a member in new organizations that were now völkisch in nature, such as the German Faith Movement, formed in summer 1933 in the context of the seizure of power.[42] In his diary, Scharenberg appeared enthusiastic about the movement's principle "to live according to German conscience, to shape life in accordance with its inner strengths, in order to become a full and complete man," in part because this did not merely mean "praying and forbearance" but "above all also working together for the public good, contributing to the shaping of public life."[43] In this sense, Scharenberg tried to become active even outside his memberships, and in summer 1933 he started a settlement project on a nearby farm and spoke at length about its progress in his diary. However, his writing dealt mostly with the difficulties the project encountered with local representatives of the Nazi regime, who, while sharing its ideological aspirations, did not accept its organizational independence. Thus, along with describing his efforts to participate in the start of Nazi rule, his diary is frequently dominated by his distinct criticism that "now only the party itself can take such things in hand."[44] This notwithstanding, Scharenberg continued to dedicate himself to the "national renewal" on his own terms.

Diaries like those of Wolfgang Söller, Charlotte Bücker, Karl Friedrich Eichler, and Wolfgang Scharenberg prove how mistaken the young student Karl Möhring was in fall 1933 in thinking that his own "fourth standpoint" was unique amid those of people who otherwise declared themselves to be supporters, opponents, or still undecided. The diaries of the 1930s generally show instead that the Germans often did not conform to the model of unqualified adherence propagated by the regime. Their relationship to the Nazi regime remained characterized by both commitment and criticism.

Self-Alignment, Biographical Reflections, and Basic Criticism

Historians have viewed the coexistence of commitment and criticism in different ways. It has frequently been interpreted as evidence that the respective persons, despite their "political naiveté," were not "wholly blinded, wholly seduced," and thus one "cannot fully fail to recognize . . . a certain distance to the regime."[45]

But by searching for a position apart from those that, as stipulated, unconditionally took a side, people were not just safeguarding residual elements of their previous personality from political demands. For many Germans, given their own specific life history, this search made it possible for them to commit themselves to the regime in the first place. It is precisely this rejection of the stipulated unconditionality that reveals their efforts to react to the two dimensions—political and biographical—of the demand for commitment: only the combination of basic commitment and specific critique enabled many Germans to adaptively react to the far-reaching social changes and transformation of social belonging after 1933 and nonetheless understand their current behavior as being consistent with their previous life trajectory and its projection into the future.

For Karl Möhring, this was the decisive issue of his intense struggle in his discussion of his position: whether or not his declaration as a "National Socialist" in summer 1993 stood "in stark contrast to [his] earlier statements." In reaction to this concern, he resolved to be a "regime-critical National Socialist."[46] Doing so allowed Möhring to identify with the Nazi regime and still see himself in continuity with earlier critical assessments of National Socialism he had made in the late Weimar Republic and in spring 1933.

In the case of the agriculturalist Karl Friedrich Eichler, the sharp criticism of the Gleichschaltung of local institutions in the wake of the start of the Nazi dictatorship, which he generally welcomed, is explained above all by the fact that he himself had long been active as a local politician. In principle, given his great enthusiasm about the first months of Nazi rule, Eichler might have asked himself whether he too was responsible for what he saw as the deficiencies now being alleviated: the political events since spring 1933 clearly called his own past activities into question. Yet insofar as his annoyance was firmly restricted to the new local functionaries and their ineptitude, he could cling to his own biography and formulate commitment to the political changes.

Even the dedication developed by the lawyer Wolfgang Scharenberg in the euphoria of 1933 was nourished both by his earlier activity in the Lebensreform movement and by his criticism of political events. During the Weimar Republic, Scharenberg had developed a specific self-understanding. As he characterized himself in 1932, "I try to work and somehow get creatively engaged, but it is not easy as an outsider to get your hook in."[47] Despite this complaint, his self-description as an outsider was centrally important to Scharenberg. As much as he welcomed the start of the Nazi dictatorship because it supported the realization of his Lebensreform ideals, in this context he also wanted to continue his creative engagement from the margins and not from within Nazi organizations. For him too, the criticism of the Nazi regime's "craving for totality" and of the fact that "the new state . . . grabs everything for itself and suppresses all cultural efforts by outsiders" possessed a strong biographical dimension.[48]

After January 30, 1933, references to personal histories were also important for party members who had already joined the NSDAP during the Weimar Republic (referred to as "old fighters" after 1933), playing a key role in these members' own self-assurance and also signaling their personal belonging. Testifying to this, for example, are the numerous surviving autobiographical reports produced by this group. In particular, the texts created in 1933–1934 invariably narrated their authors' life as part of the "movement's time of struggle," reporting on their personal journey to the National Socialist movement, their involvement therein, and their role in the victory of National Socialism. Written such that 1933 formed the telos of the authors' entire life trajectory, these stories were naturally also retrospective constructions and often highly questionable. Within the NSDAP, there were bitter struggles for influence, with belligerents castigating the "blemishes" in the life histories of their competitors.[49] Yet only in their nature as a construct could these life stories signal commitment with the unconditional adherence generally demanded by the Nazi regime.[50] However, not all contemporaries could possibly provide a corresponding interpretation of their biography. The requirement of belonging raised the question of how a person's commitment related to one's previous and future life path, and contemporaries with a different course of life could only answer it by marking a specific distance. With the help of this distance, one's view of one's own life could be harmonized with one's new political statement: persons from those broad swaths of society beyond the narrow circle of people who had been actively involved in National Socialism during the Weimar Republic could commit themselves only by rejecting the demand for unconditional adherence when determining their personal position.

The coexistence of commitment and criticism made the assertion of belonging possible even for people who criticized not merely specific phenomena but rather the system itself and were considered "opponents" by the system. Even in his earliest entries, Hans Maschmann, for example, the socialist grade school teacher who in late March 1933 "retreated" to his diary, unequivocally denounced the destruction of the Weimar Republic, the persecution of people "because of their political convictions," and the brutality of the new regime; he left no doubt about his fundamental criticism of the new regime.[51] But right from the beginning, he opposed its efforts to deny his social belonging because of his critical attitude and to view him as an enemy of the ongoing "national uprising." "They allege that republicans are not nationalistic, that they have no love for the fatherland," Maschmann began his entry on April 4, 1933, vehemently disputing this allegation in his next statements. He noted in somewhat abnormal German, "Never was a deeper love of the fatherland the motivation for the deeds of a large part of the men of 1918"—as a former member of a workers' and soldiers' council, Maschmann saw himself as one of those men. The Nazi regime, he insisted, was using the "nation" only for "party-political agitation." "We republicans," he noted emphatically, "will no more allow our love for the fatherland to be taken from us than our love for our parents, spouse, for our children.... We do not deprive other Volk comrades of this.... We do not touch the holiest in the other's soul."[52]

But it was not only in this abstract sense that Maschmann, despite his sharp criticism of the Nazi regime, still claimed belonging. Rather, wherever possible he also tried to signal his agreement with current developments. "Despite everything that I have reported here about the upheaval," Maschmann's next diary entry stated two days later, "the picture would not be complete if I did not mention the serious struggle of the völkisch movement for a clarification of the German worldview." "In the years since the end of the war," in no other political current had people "tried so hard for a renewal of German idealism." Maschmann claimed his part in this as well. As he noted in the same entry, within the Socialist movement he had repeatedly "spoken with rigid supporters of historical materialism and pointed out to them the need for the intellectual reorientation of the socialist parties.... But I was speaking in the desert."[53] And for all of his criticism of the dictatorial character of the new regime's measures, at times he also agreed with some of them. On April 8, 1933, Maschmann commented on the so-called Second Gleichschaltung Law regulating the relationship between states and the Reich with these words: "Much happens that must indeed be honestly affirmed by anyone who wants the best for the nation. Today new laws came out that brought us enormously closer to the realization of the German unified state." At the same time, he was "fully aware that this legislation is only possible through the dictatorship" and that there was "no possibility of resistance." The "consequences of the law," however, also depended on the "will that condones these laws"; in the same way, the question of "whether the nation becomes that which it is worth being according its deepest predisposition" would be answered "less by the leadership than by its own will."[54] Therefore, despite his basic criticism of the new regime, Maschmann did not want to remain aloof; rather, he definitely wanted to continue participating in political events. "I have struggled bitterly by day and in sleepless nights, and I struggle on and on, to understand what is happening," he noted briefly one week later. "I search for how the new is setting values, not merely for the sake of passive participation but to be able to give full affirmation. There is much in the movement that is consistent with intentions I've had for years."[55]

These diary entries from spring 1933 do not signal the onset of a change in attitude. Even in entries of later months and the following year, Hans Maschmann kept up his sharp and fundamental criticism of the Nazi regime, repeatedly disputing its legitimacy, repudiating its politicians, condemning its violence, and deprecating wide sections of its policies. And yet like Karl Möhring, Karl Friedrich Eichler, and Wolfgang Scharenberg, Hans Maschmann claimed belonging—despite his criticism of the Nazi regime, as categorical as it was.

There also were other critical contemporaries who, despite their obvious dissatisfaction with the system's basic structure, did not see themselves as fundamentally opposed to the new system. Consider, for example, Daniel Lotter, the Fürth gingerbread baker born in 1873 who started his diary in 1934 on the first anniversary of Hitler's appointment as Reich chancellor and henceforth used it chiefly for his critical commentary on political developments. During the Nazi dictatorship, Lotter continued to claim belonging, and not simply in strictly practical terms by still holding various honorary offices he had assumed prior to 1933. His diary entries, as well, repeatedly show that he combined his extensive criticism with basic approval and hope for improvement. As Lotter noted, for example, in April 1934, it was impossible "without violation to force the mighty flooding current of German intellectual and cultural life into the channel of the National Socialist worldview." To be sure, there were "historical moments when one must consciously subordinate age, opinion, life, and judgment to a higher ideal, a single powerful will"—here Lotter referred not only to August 1914 but also decidedly to the plebiscite on the withdrawal from the League of Nations in November 1933. But there must "also come a time again when the diverse, the manifold, the personal are able to speak and come to bear." The regime would "fail" if it did not "change the methods through which the NSDAP won its power, and what good German could wish for that."[56]

The massive support for the new regime in 1933–1934, repeatedly demanded by its representatives, was only ensured because of the coexistence of commitment and criticism in the way people defined their positions. This coexistence strongly contributed to the social dynamic of 1933 that made the radical restructuring of the political system possible in the first place. But at the same time, it subverted the regime's efforts to realign social belonging along the clear-cut division between enemies and supporters of National Socialism. For the regime was by no means prepared to accept the self-descriptions used by Lotter, Maschmann, and others to see themselves as belonging to society despite their fundamental criticism. Time and again, the regime's leading representatives highlighted the dichotomy between belonging and criticism of the regime, because, as Joseph Goebbels put it in March 1934, "National Socialism does not recognize two different views about one and the same thing."[57]

At this particular time, the regime was taking great pains to center public attention on the irreconcilability of criticism and belonging. In early 1934, the regime found itself in a difficult situation. Although all meaningful political opposition had been eliminated in the course of 1933, it faced the alarming escalation of the "structurally preprogrammed conflicts between various bearers of the seizure-of-power process"—namely, the activists of the National Socialist movement in the SA; the state and party leadership around Hitler, Goebbels, and Göring; and the conservative allies of the NSDAP.[58] In the first months of 1933, their divergent interests still remained in the background, but they were becoming more and more dominant by the end of the year. As a result, the state and party leaders found themselves confronted from within the power structure by very disparate demands regarding government strategy. Further aggravating the situation were surveillance reports on the public mood, which were now being prepared for the first time. They reported critical commentary from throughout the entire Reich and were interpreted by the regime as evidence of the population's growing loss of confidence.[59]

Facing both power struggles within the regime and the bad public mood, in mid-May 1934 the NSDAP leadership initiated a large-scale "campaign against denigrators and fault finders," whom Goebbels had already targeted with comments in March.[60] Conducted throughout the country over the following weeks with thousands of local rallies, the propaganda campaign served both to justify government policies and to discredit competitors within the regime; it was also supposed to reactivate social support that had ostensibly been lost. In his programmatic opening speech in the Sports Palace, broadcast over radio and printed in the newspapers, Goebbels established continuity between the "nigglers" and "critics," "whiners" and "denigrators" of the present with those who in the First World War had delivered the "dagger thrust"—the stab in the back—to the German Reich. "There are people," Goebbels said, "who cannot stand themselves and they are already annoyed when they look in a mirror. . . . We know this type well enough from the war." In the first months after the seizure of power, government officials "had to deal with the major tasks put to them with all their strength," and as a result, the "critics [had] assumed they could continue their laudable handiwork, just as in the war, in the National Socialist revolution as well. But they will have deceived themselves. . . . For a time we have not dealt with these people; now they will get to know us!"

Goebbels stressed that the critics would not be met with "state authority" but rather that the "Volk itself should judge." He emphatically appealed "to the confederate Volk" to "commit . . . itself to National Socialism out of inner passion" and demanded that "critics in the land be opposed face to face." They should be "made to explain themselves and revealed to the Volk in their whole criminal attitude." Goebbels's speech aimed at the clear delineation between supporters and opponents of the Nazi regime, which threatened to be blurred by "whiners" and "nigglers." And he relied on the same instrument that, from his perspective, had ensured social support for the regime during the first months of power: the massive and unequivocal commitment of the population. The regime, he proclaimed, was "starting a huge enlightenment campaign" and "mustering the well-intentioned within and outside the party against the small number of nigglers."[61]

But the campaign's activation efforts failed. While the "campaign against denigrators and faultfinders" generated wide-ranging rally activities throughout the Reich, it hardly met with any widespread enthusiasm, nor could surveillance reports write about a decline in critical commentary. It failed to trigger anything like the social dynamics generated by Hitler's appointment as Reich chancellor the year before. But to describe the "operation against the denigrators . . . unequivocally as a failure"[62] that could not stop the "dramatic change of atmosphere" that brought the "people's mood dangerously [close to] a sweeping condemnation of the regime"[63] only repeats a misconception shared by regime and other political observers. Focused solely on politics, the formal division between supporters, "enemies" and "opponents," and the still undecided can only grasp criticism and difference as indicators of opposition. Thus, it does not help us understand the central importance of difference as part of the commitment of many Germans.

For many diarists, the anti-complainer campaign, in particular, provided a reason to reassure themselves—as demanded—of their own commitment to the Nazi regime. Having already determined their relationship to the new regime through a combination of commitment and critique in 1933, people took note of it once again in their diaries in May and June 1934, even though the campaign itself often did not meet a positive response. In

June 1934, Hans Maschmann rejected the "speech and press campaign of the National Socialist party," where "the verve and enthusiasm . . . [was found] only in the speeches of the revolution's beneficiaries."[64] "The high ethical objective Hitler strove for" is "understood only by the very few, and only by those who don't first need to hear it from him, because they deeply experience it." And Maschmann counted himself among these few. Nonetheless, in this very same entry he once more recorded his relationship to the Nazi regime, which he had found in spring 1933: "My attitude is this: I want to support the fatherland, holy and faithful assurance. But I will turn away with pride and silence from anyone who does not trust me in this, even if he stands in the highest position of power. I have the purest political desire, but no political ambition."[65]

The gingerbread baker Daniel Lotter seemed just as unenthusiastic about the "protest rallies against the denigrators and faultfinders." In his diary in May 1934, he noted, "I cannot think that in this unfree air, with this constant pressure from above, anything good can result and develop in the long run." The National Socialist movement had "helped the German Volk and state achieve greater unity and solidarity" and thus done them much good. Lotter stressed, however, that "most of what is now being preserved through coercion will disappear again," and with this assessment he once again reiterated his position toward the Nazi regime.[66] And Karl Möhring reacted similarly in May 1934. In principle, the "struggle right now against the critics and nigglers" was admittedly "wholly justified, as far as the negative criticism was concerned," but he felt it was clearly exaggerated. One should "not take these philistine nigglers all too seriously" because "after all they are not basically opponents of a real National Socialist state." One should not make them feel that they are an "awe-inspiring opposition." Above all, however, Möhring maintained reassuringly that, according to his estimation, the campaign was not aimed at suppressing all critical statements. "Positive criticism," he noted emphatically, "is not only permissible but rather it is desired and necessary. Indeed, Goebbels stressed this too."[67] Thus in 1934 Möhring used the very same terms he had used the year before to define his relationship to the regime while rejecting the stipulated demand for unconditional adherence: "I am a National Socialist as I understand it, that is, I exercise criticism not to undermine the reputation of the state or rob others of their faith, but to make it better." Exercising "purely negative criticism," on the other hand, was "completely wrong."[68]

3. "Which Is Also Not What the Führer Adolf Hitler Wants": Reconciling Differences with One's Commitment to the Regime

Since in many cases the positions found by the Germans in 1933–1934 toward the Nazi regime did not meet the new rulers' demand for unconditional adherence, the regime's vigorously disseminated notion of individual commitment was already raising questions for people. The demands stridently presented in the "campaign against whiners and faultfinders," for example, forcefully asserted a strict division between supporters and opponents. This presented many people with the problem of explaining how and why in their case criticism and commitment nonetheless went hand in hand. Even though some diaries also contained commitment and differences standing side by side and wholly unconnected, such explanatory efforts played an important role when people determined their personal positions at the start of the National Socialist rule. Rejecting the unconditional adherence demanded by the regime when it came to one's own position required specific patterns of reasoning to explain why, in one's own case, criticism explicitly brought against the new regime did not call one's commitment into doubt.

To understand the positioning of people toward the Nazi regime and thus also understand the massive levels of commitment, asking about which elements of National Socialism they tended to approve or disapprove does not get us very far.[69] Such efforts to carry out retrospective opinion surveys leave crucial questions unanswered: How does one explain the situation that "for the same person, acceptance and rejection" could exist "relatively seamlessly side by side"?[70] What role did this phenomenon play in the individual's positioning toward the regime? Given the demand for definitude, how did Germans back then sustain the tense relationship between commitment and criticism?

For a historical explanation of the massive commitment to the Nazi regime, it is important to recognize that social integration under National Socialism functioned not "through homogenization" but "through the perpetuation of difference."[71] But this insight must be expanded. The positions found by contemporaries themselves remain misunderstood if one simply concludes that they were characterized "more often by inconsistency than by consistency" and then, in trying to create a classification scheme, dissolves them into the particular elements that conveyed approval and criticism.[72] It is much more precise to ask about how consensus and dissent related to each other as part of the determination of a stance. In this respect, diaries of the 1930s allow us to identify a specific system for managing differences that allowed people to perpetuate criticism and commitment at the same time and also continued to be centrally important for the commitment of large parts of German society to the Nazi regime after 1933–1934.

The Hitler Myth, the Future, and Personal Pictures of the Nazi Regime

To understand how people dealt with the tension between commitment and difference when determining their position, we need to look closely at how they described both themselves and above all the object of their commitment during this process. As Goebbels had emphatically reiterated in his speech launching the anti-complainer campaign in 1934, the regime called for a "commitment to National Socialism."[73] But instead of clarifying matters, this formulation tended more to obscure the entity that required one's commitment. Insofar as the regime maintained that the establishment of National Socialism started with Hitler's appointment as Reich chancellor, it was unclear whether the "commitment to National Socialism" was supposed to apply to an ideology, the National Socialist movement, or the new political system. Especially during the first months, the last of these had an extremely polymorphic appearance, despite regime officials' repeated avowal of the unity of the "national government."

Ever since Ian Kershaw's pioneering study on the relationship between the Führer cult and popular opinion, first published in 1980, researchers have stressed the importance of the Reich chancellor and Führer Adolf Hitler as a key pole for Germans to identify with. In this study, Kershaw focused not on Hitler as a person but on his public representation and the way he was socially perceived—the Hitler myth. And he argued that this myth possessed "a crucial stabilizing and integrating function" for the broad involvement of society during the Nazi dictatorship.[74] The Hitler myth was marked by the purposeful propagandistic staging of Hitler, on the one hand, and, on the other, its perception within society, which resulted in a major "discrepancy between the contrasting images of the Nazi regime as reflected in the popular perception of the Führer and of the Party functionaries."[75] Already emerging in 1933–1934, this distinction decisively influenced the public perception of the regime, especially after the murders of the top SA leader, Ernst Röhm, and other SA leaders, as well competitors within the regime, by means of which the state and party leadership around Hitler put a violent end to those internal power struggles already addressed in previous weeks by the anti-complainer campaign.[76]

The propagandistic stylization of the Night of the Long Knives made it possible to definitively establish the intended social perception of the idealized image of Hitler, abstracted from the everyday reality of National Socialism. This contributed to social integration because it ensured—according to Kershaw's oft-adopted theses—that existing dissatisfaction with the Nazi regime was blamed exclusively on local Nazi functionaries. With his "public image," Hitler was able to "offer a positive pole" with which "sectional interests and grievances" could be equalized and which "defus[ed] discontent."[77] The bedazzling Hitler myth provided the necessary "compensation for the criticism of everyday lived reality and the political system of the Nazis."[78]

As a matter of fact, diaries of the 1930s also dedicated plenty of attention to Hitler, which, considered against the background of the massive propagandistic staging of his person and his central position in the Third Reich, certainly comes as no surprise. Time and again, diarists devoted extensive entries to Hitler's speeches, tried to understand his lines of thought, or tied their hopes, confidence, and political approval to his person.[79] In this respect, for many people, the person of Hitler played a decisive role in their commitment to the Nazi regime, even though this person was by no means central to the commitment of all diarists. Yet the division between the Führer and the local NSDAP or other representatives of the Nazi regime frequently played a more specific role in the written position determinations in diaries of 1933–1934. It suggests that we should reassess the thesis of the Hitler myth's "compensatory function" through which a "considerable part of the dissatisfaction with the Nazi regime . . . was absorbed."[80] The diaries indicate instead that its integrative function existed not so much in compensating for negatively viewed aspects or making them forgettable as in creating the opportunity to formulate deliberate criticism while at the same time not identifying it as directed against the regime.

Walter Lindemann, the young Berlin doctor who on January 30 cheered Hitler and his cabinet in front of the Reich Chancellery, retained an enormously positive picture of the new chancellor in the months that followed. With the increasing length of Nazi rule, this ever more strongly formed the basis for Lindemann's enthusiasm for the Nazi regime, even though he noted certain aspects of the new system with displeasure. "Now I must say,"

Lindemann wrote for example in June 1933, "that I find a few of the leaders in the NSDAP very unlikeable, thus especially *Herr Göring* and *Herr Goebbels*. The former owns a 14-room apartment in the West [of Berlin], a huge Mercedes, and his own airplane (!!). And he calls himself a National Socialist. The latter talks and talks and at the same time keeps a large house with his wife."[81] In 1933–1934, Lindemann complained repeatedly, for example, that "some of the '*old, honored fighters*'" had forgotten "their modesty, which is enjoined upon them by the *National Socialist worldview*," and had become "proper fat cats."[82] At the same time, wholly in keeping with Ian Kershaw's thesis, his criticism repeatedly excluded Hitler, who "indeed stands there without any flaws."[83] "He alone is our great Führer; the others were only his sidekicks."[84]

But this does not mean that the new Reich chancellor himself and the policies of his regime were spared Walter Lindemann's criticism. Quite the contrary, their action against the Evangelical Church as early as fall 1933 but especially starting in October 1934 aroused his disapproval. While Lindemann frequently recorded his displeasure with the lifestyle of various Nazi functionaries in his diary without further commentary, in this connection he expressly emphasized his personal dissent with the regime. "I most energetically reject the *community of faith of 'German Christians*,'" he noted on October 12, 1933. A few months later in January 1934, he repeated, "I completely and utterly cannot declare my agreement with the *truths* of the *Hitler regime* vis-à-vis the Evangelical Church."[85]

At this point Lindemann stated more explicitly than in any other entry of 1933–1934 that his own assessment conflicted with the regime, and this is precisely where his idealized picture of the Führer played a central role. The community of faith of the German Christians "contradicts . . . the outlook of the Führer himself," he noted in his diary, justifying his repudiation and documenting his assessment with a footnote referencing a place in Hitler's book *Mein Kampf*, which was extremely unusual for Lindemann's diary.[86] When in January 1934 Lindemann repeated his disapproval of regime policy toward the church, he again explicitly referenced Hitler. This time, after criticizing the forced dismissal of church officials who were replaced by "wholly unsuitable and *immature* people," he quoted directly from *Mein Kampf*. Here, according to Lindemann, Hitler had written that the "task [of the Nazi movement] is not that of a religious reformation, but rather that of a political reorganization of our Volk," and that "*for the political leader the religious doctrines and institutions of his Volk must always be untouchable.*"

Following the quotes, Lindemann commented, "Unfortunately the practice has shown that the actions taken here were completely contrary to the words."[87]

While Lindemann's depiction of Hitler and the government was fundamentally positive, his criticism of the Führer and regime was no less pointed. During the Weimar Republic, Lindemann had been more of a national conservative than a National Socialist. Lindemann's displeasure with the operation against the Evangelical Church also grew from his biography and was directly related to the great importance the Berlin doctor ascribed to his religious education. For Lindemann, his commitment to the Nazi regime was supposed to be joined with the retention of his own self-image. To this end, his reference to *Mein Kampf* and what he presented as ostensibly being Hitler's actual view allowed him to reconcile his commitment and his differences with the regime pertaining to its relationship to the Evangelical Church. Lindemann was not just using the reference to reinforce his pro-church stance. He was also reassuring himself that his repudiation was not categorically aimed against National Socialism. While his differences with the regime were explicitly marked with extraordinary clarity, the reference to Hitler marked them just as strongly as not being critical of the system.

Other diarists similarly used direct references to Hitler to identify expressions of displeasure as not being hostile to the regime. For example, in his annual report in late 1933, the farmer Karl Friedrich Eichler not only criticized changes to the composition of the municipal council but also railed against the far-reaching demands raised by people "from the suborganization of the movement" against the established local politicians. Thus all "municipal leaders" were supposed to "show up in uniform for official actions, which, of course, could not be asked of many old and older officials." Then Eichler, too, added to his criticism: "which is also not what the Führer Adolf Hitler wants." In doing so, he was not merely reinforcing his personal assessment but also, despite his pronounced difference with NSDAP functionaries, marking it as not directed against National Socialism.[88] Another example comes from Franz Buesgen*, a savings bank employee from Herne born in 1911 who joined the SA and NSDAP in the mid-1930s. Like Walter Lindemann, Buesgen repeatedly used statements by Adolf Hitler so he could maintain his own religious views and reconcile them with his self-image as an SA man.[89] For example, upon noticing that more and more contemporaries were apparently no longer using the so-called German greeting because of their objection to the "hostilities toward the faith," he suggested in his diary that those who "are anxious and looking at the dark side" should look at "the Führer's *Mein Kampf*, in which the Führer often quotes 'here too we can learn from the Church' and similar places."[90]

Indeed, the pictures of the new Reich chancellor that people drew for themselves against the background of propagandistic stylization—the Hitler myth—were very important for their broad commitment to the Nazi regime in 1933–1934. As the "bearer and enactor of a myth," for many people Hitler formed a "decisive figure for identification and projection" that facilitated their commitment to the new regime.[91] But this did not mean that their criticism of the new regime was therefore "compensated" or directed solely toward local Nazi leaders. Rather, the reference to Hitler made it possible to consciously formulate criticism in the first place: as a surface on which to project far-reaching expectations and high moral aspirations, Hitler could also be held up in contrast to the concrete phenomena of the Nazi regime—in Walter Lindemann's case, even decidedly against "Hitler's regime." This allowed people to mark their often biographically based displeasure as not being fundamentally directed against the regime. With this form of argument, they could simultaneously declare their commitment to the regime and formulate differences from the regime; without such an argument, commitment would not have been possible for many people in 1933–1934.

The tension between commitment and dissent could also be bridged by other arguments. In relation to their own critiques, people often noted in their diaries, for example, that National Socialism was still just being created. As the Berlin bank employee Wolf Busse wrote reassuringly in summer 1933, "everything is still in development and an end, as well as an overview regarding disadvantages and advantages, can be surveyed only with limits." He then complained that "income from work has remained the same, whereas expenditures, notably half-ways by force, have substantially increased, so that it is increasingly more difficult for the worker to balance income with expenditures."[92] Like Wolfgang Busse, other people also mitigated their criticism by noting that National Socialism had only been established since January 30, 1933, a point frequently made by the regime as well. As with references to Hitler, this allowed people to mark their own differences as not being fundamentally directed against National Socialism. As another diarist noted, "things happen in a revolution, however, that in normal times would have to be condemned," but on these grounds they could also be ignored as deciding factors in evaluations of the new regime.[93]

For this reason, many diarists did not view the violence and exclusionary policies that accompanied the start of the Nazi dictatorship as a central feature of National Socialist rule, feeling that these policies would be overcome as Nazi rule progressed. As previously mentioned, in the elections of March 1933, the lawyer Ludwig Bröcking voted for the Center Party again despite his enthusiasm for the new regime. Along with citing his longtime affiliation with the Center Party, he justified this decision by noting his disapproval that "the new masters, especially the National Socialists, throw the Communists with the Majority Socialists *into one pot*." The arrests of KPD functionaries and members seemed justified to him because "after all they themselves propagate violence" and are "also declaratively against the German fatherland." The SPD, however, encompassed "the strata of dutiful German workers and citizens, encompasses millions of frontline fighters, Hindenburg voters." It was a major "political mistake" to now force these "masses" to the side of the Communists and "thereby also damage the idea of the *Volksgemeinschaft*, which I have always held high." Instead, Hitler should also be "*forcing* . . . the socialists too into his battlefront." Bröcking concluded his extensive criticism with these words: "I would like to hope that he can pull it off, and certainly do not want to work against it. For now, however, I cannot believe it will happen."[94] By referring to potential future developments, he too marked his explicit criticism as not being fundamentally aimed against the regime.

People distinguished between the present and a supposed future, particularly when they deliberated on the violent policies of the early Nazi dictatorship. They also repeatedly separated their basic approval of certain persecutory policies from what they saw as their unintended consequences. Curt Weber, the Freiburg businessman who in 1933 prefaced his travelogue by summarizing his political stance, named—apart from various aspects of the new regime that excited him—the "action against the Jews" as a central point of criticism. This "naturally resulted in injustices and mortifications in many individual cases that one would rather know had been avoided." But he went on to add that, "viewed as whole," the "action was . . . fully justified," and, "as is unavoidable in such operations, a few innocent people simply had to suffer for the great mass of the guilty."[95] In this way, too, differences could be marked as nonessential and, as in this case, criticism could be transformed into regret over supposedly undesired side effects; in principle, that regret was not directed against the regime and could be formulated for precisely this reason.

Ultimately, all of these argumentations were based on the same principle. They described National Socialism, the object of one's commitment, in a specific way; thus certain critically viewed phenomena of the start of Nazi rule were not ascribed to the latter and hence could be criticized without creating a fundamental distance. Naturally, this meant that the pictures individuals drew of National Socialism were sometimes very different, but those differences allowed many people to combine their commitment with their specific and often biographically based differences with the Nazi regime. Everyone could understand "National Socialism" in a different way and thus commit themselves with their specific life trajectory, which also made it possible for many who had not sympathized with NSDAP prior to 1933 to declare themselves supporters of National Socialism.

The importance of conceptual reflections for the combination of commitment and biographically justified criticism is especially evident in Karl Möhring's diary. There, the Göttingen student, who in July 1933 declared himself to be an "advocate of National Socialism," bridged his earlier critical assessments of National Socialists and his new position with very deliberate ruminations on the concept of "National Socialism." "In September of last year," Möhring wrote, referring to an earlier entry, "I stated that I am not a supporter of the conservative view of the world and state . . . but that, in contrast, I am of the opinion that people constantly change." At the time he had described Franz von Papen "as an advocate of this new community outlook, as I called it back then, and what I now call the 'National Socialist worldview.'" Naturally, Franz von Papen, "who, of course, is not a National Socialist," must now be attributed "with the National Socialist worldview," whereas "this essentially does not apply to many a National Socialist voter."[96] Möhring kept working on this unorthodox classification in subsequent entries of summer and fall 1933, coining for himself the term "National Socialist philistines" for those NSDAP members who did not adhere to the "National Socialist worldview."[97] Using this distinction, Möhring repeatedly justified his own criticism of the new regime, and it also informed his contention in late 1933 that he was a "National Socialist as I understand it, that is, I exercise criticism not to undermine the reputation of the state . . . but to make it better."[98] With its arbitrary use of the terms *National Socialism* and *National Socialist*, his argument may sound absurd, but ultimately Karl Möhring was only doing what many other contemporaries did when referring to Hitler's "real" views or to the supposed future form of National Socialism and when labeling certain results of National

Socialist policy as "actually unintended." Namely, he defined a picture of National Socialism to which his commitment applied, and this allowed him to comprehend himself as a National Socialist precisely because it marked the differences resulting from his actual political views and previous course of life as not being directed against National Socialism.

The Nation and One's Own Picture of the Nazi Regime

However, not all Germans were able to claim belonging by aligning their commitment according to their own picture of National Socialism, one that integrated criticism and rendered it nonessential. This argument presumed that they were prepared, like Karl Möhring, to conceive of themselves as National Socialists or at least as supporters of National Socialism. But people like Daniel Lotter, Hans Maschmann, and Henry Marx were only conditionally prepared to do so. When aligning themselves, they wanted to maintain their existing self-conceptions under the new system as well. In their case, the separation between an ideal and real National Socialism did more to heighten their criticism of the system than to help them successfully integrate their differences into their commitment. In February 1934, for example, Daniel Lotter, the gingerbread baker from Fürth, still speaking entirely in terms of the distinction between Hitler and local NSDAP functionaries, noted that "the pure intention of Hitler" is at risk if he "does not find the resolve to cut ties between himself and people the likes of Str."[99] The abbreviation referred to Julius Streicher, the local Gauleiter who, as publisher of the weekly newspaper *Der Stürmer*, was known as an especially radical antisemite and repeatedly drew Lotter's criticism.[100] But in Lotter's case, the distinction between Hitler and Streicher did not reconcile his criticism with a commitment to the Nazi regime, for the simple reason that, for him, it lost its credibility over time.

A few months after the aforementioned entry, Lotter learned from "Streicher's loyalty telegram to Hitler," sent and published by Streicher after the supposed SA putsch attempt in June 1934, that the hated Gauleiter "is on familiar terms [per Du] with Hitler." This, in Lotter's opinion, was a sign of the Führer's poor "knowledge of human nature"—"a fatal flaw for a statesman."[101] In the following weeks, he attentively monitored the relationship between Hitler and Streicher, as well as the Führer's role in the conflict between the regime and the church, which Lotter repudiated, before finally concluding for himself in October 1934 that "the hopes that were placed on Hitler will likely prove futile. Hitler supports . . . Streicher and a number of other big players, who without Hitler's protection and the political police would have been swept away long ago."[102] The hopes he associated with Hitler collapsed for Lotter precisely when reality failed to confirm the difference between the Führer and other Nazi functionaries. For people like Walter Lindemann, the idealized picture of Hitler had detached itself from the real person such that they could use it to criticize the conduct of the real Reich chancellor. For Daniel Lotter, what in his eyes were the wrong policies of Hitler shaped the picture he made of the Nazi regime and its leadership, thereby increasing his differences even more.

Like Daniel Lotter, other critical Germans did not merely face the problem of reconciling their own commitment with individual aspects of the Nazi dictatorship that they rejected but also had to find a form of commitment that would not simultaneously force them to conceive of themselves as National Socialists. They could do so by adopting the official interpretation of the start of the National Socialist dictatorship as a "national" event that reached beyond the National Socialist movement. Viewing Hitler's appointment as Reich chancellor in 1933 as a comprehensive "national uprising" gave many people the opportunity to deliberately assign their commitment to the nation and thus claim that they belonged to Germany without having to construe themselves as supporters of National Socialism. Nationalism, naturally, also played a role for individuals who committed themselves to the regime as self-described "Nationalist Socialists," however defined.[103] But for people outside this group, it was precisely the interpretive figure of the "national uprising" that enabled many to commit themselves to the new regime while simultaneously distancing themselves from the National Socialists. Many diarists of the 1930s not only welcomed certain developments from the first months of the Nazi dictatorship as positive for the nation but also emphatically aspired to be involved in national developments and signaled their full personal participation. Instead of merely approving, they too formulated their full personal commitment, and despite their clearly expressed rejection of the National Socialists, they claimed to be part of society and to belong to the new regime.

Born in 1883, Friedrich Ahlers-Hestermann, an artist and lecturer from Cologne who had worked at the Cologne Werkschulen (an academy of fine and applied arts) since 1928, summarized his reflections on his relationship to the new regime in 1934 on two otherwise undated pages. In doing so, he made no secret of his repudiation of the National Socialists. In March 1933, he was dismissed as per the Professional Civil Service Act from his lecturer position at the Cologne Werkschulen. Even though he found admission to the Reich Chamber of Culture just a few months later and started a private art school without state interference, by 1934 the enormous powers that the National Socialists had gained since spring 1933 had left Ahlers-Hestermann disenchanted. "As long as resistance was possible," Ahlers-Hestermann wrote to begin his discussion, "I have provided it with my weapons," whereby he meant above all his involvement in political conversations with friends and acquaintances. "But if the opponent has won along the entire line, then, stripped of all instruments of power, one needs to conclude a treaty with him." This was "no cowardice, no opportunism." Rather, "open resistance" against a "power that has all of the instruments in hand" was simply no longer possible. One "cannot raise any protest against fundamental measures of the victor with which one does not agree, for, especially in the seizure-of-power phase, it will be suffocated, along with the protester."[104]

But in the case of Ahlers-Hestermann, frustration about his powerlessness did not lead to resignation and retreat. He dismissed any thoughts of possible emigration: "If one is attached to the whole, then one wants to help work on it even under oppressive conditions and not simply evade this potentially awful fate by fleeing in order to sit in safety beyond the border." This "naturally does not apply to those who for natural reasons *cannot* have this feeling of belonging, or those who are forced [to emigrate] by the victor through political elimination [Ausschaltung]." But anyone who, like him, "could not or did not want to emigrate" but neither "wants to be shot dead or suffocated" must "do his work with every effort within the limits allowed him by the treaty." Disillusioned by the implementation of the Nazi dictatorship, Ahlers-Hestermann tried to accommodate himself to the Nazi regime out of necessity. But for him this did not mean concentrating on his painting or private life. Rather, he strongly underscored his hopes that "my knowledge and pure effort" could continue "to benefit my Volk." Naturally, the new "power" made this more difficult, and Ahlers-Hestermann noted once more that for him this was not about "making a pact" with said power. Nonetheless, he was resolved to "continue to work, to collaborate on the education of my Volk," which Ahlers-Hestermann saw as an act no less heroic and worthy than his previous "resistance": "To want it nonetheless, that is my undauntedness."[105]

Friedrich Ahlers-Hestermann clearly established his opposition to National Socialism in his deliberations. But he did not retreat into "inner emigration" in 1934, as claimed by an art historian in 1980s.[106] In his written deliberations, he not only emphasized the immensity of the regime's power, which now was insurmountable, but, referring to a more comprehensive societal awakening, also signaled his unremitting effort to continue his active involvement in the development of the "whole." Other people who felt sharply alienated from National Socialism highlighted similar intentions. The Jewish socialist student Henry Marx, for example, justified his aspiration to participate in society in a similar way. As already mentioned, he explained his intense efforts to not let himself be turned into a "second-class state citizen" by insisting that the course of the social awakening also "revealed... the value of the German fatherland," that "the nation as a unity is henceforth a fact," and he wanted to collaborate on its advancement.[107] The socialist teacher Hans Maschmann doggedly defended himself against any denial of his "love for the fatherland," and despite massive criticism of the Nazi dictatorship, he insisted on being involved and playing a part in the nation. Nor was it coincidental that Daniel Lotter, the gingerbread baker from Fürth and former Freemason, rhetorically asked "what good German" could want the Nazi regime to fail.[108]

In 1933–1934, the interpretation of the start of the National Socialist dictatorship as a "German uprising" that embraced all Germans provoked a pressure that also compelled individuals like Friedrich Ahlers-Hestermann, Henry Marx, Hans Maschmann, and Daniel Lotter to contemplate their relationship to the new regime. But at the same time, people who did not see themselves as National Socialists could also use this interpretation to continue distancing themselves from National Socialism while nonetheless complying with the demand for commitment. These arguments, too, were based on a specific definition of *National Socialism*, for they insisted that *nation* and *National Socialism* were not identical. Understood this way, the "National Socialists" constituted one political actor among others—this actor admittedly held broad powers in the new political system but nonetheless was by no means alone in advancing the nation's reconstruction. In this way, people could comply, via the reference to the nation, with the regime's demand for belonging and conceive of themselves as part of the "national uprising" and at the same time assert a distance from the National Socialists—even though ultimately the Nazi regime always benefited from their commitment.

Less than four weeks after Daniel Lotter recorded in his diary his disappointment about Hitler and the protection he provided for Nazi functionaries whom Lotter despised, rumors reached him about an assassination attempt against Hitler, which left him deeply disturbed. Lotter wrote down what he had heard. He also used this opportunity to express his anger again that, "even should it be true, hardly anything about the attack will get through to the public." At the same time, however, he ended the entry with these words: "What will become of this Germany if such plans, which doubtlessly exist, should one day become reality, now that Germany's fate rests on one person?"[109]

This reference to the nation influenced how people positioned themselves toward the Nazi regime in different ways. It could also lead people who had initially distanced themselves to draw closer to the National Socialists in their attitudes and self-descriptions, as is illustrated by the diary of Wilhelm Scheidler, a young worker and SPD functionary arrested in summer 1933 and imprisoned in the Osthofen concentration camp because of diary entries he had written up until that time. Even though security officials saw the entries as clear evidence of his hostility to the state, with respect to 1933 the diary mainly documents the rapid change of his attitude and self-description, driven by the reference to the nation. In his diary, Scheidler kept a daily list of systematic key words below the entries, beneath which he wrote brief comments. These included the times when he got up and went to bed, the foods he ate for lunch and dinner, and also a heading he called "aim in life." The notes he recorded under this heading in mid-March turned above all on the so-far unrequited love of a girl and his goal of continuing to champion his own political ideals. "Ella, I love you! Fight for Socialism!" he wrote, for example, on March 10, 1933. The next day's entry reads, "The future of the nation and the working class lies close to my heart—*Ella*." And on March 12, Scheidler wrote, "*Ella!* Fight for Socialism."[110] His daily reports were also characterized by the need to distance himself from the National Socialists—Scheidler called them "brown murderers" and referred to himself as a "fighter for Socialism, for freedom."[111]

But in the weeks that followed, his comments changed considerably, particularly under the "aim of life" heading. While he still mentioned the name of the girl he adored on a daily basis, after the end of March his political goal no longer appeared, even though the entries were still dominated by his socialist attitude. On May 1, Scheidler complained bitterly that "like in fascist Italy . . . we workers are shackled to chains" and have become "slaves again. I could cry. I can hardly find the words to express my worries and my pain." He reported that on that day "the entire assets" of the local SPD organization, with which he was involved, had been confiscated, and he noted how "sad" it was that during the National Labor Day celebrations "a number of workers, under duress, raised their hand in fascist greeting during the Horst Wessel Song." But on this day that traditionally honored the struggle of the workers' movement, under the heading "aim of life," Scheidler did not repeat his rallying cry for socialism. Instead he noted, "Ella! Germany, my fatherland."[112] The nationalist comment did not directly conflict with his socialist convictions; in March, as well, he had spoken about the "future of the nation and the working class," for which he wanted to campaign.[113] But in spring 1933, nationalist positions gained more and more importance in his diary. On April 25, Scheidler summarized matters: "In today's time I must become cognizant of my duty to the fatherland, otherwise in the state you are the fifth wheel on the wagon." Nonetheless, Scheidler reassured himself, he would remain "true to his opinions."[114]

But the entry on May 1 was the last in which Scheidler sided with the workers' movement. Instead, three days later and against the background of the police operation against the workers' movement, he deregistered from the local SPD organization in the subdistrict of Offenburg and personally declared his resignation from the party. In the days that followed, nationalist turns of phrase and argument increasingly found their way into his diary. On May 10, in honor of the anniversary of the sentencing to death of the Freikorps soldier and Nazi hero Leo Schlageter, Scheidler noted that he "loves" him because he died "for Germany, our fatherland."[115] On May 17, Scheidler reported how "enthusiastic" he had been about Hitler's foreign policy speech in the Reichstag. "I could not have wanted it to be any better and I am happy he spoke with such restraint and yet so openly," he noted, and he also commented with pleasure on how the Reichstag's SPD faction—now referred to as "my earlier Social Democratic comrades"—concurred with the declaration. "Our Volk is unified," he commented. "That is the greatest and most beautiful joy! May it only also become free."[116]

When on May 28, 1933, the city parliament was finally elected in the Free City of Danzig, Scheidler noted that he was "pleased . . . that the National Socialists won so big. I welcome the results in the interests of Germany."[117] Even in late May, Wilhelm Scheidler did not understand himself as a National Socialist. But the reference to the nation nonetheless had changed his attitude and self-image. The young Socialist had lost the need to sharply distance himself from the National Socialists, whom he had still been insulting just a few weeks earlier, and finally, by the end of May, he welcomed the NSDAP's electoral victory without devoting even one comment to the singularly bad performance of his former party. Like Scheidler, against the background of the supposed "uprising" of the entire Volk, other people too used the reference to the nation to draw closer to the National Socialists in their self-descriptions and to declare their belonging.

In contrast, for some people the reference to the nation and the accompanying definition of the National Socialists as a particular actor performed the same argumentative function as did the Hitler myth for Walter Lindemann, Karl Friedrich Eichler, and Franz Buesgen: it allowed the formulation of difference and commitment at the same time and thus combined their personal criticism with their claim for belonging. Hence, for Germans like Hans Maschmann and Daniel Lotter, criticism of National Socialism and nationalist commentary did not merely coexist in the positions they took in their diaries. Rather, they were just as interdependent as the combination found elsewhere between the idealized picture of Hitler and dissatisfaction with certain phenomena of National Socialist rule. Maschmann's central criticism against the National Socialists, which he never grew weary of formulating, was based on his opinion that they would never unify the nation as desired. Thus Maschmann's entry for May 1, 1933, which recorded his impressions of the first Day of National Labor, began as follows: "In the noise of the street, in the intoxicated cries of the masses at the resounding phrases of the speaker . . . under the compulsion and order to believe in the word that has no concepts, from the beseeching pleas and appeals of the 'Führer' to believe and to trust him . . . will all of this produce a nation?"[118]

Even though Maschmann still considered himself a socialist in spring 1933, that fact was irrelevant to the entry. He accepted the nationalistic reinterpretation of the traditional Day of Struggle of the Workers' Movement, which had been energetically promoted by the propaganda of the Nazi regime. He doubted, however, whether "a nation that is free" could arise from these coercively instituted mass events. The organized celebratory processions were "not the nation waking up," because the "best of the Volk" were living "in the prisons of this 'nation.'"[119] Maschmann expressly noted that his phrase did not refer to imprisoned politicians of the workers' parties. "I am not thinking of those who are in the internment camps. They are not the best. I am thinking of those who are from the aristocracy of the German spirit." These real nationalists (real because they were motivated by ideals, and Maschmann counted himself among them) were in "excruciating imprisonment" because the course of social events was being determined not by them but by the "malevolent spirit of the masses" instrumentalized by the political leadership. "We want the disarmament of hearts and minds, the arming of the will for peace," but just then the regime was pursuing the "arming of minds through hatred. The will for reason is being poisoned by all kinds of intoxicants, administered in large doses."[120] Yet as he had already pointed out sarcastically three days earlier when criticizing the finale of the main May celebration on the Tempelhof Field in Berlin, "one does not unify the Volk, one does not form the nation," by means of "gigantic fireworks that cost RM 250,000."[121] References to the nation brought Hans Maschmann no closer to the National Socialists. Instead, he maintained his distant stance because he was able to combine his commitment to the nation with the formulation of objections to the Nazi regime. Insofar as his criticism was based on his fear that Hitler's regime would not successfully construct the nation as promised, Maschmann formulated commitment and distance in equal measure. This way he could hang on to his criticism, thereby preserving his existing self-perspective, and nonetheless still claim not to be an "opponent" of the new system.

This was similarly the case for Daniel Lotter. The gingerbread baker from Fürth repeatedly justified his discontent about the suppression of dissenting opinions and the political monitoring of the public sphere by expressing his worries about the development of the German nation. "Without violation one cannot force the mighty flooding current of German intellectual and cultural life into the channel of the National Socialist worldview," he wrote in his entry for April 15, 1934 (the same one in which he noted that no "good German" could possibly want the NSDAP to fail). This would inevitably "lead over the short or long term to a catastrophe."[122] He also always invoked the interests of the nation when criticizing individual Nazi functionaries. "The harm Streicher has done to the German Volk is reaching tremendous levels," he pointed out on May 27, 1934.[123] In fact, Lotter was even able to refer to the nation to justify distancing himself from Hitler. In late 1934, he reported with bitter irony that the Nazi regime was "still successfully making efforts to offend all personalities of character and importance." The "famous director Furtwängler" was "prohibited from exiting Germany"; the theology professor Karl Barth, a cofounder of the Confessing Church, had been "ousted from his office by the disciplinary court." "A cultural disgrace of the worst kind!" he commented, adding sarcastically, "Why do we still need important men: after all, we have Hitler and Goebbels and Göring and our Gauleiters, one of whom (Brückner—Silesia), incidentally, has again been chased away because of homosexual transgressions."[124] Through his commitment to the nation, Lotter too managed to declare his belonging to the nation and likewise conjoin this with his distant stance toward National Socialism, thus finding an explanation for why his criticism did not signify fundamental alienation.

Even German Jews, whom the regime considered "enemies of the German Volk" regardless of their individual positions, could use the reference to the nation to still claim belonging in their self-descriptions of 1933–1934. In his effort to break out of social isolation, young Henry Marx was not alone in orienting his life plans in 1933 around his "relationship to Germany." He emphasized in his diary that the term German did not refer to lineage but to an "ideal state": "One is not born a German; one strives for this goal during one's entire life."[125] By and large, in 1933–1934 many German Jews understood themselves "inwardly as profoundly German and wanted to remain so." Diaries, in particular, show time and again how Jewish contemporaries after 1933, despite the antisemitic measures, tried with all their might to insist that they were "German."[126] This was not just an expression of widespread Jewish assimilation over the past years and of German Jewish self-images and "strategies developed in the Weimar Republic."[127] Despite unbridgeable differences with the Nazi regime, they too still endeavored to claim belonging.

Individual commitment to the Nazi regime in 1933–1934 was not a spontaneous and fully voluntary matter. After the start of National Socialist rule, the entire Volk certainly did not commit itself with great enthusiasm to National Socialism as depicted in Nazi propaganda. However, during the first months of Nazi rule, the dynamics of the seizure of power generated immense social pressure for individuals to establish a relationship to the new government. Given the fact that even just the street violence of spring 1933 clearly demonstrated that the Nazi regime equated individual commitment with social belonging, it is hardly surprising that so many people, despite their disinclinations, searched for ways to comply with this demand—including in their private reflections in diaries. The Nazi regime associated its demand for commitment with a model that made clear-cut divisions between supporters, "enemies" and "opponents," and the still undecided. But the positions we see people taking in the diaries of the 1930s often failed to fulfill this aspect of the demand. Instead, people notably founded their positions on the combination of commitment and criticism, the latter usually biographically based. In light of official demands for unconditional adherence, this required specific arguments for justifying why one's own dissatisfaction did not entail the repudiation of the regime. In this way, people could understand themselves as proponents and supporters of the new regime who set their own definition for *National Socialism*, whether by referring to the supposedly genuine views of the Führer or with other arguments. This way they could combine commitment with biographical self-conceptions. However, the reference to the nation and the interpretive figure of the "national uprising" also facilitated claims of belonging in positions taken by persons who were unwilling to conceive of themselves as National Socialists. Hence, their repudiation of the National Socialists, presented at times with striking clarity, did not need to be comprehended as fundamental opposition against the government. Rather, they could make it part of their commitment and thereby preserve their personal self-understanding.

In 1933–1934, these specific types of argument secured for the Nazi regime the massive commitment of large parts of German society by allowing people to circumvent the regime's demand for unconditional adherence. For individuals unable to fully harmonize their previous life with the requisite dedication to National Socialism, this circumvention allowed them to commit themselves to the regime with their personal biographies in the first place. The redefinition of social belonging did not create the categorical separation that the regime was actually trying to achieve—namely, between the regime and its supporters, on one side, and "opponents" and "enemies," on the other. But at the same time, the argumentative mediation between biographical self-conceptions and political views, on the one hand, and the requisite commitment, on the other, made the Nazi regime compatible with people who were far outside the circle of its own party members and supporters.

4. "When I Read the Entries of 1933 and 1934": Continuity and Change of Personal Political Positions in the 1930s

On August 2, 1934, Reich President Paul von Hindenburg died. The health of the eighty-six-year-old had deteriorated so badly in July that, in light of his imminent death, the Reich government had already passed a law the day before mandating that, in the event of the "demise of Reich President Hindenburg," the "office of the Reich president ... [would be] unified with that of the Reich chancellor" and the "previous powers of the Reich president" transferred to the "Führer and Reich Chancellor Adolf Hitler."[128] The merger of the state's two highest offices on August 2, 1934, which the Reich government then had affirmed with a plebiscite less than three weeks later, formed the denouement of the Nazi seizure of power. After the effective elimination of the Reichstag and German states, the prohibition of independent associations and organizations, and the acquisition of facilities for intervening in the judicial system, administration, and media, the last remaining institution that had served to divide and monitor political power during the Weimar Republic had now also been removed. Henceforth, all formal powers resided with the Reich government and the "Führer and Reich chancellor of the German Volk," as Hitler had himself called after the offices were merged.[129] The so-called second seizure of power in summer 1934 meant that the conquest was over and that the new state leadership had consolidated its powers, even though its more extensive social policy goals had by no means been realized at this time.[130] Nonetheless, the year 1934 formed an important juncture with respect to the demand for commitment made by the regime within the context of efforts to fundamentally reconstitute German society. Most diarists determined their individual relationship to the new regime during the first two years of Nazi rule, returning to the issue only on specific occasions in the years that followed.[131] This was particularly true of people whose diaries did not focus on the discussion of politics and who in 1933–1934 had come to an understanding of their relationship to the new regime in specially written entries.

After his entries summarizing his own position in fall 1933, Wolfgang Söller, the director of the Krupp Book Hall, returned to the subject once more the next summer, noting that "politics ... plays a larger role in today's life."[132] Thereafter, political events and the issue of his personal stance vanished from his diary. The entries of 1935, 1936, and 1937 were all about private experiences, travels, and professional developments. Not until the end of 1937 did Söller revisit the issue of his relationship to political events. In his entry of December 31, in which he "looked back and forward in the usual way," he noted that "the hallmark of 1937 will generally be: a tremendous job of development and expansion, this in Germany, in Essen, at Krupp, indeed in almost every family."[133]

Söller's basic commitment to social renewal and the regime, which, notwithstanding criticism, he recorded in his diary in 1933, informed this passage in two ways: first, in how he situated social development within the nation and family; second, in the fact that he actually made note of this observation at this particular time. The comment was not made on a whim but was instead related to the fact that in 1937 Söller felt very much moved by national developments. That summer his mother-in-law had suffered "a light accident when trying to climb into the streetcar" and, frail as she was, died from the consequences that very afternoon.[134] The death of the seventy-one-year-old relative, whom he called Oma, greatly preoccupied him in his diary. Söller dedicated a detailed eulogy to the memory of the deceased, and the incident was also responsible for his comments at year's end about the society's "development."[135] The "symbol" of development, he noted, is "ever more traffic, that unfortunately time and again claims it victims. This also includes our Oma."[136] Naturally, the move from the death of a mother-in-law, whose accident while getting on the streetcar could hardly be considered the result of a general increase in traffic, to the development and expansion of the nation was anything but obvious. That this association nonetheless came to Söller's mind reveals how much his commitment to the Nazi regime in 1933–1934 led to an awareness on his part that his own life path was intertwined with the development of the nation. This perception persisted in following years as well, shaping his annual review at the end of 1937, which interwove political and private developments without voicing regret over this interdependence. Instead, Söller took the death of his mother-in-law as an occasion to issue an admonishment with regard to further development work: "May we be allowed to be diligent and active as well as contemplative and reflective in proper proportion to our share."[137]

Even after 1934, diary writers again and again paralleled and interwove their personal life with the development of the Nazi regime, with annual reviews providing the perfect opportunity for this kind of reflection. Consider, for example, Christoph Ahrens, the former seaman who in the 1930s tried his hand as a painter and, looking back over 1934, had spoken about the "vortex of events" that pulled everyone in. In the following years, as well, he would conclude the year by writing a retrospective annual report, which always contemplatively summarized personal, professional, and political developments in equal measure, often drawing connections between political events and personal experience.[138] In much the same way, the farmer Karl Friedrich Eichler integrated political occurrences into summaries of family events and life on his farm in regular annual reports in his family chronicle. He had already been following this practice prior to 1933. Back then, however, his entries only really devoted significant attention to political developments during the crisis periods from the end of the Great War until the early 1920s and after the world economic crisis of 1929.[139] During the intervening years, which were relatively peaceful for Eichler, politics took up very little space. Thus, the fact that in the years after 1934 he kept up his detailed reporting and especially his commentaries on political decisions affecting him and his farm should not simply be seen as the continuation of existing writing habits. The new interrelationship between his personal life and political events is also reflected by the changing structure of his entries: before and during 1933, the sections dealing successively with political, agricultural, and family developments were strictly separate; after 1934, however, they became increasingly interwoven.[140]

In annual reviews, diarists in the second half of the 1930s were still expressing the biographically grounded commitment to the Nazi regime through the interweaving of political developments and their own personal lives. At the same time, however, these reviews also marked an important difference compared to 1933–1934: during the first months of the Nazi dictatorship, diarists did not need any formal reason, such as an annual retrospective, to start speaking about their relationship to the Nazi regime—instead the question of how individuals stood in relation to the new regime had been raised by the political developments themselves. This changed in the second half of the 1930s. Personal commitments still remained very visible in the diaries, but many authors no longer felt that political "happenings" were challenging them to respond with their own "commentary," as Wolfgang Söller had noted in his diary in fall 1933.

A different picture emerges in the case of diarists who made political discussions a central—or the central—component of their diary writing. They continued to deal regularly with political and social developments even after 1934. Yet even so, the question about their own position toward the Nazi regime took a step back in their writing as well. The positions they had found during the first months of the new regime still shaped their confrontation with political developments in the second half of the 1930s, but for these authors too, political occurrences after 1934 no longer triggered fundamental questions about how they stood in relation to the Nazi regime.[141] Instead, it was the other way around: arguments they developed in 1933–1934 in the context of determining their position were now, in the second half of the 1930s, determining their written commentary on political developments.

Even after 1934, the Fürth gingerbread baker Daniel Lotter repeatedly complained that the "voice of the populace . . . hardly finds expression in the public sphere,"[142] showed his frustration with "Streicher's rages,"[143] and blamed Hitler for what he saw as "coercive measures and abominations";[144] yet he nonetheless continued to uphold the claim that he was "a good German" and not an "opponent."[145] After 1934, Walter Lindemann still condemned the behavior of individual Nazi functionaries and would keep up his severe criticism of the "oppression and *violation of the Evangelical Church*" until the start of the war. But he nonetheless continued to affirm the regime.[146] Throughout his regular detailed discussions about the political situation, Hans Maschmann stuck with the position he established in 1933, based on his worry that the National Socialists would be unable to unify the nation. The struggle with the relationship between the National Socialist regime and the nation runs continuously throughout his diary. "I will make an effort and try," he opened an entry in March 1935, "not to condemn the good of the movement with the bad that it generated." But after extensive discussions, he finally had to concede that he was simply unable to do so: "It is always like this: I try to see the good fortune of the movement and this state. But as soon as contemplation proceeds from the sum of what exists, the positive sinks into nothingness." The nation "has become an end in itself and the means of power-political instincts." "Never," Maschmann noted, "were we less a nation than today."[147]

The vast growth of Maschmann's diary after 1933 shows that his effort "to be affirmative" was more than just a rhetorical strategy. Ultimately, this effort dominated almost each and every one of his entries: time and again, he tried to harmonize his own notions of the nation with the National Socialists as bearers of the government and thereby escape the discord wrought for him by the position he established in 1933—despite being aware that this was hopeless. In early May 1936, he noted in his diary that "I have undertaken to no longer worry about politics, because I experienced in myself how the daily disappointment and bitter pain about the misleading of public opinion ate at my mental and physical health."[148] Maschmann traced his health problems at the time back to the constant confrontation with politics and saw this as a warning to avoid it. But despite this intent, he resumed his political analysis in the very same entry with a detailed discussion of Hitler's speech on the May 1 national holiday and the current foreign policy situation. And in the next diary entry, three days later, Maschmann was back to his singular focus on the subject that had dominated his diary since early March 1933: "I suffer for the sake of my Volk, because such mendacity and these individuals have achieved victory over the better Germany."[149] The entry of May 1936 was not the first in which Maschmann resolved to cease his written confrontation with political events because it was making him suffer, nor would it be the last.[150] But as in this case and others, he always failed because he never fundamentally questioned the relationship to the regime he had found in 1933, which claimed belonging through the nation while at the same time asserting a distance from the National Socialists, whom he viewed as a particular actor. This position fed his perpetual problems in his diary. Yet this position was precisely what made it possible for him to claim belonging and still hold on to his own self-image. While giving it up could have brought his intense written struggle to an end, it would have required choosing between social belonging and the preservation of his self-perspective, which he was unwilling or unable to do.

Maschmann's diary is undoubtedly exceptional in terms of the intensity of his preoccupation with the Nazi regime arising from this conflict, but not with regard to the underlying intent, which was, namely, to preserve the position found in 1933–1934 during the second half of the 1930s. Despite their extensive discussions of current debates, many diarists, having established their relationship to the Nazi regime in 1933–1934, held on to it in the second half of the 1930s. This was related above all to the fact that their commitment in 1933–1934 had in fact also been a biographical decision. Many contemporaries continued working intensely on their political assessment of the Nazi regime with regular discussions of political developments in their diaries. But changing their political evaluation did not automatically challenge the basic decision they had made to declare their commitment with their own person and life history. The positions they had found proved to be astonishingly flexible, informed as they were by the coexistence of criticism and commitment, which in 1933–1934 had made it possible to claim belonging with their existing biographical self-assessments and political views. They could reconcile their existing position toward the Nazi regime not only with newly arising dissatisfaction with that regime but also with the disappointment of hopes and expectations formulated in 1933–1934; thus, in the years that followed, they could preserve the self-perspective they had gained at the start of the National Socialist dictatorship.

In the course of Nazi rule, Walter Lindemann, for example, reacted in his diary with increasing irritation to Hitler's speeches during the second half of the 1930s, specifically to the way Hitler still went on and on highlighting the differences between the Weimar Republic and the Nazi regime. "This morning, or rather at noon," Lindemann noted in February 1938, "I had to *endure one Führer speech more than three hours long*. Once again it was the usual [?]: 'for 14 years [i.e., the Weimar period], etc.; Germany is more beautiful and glorious since the National Socialist movement won this state, etc.' I breathed a sigh of relief when it was finally over."[151] Time and again, the comparison with the years before 1933 and the blatant self-praise filled him with disgust, but this did nothing to change the relationship to Hitler he had found in 1933–1934. He was still able to legitimate his criticisms—particularly of National Socialism's relationship to religion—with references to *Mein Kampf*;[152] he could still formulate disagreement with regime policy and nonetheless bow "*before the statesman's genius of our Chancellor* Adolf Hitler" when the Reich chancellor's actions conformed to Lindemann's idea of the Führer.[153]

Lindemann's frustration with Hitler's speeches in the second half of the 1930s was also related to his apparent disappointment with the way the system developed after it began and its failure to fulfill his awoken expectations. "*Not much has changed yet for the better in Germany*," he noted in September 1935, referring to the economic situation, and his disenchantment frequently showed in other contexts as well.[154] The suppression of dissenting opinions in the public sphere and various specific regime measures also drew sharp criticism. But this did not change his commitment; at most, it merely changed the arguments he used when balancing the tension between dissent and commitment. In the second half of the 1930s, alongside references to what were ostensibly Hitler's real opinions, the nation took on more importance in his diary as an argument for integrating criticism. Nationalist positions had been central for Lindemann in 1933–1934 as well, but toward the end of the 1930s, he used them more vigorously to formulate criticism of the National Socialists. When in 1938 the November pogrom devastated Jewish businesses, residences, and institutions, Lindemann—an SA man—bluntly criticized it numerous times in his diary and recorded what he had learned about the event from various places: "In Oldenburg," he noted on November 12, "the Jews were whipped through the streets by the National Socialist mob and coerced SA men; in Berlin many expensive stores were looted. The *Goebbels course* is triumphing. One is ashamed to be a German."[155]

It was much the same for the student Karl Möhring, who had declared himself to be a "National Socialist as I understand it" in his diary in 1933. Over the course of 1934, his diary entries became less regular, such that his notes were now often weeks and finally months apart. In 1935, Möhring wrote two more entries in the spring, wrote one in the summer, and then concluded his diary in November with a retrospective review of his personal development thus far. In the meantime, Möhring had completed his studies and started a teacher training program at a secondary school in Quedlinburg, but the training program caused him such severe problems that he had to break it off in fall 1935. This event provided the occasion to look back on the previous path of his life and career, which brought Möhring to speak about his political position toward the Nazi regime. Looking back, he noted that in 1933 he admittedly declared that he was "for the NSDAP, but soon thereafter had to acknowledge that much still divided me from this party."[156]

Even though in fall 1935 he no longer described himself as a National Socialist and in hindsight now considered his specific declaration to be a "supporter of the National Socialist worldview" as ill-advised advocacy for the NSDAP, this did not mean that he had therefore abandoned his commitment. Möhring was mainly doubtful about the point of having studied and "whether the expense of 10,000 Marks" for this purpose "had really been worthwhile," because looking back he was sure that he "could have filled a position in the community life of the Volk in another way more quickly and with a sense of satisfaction. For these bygone seven years [i.e., years of study] have naturally not been beneficial for the overall development."[157] Although his declaration in 1933 that he was a National Socialist seemed wrong to him in retrospect, in 1935 he was still clearly voicing his hopes to make a contribution to the "community life of the Volk," even without describing himself as a National Socialist. After 1934, Karl Möhring gained the insight that his differences with the NSDAP were too great. But in his case too, instead of changing his fundamental commitment to the regime, this insight changed the interpretation he used to explain the differences.

But disappointed hopes did not lead all contemporaries to change the self-descriptions they had developed when committing themselves to the Nazi regime in 1933–1934. One example is Erich Rahmacher, the Freiburg postal employee, water sports enthusiast, and puppeteer who had placed great hopes in National Socialism because it allowed him to pursue his favorite hobbies within the Hitler Youth. In fall 1936, after looking through his diary, he noted that "when I read the entries of 1933 and 1934 I have to laugh! How long will this capacity of mine for enthusiasm and fantasy probably last?" Everything "naturally turned out much different" than he had wanted. Rahmacher described how some of his hopes had proved to be a "very horrible flop and castles in the air" and how even more generally things were "not as easy as I thought." "Success and accomplishment," he concluded, were "in any case not at all in proportion to the very tremendous expenditure of effort and work." Although it had also brought him an "endless amount of joy," he noted, "I can no longer keep toiling like that. It is definitively over."[158]

After three years of active involvement in the Hitler Youth, Erich Rahmacher was disillusioned as he looked back and exhausted by the exertions of his Hitler Youth activities. But this did not mean turning away from the National Socialist movement or giving up his involvement in the Hitler Youth. In the same entry, Rahmacher reported that he was supposed to be promoted to chief postal inspector and therefore would probably also "(need to!) join the NSDAP."[159] Precisely by describing this in his diary as a necessity and not as a voluntary act, he indicated that his basic commitment as found in 1933 had not changed. Back then, too, he had committed himself to the Nazi movement because within it he could advance his private life plans, and this also characterized his relationship to the regime in the second half of the 1930s.

In fall 1937, he reported that transfers were pending at his post office, from which he was, however, exempted from the outset. "Apparently I am sitting pretty," Rahmacher commented, adding that "the Kreisleiter"—whom he had come to know personally by way of his service with the Hitler Youth—"and the Hitler Youth are doing me some good after all." And even though this wording once more voiced his frustration about his Hitler Youth activities, at the same time Rahmacher also took more pleasure from this work again. "Hitler Youth paddling this summer, very big!"[160] he noted in the same entry. In January 1938, anticipating the next season, he was once again making "big plans: carry over old vacation time, July with Swiss scouts down the Rhine, end of July fourteen days with 1000 Hitler Youth scouting game in the Hegau Mountains, then all the way to Ulm. . . . Punch and Judy Show is also supposed to start again. 'Hitler Youth School for Artistic Puppetry.'"[161] Although the hopes Rahmacher tied to the start of

Nazi rule in 1933–1934 had only been partially fulfilled, this did nothing to change his underlying commitment to National Socialism, which for him particularly consisted of the attachment of private hopes. At the end of the entry, when Rahmacher reported that he was currently reading the autobiography of the physician Carl Ludwig Schleich, he commented, "That guy sure had a wonderful youth. I am just now actually really starting to live."[162]

Other contemporaries, in contrast, could not integrate dashed hopes or new criticisms into their previous commitment. Walter Lohs, a trained businessman born in 1879 who managed a farm in Röhrsdorf in Saxony, had become a member of the NSDAP in February 1932. Thus he welcomed Hitler's accession to power in 1933, attaching great hopes to the new regime, above all economic ones. But by late summer 1934, he already saw that they were disappointed, which drove him to pick up his diary again. From 1919 to 1926, he had consistently kept the diary with a few regular entries per year, but thereafter his entries became sporadic, and by summer 1934 three and a half years had passed since his last entry. In his diary, Lohs now reported briefly on the past months and about Hitler's accession to power, complaining that "Hitler . . . wants to help the agricultural economy," but despite a few improvements, "we still have *exactly the same encumbrances* as under the earlier government and the *lowest* prices of the Brüning government as fixed prices." The agricultural economy was "being supported in name only, with nice words, but in reality is still being drained exactly as before."

As he pointed out in his entry, Lohs had "always supported" the National Socialist movement prior to 1933, but now "after all of the undergone experiences," he felt "complete indifference toward the party." At this point Lohs still believed that the lack of support for agriculture within the party was because "the theoreticians have too much influence" within the NSDAP and because after the seizure of power posts were given to "wholly unscrupulous people who have a big mouth."[163] In his criticism of late summer 1934—namely, that "today after one and a half years of government" the agricultural economy was still burdened with the "same encumbrances, sometimes even *higher ones*"—he also still referred to a quote from *Mein Kampf* and expressly stated that he was currently "not hostile toward the matter, but indifferent."[164]

However, this dramatically changed over the next months, during which Lohs wrote regularly in his diary while constantly observing and commenting on the burdens of the agricultural economy. "It is a very nasty lie," he noted in March 1935, "when Hitler says he wants to help the agricultural economy." Instead Hitler was considering "*only* the factory workers and nobody else." Only through "fraud and false promises did the Hitler people win the agricultural vote." Agriculturalists were no longer "free farmers anymore, but only Hitler slaves. . . . Curse Hitler and his system: we are not slaves and will not let ourselves all be squeezed into one form. Pew. Pew."[165] Walter Loh's writings were now void of arguments that could contain his criticism and reconcile it with commitment. His diary showed no sign of any effort to claim belonging despite criticism. "Better dead than a slave! Pew Hitler system,"[166] Lohs noted in summer 1935. In his eyes, the system had not gotten rid of Marxism but actually helped set it up in the first place, and he would keep on cursing it in years to come. "National Socialism," he noted a few weeks later, "is in reality the doctrine of Karl Marx, except in place of international they have put the word national in order to feign a rightwing party and capture rightwing votes. . . . A Volksgemeinschaft is feigned; and yet it is the worst dictatorship, where intrigues are the going thing. Honorable people are stamped into the dirt because they are not given any chance to justify themselves. . . . Of course, criticism does not exist and the power of the Führer guards against every attack. A glorification of educated people by the plebeian movement."[167]

Walter Lohs fiercely ranted at the existing system, but what else could he do but curse? By committing themselves to the Nazi regime during the first months of the Nazi dictatorship, Walter Lohs and countless other people had contributed to the social dynamics that enabled the new regime to fundamentally change the society and political system. Any opportunities for private dissatisfaction to influence societal developments had virtually disappeared by no later than summer 1934, with the merger of the offices of the Reich president and Reich chancellor. Given his disappointment in 1934, Lohs would surely have cast his next vote for a different party. But this was no longer possible. After 1934, even in places where dissatisfaction suddenly turned into alienation from the regime, the enthusiastic or critically minded commitment that people had found in 1933–1934 under the pressure of the social dynamics of the start of National Socialist rule was far more of an important factor in the development of history.

3

ESTABLISHING A PERSONAL STANCE TOWARD THE REGIME WHILE UNDER SOCIAL OBSERVATION

1. "Wilke and Wife Have Switched Over": Observing Others within One's Own Milieu

In mid-January 1933, Franz Buesgen finally managed to get a job in his trained profession. Born in 1911 into a four-person family from Langenberg that moved to Herne in the nearby Ruhr region in the early 1920s, young Franz had finished his schooling in 1928 with an intermediate school leaving certificate. Next, he successfully completed an apprenticeship at a bank, where he continued working for a few months before being dismissed in fall 1931. Finding a job as a bank employee was difficult for the recently trained novice. He remained unemployed for a year, apart from a temporary stint for a few weeks in summer 1932 as the supervisor of a travel group. In November 1932, he finally found work as an unskilled employee in the social welfare office of the town of Herne. Here Buesgen got lucky. After two and a half months, a position opened up at the town savings bank, and he transferred there in mid-January 1933.

Buesgen celebrated the transfer to the savings bank in his diary. However, that he wrote a diary at all was due to the interim job that brought him to Romania in 1932 as a tour guide. He would continue the diary he started on that trip until well after the war. In keeping with the specific origins of his diary as the travel notes of an unemployed person, recreational activities and the striving for his own professional advancement dominated the entries. Thus, it was extremely unusual when, on April 30, 1933, Buesgen summarized in a six-page entry the political developments that had taken place since Hitler's appointment and gave an account of his own position toward the new regime. Admittedly, he noted, for "such a small politician like I am, it is naturally [not possible] . . . to fully grasp the momentary situation of Germany." But Buesgen nonetheless wanted to "try," and in the remarkably long entry, he therefore strove to provide the "most truthful picture possible" of the start of National Socialist rule.[1]

However, the entry stood out in the diary not just because it dealt so copiously with political events but also because the text was actually not written for the diary: it was a copy of a letter Franz Buesgen had just written to his older sister Gerda. He marked this in the diary both by adding a separate heading and also by transferring the letter to his diary unchanged, including elements of direct address.

These political discussions in the heretofore apolitical diary of Franz Buesgen provide another example of how the start of Nazi rule raised questions for Germans about their own position toward political events, how it forced its way into their diaries, and how it could make daily writing a key instrument for establishing one's position. But as a copied letter, the entry also indicates that determining one's personal position in 1933–1934 was not an isolated process. Rather, in many respects it occurred through an exchange with others facing the same challenge.

One cannot help but notice in other diaries as well that determining one's position was always a social process—as when, for example, an entry reported a discussion about the political situation with friends and acquaintances. Even Hans Maschmann, who had so forcefully pointed out in his diary that it is "advisable to remain silent, even with the best of friends," repeatedly reported such conversations.[2] But the embedded nature of personal position determinations in 1933–1934 is illustrated most vividly by letters from this period in which friends exchanged ideas about political events. During the first months after Hitler's appointment as Reich chancellor, Franz Buesgen was by no means the only person who reported by mail on his thoughts and attitude regarding the new regime. The businessman Otto Kirchmann, for example, did this quite broadly.

Somewhat older than Buesgen, Kirchmann came from bourgeois circumstances, and in 1921 he completed his studies in law with a doctorate on liability insurance policies. But his professional career led him neither to the insurance industry nor to any other activity that his studies qualified him to perform. A severe eye injury suffered in the First World War made it impossible for him to read for long hours at a time. Kirchmann moved to Hamburg, where he first worked as a realtor and then in 1923 opened a pharmacy in the Winterhude district, which he still ran in the 1930s. But he continued to maintain intense correspondence with his former classmates of the Armenia fraternity, which he had joined as a student. Kirchmann inherited his deep appreciation of written correspondence from his bourgeois parental home, and that influence was still reflected in the 1930s by his equally extensive exchange of letters with his siblings and other relatives.

Compared to the letters of his correspondence partners, Otto Kirchmann's letters—always typewritten—were remarkably long, rarely less than two and sometimes more than ten closely typed pages. They contained both descriptions of concrete experiences and abstract explications on various topics, politics prominent among them. Thus it was only natural in 1933 for Otto Kirchmann to also talk with longtime friends and close relatives about his own thoughts regarding the start of National Socialist rule. Contrary to Buesgen, who largely welcomed the start of the Nazi dictatorship, Kirchmann appeared extremely critical and disapproving. He wanted to "hold on to my liberal worldview," he wrote in a letter to a distant relative in fall 1933. On six closely typed pages, he outlined his political assessment of the Nazi regime so that the correspondent would find "my stance comprehensible, which is not dictated by a rejection of the new but by concern about my beloved German fatherland."[3]

As early as March that same year, in a "family circular letter," Kirchmann had explained his position as a "liberal" to his siblings with a wide-ranging argument: "To date I have not found anything better than this worldview," even though it is now being "disparaged by the very top of the Reich."[4] This letter and others clearly show how important Kirchmann felt it was to communicate his stance to friends and relatives and how personally meaningful he considered written discussions of the political situation. When in March 1933 he likewise wrote to one of his siblings, explaining that he primarily rejected the "political turnaround, as you call it," for "purely humane and ethical reasons, especially patriotic ones," because it means "nothing good for our German fatherland," he appended his comparatively brief account with the offer to "provide [his sibling] with the carbon copies of my correspondence with the publisher of our Munich Armenian Notices," in which he had extensively laid out his position toward the new regime.[5] His comprehensive discussions of political developments in letters to various correspondents functioned for Otto Kirchmann in much the same way that diaries did for other people. In his exchanges with friends, relatives, and acquaintances, when justifying his rejection of the new regime and his simultaneous participation in political affairs, he also deployed the same arguments used by certain diary writers.

But as opposed to diaries, the arguments he articulated in letters met with direct response. His stance found only minimal acceptance, especially in his exchanges with other fraternity comrades. One such correspondent was Anton Schäfer, the publisher of the internal notices of the Armenian fraternity, with whom Kirchmann had an intense correspondence and who became a senior civil servant after the seizure of power. As early as mid-February, Schäfer noted in a written response to Kirchmann, "I do not take the *Hitler regime* as tragically as you."[6] Less than four weeks later, he wrote to Kirchmann, but without addressing Kirchmann's long discussion more precisely: "You are depressed and as a modern Cassandra do not want to endorse the given solution." Schäfer "welcomed . . . the new course," and Kirchmann should do likewise. Hence the old friend advised, "[Let] the rose- and similarly or black-colored petty bourgeoisie mourn, and look toward the future, which will bring something better."[7] But Kirchmann held fast to his critical attitude toward the new regime.

This led him into heated disputes with other fraternity comrades. In early May at a fraternity meeting in Hamburg, his position toward the new regime resulted in fierce conflicts. A number of fraternity comrades went at him sharply because of his reserved attitude, and they did not restrict themselves to well-intentioned advice. On the contrary, they issued thinly veiled threats of protective custody and denunciation. Otto Kirchmann wrote to the director of the local Armenian group the next day and told him to "save yourself the effort of inviting me in future to the Armenian evenings" because he "would not be coming for a long time hence." The "conflict of yesterday" had filled "me with such disgust and abhorrence with politics" that "in the rest of the sleepless night I decided to roll up like a hedgehog and not let anything approach me that even very remotely smells like politics."[8]

Many Germans in 1933–1934 understood the determination of their relationship to the new regime as something personal. This is precisely why so many of them talked about it in their diaries. But at the same time, establishing a position toward the Nazi regime in 1933–1934 was anything but a private process that people could work out by themselves. Insofar as the determination of one's own position to the new regime also occurred in exchanges with others, it was not enough to determine a position that did justice to one's biographical self-perception and personal political views. One also needed to find a form of self-presentation that could hold up under the gaze of friends, acquaintances, neighbors, and family members. Taking a position toward the new regime did not only affect how people understood themselves; it also shaped the social relationships they had at the start of National Socialist rule.

On the one hand, this was because of traditional conversation practices within existing friendships and acquaintanceships. As with Otto Kirchmann, in many cases the exchange of political ideas and knowledge of each counterpart's political attitudes had already been part of such social relationships during the Weimar Republic. Thus in 1933 as well, Germans made the start of Nazi rule a topic of conversation among friends, acquaintances, and colleagues. But on the other hand, the impact of people's positions on their social relationships also very much related to the way the Nazi regime, right from the outset, pressured them not just to commit themselves "to National Socialism out of inner fervor" but also to put this "commitment" on public display.[9] For the regime, the demand for commitment was not simply about people's attitudes. It sought visible public support for itself and a fundamental realignment of social relationships in accordance with the positions that individuals took. For the regime it was therefore critical that the "commitment to National Socialism" not remain a private matter but instead become publicly visible.

As early as spring 1933, it propagated an entire series of symbols and symbolic practices, whose public use was supposed to make the individual's proximity to or distance from the regime visible. These derived largely from the preexisting repertoire of the National Socialist movement, which had assigned prominent importance to symbols from the very beginning.[10] But with Hitler's appointment as Reich chancellor and the affirmation of his regime in the Reichstag elections on March 5, 1933, their character fundamentally changed, just as they in turn radically changed public space. This was already becoming widely visible during the electoral victory celebrations. Partly in the night leading to March 6 and partly within the context of rallies over the following days, local NSDAP functionaries forcefully and symbolically raised the swastika and black-white-red flags on town halls and other public buildings throughout Germany, often against the will of mayors and other local politicians. The operations arose from local initiatives but were given cover by the presiding Reich commissioner for the Prussian Interior Ministry, Hermann Göring, who instructed police that they "should not be available to prevent the forcible raising of the swastika flag."[11] Indeed, in places where mayors wanted to prevent the flying of flags, NSDAP, SA, and Stahlhelm detachments forcibly entered town halls to raise their flags.[12] In a very concrete way, raising the flags was a demonstration of power, but raising them on official buildings was also supposed to symbolically show both the existing institutions and the population who would henceforth have the say in Germany.[13]

Usually two flags were raised. But attention and opposition centered primarily on the swastika flag, even though the black-white-red flag just as clearly asserted the aspiration to make changes to the existing political system—from the perspective of its supporters, this aspiration was what the affirmation of the "national regime" in the Reichstag election signified.[14] Accordingly, the raising of the swastika flag often provoked objections not because it symbolized the start of the "national uprising" but because a "party was presuming to raise its party flag on the town hall," which, as noted in a protest letter by the magistrate of Limburg in Hesse, belonged to *"no party, but to the entire citizenry."*[15] The swastika flag had been exactly that in previous years: the flag of a political party, which as late as the election campaign of February 1933 still competed with the flags of other parties for votes. By hoisting the swastika flag, Nazi activists made their party's claim to power visible far and wide,[16] yet at the same time, this operation fundamentally changed the character of the swastika flag. The de facto elevation of both flags to the official symbol of the new state was officially affirmed one week later by Reich President Hindenburg, who for the occasion of the March 12 Day of Commemoration of the Fallen stipulated that, "until the final regulation of the Reich colors," "the black-white-red flag and the swastika flag shall be raised *together*" on public buildings.[17]

Elevated to a national flag, the swastika flag no longer merely identified a party but rather became a symbol that now also could and was supposed to publicly demonstrate—apart from NSDAP membership—commitment to the Nazi regime, even by those who were not party members. "Garland your houses and the streets of the towns and villages with fresh greenery and with the flags of the Reich," the regime called out to "the entire German Volk" a few weeks later for the May 1 national holiday. "The pennants of the national uprising should flutter on all trucks and cars!"[18] All Germans were now supposed to use the swastika flag to publicly demonstrate that they were part of the "national uprising."

Indeed, in being used to show commitment to the Nazi regime in spring 1933, the swastika became a garish presence in the everyday lives of Germans. In her diary, the Hamburg housewife Luise Solmitz reported with disgust on the "industry of tastelessness" flourishing "around the swastika," from "sofa cushions with a swastika, wool hats with a giant swastika on the back of the head. . . . Hitler or his banner on an eraser and a pencil, on blankets and handkerchiefs, on candies—the black-white-red flag appeared immediately as a 'lollie,' is being sucked on a massive scale."[19] Solmitz precisely noted the change of symbolic meaning that stood behind this widespread usage. In late March 1933, she reported that one saw "swastikas . . . now" in the soup kitchen where her husband helped out, much to the irritation of the kitchen chef, a "convinced socialist." But he "must tolerate them. The wearers [of the swastika symbol] can rightly say: that is not a party, that is the state."[20]

The fundamental change that turned the party flag into an element of "state symbolism," into a "symbol of völkisch unity and totality,"[21] also affected other Nazi symbols that had been used during the Weimar Republic to distinguish the National Socialist movement from other political players. In spring 1933, the Hitler greeting, for example, similarly evolved from a gesture documenting association with a specific political movement into the "German greeting": a general formulaic greeting that, beyond the circle of NSDAP members, was supposed to "visibly certify belonging to others in daily life."[22]

The relative importance of membership in the NSDAP also deeply changed. The NSDAP transformed from a movement party geared for independent political clout into a far-flung network of various organizations that, together with the former party organization (now called the political organization), sought to cover all aspects of social life and thus bind "the broadest possible segments of the 'Aryan' population into the multisegmented party apparatus."[23] After 1933, with the elimination or Gleichschaltung of other social organizations, membership in the party organization, its units, or one of the affiliated or supervised associations, as well as the associated emblems and uniforms, also increasingly became symbols of commitment. They were no longer only the expression "of a very specific spiritual affinity, shared ways of life, and the same willingness to sacrifice," as the *Völkischer Beobachter* had written as late as July 1932.[24] In addition, the Nazi regime created new symbols of belonging, such as the collection drives of the Winter Relief and the National Socialist People's Welfare.[25]

With its calls for flag decorations, the everyday use of the Hitler greeting, the joining of "national associations," and "sacrificing" to national collection drives, the Nazi regime established an entire range of symbolic practices that aimed at more than just urging people to publicly commit themselves to the regime. They were also supposed to make the positions of individuals visible in the public sphere. For one thing, this facilitated political surveillance by the regime itself.[26] For another, these symbolic practices were supposed to make people's positions accessible to the gaze of neighbors, friends, acquaintances, and relatives. The swastika flag, Hitler greeting, memberships, and willingness to make donations were supposed to not only secure public support for the regime but also contribute to the restructuring of relationships among the Germans, aligning them according to their individual positions toward the regime.

Many people actually adopted these practices as part of their everyday lives, thereby publicly demonstrating their relationship to the new regime. Beyond that, however, as soon as the first months of the Nazi dictatorship, they also often began attentively observing the positions established by friends, neighbors, acquaintances, and relatives. While Otto Kirchmann, for example, informed his fellow fraternity members in detail about his personal analysis of political developments, they in turn also sent him information about the attitudes of other fraternity members, sometimes warning him to be "guarded" with certain people from now on.[27] And in his letters, he also frequently reported on the positioning of common friends or acquaintances. His reports by no means referred only to members of the Armenian fraternity, whose relationships among themselves had already been partially determined by political attitudes and who, given the fraternity's potential Gleichschaltung, collectively faced the question about having a shared political position.

Kirchmann usually concluded his long political discussions with a short section inquiring about the addressee's private and familial well-being or spoke about his own personal matters. In so doing, he consistently marked the separation from his political discussions, thus emphasizing, despite all political differences, his personal appreciation for his counterpart. "But now enough of politics. . . . Finally private!" for example, began the conclusion of a letter to a fellow fraternity member in March 1933, in which he extended greetings to acquaintances and asked about the well-being of his counterpart's wife and children.[28] But even in these sections, which were clearly marked as apolitical, when reporting on his own family members he frequently spoke about their stance toward political developments. "Didn't you recently ask once about my brother Klaus?" Kirchmann wrote in March 1933, picking up on a past letter. He mentioned that his brother was "apparently well," gave a brief account of his occupational development, and then noted generally, "Incidentally, he is apparently a Hitler supporter."[29]

In spring 1933, Kirchmann began to pay careful attention not just to the stance of members of the Armenia fraternity but also to that of his siblings and other relatives with regard to the regime. In April 1934, almost exactly one year after the family circular letter in which he declared to his relatives that he was a "liberal," he summed up his observations in a new circular letter to his siblings and their life partners. He opened the letter by bemoaning that the tradition of family communication had "almost fallen asleep a bit." Hence, he briefly summed up the present status of his relationships to his siblings, focusing, however, not on his various sympathies for one or the other but rather on their political positions. With his brother-in-law he had "no connection anymore . . . Hans himself comes over to us now and then to satisfy himself about the advances made by my National Socialist attitude and to increasingly agree even with me that the people in Stettin are swimming in enthusiasm (by all appearances at least)."[30]

It was not unusual that Otto Kirchmann had already started in spring 1933 to map the social environment within his family and circle of friends according to the respective proximities of individuals to the new regime. Like Kirchmann, many Germans attentively observed the political stances taken by the people within their social milieu not only by drawing on impressions from political discussions but also by using the symbolic practices propagated by the regime to help assess the alignment of friends, acquaintances, and relatives. Thus, having suspected that his brother Klaus was a "Hitler supporter," Kirchmann saw his supposition confirmed a few weeks later by the fact that Klaus "has joined the NSDAP," as he reported in a subsequent letter.[31] Much the same applied to Annie Wächter from Saarau in Silesia. In a letter to her sister, a housewife whose husband worked as a forester in the Hammerheide in Pomerania, Wächter talked about which relatives were "now also Nazi" and how "here in Saarau [one could] observe how the people who are explicitly on the left now suddenly want to have patriotism all to themselves."[32] She likewise associated their metamorphosis into a Nazi with people joining the party. So too did Herman Schleifenbaum*, a Berlin sales representative born in 1875 who had already sympathized with the NSDAP before 1933 and now—unlike Kirchmann and Wächter—welcomed the start of National Socialist rule. In his diary, kept in the form of brief typewritten remarks, in 1933 he carefully noted which relatives had "apparently gone over to the NSDAP." At the end of the year, under the heading "Types of a Few Volk Comrades," he outlined the changed political attitudes of three acquaintances who had all aligned themselves with the regime over the course of the year.³³ Theodor Thomas, a union official from Berlin, in 1933–1934 carefully observed the "play of flags" in his neighborhood; the Hamburg housewife Luise Solmitz repeatedly noted in her diaries which neighbors flew which flags.³⁴ And Stephan Weidenbach, the teacher and town archivist in the small town of Andernach on the Rhine, used flags, in particular, as indicators to document the changes in his hometown.³⁵

Otmar Krämer, the diarist who on February 3, 1933, celebrated Hitler's appointment as a historical event and predicted that now "everyone in Germany, whether friend, foe, or neutral person, will be forced to take a stance on National Socialism," may not have outlined the developments of his hometown in his diary. Nonetheless, in May 1933 in his diary he sketched a summary of the political attitudes of his acquaintances, friends, and neighbors based in equal measure on impressions from conversations, general character assessments, and the use of symbols. "Helmut and his wife are Ludendorff supporters, Schmitt and wife old National Liberals and businesspeople, Kalli Hauer a little bit of a dabbler in everything. All have a very critical, wait-and-see, and skeptical stance toward the new development in Germany. Wilke and wife have switched over, like the Fischers. Rolf wears the swastika and is a member of the NSDAP. Tailcoat-master [Frackmeister] Goetz is an old conservative and warns against the development in the previous sense as anti-cultural. His relative Rudolf, who in times of peace was a banker in England, is detached. The Meissner siblings, enthusiastic Hitler supporters."³⁶

Thus in 1933–1934, for various reasons, people grasped the question of an individual's relationship to the new regime not only as something personal but also as a social process: many people wanted to discuss the political changes with friends and acquaintances. At the same time, the regime urged people to position themselves in public with its own symbolic practices, observe the positions taken by individuals within their own social milieu by means of these symbols, and align their behavior accordingly.

Even when contemporaries, unlike Otto Kirchmann, did not position themselves on their own initiative before their friends and family, the official demand for individual commitment challenged them in two ways with regard to their own social environment: they confronted the problem of having to delineate their position while under social observation and to justify it to friends, acquaintances, neighbors, and relatives; at the same time, as observers they themselves began to increasingly map out their social environment according to the parameters of proximity to and distance from the Nazi regime.

2. "House Flagged with Swastika and Black-White-Red": Establishing Political Positions under the Public Eye

The demand for individual commitment raised by the regime in 1933–1934 basically had two sides. It was made with regard to one's own self-understanding, on the one hand, and one's self-presentation to others, on the other, and therefore it required a personal and public determination of one's position toward the new regime. People were well aware of this. Curt Weber, the Freiburg businessman who recorded his position toward the new regime in summer 1933 at the start of his travel diary, did more than just briefly outline his personal stance toward the new Nazi regime. This itself—what he called the "internal adjustment"—was "not all that hard." In contrast, the "external adjustment to the conditions" created "more difficulties" for him, as he noted and then also demonstrated by dedicating much more space to this problem. This was because "even today [it] has not yet been solved as desired," since official bodies and acquaintances evidently did not accept that he was committed to the regime. Hence, in summer 1933 Weber was anxious not to send any signals that might have raised doubts about his commitment, not even as the result of a private vacation. "These difficulties," he reported at the start of his travel diary, had moved him "at the last minute to give up our initial plan of going to the mountains again this year." Weber and his wife had in fact planned on spending the holidays at the Austrian-Italian border with a befriended married couple. The hotel had already been found, and the cancellation of their joint travel plans at short notice led to the "disgruntlement" of their friends. But in light of the doubts regarding his political attitude, Weber did "not want to go abroad," especially not to Austria, which was "out of the question" because of "the political tensions" with the German Reich.³⁷ Instead the couple spent their 1933 summer holiday on the North Sea coast.

The relationship between taking personal and public positions—"internal" and "external adjustment," as Weber put it—has played an important role in the public and scholarly confrontation with the history of National Socialism from the beginning. Even the first interpretations of the relationships of individuals to the Nazi regime in the early postwar period faced the question of how to evaluate public behavior during the Nazi dictatorship and to what extent it can be used to make conclusions about personal attitudes toward the regime. And up to the present, discussions about the relationship of individual persons to the Nazi regime face the problem of what external behavior—for example, joining the NSDAP or publicly declaring loyalty—can tell us about "real" attitudes.³⁸

In the scholarship about Nazism, this strong focus on individual attitudes and ideological conformity with the Nazi regime has been increasingly criticized, with their significance for explaining participation in National Socialist rule coming under dispute.³⁹ Precisely by looking at social practices, numerous recent studies have highlighted that people did not need to conform to the ideological foundations of the Nazi regime in order for their actions to support its rule.⁴⁰ While the regime strongly urged unequivocal commitment, its specific practices of rule could very well integrate a large range of various motives and political attitudes. This could explain, Frank Bajohr has argued, "why German society in the Nazi period, despite its diversity of attitudes, functioned largely without friction as a Handlungsgemeinschaft [community of action] fitting in with the National Socialist regime."⁴¹ Indeed, many factors support the thesis that within Nazi society "everyday social practice . . . [constituted] *the* integration machine par excellence" and that the functioning of National Socialist society can be explained largely without regard to the personal attitudes of the Germans.⁴² But this by no means renders superfluous the question of how the adopting of personal and public positions stood in relation to each other. Rather, it can be posed in a new way. Instead of being concerned with exposing "real" attitudes, one can ask how people like Curt Weber dealt with the tension—which Weber perceived as well—between "inner" and "external adjustment" and determine for themselves the relationship between public and private positions given the rapidly changing environment.

The tension between their personal and public positions confronted individuals in this respect not only in their role as active agents being observed by friends, acquaintances, neighbors, and relatives but also in their observations of other people within their environment taking a political stance. For example, when Annie Wächter reported to her sister which relatives were "now also Nazi," she appended the observation with this remark: "Whether out of conviction or fashion I cannot determine, but I believe the latter."[43] Hermann Schleifenbaum, too, who at year's end in 1933 under the heading "Types of a Few Volk Comrades" outlined the attitudes of various persons toward the Nazi regime, finished his account with thoughts about a teacher he knew who had previously been "conservative"; "then a Social Democrat—according to reports from his colleagues a convinced socialist"; and now in late 1933 still worked as a "magisterial school inspector." "Has he changed again???" Schleifenbaum asked in light of the sketch of the man's career.[44] Time and again, when observing how individuals positioned themselves within their social environment, people seemed unsure whether their assessments of the political attitudes of others were genuine and how their friends, acquaintances, or relatives were actually aligned.

One reason for this was that the regime had made public commitment through the use of symbolic practices mandatory in many contexts. Refusals could draw repressive action by the state. Even where not legally mandated, party agencies or even just Nazi activists frequently penalized the absence of flag decorations, divergent forms of greeting, or an insufficient willingness to make donations. In summer 1933, Walter Lindemann, for example, noted an incident that took place in a pub. After an SA candidate he knew said "Goodbye, Oskar!" to the host, he was stopped by "four SA people, who what is more were in civvies. They told him, it is Heil Hitler, etc. They beat him very horribly and *the SA man Holtfort, whom I also know very well, shot at him with three shots.*" Lindemann pointed out that the perpetrators were "thrown out of the party and . . . arrested by the police" for using violence.[45] But even without the presence of violently inclined SA men, flouting the symbolic practices propagandized by the regime could have consequences. Demands that people use the new symbols to align themselves with the regime also provided numerous opportunities for denunciations at police stations and party offices.[46] This made it questionable—not only with respect to official occasions but at a basic level—whether externally displayed commitment reflected an individual's personal attitude or was just coerced.

A second reason is that in many cases the indicators elevated to symbolic practices were hardly able to adequately represent an individual's personal position. While Germans based the arguments they used to find their position toward the regime on both dissent and commitment, the symbols followed the dichotomous logic used by the regime for observing how the Germans positioned themselves. Was a house decorated with flags or not; were greetings made with "Heil Hitler" or not; did an individual join "national associations" or not; did one participate in Winter Relief collection drives or not—this was the unequivocal logic by which symbolic practices were supposed to deliver information about a person's commitment to the Nazi regime, thus leaving no room for the differentiated arguments many people used as the basis for their personal commitment.

Against this background, scholars have repeatedly argued that personal views and public behavior essentially did not concur during the National Socialist dictatorship. This interpretation has been reinforced most recently by Mary Fulbrook on the basis of an intense evaluation of largely retrospective self-testimonies. According to Fulbrook, the political monitoring of public space and the pressure on people to align themselves meant that individuals "learned to form distinctions between what they saw as their 'private' and hence presumably 'authentic' selves, and their public behaviour."[47] Fulbrook considers such "dissonant lives" to be the central characteristic of individual lifestyles during the German dictatorships of the twentieth century. But in contrast to this thesis, I find that contemporary self-testimonies indicate more that people, despite the basic tension between personal and public position determinations, tried to combine these two types of commitment to the regime.

Ingrid Thiele* was born in 1914 into an impoverished family in the Ruhr region as the second of five children. She left her parental home early on to stand on her own feet financially and support her family from the meager wages she received during her apprenticeship as a gardener. In fall 1933, Thiele had read the pacifist novel *Katherine Becomes a Soldier*—which had actually been banned after the book burnings in May that same year— which takes the form of a diary to tell of the fate of a young nurse in the First World War.[48] "Inspired by the book," she herself began recording her "everyday life of joys and sorrows" in a diary, as she noted in her first entry in early September 1933.[49] As one can assume from reading, Thiele initially distanced herself from the regime but then did in fact commit herself in fall 1933, using her newly started diary for precisely this purpose. "I now believe in Adolf Hitler," she noted in mid-October 1933. But she supplemented her confession of faith with a remark that "I did not want to proclaim this openly because I first sympathized with his opponents." She would first need to "completely penetrate his ideas before I commit myself to him out loud."[50] Like the businessman Curt Weber, Thiele also viewed taking a position toward the Nazi regime as consisting of both personal and public processes, which followed different logics. But for Thiele, taking a public stance was not just a necessary part of defining one's own relationship to the Nazi regime. It was what actually motivated Thiele to commit herself personally to the regime. "The entire standoffishness, the guardedness, I don't want it anymore," she noted in her diary, explaining her decision. "None of it does any good, the regime stands firm." Meanwhile, her initially distant stance was increasingly moving her into a social position she no longer wanted to accept. "Now whoever is not organized will gradually become an outsider, and I do not want that."[51]

Inge Thiele did not separate her personal and public positions toward the Nazi regime. As she realized that her sympathies with "opponents" of the Nazi regime were driving her into social isolation, she did not try to conceal her personal political assessments and submit to pressure only in the positions she took in public. Rather, for her it seemed that a public commitment to the Nazi regime also required a corresponding personal position. And thus in the following weeks, Thiele also enacted her personal commitment to the Nazi regime in her diary, particularly through discussions of her public position. In her next entry of mid-November 1933, she reported how, when listening to one of Hitler's speeches on the radio, she "automatically joined in with the Heil Hitler and Sieg Heil."[52] And she cheered in her diary when she was finally accepted into the German Labor Front at the turn of the year: "I am no longer standing on the sidelines."[53]

Inge Thiele was not an exception. Time and again, Germans made it clear in their diaries just how personally important it was for them to take a public position toward the Nazi regime. This is evident, for example, in places where comments about taking symbolic positions especially stood out, as in the case of a housewife and mother born in 1898, who in her brief notes, except for mentioning major political events in spring 1933, only spoke about the start of Nazi rule in a single context: when a relative brought "a Hitler shirt for Hansi," her young son, and the family henceforth publicly displayed its commitment to the regime with the uniform shirt.[54]

But time and again, the personal importance of public commitment becomes especially visible in the graphic construction of diary entries, as exemplified by the diary of Claus Behr*, a wine dealer and innkeeper from the Black Forest. Behr welcomed the start of National Socialist rule. "The election *must* turn out national," he noted with regard to the Reichstag election of early March 1933. A few days later, he rejoiced because of the "victory of the NSDAP and the 'Black-White-Red' group along the entire front" and also reported on the victory celebrations in neighboring Freiburg and in his small town, where "the swastika flag was raised on the town hall balcony" and "likewise on the district office building."[55] In the following weeks, Behr then used flags in his diary as a way to similarly display to himself his personal public commitment to the regime in spring 1933. Behr also decorated his home and inn with flags to publicly demonstrate his belonging to the regime, first on the occasion of the Day of Potsdam at the end of March but then also on Hitler's birthday in April and on the anniversary of the death of the National Socialist "martyr" Albert Leo Schlageter.[56] However, the flag decorations also meant something to him personally, as one can tell because on all of these occasions he noted in his diary that "the house is decked with *swastika and black-white-red* flags," each time also embellishing the entries with a drawing of a swastika.[57] He too enacted his personal position toward the regime in his diary with the same symbol he used to display his belonging publicly. The Berlin doctor Walter Lindemann did much the same, not only using the flag to align himself publicly but also repeatedly drawing small swastikas and black-white-red flags in his diary next to entries about key events related to the start of National Socialist rule.[58]

However, while symbolic practices meant for signaling public commitment were used in diaries to indicate personal commitment,[59] the process also occurred the other way around: other contemporaries tried using the prescribed symbols to publicly show positions they found by way of private deliberations—positions that often did not meet the requirement of unconditional adherence demanded by the regime. Luise Solmitz, for example—the Hamburg housewife who on January 30, 1933, showed such great enthusiasm for the cabinet combining National Socialist and nationalist politicians—dedicated a lot of attention in her diary to the public use of flags. Like Claus Behr, Solmitz displayed her commitment as early as January 31, 1933, and on other occasions by publicly decorating her house with flags. Unlike Behr, she did not systematically note this in her diary; however, she dealt much more extensively with the basic question about which flag could symbolize the awakening of the nation and should be elevated by the government as the future state flag. She attentively took note of the first state decrees, issued before the March 5 Reichstag election for the National Day of Mourning in Prussia, which "as an exception" allowed the raising of the black-white-red and swastika flags; she reported enthusiastically on the hoisting of flags on the town halls and official buildings during the celebrations of the electoral victory a few days later; and finally in mid-March she made a detailed statement on the question of the future national flag.[60] For Solmitz, this question was extremely tricky because she thought it could potentially produce great conflict for the "national uprising." She was of two minds in her assessment, writing, on the one hand, how she "loves black-white-red" and "welcome[s] it as a return to ... worldwide recognition" but pointing out, on the other hand, that the National Socialists would quite rightly insist on their flag, that one cannot take away "from the immeasurable swarm of the brown host the symbol by which they won, suffered, and died!"—"Get your hands off it, just leave the two flags next to each other, so nicely harmonious and united!" Solmitz implored in her diary. She suggested combining the two flags as an alternative: "How about black-white-red and the swastika in the white middle band, as has been done by many who do not want to or cannot buy new flags?"[61]

The significance Solmitz assigned to the question about the new regime's official flag was not just related to what she felt was its importance for future political developments. The question also very concretely affected her options for expressing her own commitment to the "national uprising." For Solmitz was by no means indifferent about which flag she used to decorate her house and demonstrate belonging. As opposed to Behr, who raised both the swastika and black-white-red flags, Solmitz pointed out in her diary on the day after the appointment of the new government that she had only raised the black-white-red flag, while noticing mostly swastika flags among her neighbors.[62]

Luise Solmitz did not reject the swastika flag as matter of principle—after all, she noted shortly thereafter that the swastika had in fact become the symbol of the new state. But her own particular enthusiasm about the political "awakening" referred directly to how the National Socialist movement and other nationalist forces had converged to form a government, which for her included many more players than just the NSDAP. Thus, even on subsequent occasions, Luise Solmitz and her husband always raised the black-white-red flag—the same flag they had already flown during the Weimar Republic—and supplemented it after the Reichstag elections of early March with a small "swastika pennant."[63] Accordingly, she was excited when Reich President Hindenburg actually declared both flags as national flags and that allowed to her to continue using the black-white-red flag to publicly express her specific personal position. Just how much her personal stance toward the regime determined the raising of precisely this flag was demonstrated in spring 1935, when the family had to replace its "old flag, which celebrated all victories with us and was never displaced by black-red-gold," with a new one because the old flag "has become completely unsightly, the black completely brown."[64] Even two years into the new government, which basically still met with Luise Solmitz's approval, the family did not buy a swastika flag but rather "an old new black-white-red flag," which she again merely supplemented with a "swastika pennant."[65] This combination continued to reflect the position taken by Luise Solmitz and her family toward the Nazi regime: she saw herself as part of the expansive "awakening" that had started in spring 1933 with the appointment of the new regime, and she situated herself within its nationalistic current.

Like Luise Solmitz, many people tried to publicly express their personal position with the symbols propagated by the regime; this was reflected by a broad spectrum of specific uses of the propagated symbolic practices. Some people tried to show their biographically mediated commitment not just by flying one of the national flags but also by drawing on flags of local authorities and German states.[66] Otto Kirchmann, who claimed to be a "good German" without wanting "to swear on the swastika,"[67] reported in June 1934 that many Germans were responding to "the Hitler greeting with 'Germany awake!'" and thus signaling their belonging to the nation but not the NSDAP.[68] Similarly, in spring 1933 individuals tried to express their commitment to the "national uprising"—as something separate from the National Socialists, who were seen as a particular player within the broad social awakening—by purposely joining the Stahlhelm, DNVP, or other nationalist associations and thus deliberately not the NSDAP. Accordingly, National Socialist organizations were not alone in registering large numbers of new memberships; so too did other organizations that carried the "national regime," as well as other nationalist associations—that is, until they were (voluntarily) dissolved.[69] In part, people joined other associations because of how difficult it was to become a member of the NSDAP or other National Socialist associations. But people also took it as a chance to publicly display their own personal commitment, which they meant to dedicate to the national uprising but not the National Socialists. In this way, many Germans tried to circumvent the dichotomous logic of the symbolic practices propagated by the regime even as they used these practices to take a position in public. In so doing, they found modes of behavior that allowed them to preserve their existing self-images and political views in the same way as when they positioned themselves privately.

How far such efforts might go can be seen, for example, in the case of Hans Maschmann, the socialist teacher who wrestled so intensely in his diary with his personal relationship to the new regime. Maschmann was among the very few diarists who openly addressed the changed conditions of political self-representation: the political monitoring of public space, which in spring 1933 made it seem advisable to him "to remain silent even with the best of friends," and the regime's intention to deny his "love of the fatherland" and social belonging because he was a "republican," although he nonetheless emphatically claimed both.[70] Even so, he too tried to behave in a way that best matched his personal position instead of calculating how to act adroitly in public. For him this meant, for example, not complying with official demands to fly flags. This was not a categorical rejection of the regime but rather the nature of his own specific commitment. He made this clear in summer 1933, when he wrote about a neighbor who had asked him why he did not fly flags on official occasions "despite this being requested from the top." Maschmann noted his response: namely, that his "worldview . . . [needed] no other symbol apart from the deed" and was made "of stuff more sacred" than that he should need, "on all occasions, serious and far-fetched," to "profane it with a flag cloth."[71] Regardless of whether or not Maschmann really answered his neighbor this way, the entry makes it clear that to himself in his diary he did not interpret his behavior simply as an act of distancing from the regime. Rather, it was part of his personal stance, which happened to be characterized by an intellectual elitism that per se rejected the symbolic practice of flying flags: his refusal to fly flags expressed his intellectual deportment, through which he set himself apart from the "masses" and their "materialistic" interests. Only these masses would be interested in the deliberate exhibition of personal political attitudes with flags and other symbols.

But Hans Maschmann was not always able to avoid taking a public position. Thus, parallel to his search for a personal relationship to the new regime, in spring and summer 1933 he also looked for a type of self-presentation that he could identify with while nonetheless still publicly claiming to belong. He consciously used the difference between taking public and personal positions toward the regime to present a different picture externally than the position he articulated in his diary. As hard as he tried to accommodate the changed conditions for the public expression of political convictions, at the same time he nonetheless tried just as hard to express his own personal stance. To this end, starting in summer 1933 Maschmann began presenting himself in letters and conversations as a "National Socialist [Nationalsozialist]"—a self-description that he never used in his personal confrontation with the Nazi regime in his diary but that allowed him to publicly claim belonging and at the same time communicate key dimensions of his personal self-description.[72] Maschmann interpreted the term literally, and as "a national Socialist" [nationaler Sozialist] he asserted a connection to both the new regime and his previous political opinions. In a letter from summer 1933, he described himself to an acquaintance as a "Socialist" who "in everything [feels] responsible to the larger community, which represents a reality for me not just since January 30. For every genuine Socialist of every stripe, it [i.e., this community] had indeed long since ceased to be an anonymous thing anymore."[73] In another letter written just a few months later, he similarly pointed out that "for a long time already I have internally not only affirmed the almost self-evident idea of a national Socialism [nationaler Sozialismus] but have also lived it in my personal sphere of influence."[74]

In his diary, which he was keeping at the same time, Maschmann described himself differently. And this different self-description clearly shows that this type of self-presentation was very much a response to the pressure to publicly align himself with the regime and not the result of any changes in self-understanding. In summer 1933, he wrote about stumbling into a political argument with his father-in-law. His father-in-law, who according to Maschmann was aligned "as per party orders," had placed the "blame for all of the misfortune and suffering of our Volk" on the "men of 1918." Maschmann, who had participated in the German Revolution, objected and worked himself up over the demand that he should trust the state's new leadership. Maschmann argued that if one "had shown confidence in the earlier statesmen, then it would long since look better in the fatherland, for they too only wanted the best." At that, according to Maschmann's report, "the old gentleman flared up: that is defeatism!" and described the "men of the old system" as "traitors, rascals, common grafters, and criminals" who should be "lined up against the wall." Maschmann described his reaction as follows: "I then spoke completely as a National Socialist." In this way, he clearly pointed out that he reacted to his father-in-law's threats not with his personal opinion but strategically. Yet at the same time, the summary of his answer clearly shows that he expressed a view that matched his personal position as much as possible. "I say that the demand of national ideal socialism, of the nationalization of finance capital, trusts, and syndicates had for decades been my demand as well; that ownership obligates had in fact also been a principle of the Weimar constitution. Thus I took a positive stance on the important demands of the National Socialist movement, precisely on the socialist ones."[75]

What Hans Maschmann addressed with great clarity in his diary ultimately applied to many people. They were very much aware that taking a position toward the Nazi regime required a personal and public determination of one's relationship to the regime and that these position determinations each followed their own logic. In this respect, there was a broad awareness of the changed conditions of political self-description, to oneself but above all to others. But this did not much change individuals' aspiration and effort to continue expressing themselves under the changed circumstances. Naturally, it enabled the basic distinction between taking personal and public positions, the awareness that "outer conformity was . . . clearly compatible with a sense of inner distance."[76] Diaries, however, do not indicate that Germans learned to separate clearly between public appearance and personal convictions after 1933. They show instead that, despite the radically transformed conditions of political communication, individuals tried hard to express their own stance as much as possible. Here as well, individuals looked for ways to conceptualize their own performances and opinions as a whole.

Suspicions of Opportunism and the Political Past

The problem occupying contemporaries in the early 1930s when reflecting on the positions they took in public was not so much the separation of behavior and opinions, of personal and publicly displayed positions. Above all, they were moved by the anxiety that their self-representation in public would be misunderstood. Such widely shared fears are exemplified by the concerns of the Göttingen student Karl Möhring. Having personally determined that he was an "advocate of National Socialism" with his "own opinion and independent criticism," he feared that those who were "100% National Socialist" would suspect that he was not a National Socialist at all, while opponents of the regime would suspect him of "being an opportunist."⁷⁷ Many people expressed similar concerns in their diaries, with the worry that they might be deemed an opportunist—Konjunkturritter—playing a prominent role.⁷⁸

It is not just today that the reference to widespread opportunism has functioned as a key factor in explaining the massive commitment to the regime; it was already being used by contemporaries in the 1930s in their observations about their own social environment. Although people were all exposed to state and social pressure to publicly align themselves, even in the 1930s few things were more condemnable that an opportunistic commitment to the regime. "Contemptible is he who disavows his disposition for the sake of material advantages," the Berlin doctor Walter Lindemann noted in his diary in spring 1933.⁷⁹ People might well be accepting in situations where they felt that acquaintances had succumbed to pressure and showed commitment only to avoid losing their job, for example. But where they sensed that neighbors, friends, or acquaintances had changed their political opinions to gain advantages, such as better chances of further professional advancement, there was great indignation and condemnation across all diaries.

In the case of Walter Heckmann*, a teacher born in 1890, this indignation led him in spring 1933 to take an old school notebook that had previously been used to record school grades and start a written record of the positions assumed by an acquaintance under the heading "Noteworthy Things regarding Political Life." In 1929 Heckmann had been transferred from Cologne to the secondary high school in Boppard on the Rhine, where as a local politician he had campaigned for the Center Party during the last years of the Weimar Republic. In mid-April, he was summoned by his school director, Heinrichs, who at first spoke to him about "a few new professional developments" but then used the conservation primarily to "return [to Heckmann] the membership card of the Center Party, which he carried with him," and told Heckmann "that he was leaving the party." The director said that he had "no longer known that he still possessed the card, otherwise he would have already returned it earlier, because already in the last two elections he had no longer voted for the Center Party," having long since "joined with Papen's politics." Heckmann apparently found the reason for leaving—namely, that the director no longer agreed with the Center Party—credible. In any event, he noted that they separated "on good terms with the assurance of mutual trust."⁸⁰ But less than two weeks later, he heard "from various sides . . . that Heinrichs had joined the National Socialist Party. . . . From the press I hear that his request for acceptance was forwarded to Munich. Thus a case of opportunism after all." Only then did the case seem "noteworthy" enough for him to write down.[81] Heckmann evidently saw leaving the Center Party in spring 1933 and joining the NSDAP as two separate things. While ending a Center Party membership at this time seemed to be a belated, actually superfluous, and yet nonetheless credible step, joining the NSDAP meant something different for Heckmann. He was certain that it occurred for economic reasons, out of "offended ambition," out of a fear of being "neglected for advancement despite proficiency," and not because of political beliefs.[82]

Heckmann assumed economic motives for two reasons. First, a membership in the NSDAP might provide material advantages, given the Gleichschaltung of the public administration and public life, which also involved giving preferential treatment to party comrades. Consequently, one of the key occasions when people suspected individuals of disavowing their actual opinions was when they joined the NSDAP, although accusations of opportunism were certainly made in other instances as well. They could also be leveled in connection with other symbolic practices if those practices could be linked to economic interests. Yet the identification of possible professional or material advantages as a result of a public declaration of belonging was not an especially solid basis for finding out whether individuals making such declarations were also acting contrary to their personal position. Joining the NSDAP certainly improved the professional opportunities of the director of the Boppard secondary high school. But even for Walter Heckmann, this did not mean that it was his sole motive for joining or that the director had disavowed his own political views to this end. In their conversation, the rector had described himself as a supporter of Franz von Papen, making it quite conceivable that for him joining the NSDAP was not supposed to express solidarity with the National Socialists but rather indicated his support of the new regime, where, after all, von Papen served as vice chancellor.

Heckmann's assessment that the rector had denied his political convictions when he joined the party was not grounded solely on the rector's prospective professional advantages, or even chiefly on their joint conversation. Instead, he based it on his knowledge about his superior's earlier political views and behaviors. In his report on the rector joining the party, Heckmann copied an extract from the memorandum of a school conference in the summer of 1930, which had dealt with pro-NSDAP agitation at the school by a handful of students. In this memorandum, the rector strongly argued that the instigator should be "expelled" from the school, the other participants should be severely warned, and "the German, history, and religious studies teachers, in particular," should be instructed to assert "their entire influence so that the radical currents lose their breeding grounds."[83] Heckmann even copied the rector's signature on the document, which for Heckmann clearly established that the rector had acted contrary to his political beliefs when he joined the NSDAP. In spring 1933, upon learning that other acquaintances had joined the NSDAP, Heckmann evaluated their decisions against their respective political pasts as well. In the context of the report about his school director, Heckmann noted, for example, that another acquaintance had "changed sides with [his] family," pointing out here too that in the past this acquaintance had been "suspected of separatist tendencies" and "at the start of my presence here [i.e., during the Rhineland occupation] was mentioned as being especially friendly in dealings with French officers, whose military hospital he supplied."[84]

The political past also served as the essential touchstone for other people when keeping an eye their social milieu. At the end of 1933 when Hermann Schleifenbaum used three examples to summarize his observations on the positioning of his acquaintances, it was no coincidence that in each case he outlined the person's previous background. In another entry, for example, about a married couple that had joined the NSDAP, he likewise remembered that the two of them "fought me back then because I pointed out the goals of these people [i.e., the Nazi movement] as being right and advocated them."[85] So too with Christoph Ahrens, the Hamburg seaman who in the 1930s tried to make a go of it as a painter. When he observed how acquaintances and friends positioned themselves, he frequently compared their political positions with his knowledge about their previous lives. After seeing a female acquaintance again while celebrating his birthday in February 1934, he noted in his diary that she "now belongs to the Nazi Woman's League; the contrast with earlier is absurd. One should not forget that other people have a memory."[86]

The use of the symbolic practices propagated by the regime to express one's public alignment always left questions about one's underlying personal position unresolved, creating uncertainty for the observer. This meant, in turn, that these individuals themselves were not the only ones dealing with the relationship between their own life course and their new political stance. Neighbors, friends, acquaintances, and relatives likewise began asking about how someone's political positions taken in 1933 fit with his or her previous life. When people took a position toward the regime, subject to negotiation was not just their own biographical self-image but also their image as seen by others—by individual friends, work colleagues, and the public. There is nothing unusual about Walter Heckmann reporting that he heard "from very different sides" that his school director had joined the NSDAP.[87] Time and again, the tension between people's previous course of life and the position they took in public toward the Nazi regime became an object of discussion among friends, neighbors, and other circles. Another example comes from Stephan Weidenbach, who like Heckmann was a teacher in a small town in the Rhine valley. Weidenbach documented the political developments in his hometown in his diary. In mid-February, Weidenbach reported how rumors that "Senior Vocational Teacher Froehlich . . . is flirting with the Nazi party" had become the talk of the town, and "Froehlich's conduct during the separatist period is now also being discussed again" in this context. It was generally being remembered that Froehlich had "been involved with them [the separatists] back then, but later, when they collapsed, portrayed himself and even had himself authenticated as a spy and friend of the 'Berliners' who 'sounded out' the plans of the separatists in order to report them to the regime, to betray them."[88]

Here and elsewhere in the country, people in 1933 intensely and openly scrutinized the commitment of individuals to the Nazi regime and the relationship between their personal and public alignments. These discussions took place in workplaces and not least within the NSDAP, where doubts about the political attitudes of new members—namely, the so-called Märzgefallene (Victims of March)—took on great importance.[89] Against this background, people struggled intensely to counteract any possible impressions of opportunism. The idiosyncratic use of the symbols of public commitment propagated by the regime was supposed to help, showing others that one's own commitment was very much in line with one's previous political views and biographical self-perspective. This was also the issue for Maschmann when, facing his agitated father-in-law during their discussion, he decided to speak "completely as a National Socialist": he wanted to behave as the situation required but also remain biographically recognizable with respect to what he said.[90]

Yet as much as they tried express their personal position toward the Nazi regime with the provided symbols, people could not override the latter's basic logic. At best, they could be aware of the dilemma of being forced to communicate their personal positions with symbols hardly suitable for the task. Hamburg resident Werner Kramp, who in the 1930s worked as a civil registry employee, confronted such a situation in April 1933. He had no illusions about how acquaintances would view his joining the Union of National Socialist Jurists (BNDJ), regardless of how much he tried to clarify his position. In spring 1933, Kramp still distanced himself from the regime in his diary, and he discussed quite clearly the public push to make a commitment, noting that "everyone feels pressure in his actions and speech that would have him adapt."[91] He thought of the local BNDJ group as a professional organization and "specialist association," and he was joining not because he wanted to but only under massive pressure from his workplace. He felt compelled to choose between "acquiring membership in the NSDAP (which results in joining the specialized association, but which is blocked as of 05/01 [1933]), or joining the specialized association as a novice (with a higher fee)." He deliberately chose the ordinary BNDJ membership because he saw this as "the freest form of a commitment to the regime." Nonetheless, he felt certain that he would be "condemned as a carpetbagger Nazi [Konjunkturnazi]" by his social circles. He mainly had his dentist friend in mind—Kramp had frequently gone off against "the Nazis" while sitting in his friend's dental chair, and the friend would now certainly see Kramp as an opportunist.[92]

Knowing that one was being observed by neighbors, friends, acquaintances, and relatives had a major impact on how individuals positioned themselves in public in 1933–1934. Many people knew they were being watched by members of their social milieu and tried to take this into account in their externally visible positions. But this did not necessarily separate their internal and external attitudes toward the regime. Instead, they went to great lengths to show externally as well that their commitment was consistent with their previous life path and earlier political views. That this often failed does not suggest that people of the 1930s were marked by a fundamental "dissonance." Instead, it reflects the changed conditions for the public communication of commitment, as individuals now had to use symbolic practices supplied by the Nazi regime. However, these practices were hardly adequate for expressing the differentiated positions found by many Germans in 1933–1934. In fact, they actually reflected the Nazi regime's notion of individual commitment, which basically demanded unconditional adherence, something that many protested when establishing their position. This was not a conflict that individuals could resolve: from their perspective, the tension was not so much between "internal" and "external adaptation" that arose because "true" attitudes needed to be concealed in public. Rather, their own observations of their personal social environment, which they carried out using the Nazi regime's symbols, directly contradicted their efforts to use these symbols to publicly express themselves. On the one hand, the unconditionality intrinsic to the symbolic practices of commitment became the basis for assessing the commitment of others; on the other hand, when people dealt with their own positions, they deliberately tried to circumvent this demand for unconditionality. The opposing logics that forcibly governed how the Germans positioned themselves and how they observed the positions of others could simply not be reconciled.

3. "The One Thing That Separates Me from Everyone": State Violence and Social Isolation

In 1933–1934, the massive publicly displayed commitment of the Germans gave the Nazi regime the comprehensive support that enabled it to restructure the political system to secure its power. At the same time, the effects of this commitment, wrought through the social observation of individuals establishing their positions in their social environment and the resulting conflicts, changed the web of relationships within which people routinely moved: in families and neighborhoods and among friends, work colleagues, and acquaintances. These changes thoroughly served the interests of the regime, which by asserting its demand for belonging not only wanted to secure political support but also sought to realign social relationships according to people's proximity to the regime.

The regime deliberately promoted the change of social relationships by coupling access to social resources and influential opportunities directly to the regime: implemented across all social sectors, the Gleichschaltung of societies and organizations, which were restructured internally according to the so-called Führer principle, often advanced previously unimportant members into leadership positions just because they were NSDAP members.[93] Heralded by the NSDAP, "party comrade support"—namely, material compensation for deprivations endured by party members during the Weimar Republic—was implemented immediately after the appointment of the new government, creating tangible prospects for economic betterment and greater professional influence.[94] When establishing a public position, individuals were not just committing actions that were attentively observed within their social milieu by others to whom such actions needed to be explained. For many people, these actions also aimed directly at the social fabric within which they routinely moved and claimed rights to individual betterment by indicating that they belonged to the regime.

The director of the Krupp Book Hall and the company's educational society, Wolfgang Söller, summarized his position toward the regime in his diary in fall 1933. Within this context, he noted with regard to his vocational activities that "for me personally . . . the proceedings on the cultural terrain are a kind of competitive struggle." He said, "I find the intellectuals should and must be more tolerant, more decent, less self-serving, more objective, to do right by everyone and not so quickly deny with respect to someone else that he too wants what is good and right."[95] But this wish remained unfulfilled because in his environment as well, in 1933–1934, many individuals exploited their commitment to the regime in order to challenge the existing social hierarchy and obtain advantages for themselves at the expense of others. In doing so, they forced those around them who actually wanted to avoid "competitive struggle" to participate too. Thus in summer 1934, Wolfgang Söller had to conclude not only that his professional environment had changed but also that he himself, internally, "not viewed externally," performed his job "with greater inhibitions than before, and cautiously with a certain reticence."[96]

These transformative dynamics generated by the massive public commitment to the regime affected all types of routine social relationships: friendships and neighborhoods, (recreational) associations, and workplace collegiality.[97] Above all, however, they affected relationships containing formal hierarchies that the regime could easily access. This was especially true of the workaday world. Writing in his diary in spring 1933, the Berlin doctor Walter Lindemann not only reported his observations of the political positions of his colleagues and superiors but also described how in April 1933, in the context of Lindemann's pending permanent appointment, the director of his hospital asked whether he was "also *politically reliable*."[98] According to the report in Lindemann's diary, the director indeed had other motives for the question, having had conflict with Lindemann in the past. But this did not change the fact that the question of Lindemann's political position was determining his professional future. Although Lindemann felt that the doubts about his commitment to the regime were an "impertinence" and for his part accused the director of opportunism in his diary, at the same time he nonetheless sought out witnesses to vouch for his "political reliability."[99]

The Hamburg civil registrar Werner Kramp, who ultimately decided to join the Union of National Socialist Jurists, also frequently contemplated in his diary "whether my disbelief will harm me in my profession." He was quite aware that the transformative dynamics in his office were difficult for him to assess. The professional consequences arising from how individuals positioned themselves toward the Nazi regime critically depended above all "on the degree of decisive commitment that one will demand."[100]

Another example comes from the diary of Werner Stock, a miller's son born in 1902 who in the early 1930s sold oil and calibrated pumps at gas stations for the Hanover branch of Kohle AG. Stock reported in detail about changes at his workplace. As at the hospital where Walter Lindemann worked and at the civil registry that employed Werner Kramp, the start of the Nazi dictatorship deeply transformed the existing social fabric in the large commercial corporation. Stock repeatedly noted rumors that the state might intervene in the operation, mentioning how an "old party comrade . . . has secretly called for a commissar for Kohle AG" to review the "conditions at our firm." He also wrote repeatedly about dismissals.[101] In July 1933, he noted that "the Nazis have unilaterally undertaken a 'cleansing intervention' among our tank facility staff," in which four workers were "arrested and taken away by the SS." According to Stock, they had supposedly "compared the red swastika armbands to a sanitary napkin," but he did not believe this. He pointed out instead that on the same day "a worker recently dismissed from the firm who is a member of the SS . . . was hired again 'upon instructions from higher up'" and that this employee had "filed charges" against those arrested. The "entire matter" was probably based "on slander and revenge," Stock commented in his diary. The next day he also recorded the consequences of the denunciation.[102] "Our workers were released, covered with abrasions and beaten up. We were very frightened when we heard the horrible details: Baade is limping, Dressler cannot lift one arm, Rogmann has a gaping wound on his back, and Sailer is almost crazy from blows to the head."[103]

As happened here, many contemporaries deliberately informed local NSDAP agencies, labor offices, and other authorities about places that still employed "Marxists" or other people who did not fulfill the regime's demand for commitment. They called for these employees' dismissal and, referring to their own political position, exerted pressure for better placements for themselves. But at the same time—and increasingly over the course of 1933–1934—individuals repeatedly faced the problematic fact that they were competing with others who also claimed to belong to the regime. This meant that the various commitments to the regime had to be organized into a comparative hierarchy, which became a major problem, especially within the NSDAP. Starting in spring 1933, massive conflicts arose among party members in local NSDAP formations. As a result, as early as March some Ortsgruppe chairmen had threatened to resign and dissolve their units because of the "disputes."[104]

The disputes largely concerned the commitment of new party members, especially with reference to their past. But even long-term members and functionaries of the National Socialist movement were not safe from accusations and recriminations. Helmut Böhme was a master bookbinder born in 1902 who had already joined the NSDAP in 1923 and worked for the party as a Kreisleiter since the late 1920s. In fall 1934, he reported in his diary that he had been "placed on leave because of serious accusations, which however were completely false and baseless." This left Böhme "most severely shaken," and he saw his "lifework torn from his hands and destroyed. . . . This meant a severe nervous strain. The craziest rumors were going around, and there was no scandalous deed that was not imputed to me and intentionally spread." Böhme ultimately managed to vindicate himself during the "investigations initiated by the party court and secret state police," and one month after being placed on leave, he was reinstated as Kreisleiter.[105] But the fact that even long-serving functionaries like him could be drawn into these competitive struggles underscores the degree to which altercations within the NSDAP also exploited and involved the issue of commitment.

Although Germans tried to improve their own standing by referring to their commitment, this did not mean that public commitment was necessarily based in the striving for betterment: the competitive struggles chiefly gave long-term NSDAP members the opportunity to demand betterments within their private surroundings on the basis of their political "merits." In turn, other people did not want to be outdone, and in this respect, individuals' conviction that they were themselves adherents of the new regime supported their impositions. Which individuals prevailed in any given case depended on many factors, especially since these conflicts opened the door to arbitrariness and corruption: for example, references to the biographies of individual party comrades could be interpreted in very different ways by party authorities, sometimes as helpful information about unreliable party members and sometimes as "stale news from 15 years ago" that someone was "trying to warm over" for self-serving motives.[106]

Even beyond the start of National Socialist rule, competitive struggles related to the commitment of individuals to the Nazi regime became a central feature of everyday life in the 1930s. They provoked disputes and conflict, resentment, jealousy, and dissatisfaction precisely among those people who committed themselves to the regime—whereby this thoroughly stood in contradiction with the regime's societal-political goals. Instead of leading to the promised unification of all Germans prepared to commit themselves to the new regime, public declarations of belonging helped generate new differences, particularly among those people deemed by the regime to be members of the prospective "Volksgemeinschaft," which was supposed to be free of conflict. Yet at the same time, through their competitive struggles within their everyday social environments, which sometimes were quite bitter, these very same people contributed decisively to the realization of the Nazi regime's most important societal-political concern: the social exclusion of all those Germans who had been declared "enemies" and "opponents" by the regime.

Antisemitic Violence

While the Nazi regime strongly pushed for broad commitment starting in spring 1933, it also clearly indicated from the outset that this option was not meant for everyone. Instead, existing rules of social belonging were supposed to be radically realigned according to the distinction between "Volksgenossen" and "Gemeinschaftsfremden." Especially through the massive violence deployed by state agencies and SA and SS members against political opponents (above all Communists and Socialists), potential resistance was supposed to be eliminated, while those now considered "enemies" and "opponents" were to be exposed in public, along with the fate that the regime had in store for them. At the same time, the violence of local NSDAP and SA activists also increasingly targeted those people for whom commitment was made categorically impossible: German Jews. This increase in violence was connected to the political practices rehearsed during the Weimar Republic by the National Socialist movement, which had included antisemitic boycotts and violent operations as important instruments of political confrontation. But here too, existing practices changed with the start of Nazi rule. Backed up by government resources, the NSDAP leadership for the first time organized a Reich-wide boycott of all Jewish businesses, which was supposed to extend "all the way to the smallest farm village."[107]

With the centrally organized boycott operation against Jewish shops, department stores, medical practices, law offices, and banks—"the first openly antisemitic operation organized on a large scale after the appointment of Adolf Hitler as Reich chancellor"[108]—the regime clearly showed that the NSDAP's antisemitic program would be an important component of "national government" policy. Less than one week after April 1, when SA men with signs, placards, and chants called for the boycott of Jewish shops, medical practices, and department stores, the government enacted the Law for the Restoration of the Professional Civil Service. This was the Nazi state's first anti-Jewish law, and it allowed the government to dismiss "non-Aryan" and politically unreliable civil servants from all state institutions.[109] This law also provided the context for establishing an initial legal definition of the term *non-Aryan*, which basically remained unchanged throughout National Socialist rule: *non-Aryan* now applied to anyone who stemmed from "non-Aryan, particularly Jewish, parents or grandparents," a condition that was sufficiently met "if one parent or grandparent was not Aryan."[110]

However, the large-scale boycott operation targeted not just Jewish but also non-Jewish Germans. Whereas boycotts during the Weimar Republic were supposed to generate political support for the NSDAP, this time the leaders of the boycott intended to clearly show the population what they considered to be the fundamental difference between Jewish and non-Jewish Germans. Julius Streicher, the director of the organizational committee created specifically for the boycott, formulated the expectations of the state and party leadership as follows: "Millions of Germans waited with longing for this day on which the German Volk in its entirety would be aroused, for it to finally recognize the World Enemy in the Jew."[111]

Along these lines, the NSDAP's call for a boycott stated apodictically that "no German still buys from a Jew or allows him or his backers to tout goods to him. The boycott must be a general one. It shall be carried by the entire Volk."[112] By marking businesses with placards and SA pickets, the boycott was supposed to show non-Jewish Germans which people within their social environment were Jewish and demand that they break off social relationships with them. "You are now being deployed as an educational group," said the boycott call issued by the Nazi Women's League to its members. With "tireless education work at home, at work, and on the street in front of the department stores," they were supposed to "drive it home" that "no German woman buys from Jews."[113] The boycott operation of April 1, 1933, constituted the opening round of the state's anti-Jewish policy. But it also clearly demonstrated far and wide that the regime was demanding not only that Germans show their commitment with flags, memberships, and forms of greeting but also that they distance themselves from Jewish people (and other "Volksfeinde") and contribute to the realization of the Nazi regime's societal-political goals.

For non-Jewish Germans too, the April boycott was an important event, which many perceived as drastic. Stephan Weidenbach, the teacher and town archivist in Andernach who used his diary as a town chronicle, was familiar with such actions. During the late phase of the Weimar Republic, as well as in March 1933 in the context of the campaign for the Reichstag elections and, shortly thereafter, the elections held for the town, district, and state parliament, he had reported that "'Hitler people' [stood] in front of the Tietz department store and distributed election pamphlets and shouted: 'Don't buy from Jews.' . . . 'Those who buy from Jews support the Communists,'"[114] which he interpreted as "a nice and beneficial 'campaign' that was welcomed by all of the businesspeople."[115] Nonetheless, he felt that the Reich-wide boycott on April 1 had a different quality. Weidenbach made detailed reports about the boycott on a daily basis—before, during, and especially afterward for almost two weeks. And to document what for him was evidently a historical event for the town, in his diary next to these entries he also glued one of the yellow placards marked "Jew!" used to identify Jewish businesses during the operation.[116]

Weidenbach's reports chiefly focused on how the townspeople perceived the operation. During the boycotts of the March election campaigns, he had already noted that "naturally," when facing SA pickets, hardly anyone visited the business being boycotted. But at other Jewish businesses customers had "gone in and out as usual."[117] And so on April 1 he also described in detail that "Jewish businesses . . . [were] all closed," and then on Monday, April 3, he explained that they had opened again and that "the people shopped again. Today I saw buyers going in and out."[118] Likewise, he extensively reported on how the "Jew-baiting" was being discussed in town. Already on April 1, he "heard on the street in passing: 'A shame!' 'A disgrace!' and the like; on the other hand, sporadically: 'It is good!' 'Finally the Jews are getting it.'" However, Weidenbach attributed these statements of approval exclusively to "businesspeople." "In general one perceives the boycotting against the Jews as a major injustice."[119] This impression was reaffirmed for him over the next few days, during which he spoke, for example, "with various Evangelicals [members of the Evangelical Church], also a Nazi. Everyone thought that the boycott was not right."[120]

Weidenbach's description falls in line with those of other diarists of the 1930s, as well as with scholarly assessments of the population's involvement in the April boycott. These assessments have generally maintained that "neither . . . the attitude of the rest of the German population or even of the German Jews . . . [was] uniform" and that there was indeed a spectrum of various opinions and - reactions, although given the absence of really solid sources, they are weighted quite differently.[121] In this case too, both contemporary observers and historians faced (and face) the problem that, when considering the public's behavior, it is "ultimately difficult to tell whether someone 'participated,' that is, did not buy from Jews, or actually did not participate but instead watched from the distance."[122] Hence, in his study about boycotts and other operations of antisemitic violence, Michael Wildt shifted the focus away from the people's attitudes and concentrated on the structural changes wrought by antisemitic violence. Indeed, the centrally organized boycott of April 1, 1933, the locally initiated boycotts of businesses, and the antisemitic pillory processions that stretched throughout the entire 1930s produced lasting changes in the "social, cultural, and political order" simply by virtue of the fact that they could happen.[123] Time and again, they blatantly illustrated the division between "Germans" and "Jews" in the public sphere. By also being purposely directed against the customers of Jewish stores, they clearly showed that ignoring this difference could have far-reaching consequences. Precisely because buying in Jewish stores was not legally prohibited and because the operations contravened existing statutory provisions, they contributed with lasting effect to the National Socialist transformation of the political and legal order.[124]

The public shaming of Jewish stores and their non-Jewish customers, as well as the threats and prohibitions like those pronounced by the NSDAP for its members, changed the shopping behavior of Germans and drove Jewish businesspeople, especially those in small towns and localities, into economic and social isolation. At the same time, however, as evidenced by the diaries of the 1930s, it seems doubtful that the violent antisemitic operations produced the desired "enlightenment" whereby people learned to view German Jews as "Volksfeinde" with whom relationships had to be severed. To be sure, the various forms of public violence against German Jews clearly provided a platform that individuals could use to demonstrate belonging. But many contemporaries only avoided Jewish businesses when forced to do so by the massive threats and violent terror underlying these operations.[125]

In this respect, the regime failed in its effort to make the relationships with German Jews a criterion for the social monitoring of the political positions of neighbors, friends, acquaintances, and relatives similar to those constituted by the symbolic practices propagated by the regime. Although the boycotts and violent actions sought to stigmatize non-Jewish German customers of Jewish businesses as "Volk traitors" and "opponents," the key factors people used to assess the alignment of members of their social milieu continued to be flags, forms of greeting, memberships, and uniforms. This even applied to the period after the early phase of the Nazi regime in 1933–1934. In contrast, however, economic and other forms of contact with German Jews became a factor primarily when evaluating the relationship of individual persons to the NSDAP.

In his diary on the occasion of the April boycott, Hermann Schleifenbaum, for example, noted with regard to an acquaintance that he was a "party member" and still went "to Tietz with his wife."[126] And other diarists, too, made it clear that NSDAP members were shopping in Jewish stores and then taking their leave with "Heil Hitler," pointing out that these NSDAP members could not be proper National Socialists.[127] In the diaries of the 1930s, operations of antisemitic violence were usually very firmly attributed to National Socialists and not to the government.[128] Thus diarists treated contacts with German Jews above all as a yardstick specifically when considering someone's antisemitic convictions and affiliation with the NSDAP. But they were far less inclined to see such contact as a factor for assessing an individual's commitment to the regime.

In this regard, during boycott actions diarists repeatedly discounted the distinction between "Jews" and "Germans" that the boycotts sought to illustrate. In April 1933 in his reports on discussions about the boycott, Stephan Weidenbach repeatedly noted that the operation was being repudiated precisely on the basis that "the Jews [had] . . . also given their blood in the war," that they "felt and acted as Germans":[129] "They are all Germans and had done their duty as such."¹³⁰ And even in the late 1930s, in cases where the contrast between "Jews" and "Germans" was advanced as a political slogan along with demands for direct political behavior, people could indeed still dispute the premise that German Jews were not part of the nation. When finally, in November 1938, during the second centrally organized Reich-wide operation of antisemitic violence, namely, the Night of Broken Glass, groups of NSDAP, SA, and SS members violently forced their way into Jewish homes and businesses, destroyed their facilities, abused and sometimes killed large numbers of people, set synagogues ablaze, and brought masses of Jewish men to concentration camps, the dismay of many diarists at the massive violence was also based specifically in their feeling that these actions did not conform to the picture they had made of the regime as the representative of the German nation.

"In Germany on November 10 and 11 very *strong Jewish persecutions* were carried out by the regime," noted the doctor Walter Lindemann in his diary, for example. "*Synagogues set on fire* and shops plundered. One is ashamed to be a German."¹³¹ Over the following days, he repeated this statement several times and constantly emphasized how little he could reconcile the violence against the Jews with his image of the nation.¹³² On the night of the pogrom, Paul Berger*, a doctor's son born around 1910, had watched the devastation in his home village of Epe in Westphalia and also personally cared for the injured. Along with writing a detailed report in his diary about the rampages, he described how the next morning he told an acquaintance about his "outrage." "She also found that what happened there was not right, how one can take revenge in such a way. She claimed to have had heard nothing of the actions in the night. She said she was sleeping on the alley side. And yet I had seen her indistinctly standing at the window." For the young man, the reason for this was clear: "As a Nazi advocate, she cannot, of course, admit and openly say how distressful all of this must be for her." As Berger departed, his acquaintance called out to him, "Get well!" "I wondered, did she mean by this the greeting, that I should also have taken leave with 'Heil Hitler'? I don't fully understand it yet," he noted in his diary, referring to her implicit request to not get so worked up, which was how the reference to the greeting could be understood. But this did nothing to change the fact that Berger did not share the views underlying the violence; he felt just as ashamed as Walter Lindemann. In his diary, he again stressed his inability to understand how "she cannot get upset over what happened."¹³³

The violent antisemitic operations vigorously communicated the regime's societal ideal of a clear separation between "Jews" and "Germans" by forcibly creating this separation throughout the action. In the context of the conflicts within the transformation of everyday social relationships, these operations also offered individuals opportunities to empower and distinguish themselves. But this did not mean that people began assessing how individuals in their social environment positioned themselves toward the regime based on their relationship with German Jews. And often massive violence was needed to make people comply with the behavior demanded by the boycott operations. Yet regardless of how they felt during the violent actions and how they behaved, the individuals of mainstream German society nonetheless strongly contributed to the social isolation of German Jews, as well other Germans declared to be "enemies" and "opponents." The continual observation of others and the exhibition of one's own political position in everyday life played a major role here. The boycott operations had a major part in the transformation of social belonging in the 1930s, but they could only thematize the relationship between German Jews and non-Jewish Germans for a moment, albeit very explicitly. On the other hand, because individuals of mainstream German society drew on the symbols propagated by the regime in their everyday competitions related to the social hierarchy, these competitions made the process of exclusion a less conspicuous but all the more pervasive aspect of the everyday lives of Germans.

Competitive Social Struggles and Social Exclusion

Unlike antisemitic violence, the symbolic practices to show commitment to the Nazi regime did not foreground the sharp division between "Volksgenossen" and "Gemeinschaftsfremden." But this separation was also inscribed in them. In 1933–1934 and in the years that followed, many German Jews tried in vain to publicly show their belonging with the symbolic practices provided by the regime. This is strongly demonstrated by the countless inquiries made to the Central Association of German Citizens of Jewish Faith about the use of flags and other symbolic practices of commitment.[134] The self-image that they exhibited externally was not accepted by the regime. Even though German Jews were not legally prohibited from using most of the National Socialist symbols during the first years of the Nazi dictatorship, local NSDAP units and state authorities repeatedly intervened when they displayed the swastika flag or used "Heil Hitler" as a greeting. The Nazi regime's symbolic practices of commitment were supposed to engender belonging precisely by disallowing "enemies" and "opponents" from using them. Those who aligned themselves with the new symbols were therefore using forms inscribed with the Nazi regime's societal-political idea. They ensured that conflicts related to the reorganization of social hierarchies were carried out with the exclusion of every person unable to use these symbolic practices, whether because of dissenting political convictions or because the regime prevented such use. However much Germans struggled within their everyday social structures over the reorganization of those structures, and however much their conflicts provoked dissatisfaction and jealousy, these symbolic practices, by virtue of these quarrels, united all those individuals who publicly aligned themselves with the regime. And at the same time, they excluded everyone who would not or could not do so from the struggle over the social distribution of benefits.

What this meant for social relationships between German Jews and non-Jewish Germans during the first years of the Nazi dictatorship can be most notably demonstrated by the example of organization memberships and the Aryan paragraph. In the course of the Gleichschaltung process, virtually all societies and associations took on a provision to exclude Jews from formal membership, which they adopted from the Law for the Restoration of the Professional Civil Service.[135] The diary of Luise Solmitz poignantly documents the long-term effects of this development. In May 1933, her daughter Gisela brought home a form from school, which her parents were supposed to use to confirm their "Aryan lineage"—something that diarists frequently reported but without giving it much attention.[136] In an entry written that very evening, however, Luise Solmitz marked this date as her family's "fateful day." Her husband, Friedrich, who had been an officer in the First World War and decorated for his service, stemmed from a Jewish family but had converted to Protestantism. His original religious faith had never mattered before in their marriage. "Fredy and I know each other for 20 1/2 years; as strange as it seems, never has this been discussed between us with a single word," Luise Solmitz remarked that evening in her notes. Even her daughter knew nothing about her father's original religious affiliation.[137] The next morning when, at her insistence, her parents revealed that she was non-Aryan, the thirteen-year-old girl reacted with shock. In her diary, Solmitz reported that Gisela became "pale as snow," even though her parents tried to give her courage and assured her that she could and should "carry her head just as high" as before. At the same time, however, they cautioned their daughter to maintain "strictest secrecy" and strongly warned her of "the dangerous hours of entrusting yourself, expressing yourself."[138]

In fact, this day permanently changed the lives of Luise Solmitz and her family, which had previously been well integrated into their bourgeois nationalist environment. Earlier Solmitz had already sharply criticized the antisemitic aspirations of the National Socialists, without at the same time indicating that she herself might possibly be affected. For her, the actions against German Jews were simply not part of the "national uprising." "Our entire soul was bent on the German ascendency, not on this," she noted in her diary on April 1 during the Reich-wide boycott.[139] Even in May 1933 and in the years that followed, Solmitz still wanted to be part of the "German ascendency." But ever since her husband's Jewish origins had become a family issue, in her diary Solmitz began attentively registering how her family's categorization as non-Aryan increasingly complicated their public communication of their personal commitment to the regime, and thus also isolated them in their social environment.

Less than one week later, she recorded in her diary a statement by her husband, who seemed resigned that now "all paths, all doors . . . are hopelessly closed" to their daughter and that all three of them "were now without a homeland."[140] Indeed, over the following weeks Solmitz observed, on the one hand, how her milieu increasingly aligned itself with the regime, mainly as individuals joined a wide range of different organizations, with their "Aryan" lineage being confirmed over and over again. On the other hand, she reported how she and her husband were repeatedly confronted with questionnaires about Aryan origins, and she spoke about her daughter, who "pleaded over and over: 'I would like to go to the Hitler Youth,' or become a 'Luise.' 'I don't belong to any association, but I so much want to as well! All are in.' And I need to say: 'It won't work. It really won't work.'"[141]

Apart from affecting her daughter, the expansion of the Aryan paragraphs chiefly had an impact on her husband. As a former frontline fighter and officer, during the Weimar Republic he had been a member of the German Officer's League, a veterans' association whose members were now supposed to be taken over by National Socialist organizations. In fall 1933, an "unknown unemployed person," as Luise Solmitz noted bitterly, presented him with a questionnaire related to this matter from the National Socialist War Victim's Care (NSKOV), one of the welfare institutions affiliated with the NSDAP for disabled war veterans and frontline soldiers of the First World War, which also contained "the Aryan question at the end."[142] Responding to the form's question about lineage, Friedrich Solmitz crossed out Aryan but left the word German untouched. This led to such confusion at the NSKOV that he had to make two further declarations to the institute and ultimately return the insignia he had already been issued, because, according to the NSKOV, "Aryanness is the basis and main condition, apart for being wounded, for membership in the NSKOV."[143]

He had much the same experience a few months later, when in February 1934 the German Officers' League was supposed to be taken over by the SA reserves. Luise Solmitz recorded a statement by her husband: "Like a criminal" one "searches for the clause in question" in the application form, which in this case was "not there." But in her diary, Luise was certain that "the questionnaire will follow; no one slips through the narrow mesh." At the same time, Luise Solmitz also mainly thought about the effect nonacceptance would have for her private milieu. It would "ultimately be impossible not to belong to the SA Reserve 2 without everyone finding out the reason. There are people wondering now already: not in the Stahlhelm?! Not in the SA?! It need not be said what mental torture this is for Fredy, and what worry it is for me, also about Gisela's future, marriage and profession."[144] Indeed, after the couple had held out hope for weeks, the "questionnaire" finally reached them in June 1934. "The net has no mesh," Solmitz concluded with resignation in her diary.[145]

The rejections by the NSKOV and SA did not just mean that Luise Solmitz could no longer demonstrate her enthusiasm for the regime, which, as she noted in her diary, persisted as before. Rather, these rejections also deeply changed the family's relationships to their social milieu. In early June 1933, Solmitz reported that she had hired "a seamstress through the National Socialist Woman's League." She said, "I felt like a person who wants to finagle something by illicit means and was almost afraid that one might ask whether it is also an Aryan household."[146] Regarding Aryan questionnaires, she often spoke about a "guilty feeling" that she could "not get rid of toward every Aryan fellow man with whom one has anything to do except as a customer," about how she "felt like a fraudster," and about how she trembled "at every random word, at every visit, every letter: what do they want from us?"[147]

At the same time, Solmitz emphasized in her diary that, particularly in connection with reviews of their Aryan origins, her family was mostly treated with understanding and respect. In her description of the NSKOV employees who revoked her husband's membership, she pointed out that they behaved "very properly" and "very finely and tactfully."[148] Even with regard to the German Officers' League, she stressed that the people there still held her husband in high esteem despite being aware of his Jewish origins. Because he was a former officer and wounded in the war, Friedrich's membership was legally secured by an exception provision, which was also found in the Professional Civil Service Act. Nonetheless, in February 1934 a member began making an issue of Friedrich's Jewish origins and called for him to be expelled. In this particular situation, many other members and functionaries voiced their support for Friedrich Solmitz, but for Luise Solmitz it was "clear that if the matter becomes a question of principles, no Seidel, no Büttner, no Abicht, and no Weber can save Fredy from Hitler's will. . . . We stand powerless in the current."[149] Indeed, in the months that followed, Friedrich Solmitz's Jewish origins increasingly became an issue, as a result of which his social backing also dwindled. When in summer 1934 "the Aryan paragraph was fielded against Fredy again in the German Officers' League," he was told "this time even by Mr. Abicht, 'If I were in your place, I would call it quits. Now I am saying it too,'" whereupon Friedrich Solmitz declared his resignation the very next day.[150]

One year later, as Luise Solmitz surveyed her social situation and that of her family in her diary, she nonetheless pointed out that, except in one case, "no one has yet offended" her family and she had "always found that most people are far more civil than they need to be."[151] Yet at the same time, she clearly saw the difference that had come between her and her "Aryan" milieu because of the Aryan paragraph. "The one thing that separates me from everything, all of the good and friendly relatives in Berlin and here, from all good friends. Internally, even if it is never touched upon. Yes, you! You do not need to tremble, it is all same to you whether the Aryan certificate is required. Before people were perhaps divided by difference according to rank and money. But this has never been! We stand apart from everybody and everything, an unbridgeable chasm between us. In the end one feels like a fraudster, or like someone who is tolerated if one has relations with others. One feels entirely dependent on the decency of fellow human beings. One is supposed to be inferior even to the rawest, meanest, most common, simplest, or most vapid creature, provided he merely has the certificate."[152]

People did not need to approve of the regime's antisemitic policies in order to contribute to the increasing isolation of German Jews in the 1930s, nor did they have to become actively involved in operations of antisemitic violence or personally try to advance the exclusionary process in their everyday life with denunciations or chicanery. To make real the exclusion of "enemies" and "opponents" as desired by the regime, and to institute the new rules of belonging, all that was needed was for people to make use of the particular symbolic practices prescribed by the regime in their competitive social struggles related to their commitment to the Nazi regime. Many Germans did not do so voluntarily, nor did they want this to harm others. Nonetheless, by participating in the game, in which rules stipulated by the regime established who could play, they decisively advanced the process of social exclusion and the transformation of social belonging.

The increasing social isolation of the Solmitz family did little to change Luise Solmitz's basic commitment toward the regime, which she had established in spring 1933. Despite very clearly identifying her family's situation in summer 1935 and attentively registering the intensification of anti-Jewish policy since that spring in her diary, she continued to publicly show her belonging. She flew flags on festive and memorial days: on March 1, Day of the Return of the Saar; on Hero Commemoration Day two weeks later; on Hitler's birthday in April; and on the anniversary of Hindenburg's death in early August.[153] And 1935 was also the year when she bought her new black-white-red flag and a swastika pennant.[154]

Hence, her family was all the more heavily affected by the three Nuremberg Laws enacted that very same year in a Reichstag assembly convened at short notice during the annual Nazi party rally. The most important of these was the Reich Citizenship Law. Whereas the logic of social belonging had first been stipulated in the Aryan paragraph of the Law for the Restoration of the Professional Civil Service and applied to government administrations and associations, the Reich Citizenship Law now extended this logic to state citizenship.[155] By way of "Reich citizenship," the law created a new and better status of state citizenship with exclusive privileges, such as the right to vote, and this status could only be obtained by a person of "German or kindred blood and who, through his conduct, shows that he is both willing and able to faithfully serve the German Volk and Reich."[156] The relevant implementation regulations adopted the definition of *non-Aryan* found in the Professional Civil Service Law. The Law for the Protection of German Blood and Honor adopted this same distinction and prohibited "marriages" and "extramarital relations" between "Jews" and "Reich citizens," as well as the employment of female household servants under forty-five years old in Jewish households. In addition, it stipulated that "Jews are forbidden to fly the Reich or national flag or display Reich colors."[157] This regulation referred to the third Nuremberg Law, which elevated the swastika flag as the sole "Reich and national flag" and abolished the black-white-red flag as an official state symbol. This decision was actually a response to the massive willful appropriation of the black-white-red flag by contemporaries who wanted to demonstrate their commitment to the "national uprising" but not to National Socialism. The regime no longer wanted to accept this flag and was anxious, in the words of Reichstag President Hermann Göring, to prevent "these colors and this flag from being debased" to a particular symbol "under which . . . the reaction keeps itself hidden."[158] The law now only took up the old flag of the conservative right with the phrase, "The Reich colors are black-white-red."[159]

The massive intensification of the anti-Jewish regulations and the abolishment of the "beloved" black-white-red flag hit Luise Solmitz equally hard. "Toward midnight," she reported in her diary, "the new laws were announced, our civil death sentence." In her diary, she described the new legal provisions in detail, starting with the Reich Flag Law and only afterward writing about the Reich Citizenship Law and Law for the Protection of German Blood and Honor. With resignation, she summarized the immediate personal consequences of these new legal provisions. "Our black-white-red flag is sinking for the second time. Anyone who marries my daughter will be sent to prison, along with my daughter. The servant girl must be dismissed. We are no longer allowed to fly flags. We do not know Jewish colors. We are only allowed to be state subjects, not Reich citizens. My fatherland, how I have loved you as long as I can remember. Only tolerated, I am allowed to live in you as a stranger." Solmitz nonetheless tried to work up some courage. She described it as a "feeling of joy" to see that she was bearing the burdens together with her husband and daughter, and she undertook "to no longer flinch, internally and externally, from the admission: we no longer belong to you, are not allowed to; this awareness and this intention were for me the result of the Nuremberg Reichstag."

But Solmitz was also aware that "this cannot be lived as easily as it is thought and written. A hundred times a day, the heart cringes when I see my child, loved beyond all things. . . . This child who means heaven and earth to me . . . is expelled, locked out, despised, worthless. This is what a mother must bear. No profession, no future, no marriage. What the children of relatives, acquaintances, what our domestic workers are entitled to, what they can strive for and achieve—Gisela stands apart." She finally finished her diary entry: "We now only feel like intruders, and like former convicts, for example, who are pursued by the stigma."[160]

The Nuremberg Laws intensified the social isolation of the Solmitz family, and yet they only legally cemented the situation that had overtaken the family during the last two years. A few days after the end of the 1935 Nazi party rally, two befriended married couples visited the Solmitz family and reported that they too had now acquired a swastika flag. Luise Solmitz recorded the reasoning they gave in her diary: "If we did not fly flags, we would of course be taken for Jews." Luise was unable to properly interpret the statement. "Was it thoughtlessness or was it supposed to show unselfconsciousness?" she asked in her entry.[161] Naturally, we cannot reconstruct the motives behind the statement, but it really need not have been spite. It may just have been the inconsiderate description of a logic that had established itself in the everyday life of Germans as part of the intense struggle related to dealing with the regime's assertive demand for commitment.

PART TWO

On the evening of July 5, 1933, the last of the political parties of the Weimar Republic declared its dissolution. As stated in the declaration of the Catholic Center Party negotiated in the preceding days with the Nazi regime, "the political upheaval has placed German state life on a completely new foundation, which leaves no room anymore for party-political activity, which was possible until just recently."[1]

The political system had in fact fundamentally changed in the few weeks since the last Reichstag election in early March. With the newly elected Reichstag's acceptance of the so-called Enabling Act just two days after it convened for the first time, the parties elected to the Reichstag—except for the KPD and SPD—had already agreed to their own irrelevance in late March 1933: the law enabled the regime henceforth to enact laws without parliamentary approval. This decision had been substantially influenced by the terroristic violence of the SA and police, as well as by vociferous demands for "national unity" and integration with the "national uprising." In the weeks after the destruction of the parties and organizations of the workers' movement, the regime used the tools of violence and nationalistic appeals to compel the bourgeois parties and associations to dissolve or merge with the NSDAP, last among them the Center Party in July. Its self-dissolution marked the end of the first stage of the National Socialist seizure of power, the results of which were cemented a few days later in the Law against the New Formation of Parties by the sentence "In Germany the National Socialist German Workers Party exists as the only party."[2]

Within the setting of this event, in early July 1933, Reich Chancellor and NSDAP-Führer Adolf Hitler came forth with "fundamental and pioneering" ideas about the "nature of the German revolution" and the future "task of its bearers." Speaking on July 2, 1933, in Bad Reichenhall, Hitler emphasized the need to distinguish between the different phases of the National Socialist revolution: "1. The preparation for the struggle. 2. The gaining of political power," which now is "virtually completed." This now had to be followed, third, by the "production of what is described as the totality of the state." At the beginning of his three-hour speech, Hitler had already explained what this cryptic formulation was supposed to mean. The "revolution," he had emphasized, "is only a means to a higher goal . . . namely, for the purpose of the preservation and security of the life of our Volk." This could not be achieved solely by gaining political power. The "essentials of a revolution are not the takeover of power but rather the education of man." Every "ideological revolution" must result in the "education and forming of man" and is "only successful if it puts the stamp of its spirit and its awareness not just on its bearers but also on the times." The "new state" remains a "product of fantasy if it does not create a new man."[3] On July 5 the Center Party finally announced its self-dissolution, and Hitler forcefully reiterated these ideas in a speech the following day: "The political parties are now definitively defeated." Now the "achievement of external power must be followed by the inner education of man." The "revolution is no permanent state; it cannot be allowed to develop into a steady state. One must guide the liberated current of the revolution into the more secure riverbed of evolution. The most important thing in this is the education of man."[4]

In his speeches on the occasion of the self-dissolution of the last political party of the Weimar Republic, Hitler was not just commemorating an important symbolic date in the assertion of the regime's political aspiration for total power. Printed afterward in the newspapers, his speeches themselves also marked a major turning point in the consolidation of the National Socialist dictatorship, for with his statements in early July 1933, the Reich chancellor was intervening in conflicts that had arisen between various bearers of the Nazi regime on the question of what to do next. Whereas particularly the (formerly) conservative allies of the NSDAP increasingly warned against a "permanent revolution" and demanded stronger dedication now to substantive political work,[5] calls coming notably from the SA for a further radicalization of the "revolution" had grown loud. Just a few days before the SA meeting in Bad Reichenhall, the SA-Führer Ernst Röhm took up the criticism against the coalition partners, insisting in an article for the *Nationalsozialistische Monatshefte* that it was "in fact high time that the national revolution stops," but only so that "this turns into the National Socialist revolution!"⁶

Hitler's pronouncements in early July were intended as a statement within this factional conflict. It was no coincidence that he made them in Bad Reichenhall. With his vocal advocacy for the "education of the German man," he was clearly siding against the calls for a "second revolution." Hitler tied his statement to a concrete demand. Vigorously pursued particularly by the SA in the first half of 1933, the dismissals of leadership personnel from official bodies and commercial companies to free up positions for "politically reliable" NSDAP members were supposed to stop. "One must not remove a good business leader if he is a good business leader but not yet a National Socialist," admonished Hitler. Rather, "today's situation must be improved and the men who embody it educated to the National Socialist understanding of the state."⁷ In this sense, the fourth phase of the "National Socialist revolution"—namely, the "solving of the unemployment problem"—"presupposed the education of the German man in the spirit of National Socialism."⁸ Hitler's speeches of early July for the first time conspicuously displayed the tensions that would decisively dominate the development of the National Socialist seizure of power over the following months. In the days that followed, other members of the government picked up and reiterated their message,⁹ and the conflict would not end until one year later, almost to the day, with the murder of Ernst Röhm and other SA leaders. The speeches marked the transition from the "first half of the seizure-of-power process," which had served to eliminate external opposition, to the second half, characterized above all by the state and party leadership's conflict with competitors internal to the regime.¹⁰

But at the same time, the calls for the "education of the German man" pointed beyond the internal power struggles of the Nazi regime and the political history of the process of the seizure of power. While the speeches fulfilled a strategic function for securing the achieved power position, they also clearly identified a central feature of National Socialist policy of the following years. The Nazi regime tried to realize its societal-political objectives precisely through the transformation of people and their lifestyles and through an education intended to make them "German men." Already in his programmatic text *Mein Kampf*, Hitler had paid strong attention to the "developmental and educational work of the völkisch state." After 1933, one of the most important features of the Nazi regime was its demand for more than merely political support and commitment from individuals.[11] The political changes that accompanied the start of the breakthrough into a "new era" were also supposed to find expression in a transformed lifestyle and new self-conception on the part of Germans, which would permanently secure the "life of the German Volk."[12]

Hitler's speeches in the first days of July 1933 became an important reference point for this process. Many of the Nazi regime's actors in the field of education took up the central phrases of the speeches, namely, about how the "new state" would remain a "product of fantasy" if it failed to create "a new man" and how the "revolution" had to be redirected to the "riverbed of evolution," using these ideas in their effort to propagandize and realize new lifestyles and self-conceptions.[13]

Neither did the demand of the new Reich chancellor in summer 1933 slip past Germans unnoticed. Werner Kramp, for example, a civil registry employee from Hamburg, noted in his diary on July 2 how "the last few days have again brought the ever further advance of the revolution." In his long entry, Kramp spoke at length about the Reich chancellor's speech in Bad Reichenhall. "It can be gathered from the Führer's speech that he distinguishes . . . four phases of the revolution," Kramp wrote, correctly summarizing Hitler's statements: "1. Preparation, 2. Seizure of power (almost complete) 3. Production of the totality of the state (key word of the day!) . . . 5. Solution of the unemployment problem." Despite announcing four points, his list ended up with five because he had aptly transcribed Hitler's statements with an extra enumerated point: "4. Education of the German Man in the spirit of National Socialism."[14] This item, in particular, preoccupied Kramp in his diary. As opposed to Hitler, who at the end of his speech had declared educational work to be the "noblest task" of the SA,[15] Kramp was less certain, wondering instead whether the SA was itself "in need of strict education." But even if for him, as he wrote, "the misgivings regarding the latter would not fall silent," Kramp basically agreed with the regime's aspiration that "everyone, along with his job, should serve public affairs," as well as with the project of "forming the new state citizen as the most important factor of the era." And he did so even though or perhaps because he saw the formation of new state citizens not merely as an important political issue.

Kramp was aware that the state's educational aspiration would make him a pupil as well, clearly realizing that the intention to create a "new man" pertained to him and his way of life too. The regime was promoting the political reorientation of the Germans' everyday life management and self-contemplation, and, despite his concerns, Kramp was prepared to participate by reflecting on and changing himself. But as he noted, somewhat perplexed, he just did not know "at the moment how I can shape myself into a mainstay for myself and others."[16]

In the following second part of the book, I focus on the Nazi regime's comprehensive educational challenge to individuals, whereby it urged them to change their self-conceptions and ways of life. Chapter 4 pursues the fundamental conditions of the political formation of individual lifestyles and self-contemplation in the 1930s. First it discusses the intentions and structures of the Nazi regime's comprehensive education project (1). It points out the many different educational agents involved in the project, as well as the plurality of educational initiatives, and explains why this makes it seem doubtful that previously pursued questions formulated in terms of the success or failure of such initiatives can adequately grasp their impact. To develop an alternative research perspective, in a second step I look into how the educational intentions, structures, and practices of the Nazi regime stood in relation to the individual people whose ways of life and self-perceptions were supposed to be changed (2). I show how, within the practices of the Nazi education project, individuals came to play a different, more active role than was actually conceded to them by the educational theories and instruments of National Socialism. Following up on this, I discuss how diaries can be used to access and analyze political self-transformation within the Nazi education project (3).

Against the background of these deliberations, chapter 5 directs its gaze to people who in the 1930s tried to transform their lifestyles or self-perspectives within the Nazi education project. The process here does not involve researching the reception of individual educational instruments. Rather, I look at three basic questions of individual self-description that were specifically raised by the diverse educational efforts of the Nazi regime: (1) the question about the individual's relationship to others, which arose within the Nazi education project mainly in connection with the category of "community" (Gemeinschaft); (2) the question about individuals' relationship with their own body, which Nazi education considered an especially high priority; and (3) the question about how people understood their personal origin, which achieved great importance through the racial-hygienic focus of National Socialist policies on the lineage of individuals. At the same time, both chapters examine the forms in which people worked on politically shaping their self-perspectives and ways of life.

4

THE NATIONAL SOCIALIST EDUCATION PROJECT

1. Educational Intentions and the Participating Players: Basic Conditions of Political Education under National Socialism

On Sunday, March 5, 1933, the parties of the new government obtained their own majority during the new Reichstag elections. The members of the government reconvened just two days later. The agenda did not actually include restructuring the cabinet, for the voting had served as an electoral affirmation of the government put in place by the Reich president, and the NSDAP had failed to achieve a majority on its own, which would have allowed the party to rule by itself. But when Adolf Hitler opened the ministers' meeting on March 7, he vigorously pointed out the need for "large-scale propaganda and enlightenment work," which required the building of a new "central authority."[1] Four days later, the ministerial panel decided in favor of the "establishment of a Reich Ministry for Public Enlightenment and Propaganda," which began work the following week.[2]

Joseph Goebbels was appointed to head the new ministry. He had been the NSDAP Gauleiter of Berlin and as Reich propaganda director had also played a major role in the NSDAP's electoral successes during the Weimar Republic. As the tenth minister of the "national government," Goebbels faced a novel challenge. Although awareness of the government's need for a methodical information policy had grown since the First World War, never had any regime approved a cabinet ranking for this area of responsibility.[3] In a speech to press representatives two days after his appointment, the new minister accordingly pointed out that the "establishment of the new Ministry for Public Enlightenment and Propaganda . . . is a revolutionary act of government." It documented that "the new regime no longer has the intention of leaving the Volk to itself. This government is, in the truest sense of the word, a government of the Volk [Volksregierung]," but one that wanted to set up the relationship to the Volk "in a different form than as it occurred in democratic parliamentarianism." The newly established ministry was charged with creating a "connection between the government and the Volk, the living contact between the national government as the form of expression of the Volk's will [Volkswille] and the Volk itself" and, in parallel with political developments, producing "a synchronization [Gleichschaltung] between the regime and the entire Volk."[4]

As early as spring 1933, the establishment of the Reich Ministry for Public Enlightenment and Propaganda marked an important contrast between the Nazi regime and the governments of previous decades—namely, in terms of the different demand that the Nazi regime placed on the population and individuals. Like Joseph Goebbels in his speech on the opening of the new ministry, many other leaders of the Nazi regime also spoke publicly in the following years about wanting, not to adapt the policies of the regime to the Volk, but to adapt the Volk to the policies of the regime. As Goebbels openly declared, this way the regime would "always be the executive of the Volk's will [Volkswille]," in that it would "carry out its intention of finding the necessary resonance in the masses of the Volk [Volksmassen]."[5] The Ministry for Public Enlightenment and Propaganda was supposed to ensure the alignment of "the nation solidly behind the idea of the national revolution."[6]

Goebbels's remarks on how to accomplish this goal pointed in various directions.[7] He chiefly emphasized the necessity of using coordinated publicity work to present the regime's action so that it would be understood by the entire population. "The propagandist" must always "speak the language of the people [Menschen]" and simplify "complicated lines of thought so that ultimately even the smallest man on the street understands them."[8] Goebbels seemed convinced that the question of the population's loyalty was just a matter of proper oration, with which one could "convince even the most standoffish and malignant persons that our political course is the right one."[9] This would require complete control and coordination of the government's official publicity work and all other public statements. And thus on the day after his appointment, the new minister had invited members of the press not only to inform the public about the establishment of the new ministry but also, with a mixture of threats and offers of cooperation, to make them clearly understand the conditions under which journalistic work would henceforth take place.

In the following weeks, the new ministry radically changed the working conditions for the press and for itself created far-reaching options for control. The so-called Editor Act of October 1933 created a system for monitoring journalists. The latter now had to be registered with the Reich Press Chamber, affiliated with the Propaganda Ministry; this required verification of their "political reliability" and "Aryan lineage" and compliance with the chamber's directives. Earlier, in the summer of that same year, the establishment of the Reich Press Conference had already created an instrument for controlling press content, which not only channeled "information" to selected journalists on a daily basis but also conveyed "instructions" for press reporting. "You are not only supposed to know what is happening," Goebbels had explained in his inaugural speech to the attending journalists, "but rather also know what the government thinks about it and how you can most suitably make it clear to the Volk."[10]

The Reich Propaganda Ministry secured similar options for directly intervening in radio broadcasting, whose representatives were likewise addressed by Goebbels ten days after his speech to the press and informed about the new ministry and the principles of Nazi communications policy.[11] Radio journalists, as well, had to be registered with the new Reich Radio Chamber starting in fall 1933. The dissolution of the radio broadcasting companies in the states in summer 1933 and their incorporation into the Reich Broadcasting Corporation, which was subject to the Reich Propaganda Ministry, also created direct access with respect to content.[12] With the interactions of the "press" and "radio broadcasting" sections and the section for "active propaganda" responsible for campaigns and major events, the Reich Ministry for Public Enlightenment and Propaganda held far-reaching opportunities to monitor and control political reporting in the media and the public representation of the regime within just a few months after being established.[13]

But at the same time, the monitoring and coordination initiative raised by Goebbels on behalf of the new ministry and the government in his speech in March 1933 was not limited solely to the narrowly defined area of political communications. Instead, it extended to all means and forms of public communication, including presumably apolitical areas, as associated with the other direction indicated by Goebbels's remarks about producing a will of the Volk that conformed to the government. Toward the end of his inaugural speech to the members of the press, Goebbels declared in sum that the new ministry needed to strive to "bring that consistent, national spirit into the Volk, which is, so to speak, the foundation of the new national government, so that everyone understands what we want, so that the entire Volk starts to react consistently, and so that everyone makes himself available to this government with his entire sympathy."[14]

This comment did not aim at "convincing" the still undecided. Goebbels spoke firmly in this context of "popular education" [Volkserziehung], emphasizing that his ministry should not merely change but rather profoundly shape the political views of the Germans. Upon foundation, the Ministry for Public Enlightenment and Propaganda set itself "the task of re-educating the population for a new society based on National Socialist values."[15] The regime was certain that only the transformation of personal lifestyles and self-perspectives would ensure its long-term societal support. As Goebbels also noted in later speeches, propaganda is "for us educational work, the forming of public opinion, not for today and tomorrow, but rather according to our intention for decades and for generations."[16] The distinction between the day-to-day control of the political opinion situation and the long-term education of the German Volk—the difference between influencing what were described in the 1930s as the people's "mood" and "attitude"—remained "constitutively significant" for the government's state propaganda beyond the start of Nazi rule. In this respect, National Socialist public policy consisted of "two different fields of activity, the one dealing with the short-term and the other with the mid- and long-term influencing of the population."[17]

The two-tiered job description advanced propaganda into a relatively unclarified position within National Socialist government policy. Although with his statements at the beginning of his speech Goebbels justified his ministry's importance for properly conveying the policies of the "national regime,"[18] by integrating the ministry's own field of activity with the higher goal of the "education of the Volk" he simultaneously declared propaganda to be an instrument of National Socialist societal policy. As Reich Chancellor Hitler repeatedly emphasized in the wake of his speech in July 1933, only through the effort at a "persistent and uninterrupted education of our Volk" could a "true German Volksgemeinschaft" be created. It was necessary to "educate a new man so that our Volk does not perish because of the degenerative phenomena of our time." Hitler strongly emphasized that this really required "all Germans to be ideologically educated to National Socialists."[19]

With its broad aspiration to control public communications, propaganda was supposed to contribute substantially to this endeavor, achieving, as Goebbels put it in spring 1933, the *"real* saturation of the Volk with the intellectual contents of our time."[20]

As he did with regard to the political opinions of the Germans, Goebbels proceeded from a rather vague notion also when considering the educational aspiration of his activities, albeit one that was widely shared during National Socialist rule: in principle, influence had no set boundaries and could be achieved by confronting people with new political models by means of a controlled public policy.[21] In this sense, the concept of education frequently used in this context meant an act of forming the individual along the lines of an ideal, a formation that effectively was to emerge on its own from the experience of everyday life. Within the National Socialist understanding, education was therefore not a specific social process affecting mainly children and youth in which educators tried to purposefully act upon pupils. Rather, the concept included the entire spectrum of social interactions because, as one leading education theorist put it, "whatever cause and purpose they arise from," they could always bring forth "a change, formation, and development in the participants."[22] Thus, the intended "education of the Volk" did not presuppose deliberate learning by individuals viewed as pupils. Rather, "experience" became the central concept of educational thought in the 1930s. It described the optimal form through which the regime, by way of purposefully created external arrangements, wanted to convey the new models of individual life management and self-contemplation. This is where "education" and "propaganda" met within National Socialist thought, which already understood even just the systematic announcement of political models to be an educational act.[23]

In this sense, the new propaganda ministry also identified commercial advertising and movies as an important "educational instrument" and called on representatives of the film industry to "sit together at the weaving loom of the era" and advance the "education of the Volk" through movies.[24] No longer defined by boundaries, the "educational task of propaganda" formed the crucial bridge between the various areas of responsibility of the new ministry, which, apart from departments for the "press" and "radio," had already seen the founding of sections for "film" and for "theater, music, and art."[25] Similarly, the Reich Chamber of Culture, founded in fall 1933 and closely affiliated with the ministry, had, along with the Reich Press Chamber and Reich Radio Chamber, separate chambers for literature, theater, film, visual arts, and music, which likewise needed to be joined by all who wanted to publicly express themselves. These organizations created monitoring and control opportunities similar to those used for press and radio journalists.

With these and other instruments, the regime tried in the following years to actively design all public space. It intended to create a semblance of the Third Reich that conformed to the regime's own ideological ideas and thus generate an experience that would change individual lifestyles and self-contemplations. The "beautiful illusion of the Third Reich" drawn up by the Nazi regime with its comprehensive public policy conveyed the image of a successful government that advanced the formation of the nation and therefore earned political popularity. At the same time, the aesthetic stylization of the regime's rule aimed at a change in "forms of perception and consciousness" and a "reorganization of the horizons of expectations and day-to-day living."[26] In the effort "to model collective and individual patterns of perception," the regime, with its comprehensive educational ambition, viewed the entirety of the everyday life of Germans as a "monumental educational space" in which demands and role models that were communicated in a variety of ways were supposed to achieve a new lifestyle and self-contemplation.[27]

The extent to which this ambition was realized under National Socialist rule, and how much the intensive efforts to design and control public space also actually contributed to the large-scale transformation of individual Germans, is a matter of scholarly dispute. On the one hand, numerous studies, especially those making cultural-historical arguments, have detected changes to political attitudes, moral value systems, and everyday forms of life within German society during Nazi rule. These have also been repeatedly traced back to the influence of the Nazi regime's media and communications policy, even though a precise link between public appeals and changes to individual lifestyles has hardly been pursued in any greater detail.[28]

On the other hand, investigations into the effects of National Socialist propaganda, as well as studies on the social history of National Socialism, have generally widely disputed the educational effect of the propaganda and policies of the Nazi regime. As early as 1983, a groundbreaking essay by Ian Kershaw took the regime's own goal for its propaganda—namely, "the task of educating the German people for a new society based upon a drastically restructured value system"—as the yardstick for evaluating the success and efficacy of Nazi public policy.[29] He himself rated its ability to contribute to a change in attitudes and lifestyles as rather low. A comparison of the views of Germans and the ideological concepts showed, according to Kershaw, that propaganda was successful above all in areas where it could build on preexisting opinions. By contrast, the regime was not successful in fundamentally changing attitudes. This thesis is still frequently shared today.[30]

Moreover, from social-historical perspectives, both older and more recent studies have underscored the persistence of existing social milieus even under National Socialist rule, arguing that, despite massive education efforts, attempts in the 1930s and 1940s to adapt existing identities and social loyalties to propagandistic precepts were unsuccessful. Instead, everyday ways of life were upheld even in opposition to political directives.[31]

When identifying the main reason for the propaganda's inefficiency, social historians have repeatedly pointed to the entangled competencies and large number of players that dominated the reality of the regime's public policy, in contrast to the ideal sketched by Goebbels of an extensively monitored and coordinated propaganda system.[32] They noted early on that, even in core areas of competence such as journalism, the propaganda ministry and its minister competed with other influential agencies. Furthermore, even though the Reich Ministry for Popular Education and Propaganda quickly advanced after being formed, at the same time the regime could not even reduce by similar levels the departments and employees at other state authorities also tasked with press and publicity responsibilities.[33] Within the area of public policy too, the "polycratic structure" of National Socialist rule prevented the complete realization of the monitoring and control plans of the propaganda ministry, which had been set up as the central institution.[34]

But even though the number of players dealing with the "education of the German Volk" was many times larger than that of those active in the ministry's core areas—namely, the control of political reporting in the mass media—this does not mean simply that the educational efforts failed. By looking more closely at the broad field of institutions actively involved in education and their activities, in the following I show instead that this constellation just created a different foundation for the transformation of individual lifestyles and self-contemplations after 1933 than the one assumed by the regime. Given the multitude of intensely strong-willed educational actors, it was impossible to realize the theoretical model in which Germans were confronted in an all-encompassing way with a standard role model for one's personal lifestyle and self-contemplation such that they had no option other than adapting to the ideological directive from within their everyday lives. But for precisely this reason, the real starting conditions for the transformation of individual ways of living and self-images must be reconstructed in order to appropriately frame the question about the impact of the intense efforts of National Socialist education.

The Players of the National Socialist Education Project

Instead of featuring unity and harmony, the educational efforts of the Nazi regime were shaped above all by the competition between various institutions active in this field. The conflicts started at the highest level of government. While anticipating his role after the seizure of power during the final phase of the Weimar Republic, Goebbels originally did not want to be the propaganda minister but rather the minister for public education, laying claim to competencies for "film, radio, school, university, art, culture, [and] propaganda" for his wide-ranging Reich ministry, which was supposed to be "joined with the Prussian Culture Ministry."[35] But then just two days after his appointment as Reich chancellor, Hitler appointed Bernhard Rust—like Goebbels, an NSDAP Gauleiter since the mid-1920s—as the Prussian minister of culture, ultimately also making him the Reich minister for science, education, and public literacy in spring 1934. As such, Rust aspired no less than Goebbels to decisively shape the regime's education policy and advance the "education of the German Volk" through the state educational institutions under his control.[36] Similar ambitions were held by Konstantin Hierl, who since 1931 had been the director of the Voluntary Labor Service of the NSDAP and was appointed the Reich commissar for the labor service one year later. For Hierl, it was the labor service that formed "the great educational school for German socialism, that is, for the German Volksgemeinschaft," which in its "volks-educational effect . . . cannot be replaced by any other institution."[37]

At the same time, the regime's line ministries and special commissioners, though not holding any direct competencies in the sectors of education or propaganda, also constantly aimed at the transformation of personal lifestyles and self-perspectives. In the 1930s, for instance, the state's health and sexuality policy was by no means limited to creating new instruments with which the Nazi regime could prevent the generation of progeny that were ostensibly a "danger to the Volk" (volksgefährdend)—namely, by means of forced sterilization, the prevention of marriages, the prosecution of so-called racial defilement offenses, and ultimately direct killing.[38] It also aimed at the education of the Germans. Formed within the Interior Ministry, the Expert Advisory Council for Population and Racial Policy supervised legislation in this area. Also created within this expert advisory council in summer 1933, alongside two work groups more strongly focused on administrative and legislative problems, was a Work Group for Education—Maternal Issues and Welfare. This work group was supposed to develop "recommendations for the support of hereditarily healthy families and for the preparation for marriage" and for the "education of women" and their "spiritual renewal."[39] Hence, as early as fall 1933, the Reich Propaganda Ministry, with its huge "propaganda campaign for population policy," was not alone in promoting individual partner selection and family planning according to the new genetic criteria. Also doing so was the Reich Interior Ministry, which played a leading role in this policy area.[40] Insofar as the health and sexuality policy of the regime was largely shaped by the fact that "the basic assumptions of racial hygiene and eugenics" always led to "the imperative to influence procreative behavior through education and enlightenment," this educational imperative demonstrates a general feature of the National Socialist style of policy, which characterized other policy areas in a similar way.[41]

Thus, while a multitude of state institutions aspired to play a leading role in the "education of the Volk," the "dualism of state and party" that permanently characterized the entire system of Nazi rule was especially important within this field.[42] Hitler's appointment as Reich chancellor and the elimination of political opposition signified for the NSDAP the longed-for success of its political efforts of the past years but at the same time also raised the question of what role the party should now assume in the National Socialist state. Its new responsibility, as repeatedly emphasized by the NSDAP-Führer and Reich Chancellor Hitler since summer 1933, must now be the "education of the entire Volk in the sense of the ideas" of National Socialism, to "educate, for the National Socialist state, the National Socialist Volk that carries it."[43] Accordingly, many party agencies also claimed a prominent role in the comprehensive education project of National Socialism. This applied in equal measure to the party's leadership staff, where various Reichsleiter held education and propaganda competencies,[44] and to their local structures on the ground. After 1933, the activities of NSDAP

Ortsgruppen, in particular, were determined by the goal of "forming the thought of Volk comrades and party comrades according to the idea of the Führer and in this way to achieve a way of life that can exist before the Führer in good conscience."[45] Also at this level were multiple offices for functionaries entrusted with propaganda and education tasks, whose holders undertook operations for the education of party members and nonmembers within their own districts, both as commissioned by various Reichsleiter and on their own initiative.

At the same time, the formations linked to the NSDAP and the societies it supervised also considered working on the "education of the German Volk" to be one of the main functions of their activities. This particularly applied to the Hitler Youth, which dealt with children and young people. But National Socialist People's Welfare, the National Socialist Women's League, and the National Socialist Doctors' League all claimed control over the "health maintenance of the Volk in the area of their worldview-related political education work" and made an effort in parallel with state authorities to propagate new racial-hygienic principles for individual preventive health care measures and the personal structuring of sex lives.[46] The same applied to the other organizations affiliated with the NSDAP, which additionally devoted much of their energy to the ideological education of their own members, a great many of whom had only joined after Hitler's appointment as Reich chancellor. Even within the SA, which had defined itself through confrontation and violence in the Weimar Republic, intensive efforts were undertaken after 1933 to make the "education of the Volk" a core aspect of the organization's modified self-understanding.[47] And *Das Schwarze Korps* (the Black Corps), the official newspaper of the elite SS, understood itself as nothing less than the "mouthpiece of a state National Socialist mission consciousness" and worked with a "self-appointed educational responsibility on the dissemination" of new lifestyles and self-conceptions.[48]

In addition, after 1933 a multitude of new special offices and institutions emerged within the NSDAP for the "education of the German Volk." Apart from various training centers, such as the National Socialist Order Castles (NS-Ordensburgen) and Adolf Hitler Schools set up by the party in 1937 alongside the National Political Institutes of Education established by the Reich Ministry of Culture,[49] these also included new guidance and education institutions, such as the NSDAP Office of Race Policy, which was supposed to coordinate and perform "educational and training work . . . in the area of human heredity studies, racial studies, hereditary health, as well as racial care and its border areas."[50]

According to Hitler's outline, the collective skillful interweaving of the multifarious educational efforts of the different party agencies was supposed to ensure the comprehensive and lifelong education of the Germans. "We have undertaken," noted Reich Chancellor and Party Führer Hitler at the NSDAP party rally in 1935, "to educate this Volk through a new school, to give it an education that already starts at youth and shall never end. In future, the young man shall be raised from one school to the next. It starts with the child and shall end with the old fighter of the movement. No one shall say that for him there is a time when he can be left entirely to his own devices."[51]

New controlling institutions, such as the Office of the Führer's Commissioner for the Supervision of All Intellectual and Ideological Training and Education of the NSDAP, held by Alfred Rosenberg since January 1934, were supposed to ensure smooth cooperation among party agencies.[52] But as with the Reich Propaganda Ministry, its unifying influence remained minimal. Like the state institutions, the party institutions participating in the Nazi education project as "schools" in Hitler's sense of the word found themselves in a "bitterly waged battle of the 'educational powers' for influence on the National Socialist education system."[53] This battle was not restricted solely to power-political disputes over competencies but rather also arose from the individual party agencies' and state institutions' different ideas about the proper ideological education for Germans. Instead of forming a "unified system of education," in practice their efforts generated "a conglomeration of values, guiding principles, prejudices, demands, and slogans in the pedagogical field."[54]

Robert Ley, the leader of the German Labor Front, who as the NSDAP Reichsorganisationsleiter (Reich organization leader) was also largely responsible for advancing the party's realignment according to its educational responsibility, noted self-critically in a speech in 1936, "We are chaotically confusing and mixing up the terms training, education, propaganda, leadership; when we talk about education, we express ourselves incorrectly when we use the word school and training. . . . All of this must someday be clearly sorted out."[55] But it never came to this. To be sure, both state and party efforts at "Volkserziehung" referred to the same set of ideological terms and textual references, particularly Hitler's programmatic book

Mein Kampf. But instead of creating the intended unified education state, the various educational endeavors formed a much looser framework. The participating actors agreed on the basic objective of this framework, but within it they pursued their own educational intentions and ideas.[56]

The regime's educational agents were not just each on their own looking at very different aspects of everyday lifestyles and personal self-contemplation. They also had profoundly different ideas about how to change them, since it was hardly possible to derive any definitive lifestyles from the hazy ideological principles of National Socialism. The educational ambition of the Nazi regime raised the problem of translating the vague principles of National Socialist ideology into concrete demands on the personal lifestyles and self-conceptions of Germans. Appeals mounted by various players with respect to the same areas of life could differ quite significantly even just depending on whether, for example, they drew on the concept of "race" or "Volk," both equally central to National Socialism.[57]

These educational endeavors varied strongly in their details, but they were unified by the aspiration to contribute to the creation of the "new" (or also "National Socialist," "national," "political," or "German") man.[58] This utopian figure formed the central reference point of the Nazi education project. It was supposed to become visible in the near term in the respective educational practices and permanently realized through people's internal conditioning. The vociferous demands for the transformation of everyday ways of life always aimed at the individual's pervasive internal transformation. What distinguished the "new man" was not just a "new" way of life. He was also supposed to be "remarkably conscious of history and the moment of its delinquency" and, from this awareness, orient his everyday lifestyle according to political categories. In terms of its aspiration, the figure of the "new man" opened up "paths to self-development in which the Self fused with the course of history."[59]

With respect to publicly propagated models, however, in the 1930s the regime's educational demands merely drafted a broad spectrum of new behavioral ideals and social roles, each presented as an expression of the "new man." While the National Socialist education project actually tried to achieve the ideological uniformity of individual self-perceptions, by proceeding this way it opened up "a wide range of legitimate subject positions," which were "juxtaposed" and yet all "safely within the ideological framework of Nazism."[60] Despite the common goal of creating the "new man," the various party and state actors each advocated their own interpretation of what should follow from the principles of National Socialist ideology for the lifestyles and self-conceptions of Germans.

Moreover, the resultant "diverse contradictions and ambivalences, which members of National Socialist society" faced within the Nazi education project,[61] were significantly amplified in the figure of the "new man," which was anything but an invention of the Nazi regime.[62] Despite aspiring for comprehensive surveillance and control, the regime by no means managed to monopolize this figure in the 1930s. As strongly as leading politicians frequently emphasized that the "new era" initiated by the "national uprising" had created the need to educate a man appropriate for the era, with respect to its key referential figure the National Socialist education project fell very much in line with longer-term developments reaching back to the turn of the century. The question about the individual's relationship to economic, cultural, and social changes had emerged as a problem in the 1880s, garnering broad social attention and leading to a kaleidoscopic spectrum of reform movements, "each in a specific way [aimed] at the reformation of the life of the individual and the lifestyle of men."[63]

In reaction to the broad destabilization of traditional ways of life and interpretations of the world, the quest for a new orientation intensified within newly founded associations, societies, and publication media, grasping out in very different directions. These explorations occurred outside established political structures but were not apolitical. Instead, they strove for "the transformation of the individual so as to have ultimately reshaped the society as a whole by means of multiplication."[64] This concept of social change, within which the "new era," "new man," social change, and self-transformation blurred together, constituted the common identifier for this decidedly pluralistic spectrum of organizations and media. Within their gamut, they included endeavors related not only to nudism, naturopathy, nutritional reform, and vegetarianism associated with Lebensreform but also to the women's and youth movements, the emerging racial hygiene movement, and the establishment of adult education centers.[65] In many ways, the movement and rule of National Socialism also followed in the tradition of turn-of-the-century reform movements; and in terms of their political style, which sought the "renewal of the Volk" by means of the transformation of the individual, they were profoundly dominated by the reformist approach.

Meanwhile, many of the ideas promoted after 1933 by the party and state educational players of the Nazi regime had already been pursued decades earlier by innovators who often advocated other political ideas. After 1933, the Nazi regime infused the activities of these previous innovators with its own ideological premises, such that they now often persisted only in ways that distorted their original meaning. Yet even so, these constellations opened up opportunities for many older educational players to continue their work related to the "new man" even after 1933. Accordingly, proponents of widely different reform movements saw the start of National Socialist rule and its education project as the fulfillment of their own hopes and a chance to realize their long-nourished ideas. Thus in spring 1934, the health-food sector industry newsletter *Branchenblatt der Reformwarenwirtschaft*, for example, proclaimed, "We see our ideas everywhere and are happily monitoring their advance."[66]

Naturally, the Gleichschaltung policy of the Nazi regime also affected these organizations. Many societies and associations were dissolved and periodicals banned. But the regime did not in principle put a stop to their previous activities. In the Lebensreform area, for example, the regime banned "a few groups that did not fit with its worldview." Others "dissolved voluntarily . . . under the pressure of National Socialist propaganda," while "sufficiently pliant" associations could continue their activities under new umbrella organizations.[67] The Nazi dictatorship likewise sent many progressive pedagogues into retirement, imprisoned them, or forced them into exile. Others, however, including leading members of the progressive education movement, like Peter Petersen, were able to continue using concepts they had already developed in the 1920s after adapting them to the new conditions of National Socialist rule.[68] Where earlier goals and activities managed to fit within the political framework of the Nazi regime and could tie into its ideological concepts, progressive endeavors could be continued even after 1933 within the National Socialist education project, albeit often in new organizational contexts.

At the same time, the National Socialist education project was also compatible with players who were not motivated by pedagogical intentions. Through its advertising, even the consumer industry, for example, formulated and disseminated new principles, according to which, for example, a "National Socialist" lifestyle and a corresponding self-understanding were demonstrated above all by drinking the right brand of coffee or visiting the proper restaurants.[69] Thus, in the 1930s, the act of living "German" could also already be expressed by consuming the right products.[70] The propagated models of a "new," "National Socialist" way of life by no means always required adaptations as radical as those called for by the health and sexuality policies of the party and state, for example.

The diversity of activities related to the transformation of personal lifestyles and self-conceptions and the different actors planning them had fundamental implications for the look, feel, and purported educational effects of the National Socialist public sphere. The large number of state, party, social, and economic actors involved in transposing the Nazi regime's ideological principles into new models for lifestyles and self-contemplation did much to ensure that public space did not exhibit to Germans the kind of consistency and control intended by Joseph Goebbels and other representatives of the regime.

Political and police monitoring, as well as the control of political reporting, admittedly made it impossible to publicly advocate any political standpoints other than those of National Socialism.[71] But concealed behind the uniformity of National Socialist symbols and terms was a broad spectrum of diverse and competing ideas about their significance for the lifestyles and self-contemplation of Germans. Although the Reich propaganda minister repeatedly portrayed the public sphere as being directed from above and tried to give public space a uniform appearance, the Nazi regime itself, with its comprehensive educational ambition, helped guarantee that even after 1933 this space was still being shaped by a multitude of actors representing various positions and opinions.[72]

The transformation of individual ways of life and self-conceptions could therefore not occur in the fashion intended by Goebbels and other leading regime representatives. With so many actors variously demanding that Germans adapt to the new political principles, individuals were not presented with any consistent model through which to align their everyday life and associated opinions by way of simple "experience." Urgently demanded and intensely promoted, the "new," "National Socialist" man remained an extremely polymorphic and contradictory figure throughout the period of Nazi rule. This alone ensured that the highly technical conception of education as formation would fail. Instead of having to be brought into line with precise ideological specifications, conformity of an individual's life according to the new principles of the Nazi state could be produced and publicly demonstrated in a variety of ways, even though the coexistence of divergent models was "by no means unproblematic, but rather highly strained if anything."[73]

This situation also has implications for researching the effects of the Nazi education project. Given the pluralities of participating actors and asserted demands, it seems to make little sense to orient one's gaze too closely according to the official claim of the propaganda. Little is gained from asking about success or failure by comparing targets and accomplishments, as was suggested by Kershaw and done repeatedly in studies ever since: the plurality of educational actors and advocated models are then only interpreted as a barrier to the regime's own efforts to transform individual ways of life and self-conceptions. Yet this overlooks the fact that the asserted educational aspiration was formulated so forcefully precisely because of the multitude of participating actors; it would otherwise hardly have been possible even with a functional state propaganda apparatus. Because the project for the "education of the German Volk" involved not just the regime but rather a multitude of actors, individuals under Nazi rule were constantly confronted in their daily lives with the question of whether and how their self-image and personal lifestyle conformed to the political principles of the state—in speeches of leading politicians, during local party rallies, on product packaging, or in magazine articles.

To be sure, the fact that the actors participating in the education project were not brought under centralized control undermined the regime's methodological plan, but it did not compromise its aspiration to politically influence individual ways of life. Disunity and competition do not mean that the National Socialist education project simply had no consequences. They merely created a different starting situation, such that the project's effects can hardly be grasped by way of the abstract question of success or failure. Because the transformation of individual lifestyles and self-images did not occur as the adaptation to an ideal as intended by the regime, it is also not possible to reveal the effects of the regime's propaganda and education efforts simply by comparing the propagated demands to the realities of the lifestyles and self-images of Germans. Rather, to develop a more precise understanding of how the Nazi education project functioned, one needs to ask about the agency actually assigned to the people declared as pupils.

2. Formative Education Instruments and Individual Agency: The Individual in the National Socialist Education Project

In August 1933, eighteen-year-old Rudolf Briske started a new chapter in his diary entitled "Thoughts." Briske was born in 1915 near Berlin and grew up in a bourgeois home with nationalistic parents. At age twelve, he became a member of the right-wing conservative Großdeutscher Jugendbund (Greater German Youth League), participating in numerous trips during holidays, first in the environs of Berlin and later in more distant parts of Germany. Briske's travels led him to start keeping a diary at age fourteen with a volume about a ski vacation in the Alps. He routinely kept diaries of his holiday travels in following years as well. In 1931 he attempted to keep a general diary in a separate notebook, resolving on January 1 of that year to "unconditionally carry through with diary writing for the entire year of 1931."[74] But he stopped writing in April.

Briske intentionally wrote his new chapter on "Thoughts" in his youth league "logbook" because, as he noted in the opening, "most of the records will be . . . related to the league," even though they also might relate to "school, family, politics, etc. . . . and any other thoughts there are in life." He outlined the purpose of the new chapter as follows: "One often ponders over some problem, a result: one develops thoughts about it. One could actually write them down sometime. Thoughts about problems, ideas, worldviews are always confused; one evolves, after all, and it would be strange if at this age one already had a fully formed worldview. This is how these writings should be assessed: not philosophical observations, but rather thoughts suddenly sprouting from the day."[75]

Briske's last comment did not just indicate the goal of his explications. It also accurately described the reason he was starting to write down his "Thoughts" during this particular August of 1933. A few days earlier, the youth league to which he had belonged for six years already, and where in spring 1933 he had become the leader of a boys' group, was dissolved and taken over by the Hitler Youth. The event was also the subject of his first entry, which followed the words introducing his new chapter. Briske did not describe the compulsory Gleichschaltung, dealing instead with more fundamental reflections. Above the entry, he wrote the headline "Form and Attitude." And using this distinction, he argued that he and his longtime colleagues were "now as a group changing our form" but "by far not yet our essence and internally our attitude." To be sure, they now had the duty "to wear the brown shirt honorably, because everybody is looking at us, since we are the future of the nation, since internal and external opponents predicate their view of the Third Reich on our conduct." However, they could "consciously retain the old [essence]." And even within the new organization, they could continue to pursue "our goal . . . of creating the German man through small communities such that later he is a useful member of the state."[76]

More because of their structure than their substantive assessment—only a few weeks later, Briske would feel that the Gleichschaltung was "necessary"[77]—these first "Thoughts" were quite typical of the other entries the young man would write in this part of his diary over the weeks that followed. Many referred to the political events of 1933, but instead of reflecting on the events themselves, they proceeded from a subject heading and scrutinized what the changes to the political situation personally meant to Briske. In the process, he took up numerous key words—such as *duty, life, serving, passion, leadership,* or *optimism* and *pessimism*—that played an important role in the efforts to create the "National Socialist man," and he contemplated them in relation to his own lifestyle and self-conception. "I say: one must become aware of one's contradictions," he wrote in September 1933, programmatically describing the purpose of his writing under the heading "Men" [Die Menschen]. "And then overcome them. Through struggle. Through life."[78] Briske also stuck to his goal when he finished this chapter of his diary in October 1933 and picked up his general diary again, which he henceforth kept on a regular basis. When ending his lengthy review of 1933 in his general diary with brief comments about the coming months, he concluded: "I am happy that this year turned out as it has, for Germany, not for me or my family. The task for next year is in short: . . . combine worldview with my Self! Heil, 1934!"[79] For Rudolf Briske, the start of the Nazi dictatorship in 1933 was more than a political event. His "Thoughts" did not turn on the problem of a political evaluation of the new regime: he did not question his basically positive assessment, and in fall 1933 he described himself as a "National Socialist."[80] He was preoccupied instead by how his way of living and associated self-perspective would fit within the transformed context of Nazi rule.

The efforts of Rudolf Briske and the resulting diary were unusual. Very few people so thoroughly questioned themselves with the propagated models for individual lifestyles and self-contemplation. Instead, diaries of the 1930s generally suggest that the regime had only a marginal capacity to move Germans by means of public appeals and propagandistic advertising to adapt their life and self-perspective to political categories. In any case, they show again and again that diarists dealt intensely with both their lives and political events (even approvingly) but did so without raising the question of how these two dimensions related to each other. Individuals' efforts in 1933–1934 to cling to their personal biography when making their required commitment to the Nazi regime indicate that many Germans were far less interested than Rudolf Briske in changing their everyday way of life and self-contemplation.⁸¹

Daniel Lotter, the Fürth gingerbread baker born in 1873, for example, saw political events above all as threatening his way of life. In his diary, he pointed out, for example, that without violence one cannot "force the mighty flooding current of German intellectual and cultural life into the channel of the National Socialist worldview" and complained when "again a piece of German intellectual and cultural life has fallen to the brown flood."⁸² And even when diarists directly addressed the regime's educational ambitions, doing so did not necessarily lead to the expected adaptations. Born in 1882, Wolfgang Söller, the publisher and director of the Krupp Book Hall, in summer 1934 described as a feature of recent months that "politics . . . plays a bigger role in life today insofar as the German Man is supposed to be a political one. Was I one in the past?" In his diary, Söller limited his answer to the determination that, while not having "the fanatical aspect" for the "one-sidedness" demanded by the regime, he had "certainly not been a typical apolitical person."⁸³ This brief comment was not the only way he underscored his lack of ambition to change his lifestyle and self-perspective because of Nazi rule; he also did so simply by never mentioning the issue again in his diary.

Particularly when compared to the regime's demand for political commitment from individual Germans, the aspiration to change personal lifestyles and self-contemplations was substantially less binding and coercive. Since there was no definitive image of the "new man" to hold up against the real ways people lived their lives, a clear determination of whether actual persons lived "National Socialistically" was often impossible. Comparatively speaking, this situation gave people plenty of maneuvering room when faced by the question of whether the propagated terms and political slogans pertained to their own life and how they understood it. Moreover, existing lifestyle habits often hardly needed any adjustment, because the ideas about life in the "new era" disseminated within the education project were largely compatible with existing lifestyles, even those that were typically bourgeois.⁸⁴ Admittedly, this constellation led people "in National Socialist society to eye others with mistrust as to whether they also conformed to the normative requirements of the *Volksgemeinschaft*."⁸⁵ But because of the lack of undisputable norms for a "National Socialist" way of life and self-contemplation, Germans could frequently avoid the demands raised by individual educational actors or construe such demands in ways that made sense to them. Private self-contemplation after 1933 did not necessarily need to occur with the political models provided by the regime for the creation of a "new man." It also remained possible in the 1930s to examine oneself using criteria different from the new political ones.[86]

But despite the broad inability of the National Socialist education project to successfully motivate individuals to engage in political self-formation, diaries of the 1930s show that after 1933 many people nonetheless started to reflect on themselves and their lifestyle using key political concepts of the Nazi regime. It is difficult to determine which population groups and how many Germans did so. Diaries do not enable any direct conclusions. But they provide information about the constellations under which individuals primarily began to orient themselves according to the new models for individual lifestyles. This too provides insights into what role the individual played in the Nazi education project and which particular people attempted to reorient themselves as demanded. Above all, the constellations allow us to understand why in the 1930s individual self-images and ways of life were often shaped by efforts related to the "new man"—even though the educational aspiration never generated the same dynamics as the demand for commitment.

Constellations of Political Self-Formation

Important evidence of the ways in which the Nazi educational project shaped individual self-images and lifestyles can be found in the diary of Rudolf Briske. Since August 1933, his entries dealt with the regime's ambition to educate the German Volk. But they were not motivated by the regime's appeals. Rather, his reflections dovetailed with personal developments that had already shaped his life and diary writing in past years. The goal of creating the "German man" had already occupied the young diarist before 1933, namely in the context of his youth league activities, and not only as a political problem. It had also been a guiding principle for leading his personal life. Thus, even though the political change may be the reason Briske started writing down his "Thoughts" during the particular summer of 1933, his diary reveals anything but an author defined by external demands who simply adapts to ideological precepts. In contrast to the vision of the regime's education plan, Briske was not overwhelmed by the new images of a "National Socialistic" lifestyle. He took up the question about the connection between "worldview" and "my own Self" in the transformed social and political context on his own initiative. The autonomous nature of his efforts is shown by Briske's refusal to be led astray by the fact that his father converted from Judaism to Christianity as a young man and that he himself was therefore deemed Jewish. The images of the "new," "German man" persistently formulated in the propaganda of the Nazi regime were not meant for him. But Briske would not let this deter him. Construing himself as a "National Socialist," he intensely examined himself and his own lifestyle using the political guidelines of the National Socialist education project.

Despite the Jewish identity ascribed to him by the regime, in working on himself Briske was no different from Germans who were considered "Aryan." The personal interest in political reflections on lifestyles and self-conceptions that stands out so prominently in his diary also appears in the private notes of other contemporaries. Entries in which authors reflect on themselves and their personal lifestyle using the political categories of the Nazi education project are especially frequent in the diaries of youths and young adults. In this respect, Briske's comment that at his age he does not yet have a "fully formed worldview" points quite aptly to a crucial motivation that, in the 1930s, led people mainly born around 1910 and later to pick up on the public discussions about the political realignment of lifestyles and self-conceptions.

This is exemplified by the diary of Kurt Frackmann*, which he began writing in spring 1934. Frackmann was born in Frankfurt in 1910. Unlike Briske, at the start of National Socialist rule he was not completing his secondary high school degree but going through an apprenticeship. In his relatively sporadic series of entries, Frackmann too always combined brief comments on his everyday life with reflections about himself, his lifestyle, and its relationship to the political circumstances of the time. The diary is characterized by numerous retrospective and forward-looking notes about his life in which he repeatedly assessed his past and future development against political categories. "I live life differently now than two—indeed even just one—year ago," he noted with satisfaction in November 1934, while simultaneously explaining, in connection with a lecture by Alfred Rosenberg, how he wanted to continue shaping the future course of his life.[87] Six months later, Frackmann outlined the ideal he was following under the heading "My Life Goals" with these words: "To form out of myself a firmly consolidated personality that can stand above everyday things, that does not founder on the banalities of life, but rather always looks toward the greater whole, yet in the struggle of life always firmly mans up." At the same time, his statements leave no doubt about what he meant by the "greater whole": "But above all to never forget one thing, never let it out of sight: to be able and allowed to serve Germany and thus Adolf Hitler and the German Volk with *all* abilities."[88]

Herbert Wiebus pursued similar goals. In fall 1936 while taking part in a Wehrmacht maneuver, the young man had been quartered in a Hessian village with the Köhl family, and he began exchanging letters with the fifteen-year-old daughter, Marianne. In his tentative love letters, Wiebus spoke about how nice it was to think about "what our Volk will look like one day when the goal of all of the National Socialist and German labor is realized: the new German Man, which we are summoned to form and educate. Or at least we are attempting it. And [we] must start with ourselves, every individual."[89] Moreover, he also always dated his letters written in 1936 and 1937 with old Germanic month names (Julmond, Nebelung, Hornung) and identified the year as "in year 4" or "year 5 of the Third Reich."[90]

Questions about the significance of the Nazi regime for one's personal life and about its conceptions of a "proper" lifestyle also frequently informed the diaries of young people that were not only kept for the purpose of political self-contemplation and self-formation. Born in 1914, Inge Thiele, for instance, came from the Ruhr region and supported her family with her wages as an apprentice gardener. In her diary, she wrote chiefly about her everyday life, reporting on her daily routine, as well as on excursions and recreational activities she undertook alone or with the League of German Girls. Above all, however, her diary dealt with growing up. Thiele repeatedly celebrated her youth, thirst for action, and passion to discover the world. These themes had already shaped her entries before she started discussing political questions and dedicating herself to the Nazi regime. Yet her reflections on her youth became increasingly intertwined with the models of the National Socialist education project. Thiele was not merely joyful about being young; rather, she was joyful about being a young person during precisely this era. "Downstairs the Hitler Youth is playing on the radio, briskly. It overcomes me like an intoxicating joy, still to be young. I just saw myself in the mirror, still the colors of youth, can it ever change? Inconceivable! I want to start again as a young girl! At my age one can already be a woman, but I don't want to yet. I still want to march with the girls, still belong to the Hitler Youth."[91] And thus in the case of Inge Thiele's diary as well, reflections on growing up often tied into the regime's political educational ambitions.

Marianne Köhl, the young woman addressed by the love letters of the soldier Herbert Wiebus, started her diary in early 1936 after her class teacher recommended "a diary for developing our style."[92] Like that of Thiele, Köhl's diary was at first a completely typical young person's diary that talked about everyday experiences—visits, school report cards, holidays and activities that Köhl undertook with the League of German Girls. After Wiebus was quartered in her parents' home in fall 1936, and as result of her correspondence with him, she gave politics more weight. Above all, apart from just recording political events, Köhl began to query herself using political categories. "I am writing 1937 in my diary for the first time. What will the new year bring?" asked the young woman almost one year after she started keeping her diary. She confessed, "We don't know, but we can and should have the will to work on ourselves with eagerness and perseverance, so that, when someday life really comes at us, we can be good, solid German men [Menschen] who also in their place do something for the good of our Volk and fatherland."[93] The diary clearly showed how the correspondence with Herbert Wiebus and his exhortation to start with oneself in achieving the "new German man" had prompted Köhl to reflect differently about herself. As early as October 1936, she reported to Wiebus that the people in her village noticed "precious little about the many political events. The girls are all extremely petty and always just talking about wretched school stuff." She often wished that she could "speak with you again like on that evening."[94]

As young people in 1930s, diarists born just before or during the First World War found themselves in a situation where, simply because of their age, they were challenged to search for their place in the world and their type of lifestyle. Like Rudolf Briske, they intrinsically possessed a strong impulse to deal with themselves—it did not need to come from the regime. They thought on their own accord about the same problems and questions that also preoccupied the educational actors of the Nazi regime. And yet at the same time, their personal search in the 1930s was often closely tied to the propagated models of a "National Socialist" lifestyle and self-perception.

In the 1930s, however, the scrutiny of one's own self-images and ways of life using the political categories of the Nazi regime was not limited to youth and young adults. Corresponding efforts can also be traced in many diaries of older writers. Take, for example, the Hamburg civil registry employee

Werner Kramp, who with approving commentary had so accurately summarized Hitler's speech at the SA leadership meeting in Bad Reichenhall in early July 1933. That was not the only occasion when he looked at his own life and its political quality. Born in 1893, Kramp was one of four children in a farming family in Barmbek. Nonetheless, after completing school he was able to begin studying law in Tübingen, but he interrupted his studies after the first semester to volunteer for military service at the start of the First World War. After just a few months, he was severely wounded, and he lay for a long time in a military hospital because of a head injury before finally being discharged from the military in spring 1918 as unfit for service. The wound left a prominent scar on Kramp's face.

It is unclear how much the injury contributed to the failure of his law career to develop as desired, despite his having resumed his studies after the war. But the First World War precipitated a turning point in his professional career. He managed to pass the first state exam on his second try in 1922, but he failed the subsequent legal internship. In 1926, he had to give up his dream of becoming a lawyer. Fortunately, he nonetheless managed to find a position as an administrative secretary in the civil registry in Hamburg, where he worked until long after the Second World War. Measured against his social origins and compared to his siblings, this job still represented social advancement. Yet this did little to change the fact that in his diary Kramp repeatedly regretted the failure of his legal career and seemed largely unsatisfied with his living situation in other ways too. In the early 1930s, he was not quite forty years old and still lived with his mother, with all of his plans to find a wife and start his own family having failed. His earnings and living situation hardly met his expectations, and Kramp also frequently doubted himself in other ways, which he expressed in his diary through recurring discussions about his own life course and many failed good intentions.

With the start of National Socialist rule, political yardsticks and categories began working their way into these deliberations. In August 1933, for example, Kramp again seemed disappointed that he was still alone. He had "been able to put the first 100 RM into the savings account, while in high summer one of the unused vacations still awaits," and he felt that "something should be thought or done that, for a start, actually gives this life its meaning." To be sure, Kramp confessed, he was thinking "more than ever about the constrained framework of marriage," but he did not feel this would resolve the problem of his inadequacies, which he had been dealing with in his diary for years. In summer 1933, however, he also noticed in this context that he was not well suited "for public responsibilities" because he lacked "adaptability . . . and the will to lead," which Kramp traced back to the same causal factor that explained why he was single: "I do not bear within me the value of the greater or lesser multitude"—that is, under the new political circumstances he was not well suited as either a leader or a follower.[95] Even though, as on the occasion of Hitler's speech in Bad Reichenhall, Kramp was expressing regret about his difficulty fitting in with the "new era," this sense of personal inadequacy repeatedly made him ask—here and also in the years that followed—whether his lifestyle was appropriate for the times. Just as his dissatisfaction with his personal living situation had repeatedly led him to reflect on his life already before 1933, after that year the sense of leading an "anachronistic" life likewise ensured that the comparison between himself and the life ideals publicly propagandized during the Nazi regime became an important part of his private self-perception.

In terms of their nature and substance, the diary entries of Werner Kramp were markedly different from the deliberations of young people like Marianne Köhl, Inge Thiele, Kurt Frackmann, and Rudolf Briske. However, like the younger diarists, Kramp did not come to deal with himself in the 1930s because of political motives. By and large, these individuals devoted so much attention in their diaries to their ways of life for personal reasons. Yet in this context, they also picked up on the public demands for the ideological transformation of individual lifestyles and self-perspectives and combined them with their own purposes. However much the actors of the Nazi education project tried to stimulate Germans to engage in political self-formation, their success depended on having Germans take up these political precepts out of their own interest—something that was strongly abetted by the plurality of propagated models. The diversity of the new lifestyle ideals did not just allow Germans to circumvent those associated with political demands that they felt threatened their way of life. For people who were open to them, it also created many more points of attachment for private self-contemplation than would have been possible with a single standardized ideal. Personal political reflection on how individuals led their own lives and viewed themselves could only become a widespread phenomenon in the 1930s because the Nazi education project in its plurality allowed many individuals to link their private self-examination to the political educational ambition of the regime.

This connection could take various forms, which are by no means fully covered by the examples shown here. For Wolfgang Scharenberg, the lawyer born in 1883 who had already been involved in the Lebensreform movement in the 1920s, the start of Nazi rule signified support for his own goal of the radical reformation of man, which allowed him to politically affiliate himself with the regime.[96] But he also understood the vociferous demands for the realignment of individual lifestyles as strengthening his own efforts at a self-aware lifestyle; accordingly, after 1933 he also frequently related his efforts to discussions of politics.[97] The doctor Walter Lindemann, born in 1906, was preoccupied with the call for a "new" faith, not just in connection with his political assessment of the regime but also with regard to his own religiosity.[98] Lindemann had already understood himself as a Christian and nationalist during the Weimar Republic, but he rarely dealt with his Protestant faith in his diary. He was only prompted to deal with his religious views in writing and practice his faith more strongly in public because of the state's intervention in the Evangelical Church and the associated demands for a new "völkisch" faith. Particularly starting in February 1935, he began to routinely note in his diary his attendance at church, which henceforth became a fixed part of his everyday life and went hand in hand with a constant discussion of religious issues in his diary. Walter Lindemann grasped the conflict between church and state not just as a political problem that needed to be integrated into his commitment to the regime but also as a challenge to the way in which he lived and thought about himself.[99]

However, his renewed attention to his own religiosity did not mean that Lindemann refused to adapt to the "new era" or to have the latter affect his religious ideas. Instead, in his diary he addressed his criticism specifically to those who felt "themselves as Germanic sons of heroes" whose "religion is blood, race, and soil"—thus aiming at certain actors in the discussions about the relationship between National Socialism and religion. Far from categorically rejecting this debate, Lindemann actually staked a position within it, as shown by his repeated emphasis that his own religious convictions were plainly more in line with the "new era." According to Lindemann, the "most unadulterated socialism" preached by Christ was also the goal of the Nazi regime, and therefore the völkisch religious persuasions were going astray. "Christ is and was the socialism considered most noble before God and men."[100] In his case, too, the personal significance of his own religiosity, set off against the background of publicly propagated demands for reform, made him think about the political character of his everyday way of life.

Regardless of the motives responsible, the dimensions of life being examined, or the results of these self-contemplations, these activities meant that many Germans in the 1930s started picking up on the political discourse related to the transformation of individual lifestyles and self-conceptions and absorbing it into their own thoughts. This appropriation at the level of individuals has never received much attention before in the literature on the Nazi education project, which has looked heavily into governmental institutions and their intentions and techniques.[101] Important here, however, is not just that the efforts of diarists to connect their personal life to the diverse images of the "new man" constituted a major part of the real effect of the Nazi education project. These efforts also reveal quite a different view of the individual's role in National Socialist education from those of previous research theses. Studies on educational thought and education organizations have always referred to the "totalitarian and thus repressive character of National Socialist education,"[102] which aimed "for a totalizing of the individual's memberness in the organizations of National Socialism that eliminated individuality."[103] This accurately describes the educational intentions of the Nazi regime. Yet the transformation of personal lifestyles and self-contemplation did not happen this way. The multitude of ideological demands and models required individuals to play an active role: faced with the broad spectrum of transpositions that converted National Socialist worldviews into models for everyday lifestyles, they had to choose and appropriate certain ones and relate them to their own person. In the practice of the Nazi education project, the models intended as instruments for the formation of appropriate lifestyles turned into a range of options.

Yet even this situation meant that the political ideas disseminated by the regime in the 1930s found their way into personal self-conceptions and lifestyles. Regardless of which option they chose, individuals always applied to their life the political categories, principles, or models stipulated by the state, party, social, and private educational agents of the Nazi regime. In this respect, occurring simultaneously within personal confrontations with the propagated models of everyday lifestyles and self-contemplation in the 1930s were both a privatization of political educational demands and the politicization of private self-contemplation and everyday ways of life.[104] Even if this did not happen as intended—namely, as an adaptation to ideological precepts—but instead actually required active effort on the part of individuals, the political categories of the Nazi regime shaped the way many Germans understood themselves and led their lives in the 1930s.

Formative Educational Instruments and Their Appropriation by Individuals

In my previous remarks, I limited the focus solely to the propagation of new models of "National Socialist" lifestyles and self-contemplation because here we can clearly see the important role played by the individual in the "education of the German Volk": people did not have to take up the educational precepts addressed to them, and when they did so, it was largely because of their personal interest in reflecting on their own self-conceptions and lifestyles, which decisively influenced the transposition of ideological precepts into their own life.

But naturally, the educational agents of the Nazi regime did not limit themselves simply to presenting their ideas on how to live appropriately and hoping they would be accepted. Instead, they used various educational instruments to strengthen their demands and control their reception. The Germans were not free in the appropriation of the new models of a "National Socialist" lifestyle and self-contemplation but rather subject to many different influences. But if one looks more closely at the intrusive educational instruments of the Nazi regime and their application, it becomes apparent that they did not displace individuals from their active role in the education process and mold them into passive pupils as desired. Despite massive efforts at exercising influence, individuals retained a large degree of control over the ideological shaping of their own self-images and lifestyles.

Publications were among the Nazi regime's most important education instruments. Books, brochures, journals, and similar publications received attention only on the margins of discussions about propaganda during the 1930s. In particular, they hardly played a role in controlling the mood situation. Yet they constituted the most widespread and often most practicable form of ideological influence on self-images and lifestyles and were valued accordingly by the Nazi regime. As an "extremely valuable means of forming the Volk [Volksgestaltung] and education," as Joseph Goebbels pointed out in 1938, books were centrally important to the "long-term goals of National Socialist propaganda" and were supposed to help "solidify the deep-down attitude of the population."[105] These are the lines along which one must understand the following sentence by Goebbels—already expressed in November 1934—which referred to Hitler's speech on education during the dissolution of the Center Party in July 1933: "Revolution is governed by the speech; in evolution the book then takes its old place again."[106] The propaganda minister was not alone in considering the book to be the ideal instrument for the "pervasive and enduring control of the worldview of the German population." Rather, it was "considered the central medium for the 'education of the Volk' [Volksbildung] by the agencies of political control."[107] As stated in an essay in 1938 in the journal *Buch und Volk*, "we witness through the book the German Man in his many manifestations.... The book lets every individual take part in völkisch life and calls upon him to help work on its formation."[108]

To ensure that as many individuals as possible heard the call of the book, the regime implemented an intensive subsidy policy that was supposed to bring the "good book" closer to the nonbourgeois classes in particular.[109] These efforts did not only apply to political literature. As Goebbels pointed out in his speech of November 1934, books with fictional and narrative content were supposed to "address the Volk directly" and help shape it.[110] This led, for example, to the emergence of a broad spectrum of new "subgenres of the novel," such as the "Strength through Joy book," the "SA novel," and the "Race novel."[111] They centered on "experience," which generally developed into the "key concept of literary criticism as a whole," and, as mentioned, it also formed the central concept in the educational thought of National Socialism.[112] Autobiographical genres were considered especially well suited for allowing readers to participate in supposedly authentic experiences, which readers were thus meant to "internalize."[113] Thus even novels and other narrative works were supposed to have an "exemplary quality" for their readers and "effect the transition in emotion and deed from the individual to the völkisch."[114] In this respect, many educational actors frequently propagated their ideas of everyday lifestyles and self-contemplation in narrative texts as well.

However, to exercise greater influence on the individual appropriation of these ideas, educators needed to address Germans as directly as possible, which narrative literature could not accomplish. This need formed the basis for the enormously successful nonfiction literature of the 1930s.[115] Not only did these titles undergo a veritable boom in terms of the vast number of new publications, but with respect to sales figures they counted among the "most successful type of books in the Third Reich."[116] Falling under this category was first and foremost advice literature, which allowed educators not only to propagate their own ideas about the "new man" but also to disseminate specific instructions on how to implement them in everyday life. Thus nonfiction books were especially popular, used by NSDAP offices as well as state and other actors.

In summer 1933, the Reich Education Office of the NSDAP and the German Labor Front began publishing the so-called *Schulungsbriefe* (Training Letters), which were primarily addressed to the large number of new party members and were supposed to convey to them, "in a clear and easily understood form, basic ideological statements and positions of notable leaders of our Volk on the events of the ongoing revolution." It is the "self-evident duty of every National Socialist," noted Reichsschulungsleiter (Reich Education Leader) Otto Gohdes in the first edition, "to engage with these observations in detail."[117] Accordingly, as early as 1934, the *Schulungsbriefe* advertised "binders" that could be used to collect editions of the letters and compile them into "manuals of our worldview," which all "fighters" needed.[118]

But large quantities of similar advice materials and political brochures were also produced outside party offices and state institutions. During the first months of Nazi rule, but also later in the 1930s, many authors—on their own initiative or at the urging of publishing houses—published their own interpretations of lifestyles and self-contemplations that were appropriate for the "new era." Against this background, the Reich Propaganda Ministry and other controlling institutions of the education project complained repeatedly about the need for a wholesale war against "opportunistic writings"—understood as all political writings by authors with allegedly careerist rather than educational motives. But at least with respect to political writings, the regime never managed to achieve the control it desired.[119] Quite the contrary, some of the best-selling books of the 1930s, such as Johanna Haarer's *Die deutsche Mutter und ihr erstes Kind* (The German mother and her first child) and Hans Surén's guidebook on naturism, were not produced directly on behalf of state and party educators, and some were published before 1933.[120]

To help people find their bearings among the large number of publications, just a few months after the start of National Socialist rule, state institutions and party offices began creating guides meant to draw the attention of readers to works considered important. Thus in fall 1933, for example, Rudolf Benze—at this time the freshly appointed division head in the Prussian Ministry of Culture before advancing in 1934 to become a ministerial counselor in the Reich Ministry for Science, Education, and Public Education—published a brochure entitled *Einführung in das völkische Schrifttum* (Introduction to Völkisch writings). For the "many German Volk comrades... who surely hear the rushing of the torrent of völkisch renewal and feel its power, but cannot tell where it is coming from and where it is heading," the brochure provided an annotated bibliography as a guide to "völkisch literature," which "after the victory of National Socialism" had swollen to an "inestimable torrent."[121] Along with similar lists of selected books, guidance was also provided by the *National Socialist Bibliographie*, which the party's official Examination Commission for the Protection of National Socialist Writing began publishing on a monthly basis in 1936. On the one hand, it offered a "systematic summary of available writings on the question of National Socialism" for party functionaries charged with training responsibilities; on the other hand, it was also meant for "those who want to find access to the National Socialist body of ideas."[122]

After 1933, many educational actors tried to use literary works, nonfiction books, advice literature, or political texts to not only stimulate but also directly influence personal reflections on lifestyles and self-perspectives. Compared to the spreading of ideological concepts, the guidelines they formulated gave far more concrete instructions. But even so, success still depended on the appropriation of those guidelines by individual Germans, who clearly noticed the politicization of the landscape of books that accompanied the Nazi education project.

Not all people welcomed this politicization. In fact, this was why Clara Hacker, for example, categorically rejected the literature of the 1930s. Born in 1885, Hacker had worked as an editorial secretary for the Social Democratic *Schleswig-Holsteinische Volkszeitung* during the Weimar Republic; in 1908, she became the first woman in Mecklenburg to join the SPD, and in 1919, she switched over to the Independent Social Democratic Party of Germany (USPD). Still clinging to her socialist attitudes, in 1936 Hacker noted in her diary that when one "gets books from the public library," one always has to check "when the book was written, that is, printed or published." Anything created since the start of the Nazi dictatorship "need not be carried home, it isn't going to be read anyway... whether novel or scholarship, except for a few foreign authors." Even "books about animals and other natural-science works" could "not be read with pleasure." Speaking with regard to Hermann Sudermann's 1926 novel *The Mad Professor*, which she had recently read, Hacker noted that when one gets one's "hands on a book that should actually have long since been burned," upon "reading this book one realizes for the first time how to gauge the large chasm between the past and present."[123]

Other people, however, were more open to the new political writings. For instance, Charlotte Bücker, born in 1873, in summer 1933 found herself forced to buy a brochure about the "goals and purpose of National Socialism" from an SA man: "I could not get rid of the obtrusive person; I had to buy." Even though Bücker had not actually wanted to purchase the brochure, she read it with great approval and noted in her entry that she would keep it "on the last page" of her diary.[124] In contrast to Bücker, Franz Göll, a white-collar employee in Berlin born in 1899, made a deliberate effort to obtain reading material from the National Socialist education project. Along with keeping a diary since he was sixteen years old, Göll kept meticulous notes on his readings, collecting excerpts in a separate notebook. Included among the books he read from 1934 to 1939 were many political texts, such as *Aufbau einer Nation* (Building of a nation, translated as *Germany Reborn*) by Hermann Göring, *Mein Kampf* by Adolf Hitler, and *Der Mythos des 20. Jahrhunderts* (*The Myth of the 20th Century*) by Alfred Rosenberg. Also listed were many advice and nonfiction books that dealt with various life management issues: "character studies," the "building blocks of the corporeal world," "genius and race," "self-awareness and personality-awareness."[125] These books were less definitively aligned with the new regime, but they too combined questions about life management and self-contemplation with new political principles and concepts, as well as providing Göll with new ideas that frequently appear in his extensive dealings with himself in his diary.

Whereas Franz Göll's readings also reflected a great interest in scientific studies and general nonfiction that reached back as far as the 1920s,[126] other people in the 1930s not only used political books as reference points for their own self-perception but by reading also situated themselves and their lives in the new era. Born in 1909, Wolfram Kroll*, for example, worked in the early 1930s as a commercial clerk at a Hamburg spice mill. In summer 1934, he enclosed a newspaper clipping with a travel report from Moscow in a letter to his girlfriend. "The author is probably Dr. Klaus Mehnert," he wrote, "whom you perhaps know and who has written the book, *Die Jugend in Sowjet-Rußland* [Youth in Soviet Russia]. A first-rate book, written entirely in the new spirit that we are also looking for in Germany. A small sample is shown in the enclosed expositions. Please save them for me."

Kroll thought his girlfriend, who at the time worked as a substitute teacher in Hamburg, would find the book interesting "from a pedagogical standpoint as well, even if one cannot transfer it to German circumstances. For us, the critical aspect of this is the mental attitude."[127] But this example, in particular, shows that reading even comparably unambiguous political nonfiction and advice books could be quite ambivalent. In 1934, Kroll used the book by Klaus Mehnert to demonstrate that he and his girlfriend—as he emphasized elsewhere in the letter—were "political men" and that they had adjusted their life management and self-images in accordance with the changed circumstance of the era. But *Die Jugend in Sowjet-Rußland* had already been published in 1932.[128] Even though it was not Soviet propaganda and the author emphasized at the end of the book that Germany should not simply copy the Russian model, he expressed clear sympathies with the young Soviet Union and the youthful generation driving it forward. It is doubtful that the Nazi regime considered this book to be appropriate for demonstrating one's personal affiliation with National Socialism.

One frequently finds such contradictory readings in the diaries of the 1930s, as in the case of Inge Thiele, the gardener's apprentice who started her diary after reading the novel *Katrin wird Soldat* (*Katrin Becomes a Soldier*). This novel by Adrienne Thomas about the story of a Jewish wartime nurse during the First World War was one of the most important pacifistic books of the Weimar Republic and thus was already condemned by National Socialists before 1933. In May 1933, it was publicly desecrated at book burnings and subsequently banned.[129] The deep impression this book made on Thiele is evident not only from the fact that it inspired her to write a diary but also from an entry she wrote a few days later about a town festival. In this entry she wrote about the many "brown and field-gray uniforms" that dominated the festivities. "How upright these boys go about, they mean something, their eyes, their demeanors demand it. I immediately must think about war, imagine these same faces in battle under cannon fire, no, it cannot be. But why are they already training the smallest ones? Hammering patriotism into them?" Yet despite the deep impression left by her reading, Thiele deliberately made the new regime's militaristic views and principles her own. "I believe," she immediately added to her worried sentences, "the book *Katrin wird Soldat* is floating around too much in my head. And this book has come under censorship, understandably, because these books raise pacifists."[130]

The efforts of various educational actors to control the political self-formation of individuals by means of books and texts were not just opposed by misunderstandings or capricious interpretations. Individuals also frequently made deliberate use of publications to distance themselves from certain claims or models and to insist on their own ideas. In June 1933, a few days before Hitler's speech at the SA leadership meeting in Bad Reichenhall, Werner Kramp had noted in his diary that he could not yet decide "on the purchase of the newest texts, that is, National Socialist educational and glorification literature . . . first, because one wants to save, and then, because one fears bland disappointment." Nonetheless, he was still concerned about whether his readings were in keeping with the times. In the same entry, for example, Kramp noted that the novel he had read most recently fell "outside the framework of today's readings" because it was "typical of the individualism of the past era." And a few lines later, he regretted not having subscribed to any "newspaper of quality during this eventful spring" but instead only "occasionally [spent] afternoons at the museum, which has since been cleansed, but *Die Tat* and *Deutsches Volkstum* are still available."[131]

A few days later when Kramp heard Hitler's appeal for the "education of the German Volk in the spirit of National Socialism," in discussing the call for education he compared Hitler's statements to an article from the latter journal, *Deutsches Volkstum*. He singled out the ideas developed in the article as "more valuable for my own 'attitude.'" Kramp then briefly summarized the piece, gleaning from it mainly that the point was to combine "the highest artistic performance with the highest responsibility to the Volk [Volksverantwortung]," which was why one needed to watch for this amalgamation as the "final and most profound symbol of [the Nazi] movement." Finally, he also took this appeal to heart for himself, writing, "I believe I must look deeper and more faithfully."[132]

Werner Kramp also used published texts to examine himself and politicize his own lifestyle and self-contemplation. But in doing so, he made a deliberate choice about which publications to use. As with the state and party actors, in light of the vast growth of literature dealing with politics and questions of life management, he attempted to be organized and distinguished between a new "National Socialist" literature and an older literature that continued to exist. He prioritized the latter when dealing with the relationship between his own way of life and the regime's political aspirations. In his effort to find his place in the "new era," Kramp drew on texts that supported his existing views and that frequently could be used against other political claims.

Thus the effects of the propagated models of personal life management and self-contemplation remained dependent on individuals. Moreover, as can be observed in diaries time and again, this dialectic between ideological stipulations and the individual's own self-understanding, motivations, and way of life also manifest itself with regard to specifically formulated instructions. In the case of Kramp, this is shown particularly clearly in relation to the many political lectures he attended. In the 1930s, educational agents often used speaking events and seminars to promote their ideas of National Socialist life management and self-contemplation. As early as the 1920s, the Reichsleitung of the NSDAP had paid attention not only to the propagandistic design of the "Führer speeches" but also particularly to the oral presentations of lower-level party functionaries and had started to develop systematic training for speakers. Looking back, Nazi Party leaders felt this training had been a decisive factor for the achievement of political power; hence, they now viewed speeches and lectures as an important vehicle for the current task of "educating the German Volk."[133]

Systematic speaker training was therefore thoroughly reorganized in 1934, with "propaganda speakers" being obliged to constantly undergo further training and have their work evaluated. The introduction of speaker credentials ensured that only specially trained functionaries spoke for the party in the 1930s.[134] Special training material for the party's speakers was supposed to standardize as much as possible the form of lectures held in the name of the NSDAP. At the same time, however, other educational actors carried out a multitude of seminars and speaking events in which those who were not specially authorized personnel also had a chance to speak. Adult education centers, for example, offered speaking opportunities even for ordinary party members who considered it their "duty of honor" to help in the political education of Germans by way of "worldview-ideologically oriented events."[135]

Werner Kramp attended the very "first course of the National-Socialistically organized adult education center [Volkshochschule] in Altona" in May 1933. Kramp knew that the course was supposed to function as an "introduction to the new world of ideas." In his diary, he pointed out that "not even a single lecturer from the earlier [school] was taken over" by the adult education center and noted, given how the course was introduced "with emphatic strictness, that the new state will no longer allow everyone to seek heaven in his own fashion." The course instructor admonished the participants to obtain "certificates regarding successful attendance at the end." But this did not bother Kramp. He attended the course, which was dedicated to the topic of "un-German art," precisely out of a desire to gain a better understanding of the new political principles. With this in mind, he summarized the lecture in his diary as follows: in art the "criterion for every artistic work and art appreciation is now native-alien [arteigen-artfremd], whereby the former has a stronger accent on history and the latter is more rational." Kramp seemed quite satisfied with the explanations he had heard. The only thing that displeased him was that the speaker wanted to "recommend only instinctive receptivity to us [listeners]."[136] But by no means did Kramp consider himself a passive receiver.

Ten days later, he reported in his diary that on the previous Sunday he had "gone to the art gallery. For me it was about the discovery of German art," which he wanted to explore "from a place of feeling" using the new categories from the lecture. Kramp reported his perception of the works of art in detail, although he realized he was having problems applying the criteria he had learned for art appreciation. With regard to portrait painting, Kramp had to conclude, for example, that "actually only Liebermann managed to pull off big portraits." In light of the principles he had learned, Kramp was evidently irritated by Liebermann's Jewish origins, and he pointed out that "compared to him" Kramp would have to "name the smallest self-portrait of Toppen as the best try of German portrait art." He was equally unsure about how to understand the works of Paula Modersohn-Becker, asking himself in his diary: Was her art the "irrational expression of the soul of our Volk [Volksseele]"? According to the new standards, this would make it an ideal work of the so-called new era. "These solid coagulated peasant heads could certainly not have been painted at a different time (or perhaps by Rembrandt, Hals?)." And Kramp even had problems with modern classical works. "One generally rejects Expressionism as alien [artfremd]" in form and as "conceptual art," he noted in his diary. Yet "in just the last course session, mentioned by the lecturer as the one certain artifact of the Germani, were ornaments that have pronounced symbolic, conceptually 'intended' meanings." "But this says nothing to me," Kramp soberly concluded. "So perhaps I do not live in our era, or the artfulness of our era has not yet been clarified."[137]

The episode of the lecture at the adult education center and the visit to the Hamburg art gallery remained ambivalent. When visiting the museum, Kramp tried to adjust his perceptions according to the political categories he was prescribed: by attending the course at the adult education center, he made a deliberate effort to understand the principles of the new regime, and when proceeding through the art exhibition, he also tried to adopt them as standards for his own appreciation of art. The regime could hardly have asked for anything more. Yet at the same time, this required a willingness and involvement on the part of Werner Kramp, and that, in turn, meant that he was not a passive recipient of the new propagated principles as desired by the regime. Even as he tried to make the ideological standards his own, Kramp did not adapt to them without reflection. On the basis of these standards, he developed his own thoughts, which did not conform to the propagated assessments and thus made him uncertain as to whether, despite his efforts, he "might not be living in our era."

Kramp's art episode again shows clearly why trying to ascertain the effects of National Socialist educational efforts in terms of success or failure is not enough. The many endeavors by various actors of the Nazi regime to realign lifestyles and self-images within German society did not lead to the goal they actually envisaged. But for many people, these efforts lastingly changed the forms and content of private self-contemplation, whereby the politicization of individual ways of life and self-contemplation and the privatization of ideological precepts conditioned each other. Notwithstanding the intrusive instruments of the National Socialist education project, the transformation of Germans with new political categories did not work as intended by regime, namely, through government control and top-down formation processes, but rather through the massive appropriation of ideological models at the individual level.

This even applies to the strictest instrument for the ideological shaping of individual lifestyles and self-contemplation: the many training and education camps of various state and party institutions. During the 1930s, practitioners and theoreticians of the Nazi education project already viewed the camp as the "most appropriate, surest, and natural manifestation for the elaboration of the German man."[138] In the historical scholarship as well, the camp is considered "the most important organizational form of National Socialist education" and is assigned "prominent importance" for "today's understanding" of the National Socialist education project.[139] According to the project's own aspirations, the training camps were supposed to serve the "awakening of the German man through the conceptual content of National Socialism" and help ensure "that all talents and abilities of each individual German Volk comrade, physically, mentally, and temperamentally, unfold in the best conceivable way for the good and prosperity of the German Volk."[140]

The fact that the camp was deemed an especially well-suited instrument was directly related to the National Socialist concept of education. Even though the Reich Propaganda Ministry considered all environmental influences on the German people to be educational and therefore organized its activities according to the ideal of fully controlling and comprehensively shaping them, the educational actors of the Nazi regime were very well aware that this sweeping aspiration could be realized much more effectively within a smaller framework. From the perspective of educational actors, the collective accommodation of participants, often in remote locations; their separation from everyday routines (and thus from other "educational" influences); and the fully configurable daily program within this environment provided all the preconditions for a coordinated experience that would sustainably transform camp participants.[141]

Training and education camps became a mass phenomenon in the 1930s. Many agents of the Nazi education project established such training facilities, which as a result addressed "almost all age groups and population strata of the 'Reich.'"[142] A correspondingly huge number of Germans passed through these facilities, largely because in many contexts participation in the training camps was mandatory. As opposed to publications and most lecture events, the camps did much more than offer Germans an opportunity for voluntary self-reflection: with greater or lesser coercion, they obliged their participants. It was significantly more difficult for people to elude the camps and their educational practices than to ignore public appeals. Yet nonetheless, even in the camps, whether a camp stay actually changed personal self-perspectives and ways of life still critically depended on the willingness of the individual. To be sure, the theoretical literature on camp education in the 1930s was convinced that if "the camp was right and the camp leader genuine," even the "dyed-in-the-wool doubter will find it difficult to shake off the compelling camp experiences": "No baulking and agitation can prevent it."[143] Yet at times even proponents of camp education, such as the Reich labor leader Konstantin Hierl, conceded that "the education by others" must be joined with "self-education": "Without the willingness of the individual to be responsive to the educational effects and work on himself, there is no educational success."[144]

This assessment was a much better reflection of reality. Unsurprisingly, "the camp . . . [affected] each person differently," which in countless cases also included adverse reactions.¹⁴⁵ Moreover, the specific advantage of the camp was also its greatest disadvantage: after the camp stay, participants were released again into their daily routines, and camp organizers could do little more than hope that the experiences they had made would have a lasting influence in daily life. Certainly, they made an effort during the camp stay to convey a certain image by which participants were supposed to remember the camp.¹⁴⁶ But after camp had ended, whether people actually made an effort to adjust their everyday life management and self-contemplation—as Werner Kramp had done with his museum visit following the lecture at the adult education center—ultimately depended on the individual. Like the public promotion of new life principles, the training and education camps of the Nazi regime also required "joint work on the New Man" by educational actors and the individuals declared as pupils. This was not just because, as Kiran Patel has pointed out, residents and staff were "equally subject to the total aspiration of the camp" and even camp organizers constantly had to examine themselves.¹⁴⁷ It was also because individuals had to play an active role if the camps were to contribute to the long-term transformation of personal ways of life and self-conceptions that went beyond the merely external adjustment of behavior during the camp stay. They needed to integrate experiences made at camp into their personal everyday lives and combine the conveyed lifestyles with private motivations.

When looking at the education camps, we see the same dynamics that governed the intensive educational efforts of the 1930s as a whole. The instruments and methods of the Nazi education project were set up to "form" the Germans according to a supposedly clear ideal and for this purpose turn them into passive recipients of new models for personal life management and self-contemplation. But this notwithstanding, even in the 1930s, the actual transformation of self-perspectives and ways of life required the individual's active collaboration. Only if political precepts were picked up and appropriated could the models of a "new" way of life actually become efficacious. For historians, this means they should be "researching the creation of the New Man in practices and on the concrete individual."¹⁴⁸ This makes diaries an important source. But before we use the diaries of the 1930s to look at concrete educational events, we should first examine how this medium related to the Nazi education project and to what degree diaries themselves constituted an instrument for political self-formation in National Socialism.

3. Experience and Reflection: Diaries in the Nazi Education Project

With regard to the historical development of the diary, it is hardly surprising and yet simultaneously astonishing that diaries of the 1930s often provide information about individuals' efforts to scrutinize their own ways of life and self-perspectives against the background of the new ideological principles. On the one hand, the diaries of this decade, too, followed in a tradition that was already more than two centuries old; from pietism in the early eighteenth century to the bourgeoisie of the nineteenth century, this medium had developed into one of the key instruments for modern self-contemplation and self-formation.[149] Between 1933 and 1945, this history was neither forgotten nor suppressed in the National Socialist public sphere. Gustav René Hocke, for example, who in the early 1960s presented a standard work on the history of the European diary that remains important to this day, had already published a rough outline of his thoughts on the motivations for keeping a diary during modern times in a literary journal in 1938. As early as this essay, entitled "Über das Tagebuchschreiben" (On diary writing), he characterized the diary as a "technique, through uninhibited speaking with oneself, for reaching the depths of one's own being," and for the "modern diary," he presented the notations of Friedrich Hebbel and Stendhal as the "ideal model" for self-examination and soul-searching.[150]

Gustav René Hocke was not alone with this understanding of the diary. Hebbel's diaries, which even before 1933 were often considered model specimens of the form, appeared in a new edition in 1935, and various academic studies in the 1930s testify that the classical function of self-contemplation and self-formation was still being attributed to the diary during this era.[151] This attribution was tied into what the youth studies researcher Siegfried Bernfeld had a few years earlier called "knowledge about diaries." In a study published in 1931, Bernfeld looked into the public image of the diary and the forms of its transmissions from generation to generation, which he ascribed less to specific instructions and more to the knowledge existing in society about the diary format.[152] The "notion of a historically grown norm of the diary: to collect meaningful current-personal inscriptions,"[153] is conveyed by the "literary fact of the diary, the social practice of keeping a diary" itself. Instead of specific instructions, the knowledge about diaries "influences children, youth, and even adults in a complex way."[154] Even the start of the Nazi dictatorship two years after the publication of Bernfeld's study did nothing to change this; thus in the late 1930s, the diary's use as a traditional instrument of self-contemplation still very much suggested itself.

On the other hand, the medium was closely linked by its tradition to various concepts of life management and self-contemplation—individualism, bourgeois culture, privacy—that were repeatedly stigmatized in the 1930s as values of the bygone era that were supposed to be overcome by the National Socialist education efforts. In his classical interpretation of the diary, for example, Hocke spoke about how, with the diary, "no disguise through the bias arising from the duress of sociological constraint" was necessary; the "blinkers of the social environment fall away."[155] Yet the Nazi education project was based precisely on the idea of a systematic shaping of individual lifestyles through purposely designed environments, for example, in deliberately created "camp communities." In this respect, it needs to be explained why diaries in the 1930s were suitable not only for personal self-inspection but also for the project of political self-formation with the Nazi regime's new models. To illustrate why diaries as historical sources can provide insights into the effects of the National Socialist education project, in the following I pursue the relationship between the diary and National Socialism.[156] I first ask about the notions of the diary on the part of the Nazi regime and then turn my attention to the diary's role in the National Socialist education project.

National Socialist Ideas of the Diary

The first indication that diary writing and National Socialism were not fundamentally opposed comes from the number of diarists at the top leadership level of the Nazi regime. The Reichsführer of the SS and head of the German police, Heinrich Himmler; the Reich commissioner for aviation and commissioner for the Four-Year Plan, Hermann Göring; the Reich minister without portfolio and later governor general of occupied Poland, Hans Frank; and also the authorities Alfred Rosenberg and Joseph Goebbels, who were specifically concerned with the education of the German people, all kept diaries, some during their youth but especially also when politically active.[157] The same applies for various other first-phase NSDAP members. Max Dingler, who was involved in the 1923 Hitler putsch but did not play any important roles in the 1930s, kept a diary throughout his life. So did Karl Friedrich Kolbow, who in 1922 established one of the first NSDAP Ortsgruppen outside of Bavaria and was a state governor of the Province of Westphalia during National Socialist rule.[158] Many subordinate functionaries of the regime also kept personal diaries in the 1930s,[159] which the NSDAP leadership also expressly did not see as a sign of a "non–National Socialist" lifestyle. For example, when in 1935 the central archive of the NSDAP appealed to "old party comrades" and other Germans to turn over documents from the "time of struggle," the text explicitly mentioned diaries written during this period as potential collectibles, along with reports, documents, placards, photos, and insignia.[160]

The most prominent diarist among the functionaries of the Nazi regime was Joseph Goebbels, who, as mentioned, had already kept a diary sporadically as a youth. In 1923 at the age of twenty-six, he began to write his diary regularly, and he continued to do so until his suicide in April 1945. In the process, Goebbels's diary evolved in close connection with his political activities. With "the start of his political career," his previously irregular writing grew more systematic until, "with the takeover of the ministerial office and ultimately with the start of the war," it incrementally developed "into the regular daily duty of a chronicler."[161] Goebbels's diary did not stand in contradiction to his political views and functions; rather, the Reich propaganda minister ascribed to it an explicit political importance—much as Rosenberg did with respect to his own writings.[162] With his political success, Goebbels increasingly considered it his duty to document in his diary the events of the rise, establishment, and rule of National Socialism and his personal part in this process and to preserve it for posterity—an aim that also found expression in his efforts to protect the diaries from destruction in the world war.[163]

But at the same time, even in the 1930s and 1940s, the diary continued to be a personal document for Goebbels. The function that had induced him to keep a diary in the early 1920s, before his political career, remained important. At that time, the young Goebbels was moved to keep a diary chiefly by supposedly typical bourgeois motives. In 1923, he characterized his diary to a friend: "I feel the need to give an account of my life. This can happen in no better and more forceful way than if I hold a day of court over myself every evening." And with his variation on the words of Henrik Ibsen, "Poetizing—holding a day of court over oneself," he deliberately placed his diary into a tradition of the educated bourgeoisie.[164] Entirely in keeping with the nineteenth-century bourgeois diary focused on one's own internality, it served young Goebbels as a "father confessor" or "conscience doctor," and thus the opening of the second volume of his diaries in June 1924 reads like an almost typical beginning of introspective reflection:[165] "May this book contribute in making me clearer in spirit, plainer in thought, greater in love, more confident in hope, more ardent in faith, and more humble in speech."[166] These motivations of self-contemplation and self-formation, which also, for example, characterized the diary of the youthful Heinrich Himmler,[167] never disappeared in the case of Goebbels, even in the later years of his political activity in the NSDAP and as Reich propaganda minister. They were only supplemented by politically motivated aims of documentation. As late as 1937, Goebbels still viewed his diary as a "place of refuge."[168]

Goebbels's diary is thus instructive in two ways for the relationship between National Socialism and the diary. First, it shows that political motives might very well have led authors to keep a diary in the 1930s and 1940s. It was along these lines that the monthly journal *Die Tat*, published since 1909, printed the challenge in June 1933 that "those who can do it [should] occupy themselves with the diary again." The text noted that "those alive today" have "a huge responsibility vis-à-vis the coming centuries," which consisted of "copiously and immaculately collecting and preserving material" for "future historians." This was also supposed to specifically include "personal and most personal writings, documents, and memories," even though in light of the "total mobilization, which spares no one and rushes everyone breathlessly through time," it was difficult to find "the distance and above all the tranquility, time, and independence to be able to leave behind impeccable commentary on current events."[169]

Second, Goebbels's diary also documents what Moritz Föllmer has highlighted as the "partial overlap between Nazism and bourgeois values"[170] that existed particularly with regard to the diary's central values of reclusion and internality—despite all of the anti-bourgeois propaganda put forth by the regime, especially by Goebbels. Within the National Socialist public sphere, according to Föllmer, the preoccupation with one's own internality was presented time and again as "old-fashioned and peculiar," whereas "others insisted that spending some time by oneself was crucial to personal regeneration. Only then could one hope to contribute meaningfully to the community."[171] In keeping with this, the appeal by the NSDAP archive also stressed that for diaries "confidentiality... shall be expressly assured," thereby adopting a traditional bourgeois understanding of the diary.[172]

Against this background, the tension between the traditional image of the diary and the ideological intentions of the regime turns out to be less severe than may appear at first glance. Symptomatic of the political view of the diary in National Socialism was, for example, the criticism leveled at Charlotte Bühler by the chairman of the German Society for Psychology, Erich Jaensch, at the society's annual meeting in 1938. In the 1920s, Bühler had cofounded adolescent psychology with her studies of diaries. In his report on the "development of adolescents and the new formation of German humanity," Jaensch rejected Bühler's thesis because "the diarists on whom she based her psychology of the maturation period belong to a 'countertype,' that is, the type that our German movement rejects."[173] Thus he specifically justified his criticism not with the medium of the diary per se but rather with the "diarists" and therefore with the personality of the authors. The political evaluation by the regime did not hinge on whether somebody kept a diary; instead, the value of a diary depended on the political attitude of its author.[174]

Yet Goebbels's diary does not just illustrate how easily bourgeois values linked to the diary could be combined with a National Socialist worldview or, conversely, how political motivations also prompted the keeping of a diary. Indeed, during Nazi rule Goebbels deliberately staged himself in public as a diary writer, and in this way his diaries point to the role of the diary form in the self-presentation of the Nazi regime. In 1934 on the first anniversary of Hitler's appointment as Reich chancellor, Goebbels published the book *From the Kaiserhof to the Reich Chancellery: A Historical Diary*, consisting of heavily revised and stylized excerpts from his diary covering the period from 1932 to spring 1933. He claimed that they were "written in the urgencies and tempo of the days and sometimes nights" and "still alive with the heated thrills that the events themselves brought with them."[175] But these statements only concealed Goebbels's post hoc interventions and preserved the character of the written account as a diary, which became a best seller and appeared in forty-two editions over the following years. They made Goebbels publicly famous as a diarist.

Goebbels's decision to report on the seizure of power in the form of a diary followed a tradition within National Socialist literature in which authors, even early on, frequently took deliberate recourse to the diary. This was not just the case for the novel *Michael: A German Destiny in Diary Form*, published by Goebbels in 1929 and still clearly identified as a literary work.[176] Hermann Göring, for example, had already published excerpts from his war diary in 1923 in an anthology.[177] During the Weimar Republic, (supposed) excerpts from diaries were frequently printed in National

Socialist brochures and newspapers. And above all, what was "in a certain sense the first National Socialist manifesto," the book *My Political Awakening* by Anton Drexler, claimed in its subtitle to be "from the diary of a German Socialist worker."[178] Texts configured as autobiographies—including diaries—played a key role within the National Socialist movement in the 1920s for self-description, self-understanding, and self-assurance.[179]

This tradition continued after the start of Nazi rule. In the years after 1933, an entire series of propagandistic texts reported on the bygone rising of the National Socialist movement "from the diary of an SA man" or "according to the diary of the comradeship leader." As with *From the Kaiserhof to the Reich Chancellery*, they were supposed to be a "memorial for the fighting party and the SA" of the Weimar period.[180] Along these lines, the press also frequently printed excerpts from the diaries of "old fighters." In the run-up to the Gau rally of 1935, the *Essener Anzeiger*, for example, drew quotes from "an old National Socialist's diary-memories of the time of struggle" to publish an entire series of articles entitled An Old Fighter Recounts, which included pieces such as "An Old Fighter Looks Back through the Pages." And after 1933, articles also repeatedly appeared in the *Völkischer Beobachter* that reported, for example, "from the diary of an unknown Hitler speaker" of bygone years.[181] Meanwhile, other publications in diary form directly picked up on this tradition and also tried to make the genre useful for the NSDAP's current responsibilities, which had arisen from the party's realignment as the "educator of the German Volk."[182]

The Ambivalence of Diaries as Instruments of Political Education

As a literary form, the diary played an important role not just for the self-assurance of the National Socialist movement but also for propagating the new models for individual life management and self-contemplation. It was counted among the so-called experiential books, which were meant to appeal "to the emotion of the reader" and, "in the seemingly authentic guise of personal testimony, bring to the reader experiences that can be politically instrumentalized, which he internalizes and are supposed to radiate on his perceptions and actions."[183] The subjectivity of the diary form was considered especially suitable for allowing readers to participate in the supposedly "authentic" experiences of the author and thereby politically educating them. "One cannot read this book without experiencing it in one's innermost being," stated a review of Goebbels's *From the Kaiserhof to the Reich Chancellery*, for example. The review went on to emphasize that the book did not just convey events from the past; from the diary, readers could also "get to know and comprehend the roots of the strength that will sustain the National Socialist state in the coming centuries."[184]

Even published diaries that did not describe the rise and development of the NSDAP demonstratively highlighted their educational aspiration in these terms time and again. "We do not want to read this book like things from old times—we want to *relive* them," stated the afterword of a "book of honor" published in 1936 that collected diary writings by German nurses from the First World War. As did similar publications, it presented the women's "bravery," "self-discipline," and "fulfillment of duty" as exemplary ideals.[185] Other published war diaries from the past war, and later also from the new war in the 1940s, emphasized analogous points.[186] And the author of the published diary of a "pieceworker" from the late Weimar period similarly underlined that the diary was supposed to "shake the conscience" of those who had "not yet grasped that we share responsibility for the entire Volk, but also the conscience of those who have not grasped anything about this Volk's return home to itself."[187]

While the diary format was frequently used in this way for propagating politically desirable lifestyles and self-conceptions, the close connection between diary literature and the regime's educational efforts was clearly apparent in the (supposed) diaries published by the central National Socialist education institutions themselves. Published independently or as newspaper or journal articles, diaries from the training and education camps of various Nazi organizations or the Strength through Joy tours were considered particularly well suited for providing insights into a "National Socialist" lifestyle and self-contemplation because they did not need to be transferred to the present of the 1930s.[188] Moreover, these texts were also meant to promote very directly the central instruments of National Socialist education and demonstrate their appeal. In the mid-1930s, the young gardener Inge Thiele read such an article about a Strength through Joy sea voyage, which impressed her so much that she wrote about it in her diary. "Last week the 3,000 vacationers came back from Madeira," she noted in spring 1935. "Workers went to the South, wandered under palm trees. Three steamers were provided for our Volks comrades. . . . The diaries of the travelers, which in part were printed in our newspapers, testify to the receptivity and gratitude of German workers, who culturally stand above the entire world. We can be proud of this. A vacation ship has now steamed off to the Azores; if things keep going this way, perhaps someday I will have a turn."[189] Thiele's entry was quite telling as to the purposes of these texts, which were always supposed to convey a picture of a conflict-free time on a voyage or in camp and told the story of a successful transformation in which participants who were previously strangers became a community.

Although we can question the extent to which the descriptions in these publications, which always portrayed camp experiences in the ideal-typical terms of the regime, were based on real participants and real diary entries, many diaries were in fact written in the training camps of National Socialism. In part this was because individual camp participants who were otherwise keeping diaries often wanted to continue their private diary in a separate notebook. Rudolf Briske, the young secondary high school graduate who in fall 1933 had recorded his "Thoughts," departed in spring 1934 for a half-year stay at a Voluntary Labor Service camp north of Berlin; he started a new diary volume for describing and commenting on the camp routine, writing daily at first and later a few times a week. But many contemporaries who did not write privately also kept camp-stay diaries. This was true for all forms of education camps, from the hiking camps of the Hitler Youth and the work camps of the Reich Labor Service to the education camps of the various Nazi professional societies and the Strength through Joy tours. Diaries were even written in the elitist Lebensborn residences of the SS and the regime's elite schools.[190]

The ubiquity of diary writing was related, on the one hand, to the long tradition of travel and war diaries. In past decades, vacations and periods of military service had also given many people a special reason for writing diaries.[191] Thus, against the background of closed-group accommodations in an unfamiliar place, the idea of transferring this established and temporally and thematically circumscribed type of diary writing to the Nazi education camps suggested itself. On the other hand, frequently camp organizers themselves also purposely encouraged the participants to write diaries—and not just by way of published camp diaries, which for their part helped motivate people to write their own. Rather, the keeping of a diary was also promoted directly. In 1935, for example, the Breslau district chapter of the National Socialist Teachers' League published the text *Jörg schreibt sein Hitler-Tagebuch* (Jörg writes his Hitler diary), which printed a fictional diary of a Hitler Youth member from a stay at a tent camp. Not only with the invitational title but also with the supposed text of the diary itself, the brochure, which was meant as a "reading and work sheet for the German school," encouraged students to emulate Jörg with their own notes. At the same time, the text also gave young readers an exemplary template for a camp diary in the same way that other published diaries functioned as practical models.[192]

Alongside such literary models, also published in the 1930s were various preformatted diaries targeted at young people and adults alike. Integrated with the Hitler Youth, the Reich Association for German Youth Hostels, for example, published the *Jung Deutschland Tagebuch* (Young Germany diary), a blank booklet whose title page featured a photo collage with children and adolescents on Hitler Youth trips.[193] Also published were preprinted albums with titles such as *Mein Landjahr* (My year in the Land Service) and *Meine Arbeitsdienstzeit* (My Labor Service time), which could be used equally as photo albums, memory books, and diaries for one's time at camp.[194]

Beyond writing templates and propaganda brochures, camp leaders often directly urged young camp participants, in particular, to write diaries. In the Bensburg National Socialist Educational Institute, pupils had to keep diaries, which were monitored by unit leaders; something similar also occurred in Hitler Youth camps.[195] A memorandum of the governor of the Rhine Province related to the National Socialist training courses set up in 1935 for pupils of high schools made it mandatory to keep a diary during the camp stay, a task for which the standardized daily timetable set aside half an hour every evening.[196] The same applied to the standardized daily schedule of the Landjahr, in that keeping a "diary that is to be organized as a 'camp chronicle'" was officially prescribed.[197] But also in camps of the National Socialist Teachers' League, which were supposed to educate teachers rather than pupils according to the intentions of the regime, participants were urged to take turns writing a daily protocol that recorded the day's agenda and special events.[198] Participants in the camps of the Reich Labor Service, many of whom were adults, were asked at least at the start of the camp stay to write a brief biographical outline of their life's journey and social environment, which was meant to help them get to know one another but which they also used to scrutinize their personal identity.[199] In this respect, contrary to various assumptions in the historiography, it was not the start of the war that first led the regime to purposely promote the writing of diaries and use them for propaganda.[200] Various actors were already advocating the writing of diaries in the 1930s, above all in connection with the education and training camps.

In light of the various ways diaries were used in the Nazi education project, it is quite surprising that theoretical discussions about the concepts and techniques of National Socialist education hardly paid any attention to the diary. In contrast to discussions on political education taking place in the Soviet Union at the same time, in Germany the diary never became a subject of systematic discussion, and at most it came into view on the margins of pedagogical debates.[201] In connection with the organization of leisure time in camps, Wilhelm Decker, for example, a Generalarbeitsführer (general labor leader) in the Reich Labor Service and lecturer for the labor service at the University of Berlin, pointed out in the *Völkischer Beobachter* that even in camps "everyone needs free time in order to be alone with himself, in order to write something from the soul, in order to read a good book for himself."[202] Yet this comment was no more than a side note.

However, there are barely any pedagogical texts that asked directly about the value of the diary for teaching new lifestyles and self-perspectives. In 1934 at the congress of the German Society for Psychology, the psychologist Georg Schliebe presented ideas on the functionality of "community diaries," in which he specifically praised how they overcame the "'internality' of the individual diary" and stressed their importance to a group's identification with a "we-ideal."[203] But his deliberations were hardly taken any further in pedagogical discussions.[204] Conversely, however, virtually no published articles rejected the diary as an educational instrument for political or pedagogical reasons. Referring to his own experiences, the secondary school teacher Wilhelm Schuwerack, for example, admittedly spoke out in an essay against the pressure to write diaries in National Socialist training camps because "no genuine diary is written at command, but rather a wished-for diary." Where a "diary is sometimes demanded by a camp leader or an attending teacher . . . the point of this arrangement is completely worthless."[205] But this assessment, too, remained an isolated comment, and it did not even speak out in absolute opposition to the diary as an educational tool. Even though the diary format was deliberately used time and again for education purposes, diaries were neither an intensely debated instrument within methodological discussions on Nazi education nor something that provoked political opposition. They simply received hardly any attention.[206]

This lack of attention should be seen in connection with the general focus of pedagogical discussions, which as a whole focused primarily on the objectives and fundamentals of education and much less often touched on methodological issues.[207] At the same time, however, it was also related to the basic assumptions of the Nazi education project itself, according to which education did not occur through deliberate appropriation but through nondeliberate experience. Proceeding from the idea that individuals could ultimately be educated indefinitely through purposely designed experiences, the diary constituted a good literary form for making the experience of concrete persons accessible to readers through its subjective and temporally immediate perspective. At the same time, however, this was also why the diary was not seen as an especially suitable educational tool. Diary writing could not create or intensify an experience for the author because the experience was supposed to arise from the physiological feeling of the moment and not from its subsequent rendering into text or reflective thought.

The relationship between the diary and National Socialism was indeed quite strained, although differently than may appear at first glance. On the one hand, there was no basic contradiction between them: through its tradition, the diary format was admittedly closely tied to bourgeois self-conceptions and lifestyles, and the Nazi education project promoted new forms of individual life management and self-contemplation very much in direct contrast with these bourgeois aspects. Nonetheless, keeping a diary in the 1930s was not considered a sign of an anti–National Socialist attitude or lifestyle. Contemporaries could write diaries even as a "National Socialist" or if they wanted to become one. Within the endeavor to transform individual lifestyles and self-perspectives, diaries were frequently deployed for educational purposes. On the other hand, however, the educational use of the diary remained unsystematic because textuality hardly fit with the basic assumptions of the Nazi education project. The transformation of individual lifestyles and self-perspectives was supposed to result directly from experience and not through retrospective reflection on those experiences. For this reason, diaries received little attention in the intense debates about the creation of the "new man," which meant that, from an official standpoint, the question of precisely how the diary and the self-formation of one's personal lifestyle and self-perspective related to each other remained largely unresolved.

For people writing diaries, this was especially important. In contrast to the Soviet Union of the 1930s, no specifications or guidelines for a politically orthodox method for keeping diaries emerged under National Socialism. Thus diarists in Germany found themselves facing not just the question of how well their type of life management and self-contemplation conformed to the "new era" but also the unresolved question of how their diary writing fit in with these times. The civil registry employee Werner Kramp, who made an intense effort at political self-education in the Hamburg art gallery, started a new diary volume in November 1933 with the intention of very precisely transcribing his "timely observations on the 1933 'German revolution.'" While not completely clear as to the purpose for doing so, Kramp hoped to gain "precision and clarity from the compulsion to write." But at the same time, he was unsure whether this was a good decision. "The new era, however, wants not to be understood but to be felt," Kramp noted directly thereafter, thus drawing attention to the contradiction between National Socialism's experiential paradigm and the diary's textual reflections.[208]

Diaries are a good source for studying the effects of the National Socialist education project, and not just because they allow for a precise look at individual Germans. Insofar as questions such as those raised by Werner Kramp needed to be resolved not officially but by diarists themselves, one can investigate how individuals politically reflected on and formed their self-perspectives and lifestyles not just in specific entries but also particularly by changing the diary format. In the 1930s, many people examined themselves in their diaries using the political ideas of the Nazi regime while at the same time trying to keep their diaries in a way that conformed to the conditions of the "new era." Thus diaries of the 1930s do not just demonstrate political self-formation; rather, for their authors they were also intrinsically an important component of this work.

5

POLITICAL SELF-FORMATION IN THE NAZI EDUCATION PROJECT

WITH THE COMMON GOAL OF CREATING THE "NEW man" and, to this end, "grabbing [the existing one] at the deepest place of his being and fully remodeling him,"[1] the various aspects of the National Socialist education project consistently aimed at the personal self-contemplation of individuals. Germans were supposed to be moved not only to change their routine lifestyle habits but also to adapt their self-images to the propagated conceptions of the "new man."

With its efforts to educate the German Volk, the Nazi regime set its sights on important basic questions of human existence, which were also crucially important to the self-perspective of people in ways that extended beyond the political reconfiguration of individual lifestyles and self-contemplation. In this respect, there were three critically important problem areas: the relationship of the individual to others; one's relationship to one's own body; and one's conception of one's own origin. In the 1930s, various efforts related to the political transformation of individual lifestyles and self-images affected these basic questions for personal self-contemplation, although it always was possible for certain educational endeavors to address more than one of these questions. People who picked up on the basic impulse of the education project and became occupied with the demanded political reconfiguration of their person also had to find their own answers to these basic questions of individual self-description. Thus these questions recommend themselves as good starting points for pursuing the larger question of how people in the 1930s dealt with the political interpretation and transformation of their own person.

In taking this approach, my perspective differs from those chosen by previous studies, which have focused on the reception history of individual education instruments. Aligned in this way, historical scholarship has hitherto mainly investigated how specific education practices were accepted by the respective persons for whom they were meant. This stands to reason, but, in light of the individual's active role as outlined here, it always produces the same results: that, for example, the training camps had different effects on individual participants and the "camp experience" must be understood "as ambivalent"; that the "attempt to functionalize school for the ideology of National Socialism . . . did not succeed as seamlessly as it was intended"; and that those aspects of propaganda that stuck with people were determined by the "concrete contexts" of the reception.[2]

For the question about the extent to which the intended transformation of individual self-images and lifestyles succeeded, this finding is unsatisfying on two levels: first, because this approach hardly makes it possible to describe the reactions themselves, and, second, because it directs the focus mainly to the role of the education project in the consolidation of power. The analysis of the spectrum of contemporary reception with respect to an individual education measure is usually linked to the goal of identifying the contribution of that measure to the "social attractiveness" of the Nazi regime. In this sense, scholars have assigned great importance to the education camps or the educationally intentioned aestheticization of public space for the "fatal attraction of National Socialism" even while simultaneously pointing out that these operations did not delight all Germans in equal measure.[3]

Diaries can hardly contribute anything to the question of how many people were responsive to or repulsed by the Nazi education project. But they allow us to focus more strongly on the educational actors' self-imposed aspiration to effect the political transformation of individual Germans. They make it possible to investigate how people who actively picked up on the pedagogical objective dealt with their own self-formation. They can be used to analyze the forms, complexities, and tensions that accompanied this attempt to convert the propagated ideological models into internalized self-images. This perspective does not bring into focus the entire variegated spectrum of reactions to the Nazi regime's educational demands. Coming into view instead are those individuals who wanted to fulfill the education project's basic intention of political self-formation. As we have seen, not all Germans had this desire—by no means should we overlook the fact that many of them were unwilling to change their lifestyle and self-perspectives, that they rejected the educational demands, and when forced to comply with them they reacted by (temporarily) adjusting their behavior. This chapter looks only at certain individuals. But their diaries make it possible to shift the focus from those aspects of the education project that consolidated power to an investigation of the specific functionalities and paradoxes of political self-formation in the 1930s.

1. "The Community Is Starting to Have an Effect in Me": The Individual's Relationship with Others

Within the Nazi education project, the question about an individual's relationships with others and their significance for one's own self-perspective was invoked most prominently through the various conceptions of community that "made up a large part of National Socialist educational thought."[4] The aspiration to create a community of Germans—or one that would officially be considered as such—and thus overcome the individualism of the past decades formed the central societal-political goal of the Nazi regime. Within this objective, the regime vigorously demanded that individuals behave in everyday life in accordance with the changed rules of social belonging.[5] Various actors in the education project, however, also understood this political goal as a central aspiration for the self-perspectives of Germans and for their own pedagogical activities: the sole "reason" for "education" in National Socialism had to be to promote "the development of that personality which through insight, recognition, and will is bound to the community."[6] Accordingly, much of the education effort was directed toward the "cultivation of personality for the idea of the community."[7]

As per the educational aspiration, the conveyance of a subjective consciousness of being part of a community was supposed to contribute to the formation of the "new man" by setting the "new man" apart from the "individualists," a personality type attributed to the "liberalist" past according to which man is solely interested in maximizing his own interests and not in the common good. At the same time, however, this consciousness would also distinguish the "National Socialist man" from the "man of the masses," who, as with Communism, lost his personal uniqueness to be part of the collective.[8] The educational theorists of the Nazi regime did not place individuality and communality in opposition to each other. Rather, they believed that the internalization of the oft-used slogan "common interest takes precedence over private interests (Gemeinnutz geht vor Eigennutz)" would form the precondition for personal individuality. "Communality" was therefore understood not only as a condition of inner bonding among the members of a group but also as a personal quality of the "new man," who would comprehend himself as part of a community and from this self-understanding readily align his individual lifestyle in accordance with the collective. The "bringing forth of the authentic self through the new collective contexts" formed "a central theme of National Socialist rhetoric," and thus the Nazi education project focused on the promotion of an awareness of one's own embeddedness in the community of the nation.[9]

Within this goal, the educational aspiration with regard to personal lifestyles and self-contemplation encountered individuals in very different contexts that often at first glance did not seem to pertain to the individual's relationship with the collective. Wolfgang Scharenberg, the Mecklenburg lawyer born in 1883 who had already been involved in the Lebensreform movement before 1933, discussed the propagated expectations of a collective lifestyle in spring 1937, for example, as he looked back over the past "winter of sports." During this year, a long spell of cold weather and ample snowfall had created widespread opportunities for winter sports even in northern Germany, which Scharenberg wrote about in his diary. Adding to the description of his own sports activities, however, he noted that "nobody" from the NSDAP's "'regional leadership' . . . [had gone] skating or snowshoeing. Such things are only done in columns as training, but not individually or in pairs for pleasure, that would be 'liberalistic.' One also does not go hiking or take walks, rather now one only marches. That is what one could [read] in an official article by the 'Gebietsführer' [regional leaders]."[10]

Much as here, the aspiration for community-oriented lifestyles and self-contemplation could raise questions about virtually all everyday conduct. This circumstance found expression in the diaries of the 1930s above all in the fact that authors ruminated or reassured themselves about their own group affiliations and communality in various contexts—oft-used opportunities for this being provided, for example, by trips or weekend excursions. In particular, the Nazi association Strength through Joy, formed within the German Labor Front, had declared the recreational and vacation behavior of Germans to be an important field for the National Socialist education project, which was supposed to help "anchor the new Volksgemeinschaft in the hearts of all Germans."[11] First and foremost, Strength through Joy was making an effort to establish new, collective forms of travel. Thus the individual could "spend his vacation in a form that above all gives him the consciousness . . . of an equal member of a large Volksgemeinschaft."[12] Organized group travels would "allow" fellowship with co-travelers "to become an experience" and thereby lead participants "into the large all-encompassing Volksgemeinschaft"[13] by communally shaping their self-conceptions.[14]

Against this background, travel raised questions for many people about their own communality and induced reflection even on the part of diarists who were unwilling to politically change their lifestyle and self-perspective. At the beginning of his travel diary for a privately organized sea voyage in spring 1934, Wolf Busse, a bank director from Berlin born in 1887, spoke about the reproach that the voyage was "after all a luxury, it is treason against the fatherland, one could have given it to the Winter Aid program," as had been formulated by "enviers," "allow-you-nothings," and "friends of the fatherland." "Seen from this standpoint, one could say I acted egoistically," Busse wrote, summarizing the criticisms, which he also did not dispute. "I admit that," he noted, "in contrast to many who do not admit it but are [egoistical] nonetheless." He then went on to justify the trip, emphasizing that he could not have invested his self-earned money in a more meaningful way. Busse evidently did not want to change anything about his own self-perspective, which was marked by pride in his personal achievements; he rejected only the political accusation of treason. Precisely because of the trip, he wrote, "I can view myself as friend of the fatherland, because ship voyages support seafaring, they are travels on German terrain."[15]

Individual travel, however, cannot be categorically interpreted as indicating individualistic self-images, as scholars have sometimes suggested.[16] Rather, other actors apart from Strength through Joy had already made it publicly clear that an awareness of one's own embeddedness and communality could also be expressed through travel in other ways. Under certain circumstances, even individual travels could be understood as part of a new "Nazi travel culture."[17] Thus, for example, political travel guides such as the brochure *Potsdam: Die Geburtsstätte des Dritten Reiches* (Potsdam: Birthplace of the Third Reich) or the city guide *Wir wandern durch das nationalsozialistische Berlin* (We wander through National Socialist Berlin), which guided individuals to the commemorative sites of the NSDAP and the new state, suggested an alternative model for community-conscious travel, which many diarists used in the 1930s.[18]

As part of a larger trip, the teacher Ludwig Lindholm, born in 1884, undertook two one-day excursions with his wife and son to Berlin and

Potsdam, which he described in detail in his travel diary. As a history teacher, Lindholm was particularly interested in the structural evidence of the past, which accordingly was also the focus of his city tours. But for him this did not mean just the architectural remnants of past centuries but rather, in particular, also the important sites of National Socialism. In Potsdam he visited the Garrison Church, where he was equally reminded of Prussian history and the Day of Potsdam, which had unfolded there. "The entire blessing of historical happenings comes over me."[19]

Likewise, along with the historical sites of the cathedral, Museum Island, City Palace, and the prestigious boulevards of Unter den Linden and the Siegesallee in the Tiergarten, the stations of the city tour on the next day's visit to Berlin also included important buildings of the new state.[20] The degree to which Lindholm understood visiting these sites as reassuring and expressing his communal attitude is revealed by the description of the visitation program in his diary, which dedicated abundant space to the hardships of the walking tour. This notwithstanding, Lindholm noted, he and his son set out again in the afternoon while his wife rested at the café. "Out of the question that we, as National Socialists, would not have seen the Reich Chancellery, Kaiserhof, and the nascent Aviation Ministry. Admittedly, it was not easy for us in our condition, but to have not seen the places where the Führer worked simply would not do."[21] It was not just curiosity and sensation seeking that drove Ludwig Lindholm to see the new buildings of the new state. Rather, visiting them was for him both evidence and an expression of his awareness of his own communal embeddedness.

In the 1930s, the commemorative sites of National Socialism also helped other individual tourists situate themselves within the community. On the one hand, this applied to trips to central theaters of NSDAP party history such as Potsdam, Berlin, Munich, or Nuremberg. In such places one could, for example, visit the NSDAP rally ground; the "Brown House"; state institutions such as the Reich Propaganda Ministry, the Reich Aviation Ministry, or the Secret State Police Office; and other key sites of the new state.[22] On the other hand, rural regions were no less important, as shown, for example, by the diary of the young gardener Inge Thiele, who in the 1930s frequently undertook excursions to eastern Westphalia. Thiele visited, for example, the Hermann Monument near Detmold and the sandstone rock formation Externsteine, which she celebrated as a "main cult center of our heathen ancestors."[23] During a "side trip to the Löns Monument, to the quiet Hermann," she gathered around the monument with young people she had met on the hike, and together they sang the songs of Hermann Löns, a poet who had been declared an intellectual pioneer by the Nazi regime.[24] And in September 1936 she visited the Wewelsburg near Paderborn, which was being "grandiosely... expanded as an SS leadership school" and where "the SS guard showed us the passages and dungeons."[25] Thiele too firmly understood these excursions as an expression of her communal attitude. "All of this has gained significance in the current time, has become a pilgrimage site," she noted—and by making a pilgrimage to these places, in her individual travels she affirmed her consciousness of her own embeddedness in a large collective.[26]

When individuals situated themselves within community in the context of trips and excursions, the "community" referred to was largely undefined, which also was true of other everyday occasions. These practices therefore fit within National Socialism's broader discourse about community, where community constituted not simply concrete experience but an expansive conceptual construct that could not be directly experienced.[27] This created opportunities for people to individually affirm their own communality without having to engage directly with the community's actual members. At the same time, however, within the framework of its education project the Nazi regime tried to produce actual encounters among Germans within smaller contexts and declare that these local communities reflected the abstract "community of the Volk."[28] Local NSDAP groups and organizations affiliated with the party were in this sense also "communities," just like other groups and assemblies of people.[29] First and foremost, this was the underlying reason for the preeminence of the training and education camps in the Nazi education project, which were stylized as the "symbol of the National Socialist worldview" because of their tangible "community life."[30] Since people directly encountered a community within these contexts—in the form of other members—they were specifically confronted here with the question about whether their own lifestyle and self-perspective satisfied the requirements of the "community." As a result, diaries addressed the questions of their author's personal communality specifically in association with Nazi organizations or education camps. At the same time, they show how people who picked up on the aspiration of the education project on their own accord deliberately sought out these contexts and encounters for communal self-formation.

At the turn of the year from 1933 to 1934, Karl Möhring, for example, the student born in 1908, voiced concerns in his discussion-filled diary that one "cannot become a true National Socialist through a rational analysis and through an individualistic ability to empathize." As he put it, "It is readily obvious. The community must be experienced." Möhring regretted that "for me the experience is not yet there." Therefore he wondered whether he "should not have taken an opportunity now in order to achieve this experience," even if the requisite encounter with others should turn out to be "negative at first."[31] Möhring was thinking here about joining the labor service, which was still voluntary at the time; he had registered with the service a few weeks before.[32] He had commented on his registration with the pithy statement that "in this era even the individual must make decisions," but he was declared unfit by the obligatory medical exam required for acceptance.[33] The labor service and the SA "do not come into consideration for me because of health reasons," Möhring concluded at the turn of the year, "but I will join any other community as soon as the opportunity arises."[34]

Similarly, in the 1930s Inge Thiele used both her private travels and also, in particular, her activities in the League of German Girls (BdM) to conceptualize herself as part of a collective. On being accepted by the league in spring 1934, she welcomed this in her diary as more than just a visible sign of her belonging to the National Socialist movement, as she had done just a few days earlier on joining the German Labor Front.[35] Regarding the first home evening of her BdM group, she vigorously emphasized that "particular value is placed on esprit de corps," "everything [is] based on *Du* [informal address]," and they had "jointly practiced wonderful new youth marches and old folksongs." "Best of all," Thiele added by way explanation, "is that all of Germany will soon sing these songs, because they are on the program in every smallest local chapter: an external sign of our unity!"[36] In her other descriptions of her BdM events, as well, Thiele repeatedly used these activities and her participation in many trips and camps to vouch for her own embeddedness in a greater community and her consciousness of this fact.

Communal Self-Formation in Camp Diaries

While in diaries of the 1930s, personal involvement in Nazi organizations and participation in training camps often provided the occasion for individuals to think about their own communality, their efforts at communal self-formation can be tracked especially clearly in diaries produced in the education, training, and travel camps themselves.[37] Time and again, individual Germans deliberately sought out camps not only to affirm their communality but also to put it to a practical test. The diaries created in these venues strongly reflect that process because their authors repeatedly used writing itself as part of the effort at communality. Thus it would be misleading to understand personal writing in camps first and foremost as a "private niche" that allowed people to retreat from the prescribed communality of the camp routine.[38] This was admittedly true for camp participants who deliberately wanted to refuse the intended education. But for individuals who encountered the educational intentions more openly or signed on with camps for their own political self-formation, the diary, whether kept on their own initiative or at the behest of camp leadership, was often a central element of this political self-education. Their writings therefore lend themselves well for understanding how people in the 1930s tried to communally shape their own lifestyles and self-images.

With the diaries, we can observe the endeavor to create a consciousness of one's own embeddedness in the collective and a lifestyle established on this basis—we can see it not just in the specific diary entries but even in the diaries' external form and design. In various ways, their authors adapted them for the effort at communality, as shown especially clearly by diaries initiated by camp leaders. In August 1936, for example, a Soest Hitler Youth excursion brought thirteen male members to East Prussia during summer holidays. The group also included Erwin Sylvanus, born in 1917, who later in the 1950s gained international fame as a playwright with the success of his play about the Polish Jewish pedagogue Janusz Korczak, who was murdered at Auschwitz; in 1958, Sylvanus was honored with the Leo Baeck Prize.[39] However, Sylvanus started his work as a writer in the mid-1930s with journalistic and essayistic articles in the local press about the activities of the Soest Hitler Youth, where he headed up the press office. In this capacity, Sylvanus also took part in the aforementioned trip to East Prussia and kept a diary where he recorded the trip with detailed descriptions.

Sylvanus's literary aspiration becomes clear right at the beginning of the diary, to which the author later added a foreword beginning with "East Land calls!"[40] "East Land has always called in German history when it has been led by strong men, and the youth in the Reich have heard this call and have joyfully followed it. They have moved off from their homeland, which has become too confined; they have followed their yearning . . . toward a distant goal: to East Land! An old song flew jubilantly from their lips, a song that resounded in the blood: 'We want to go to East Land.'"[41] The line was from the "Song of the East Land Trekkers," a Flemish emigration song originally from the twelfth century. And the author repeatedly took it up in subsequent sections as well, thus integrating the group's trip into a historical tradition that was now being continued under the new political circumstances of the 1930s.

But at the same time, Sylvanus also used this motif in a literary sense at the start of his descriptions to introduce the location and dramatis personae: "East Land calls!" repeats the last paragraph of the foreword, "and it has called us, a small group of Hitler Youth boys in Westphalia Land." He subsequently describes the group members with a few brief words. The "call became for us a command," the opening remarks conclude. "We saved and worked, and then the money was gathered, and now we will leave our old beloved small hometown, as our fathers once left this Westphalian soil; we will travel to East Land. And already today, it sings and sounds within us: 'We want to go to East Land!'"[42]

The remarkably ornate stylization of the diary was not just due to the young literarily ambitious author's use of the travel description for his first attempts at writing. Rather, from the very first, the "Diary of the East Prussia Trip of Bann 132 of the Soest Hitler Youth" was not a personal document written for the author himself. As head of the press office, for the trip Sylvanus had taken on the function of a reporter who was supposed to document the journey in daily reports and afterward provide the results to all of the participants. Having returned, he therefore made a clean copy of his entries using a typewriter, furnished them with a title page, and made copies of the thirty-six-page transcript for the other travelers.

Other trip and camp organizers also appointed individual participants to write a diary as a record for the "community." Thus, for example, the various trips undertaken by a Hitler Youth group from Herne between 1935 and 1939 were in each case documented in a communal "Diary for Trips and Camps" by a participant acting as a reporter.[43] And in a labor service camp for female youth, an official from the camp leadership apparently used an elaborately designed diary to document the experiences of work crews, each of which served a six-month term. Even though the diary itself remained in the camp, the entries were presented to the respective participants when they completed their service period, as reflected in the diary by the respective completion pages, which all participants signed.[44]

While officially appointing a reporter led to a substantially larger readership than that of a typical diary written by an author for him- or herself, other camp leaders went even further and made arrangements for collective authorship. The leader of a Hamburg Hitler Youth group, which in summer 1939 traveled to Saxony and the Sudetenland (the latter had become part of the Reich just a few months earlier), organized the writing of a "Diary of the *Great Journey* of Gefolgschaft 11/88," which was subsequently printed and copied for the participants. In the foreword, the "leader of the Gefolgschaft" pointed out that "the text was also not written by one reporter but rather each day was recorded by a different comrade."[45] Thus, of the forty participants, at least sixteen took part in writing the diary. The printed version of the diary included a list of the participants but did not identify the authors of the respective entries, further enhancing the idea that this was a collective work.

The elite schools of the Nazi regime also kept collective diaries according to this model. In the National Political Institute of Education in Bensburg, the "Diary for Platoon 2, II Centuria" was started at the beginning of the 1936 school year—apparently by the platoon leader—with an entry invoking the desire that "we are one day capable and worthy of accepting Adolf Hitler's legacy, protecting and expanding it." To this end, he wrote at length about "how the Führer wants to have us" and quoted extensively from a speech in which Hitler had emphasized that "a real Volksgemeinschaft" could only "arise from [an] idealistic attitude" if everyone did not think "only about himself." Accordingly, Hitler called for young people to "take on concerns not for the individual, not for you alone ... but for a community small and yet so large."[46] The diary did not just feature the platoon leader's prelude with Hitler's appeal. It subsequently contained entries written in turn by various platoon members, who in this case were identified by name, giving them a direct opportunity to show that they were taking on communal responsibilities and to portray the school day's events from the perspective of the collective and thus live up to Hitler's expectations.[47]

Camp leaderships that guided the production of an official camp diary tried to make these writings part of the envisaged communal education and thereby markedly recast the diary's classical form. The change of readership, on the one hand, and authorship, on the other hand, both aimed at making the experiences of the community, rather than the personal experiences of the individual author, the subject of the diary. In this way, they were supposed to help convey communality. Nonetheless, diaries also presented problems for the envisaged communal education because the narrow focus on the experiences of camp community also unintentionally drew attention to the fact that this community was very much a temporary collective. Just as camp diaries began with final preparations or the arrival at camp, so they also ended with the final day of the stay. At the same time, dismissal and the return to daily life were frequently staged in a special way. In the diary of the East Prussia trip of the Soest Hitler Youth, Erwin Sylvanus, for example, described the end of the trip in a literary form similar to that of the trip's start—he dramatized the homecoming, which also embodied the individual's transition from the community of travelers to personal privacy: "Paderborn—Gesecke—Lippstadt—we are home again. A familiar sign greets us with 'Soest.' The town is still asleep, and the empty alleys lie lonely before us. . . . 'Are you glad that you are coming back to mother again?' 'Oh, no . . . [ellipses in the original]' A handshake: Heil Hitler! Yes, and we live over there." Here in Sylvanus's description of the arrival in Soest is his first use of the collective pronoun to refer to someone's family and not to the community of travelers. In his entry, Sylvanus depicts himself as saying, "Mother, I am here again. And I have brought you a kiss!" when entering his parents' home. And in the diary, which was meant for all of the journey's participants, he commented, "Oh well, the others are not here,"[48] thereby clearly marking the fact that the community of travelers had dissolved upon its return.

This was a central problem for camp organizers. The camp and travel communities were supposed to help transform the participants' self-conception, not just alter it for the duration of the respective community. Participants were supposed to tangibly experience communality in everyday camp life, but even so, these experiences were not supposed to stay confined to camp. The official camp diaries were therefore embedded within an elaborately pursued policy of memory, which was meant to ensure that participants memorized a certain picture of their camp stay.[49] This memory was supposed to make the communality (presumably) experienced by participants in camp available to them permanently. Hence, it was by no means coincidental that the last entry in the diary of the Soest travelers to East Prussia did not just mark the end of the community of travelers but also evoked what would remain from the trip and shared experiences. Sylvanus introduced the final sentences of the diary with his mother's admonishment directed at him as an overtired returnee: "'But now march off to bed, and when you wake up again you can tell more . . . [ellipses in the original]!' 'Actually . . . [ellipses in the original]' But then I am lying in my bed again, oh, and everything is as it was three weeks ago when we set forth.

And tomorrow the teacher will continue again with verse 287 of the sixth book of the Iliad, because before the holidays we stopped at verse 286. And between them lies a wonderful eternity. It was beautiful in East Prussia."[50] Sylvanus clearly highlighted what remained after the community dissolved and everyone returned to private everyday life—what, despite all of its similarities with the period before the trip, set the post-trip period apart: the (nostalgic) recollection of the travel community.

The official diaries handed out to all of the participants after the end of a camp or trip were supposed to contribute directly to this memory. "The experience lies behind us, but the memory remains," wrote the leader of the Hamburg Hitler Youth group in the beginning of his foreword to the "Diary of the Great Journey" to Saxony and the Sudetenland. His next sentences evoked the experiences of the past trip and commended the diary as an important memory aid: "Let this diary not fail in its purpose of reawakening, in later times, memories of the sixteen beautiful days for each of the forty participants and letting them experience many things once more in thought."[51] The official diaries of the camps were not just supposed to clearly illustrate one's embeddedness in the group during their authors' stay. Rather, they were meant to lastingly contribute to the communal character building of camp participants by conveying a specific picture of past experiences that focused not on any individual's own impressions but on the collective experience of the camp or travel community.

Apart from changing authorship and readership, these attempts to use the diary for communal education also altered the constitutive temporal structure of the diary's textual form. While this form is basically distinguished from other autobiographical literary genres by its creation in the face of an incalculable future, camp diaries increasingly abolished this distinction between diaries and retrospective autobiography.[52] Even in the 1930s, private diarists were well aware of the temporal constellation of their writing. They frequently recognized in their own entries that, although they were trying to align current events with past developments to sound out what would come, ultimately this did not let them calculate the future and the biographical significance of the present.[53] Many authors felt it was important to create entries of enduring value, but they knew that whether they achieved this goal would only be revealed by a future autobiographical retrospective. Official camp diaries, in contrast, purported to be extremely certain of the future. They did not want to leave the significance of experiences made in camp dependent on future autobiographical recollections. Rather, they wanted to codify the meaning of the camp stay in the present.

While diaries written in camps by individual authors for themselves did not undergo changes of readership and authorship, they too exhibit similar efforts by their authors not to limit themselves to interpreting their present experiences but rather to establish a specific memory of the camp stay. Rudolf Briske, the young man born in 1915 who in late 1933 undertook to "combine [the new] worldview with my Self," followed up on this intention a few months later by reporting to the Voluntary Labor Service. As he wrote in his last entry before starting his term, the service had a crucial part in forming a "new type of man," the "type of the socialist . . . the youth, and the future" because of its communal accommodations.[54] When Briske finished his labor service in October 1934, he concluded his camp diary with an entry that contemplated the significance of the past few months for the future: "We will only notice the true value of the labor service later, after years," Briske noted in early November. "We have experienced so much; much, much more than we all think."[55]

But Briske did not just essentially evoke the enduring value of the past experiences; rather, at the end of the entry, in his description of the trip home, he immediately introduced the future recollection: "The discharge was actually quite nice. On the return trip I spoke about motorcycles in order not to think about Groß-Mutz [the labor camp]. They were actually beautiful days. Rugged days. We will think of them often. We will soon appreciate what they gave us: we see the comrades, their worker's hands, and see among them the lads next to the common stiffs . . . [ellipses in the original] whipping rain, our lock step thudding in the puddles, soaking wet, we are singing, are happy." Briske's vivid description, consolidating various impressions of the previous months, climaxed in the remembrance of a situation in which eight of the eleven men in his troop were supposed to be punished. "Two of the old ones report as well. Only the one new person is left. Looks at us. 'Do you want to stay here by yourself?' says someone. He reports as well. He has gotten the meaning of our camaraderie. All of this was given to us by the labor service."[56]

This final picture, which concludes the camp diary, did not stand in contradiction to Briske's entries of the past months. But in his daily entries, along with evoking the "camaraderie among the working men," he frequently recorded other impressions, frustrations and conflicts with superiors and comrades. The concluding memory picture suppressed them and deliberately grasped only part of his experiences: the part that Briske wanted to take from camp as a lesson, which was supposed to stay internalized. Briske also openly formulated this quintessence of his camp experience: "Our goal must remain community among the positive forces of all strata of the Volk against the negative: against the materialism among the 'educated,' against the egoists and those only living compulsively among the workers."[57]

Like Briske's diary, those of other authors who wrote for themselves in camps were dominated by the authors' attempt to think of themselves as part of a community by deliberately staging a communal memory, not only with the diary's content but also in terms of its structure. Even private diaries consistently established the picture of a harmonious camp community. In many cases, this effort took on far broader dimensions than with Rudolf Briske. Like his camp diary, the diaries of other participants consistently ended with the last day of the camp stay and the return trip. But work on the camp diary by no means stopped there. Like the writers of official camp diaries (which for copying purposes required at least a typewritten transcription of the entries after they returned), even authors of diaries written for themselves frequently not only wrote a final summarizing entry but also elaborately reworked their diaries.

This was the case with the theology student Karl Leisner, for example, who had kept a diary during his stay with the labor service from spring to fall 1937. Leisner was twenty-two years old at the time and had already been active in the Catholic youth movement for a few years. As a Catholic youth functionary, Leisner repeatedly came into conflict with the Nazi regime during the 1930s, began to be systematically monitored by the Gestapo in October 1936, and during the war was finally detained in the Sachsenhausen and Dachau concentration camps, dying just a few weeks after the liberation of the Dachau camp because of the conditions of his detainment.[58]

Although he was politically distant from National Socialism and found the camp routine restrictive, when he finished his term of service Leisner nonetheless still gave the labor service a positive assessment: "Last handshakes in the troop. Serious, but yet I am happy to be allowed once again to freely arrange my life on my own. Under no circumstances do I want to be without this time. It was a hard school of life, but was weathered well. It gave you a lot about human beings—and above all also self-knowledge. . . . And despite the bitter disappointment . . . —despite everything, I have become very deeply fond of my Volk."⁵⁹ This assessment made at the end of camp also found expression in the clean copy of the camp diary Leisner later compiled in an official album, its jacket decorated with a spade and the identification number of his labor service camp, with a title in large letters indicating the camp's location. Leisner did not transfer the diary into this album word for word. Instead, he rewrote the original entries, which often only recorded the stations of the day's routine and logged his impressions, into lengthy descriptions. Moreover, he also put great effort into designing the album, providing a separate title page and adding numerous photos he had taken during his time at camp.⁶⁰

Other diarists also similarly worked on their notes when they returned from camp—even today, these diaries show the effort that went into their elaborate design. Else Dietrichs*, a seamstress from Berlin born in 1911, voluntarily reported to the Reich Labor Service of Female Youth in fall 1936. After returning, she wrote short reports in a preprinted diary about the various stations in the daily camp routine and particular incidents during her time at camp. She organized her entries chronologically into a comprehensive account of her camp stay made up of individual chapters, added headings, and illustrated the diary with numerous photos, self-made cut-out silhouettes, newspaper clippings, and postcards. The post hoc effort Dietrichs put into her diary to fix her future memory of her labor service is also evident in the clean and even handwriting of the work's extensive text, which spans multiple volumes. As a prelude to her book, she stated the work's guiding narrative in awkward verse: "Der Sinn für Kameradschaft lebt noch fort, wenn wir längst sind zerstreut und treffen wir uns mal an einem Ort heißt es 'FAD,' du schöne Zeit" [The sense of camaraderie still lives on when we are long since scattered, and if sometime we meet some place, we will say: 'FAD,' thou lovely time].⁶¹

In a similar way, the secondary high school graduate Heinz Korsch*, who reported to the labor service in spring 1933, assembled his diary "*after the departure from the labor service . . . from a chaos of notes, newspaper reports, printed matter, and photos,*" as he commented in a postscript.⁶² Along with extensive reports of camp experiences, which he also organized into various chapters with headings, his diary, like those of Leisner and Dietrichs, also contained his own drawings and numerous photos, which expanded the diary to an "unintentional" length.⁶³ Heinz Korsch directly spoke about how working on his diary did not mean merely creating a clean copy of illegible notes but rather scrutinizing his own communality.

He saw his follow-up work on the diary as "stylistic practice"; above all, however—and this, he noted, was "what makes the work important to me"— he did it to "fully recognize the scope and difficulties (especially of the internal kind!)" of what he had gained from the experience of cohabitation in the labor service. He wrote, "I believe that I will utilize those insights again!"[64]

In terms of their structure, the official and private diaries from Nazi education camps were often predetermined by the efforts at communality. Accordingly, they drew a strongly idealized image of camp stays. Thus, the diaries do not provide for an undistorted view of daily camp routines and participants' perceptions of them, meaning that they cannot simply be read as evidence for the success of National Socialist camp pedagogy. Camp diaries are not simple textualizations of experiences generated for participants by camps through purposeful arrangement. Insofar as many diaries from camps of the National Socialist education project elevated the emergence and development of the camp community as their guiding narrative and already used this narrative as the reference point for their form and design, they do not just report on the communal self-formation that occurred in camps. Rather, with the temporal structure of their text and the different kind of readership and authorship, camp diaries were themselves part of the effort to make participants aware of their own embeddedness in the community and to make them draw consequences from this for their lifestyle and self-contemplation.

Assimilating with the Community

Since diaries in camps were often closely tied to efforts of communal self-formation, they are thus especially good for following how individuals tried to make themselves communal. This did not necessarily require discussions as explicit as those recorded by Elli Wintgen*, born in 1917 into a family of the Bremen bourgeoisie. *"In the labor camp in Rehde. I have been here for three days. The community is beginning to take effect in me,"* she wrote, beginning her diary from the period of her voluntary labor service in 1936. In this particular case, the diary obviously conformed to the author's social origins, in that it entirely lacked any description of daily camp routines and instead reflected her inner experience, as would a "typical" bourgeois diary.[65] Even so, Wintgen tried in this way to detach herself from the "bourgeois culture of the parental home," from which she was "alienated" and which in her diary she compared with her impressions from the labor service.

"In the endless expanse of the landscape, the personal self loses its significance. To want to do something for others is a natural need." In written self-contemplation, Wintgen tried to educate herself to communality, which in the diary found expression as self-criticism and purposeful resolutions: "I was too caught up in my own dreams and wishes. Judge other people according to my own ideas and standards. I must become stricter with myself, but more understanding toward others. Only when others can understand my ideas do they have substance, only then can I exist in the community."[66]

But generally speaking, such entries, which call to mind bourgeois introspection and Soviet self-criticism in equal measure, were rather unusual.[67] In the diaries from the Nazi education camps, the effort to become conscious of one's communal embeddedness and to make this the basis for one's own self-contemplation mainly found expression in a specific narrative perspective. Corresponding to this was a use of language that could demonstrate and produce communality even without more extensive reflection.

The effort at communal self-orientation is evident in camp diaries above all in the way that even those written by individual authors for themselves consistently followed, along with the author's experiences, the experiences of the collective. In this sense, they were similar to official camp diaries. Like these, the diaries of individual camp participants made the camp community the central topic of their personal entries. In diaries that were reorganized during the revision process, this became clear from the chapter structure, which often closely followed the formal structures of the camp. Else Dietrichs, who so elaborately designed the diary she wrote for herself during her time in the Labor Service of the Female Youth, began her account with a chapter entitled "Camp House." Here she described the Königshorst labor service camp, which was accommodated in an old farmhouse, as well as the purpose of the labor service: "To lead girls to camaraderie."[68] She went on to talk about her own arrival at the labor camp in the next chapter only after writing this general opening. It was symptomatic for her entire diary, which reported not only about her but also about the structures and processes of the labor service. She did not describe the latter simply to make her own experiences comprehensible; rather, the regular processes and events in the labor camp during her attendance formed a central and equally important topic on their own.

In the section "The Flag Ceremony," which Dietrichs used to start describing her camp stay, she reported on her first morning flag raising, which for her would "remain unforgettably remembered." She was the last person to join the group, which had already assembled around the flag. "The leader and the rest of the girls already stood ready to start and reached their hands to each other in a closed circle. I quickly stepped into the circle too, but immediately had a bad conscience because of my 'tardiness'; but neither the leader nor the subleader reprimanded me for this." Nonetheless, while later sitting across from the camp leader during the breakfast, Dietrichs could "not appease my bad conscience; I first had to describe to the leader my reason for the 'tardiness.' She just laughed and Lo, in her comical way, said: 'Oh, just let it go, Else, nobody saw it!'"[69] As in this case, in her report Dietrichs repeatedly linked her own experiences (acceptance into the camp community) with the general presentation of the daily camp routine and its important stations (flag ceremony).[70] The next chapter provides an overview of the "Daily Routine in the Voluntary Labor Service," followed by a number of sections dedicated to the work ("Among the Settlers," "The Production of the New Green Uniforms," "The Kindergarten," "The Kindergarten Party at Our Camp"). She likewise also reported generally about the various work sites where participants from the Königshorst labor service camp were deployed and about the work she performed. In the next chapters, Dietrichs also focused on the communal education purpose of camp as the subject of her text, using many episodes to indicate that it was "not very easy for the individuals to completely and utterly adjust themselves to the generality" but that they "gradually succeeded . . . in creating a comradely unit."[71] Other diaries also did not restrict themselves to providing only the information needed to understand their author's personal experiences. Like Dietrichs, when subsequently revising his labor service diary, Heinz Korsch, for example, also organized it into chapters under headings such as "Unit and Idea," "The Röhn Camp," "The Course of a Day," and "At Work," similarly embedding his own impressions and experiences within the general information he provided about the structure and processes of the daily camp routine.[72] Thus the memory book he compiled, too, was both a personal report and a general account of the camp stay.

Retrospectively revised diaries were not the only ones whose accounts were strongly shaped by the camp itself. So too were diaries written during the camp stay, like that of Rudolf Briske. They show a strong alignment between notes written on a daily basis and formal camp structures, especially with the standardized daily routine. For May 11, 1934, for example, Briske noted in his diary, "After wake-up and gymnastics, six-kilometer march to the workplace. Shoveling a ditch. In between, back peeling potatoes, get breakfast for the entire platoon. Not easy. A few blisters. Never mind. When exercising, indeed like always, standing idle doesn't work. . . . Afterward 'Lesson on State Politics.' Schirach's 27th birthday. . . . During free time read, talked about philosophy, played chess. Besides, one is always bone tired in the evening."[73] Even two and a half months and many diary entries later, the incremental recounting of the day's routine still dominated his notes: "In the morning especially rugged sports under Senior Troop Leader Böhm, then flag parade, next cleaning of quarters. Was naturally given shit because there was still some dust in the corner of my cubicle. . . . After approval, washing of socks, footwraps, etc., then writing, readings, lay down after lunch."[74]

Briske's diary shows that the close attention to the camp's formal structures—also evident in other diaries—did not simply arise from the form of the diary. To be sure, private diaries too could consist chiefly of brief notes that meticulously registered the daily routine. Yet this was certainly not how Rudolf Briske had previously kept his diary. There he had used his entries above all for the comprehensive discussion of various problems that occupied him and in doing so disclosed his thought processes in long deliberations. The section of the diary entitled "Thoughts," which he started in 1933, was wholly characteristic of his diary writing outside camp. Only during his camp stay did the expansive discussions largely disappear, replaced by the incremental notation of the day's events.[75]

By way of the orientation of the diarist's descriptions according to the camp's formal structure, the main subject of the diary became what also stood at the heart of the educational undertaking. The concept of camp education was based on assembling participants at a place as far removed as possible from disruptive influences, where the "daily routine of the personnel" would be subject to "a rigid order" so as to "standardize the everyday life of the occupants." Participants were supposed to be educated to community not so much through the camp training sessions but rather through their "continual integration in groups," which resulted from the day structure. And this was supposed to make it impossible for them to "individually process the impressions of camp life."[76] Scholars have rightly pointed out that the comprehensive shaping of everyday life as imagined at the theoretical level could hardly be realized in such totality.[77] However, for participants, the structuring of camp life, which even included leisure time, is what most sharply distinguished camp from everyday life. Yet the different nature of the daily routine does not in itself explain why authors who were willing on their own accord to engage in communal self-formation paid so much attention to the day structure in their diaries. We see this in the continuity with which Rudolf Briske and others reported month after month on a daily routine that always stayed the same. Indeed, the individual's communality in the education camps found expression precisely through his or her conscious integration into the organized daily routine, both within and external to the diaries.

Diaries frequently talked about this. For example, at the end of his chapter "The Course of a Day," where he gave a detailed tabulated overview of recurring daily stations, complete with specific times, Heinz Korsch pointed out that the "total duty so amply fills up the time that 'liberals' as well as 'individualists' cannot develop."[78] And he opened the chapter "Camp Life" with the finding that the labor service volunteer "must renounce old interests; that is the first experience. But the more someone is an individual, he will create new ones within the framework of camp life. But everyone will somehow bend in *one direction*, according to the one law—the *community law*." His revised diary also did not conceal the fact that this integration into the new structures of camp was clearly difficult. "At the beginning," nobody found it "easy to come to terms with it," and "some agonized at first! For the first while, on free evenings I need [sic] to run in the woods as per old practice . . . [ellipses in the original] 'Just to not see the camp for once, think of something else!'"[79]

Korsch seemed all the more satisfied that he nonetheless made friends and adapted to the procedures of camp. He and others, like Briske or Dietrichs, also documented and accomplished this integration by aligning their diary entries with the formal elements of the daily camp routine. To be sure, organizers did not always manage to design the operations in the training camps of the National Socialist education project in such a way that the permanent embeddedness of participants in groups actually prevented them from individually processing camp life. But even so, the model of the ideal daily routine—despite any shortcomings in its realization—gave participants who were working on their own communality an important reference point for inscribing themselves into the community.

In this sense, even those camp diaries whose entries consist of little more than the brief listing of daily stations can be read as expressions of a communal self-understanding. Emil Kuhn, a secondary high school graduate from Koblenz born in 1918, used daily entries to document his stay in a two-week national-political training course, which he completed as part of his schooling. For November 22, 1934, for example, he noted: "7:30 Get up, early-morning exercise, wash, get dressed, tidy beds. 8:00 Coffee like always. 9:00 Decamp toward Bollenbach. There practice fanning out and stalking. 12:30 Lunch. Soup with meat and potatoes cooked together with vegetables. Then free until 4:00. Four o'clock coffee like always. 5:00 Lecture on the six primary points of the party. 6:00 Lecture on art and on Dürer with photographs. 6:30 Photographs of borderlands. Alps with Austria. 19:00 Supper. Sausage sandwiches with tea. 8:00 we departed for a tavern where we met with a choral society. Together we sang the song 'The Watch on the Rhine.' 10:00 sleep."[80]

Kuhn documented the other days in the same way, and this was also how other Germans described camp stays. Like Kuhn, they largely dispensed with their own commentary on daily events or with recording their impressions or personal experiences within the rigid daily framework. Thus, for example, the diary entries recorded by Anton Gloeckner* in a Hitler Youth tent camp in summer 1935 likewise consisted only of key words related to the day's routine: "5th day, Thurs. 22nd, 6:00 Wake up, etc. Morning ceremony. Slogan: honor! Grub: 'coffee' and bread with fruit pulp. Service community: reconnaissance patrol disbursement! Grub: cooked beans + potatoes + one meat sausage for everyone. Rest. Shooting in Bammental. 3 shots prone supported = 18 rings. In camp, practice for evening. Grub: pea soup + potatoes + meat sausage. Rally in the village. Lowering of the flag, etc."[81] And likewise, Doris Becker*, born in 1924, noted her participation in 1938 in a training course for Young Girl Leaders in log-like entries: "8th day January 25, 1938. 7 o'clock Wake up, Wash, Get dressed, etc.—8 o'clock Flag raising, Breakfast.—9 o'clock Woodwork.—1/1 11 o'clock Singing at Trudel.—12 o'clock Food: Oxtail soup, Fried potatoes, Russian eggs, Field salad.—1 o'clock, Bed rest.—2 o'clock Free time.—3 o'clock Training: Nuremberg Laws.—5 o'clock Sports.—7 o'clock: Supper: Apple rice.—8 o'clock Flag lowering, Home evening: You are a chain without end.—10 o'clock Camp rest."[82]

While this last example, in particular, may seem quite inexpressive and impersonal when considered on its own, it nicely demonstrates that even this kind of diary, and likewise the more extensive descriptions by Else Dietrichs, Heinz Korsch, and Rudolf Briske, can be understood as a deliberate integration into the structure of camp. Apart from recording every day at the training camp in this way, before each daily entry Doris Becker also wrote down the general model of the camp's standardized timetable under the heading "Order of the Day": "7 o'clock Wake up. — 7-7¼ o'clock Early morning exercise. — 7¼-8 o'clock Wash, dress, make bed, etc. — 8 o'clock Room roll call. 8:05-8:15 o'clock Flag raising. — 8¼-9 o'clock Breakfast. — 9½-10 o'clock Singing. — 10½-11¾ o'clock Sports. — 12-1 o'clock Lunch. — 1-2 o'clock Rest period. — 2-3 o'clock Free time. — 3-5 o'clock Worldview training. — 5-7 o'clock Woodwork. — 7-8 o'clock Supper. — 8½-9 o'clock Newspaper report. — 9½-9:40 o'clock Flag lowering. — 9:40-9:50 o'clock Wash, undress, etc. —10 o'clock Camp rest."[83] As absurd as the constant repetition of the same unchanging schedule may seem, this placement of the "Order of the Day" before each daily entry clearly illustrates that Becker deliberately made the general camp structure, and not her personal impressions, the subject of her diary.

Even though we do not clearly know the specific circumstances in which the camp diaries of Emil Kuhn, Anton Gloeckner, and Doris Becker were written (at least one was probably created at the direct instruction of camp leaders[84]), we cannot interpret these diaries simply as the minimal fulfillment of an obligation, whereby the participants reluctantly responded to a mandatory writing assignment. As stereotypical, impersonal, and interchangeable as the various diary entries may appear—not only within each diary but also from one diary to the next—this can be understood as precisely the form in which the authors (voluntarily or involuntarily) recorded the experiences of the community in their personal diary: that is, day in and day out, by virtue of the daily routine shared by all of the participants—and, namely, not their own personal experiences, which differed from the group experience. In this respect, these diaries need not be interpreted as documents that "*merely logged*" and did not "*reflect on*" the camp experience, as has been argued, for example, by Andreas Kraas with regard to the camps of the National Socialist Teachers' League.[85] Rather, the log format itself can be understood as an act of reflection in which, by focusing on the general structures of the camp, the subject of the diary became the community and not the diarists' personal experience. These camp diaries too featured a narrative perspective that documented communality, but without the kind of explicit discussions recorded by Elli Wintgen, the young daughter of bourgeois parents from Bremen.

Further indications that these log-like diaries should be interpreted as part of a process of communal self-formation are found in the specific linguistic usage of the personal pronouns *I* and *we*.[86] This is quite clearly illustrated by the diary of Anton Gloeckner from the Hitler Youth tent camp: "In the afternoon we departed for Bammental. We swam in the pool. When we came home there was buttermilk," Gloeckner noted in typical fashion about the activities on the second day of camp.[87] All of the entries in his camp diary consistently use first-person plural to identify his own narrative voice and simultaneously present the author as part of the collective. In contrast, *I* is used only once, on the seventh day of camp: "Then removal of the performance badge in terrain sports. I failed at camouflage. We did not get back to camp until 14:30."[88] It is no coincidence that Gloeckner came to speak about himself precisely when he stood out from the group because of his poor performance. Authors of other camp diaries also spoke in their entries consistently in terms of *we* and *us* and did not use *I* until they deviated from the community.

This applied equally to both private and official camp diaries. One such diary was the "Logbook of the Camp and Trip" of a BdM group that traveled by bicycle to the Bodensee for a multiday camp. The diary was created by an unknown author, who wrote it in the *we* form. Thus she reported as follows, for example, on waiting for the necessary leave from school one day before departure: "Today we also had no desire to learn because of all the agitation, for it was not yet clear. At the last moment we got the permission; it was a miracle that we did not jump with joy. After school there was still much to discuss. Here is when it first occurred to us that we had not yet packed. Packing went relatively fast, but in the meantime it had nonetheless become evening. Now quickly to bed, because turning up bleary eyed tomorrow is not allowed."[89] The unknown narrator did not only use the *we* form to describe what the girls did together on this day. She also indicated feelings and thoughts collectively with *we* and even conceptualized packing at one's own home and going to bed in nonpersonal formulations and thus in a general statement that applied to the entire group. The next day as the group got underway with the bicycles, however, the author realized that she could not keep up with the others. This brought her to speak of herself in the diary firmly in the *I* form: "Now came the pedaling. Over time the pedaling went right into my stomach and while riding I was given the first valerian drops." As the car carrying the luggage caught up with the group, the young woman was "suddenly called forward and it was said, I should get in. . . . I was happy that I could hitch a ride, because had I still pedaled along we would not yet be in Donaueschingen today."[90]

The "Diary of the Great Journey" of the Hamburg Hitler Youth boys to Saxony and the Sudetenland was also written by the various authors in the *we* form and only mentioned individual participants if they stood out from the group or fell out of ranks: "We had to climb over steep heights and hike through deep chasms.... The mountains so enticed one comrade that he had to climb around on them and afterward could go neither forward nor backward. As a reward for this he received five days of kitchen duty!"[91] Along these same lines, in the diary of the East Prussia trip of the Soest Hitler Youth boys, Erwin Sylvanus, too, only spoke explicitly about himself when he appeared in his capacity as a member of the trip leadership; otherwise, he used the collective *we*.[92]

In camp diaries, the dominant perspective on the experiences of the community and one's relationship to the collective found its lexical equivalent in the specific use of the *we* and *I* forms. The diaries of Anton Gloeckner and the unknown participant in the trip to the Bodensee report on group events in the same way as the logbooks of the Hitler Youth groups from Hamburg and Soest, whose authors consistently identified themselves as members of groups with the use of *we* and presented the group's experiences as their own. Nonetheless, the use of the *I* form for the deliberate identification of one's own deviation from the group also reveals that the diarists always had their own communality very much in mind.

As the lexical equivalent to the narrative perspective of the camp diaries, this grammar of personal communality also characterized diaries in which authors generally spoke more strongly of themselves, but it did so in a more hidden manner. Rudolf Briske often used the *we* form in his entries, for example, to describe his final memory picture as something that "we will often think" about, but by the same token, he also recorded personal experiences and impressions marked with *I*.[93] Yet Briske's efforts at communal self-formation, too, were reflected in his linguistic usage, as shown, for example, by his account of the difficulty he had adjusting to the formalized daily schedule. Before joining the camp, Briske had firmly welcomed the structured daily order and probably for this reason also aligned his diary writing according to daily recurring elements. Nonetheless, at first he had difficulty getting used to the small amount of sleep. Around one week after commencing his duties, he noted in his diary: "Get up at 3:30. Somewhat early. One doesn't actually complain here . . . about anything: but one thing is wrong without question, the too-little sleep. Six hours is not enough for a 20-year-old person! But one doesn't make anything of it."[94] As in this entry, Briske repeatedly recorded his displeasure and difficulties in his diary in a form that consistently transformed them into general experience. Also, when he complained about tiredness in other entries, he did so with the impersonal *one*, indicating generally applicability. "One is damned tired again," he began his entry two days later.[95]

Else Dietrichs also wrote broad sections of her entries in the *we* form, but she did not sustain this throughout her entire report. Yet in her diary, the idea informing this grammar of personal communality, which associates individuality with deviation, found remarkably clear expression in some of the things she described. Dietrichs followed her chapter on the production of camaraderie among camp participants with a section on "Jokes and Teasing That We Permit Ourselves with Individual Girls." In the style of humorous boarding school stories, in this section she extensively described how the community chastised those particular girls who through their "insolence and non-camaraderie . . . brought us so much disgrace . . . during the FAD time."[96] Included in this section was a chapter called "The Nighttime Washing of Eva Schmidt." Here Dietrichs described, for example, how at night she and her "comrades" jointly forced a new camp participant who allegedly did not wash herself to perform physical hygiene. In the process, the supervening camp leader helped them carry the bed with the delinquent, who in her anger over being harassed was ranting about the labor service, out of the dormitory and into the hallway, where they continued to watch over the girl, catching her again when she finally wanted to run away and guarding her in turns until morning.[97]

Elaborately described, this episode was not the only "teasing" of this and other girls recorded by Dietrichs in her diary. She identified them by their full names and characterized them in detail in her entries. In contrast, she did not devote any separate entries to her "comrades." Thus in her diary as well, individuality occurred as deviation from the group. For Dietrichs, the other members of the labor camp seemed to have been adequately described by the general account of camp routines.

In the camp diaries of National Socialism, the effort at communal self-formation did not lead to much explicit discussion. Instead, these diaries had their own distinct narrative perspective whereby the account's orientation according to camp structures made community the main subject. The author's own experiences were integrated within this framework or receded behind the collective. This perspective carried over to the linguistic-grammatical level in a specific usage of the *we* and *I* forms, a specific grammar of one's own communality.

Diaries from the training camps of the Nazi education project therefore show how individuals in the 1930s made an effort at their own communal self-formation and how writing was part of this effort. Thus in the camps, people also often learned a certain communal form of written discussion, which after camp stays one could also use privately. In summer 1935, as seven Dortmund youth departed for their private holiday at the North Sea, they jointly documented their trip in a "Diary of the North Sea Camp," which meticulously transferred the communal techniques learnable in the camps to their friendship. The friends wrote the entries in turn, all of which were written in the *we* form, and the diary spoke about *I* only in the particular entry dealing with a "large tiff" because individual participants did not perform their chores for the group (washing dishes, making breakfast).[98]

The entanglement of efforts at communality with diary writing itself is especially close in camp diaries, and it is here, more so than in other contexts, that we can clearly see how people tried to transpose the ideological model of the "communal man" into their own self-images. Drawing on the range of communities offered by the camps, they used their diaries above all to integrate themselves—also through writing—into collective structures and thereby to comprehend the experiences of the group as experiences of their own. Hence, for many Germans individuality still appeared, but chiefly as a negative deviation from the community.

Communal Self-Formation and Personal Interests

Arising in the camps of the Nazi education project was a specific form of communal self-formation that translated models of a community-oriented lifestyle and self-conception into tangible practices of life. Can one therefore conclude that the Nazi regime's intentions related to communal education were successful? To answer this question, it should first be reiterated that only certain individuals made an effort at political self-formation and tried to develop a communal lifestyle and self-perspective. Second, even the diaries of authors who did so reveal that this effort to achieve personal communality remained inscribed by many hindrances and paradoxes. We can also use these diaries to trace how self-education to communality—with its aim to integrate into the collective—remained bound to a specific dialectic in which the practices guided by the propagandistic models of the community made up only one side.

Even concentrated efforts at personal communality did not directly create the "community man." This is already illustrated by examples where individuals purposely entered into community but in their diaries ultimately had to concede the failure of their efforts. Such was the case with Wilm Hosenfeld, for example, a village schoolteacher from Thalau in Hesse, born in 1895, who joined the SA and National Socialist Teachers' League in 1933 and in 1935 also joined the NSDAP.[99] In his diary, Hosenfeld frequently addressed his relationship with others in the context of these Nazi organizations. In September 1936, when he was taking part in the national party rally in Nuremberg, the tent camp accommodating him and other SA men particularly inspired him to write in his diary about his own communal embeddedness: "SA camp Langwasser. Here in Nuremberg one first gets an idea of the SA. As Rudolf and I went through the evening camp pathways, he said: 'It is like a walk through Germany.'" Accordingly, Hosenfeld also experienced the end of the camp as a return from the community back to his own private life: "We [he and his brother Rudolf] had to fill the day ourselves. The Reich party rally is over. The camp is emptying out."[100]

Just a few weeks earlier, Hosenfeld had been at a multiday National Socialist Teachers' League training camp, where he likewise had dealt with his relationship with the other participants. But in this case, he had to conclude that "many colleagues . . . are not worth much as characters. Sure, within their domestic environment; but detached from this they are just a mass. I relate to no one."[101] Above all, Hosenfeld disapproved of the evening get-togethers organized by camp leaders to heighten camaraderie. "Intellectual nadir of conviviality. Caterwauling and inanities make up the entertainment. A lot of beer," he noted in his diary. At the same time, this led Hosenfeld to a more basic assessment: "Why do I fit so poorly in the large community of such a training course? The colleagues are so foreign to me."[102] Despite his desire for communality, Hosenfeld had to conclude that he was "just not a person for these banalities and the inane babble." Nor did this just apply to the "camaraderie evenings" of the teachers' league training camps. Later too, he noted in his diary that when "the entire comradeship streams into the tavern," he "stands apart. This type of conviviality and comradeship does not suit me. So I am always viewed as an outsider."[103] This was also the case with the SA, whose camp at the Reich party congress had impressed him so much. In spring 1938, on the occasion of a "camaraderie evening" (which, according to his diary, he actually looked forward to), Hosenfeld noted, "The opinion of my Sturmführer and other comrades about life and life formation is one so different that I cannot agree with them at these social occasions. On duty things go very well."[104] Even when people consciously worked at their communality, particularly also in the context of arrangements established for this purpose as part of the National education project, their efforts could have the opposite effect and therefore highlight all the more starkly the differences that still prevailed among participants.

The encounter with others in the political context of the education camp or within Nazi organizations did not necessarily bring participants together, even if they themselves were making an effort at communality. While educational actors always interpreted the relationship between participants as an expression of the communality they achieved, for individuals the camps could also make existing differences really obvious for the first time. Significantly, however, diaries from the education camps of National Socialism show that this registration of difference did not just occur in cases where individuals criticized their lack of communality. To me it seems that this fact must be central to our understanding of communal self-formation. Even though Wilm Hosenfeld seemed resigned in his diary, his perception of differences was very much a constitutive component of his effort at communality. It established the specific dialectic to which the striving for communal self-formation always remained tied, despite efforts to integrate with the collective.

Even for people who seemed more optimistic than Wilm Hosenfeld and drew the picture of a successful communal relationship in their camp diaries, the camps starkly highlighted existing differences. In his daily entries, Rudolf Briske, for example, frequently noted problems with the camaraderie among camp participants—problems that he consciously suppressed in his final memory picture.[105] In the case of Heinz Korsch, on the other hand, such problems still remained part of his retroactively revised camp diary. The newly minted secondary high school graduate first reported on the relations between labor camp participants in the chapter "Secondary High School Graduates in Practice," which followed directly from his account of how he reported to the labor service and arrived at camp. "A secondary high school graduate, despite his *school leaving* exam . . . is most unready and immature when he steps into the battle arena of life," Korsch wrote at the start of this chapter, referring to his own willingness to work on his communal self-formation. "We [graduates] are now joining the labor service, voluntarily!, and have the best intention of showing that we are neither 'vain prigs' nor 'educated pigs,' and ardently want to stand up for a transcendence of the old class differences."¹⁰⁶ But at the same time, he thereby allocated himself to a specific group of camp participants, which was critically important for his further thoughts about the camp community. "We find in the camp mostly unemployed SA men who cultivated their own mind," he continued with his description. And he repeatedly came to speak about this difference, which was based on the social origins of the individual workmen, in connection with the question about communality among the participants and his relationship to them. "The work at the sports field in the tough clay and damp cold certainly did not come easy to us [graduates]," he noted in the same entry, yet they had "worked no less than the others. But when a secondary high school graduate stopped shoveling or sometimes had to disappear, then sure enough it is seen by one hundred eyes. They are perhaps just waiting for the chance to say pityingly: 'Oh well, he is of course a secondary high school graduate!'" ¹⁰⁷ A little later Korsch reported that at camp he had doubts about "whether camaraderie and Volksgemeinschaft *while retaining one's own pride and feeling of personality* is even possible." Yet this conflict nonetheless dominated his relations with other camp participants and the ways in which he viewed them until the very end of his service period. "Spies, secondary high school graduate from Eisenach, Glaser, the headstrong farmer from 'Seunde,' are newcomers," Korsch wrote when noting the arrival of new camp participants.¹⁰⁸

Similar things appear in many camp diaries, whereby an individual's personal perception of other camp participants was chiefly determined by their profession and regional origin. Rudolf Briske also distinguished in this way between secondary high school graduates and other labor service workers, although it especially annoyed him that "particularly among secondary high school graduates [there were] uncomradely people who . . . the entire livelong day sit on the shovel and only work when a leader comes by. Such ass-kissers, who in near future will naturally get beaten up, have not comprehended the new spirit."¹⁰⁹ The theology student Karl Leisner likewise kept an overview of the fellow members of his troop in the diary he wrote during his term with the labor service, noting not just their addresses but also their professions. His characterizations of individual camp participants and of the entire group indicate that this concealed a specific perception of difference. "Am in troop 2. There are eighteen of us with leaders," he wrote, describing his closest comrades. "Two are from Saarland. One NDer. He is a secondary high school graduate. One more secondary high school graduate (Saxon). Two Bavarian farm lads. The others Saxons."[110] But Leisner also addressed the differences between participants directly, especially in areas where he tried to overcome them. "In the camp I will soon generally be called 'the pastor,'" Leisner noted in his revised entry of April 7, thus coming to address the particular personal characteristic that, in his opinion, distinguished him most clearly from the other camp participants. "Sad, what notion the Saxons have about the religion of Christ. Abysmal!" Leisner added, while at the same time emphasizing: "But nonetheless: they are all my comrades!"[111] And a few weeks later, Leisner reaffirmed the point, noting that it was also necessary to establish "comradeship with an 'evil man.'"[112]

When introducing the participants in the trip to East Prussia in his introduction, Erwin Sylvanus too emphasized the group's heterogeneous composition. "East Land calls! And it has called us ... Paul, who stood at a lathe and forged a steam boiler, Günther, who is now going to the academy and wants to be a painter, Jupp, who stood in the fields and mowed the ripe wheat, Bruno, who swung the hammer and had to tame and form glowing steel, Winner, who goes to a secondary high school and is learning Greek and Latin."[113] Another example comes from the diary of a woman from the Ruhr region who took part in a trip to the Allgäu organized by Strength through Joy. She decided to write her travel report under the heading "Holiday from Myself," a title that she borrowed from a popular book and movie and that aptly characterized the official purpose of the trip. The report was marked by its particular attentiveness to the peculiarities of southern Germans, as evinced, for example, by the constant noting of unfamiliar expressions and pronunciations.[114]

Insofar as people directly dealt with their own communality in the camps of the National Socialist education project or were challenged by these camps to do so, the education camps also produced an unintended consequence: they fostered a particularly acute awareness of social differences among participants. This can help explain the rather numerous conflicts between groups of participants from different regional or social origins, as have been documented with regard to both Strength through Joy trips and education camps.[115] But these conflicts need not necessarily be seen as evidence that educational actors failed because people remained "fissured into groups" and never managed "to stage the conflict-free Volksgemeinschaft" in the camps.[116] Official camp accounts and other forms of staging community constantly showed a picture of harmonious togetherness, and the analyses of conflicts have been carried out with this in mind, mainly on the basis of reports written by participants immediately after they returned from camp. But these descriptions always described the other participants as members of certain social or regional groups, not as individuals. They did not trace conflicts back to personal but rather to social factors. Thus, ultimately these texts show how much the authors themselves appropriated the communal perspective of the educational actors—especially when they talked about conflicts. The perception of the other participants not as individual persons but as representations of social categories fits within the grammar of one's own communality, which perceived individuality primarily as deviation—and at the same time joined with the underlying intentions of educational actors.

To bring Germans of various social and regional origins together: this is what camp leaders saw—and what was also publicly proclaimed—as their educational contribution to the formation of the national "Volksgemeinschaft." For everyone involved, speculating about the success of these efforts and the degree of communality among participants meant repeatedly and decisively identifying the various origins of participants. "Whether unemployed person, lawyer, or secondary school graduate, all feel it the same way—the good fortune of community. Nobody is looking for anything else at the moment," Heinz Korsch noted in his diary, for example.[117] The perception of difference played a direct part in how one dealt with one's own communality and with the communality that existed among the participants. The agents of the National Socialist education project constantly described the engendering of community as an act of transformation—the education of Germans "from I to we." And yet the concrete efforts to translate ideological models into individual self-images remained trapped in this paradox. References to the social diversity of group members made it possible to sharply highlight one's own communality or the good "camaraderie" within groups, and yet at the same time, this did not abolish but rather reinforced the differences between group members.

The dialectic of communal self-formation, which along with the awareness of one's own embeddedness in communities simultaneously accentuated the differences between its members, meant that communality during the 1930s did not constitute the hoped-for conceptual alternative to individualism, the pursuit of self-interest ascribed to the "liberalist" past.

To be sure, efforts at communal self-formation with the aim of communal integration were based on such an opposition. But they also strengthened the awareness of differences and idiosyncrasies of others and oneself. Thus, communality did not impart the self-understanding of a radically "new personality"; instead, it chiefly provided a special mode for thinking about oneself.

This is also clearly shown in diaries where the effort at communality repeatedly combined with the self-conscious pursuit of personal interests. Consider Inge Thiele, the young gardener who reassured herself of her own communality with her numerous private trips throughout Westphalia, as she also did when accepted into the League of German Girls. In her diary, she also made particular use of her regular attendance at BdM camps to highlight her own embeddedness in a larger community. In 1934, while participating in her BdM group's "Easter trip," she described being at the "flag consecration at the Easter fire" and seeing other fires on the night-time horizon as "the most beautiful experience." She noted, "Young people were standing there as well, tanned German youth. Everywhere the same picture, it makes you joyful and strong thinking about it."[118] As she did here, during camp Thiele frequently assured herself of her awareness of being part of a community and at the same time also stressed that this went hand in hand with "constraint" and "discipline," which were needed for the community to be "held together."[119] In contrast, at the beginning of her account of the trip in spring 1934, she had not stressed the necessity of her own integration: "So, Easter trip! It was always my secret longing to take a haversack on a trip sometime . . . to go sometime for multiple days with a stove and cooking utensils in a singing marching column with a flag and guitar accompaniment, for I felt that is my world, here I will find satisfaction."[120]

As here, Thiele repeatedly made it clear that community was not just about fitting in; it also created opportunities for her to realize her own interests. Weeks earlier, commenting on the home evenings of her BdM group, she had similarly noted, "What interests me, I find there. Politics, free expression, comradely exchange, sports, literature, singing, music, admittedly everything limited because of the small amount of time, but offering all of us support. We now belong together, conversing, enjoying, learning together for a goal: the reconstruction of Germany."[121] In the 1930s, Inge Thiele made an effort at communal self-formation on various occasions. But this by no means conflicted with her personal interests. Although she worked hard at integrating with the collective, this also gave her personal satisfaction.

We see the same sort of thing in other diaries whose authors, despite their efforts at communality, at the same time also used camp stays for private purposes. Karl Leisner, the young theology student whose faith had already repeatedly brought him into conflict with the Nazi regime, did not just view his camp stay during his labor service as an opportunity to purposefully practice communality in the encounter with others. For him, camp was also a time for seeking clarity about his own life path. In the curriculum vitae he had used for registering for his school-leaving exam in 1934, Leisner had already noted that he wanted to join the labor service "to work there in union with the productive youth for my Volk and at the same time test and steady myself for the difficult profession [i.e., the priesthood]."[122] Three years later, this twofold goal still informed his term in the labor service, which he also used to weigh his decision on whether to be a priest. At the end of his service period, when he wrote in his diary that "under no circumstances do I want to be without this time," which had "given" him so much, "above all also self-knowledge," this finding referred, on the one hand, to his having "become very deeply fond of my Volk." On the other hand, however, Leisner also pointed out that "perhaps . . . this deep feeling of compassion [i.e., for the Volk] . . . was one of the most decisive ones (seen in human terms) that actually in the end strengthened the longing for the priesthood so much and led to the final decision and hard-won resolution to take this life path."[123] During his time with the labor service, Karl Leisner, too, purposely joined with the community, but at the same time, he used his stay to pursue private goals that stood in basic conflict with those of the labor service.

In the case of Leisner, we can clearly see the interrelationship between the communality consistently promoted by the educational actors of the Nazi regime and Leisner's private interests, which in the months after the completion of his labor service brought him into more and more conflict with the regime and ultimately into a concentration camp. It illustrates with remarkable clarity what applied in general to the efforts of individual Germans to develop communal self-conceptions and lifestyles—efforts that were sometimes quite intense. Contrary to the aspiration voiced by the regime's repeated public demands, the Nazi education project's models of a communal lifestyle did not lead straightaway to overcoming an individuality based on the pursuit of personal interests. Rather, educational influences and individual practices of self-formation turned communality into a special mode of individual self-contemplation and individual behavior that, along with the awareness of one's own embeddedness, also underscored the idiosyncrasies of individual Germans.

In this respect, the Berlin banker Wolf Busse was not wrong when bitterly noting in his 1934 travel diary that he was not alone in being "egoistic" but that others just did not admit it. And yet this assessment misses the essential point. Efforts at communal self-formation did not, in fact, eliminate the pursuit of one's own interests, even though the underlying models of the Nazi education project often denounced such conduct. Even after 1933, people who made an effort at a communal lifestyle and self-perspective continued to make self-serving decisions. But at the same time, they increasingly brought such decisions into the immediate context of an awareness of group embeddedness and group interests, whether on individual trips or in other situations. Directly following her Easter trip with the League of German Girls, Inge Thiele found herself in conflict with her parents, who because of her father's unemployment were once again asking for financial assistance from their poorly paid daughter. In past months, Thiele had already repeatedly supported her parents, helping pay, for example, for butchering the pig they kept in their garden so they could sell the meat. But this time Thiele did not want to give them anything: "Always just money. Money is what they want from me. And for me it is hardly enough to keep pace with the others, and to stand on the margins again like before?" Although she raised this question in her first entry after having described her Easter trip, she was referring directly to the fact that she was already saving for another trip planned for Pentecost. She answered her own question: "No!" And she continued: "Loveless egoism? Aunt Helga and Uncle Herbert call it healthy egoism!"[124]

As in this case, Thiele repeatedly assessed everyday decisions against the model of a communal lifestyle and asked herself whether she was acting egoistically. She devoted herself quite extensively to this problem when she finished her apprenticeship and voluntarily registered with the labor service. On the one hand, Thiele saw the labor service as a place where communal life was possible in a special way, and this made it worthwhile to participate. "When I listen to the Führer, who wants to give all of us a standardized school for our Volk, then one gladly sacrifices the half year; after all, it is for life," Thiele noted in October 1936. Having personally visited a labor camp in Dortmund, she added this joyful assessment: "Emanating from here is a unique attitude to life, self-discipline, and service!"[125] On the other hand, she was pressured, particularly by her parents, to earn money instead, which also seemed important to the young gardener. "Often my mood is such that I actually want a rejection so that I look for a different job somewhere," she noted indecisively in early December 1936 while waiting for the labor service to respond.[126] In February 1937, after the question had finally been resolved with much to-and-fro, Thiele noted, "Rarely have I been this indecisive." Once more, she summarized the conflict that had preoccupied her in recent months: "Two worlds intersected, the community of the labor service, which I had so desired, and earning money, which I so need."[127]

By no means did all Germans in the 1930s deal with such thoughts. Only a fraction of them began thinking about their embeddedness within the collective and what that meant for their personal lifestyle and self-contemplation in light of the demands for the "communal man" propagated by the National Socialist education project. The occasions on which individuals asked themselves these questions varied, although the education and training camps played an especially important role. Time and again, contemporaries deliberately sought them out as places where they could work on their communal self-formation. How they did so is shown, in particular, by diaries that were created in the education camps and that did not simply report on efforts at personal communality but whose form and content were also strongly shaped by these efforts. Taken as a whole, they document how the attempt to make community the basis for personal ways of life and self-conceptions was very much determined by the effort to consciously integrate oneself into the collective and its structures, whereby individuality was associated above all with deviation from the whole.

Even though the practices of communal self-contemplation that emerged from the interaction between camp participants and the educational efforts of camp leaders aimed at having the individual recede behind the collective, communality in this form could not be seamlessly realized: the visualization of one's own embeddedness in communities at the same time created an intensified awareness of social differences between their members and the idiosyncrasies of individuals. This dialectic prevented the effort to achieve a communal lifestyle and self-perspective from actually overcoming the pursuit of personal self-interest. At the same time, for these individuals, it made "community" part of their own life management and self-contemplation. Thus, Thiele's ultimate decision to take a new job instead of joining the labor service in 1937 should not be interpreted simply as a sign of insufficient communality. The education project's demand in the 1930s for communality in the concrete living practices of individual Germans was reflected not in the result of her decision but rather in the specific mode in which she thought about it.

2. "I Am in the Best Shape of My Life": The Relationship to One's Body

Bodies and the relationship to one's physique played a prominent role within the National Socialist education project. "If Russian ideologues of the New Man worked on their souls, their German counterparts worked on their bodies to serve the nation," wrote Peter Fritzsche and Jochen Hellbeck, underscoring the central importance of the body in the diverse efforts of the Nazi regime to create the "new man."[128]

This had various reasons. First, using informational events, publications, and specific educational practices, many educational actors of the Nazi regime worked intensely to promote new forms of dealing with one's body as well as a transformed awareness of one's own physicality and to establish them among Germans. Given that the fundamental reconstruction of German society was not supposed to just serve the communal integration of individuals but also ensure their supposed racial hygienic purity and homogeneity, many educational actors firmly viewed the body as a "politicum," for "through his body" the individual was "bound with the total body of his Volk," as pointed out here by Alfred Baeumler, one of the leading theorists of the National Socialist education project.[129] Thus, the creation of a healthy "Volkskörper" (body of the people) was also supposed to be achieved by ensuring that "the individual's bodily care, bodily exercise, and bodily discipline . . . are no longer a matter of a private man who is concerned about his personal well-being"; rather, they were to be redeveloped "under the aspect of the health and strength of the whole": "It is no longer left to the individual, whether he wants to be healthy or not. How high he wants to go in the training of bodily skillfulness is no longer left to his subjective discretion."[130] Nazi physical education was set up to serve collective goals, but this purpose also meant changing the individual's body and body awareness. From the perspective of many actors of the Nazi education project, the "way to the New Man" led specifically via "the self-reform of the body by means of individual bodily practices." For this reason, they attempted to guide people to this reform by conveying information and practical exercises.[131]

Second, underlying this dedication to physical education were notions of the ideal National Socialist body that also more generally dominated the public self-representation of Nazi rule. The Nazi regime visualized its own rule and the utopian ideals of its policies through representations of idealized individual bodies or the staging of masses of bodies, above all in photographs, films, sculptures, pictures, and mass events.[132] Consequently, in the 1930s the populace was "constantly confronted with the iconography of the perfect body," which was supposed to exemplify the "new" Germany.[133] Within the Nazi regime's public policy, the body functioned as an "important carrier of ideology." In this respect, the Nazi regime always described itself with pictures of beautiful, healthy, and strong bodies, "while all kinds of images of the enemy were made palpable in pictures of the imperfect body."[134] The pictorial representations were supposed to attest to and support the attractiveness of the regime but at the same time also "function educationally on the inner pictures of the individual."[135] They formulated a "targeted appeal to the observer," who was supposed to understand them as "instructions on a certain approach to one's own body."[136]

Third, the relationship to one's body was also addressed in many educational contexts that, while not directed at the body itself, still considered the body to be the main starting point for the transformation of individual lifestyles and self-perspectives. With his thoughts on the "educational principles of the völkisch state" in his manifesto *Mein Kampf*, Hitler himself justified a "pedagogical theory of value" that stipulated a "hierarchy of body-character-spirit."[137] National Socialist education basically aimed for a comprehensive "holistic" shaping of the individual but in doing so assigned crucial priority to the body. "Bodily education" is "not a thing in itself," stressed the Reichssportführer (Reich Sports Leader) Hans von Tschammer und Osten, for example. "The body is not the goal but rather the starting point and most important tool of education."[138] In keeping with the basic experience-oriented focus of pedagogy in the 1930s, many educational actors therefore viewed physical education and "bodily exercises" as "general principles of education."[139] Bodily exercises were presented as an "outstanding component of overall education, and, namely, for the youth and adult education of both sexes," which was supposed to lead to "performance ability, resilience, strength of will, and toughness, to courage, decisiveness, and discipline."[140]

Physical education practices therefore did not aim only at the body and the individual's experience of the body. As an outstanding "medium of the educational efforts" of the Nazi regime, the many activities for influencing the body were never only about changing the bodies of the Germans.[141] Rather, by means of their bodies, the regime wanted to shape them politically by having them link bodily conduct and experience with prescribed meanings and models. This was the reason for the body's prominence in the National Socialist education project, but also a central challenge. Thomas Alkemeyer has noted that "the individual was to be formed from the outside inwards," characterizing what he describes as "the very crux" of Nazi physical education, which proceeded from the assumption that "through the adoption of prescribed poses or positions one could induce people to take up certain inner positions."[142] Within the education project, political self-formation was also supposed to mean developing a new consciousness of the body, which in turn would bring about a lifestyle and self-contemplation appropriate to the "new era."

Many historical studies have pursued the ideological notions of the body, as well as the visual representations of the body and specific bodily practices of the 1930s they supported. However, far less attention has been given to the question of the extent to which efforts related to people's bodies brought about the desired self-formation.[143] Although we can reliably estimate the immediate physical consequences for people in the form of "invigoration" and enhanced sportiness,[144] it is much more difficult to determine the education efforts' impact on the body awareness of individuals. This notwithstanding, historians have variously assumed that "in sporting activities that were hardly experienced consciously, the values and norms of the sport were also individually inscribed in the bodies" and that "standards of value" mediated by body images and bodily exercises "were largely received without reflection."[145]

Then again, other authors have been much more skeptical. Barbara Keys, for example, has pointed out that even today "detailed knowledge of precisely how physical exercise affects psychological states is lacking." The results of modern sports psychology, however, primarily indicate that "different forms of physical exercises can have very different psychological effects on participants." Without question, "physical education and sports" were "important elements" for the "popular support" of National Socialism, but, as Keys points out, "claims that physical exercises could be used with precision to reshape not only the human body but human nature as well should be treated with skepticism."¹⁴⁶ Daniel Siemens has likewise noted that the "full-automatic fire in media" of body-related discourses in the 1920s and 1930s did not necessarily need to be read as evidence for their success but could "also conversely [point to] a widespread resistance to new concepts of the body." Therefore, it is necessary to compare "individual bodily experiences . . . with the discourses about physicality."¹⁴⁷

To this end, Siemens himself has called for "a stronger analysis of ego documents,"¹⁴⁸ although at least with diaries of the 1930s this proves to be much more difficult than may appear at first glance. They are much less informative for questions about their authors' physicality than about the communality demanded by the regime. They do not provide particularly good access to the individual body experiences of authors, since diarists did not usually address their own physicality in their daily entries. A striking example is the diary of Wolfgang Scharenberg. For Scharenberg, purposefully a vegetarian and Lebensreform advocate, the body was undoubtedly especially important, even politically. This also repeatedly manifested itself in his diary. For example, when in spring 1934 he learned that a neighbor, after giving birth, had fallen critically ill because of a lack of knowledge about breastfeeding, Scharenberg reported on this in his writings and addressed this problem to the Nazi regime, which after all supposedly paid so much attention to the body. He asked, "Where is the Nazi People's Welfare? Here there would really be something to be done for the improvement of the race, namely, at once and very effectively across the board."¹⁴⁹ Yet he did not write in his diary about the understanding and experience of his own body. His entries frequently touched on the body as a general political problem of the times. But in his diary, he did not reflect on his own physicality.

This was very much the case for many diaries of the 1930s. Their authors spoke often about bodies yet far less about their own body. This makes it much more difficult to pursue Germans' perceptions of their own bodies than to examine their general ideas about the body. Naturally, individual diarists wrote about bodies on various occasions: for example, in connection with diseases or sexual experiences.¹⁵⁰ However, in the 1930s an individual's own physicality broadly and regularly became the subject of daily writing in places where diarists not only took notice, like Scharenberg, of the body images of the Nazi regime but also, unlike Scharenberg, deliberately picked up on educational aspirations with respect to their own body. Thus diaries from this period hardly make it possible to approach the "epoch-specific experiential form of corporality"¹⁵¹ because they do not give expression to approaches to the body that were typical for the time; instead, they mainly give expression to a certain contextually framed approach. For many people, Nazi physical education gave them their first reason to deal with their own physique in their writing. Thus in the diaries of the 1930s, efforts at the political self-formation of one's own body come up more often than other forms of individual physicality. Therefore, they do not allow for a general "investigation of the experience of the body of a bygone time," not even of the Nazi period.[152]

But for the question raised here—namely, about how the models of the Nazi education project were translated into concrete lifestyles and self-images—diaries provide a good source. As in the case of communal self-formation, so too with regard to individuals' relationship to their body; for diarists who worked at finding different ways of interpreting their bodies within the context of the Nazi education project, one can investigate how body-related self-formation occurred and above all which elements of National Socialist ideas of the body they used. In light of the multitude of ways to approach the body and the many actors involved in physical education, it is hardly surprising that, in this field too, various ideological conceptions of the ideal body and "various practices of physical education coexisted in the Third Reich, some of them competing with each other."[153] This was true for body-related self-formation within the framework of the National Socialist education program as well; there were no clear standards that individuals could have adopted from their own experience of the body. Here too, we can only acquire an understanding of the political transformation of individuals' relationship to their own body by closely examining how individuals dealt with the propagated models of personal physicality.

Political Interpretations of One's Own Body

When did diarists in the 1930s actually come to speak about their own body and the educational aspirations addressed to their body by the regime? This basically occurred—hardly surprising at first—in very different contexts and addressed widely different dimensions of personal physicality. In her investigation of early-childhood education in the twentieth century, Miriam Gebhardt, for example, has shown by way of parental diaries that in the 1930s the "implementation of up-to-date scientific care and education . . . [was] anything but smooth." Nonetheless, the practice of education aligned itself with a "concept of a physical ideal" that featured clear parallels with the body images of the Nazi regime, in that this practice too focused on "psychological and bodily robustness, visible strength and resilience."[154] On the basis of a comparably small number of ego documents, Geoffrey Campbell Cocks has drafted theses about contemporary experiences of the body in cases of illness. Where Gebhardt gives greater emphasis to the orientation according to the new models of the Nazi education project, Cocks argues that, in National Socialism's so-called health dictatorship, illness offered people refuge, which they deliberately used to escape collectivism. Physicality in cases of illness was therefore experienced not so much in accordance with ideological categories but rather mainly in private.[155]

Along with childhood education and illness, one can find other occasions in diaries of the 1930s where individual authors came to talk about their relationship to their own bodies: genderedness, sexuality, and age, for example. In particular, we can find written confrontations with one's own body in places where the Nazi regime not only propagated its notions of the ideal body but also worked with specific physical exercises on the transformation of Germans. Above all, sports and "physical education" (Leibeserziehung) provided an occasion for many diarists to record thoughts about their own body. Entries on this subject are found in many diaries—in some cases, sports actually constitute the main reason for diary writing. In this respect, this thematic focus provides a good foundation for pursuing the logics of physical self-formation within the framework of the National Socialist education project. It allows for a more precise understanding of the ways in which propagated body images and pedagogical practices could shape the individual experience of the body in the desired way.

Consider Heinz Korsch, the eighteen-year-old graduate who voluntarily reported for labor service in spring 1933. In his camp diary, which he revised after completing his term of service and rearranged according to subjects, he gave "Sports" a separate chapter, entitled accordingly. Here Korsch collected his diary entries about sports-related practices and especially the sports festivals and competitions he participated in during his term of labor service. He also decorated this chapter—just under twenty pages—with newspaper clippings and added photos that mainly showed him at sports competitions. In the text, Korsch meticulously described the course of the various sports festivals and the associated preparations, in which he himself was sometimes substantially involved. At the same time, he used this chapter to outline his physical condition. "I am in the best shape of my life," Korsch noted in the description of a competition, underscoring his claim with a comparison to his time at school, only a few months in the past, when he was admittedly "thoroughly fit, but mostly overtrained and weakened." Not until he was at the camp did "a quarter year of work create the balance. Now I even have the necessary strength for the throwing practices."[156] Even outside this special chapter, physical exercises frequently provided an opportunity for Heinz Korsch to write about his physique in his diary. "Noticeable the stiffness and inflexibility of most of the comrades. Product of their own lifestyles," he noted, for example, when talking about early-morning exercise while introducing the camp's standardized daily routine. "My critical athlete's eyes miss the healthy average of athletic bodies," Korsch commented, making it clear how very much he perceived and described his own trained body precisely in terms of its difference from other people engaged in sports.[157]

Like Heinz Korsch, other diarists also used their sports activities as an opportunity to deal with their own body in writing. This applied chiefly to adolescents and young adults like Heinz Korsch, and not just because this age group was particularly active in sports. Rather, through its youth organizations, the regime made deliberate efforts to encourage Hitler Youth boys and BdM girls to both engage in sporting activities and also write about physical exercise. In summer 1938, the Reich Youth Leadership published a booklet entitled *Sport-Tagebuch der deutschen Jugend* (Sports diary of the German youth), which was meant to be distributed through local organizations to "every boy and girl within the Hitler Youth."[158] The first page of the sports diary prompted its respective owner to fill out his or her name, address, and organization identifier, while the diary itself basically consisted of preprinted tables for recording sports achievements. Using headings, the recurring tables were each assigned for one year of life, ideally starting at age eleven and continuing until age nineteen. Above the table, body size and body weight were supposed to be entered as at the key dates of April 1 and October 1. The lines of the table provided fields for various sports disciplines (such as running competitions, high jump, long jump, shot put, and endurance swimming) for recording and dating up to four different results, as well as a final column for recording the year's best performance. Under the headings "I Have Participated in the Following Trips" and "I Have Participated in the Following Camps," the booklet also contained some limited space for corresponding remarks.[159]

With its various fields and rubrics, the *Sport-Tagebuch* referred to the requirements for the achievement badges of the German Youngsters and

Young Girls League (starting from age twelve), as well as the Hitler Youth and League of German Girls (starting from age fifteen), explanations for which were appended to the blank tables.[160] As with the sports badge of the SA, which could also be earned by nonmembers, the various achievement badges of the Nazi youth organizations were newly created at the start of National Socialist rule. Meanwhile, the Reich Sports Badge and Reich Sports Youth Badge, which already existing during the Weimar Republic, were inscribed into the new political context by being renamed after 1933. Together these badges were supposed to motivate young people and adults alike to intensify their sports activities. The ideal biography as envisioned by the Nazi regime, which began by joining the German Youngsters or, respectively, Young Girls League and then advanced through the various organizations of the NSDAP, also always included sports requirements, which were marked by annually recurring achievement badges and competitions. Taken as a whole, these requirements were one of the key elements of National Socialist physical education.[161]

The *Sport-Tagebuch der deutschen Jugend*, as well as other so-called achievement books that emerged in connection with the various sports badges in the 1930s and similarly served to record best times and distances in sports, were an important component of this educational practice.[162] They documented the results of sports competitions and formed the basis for issuing achievement badges. Apart from this administrative purpose, logging one's competition results was also supposed to have a self-educating effect. The achievement badge was intended not just as an "incentive" but rather, by means of the achievement book, also "a type of healthy fun against which physical development [could be] measured."[163] Read over the course of time, the *Sport-Tagebuch der deutschen Jugend*, with its entries for weight, size, and annual performance results, documented both the physical growth of its adolescent author and, ideally, his or her increasing fitness and strength. "Enter into this booklet the best sports performances that you achieve in the course of the year," urged Reichsjugendführer (Reich Youth Leader) Baldur von Schirach in the foreword to the *Sport-Tagebuch*. "You will later follow the results of your athletic development with pride and joy."[164] The achievement books were designed to encourage conscious, formative access to one's own body, with the recorded results of one year meant to function as an incentive to achieve better values in the next. "Youth dedicates itself to *performance!*" Schirach proclaimed in the opening of his foreword. He went on to emphasize the connection between the enhancement and documentation of performance: "Already during the first years of Hitler Youth service, every *kid* should himself render account. Get to know your weaknesses and overcome them. You need to know what you have learned on the sports field and turf. Every success inspires you to new achievements."[165]

In contrast to what one might assume from these pithy words, Schirach was addressing a critical and highly controversial point within National Socialist physical education. The Reich Youth Leader conceded that some young people might "perhaps not be able to achieve peak performances" because they lacked natural gifts, but he insisted that through "tough training" they could nonetheless attain their "own best performance."[166] Other actors within the Nazi education project, however, found sports concepts geared "toward 'physical fitness' and the formation of the 'Volksgemeinschaft'" difficult to "reconcile . . . with the achievement principle of competition and club sports based on competition, comparison, and individualization."[167] It was along these lines that the Nazi sports official Bruno Malitz issued the call to fight "liberalism, the liberalist idea in sports," in an influential text in 1933.[168] At the start of National Socialist rule, this led to calls to abolish elite and high-performance sports. Particularly the "tense relationship between high-performance sports and general physical education" showed that the connection between the far-reaching goals of Nazi physical education and the striving for athletic achievement was still problematic.[169] Education practitioners and theorists frequently saw sports geared toward achievements as a salient feature of "liberalistic policy, which [leads] to the striving for records, to unhealthiness in sports, to the destruction of the community's morale for sports."[170] "Political physical education as character training," emphasized Alfred Baeumler, "therefore cannot be based on the purely athletic achievement principle. Rather, one must proceed from a principle external to the purely achievement-related. We see this principle in the politically oriented team."[171]

Nonetheless, the annual numbers of participants in competitions for the various sports and achievement badges of the Nazi regime—events dominated by solo rather than team disciplines—were very high. And these numbers are not alone in suggesting just how important individual performance and the striving for achievement still was for many people and their understanding of the body under National Socialist rule.[172] The descriptions of sports activities in diaries of the 1930s also show how authors linked above all their individual pride and effort to improve performance to sports and physical exercise. Heinz Korsch, for example, after determining in his diary that he was "in the best shape of my life," went on to give a precise account of a sports festival, describing his own achievements in detail and repeatedly comparing them to results of other comrades. "Jensch cannot be beaten in his special field. Puts the *shot* over 11 meters. A bull of a guy . . . pushes me to third place. Participation is always very strong, but the average is definitely missing," he reported on the shot put, for example.

After accounts of the long jump and javelin throwing, his report finally climaxed in an especially detailed description of the high jump competition, in which Korsch soon left the other participants behind. "I am now jumping only by myself, take my time to concentrate. I do 1.73 [meters] cleanly. The 'old man' himself measures. Then he announces: 'height of jump 1.78 meters'—crowd of people," Korsch writes, denoting the large interest of the spectators, which include not only his labor service comrades but also residents invited to the sports festival. Even so, he has "never been as calm as now." Korsch fails the first two attempts at the new height, "then carefully up and over . . . and the 'old man' bellows again: 'Jumped clear. Height—1.78 meters.' 1.83 meters. Measure out the approach and takeoff, concentrate myself. 'By thunder, you're supposed to clear your own height?' It is eerily still. The liftoff is good, but, in the rotation, at first I think I've lost and just hollow my back (scissors jump . . .). Cleared it totally cleanly. I try 1.88 meters once, then give up, am too tired. It is my nicest sports victory," wrote Korsch, finishing his report on the sports festival. With its simultaneous emphasis on the audience's reception and his body control, the report leaves no doubt that he greatly prized his victory and attributed it to himself and his trained body.[173] For confirmation, he pasted a newspaper article, the passage about his high jump victory duly marked, into the diary next to his report.

How much other diarists viewed sports as an expression of their own physical ability and body control is evident not only from similar descriptions in other diaries but also from the way authors in their private diaries frequently adopted the practice of precisely logging their achievements as suggested by the achievement books. By no means did this need to be as puristic as in the case of Doris Becker, born in 1924, who time and again punctiliously logged the results of her sports competitions: "Women's Leader Triathlon in Durlach in the open-air gymnasium. Emma Gerlach and Mimi declined. Three competition types: 75-meter sprint, slingshot throw, and high jump.—Sprint = 10.9 seconds—Throw = 24 meters—High

Jump = 1.10 meters. Total points: 1887."[174] Around the same age as Becker, Inge Thiele, the gardener from Solingen, joined her transcriptions of sports accomplishments with unabashed expressions of personal pride—even though her diary also includes this copied statement from the NSDAP sports official Bruno Malitz: "Being a sportsman" does not mean "achieving brilliant victories over others" but rather working "tenaciously and diligently on yourself."[175] With regard to the BdM sports badge, however, Thiele nonetheless noted not only that she was "internally happy that I am so far in this and everything worked out" but also that she wanted to be "with the first [badge] wearers in Solingen." And alongside the "very good average achievements" on her part, she situated the results of a friend, who "still does not yet always reach the minimum."[176]

Anton Gloeckner, who completed the tests for the Hitler Youth achievement badge for the first time in 1935, did not just note the results of his sports tests in the official achievement book but also frequently used them as an opportunity to talk about his personal sports activities and successes in his private diary. "This morning at 10:00 o'clock we had to muster in the market square. For the achievement badge we had to do shooting and the mallet throw. Those who had not yet done the pack march actually had to start at 5:00!" he noted in early September 1935, for example. As in this case, his entries always illustrated how membership in the Hitler Youth obliged him to engage in sports. But they also show how personally important these tests were for him. "Target throwing gave me little concern," he went on. "But the shooting at the Molkenkur shooting range lay on me like a nightmare. Results: Target throwing: 5 throws, 3 hits. Shooting: 5 shots—total (shots placed!) 35 rings. Including an 11-ring shot placement! I was not a little proud of it! Half failed!"[177] When it came to the oft-discussed tests for the achievement badge, Gloeckner more than once highlighted his athletic achievements and the satisfaction they gave him. And when in late November, having completed the tests, he sent his "achievement book into the oh-so-long official channel," he summarized again: "Hopefully I will get the badge by Christmas! I am not a little proud of it!"[178]

In individual cases, written monitoring of one's own athletic achievements could also become a key inspiration for keeping a private diary, as in the case of a school student from Württemberg who in her Nazi youth organization was intensely involved in aquatic sports and kept track of it in her diary. Written in a blank notebook, her "Swimmer's Diary" consisted almost exclusively of descriptions of competitions and her swim times in competitions and training. "At the 1938 Bann sport meet I swam in a competition for first time, namely, in the young girls' 50 breaststroke in 1:08 minutes. That I came among the 'also ran' did not annoy me. And so at the 1939 Bann sport meet, which again had its aquatic sports function in the Tailfingen outdoor pool, I started in the young girls' 50 meters breaststroke. And I won in 52 seconds. My toughest rivals were Lisa Goetz and Lotte Enzler. So this was my first victory," the author wrote, summarizing her previous swimming career in the beginning of her diary and thus setting the focus on the improvement of her personal physical performance and successful competitions right from the outset.[179]

Individual pride in one's own performance and body can even be observed in entries in which diarists reported on team competitions and other collective exercises—areas that, according to critics of the pursuit of athletic achievement, were better than individual disciplines for conveying values such as commitment to the community and camaraderie. In July 1934, for example, Rudolf Briske extensively reported in his diary from the labor service about a relay race in which his Groß-Mutz labor camp competed against a neighboring camp. "Hilgen, an ADW sports director, Noeske, and I were, so to speak, race management," Briske wrote, identifying his role in the relay race at the beginning of his report.[180] He then gave a detailed account of the "preparations . . . that is, the exact division of the route, the runners, etc. The route was 40 km, four times around a country-road triangle, there were 100 men running. . . . We allocated: a few 800- and 600-meter runners, most of them 400 meters, and a few short-distance ones. Everyone received a slip with a number, name, route, distance from ___ to etc., because you always need to reckon with maximum stupidity. The route was quite a good country road with a little gradient, which is where the short-distancers were deployed." By comparison, the actual description of the race was rather brief: "Our runners were out front right from the start, and with one exception we remained so until the end. Nonetheless an exciting struggle in which everyone gave his utmost, for our lead lay between 50 and 500 meters, which is not much for such a long route. We won with a lead of around 200 meters. . . . Result: Groß-Mutz, 40 km in 1.49 and a bit."

However, what best reveals Briske's desire to emphasize his own particular part in the group's achievement is not the comparative weighting of the preparation and race itself but his final comments. The division of labor in the organization of the race may have conformed almost ideally to the educational model that served as an alternative to the pursuit of individualist athletic achievement, yet Briske explicitly pointed out that "apart from faultless runners, the victory . . . is essentially thanks to good organization; we gave everyone the distance he was capable of, whereas the opponent had everyone run the same distance."[181]

Briske's awareness of the obvious tension in the entry between individual achievement and collective success is illustratively suggested by a diary entry a few weeks later that reported on daily work, which in the labor service was used along with sports as an instrument for physical education.[182] In late September 1934, Briske transferred back to a work site where he had previously helped dig a ditch. Nothing about this job had changed in the meantime, but the process certainly had. "New is: everyone is given a fixed section that he needs to manage," Briske noted after a few days of work. He was uncertain about how he should feel about this arrangement compared to the previous one, where the entire work troop had to collectively complete a certain section of the ditch per day. "Advantage: much more is accomplished than before. Disadvantage: community is not promoted, camaraderie undermined, since everyone just thinks of himself," Briske explained in his diary. Nonetheless, while Briske otherwise worked very hard on his own communality, here the young man pointed out, "Since from an economic standpoint something must be accomplished, and the joy of working increases a lot with individual work, I would like to decide in favor of it [the new rule] after all." As if to make it clear that he was referring to no one but himself and his own performance ambition, Briske expanded this assessment by reviewing workdays of the past: "Gradually one figures out how to accomplish a lot and finish early without wasting too much strength. There is no boredom, working is much more fun than forever standing around . . . like before."[183]

In emphasizing their own physical accomplishments, many people who wrote about dealing with their bodies within the context of the National Socialist education project were certainly not fulfilling the expectations addressed to them by many of the Nazi educational actors. These actors expected sports and work, in particular, to be linked to community and integration instead of individual pride. Even so, an achievement-oriented experience of the body did not mean the rejection of political aspirations for one's body. Such a perception of the body was actually congruent with images of the body drawn up by other educational actors with demands for performance improvement—for example, by Baldur von Schirach. Moreover, a deliberate focus on one's body within the framework of the

Nazi education project also found expression in reports about athletic accomplishments in general, in that many Germans felt the need to shape their physique. The example of Rudolf Briske's zeal for work clearly shows the degree to which the individual's private interests frequently combined with the regime's efforts at education. Even though his entry strongly gave voice to personal ambition, at the same time one of the main goals of work-related physical education was to impart body control to labor service participants. By means of body control, they could learn to achieve "the best possible work performance with the least physical exertion," as stated in a 1938 manual for German youth in the Reich Labor Service.[184] Briske's comment about understanding more and more how he could "accomplish a lot and finish early without too much waste of strength" was informed not only by personal pride and ambition but also by body-related models of the National Socialist education project.

Plurality of Body Experiences

As in the case of Rudolf Briske, when other writers approached their bodies, they often used individual values and principles of National Socialist physical education and its idealized images of the body. Thus Nazi educational actors were actually quite successful in conveying ideological notions with bodily activity as intended.

Yet diaries also show that different individuals could link very different ideas and experiences to similar physical activities. Whereas Briske in fall 1934 in his diary linked excavation work less to communality than to effective body control, letters sent around the same time by Wolfram Kroll, born in 1909, to his fiancée expressed, in particular, the experience of camaraderie that came from heavily working the terrain. In this case, employed as a business clerk at a Hamburg spice mill, Kroll was not writing his girlfriend from an education camp where work was also supposed to convey communality. Rather, he was just starting to clear and prepare the property on which the two of them wanted to build their home. Their relatives viewed the project with skepticism, describing "our goal as reaching too high," as Kroll wrote to his fiancée. But at the same time, he emphasized to her that "man, as long as he is young and able to do so because of his work wages, sets himself tasks that sometimes appear insurmountable." In this sense, private life was "exactly like the Third Reich," which also "previously was a goal and after the takeover of power was also not finished overnight, but rather the completion was set back again into a future as the greatest goal."[185]

This comparison was not the only place where the letters of Wolfram Kroll reveal how much he and his fiancée were trying to "live the New Man" the way "the two of us have always vowed."[186] It also came through in his descriptions of working the terrain. "It is a liberating feeling, this work, I cannot even describe it to you," Kroll reported after he and a friend began by setting up a fence around the property. "This sound of the saw and the tension of the muscles, then digging again and the heaving blows of the axe. . . . Those were the beats in this duet," Kroll raved in his letter about the hard work. It had him "thinking involuntarily about Lersch or Bröger," two working-class authors with high print runs during National Socialist rule, and Kroll enclosed one of their poems with his letter. But he also thought about his helpful friend, "this camaraderie toward each other," and the "satisfaction that he too finds in the work."[187]

In his next letter, Kroll emphasized more clearly that the "beautiful work on our land" revealed to him a "deep profound meaning in working and being connected to the soil," which he saw particularly in the communality he experienced through the work. "It is the deep meaning of the work. I believe it is the start from the very beginning, this clearing and plowing. Perhaps it is also the honesty that confronts you in this work and that, quite especially for me, becomes consciousness, in contrast to my office work. Far from any economic expedience and going far beyond that which one calls striving for the future and the family. This work is truly furthering community."[188]

Heinz Korsch, who in his diary from the Reich Labor Service reported not only about sports but also copiously about the physical work, focused above all on the opposition between body and spirit—this is already apparent in the earlier quote from Kroll. This dichotomy underlay the education project in general, with its orientation toward experiential pedagogy, and the attempt to inscribe ideological models by means of physical education did this more specifically. The "new man" was supposed to emerge not from reflection but rather from physical activity. Heinz Korsch thought about this principle during his work at the labor service camp, which consisted primarily of breaking apart and removing boulders that were strewn across the meadows and pastures around the camp. It was difficult but mindless work during which one could "so nicely entertain ruminations and thoughts, which is not possible with other work."

This statement was meant ironically, because rumination was for Korsch a central problem, one that he felt affected him and the other secondary high school graduates in the camp "who cannot refrain from *thinking*." A "good labor service man *is not allowed to think*," Korsch noted, formulating an ideal of physical labor that took up models of the education project and that he himself tried to follow. It had been especially difficult during the first few weeks, he reported in his diary: "One can probably concentrate on the work for one to two hours, but then an irresistible rumination frustrates productivity. I cannot with moronic happiness carry out the same movement for many hours (this happens to everyone who previously was not physically but rather mentally drilled)." Thus, for secondary high school graduates the "'spice' of work" lay "not in physical exertion, as widely presumed, but rather in the inability to mentally disconnect." Yet for him there had "also [been] in this ... an '*upward* trend'": "After four months of labor service, I am blunted and acquiescent enough so that I can pound hardcore or gravel or carry handbarrow after handbarrow with stones to the construction site for hours."[189]

In contrast, other people saw physical activity as a "glorious school of the body" in which the "entire corpus is thoroughly trained."[190] We see this in the case of Anton Gloeckner, for example. After passing his tests for the Hitler Youth Achievement Badge in fall 1935, he joined the local sports club the following spring so as to "strengthen my body so that I become a good sportsman and later do not fail the test for the officer career path."[191] His decision reflected a speech Adolf Hitler gave on the Day of National Labor just a few days earlier on May 1, 1936. Commenting on the speech in his diary, Gloeckner had noted, "Three demands: be willing to sacrifice! Be strong in character! Be hard!"[192] To this end, in Olympic year 1936 he completed not only the Hitler Youth Achievement Badge again but also the Reich Youth Sports Badge and various club competitions, which he still proudly related to his own performance but also to the goal of strengthening his body. "Now the beautiful summer is over and it is getting cold. Two weeks ago we did the club championships again. 1500 meters 4.46 minutes; 100-meter hurdles 16 seconds. Improved once again," Gloeckner noted in late September in his diary, looking back over the past few months, which had been filled with sports. Looking ahead, he added, "Over the winter I want to strengthen and steel my body."[193]

"Hardness" and "self-mastery" also often figured as values for diarists who reported less about their enthusiasm for sports than about chicanery, drills, and physical duties. In letters to his parents, for example, Hans Stelzer*, born in 1917, was by no means passionate about the obligatory physical activities he had to carry out in the labor service in spring 1936. "I thought I was a monkey's uncle when yesterday at 4:30 the whistle blew to get up," Stelzer began one of his letters of April 1936, which reported in detail on the chicanery of early-morning exercises (Frühsport), which they now just called "freezing sports" (Friersport) at camp. "As I became properly awake, I noticed I was already in gym and sports clothes and chasing after the person in front like a wild forest donkey. It was still pitch dark and in the wild running to and fro one usually ran into objects that were harder than our skull. Now and then someone also went flying and immediately always two and three on top."[194] But at the same time, Stelzer did not reject per se the service's physically demanding and painful obligations. "Just don't have any worries and doubts and anxieties and migraines and devil knows what else," he admonished his parents in a later letter. "Our era simply demands steel-hard men, ironclad in internal and external bearing. Firmly clenched my teeth, worked, and did even more than required."[195]

Understood this way, labor service with its physical hardships was admittedly unpleasant but meaningful and necessary. It was no coincidence that a few days later, after describing the morning run through the forest, Stelzer explicitly emphasized that he and his comrades had since become "accustomed" to the early-morning exercises "and already no longer think anything of them."[196] He also invariably commented in much same way on physical hardships in other contexts but then also pointed out that they had their positive side: "Then at 6:00 to the construction site, where we then toil in the ditch until 12:00. The ditch must be finished by this time, otherwise there is overtime! Recently I had violent back pain (the others have it now), but I clenched my teeth, continued shoveling, even though I wanted to scream with every throw, and now I no longer feel anything. 'In the ditch' means for us the same as 'in the bone grinder.' Hopefully we will get different work soon. We are certainly becoming tough in the process—it can't do any harm."[197]

Inge Thiele, too, extolled her sports and other physical activities because of their toughening effect. At the 1935 Reich party congress of the NSDAP when Hitler formulated his well-known challenge to the German youth, Thiele enthusiastically took it up in her diary. "At the Nuremberg party congress the Führer made a striking statement on how he wants the youth to be: 'lithe and lissome, sleek as greyhounds, tough as leather, hard as Krupp steel!' I want and must become like that. Führer, we understand you!"¹⁹⁸ But unlike Stelzer, Thiele did not associate this ideal with ruggedness and falling into line but rather saw it more as a healthy, natural lifestyle. "How beneficial it is to freely surrender your limbs to the bitter forest air," she had already noted in spring 1934 when describing BdM activities. "Everything to improve the health of the youth. Sissification must be thoroughly extirpated. Steeled, resilient people are the foundation pillars of the state."¹⁹⁹ And Thiele also aspired to achieve this by taking care of her body. "I want to remain healthy and become very old doing so," she noted a few weeks later in her diary. "Make the latent powers of nature useful to me, let the sun heal injuries that have occurred, clean nourishment, etc."²⁰⁰ And in fact Thiele's efforts at the self-formation of her own body, which she felt was still growing, did not just include her sports activities. She also tried in other ways to lead a healthy life and not become a "citified person."²⁰¹

The ameliorative aspiration of National Socialist physical education also made physical activity quite meaningful from the perspective of older diarists and could direct their attention to their body.²⁰² The Hamburg civil registry employee Werner Kramp, who rarely discussed his body in his diary, talked about it in greater detail for the first time in winter 1933–1934, when, "after certain passing pain symptoms in the back, in the side above the pelvic bone," he had other "still persistent ones in the diaphragm and lungs." When the doctor only diagnosed "pain from muscle strain," probably from carrying a heavy suitcase a few days earlier, Kramp recorded in his diary the "not very pleasing finding that one is entirely unaccustomed to physical activity." His additional comments illustrate that this impression was directly linked with the public promotion of a different kind of physicality. Thus Kramp observed who among his acquaintances, for example, "Alph. Maler (68 years, senior educational counselor), still takes part in gymnastic exercises" or has "gone to the SA" where he regularly does athletics. "In the interest of my health, I probably ought to do something similar," Kramp concluded in his diary, but then he noted at length all of the bad things that he "hears about the SA service," which was a "waste of time" and "unbearable" and which he therefore refused to join even for the sake of improving his personal health.²⁰³

The diaries and letters of Rudolf Briske, Wolfram Kroll, Heinz Korsch, Anton Gloeckner, Hans Stelzer, Inge Thiele, and Werner Kramp each show in their own way how Germans began dealing with their body within the framework of the National Socialist education project and thus took on values and interpretations that educational actors explicitly wanted to convey. People experienced physical activity as domesticating their body and spirit, as expressing their communality, as enhancing their physical capabilities, as increasing their endurance, or as improving their health—in accordance with various images of the body and physical education practices.

This by no means fully outlines the spectrum of individual bodily experience in the 1930s. But this diversity already indicates that the values specifically associated with the body did not emerge from the educational practices themselves. Rather, they were fundamentally dependent on the individual interests and needs of the respective writer. With his efforts at unthinking labor, Heinz Korsch perpetuated the separation between secondary high school graduates and other labor service participants that strongly shaped his overall perception of camp.[204] Anton Gloeckner worked on strengthening his body precisely because after finishing school he wanted to become a Wehrmacht officer and was worried about the qualifying examination. "I want to become an officer in antitank defense," he noted in his diary in spring 1936. "If only the athletic ability is enough!!"[205] And having concluded that working on the land for his future was "truly furthering community," Wolfram Kroll went on to say that it was "precisely this garden work" that helped him "get over the gray everyday routine" and endure the dismal work he did on business days.[206]

While educational actors schematically assumed that Germans would link ideological notions to their experiences of the body solely through physical actions, the diary of Inge Thiele clearly shows instead that this connection depended deeply on the individual's respective needs, interests, and experiences. Very few diarists in the 1930s dealt as intensely in their writing with the political interpretation of their own body as did the young gardener. Thiele repeatedly vowed that she and her sisters wanted to live life "as just natural people," emphasizing how she was "drawn to the soil, to land and nature, to shed this urban whitewashing, to throw off fashionable clothes like ballast, that is who we are."[207] As late as summer 1936, she proudly declared that a friend who was "too much accustomed to sated, comfortable bourgeois life" and, in Thiele's opinion, should live "more for the benefit of her health and less genteelly," had called her a "picture of health and sportiness." Thiele's ideal of how to deal with one's body in a healthy and natural way—a way "bought with deprivations, etc."—was filled with countless ideological terms and figures of thought that were intrinsic to the National Socialist physical education program. But at the same time, it also conformed to her situation in life as a gardener's apprentice with a meager income in the comparatively rural outskirts of Solingen.[208]

However, in spring 1937, having decided after long deliberation against joining the labor service,[209] she started a new job in Kassel, where she now earned more and worked in what to her seemed an unmatched urban environment. This had an immediate impact on how she dealt with her body. On learning at her new workplace that "I now earn 40 marks," she noted that she "almost threw herself around the neck" of her new boss, "so surprised was I with joy, all kinds of nice things I could buy myself were already fluttering before me."[210] Indeed, during the next week she plunged enthusiastically into the consumerism of an urban life. "I need to have that many things if I want to be more or less presentable," she noted barely one month later, reporting time and again in the following weeks about buying fashionable clothes and trying a new hairstyle—"perhaps even the now-so-modern Olympia curl."[211] "My life is now actually very different from what it was in Solingen; there I placed too little value in clothes," she finally determined in fall 1937.[212]

As she became part of an urban life that she had previously rejected as unhealthy, statements such as those made just weeks earlier, which still promoted a healthy and natural way of life, increasingly disappeared from Thiele's diary. She would speak about her body far less often than in years past, yet without giving up the aspiration for a healthy life. As late as January 1939, she seemed satisfied to have "brought my body healthily into the 25th year."[213] But the diary entries no longer reflected her earlier understanding of healthiness, which had been so closely tied to a rural and natural way of life. In late October 1937, after taking a trip for her garden center into Kassel's surrounding forests to cut down fir trees, she noted in her diary, "We drove through crooked narrow villages. I would not like to live there, they lay there so dead. There is something to city life after all, so familiar; one drives back again into the light-filled city with the feeling of home."[214] And one year later, when she took a bicycle trip through the surroundings villages again, she now found the "natural" life in the countryside entirely inconceivable: "How must these people all live, I have to think, far from the bright big city?"[215]

With its specific practices of physical education and the propagation of its own ideas of the ideal body, the National Socialist education project accomplished more than merely the athleticizing of individual bodies. By providing interpretive models and categories, it also managed to motivate certain individuals to confront their physicality more intensely, as per the far-reaching aspirations of education theory. In its endeavor to convey political values, Nazi physical education could be quite successful. But contrary to the hopes of Nazi education theorists and practitioners and the presumptions of historians, this success did not come from the physical activity and the associated lived experiences themselves.

Instead, as shown by the diaries of the 1930s, the project mainly succeeded in cases where individuals concentrated on their bodies as part of their personal political commitment and could link ideological conceptions of the body to their own respective life situations and individual needs, interests, or experiences. As with the Nazi education project in general, efforts at body-related self-formation combined the educational measures of the regime with the existing physicality of the respective persons. Not even by way of the physique could educational actors of National Socialism "inscribe" ideological value propositions and interpretations "into the body," even when people made efforts on their own accord to engage in the political self-formation of their physicality.[216]

Body and Race

Looking at National Socialist physical education reveals something applicable to the Nazi education project as a whole: even under the conditions of the Nazi dictatorship, the political formation of individual lifestyles and self-perceptions remained largely dependent on individual Germans. But with regard to the contemplation and formation of an individual's own body, this finding takes on a certain specificity. Not all values and conceptions of the body that were supposed to be conveyed through educational models and practices were equally compatible with individual practices of formation and contemplation.

Thus, it should not by any means be understood as a coincidence that the intensely propagated concept of "race" and its associated categories were seldom used—or, more precisely, were used only in a very specific way—in efforts related to the political self-formation of the individual's own body. Yet representations of the body and body practices were very important for the regime's many different racial policy measures. Since the establishment of the category of "race" as a scientific concept in the eighteenth century, it had been defined by means of physical features.[217] The features used to establish a person's "racial quality" admittedly changed many times in the nineteenth and early twentieth centuries. But even in the 1930s, it was precisely the individual body that was supposed to function "as the sign for 'racial' belonging."[218] Educational actors worked with corresponding intensity to popularize the concepts and categories of racial science, which Germans were to use to racially interpret their own and other bodies. National Socialist physical education was also concerned with educating individuals in the "racial-physiognomic evaluation of the body," whereby the body's "racial quality" was supposed to be identified by its external appearance.[219]

Especially significant in this regard were the heavily illustrated books by Hans F. K. Günther. Günther was one of the most popular researchers of race, and his books were often used not only as training material but also as templates and starting points for many other publications of the education project.[220] Already in publication since the 1920s, Günther's works not only aimed at marking the difference between "Jews" and Aryans" but also outlined a more comprehensive "racial knowledge of the German Volk." They presented a differentiated classification model that identified six different "racial types" in the "German language region" and illustrated them with photos: "Northern," "Western" "Eastern, "Eastern Baltic," "Phalian," and "Dinaric." The "Jewish" race was not counted among the "German" races. The pictures were supposed to provide an "iconographic model for the 'racial' evaluation of the body" and imprint themselves "as iconographic memories of the various 'racial types' in the memory of the observer."[221] This was the way that many pedagogical texts of the 1930s tried to provide a guide for "racially knowledgeable seeing and understanding."[222] Based on photographs taken directly from Günther or following from his pictures, lesson materials tried to teach what one could "search for and find in a man's face when looking at him."[223] This was supposed to achieve the "awakening and development of the ability" to independently apprehend "the specific type of man in his main features and to evaluate this type according to its significance in the organic structure of the German Volksgemeinschaft."[224] At the same time, the pedagogical texts repeatedly pointed out that this required practice. Thus, a book aimed at teachers suggested giving "children the task of observing the Jew outside in life" and to have "these observations entered in the newly designed 'Jew notebook.'"[225]

"Günther's classification and the associated 'race portraits' became a solid part of school education and training in Nazi organizations," and other practices (related to sports education, for example) were also supposed to contribute to "racially conscious self-education."[226] But even so, the categories provided for the evaluation of bodies hardly had any impact on what we can see in diaries as efforts at the political self-formation of a person's body. Naturally, the values adopted by Germans from the options provided by the education project were often closely connected with the Nazi regime's racist picture of the world. *Performance* and *hardness* were terms directly associated with the social Darwinist assumption of a struggle between various peoples and races. Health as a category was also always linked to notions of a "Volksgemeinschaft" made healthy through racial homogenization and of a person's associated obligation to cultivate his or her own racial qualities. In this respect, looking at parental diaries under National Socialism, Miriam Gebhardt writes with good reason that "even if the word 'Aryan' does not occur . . . the physical attributions sometimes attested to a corresponding body of ideas."[227]

Nonetheless, it is significant that the body-related categories of racial studies hardly show up in the diaries of the 1930s, and when they do, this happens above all in a very specific context. Such concepts appear in diaries mainly as the subjects of lectures, training courses, or schoolwork that their authors were dealing with voluntarily or out of necessity. Born in 1918, Henriette Weiss*, for example, came to talk about the racial studies concepts of the Nazi regime in an entry in her diary when reporting at length on a "political training evening for the assistant's exam," which dealt with the difference between "Germans" and "Jews."[228] The doctor Walter Lindemann reported in his diary about giving lectures for the SA in 1934 on "hereditary and racial studies," noting too that the laws of heredity are "also indeed very important and their strict observance must be one of the foundational pillars of the National Socialist state."[229] Even so, in his diary he spoke about racial studies only in relation to his lectures. This was likewise the case for the teacher and SA member Wilm Hosenfeld, born in 1895. In late 1938, while commenting on the importance of biology classes, he too emphasized that the new knowledge of racial studies should not be confined to "theoretical-scientific understanding" but needed to "have practical implications for human dos and don'ts."[230] But he also did not combine his plea with concrete actions. At least in his diary, where Hosenfeld reflected intensely on himself and his everyday life, the categories of racial studies had no relevance. Only in a single entry in fall 1938 did he record brief comments on "racial care," which referred, however, to the political program of the Nazi regime and gave his assessment of the matter.[231] As in other diaries of the 1930s, for Hosenfeld, the terminology of racial studies remained a set of alien scientific categories that he did not use with reference to his own body or the bodies of other persons.

Nor did Inge Thiele come to speak about racial studies knowledge until the summer of 1934, when she reported on an "interesting lecture" in the League of German Girls. "My brain is immediately receptive to all research work. The Jewish question was dealt with and the racial mixing of the German tribes [Volksstämme]. I was able to follow and even add things and was allowed to ask questions; I love lectures then, especially if it [sic] is not set up like in school."²³² Even though Thiele strongly emphasized that she understood the racial studies lecture well, in her diary she did not bring this learning to bear on her regular dealings with her body. Not until September 1935 did the concept of race reappear in her diary—namely, on the occasion of the passing of the Nuremberg Laws. Other diaries also used *race* in the context of antisemitic statements and to mark the difference between Jews and non-Jews, but in this context, they did not use it for the concrete perception of bodies. Neither did statements about how a person looked play a role in describing Jews or in clarifying whether a person was Jewish, nor did the term *Aryan* form a category that diarists used to describe themselves in the 1930s. The latter was used almost exclusively in connection with the Aryan certificate, with the Aryan paragraph, and in its negation as *non-Aryan*—thus, it was used when determining the boundary between Jews and non-Jews but not when reflecting on one's own physicality.

In contrast, diary entries that firmly operated with racial studies categories when dealing with the body are found extremely rarely and really only among a specific group of persons. The youth Kurt Frackmann, for example, who wrote his diary for his own political transformation and in summer 1935 described his "life goal" as becoming a "firmly consolidated personality" and serving "Adolf Hitler and the German Volk with all abilities," reported in fall 1934 about getting to know a family "through my business activity". He noted that "despite—or precisely because of?—the only superficial acquaintance," the family made "a good impression on me. The woman large, slender, and blond, a typical Nordic appearance, pushes me again a little bit in the direction of that Nordic type of woman. The children, light blond, spoke a beautiful clear German. The man seems to be an Eastern Balt, speaks Russian, Polish, and French."²³³

Similar discussions also appear in the diary of Wilhelm Bollmann*. "I am proud of these two children, for they are dutiful people, big and strong," he wrote, portraying his own offspring at the beginning of his entries.

"Elizabeth is a calm, well-balanced person like her mother (Phalian-Nordic). Also like her mother externally! Werner is lively, downright Nordic with a dark element like his mother, but otherwise with my face and my body-build."[234] And writing a few months later about an acquaintance, he noted that she was "gorgeous. Large, Nordic, a fine person. I like her and her husband."[235] But Wilhelm Bollmann also differed from most diarists of the 1930s because of his proximity to the Nazi regime and the great lengths to which he went to live according to its ideological principles. Born in 1896, the trained locksmith had already joined the National Socialist movement in the 1920s, and after Hitler's appointment as Reich chancellor, he made a career in the NSDAP. He had become the mayor of a small locality in the Münster region but since 1934 had worked chiefly in the Westphalia/North Gau training office, and in the late 1930s he directed the Schloss Nordkirchen Gau Leadership School. Bollmann was himself an agent of the Nazi education project and called for the propagation of a racial physicality; assisting in the "proper education and support of our Volk" filled him with pride.[236]

In that their political engagement was also supposed to find expression in their private life, Bollmann and Kurt Frackmann had a specific personal interest in a racial reading of the body. Thus even these diary entries ultimately indicate the extent to which ideological aspirations and someone's concrete ways of life had to merge for people to adopt the regime's ideological concepts. And even though these entries used racial studies categories to describe individual bodies, ultimately they too show that they basically remained scientific categories. In both diaries, the quoted entries remained largely isolated. Kurt Frackmann never used the categories in any other entry. Wilhelm Bollmann described tangible bodies with concepts from racial studies in only a handful of other places. Moreover, in each of these entries—as in the quoted passages—he took on the (quasi-scientific) role of an observer.

Ferdinand Beier, a lawyer and notary born in 1878 who lived in Coesfeld during the 1930s, accentuated this observer position in the single entry where he came to speak explicitly about the categories of racial science. "Since one now lives in the year 1938 and ... has read his Günther, one carries out racial observations," he noted in a long report about a Strength through Joy trip to Tyrol, intended above all as a skiing trip. "Along with Dinarics with Nordic elements, Tyrol types, the freedom fighters and hunters of the Defregger pictures, one sees people with a strong Eastern element.

Our innkeeper and his wife are such types in whom the Eastern aspect is strongly represented," Beier noted, seeing here an explanation for what he felt were unsatisfactory meals. "Unfortunately, the racial doctrine that states that the Eastern person has a strong savings and acquisition drive proves true, because for the ___ RM that they received for every KdF traveler, our innkeeper and his wife provided a meal for which the profit is large but the food very frugal."[237]

Similarly, in the only entry in which he used racial studies categories, Rudolf Briske, who in his diary from the labor service was intensely concerned with political self-formation, explicitly noted that he was "conducting racial studies." Here Briske summarized "observations" he made over a longer period about the various troops at the camp, which he thought he was "able to explain racially." "The two main races are Nordic and Eastern: first platoon predominantly Nordic, second platoon as well, third platoon mostly Eastern," Briske explained at first (concealing his own so-called racial status as half-Jew with the adverb *predominantly*). He went on to interpret various phenomena with these categories in mind: "Washing: every time after work we shower. The entire platoon. But one rarely sees anyone from the third platoon in the shower. Conclusion: the Nordic race is more for cleanliness."[238] As if writing a research diary, Briske organized his recorded observations according to various phenomena.

The contrast between this entry and Briske's confrontations with his body elsewhere in his camp diary pretty much showcases the fundamental logic of body-related self-formation within the National Socialist education program. In the 1930s, Rudolf Briske and other individuals drew on the disseminated images of the ideal body and on a corresponding perception of the body to work at the political self-formation of their own bodily experience. This occurred primarily in connection with physical exercises that various Nazi educational actors hoped would contribute to the political transformation of Germans. In this respect, the attempt to convince individuals to link bodily experience with ideological interpretations that corresponded to propagated models of individual life management and self-contemplation was thoroughly successful. But this connection did not arise directly from physical activity but rather remained largely dependent on the interests of the individuals and their experiences of the body. Rudolf Briske could tie the experience of his performance capacity to athletic activities and to his work at the labor service camp, and this enabled him to integrate both his personal interests and the political models of the Nazi education project within this experience. The vigorously popularized categories of racial studies, on the other hand, were less compatible with the body experiences of Germans. They could very well be used for "scientific" observations of the body, as recorded by the young man in an isolated entry. However, like most other diarists, Briske reflected on his own physicality using other concepts from National Socialist physical education that related more readily to his own experience.

3. "My Own Hereditary-Biological Mooring": Envisioning One's Personal Origin

The concept of "origin" held overarching importance for the Nazi education project. With the effort to create the "new," "National Socialist" man, the Nazi regime directed its various educational endeavors at the existing self-images of Germans. Individuals constantly faced the demand to stop orienting their lifestyle and self-perception according to their previous biographical experiences and knowledge of their personal life path; instead, they were supposed to use the new political categories being propagated by educational actors in the 1930s. In the training camps, the "differences of origin, levels of education, vocations, and commitments" were supposed to be bridged and "conceit and enviousness" overcome. "Taking their place was the recognition that the only standard for the human evaluation of the Volk comrade is his value to the community."[239] And Nazi physical education, too, aimed at a "transformation" in which new ideological ideas were supposed to replace the experience of the body arising from the previous life path.[240] The creation of the "new man" required detaching Germans from the influences of their origin and establishing new reference points for self-contemplation and life management. This often affected and challenged existing notions of the individual's personal origin.

At the same time, however, the transformation of ideals about one's personal origin formed a particular subsection of the Nazi education project that emerged from the comprehensive "biologizing of the social" in National Socialism.[241] The educational actors of the Nazi regime did not understand the concept of origin just in terms of social origin—that is, those family and social circumstances within which individuals grew up and whose influence on their self-perspective and lifestyle needed to be broken for the creation of the "new man." Rather, they also grasped origin in the sense of lineage and heredity and thus often used it with a still relatively new conceptual meaning. The concept was not inscribed with a biological meaning alongside its social meaning until the "biological revolution" at the close of the nineteenth century. Its aftermath included the rediscovery of Mendel's laws of heredity around 1900 (they had already been developed forty years earlier) and, a few years later, their application to human beings. With this biological meaning, origin referred to a person's predecessors and the hereditary factors they passed on.[242]

The new knowledge of heredity in the early twentieth century had wide-ranging consequences.[243] It provided the basis for biology's ascendence into a "leading science" of the following decades and established the now scientifically oriented field of racial studies as an important reference point in sociopolitical discussions. Whereas racial research in the nineteenth century had primarily been a domain within an anthropology focused on external appearances, it was fundamentally changed by Mendelian rules, which "detached the concept of race from external appearance" and attached it to "inherited and heritable genetics."[244] This led anthropology out of the blind alley it had stumbled into during the late nineteenth century, when it turned out that the massive numbers of body measurements undertaken in previous decades could not be used to clearly identify races. Understood as heritable units, which according to biological rules of inheritance always appeared in reality only in mixed form, the new concept of race solved the problem of not being able to use measurements of bodies and skulls to demonstrate something that science nonetheless firmly believed existed. If present humans were conceptualized as the product of their biological origin, then it was no longer surprising that race could not be exactly demonstrated through the observation of physical externalities. As per Mendelian rules of inheritance, it was only logical that appearance and heredity picture—the phenotype and genotype—did not match.

However, older conceptions of race were not simply abolished by the new knowledge of heredity. Body images and body visualizations that claimed to be definitive remained a fundamental part of racism in the twentieth century as well; as shown, they continued to be a major influence on Nazi physical education in the 1930s. But at the same time, the focus on lineage gave racism a new dynamic, which starting in the early twentieth century moved "social Darwinist selection theory to the center of the racist paradigm." This paradigm could be used to draw directly applicable conclusions from scientific findings.[245] Established around the turn of the century both as a new science and as a social movement, racial hygiene thus traced widely different social problems and undesired behaviors back to "bad" or "pathological" hereditary factors. Yet the biologizing of the social did not consist solely of now using natural scientific causation to explain social phenomena. In conjunction with Darwinian theories of evolution and selection, racial hygiene also initiated new strategies for eliminating social deficiencies by arguing that these problems could only be eradicated through the state control of human procreation. The natural course of such procreation was disrupted by economics, politics, and society. If the state did not take countermeasures, then the German "Volk" would meet its biological downfall because of the supposedly more vigorous procreation of its "degenerated" and "diseased" parts.[246]

With the start of National Socialist rule, this principle of racial hygiene became the overarching guideline of total policy. Proceeding from the conviction that social deficiencies were hereditarily determined, in the 1930s and 1940s "the elimination of social problems by the elimination of those seen as causing these problems" was pursued ever more radically.[247] The destruction of the European Jews, the Sinti and Roma, and the disabled; the persecution of gay people and the sterilization of so-called antisocials and hereditary defectives—these had their common starting point in the biologizing of the social.[248] Thus "heredity" became an important "basic ideological question" for the Nazi regime.[249] This also applied to the entire Nazi education project because the control of procreation was supposed to extend not just to the prevention of "bad" but also to the promotion of "good" progeny. But as pointed out, for example, by the director of the Race Policy Office of the NSDAP, Walter Groß, the latter was not really an area where the state could directly intervene. It could "cut off on lineages and bloodstreams what is undesired, in that it sterilizes or institutionalizes ... or in that it puts heavy pressure on what comes from a hybrid family."[250] But when it came to promoting genetically healthy progeny, state institutions were almost exclusively reliant on the education of the individual: "No other method leads us basically beyond the situation of today, which moves ever closer to our biological death, apart from the attempt to reawaken the submerged and buried life-affirming instincts of the nation."[251]

As a result, both the aspiration to overcome social origin to create the "new man" and the creation of a consciousness about one's biological origin formed overarching reference points for the Nazi education project. This consciousness was addressed in various contexts, such as when physical exercise and sports were lauded as contributing to the "reconquest of our Nordic character and racial strength" or when shared "blood" was said to be experienced in the community of the training camp.[252] But at the same time, various educational actors of the Nazi regime also addressed the question of personal origin directly to individual Germans. They were supposed to think about their biological origin and understand themselves as the product of their ancestry, thereby changing their self-contemplation, according to which they should realign their lifestyle. "We have the damned duty and obligation," stated a brochure at the start of the Nazi dictatorship, "to remember our origin and do everything so that we achieve clarity about who we actually are."[253]

These efforts by the Nazi regime "to get Germans to accept their racial responsibilities as Aryans" were part of the comprehensive "racial grooming,"[254] which in the 1930s affected not only those people whose lives were threatened by Nazi racial policies. Even though this context was already highlighted in the 1980s with influential studies by Detlev Peukert, Gisela Bock, Hans-Walter Schmuhl, and Ulrich Herbert, the ramifications of those racial policy efforts of the Nazi regime that aimed not at destruction but rather at educational measures for the solution of social problems are still largely underexposed.[255] As expansive as historical knowledge about the exclusionary and destructive dimension of National Socialism and its scientific and ideological underpinnings has now become, researchers are still just starting to deal with the question of whether and how Germans in the 1930s and 1940s integrated the ideas and categories of racial hygiene into their self-conceptions and lifestyles. The following chapter pursues this question, and here too I am primarily interested in how during the 1930s the Nazi regime's racial hygienic models could be transposed into individual self-images and lifestyles.

The Hereditary Dispositions of the Individual

On the basis of new findings about heredity and selection, starting in the early twentieth century racial hygiene outlined wide-ranging predictions on the development of society and the imminent "degeneration of the German Volk" because of its "hereditarily defective" parts. Yet options for determining the "racial quality" of individual persons were very limited. By the 1930s, nothing in this respect had changed. Even though the Nazi regime aspired to shape reality in accordance with fundamental natural laws, scientific methods for directly verifying an individual's "racial belonging" were lacking.²⁵⁶ As a result of biological figures of thought, the application of the laws of heredity on humans admittedly quickly changed the concept of race and the worldviews it supported. But this development had not kept pace at the methodological level, and no scientific techniques had emerged with which "blood"—seen as the carrier of hereditary factors—could be analyzed for its "racial components."²⁵⁷ Instead, racial hygiene had introduced family studies—and thus what were actually the techniques of historical scholarship—to biology.²⁵⁸

Until the end of the nineteenth century, genealogy had amounted almost exclusively to researching nobility. But around the turn of the century, scientific knowledge of heredity fundamentally changed this branch of scholarship as well, which was now reformulated "as a 'borderland science' between history and natural science." As a result, "family and ancestry research" was democratized. It had developed in close connection with racial hygiene from a "family studies movement" with "tens of thousands" of proponents "recruited in equal measure from the bourgeoisie and aristocracy,"²⁵⁹ proceeding from families—now also including non-aristocrats—who were interested in the new biological knowledge and no longer just in the male line. At the same time, it was shaped by the sustained "biologizing of genealogical thought," through which the "new science" of genealogy took on a key role in determining the "racial quality" of the individual:²⁶⁰ since hereditary factors could not be directly determined, they were to be inferred from a reconstruction of hereditary processes, even though this procedure remained uncertain and, with respect to heredity, specific features could be interpreted in different ways.

Yet the proof of the validity of the Mendelian laws of heredity for human procreation had already been delivered by this "method of ancestor and kin research based on church books" in 1913. And "a quarter century later," this same method "still formed the technical basis" for the racial policies of National Socialism.²⁶¹ To be sure, the prohibition of marriages and extramarital sexual relations between Jews and non-Jews, passed in fall 1935 during the Nuremberg party congress, could be justified by saying this was necessary for ensuring the "purity of German blood," which in turn was the "precondition for the continued existence of the German Volk."²⁶² But there was no method whatsoever for "verifying an individual racial blood difference" that could serve as a basis for determining who counted as Jewish under the law.²⁶³ Instead, the determination was made according to the individual's family origin with direct reference to the logic of hybridization worked out by Mendel.

The National Socialist education project's endeavors to create an awareness of one's own hereditary dispositions were also affected by these methodological complications, such that the broad popularization of biological knowledge about the "laws of heredity" and genealogy took on substantial importance. The question about the individual's origin was thus developed within the available genealogical paradigm as both a present and a future problem: the practical experiences acquired by the genealogical movement since the 1920s, and in particular the many complications involved in gathering information about one's ancestors, fostered extensive efforts during National Socialist rule to make the process easier for future generations. The forward-looking aspect of the question about the individual's origin was reflected, for example, in comprehensive projects like the plan for a Reichssippenkartei (Reich Kinship Card Catalog), intended to centrally document the family relationships of every single German.[264] At the same time, however, within the Nazi education project, the German people themselves—especially parents—were called on to perform this task.

With his advice book entitled *Vererbung und Rasse* (Heredity and race), for example, Gustav Franke presented an "introduction in the doctrine of heredity, family studies, racial hygiene, and racial studies" written "for *every* Volk comrade" as early as 1934, and four years later it appeared in a second edition. Franke was a Gau specialized employee for racial questions and author of the official NSDAP series Schriften der Bewegung (Writings of the movement). In the section of *Vererbung und Rasse* that dealt with the "application of the doctrine of heredity on man," his advice book focused exclusively on "family studies." Here he strongly noted that it was "to be urgently requested that parents start making records of the development [Werdegang] of their children as early as possible. A life book for every child should actually be started already at birth."[265] The child's physical growth, as well as "the first attempts to walk," "how the child learns language," and indeed "everything that father or mother themselves consider noteworthy," was supposed to be logged in this book. "First drawings and writing attempts, in addition photographs indicative of a human's individual stages of development, are not just lovely memories but rather also have great value for family studies." He suggested that parents later "make a gift" of the resulting "small collection" of descriptions and materials for their progeny, "and they would thereby also be laying the best gift for their grandchildren in the cradle," Franke wrote, clearly emphasizing the material's relevance for future progeny planning. In conclusion, he stressed once more that the "exact developmental history of the individual family members," which was to be started by the parents, should "be described as nothing less than the basis of a serviceable family studies of the future."[266]

Similar ideas were also propagated by the journal *Neues Volk*, published by the Race Policy Office of the NSDAP, which in 1938 promoted the creation of private "family archives." These archives were to organize and safeguard documents collected during genealogical research for the family's progeny. The article lauded the "family diary" as an "important component. . . whose value, unfortunately, still gets far too little respect." "The mother as the stationary pole, around which circles the family's entire life," outlined the idealizing text, "has taken it on to maintain the records that are kept as important events in the life of a family." Meant here were chiefly the birth and growing up of her children. The mother "will record every first babble, every movement, every first step, she will write down and describe the life and development of her children in the way that only the eyes of a mother is able to see it."[267] In so doing, the authors were supposed to realize that they were forming the basis on which "the next generation . . . will look back with reverent love at the developments that speak so brightly and near-to-life from the mother's records": "Arising here is the document of a family's mental attitude, which . . . can provide information again and again about the inner value of a clan."[268]

The demand to precisely document the growing up of one's children for their own future research into their origin followed directly from the tradition of bourgeois parental diaries that emerged in the late nineteenth century, which doctors and pedagogues had used ever since to try to guide early-childhood education. The diaries retained this control function in the 1930s as well, in that they were supposed to help disseminate ideas from National Socialist early-childhood education, as Miriam Gebhardt has worked out by looking at changes to preprinted parental diaries in the early 1930s.[269] At the same time, however, after 1933 preprinted diaries did not just change in accordance with evolving ideas on the proper encouragement of child development during the first years of life. They were also set up for the long-term documentation of origins and thus for later reading by the respective children. The preprinted diaries now referred to how they were establishing the "basis for a health-related family history of the broadest strata of the Volk." And, as per the "high importance of hereditary doctrine," they now contained an ancestry chart and an analogous chart about the "little one's first becoming" that was supposed to document developments in the months before birth.[270]

Even where parents did not reach for such preprinted diaries but wrote in blank notebooks instead (as recommended by Gustav Franke in his advice book),[271] parental diaries of the 1930s for small children or prenatal babies frequently show that these endeavors on the part of educational actors were often joined by corresponding efforts on the part of the (soon-to-be) parents. In January 1936, for example, Julia Bergerhoff*, a kindergarten teacher born in 1911, apparently began a diary for her unborn child immediately after learning about her pregnancy. Already the diary's first entry indicated that the self-selected title, "The Diary of a New Man [Menschen]," did not simply allude to parental expectations of progeny but instead bore solidly on the political education project of the Nazi regime. Here the author opened with a statement by her husband: "Children, many children, and again and again children, the greatest wonder of this world! These few words are to be the first greeting to you from your father. From them you will one day realize how much he loved you already long before we were allowed to think about you," the text noted, emphasizing the value that the words would have someday for the child's later research into her personal origin. "Someday you shall know, without distortion, what you mean to us now already. You shall know how your life began. You will see what kind of people we are," wrote the author, addressing her future daughter, wanting even now to reassure her through the diary that "you . . . arose from the great will for the creation of healthy progeny."[272] Even though this diary did not include an ancestry chart and the entries of the following years never directly referenced the categories and concepts of the science of heredity, this opening always turned the subsequent descriptions of growing up into a record meant to enable the author's daughter to make an exact picture of her origin.

Far more urgent than preparations for one's children's future recollections was the Nazi regime's requirement that individuals look back at their own ancestors, which arose particularly from the need to verify one's non-Jewish lineage.[273] The question of who was to be considered "Aryan" was already regulated in the Law for the Restoration of the Professional Civil Service of April 1933, which provided for the dismissal of state officials who were "not of Aryan lineage," defined as persons with "non-Aryan, particularly Jewish, parents or grandparents." Hence the religious affiliation of one's predecessors was considered the decisive indictor.[274] Therefore the definition based on family origin was established directly at the start of National Socialist rule, and two years later it would serve as the foundation for the radical modification of state citizenship by the Nuremberg Laws. As of September 1935, only Germans "of German blood"—that is, Germans without any Jewish grandparents—could now be "Reich citizens" and thus fully entitled state citizens, while Germans with three or four Jewish grandparents were declared to be "state subjects" with fewer rights. Germans with one or two Jewish grandparents were considered first- or second-degree "Jewish hybrids," even if they themselves had no direct relationship with Judaism. Their legal and racial status remained disputed.[275]

In the 1930s, this linking of citizenship rights and state benefits to non-Jewish lineage was advanced and sustained by further regulations. Concomitantly, after 1933 the investigation of one's personal family origin transformed "from a voluntary hobby . . . to a compulsory exercise for virtually the entire population," whose members were supposed to prove their "racial quality" to authorities precisely by means of genealogical research.[276] Non-Jewish origin was basically to be proven with documentation at the competent office—for admission as a student, doctor, lawyer, or soldier; when joining the NSDAP or one of its affiliated organizations; as an employee in state institutions; for participating in training camps; for applying for one of the popular marriage loans provided by the state; and in numerous other contexts.[277] Thus millions of Germans set about searching for the birth, baptism, and marriage documents of their predecessors in parish offices, state archives, and civil registries.

This was an incredibly time-consuming enterprise, which required that people, who mostly were "completely inexperienced in family research," become personally involved and know where and how to search for the corresponding documents.[278] Born in 1917, Alfred Wiese, for example, did not belong to the demographic that fed the genealogical movement of the Weimar Republic. Wiese's father, Anton Wieczerzycki, had a farming background, but he never took over the parental farm, becoming instead a laborer for the military. He had worked for the Topographical Department of the Royal Prussian Land Survey, as well as in Spandau in the army cannery and the artillery workshop. Nonetheless, in the mid-1930s Alfred Wiese, too, started collecting birth, death, and marriage records in the family's possession and acquiring missing documents for his parents, grandparents, and great-grandparents. This was not an easy task, for the family first came to Berlin because of Wiese's father's work for the military. They were originally from West Prussia, as was also suggested by the surname Wieczerzycki, which his father only changed in the 1920s. Thus well into the war, Wiese corresponded with various civil registries and parish offices in the old homeland, requesting information. In this way he reconstructed his ancestral line back to his great-great-grandparents, compiling their dates of birth and death and also baptism certificates, which confirmed his non-Jewish lineage.[279]

The search by people with no experience in family research was supported by numerous advice books with titles such as *Erbbiologischer und eugenischer Wegweiser für Jedermann* (Hereditary-biological and eugenics guide for everyman) or *Wie finde ich meine Ahnen? Anleitung, wie man schnell seine arische Abstammung nachweist* (How do I find my Ancestors? Instructions on how one quickly verifies his Aryan lineage).[280] The new interest in investigating one's personal origin was also intensely promoted by many lectures, training courses, and exhibits, mainly arranged by genealogical associations that had already emerged before 1933. And even where other actors discovered the subject for themselves after 1933, the countless publications related to ancestral studies in the 1930s converged directly with the promotional efforts of the genealogical and racial hygienic movements in the Weimar Republic.[281] In addition, local NSDAP offices, genealogical associations, and city archives set up advice centers that people could turn to personally and ask for assistance in the search for their predecessors.[282]

The many different publications sought generally to promote personal involvement with one's lineage but at the same time also tried to clarify the methodological basics needed for family research. Following an introduction on the significance of the Aryan certificate, the guidebook *Ahnenforschung leicht gemacht: Wege zur Ahnentafel und Familienkunde* (Ancestral research made easy: Paths to the ancestry chart and family studies), for example, provided illustrative references on how to acquire the certificate, explaining which documents were required and where they could be obtained, as well as providing, by way of examples, suggestions for formulating written requests for birth, marriage, or baptism certificates. In addition, it explained how to properly indicate names and birth dates and then spoke extensively about what to do if complications arose, such as ambiguous place names or—as in the case of Alfred Wiese—altered surnames. The explanations were also supplemented with comprehensive lists of genealogical resources, important archives, and further useful addresses.[283] Like other guidebooks, this text also put a lot of effort into explaining the system of genealogical notation for readers. Using many graphics, it illustrated the difference between genealogical and ancestry charts, their underlying principles, and the generally common symbols for "born out of wedlock," "married," "divorced," "suicide," or "extramarital relation."[284] A *Rassenhygienische Fibel* (Racial hygienic manual) for children and adolescents also dedicated to this problem a separate section entitled "How You Can Best Write That Down," which explained even to young readers how best to set up an ancestry chart, in which men are symbolized "as a quadrangle, the women as a circle," and how relationships between them should be graphically represented.[285]

Proper notation was also conveyed with various preprinted forms, which different actors had already started publishing in 1933. Using preprinted tables and written explanations, they were supposed to provide immediate practical assistance in writing down discovered information.[286] The most influential of these forms was a booklet entitled *Ahnenpaß* (Ancestral passport) created by the Reich Association of Civil Registrars, which was closely involved in the large-scale verification of non-Jewish origins. The *Ahnenpaß* contained fields where information about birth dates, religious faiths, and affinity circumstances could be entered and officially certified by civil registrars or church book clerks. They were preceded by a blank ancestry chart that, when completed, was supposed to provide clarity about the relevant person's family relationships at a single glance.[287]

In the 1930s, the *Ahnenpaß* evolved into a quasi-official document, which was supposed to obviate the need to always present various authorities with the individual documents that were collected for each parent and grandparent. As noted by a specimen from the NSDAP's own publishing house, the Franz Eher Verlag, "sooner or later" it was supposed to become "a mandatory identification document for every Volk comrade."[288] But by the end of the Nazi dictatorship, this had still not happened. Until the very end, the preprinted forms were not distributed by state officials but rather sold in bookstores and stationery shops. Accordingly, many commercial publishers offered different versions of ancestral passports and family registry books in a number of ostentatious or minimalist designs and directed at various consumer classes, large quantities of which were sold overall. The 31st print run of the *Ahnenpaß* of the market-leading publishing house of the Reich Association of Civil Registrars appeared in 1937; the 136th print run occurred just one year later. For the entire period of Nazi rule, "total sales of *Ahnenpässe* in the millions is almost certain, and in the tens of millions is probable."[289]

Even so, the large sales figures of ancestral passports should not be allowed to hide the fact that, in practice, realizing the aspiration to genealogically verify non-Jewish lineage to the degree actually envisioned by the Nazi regime was impossible. Thus, in 1935 the family researcher Georg Nahnsen, who had already been bustling about during the Weimar Republic, complained that genealogy was still not a "self-evident concern for all Volk comrades."[290] This was quite true and related to the fact that, in light of the laborious procedure, in many administrative contexts—even for state administration employees—the documented verification of lineage was replaced by solemn declarations or the simple affirmation of non-Jewish origins "to the best of one's knowledge." As Eric Ehrenreich has noted, this "easing of the ancestral proof requirement" meant that "the majority of Germans probably made an ancestral proof by oath" and not by way of findings from family studies.[291]

Despite the complexities revealed by the practice of enforcing the genealogical verification of non-Jewish origins, during its entire rule the Nazi regime held fast to the principle that people had to provide this verification themselves. The Interior Ministry's "expert for racial research," created by the Professional Civil Service Act in spring 1933, and the Reich Agency for Kinship Research that emerged from this office in the mid-1930s, were only supposed to intervene in cases where the matter could not be resolved locally between the individual and the relevant authorities—for example, because the submitted documents were called into doubt or insurmountable obstacles arose in the search for documents.[292] For one, there were practical reasons for self-verification, since an official review of the family relationships of every German would have overwhelmed the capacity of the state. For another, the ancestral passports were not just supposed to be used for the identification of "Jewish" and other "alien" Germans; rather, they were also meant to encourage individuals to confront their own origin. As much as they were used to decide whether to grant state citizenship rights or state benefits, having people produce their own ancestral passes was also very much understood as an educational measure.

This is illustrated, for example, by the many preprinted ancestral passports for children, such as those Frank Maik, an Essen factory worker's son born in 1935, filled out as part of his school lessons in 1935. Starting with an ancestry chart extending from parents to great-grandparents, the booklet *Meine Ahnen* (My ancestors) also contained a form with blanks that asked for biographical information—birth dates; vocational information; marriage dates; "physical characteristics" such as height and hair color; "illnesses (type of illness and time)"; and "mental qualities." Also provided were empty pages with the headings "From the Life of My Father," ". . . My Mother," ". . . My Grandparents," ". . . My Great-Grandparents," on which Frank Maik wrote out accounts of the lives of his predecessors.[293]

As with such child-appropriate preprinted booklets, the proper ancestral passports were also meant to have an educational effect. As a result of "lineage verification" and the work this entailed in the "fields of family research," "all strata of our Volk" would be led "in prosaic everyday life to think now and then about the existential connection to the ancestors," stated, for example, a "Guide for the Issuance of an Ancestral Passport," which was appended to an elaborately designed preprinted form from the Franz Eher Verlag.[294] And another family lineage book pointed out that the entries would "situate every . . . person in relation to his predecessors and descendants. It will be brought to the individual's awareness that he is just a connecting link in a long chain of generations."[295]

Thus the Nazi regime's educational intentions of motivating individuals to confront their personal origin and adapt their lifestyles accordingly were not the reason genealogy attained its central position in the 1930s. This had more to do with the shortcomings of racial studies and racial hygiene, which, although developing new ideas in the early twentieth century about heredity in the process of human procreation, could not find a scientific method that could prove the purported hereditary components. Notwithstanding all of the rhetoric about "blood" and "natural laws," there simply was no technique more precise than that of making inferences about the individual's hereditary dispositions on the basis of genealogical reconstruction. Yet insofar as Germans were obliged themselves to work at clarifying their lineage through family studies, this method was at the same time much more useful for imparting to individuals an awareness of their personal origin than would have been possible with medically certifiable findings. It made the individual's own involvement with lineage a necessity, which for the educational actors of National Socialism held the promise of having a profoundly formative impact on the people.

Biologizing Individual Self-Conceptions

Various actors of the National Socialist education project hoped that ancestral passports and ancestor research would greatly contribute to the transformation of personal self-perceptions and lifestyles. Yet even though Germans had to collect the information themselves, the ancestral passport functioned in the 1930s as a quasi-official document. So it was far from obvious that it would take on the desired personal meaning for individuals, nor did this actually happen for all of the Germans who in the 1930s sought out the family historical documents they needed to verify their lineage. Otmar Krämer was a domain counselor born in 1879 who became an NSDAP race warden in 1934 and in this capacity helped, as he put it, the "Thuringian Office for Race Matters in detecting Jewish grandmothers or Aryan great-grandfathers." With respect to his job, he knew that "people are not always immediately willing, accommodating, and approachable." They came above all because "without a kinship chart from the Thuringian Race Office" there would be "no marriage loan."[296]

Many people no doubt viewed the verification of their lineage in these terms—namely, as an official matter for obtaining state benefits.[297] Yet for other persons, even if they were forced to deal with their own predecessors for external reasons, doing so very much changed their existing notions of their personal origin. As Peter Fritzsche has emphasized, in many cases this is evident from the documents themselves. Time and again, "*Ahnenpässe* . . . [formed] the foundation of personal archives," insofar as "private papers gathered inside the pages." Marriage and birth announcements, letters, vaccination certificates, restaurant receipts, and other things were preserved inside the ancestral passports.[298] One also frequently finds photos glued into ancestral passports.[299] Moreover, the official requirement to provide information about one's predecessors often inspired individuals to engage in further research, even beyond the prescribed degree of kinship.[300]

Just a few weeks after the promulgation of the Nuremberg Laws, the Munich resident Klara Schötz had the birth, death, and baptismal information of her parents and grandparents certified by the civil registry. Thus she provided the necessary information to verify her non-Jewish lineage. However, later she independently supplemented this with further information about other predecessors, which she did not have officially certified, which in turn highlights the fact that she attributed more than merely functional importance to her ancestral passport.[301] One can presume that something similar was behind the kind of extensive research carried out in the late 1930s by Paul Krumbholz, a lecturer at the Military School in Munich born in 1897. One of his uncles had already started genealogically researching his own family in the late 1920s, and in 1931 he sent Krumbholz an ancestry chart as a "Christmas present," which did not interest him very much at the time. Hence, later in the 1930s the uncle was all the more pleased to learn from his nephew that "you also find pleasure in ancestral research, which I devoted myself to when it was not yet modern."[302] Indeed, Paul Krumbholz enthusiastically dedicated himself to ancestral research. On the basis of his uncle's prior work, he researched a total of 183 of his ancestors back as far as eight generations, to the early seventeenth century. He organized the information collected about himself and his wife according to a system developed in the field of genealogy and filed them in two large folders. At the same time, he also prepared ancestral passports for himself and his wife, making use of supplemental forms provided by ancestral passport publishers for documenting ancestors beyond the fourth generation.[303]

Notwithstanding their formal design and official character, ancestry charts, ancestral passports, and the requisite family studies research provided some Germans with a model of biographical self-interpretation and self-representation that could be used in both official and private contexts. Consider, for example, Hans Drescher*, who was born in 1889 and was an NSDAP member and block leader since 1933. In 1937 he was up for appointment as cell leader, for which he had to provide personal documents. Along with the obligatory ancestry chart, he also submitted the necessary curricula vitae, in which he consciously situated himself in the line of his predecessors. "Anyone who wants to talk about his life must start with those through whom the bloodstream of his own life flowed. The paternal ancestry chart can be traced as far back as the year 1623 and lists a continuous succession of wine growers and farmers who lived in Winterbach in Remstal, mostly in miserable circumstances," Drescher wrote, beginning the account of his life path, which he tied directly to the line of his predecessors. "The chain broke with my father; he became a missionary with the Basel Mission, which sent him to China in 1883. After his marriage in 1888, I as the first child was born in Hong Kong on 10/27/1889."[304] These few sentences show that Drescher traced the line of his predecessors far beyond the key date of January 1, 1800, that was required for NSDAP members and functionaries—a date that, in turn, was much further back than the information about the parental and grandparental generations otherwise required for the Aryan certificate.³⁰⁵ At the same time, when preparing the ancestry chart, he did not limit himself only to the information about the degrees of kinship and religious affiliations of his predecessors that was needed to verify his non-Jewish origins; instead, he also compiled additional information about occupations and lifestyles to draw conclusions about himself.

The ancestral passports themselves encouraged this kind of "evaluation" of one's personal lineage, with pages that, under the heading "Dein Blut, dein höchstes Gut" (Your blood, your greatest asset), asked the person to fill in specific information with respect to average size, average age, average age at marriage, average number of children, and the distribution of physical features such as eye and hair color. And the advice literature also frequently emphasized that "statistical evaluation" was what first turned "generation studies" into "völkisch family studies," which "is not content with the fullest possible graphical compilation of family and kinship" but "rather must, beyond that, record information about physical and mental particulars as well." Only then was it possible to trace "how normal or abnormal physical qualities, special aptitudes or abilities as well as illnesses, among others, are *inherited*."³⁰⁶ When the Munich resident Klara Schötz prepared her ancestral passport, this principle guided the way she arranged the various slips of paper on which she had compiled names and information about dates of birth and death, along with notes about vocations and above all causes of death, as well as illnesses and hospital stays.³⁰⁷ Drescher had proceeded in a similar fashion, concentrating above all on the vocations of his ancestors, which according to one advice book could be "of special significance; because the vocation is usually related to a particular aptitude or at least propensity of the practitioner."³⁰⁸ An accumulation of certain vocations was a sure sign of a certain familial talent, and it was precisely against this background that Drescher interpreted the line of his predecessors, even though neither his father nor he himself, a teacher, had continued this tradition.

The opening of Hans Drescher's curriculum vitae, despite its official character, must be interpreted as more than just the expression of an instrumental discursive strategy vis-à-vis the party authorities. This is also shown, for example, by private discussions in diaries like that of Wilhelm Bollmann, a Gau training lecturer born in 1896, who in contrast to

Drescher had already been active as an NSDAP functionary in 1933. In 1936, after taking a break from writing for a few weeks, Bollmann resumed his notations in January 1936 with a retrospective look at a "race lecture" from almost two months back. It had been an "average lecture," Bollmann commented, although it nonetheless prompted him to "philosophize": "Where do I come from? Where does my Lore come from?" he asked with regard to his children, with whom he and his wife had "continued the chain of our ancestors." He continued: "It appears as if our children have good hereditary material. What is somehow good and bad from the thousand-year chain will continue in the same direction. My family tree leads to Hesse and Waldeck. The paternal side gets lost . . . [ellipses in the original] From mother's type, strong and weak decedents arose, as [I] also was before. . . . [ellipses in the original] This must become an average mixture in the long run. But now and then a genius will break out of this horde, and similarly one who goes to rack and ruin."[309]

This insight gained from family research also provided Bollmann with an explanation of his previous life as "naturally predetermined." "Ever since my maturity as a human being, my innerness pushes from deeds to deeds. Viking blood wants to raise the world from the ruins. One thing prevents me again and again from doing this. That is the hereditary material of the warrior to subordinate himself," Bollmann wrote, identifying the principle inherited from his predecessors that had determined his life thus far. "What drew me out as a 17-year-old war volunteer to the army of the Germans, where there was hardship and suffering, death and ruin? What let me endure for four long years? In the ranks I was also an outsider who, disdainful of death, went into combat voluntarily many a time. One single drive propelled me, my hereditary material!" The tension between subordination and independent initiative, between perseverance and the urge to act, which Bollmann situated in his genetic material, was something he recognized in his professional career after the end of the war, when he first worked "in the pay of Jews" and then "bared his teeth to them . . . after all" and created "a new platform" for himself. "Others made themselves comfortable, I needed to learn." This was the way he explained his life trajectory on the basis of his inherited material. As a locksmith during the Weimar Republic, Bollmann had upgraded his education to become an engineer and set up a small, albeit unsuccessful workshop. Even though these were difficult times and he was not "always completely honest" with his later wife, he had had no other choice: "The blood had me go this way."[310]

Family studies could provide a new model for biographical self-contemplation even for individuals who were not functionaries or members of the NSDAP, motivating them to deal with their own origin. As a civil registrar employee, Werner Kramp, born in 1893, often came into contact with the political renegotiation of personal origins as part of his work.[311] But he also launched his own private examinations. In the winter semester of 1933, after his course on National Socialist art appreciation in summer that same year, Kramp attended another event at the Altona adult education center, where the "family researcher Nahnsen" was to "demonstrate the techniques of this research in a long-winded manner."[312] Even though Kramp felt that "Nahnsen's explanations on family research ... fell below expectations," he also continued working on his own origin over the next weeks outside the adult education center.[313] He made a family tree as a gift for his sister Helma and her husband, whereby he naturally also identified his own ancestors.[314] He indicated that this also held personal meaning for him when, writing about the holidays in his diary, he noted that their family celebration of Christmas that year was "expanded in consideration of deceased members and genealogical ancestors."

Yet, occasioned by his family studies activities, Kramp in his writing also thought more deeply on his ancestors and their meaning for his own life. "In terms of vocation, there is no consistent line," he noted, analyzing his succession of ancestors. "Dominated by agriculture, but a merchant and industrialist also occur, then three construction tradesmen, the Grüttners probably simple bricklayers from the Verden region. Grandfather R. as a successful building contractor, and the first Arnold we know of as an imperial master builder. One might have expected healthy progeny in us and must actually recognize in ourselves the dying branches of a well-founded tree."[315] With the last sentence Kramp came to speak about his oft-recurring complaint—namely, that at forty years of age he still had neither a wife nor children—a complaint that had received new nourishment just weeks before. By chance, Kramp had met a woman in November, which gave him hope that she might be the answer to his bachelorhood. But after just a few days, he got the brush-off. The woman was already engaged, and Kramp was deeply hurt by the rejection. As late as New Year's Eve, he spoke in his annual review about how, after the "approach of a girl and ... awakening of hope," the swift disappointment that followed had given him a "hardening of heart."[316] Along with the course at the adult education center and the Christmas family festival, the brief romance too had helped encourage his genealogical work, which, as Kramp wrote in his diary, "before seemed justified to me . . . only in the event of [my] own procreation." Emerging "hopes of this kind" were what "had him envisage this further plan."[317] His disappointed yearnings for a wife and children had informed his thoughts about his personal origin almost as a matter of course. And how he bemoaned his disappointed love was indeed closely related to his racial knowledge about heredity. "But now I hardly have hope anymore of leading the small matriarch home," Kramp noted with resignation in his diary shortly before Christmas. And yet "from a blood standpoint, the choice would certainly have been advisable, because then an additional Lower Saxon element of the Altmark would have mixed with blood groups of Eiderstadt (Friesen?) and Holstein."[318]

In the 1930s, Franz Göll, born in 1899, also used family studies to look into his origin. Working at the time as a printer for the Julius Springer Verlag in Berlin, Göll had already shown a marked interest in scientific questions during the Weimar Republic. This interest had also guided his search for the reasons for his own frailty and lack of self-confidence, subjects of routine complaint in his diary. Even back then, Göll had been convinced that the human being does "not stand outside of nature as a special being, but rather is permeated by it in all of his parts," an assessment he often reiterated after 1933.[319] However, only against the background of the massive popularization of genealogical techniques and biological knowledge about heredity during the Nazi dictatorship did he begin to understand himself as the hereditarily determined product of his predecessors and to identify his lineage as a possible reason for his allegedly inadequate personality. Particularly starting in summer 1933, Göll dedicated many extensive diary entries to dealing with his lineage, trying to determine the influence that his predecessors had exercised on him.

"The frail psychological constitution in our family is to be traced back not just to paternal influences but also to influences on the maternal side. Thus the father of my mother was a psychological weakling, a person who knew little or not at all how to assert himself vis-à-vis others," Göll wrote in late July 1933, starting his first "family-biological" sketch in his diary.[320] Above all, he dealt here extensively with the bad moral conduct of his mother's brother, admonishingly illustrating where the family's hereditary disposition could lead in unfortunate cases. With regard to his own life situation—unmarried despite having had various intimate relationships—Göll apparently considered it "worth mentioning, with regard to family biology, that my grandfather only married comparatively late. While his brother Gustav died as a bachelor. One brother who emigrated to America supposedly also lived as a bachelor. The marriage of the sister Maria . . . remained childless."[321]

In his entries over the following months, Göll spoke frequently about his lineage and the "main biologically essential feature in our family," which he identified as the "predominance of an asthenic element."[322] In summer 1934, he again dedicated an extensive "hereditary-biological study" to his uncle's family, describing which "hereditary material" had "unmistakably manifest itself" in each of his uncle's various children.[323] Then in two long entries in November 1934, he analyzed "my own hereditary biological mooring,"[324] wrote in detail about what he felt were the identifiable hereditary dispositions of his parents and grandparents, and thought about which of them had "transferred to me."[325] The "biological hereditary material of my mother," for example, Göll noted, "including the latent hereditary dispositions," corresponds to "the genotype of the Schöppke family," and therefore the line of his mother, although he related this above all to her "physical constitution." She had inherited the "psychologically predominant factor" from her father.[326] Göll could only "report comparatively little" about his own father, who had already died in 1915. "He was of a small, stout form, physically in a well-nourished condition, but of a slack constitution; otherwise without special features. In an intellectual-psychological regard, he was a stolid character."[327] Although Göll seemed skeptical about the degree to which this properly allowed him to "evaluate Father as a hereditary-biological factor for me," he believed he had "inherited from him the stolid-melancholic dispositional basis," while he felt that physically he descended more from his mother.[328] Distilling his discussion, he wrote, "In summary, from these statements one can probably draw the conclusion" that, in light of the very unfavorable preconditions of his predecessors, "in my case a phenotype has crystallized that without doubt towers above the [family] average," whereby he once more threw a side glance at his uncle's family.[329]

Like other Germans at the time, in the 1930s Klara Schötz, Werner Kramp, Franz Göll, Wilhelm Bollmann, and Hans Drescher did not merely start collecting the information about their parents and grandparents that they needed in various official contexts. Rather, in keeping with the popularized knowledge of heredity, they understood their ancestral lineage as an important source of self-knowledge, sometimes tracing it back far beyond the third generation. Thus, by way of the question about origins, the widespread biologizing of the social under National Socialism found expression in the biologizing of individual self-perspectives, which some people now organized according to new knowledge about their lineage. This required an exploratory focus on one's own predecessors, which produced this knowledge in the first place and was deliberately supported by writers of advice literature, family researchers, and many additional actors, who popularized genealogical techniques. Diarists like Werner Kramp, Franz Göll, Wilhelm Bollmann, and Hans Drescher appropriated these techniques and made them an important foundation for their own self-contemplation.

Germans were better able to apply racial hygienic figures of thought and racial studies concepts to themselves when dealing with their personal origins than from within the context of Nazi physical education. As has been shown, in their efforts to ideologically influence body experience, the educational actors of the Nazi regime faced the problem that linking categories of racial studies to individual experiences of the body was invariably difficult. Accordingly, acceptance of the categories remained limited, and they were used above all in areas where people consciously assumed the role of an observer to "conduct racial studies." The goal of having Germans grasp the scientific categories of racial studies not as foreign but as relevant to themselves also informed the effort to motivate individuals to confront their personal origin. This was more successful than efforts within physical education because the propagation of genealogy offered contemporaries a concrete method they could appropriate. By means of ancestral studies, Germans could still see concepts from racial studies and heredity as scientific knowledge while at the same time using them to initiate a process of self-confrontation, one that could incorporate scientific concepts because they did not need to be felt but rather provided instruments for self-research.

Scientificity formed a central precondition for the biologizing of individual self-perspectives in the 1930s, asserting that the applicable terms and concepts from racial studies had a clear and unambiguous meaning. Yet even so, people could not be prevented from arriving at their own very particular interpretations of their origin.[330] The corresponding deliberations on the part of individuals often did not convey the sense that scientific methods were being applied. Werner Kramp, Franz Göll, Wilhelm Bollmann, and Hans Drescher, for example, each saw very different things as being inherited from ancestral "blood." For Hans Drescher, ancestors passed on talents, which he deduced by looking at the vocations of his predecessors. For Wilhelm Bollmann, in contrast, they did not transfer any specific ability but rather a basic attitude toward life that decided whether one was defined by dynamism or acquiescence. Accordingly, he believed he had received "Viking blood" and a "warrior's heredity" from his ancestors. Werner Kramp, meanwhile, more closely followed the categories of racial studies as disseminated by Hans F. K. Günther and other popular race researchers who identified various races according to the regions where they originally settled—for example, as "Nordic" or "Eastern." While Kramp did not adopt these concepts, at the very least he invoked the idea of a close link between geography and heritable dispositions in his comment that his hoped-for relationship thwarted by unrequited love might have mixed the blood of the "Altmark" with the "blood group of Eiderstadt." Franz Göll ultimately found entirely new forms in his deliberations, declaring both families from which he descended as separate "genotypes."[331] Accordingly, he used family names like scientific names for types. With regard to his uncle's children, for example, he determined that three of them showed "the influence of the Amboß family in their physical and psychological constitution, two . . . a Liskowian factor," and one "a mixed type (physical = Liskow, psychological = Amboß)."[332] In their deliberations, Kramp, Bollmann, Drescher, and Göll all similarly applied scientific knowledge of heredity and its fundamental rules to themselves. But they had very idiosyncratic ideas as to what exactly had been passed down to them, which only very loosely corresponded to the scientific categories of racial studies.

In his investigation of the Aryan certificate, Eric Ehrenreich has argued that such discrepancies should actually have revealed to people the senselessness of their actions and led them to reject the Nazi regime's policies of racial hygiene.[333] To me, however, it seems that these inconsistencies reflect an essential condition for allowing individuals to apply the basic ideas of racial hygiene and hereditary science to themselves. Precisely because in the 1930s there was no clearly defined scientific understanding as to which and how physical and temperamental features were inherited, contemporaries were able to apply the knowledge they obtained from their genealogical family research to their own self-perspectives. It is no coincidence that the findings they gained from family research dovetailed so smoothly with the ideas about themselves that Franz Göll and Werner Kramp had been recording in their diaries for years, or that Wilhelm Bollmann discovered in the blood of his ancestors the principle that seemed to structure his entire life—namely, the difference between compulsive action and resigned perseverance. Their diaries and those of others in the 1930s show that, in the concrete application of ancestral research, one's own self-perspective and knowledge of heritability deeply influenced each other. Basically, once a one-dimensional mode of operation was asserted using the principle of biological heritability, the "bloodstream" flowed from the ancestors of the past to the progeny of the future, passing on the respective characteristics from one generation to the next through the process of heredity. In the 1930s, people could identify supposedly heritable characteristics only by comparing themselves to the accumulated information about their own predecessors. The perspective of genealogy faced directly opposite to the concrete principle of heredity, and for this reason, when researching their ancestors, people did not merely identify the residual influence of their predecessors within themselves but also projected their own ideas about themselves into the past. It is not surprising that the efforts in ancestral studies undertaken by Franz Göll and Werner Kramp did little to change their criticisms of themselves and others, which they had also expressed in other diary entries. Instead of finding within themselves the "blood" of their ancestors, they mainly discovered their own inadequacies in their family past.

Nazi Racial Policy and Individual Self-Contemplation

Even though Germans in the 1930s used techniques prescribed by the Nazi education project to biologize their individual self-conceptions, they did not necessarily adopt the racial studies categories propagated by the regime. Given the weaknesses of genealogy when it came to identifying specific hereditary factors, in the 1930s individuals' confrontation with their own origin was inevitably open to their own interpretations. These did not necessarily have to correspond to the popularized categories of racial studies. The scientific nature of the biologizing of individual self-conceptualizations did not simply lead people to adopt scientific findings. At the same time, however, very specific appropriations of genealogical findings about personal origin occurred in the context of the state's racial policies. As intended by educational actors, Germans were influenced by and integrated into racial policy. The new knowledge about one's ancestors made people support the Nazi regime's racial policies in two ways.

First, personal life decisions, particularly related to sexuality and partnerships, were now supposed to be aligned with one's personal hereditary factors. This is shown, for example, by the diary of the young gardener Inge Thiele, even though she rarely dealt much with her lineage in her writing. She did not engage in genealogical self-contemplation. But her hereditary disposition repeatedly played a role in her detailed discussions about a healthy lifestyle and her thoughts about the choice of partners, sexuality, and the desire for children. "Wading through streams, climbing, resting, paddling, swimming and joyful healthy youth nearby, nothing of illness and decay. That is how my future must be and that of my offspring," Thiele maintained in May 1935 as part of her description of an excursion. And four years later, when noting with pride that she had "brought my body healthily into the 25th year," "unspent and athletically steeled," she immediately added with a glance at her future, "Now I long for a lovely man and a healthy child."[334] Whether and how people shifted their own life decisions into a context with their lineage strongly depended on the individual case.

More fundamental insights into the relationship between the biologizing of individual self-images and the state's racial policy can therefore be found by looking above all at the second objective that was supposed to be achieved by popularizing genealogy and knowledge of heredity: the procurement of broader social acceptance and approval of racial policy measures. Viewed against this background, diaries of the 1930s frequently show that even the idiosyncratic application of family research and the scientific principles of heredity to one's own future could foster approval of the Nazi regime's racial policy.

This connection between genealogical self-reflection and the acceptance of racial-hygienic practices is exemplified by Werner Kramp, who already saw his professional work at the civil registry as "serving racial thinking."[335] In mid-February 1934, just a few weeks after his family studies work at Christmas, Kramp reported in his diary on a meeting of the student fraternity he had joined while studying at university and whose events he still attended even after his legal career failed. This time the meeting was especially lively, and its agenda included the "demand to eject Jewish hybrids from the league." As he emphasized in his diary, during the meeting it had been quite clear that "a refusal" could result in "the dissolution of the league." "Nonetheless, the mood of the people from Hamburg was heroically set on rejection [of the demanded exclusion of the so-called Jewish hybrids]—for reasons of loyalty." On the basis of the special bond between fraternity brothers, various speakers had spoken in favor of keeping the two affected members, whose names and "kinship circumstances" (the number of Jewish predecessors) were unknown, at least to Kramp. Even though he lacked more precise knowledge, he criticized the final decision to retain the affected fraternity brothers. Although he did not dispute the special loyalty of fraternity, he asserted that "a biologically determined duty for disloyalty" required the exclusion of the so-called Jewish hybrids.[336]

The connection between National Socialist racial policy and the contemplation of one's own origin is also evident in the diary of Inge Thiele. Apart from deliberating about her body and future offspring, the young gardener came to speak in detail about her lineage in one single but very long entry after the promulgation of the Nuremberg Laws, which she had praised as "wonderful laws" that "penetrate the secrets of the blood, make them rules of faith."[337] Less than one week later, she and her sister visited a previously unknown "cousin of Dad and Uncle Hubert," and against the background of the knowledge of heredity that had just been elevated into law, she began interpreting the process of getting to know her second cousin—named "uncle"—by focusing on their common predecessors. "We felt at home with each other so quickly, as if the voice of blood had spoken. Or was the amiable, eloquent Uncle Wolfgang to blame for this?" Yet ultimately, it was their shared lineage that for Thiele primarily explained why she liked her previously unknown relative. In the "speech" and "mode of expression" of her second cousin, she recognized the brother of her father, "just more nervous, hastier, a really excited businessman." She noted, "It is peculiar that we are talking with people who are actually strangers to us, yet above all about things that concern us both. If we look back at our predecessors, we draw much closer to each other; there still is blood relationship, tight village community. Suddenly one is no longer a stranger, the same predecessors, the same home ground."[338] The extent of interdependence between antisemitism and the view of her own origin is not shown merely by the chronological proximity of the promulgation of the Nuremberg Laws. In her description of the visit, she also noted that her uncle lived in a house on "Elberfeld's most important business street" and explicitly added, "It reeked everywhere of Jews. Uncle Wolfgang had just previously taken over this business from a Jew."[339] Never before had Inge Thiele, who undoubtedly held anti-Jewish sentiments, recorded such an openly antisemitic comment in her diary, nor did anything like it appear again in the following years until the start of the war. In her case, it was only the hereditary-biological look at her own future prompted by the promulgation of the Nuremberg Laws that created the framework for the comment.

At the same time, genealogical self-exploration did not inevitably go hand in hand with approval of the regime's racist policies. Forming an opposite pole to diaries such as those of Werner Kramp and Inge Thiele are diaries like that of Franz Göll. Very much in keeping with his long-standing interest in natural sciences, in his diary in spring 1934 he too praised "our present population policy" for standing in "harmony with natural law."[340] Nonetheless, he was unable see many benefits in the Nazi regime's efforts at racial hygiene. As early as summer 1933, he viewed the fact that Adolf Hitler was a "borderland German" and that other "leaders of the Volk [Volksführer]" had grown up "on the country's border" as evidence "against the now predominant scientific-dogmatic view of the supposedly exclusively political influence of racial purity." Hitler and the other leaders of the Volk "precisely revealed, after all, the strong influence of racial mixing."[341] And even in Göll's later entries, the efforts by the regime to achieve racial purity met with disapproval. In spring 1938, he formulated his aversion in an elaborate dystopian vision that he wrote down after having seen film footage of a "home for mothers" at the movie theater. He could "not ward off the thought of having taken a look at a human breeding facility," Göll noted. "Here nascent human beings are being expertly raised according to a coordinated and standardized schema for their later exploitation and utilization," and "the knowledge of the laws of heredity [was being] harnessed" to do so, he remarked with horror.[342]

In this respect, it is not enough simply to see the significance of genealogy—which was also personally significant for many people—as direct evidence for the "widespread acceptability of racist policy."[343] Understanding oneself as the product of one's predecessors did not necessarily mean approval of the Nazi regime's racial policies. But it is also wrong to believe that it was possible in the 1930s to separate genealogical "research free of biological or antisemitic elements" from ancestral research conducted "in zealous obedience aimed at unveiling any non-Aryan lineage."[344] Not all people who explored their origin searched for "Jewish" or "alien-racial blood" and endorsed the racial-hygienic conclusions drawn by the Nazi regime from the knowledge about heredity and lineages. But even if people did not do so, the knowledge of heredity that had inscribed genealogy since the turn of the century contributed to the biologizing of personal self-perceptions. To understand oneself as the product of one's forebears inevitably meant internalizing figures of thought that also supported the racial-hygienic politics of the Nazi regime.

This can be traced particularly well in the diary of Franz Göll. In the detailed discussions about his lineage written by the Berlin white-collar employee at the start of Nazi rule, apart from the character traits and physical features of his parents and other predecessors, he also spoke about growing up. As much as he reflected on what he had inherited from his ancestors, he also very much saw his lack of strength of character and his problems in dealing with life—which he constantly complained about in his diary—above all as the result of an unsuccessful upbringing. His mother simply possessed "no parenting qualities," Göll emphasized in the context of his "family-biological" discussions. "The temperamentally nervous influence of my mother with the intellectual-psychological inhibitions impacted me very unfavorably, disadvantageously, and repressively in my years as a youth," he noted in his deliberations. He had to "first instinctively paralyze" her "repressively acting influence" in order "to uncover the driving forces of the development of my own personality," which ultimately led him to the "above average" "phenotype," which Göll affirmed for himself in the same entry.[345]

In light of his wide-ranging genealogical deliberations and repeatedly noted dissatisfaction at not having enough information to explain all of the "distinctive characteristic traits, like my hoarding, my inclination toward philosophical broodiness" from his own lineage, it would have been obvious to suspect that the heritable influence of his predecessors stood behind his personal inadequacies. In an earlier entry Göll had, of course, already identified an "asthenic element" in his "ancestral line," and overall he did not draw an especially favorable picture of his forebears.[346] But in the entry that summarized the results of his "own hereditary biological mooring," he vigorously blocked this interpretation, pointing out that the assessment of having been "altogether wrongly raised" was not only "a claim made up by me" but something that had "been told me by multiple doctors." Despite private efforts to comprehend himself in his diary as the product of his lineage, Göll insisted that his mother's incapability had critically disrupted his "intellectual-psychological development and maturation into a personality" and that the weaknesses he bemoaned were not inherited.[347]

While not at all inclined toward the positions and measures of racial hygiene in his diary, he also unerringly and vigorously declared that his own inadequacies were caused by social and not heritable factors. He thus moved exactly along the dividing line that, with the racial-hygienic orientation of National Socialist policy, determined the boundary of the Nazi education project itself. The biological concept of origin was so important to this project in part because it called into question the idea of education itself. "Why education instead of heredity?" asked the title of a popular-science book by the pedagogy professor Gerhard Pfahler in spring 1935. It was a response to the challenge that the idea of a wholesale heritability that included physical and temperamental features posed to any attempts at exerting an educational influence. Pfahler's book was meant as a guide for teachers and parents, intent on answering their questions as to "how far heredity [reaches] in my child" and where the "space of freedom, of formation" exists.[348]

Even as a pedagogue, Pfahler did not turn against the idea that family lineage extensively shaped personality. Rather, he argued that a precise knowledge of one's origin formed the basis for successful education. Heritability, Pfahler pointed out, situated "the human being in a firmly bounded space" from which one could "never break out" in one's life.[349] In this respect, the "doctrine of heredity" determined the "field of education," which was "possible only in the framework of the boundaries staked out by race and heredity."[350] Thus Pfahler formulated a position shared by many pedagogues in the 1930s. Other experts such as Alfred Baeumler noted that only through knowledge about heredity could one grasp the "true principle of educability"; the point of education was to help hereditary dispositions achieve their best possible expression.[351] Göll's discussion of his own origins and the interpretation of a "development of personality blocked by wrong parenting" were inscribed precisely along this dividing line. Even though Göll did not trace his family lineage to verify his non-Jewish origins, and although he repudiated the Nazi regime's racial-hygiene measures in his diary, by interpreting his own deficits as the result of bad parenting—and not the result of his inadequate hereditary dispositions—he adopted a key figure of thought that underlay the Nazi regime's policies of racial hygiene.

Franz Göll was not merely appropriating an ideological notion whose validity he affirmed even though he repudiated the racial policies. By emphasizing his educability, he also set himself apart from people whose educability the Nazi regime denied and who therefore also were not meant to participate in the formation of new lifestyles and self-contemplations by way of the education project. At the start of his book, Gerhard Pfahler had emphasized that the knowledge of heredity pointed in two directions. Along with the "hereditary occurrence with completely or almost healthy human beings" there was "degeneracy and disease."[352] The latter were decidedly not the subject of his suggestions about a proper education that brought hereditary dispositions to account. Pfahler offered only one piece of advice for the individual affected by the "terrible severity of what heredity can mean" because of "degenerate," "diseased," or "alien" hereditary elements: to break "the chain of his lineage out of free resolve." Only by forgoing progeny of their own could these people still "provide a building block for the construction of the Reich" and "make [their] lineage 'full-value' again in its demise, in the sense of what is valuable for the nation according to the new German image of man."[353]

Pfahler openly indicated how very much the National Socialist education project's boundary along the question of one's origin was also supposed to form the boundary of community membership itself and what, for the Nazi regime, followed from ineducability due to heritable factors: the expulsion of such persons from the "Volkskörper" (body of the people) held together by heredity. These persons were no longer under the purview of the educational actors of the Nazi regime but rather under that of its security and health officials. And the latter did not rely on the affected person's "awareness of responsibility" as evoked by Pfahler. Instead, with massive violence, by means of sterilization and murder, they pursued the "elimination" of all those persons imputed to have a "hereditarily harmful" influence on the "German Volk."[354]

The question of whether one's weaknesses were learned or inherited did not just constitute a scientific problem that could be figured out with the (inadequate) methods of family studies. Instead, for individual Germans, the answer to this question had immense consequences for their personal life in the present and for its future trajectory. In the 1930s, the question about origin was so relevant to how people conducted their life, not because educational actors repeatedly proclaimed that life decisions were henceforth to be oriented according to one's personal lineage, but because this question could simply not be avoided in light of the constant threat emanating from the racial-hygienic distinction between heredity and education.

This is shown quite powerfully in situations where the biologizing of individual self-perceptions did not occur through self-directed research into one's personal origins but came about when doctors and other official bodies forcibly confronted individual Germans with the finding that they had "diseased" hereditary dispositions. Born into a Catholic family in 1918, Thomas Vossen* kept his diary in the mid-1930s as a school student in a small Westphalian town; he came to notice these repercussions quite drastically with respect to a friend. In December 1935, he met a friend he had not seen in a long time, and this friend behaved strangely. "He seemed to be fighting an internal struggle," Vossen noted in a lengthy diary entry, describing further how the friend had suddenly lunged at him and choked him when Vossen talked about the girl that his friend adored. The reason for the attack, however, was not jealousy or disappointed love. "With pain and difficulty," Vossen reported, he brought his friend "to us in the apartment," where "he told me . . . his entire life." Vossen noted "the terrible state of his family. For him, the hereditary burden came to light in the sexual area. He is fighting against masturbation and is succumbing until a pure friendship with a girl liberates him from it."[355] Vossen's description noticeably reflected sexual notions and redemptive hopes shaped by Christianity, which also marked his diary in other contexts—he had introduced the diary with the epigraph "Live God's work and life is a testament to the spring-clear pure idea of God-Life."[356] But the episode does not just indicate that the popularized biological knowledge of heredity could be joined with notions strongly shaped by religion. It also clearly illustrates how the knowledge of the "laws of heredity"—and hence of being different from what one actually wants to be because of lineage—could provoke profound uncertainty and anxiety.

The difficulties created for people upon the revelation of a supposedly hereditary illness in their family can also be traced in situations where such difficulties were self-consciously and successfully integrated into one's own self-conception. This is illustrated, for example, by the diary of Fritz Funk*, who lived in Duisburg. During the war, when, after having had two boys, he and his wife also got the girl they had been longing for since the 1930s, the proud father took this as an occasion to implement his long-held plan "to keep a family diary." Funk opened the diary with a section titled "My Memories," in which he recorded "What life gave us . . . good and bad."[357] He began with his youth, telling about how after grade school he had wanted to be a confectioner but then completed an apprenticeship as a machinist; how, having then become unemployed, he tried to get various jobs and in 1933 finally went to the labor service. During this period, he came to know his wife, who worked in a Duisburg cable factory. From this point onward, in a report organized in a number of dated entries, he concentrated on the history of their marriage, describing key events: the wedding, which was made necessary because of an unintentional pregnancy and caused difficulties with their respective parents because Fritz was baptized as a Protestant and Käthe as a Catholic; the tight living conditions with his parents-in-law, where the young married couple had to live because they could not afford their own apartment; the move to a three-room apartment, which only became possible more than two years later through state mediation but was nonetheless described as a great triumph, even though at first they had "furniture . . . for just barely two rooms"; and finally the birth of their two sons in 1935 and 1937.[358]

The material difficulties at the center of this sketch-like account were also specifically related to their having been denied the state's marriage loan—financial support for newlyweds introduced in 1933. Funk expressly pointed this out in his report. Although the entry was written in retrospect, in describing the marriage he first highlighted how, even though "the times . . . [were] not rosy," he decided to marry because he was sure they would get the state loan. He did not report that their application had been denied until the section dated the following month.[359] "The reason will probably be," Funk noted, that "Käthe's sister Gisela is in an institution in Essen and the institution's doctor is treating the affliction . . . [as] heritable."[360]

With that Funk began talking about the second plotline dominating the description of their years of marriage, apart from the report about their economic circumstances. The importance of his wife's evidently problematic lineage in the account of their joint story in the diary is shown by that fact that, after the typical stations of a marriage biography (getting to know each other, wedding, births, moving into a shared home), under the date "September 1935" Funk now spoke only about this one other event: "Receive a decision notice from the health court, according to which, because of Gisela Tönjes and the liability of other family members on Käthe's side, sterilization is supposed to be performed on my wife." The text noted that they opposed this "with might and main," with his wife having to "prove that she is effective as a useful member of the Volk [Volksglied] in all respects." Within this context, Funk had apparently dealt quite intensively with his family's hereditary "liability," "but," as he wrote, this should "be of no further interest here." In retrospect, for the family history it seemed sufficient to note that "Käthe . . . solved her problem well." She was "recognized as a useful member of the community." Continuing for emphasis, Funk added that she "proves to me anew each day that she can keep house, understands saving, and above all knows things for which she strives and lives."[361]

Despite the danger threatening the marriage and their plans for children, which in 1935 were still unresolved, Fritz Funk addressed the problematic lineage of his wife, Käthe, in his account in the family diary, which was later supposed to help the children reflect on their origin. In the diary written retrospectively after the start of the war, this was not merely an expression of insecurity and anxiety. Precisely because they had managed to avert the sterilization, Funk could have simply concealed his wife's origin, which in the 1930s and 1940s was a threat to his family. That he did not do so and instead made his wife's hereditary "liability" the second plotline of the family diary shows that he reacted to the threat by trying to find an interpretation that could accommodate the hereditary "liabilities." Thus Funk too engaged in the biologizing of his own self-conceptions, although he did not reflect on his forebears on his own initiative but rather under duress.

However, Funk's interpretation was likewise based on the circumstance that no method existed for directly and unambiguously identifying hereditary dispositions. Funk himself noted in his diary that since there "merely existed states of illness in Käthe's family," these could be "construed in different ways."[362] Thus he could develop a self-conception of his family that integrated the "liabilities" of his wife, even though in this respect—just as with the decision to have further children—he did not comply with the expectations of educational actors concerning his "awareness of responsibility." This was only possible because the threatened sterilization was ultimately not performed. Yet at the same time, Funk did not view this official decision as proof of his wife's health. During his account of the wedding, when speaking about his parents' concerns about him marrying a Catholic woman, he insisted even in retrospect that religion was just a "matter of the heart" and that therefore it was of "no further importance what the offspring know about religion. They are German." But something else seemed more important to him. Adding his own anxieties to those of his parents, he noted, "If they have something from my blood," then he was sure that his children would "put aside the nonsense" coming from the hereditary dispositions of their mother. "Good [blood] enhances them," he concluded hopefully.[363]

The example of Fritz Funk shows that even if the biologizing of individual self-perceptions was coerced by the confrontation with "hereditary liabilities," the ambiguities of the knowledge of heredity opened up interpretative spaces that individuals could use to reconcile even problematic lineages with their own self-images. But the example illustrates more than that. It also points toward threats, fears, and worries that unverified knowledge could trigger. However much Funk hoped that his own "good" genotype would have a formative influence on his children, people could have little certainty—despite precise genealogical research—about the concrete effects of their hereditary dispositions. This was also the background for Werner Kramp's comments in his diary around Christmas 1933, which noted that he read "all sorts of biological material, but just not with sure understanding and consoling expectation," and emphasized that he was starting to "fear the pitfalls of the blood, of the hereditary mass."[364] For him too, there was an external reason to worry. Following the statement, he asked, "Where could the epilepsy of the brothers come from?" He continued: "One would like to have oneself examined someday, but this too is always prevented by the wretched question of cost. The blood makes its presence known."[365]

For Kramp, the uncertainty about the state of his own hereditary disposition held immense potential to lastingly change his self-image. To be sure, his preoccupation with bachelorhood and the longing for a partnership and offspring continued to dominate his diary. But at the same time, driven by anxieties about his own origin, Kramp now began to view these topics increasingly within the context of his possibly problematic hereditary disposition and to distrust his own body. Immediately around the time of his genealogical endeavors, Kramp wrote the entry in which he spoke about his body by way of the "pain symptoms in the back" he developed after carrying a suitcase and thought about getting involved in sports "in the interests of health."[366] The unpleasantries of collective gymnastics in the SA or other Nazi organizations and his unwillingness to expose himself and his body to their disciplinary treatment constituted only part of his reason for not doing so. He also noted that the enterprise was probably completely pointless because "if my healthy blood fails . . . I am finished anyway."[367]

A few months later, in November 1934, it seemed to him that this had actually happened, as he reported in his diary that one of his brothers had agreed to his own sterilization. Kramp commented that he himself had only sparse "hope for procreation," since it was certainly an obstacle for marriage "that my brother is mentioned as being hereditarily diseased. According to the views now just gaining acceptance, one can never get rid of such a defect."[368] Expressions of despair about ever being able to found a family were not uncommon in Kramp's diary and had marked his entries for years. In this respect, his brother's sterilization and the implied official confirmation of his worries about his own hereditary disposition also fit with his existing self-image. But at the same time, the biologizing of his person decisively changed the nature of his dissatisfactions and anxieties. Now they basically could no longer be changed; instead, they were determined by his origin. "The Mendelian laws are confirmed even for critics" of racial-hygienic policies, Kramp wrote, reflecting on the hopelessness of his constant complaints about his bachelorhood—a hopelessness that was previously unknown. "We cannot avoid our time, even if we retreat from its pressure into ourselves."[369]

This was even more so the case for Germans whose lineage gave them no maneuvering room whatsoever for willful interpretations, as was true for young Rudolf Briske, for example, who in his diary and in the labor service worked so hard at "combining worldview with my Self." In his effort at political self-formation, Briske did not personally assign much importance to his lineage. But as the son of a father who had converted from Judaism to Christianity as a young adult, he unavoidably faced the coercive biologizing of his person by the Nazi regime. This is also documented by his diary. In fall 1933, Briske ended the chapter on "Thoughts" in his diary, which he had started a few weeks earlier and had organized according to key words, when his sister came home with the news that she had been ex-matriculated as a student because of her origin. In its place, he started a new diary with regular entries about his everyday life and began by noting his intention from then on to "keep a diary again for an indefinite period" because now "everything must be prepared for idea and struggle—especially for me in my situation."[370]

Briske noted more clearly than before that the political events since spring 1933 did not just open up opportunities to him for political self-contemplation, where he personally could situate himself with his "thoughts." Rather, as the result of the Jewish lineage ascribed to him by the regime, political developments affected him far more directly, to which he reacted with a different kind of diary writing. Here he spoke very directly about himself, even though he was still occupied by the question about how his lifestyle and self-perception stood in relation to National Socialist rule.

His subsequent entries repeatedly turned on a problem that Briske had already identified in the opening entry of his diary—namely, that for him and his sister it was being "made difficult to remain National Socialist. Especially because of course one does not want us to be National Socialists."[371] Briske felt the immediate impact of this in his everyday life. He was no longer allowed to participate in the Hitler Youth, which in summer 1933 had taken over the Greater German Youth League where Briske had been an active member for years. Other members spoke out against him as a "Jew." For him this was a profound rupture. "Until now one always had something to do, especially in the league," Briske noted in his diary in November 1933. All his friends were "active in the movement and no longer have any time for one. One has abundant energy—and yet is more lonely than ever before."[372]

And yet Briske thought the actions taken against the Jews were basically needed. "For us, a pity that it came," he noted upon his sister's exmatriculation, "but it is right. It had to come this way. Revenge against Marxist Judaism is being taken out on us."[373] In the following months, Briske frequently affirmed his approval of the regime's antisemitic policies, emphasizing that "questions of heredity . . . particularly interest[ed]" him. With regard to his situation and his parents, he also repeatedly spoke about the "horrible crime" his mother had committed "by marrying a Jew."[374] This led to severe conflicts with his parents, which escalated as early as November 1933. Asked by his father whether "or not this state [has] stripped me and my predecessors of honor," he responded, "Yes, it has taken away the honor of a small number of Jews, but in exchange has given it back to millions of Volk comrades."[375]

In the fierce conflict that followed, Briske's father threw him out of the house, and he ran away and declared that he would only return once his father gave him "his word of honor" as a "World War officer" to "no longer speak against my National Socialism." Commenting on the apology, Briske wrote, "Pity that this man is a Jew," underscoring that he was well aware of the tragedy of the situation. It is "terrible," he wrote, that "Father and Mother . . . through this marriage wanted the best for Germany, without knowing that they thereby plunged themselves and their children into ruin and are thereby committing a crime against the Volk!"[376]

In the 1930s, the biologizing of personal self-conceptions did not just occur by researching one's own lineage as propagated the regime, an activity many people pursued beyond what was needed for verifying their non-Jewish lineage. Rather the racial-hygienic policies of the Nazi regime also forced personal self-conceptions to include the individual's personal lineage by confronting them with their "hereditarily diseased" or "alien" dispositions. Time and again, the ambiguities of the scientific knowledge of heredity created room for specifically adapted interpretations. Cases like that of the Funk family acutely show that, despite all scientification, the biologizing of personal self-perceptions in the 1930s allowed for readings specifically adapted to oneself. Therefore we cannot conclude that biologizing interpretations indicated an approval of Nazi policies of racial hygiene. But at the same time, even idiosyncratic interpretations of one's lineage confirmed the central principles of racial hygiene in one's own case. People could not circumvent the "laws of heredity." Given the absence of methods for the exact verification of hereditary pathways, they could only find interpretations that rejected the influence of potentially harmful hereditary dispositions and conformed to their existing self-images.

Hence, even this kind of biologized self-perception ultimately promoted the state's racial policies. This did not require people to deliberately and willingly include knowledge of their origins in their life planning, as did the young Inge Thiele, for example, when thinking about her future offspring. With the biologizing of personal self-perspectives, even Germans with their own ways of reading their lineage could not avoid the fact that they were supporting the Nazi policies of racial hygiene, whether they wanted to or not. Its principles came to pervade society precisely because the scientific knowledge of heredity could be linked in such different ways with one's own self-conceptions. Even though many people construed the scientific knowledge of heredity and race in their own willful manner, they thereby nonetheless affirmed the basic assumptions of racial hygiene. It thus became impossible, especially for individuals with a supposedly "alien" lineage, to evade the biologizing of their person. "Again a terrible day, like everything in my life thus far. Caused by this terrible crime of a Jew and a German woman marrying each other," Rudolf Briske noted in late November 1933 in his diary, deep in despair because his origin forced him to be someone different from who he actually wanted to be. "To have to be Jewish by blood and internally German: that is terrible. . . . I ask myself: What meaning does my life have? I know none. And why am I still alive? This is known only by someone higher than me. I can only say: pity that I was born."[377]

Political Self-Formation between Origin and Future

The case of Rudolf Briske is not typical of the reactions of Germans deemed to be Jews by the regime. Yet for precisely this reason, his case provides for some key insights with regard to the National Socialist education project because Briske, despite his origin, intensely worked on his political self-formation with the new models of personal lifestyles and self-contemplation. Even while clearly recognizing his origin as an insurmountable barrier, he struggled so as not to succumb to the role prescribed by his lineage and to still participate despite his origin—not only by politically forming his way of life and self-contemplation according to ideological models but also on an organizational level.

In thinking about his professional future after graduating from secondary school in spring 1933, he pointed out that studying abroad in Austria would perhaps allow him to "enter into relation with National Socialist organizations and prove himself there."[378] By way of leaders of his former youth league, Briske also sent a "request for recognition" to the Prussian minister president Göring to find acceptance in the Hitler Youth, SA, or other organization. But at the same time, he repeatedly noted in his diary that he did not want to make his involvement in National Socialism contingent on official recognition. In his year-end review for 1933, he explained his goal to "combine worldview with my Self" more precisely: "If possible, deployment in the state. Otherwise work for the state, even if it is not wanted." And he thus clearly underscored how much he still wanted to participate even if he was denied an exemption regulation.[379]

Briske was quite successful in this effort. In the 1930s, he did not just *want* to be part of the Nazi education project, in which many actors worked on the realization of the "new man" in the interest of the Nazi regime—he unquestionably *was* part of that project. This was not only because he ultimately received an exemption regulation (this notwithstanding the failure of his appeal to Göring) and found acceptance in the labor service. What made him part of the National Socialist education project was above all his strong and emphatic dedication to the political formation of his own physicality and communal self-perspective. Even if their appeals were not actually directed at him, in the 1930s Briske did exactly what educational actors demanded from the Germans: he related his own ways of life and self-perspectives to the propagated models. Participation in the Nazi education project did not depend on formal membership in Nazi organizations or educational establishments but on the concrete behavior of individuals.

The personal effort at political self-formation within the framework of the many different measures for the "education of the German Volk" was not determined by the lineage of individuals, yet having an "alien" origin or "hereditary liability" raised particularly striking questions as to why someone would try to adapt to the Nazi regime's propagated models. Rudolf Briske raised them as well, thinking about them extensively in his entries on the relationship between lineage and self-conception. "One will, perhaps rightly, prohibit us from professing ourselves as National Socialists, from professing outwardly," Briske noted as early as fall 1933, defiantly underscoring his aspiration to participate. "But political attitude, worldview, cannot be forbidden."[380] His further statements are especially informative with regard to the question of the individual's ideas of one's origin because they deliberately took up the other conceptual meaning of *origin*: the social context from which a person derives. Time and again, Briske reassured himself of his self-image as a "National Socialist" by referring to his previous course of life, which he opposed against his "Jewish" lineage. On the occasion of January 30, 1934, for example, he basically argued that "the best National Socialist is not he who came over with flying flags and previously was somewhere else . . . but rather he . . . who out of love for the Volk has first brought himself to this idea and then fights for it, because at heart he must." Referring to himself, Briske added, this could "also be someone who earlier did not stand in the National Socialist movement but fought elsewhere for the Volk."[381] Along these lines, Briske in his diary repeatedly referred to his past years' activities in the Greater German Youth League, an organization whose "heritage" had now been taken over by the Hitler Youth. His "works" had "not [been] for naught," noted Briske, who also saw his own work preserved in the Hitler Youth Fähnlein that emerged from his earlier youth league unit. There would be "nothing . . . without us, without yesterday," he noted in his diary.[382]

References to a person's own past were nothing unusual in diaries of 1933–1934. Indeed, many people tried in this way to profess belonging to the Nazi regime and at the same time document that doing so did not mean they were denying their previous political views.[383] In a certain sense, Briske's reiterated reference to his political involvement prior to 1933 was supposed to perform the same function. But at the same time, he clearly understood that, in light of his origin, he "had to stand apart, that one does not need me," as he remarked in his diary when he received the rejection of his plea to Hermann Göring.[384] For Briske, this was not about commitment, which always had two sides, which had to be justified within and displayed without.[385] He knew that he could not publicly claim or display belonging. In his diary, he searched for a justification to still consider himself a "National Socialist" despite his origin, even if he "could tell it to no one."[386] In this respect, for Rudolf Briske, references to his life path prior to 1933 were also an expression of a way to contemplate his life and origin that would integrate him into the Nazi education project, beyond his efforts at political self-formation.

Without doubt, the efforts at biologizing personal self-perspectives through genealogy and the knowledge of heredity stood at the center of the endeavor to motivate people to confront their own origin. However, educational actors also worked at using new political models to influence how people imagined their life paths starting from birth. Contributing to this, for example, were the many novels, brochures, and educational materials that described the life of the "martyrs of the movement" as a "meta or collective biography." By representing the fate of their protagonists as "standing in for the fate of the German Volk," they did not just present their life story "in an idealized manner as a guide to action."[387] With their "remarkable uniformity with regard to substantive structure," the publications also offered a specific model for how to contemplate one's own life.[388]

The diaries of young people that were first started in the 1930s illustrate particularly clearly just how purposefully this model was deployed to shape ideas about one's origin. Such writers frequently began their diaries with a detailed description of their previous life path. Anton Gloeckner, for example, was born in 1920 and in fall 1933 had attended a Hitler Youth camp, where he wrote a camp diary. He went on to keep a private diary, which he began by "recording my experiences as a tiny tot."[389] Gloeckner began with his birth, spoke about numerous episodes from his childhood, and reported on his school career. The focal point of his descriptions, however, was his involvement in the Hitler Youth. With reference to "many a trip, home evenings, marches, scouting games, liturgical masses, and camps," he drew a direct connection from his activities in the Catholic youth organization League of New Germany to his current Hitler Youth activities.[390]

Above all, however, he integrated into his biographical sketch, which thus far had only been about his own life path, a few remarks about the "party struggles" of the late Weimar period, during which he "eagerly gathered all of the leaflets" even though he could "not figure anything out . . . from their content." "I was not committed to any party," noted Gloeckner, "yet after the National Socialist revolution I joined the Nazi Schoolchildren's League," "zealously" wearing its "badge with the inscription: 'Now more than ever!'" He wrote, "I still have a good recollection of the election campaign for the Reich-presidential election. In it I passionately took the side of Hindenburg."³⁹¹ After this account of his political position around 1933, Gloeckner devoted the last section of his multipage description of his life to his joining of the Hitler Youth and the special events he had participated in as a member so far—above all, camps, rallies, and cultural events. "Now I am finished with my toddler's history," he wrote at the end of his introductory life sketch, closing with the declaration that he had "come to be a vain boy" who "someday wants to join the Reich Army as a doctor or officer."³⁹²

Similar interpretations of the diarist's own life are also found in other diaries of young people of the 1930s. Inspired by the prototypical biographies in books and brochures, young diarists wanted to portray their previous life trajectory as a path toward the National Socialist movement. Born in 1920 like Anton Gloeckner, Henning Zeng* introduced the diary he started in spring 1938 with a description of his life that likewise first told about his growing up before culminating with an account of his personal political development, which ended with his acceptance by the Hitler Youth. Zeng was similarly anxious to show that during the Weimar Republic he had already been a "German boy" who had admired Hitler and only failed to become a member of the Hitler Youth because his area did not have a local chapter. "So we could only witness in spirit what others felt firsthand," Zeng noted retrospectively. As evidence of his political attitude back then, he added, among other things, a story in which he and some other boys had asked a farmer for "a couple of apples": "'Only whoever is communist gets some.' We stood up at the bridge. Two, three men stepped forward and then gloatingly showed us the apples. We laughed!" Zeng noted emphatically, adding, "And had we fallen over from cravings, we would not have betrayed ourselves."³⁹³

What is telling is precisely this seemingly absurd seriousness with which Zeng stylized the rejection of the apple as an expression of his political attitude. For Henning Zeng actually had no need to prove his belonging, and neither did Anton Gloeckner. At the start of the Nazi dictatorship, they were still under thirteen years old, had no political past in the Weimar Republic, and as members of the Hitler Youth in the present of the 1930s were firmly integrated into the National Socialist movement. What we see in their vigorous efforts to situate their National Socialist attitude in the period before 1933 and to present their own childhood as part of the rise of the NSDAP is not a struggle related to the sort of commitment claimed by many adults in the 1930s using biographical arguments. Instead they tried to interpret their lives by way of a prototypical National Socialist biography that was actually modeled on the role of the "old fighter," namely, NSDAP members who as adults during the Weimar Republic were instrumental in the ascendance of the NSDAP.[394] The intended transformation of the individual's ideas about his origin within the National Socialist education project was therefore not just determined through biologization but also through politicization. Whereas genealogy disseminated practices and knowledge that individuals were supposed to use to grasp themselves as the product of their ancestors, educational actors also popularized new models of biographical self-contemplation through which the individual's life path starting from birth was supposed to be contemplated according to the question of what the individual would have done for the National Socialist movement and "his Volk." This way even Rudolf Briske, despite his "Jewish lineage" but with his longtime involvement in the Greater German Youth League, could grasp himself as part of the National Socialist movement.

In the double perspective of biologization and politicization, the redefinition of individuals' ideas about their origin generated a paradoxical but crucial effect for the educational endeavors of the Nazi regime. Despite all of the forceful demands for foundational transformations and "new" lifestyles and self-perspectives, the specific nature of the reconfiguration of the ideas about personal origins always also defined individuals in terms of what they already were by virtue of their lineage and previous course of life. "I cannot get rid of my past," the Berlin white-collar employee Franz Göll complained repeatedly in his genealogical discussions about his family in his diary over the following years. "Sometimes it seems to me as if my life had not yet begun," he noted in spring 1938, for example, "as if I still need to first overcome the past (seen in terms of hereditary biology)."[395] The Gau training director Wilhelm Bollmann noted something similar when looking back in his diary over his involvement in the NSDAP since 1929, concluding with satisfaction that the "erstwhile ridiculed and besotted Nazi" had turned into a respectable and influential functionary: "Officers and honors of all kinds have not [been able] to delude or change me and my own."[396]

Whether people bemoaned not having changed or made this the basis for their pride, either way, they failed to see that the question of change or continuity was not about individual strengths or weaknesses. Despite all appeals for renewal, the persistence of one's own life—by way of the question about one's origin—was instead a fundamental part of the National Socialist education program. Paradoxically, the regime asked individuals to be completely different in the "new era" but at the same time also to be what they always were with regard to their forebears and previous course of life. This paradox also helps explain why the existing self-perspectives and lifestyles of Germans were so immensely important to political self-formation in the 1930s. It was not just that individuals, when striving for political self-formation, always also brought themselves with their prior life history into the Nazi education project. Through the question about personal origins, the project itself demanded that one adhere to existing self-conceptions and lifestyles.

For this reason, the oft-observed persistence of individual lifestyles and self-images in the 1930s should not be grasped simply as proof of the failure of the Nazi regime's educational aspirations. In fact, as Ian Kershaw and then many other studies have emphasized, efforts to change people's self-contemplation and life management became effective above all in areas where the models advanced for this purpose harmonized with existing views and lifestyles.[397] But this does not, in fact, point to the lack of effectiveness of education propaganda, for example, but rather to the central feature of the political change of individual self-perspectives and ways of life in the 1930s. The educational efforts did not just reinforce existing convictions, as has often been stressed in the scholarship. Rather, they led many people, at least in individual contexts, to begin aligning their life management and self-contemplation with the new models prescribed by the Nazi regime. This did not mean implementing forms of everyday life and thought that were completely new. Rather, the effect of the Nazi education project lay precisely in the ability to factor the Germans and their individuality into the process of political self-formation. A combination of political models of the "new man" and the individual's own experiences and views emerged, the results of which can hardly be explored through external observations because existing lifestyles were not simply replaced by new ones. The Nazi regime did not manage to directly achieve its utopian ideas in the education for communality, in the realization of its own conceptions of the body, or in the biologizing of individual self-perspectives and lifestyles. Yet nonetheless, for many people the efforts undertaken for this purpose led to a situation in which their relationships with others, their relationship to their own body, or their idea of their personal origin were shaped and transformed by the political categories of the Nazi education project. Though often not in the manner envisaged by educational actors, with its intensive efforts to create a "new," "National Socialist man," the Nazi regime actually managed to politically shape individual self-perspectives and ways of life. Admittedly, not to the degree called for by the regime's utopian models, and certainly not with respect to all Germans. But even though in the 1930s the "new," "National Socialist man" could not be had apart from the paradoxical interpenetration of political aspirations asserting newness and existing self-images of individuals founded on earlier experience, diaries of the 1930s clearly show how very much individual self-conceptions and ways of life were changed within the framework of the education efforts pursued by the Nazi regime.

PART THREE

On the evening of October 14, 1933, the late editions of newspapers announced in huge headlines that Germany had withdrawn from the League of Nations and pulled out of the disarmament conference in Geneva. The representatives of sixty-four states had started negotiating the coordinated worldwide reduction of war materials in February 1932. The Hitler government took over Germany's negotiation mandate one year later, and during the first months of its existence saw the Geneva conference as an important forum in which to distinguish itself on an international stage. The new Reich chancellor had always publicly asserted his interest in international reconciliation and commitment to peace, even though just three days after his appointment he had openly presented his foreign policy objectives to top Reichswehr leaders as "strengthening the will to fight," the "reconstruction of the Wehrmacht," and the "conquest of new Lebensraum in the East."[1]

For the new regime, the disarmament conference was primarily supposed to reinstate the military balance between Germany and the victorious powers of the Great War. Accordingly, in his "speech for peace" in May 1933, Hitler had announced that if the perpetuation of separate armament regulations resulted in an "eternalization of Germany's disqualification," then "it [would] be ... difficult for us to continue belonging to the League of Nations."[2] In fall 1933, it became increasingly apparent within the Geneva negotiations that above all Great Britain and France were unwilling to allow the partial German rearmament that the Hitler regime considered necessary to achieve parity with other states, and Germany left the armament conference and League of Nations in mid-October.[3]

The extensive activities through which the regime informed the German and international public on October 14 about its decision showed the immense importance it placed on this step in terms of foreign and domestic policy. Along with an official announcement and a "Call of the Reich Government to the German Volk" disseminated through mass media and placards, Reich Propaganda Minister Joseph Goebbels also held a press conference on this day, where he read a further "Call of Hitler to the German Volk." In addition, for that evening he organized a radio address in which the Reich chancellor turned directly to the Germans and the representatives and publics of other countries.[4] In the radio address, Hitler underscored that the government and population were fully at one in the decision to withdraw, something that had already been vigorously maintained in the texts published earlier that afternoon. The "Call of the Reich Government to the German Volk," for example, began with the determination that "the German Reich government and the German Volk are at one in the will to engage in a policy of peace, reconciliation, and understanding," which the text subsequently emphasized even more by starting each additional section with this formulaic expression of unanimity: "The German Reich government and the German Volk renew the commitment to gladly agree to any actual disarmament of the world. . . . The German Reich government and the German Volk are filled by the same concept of honor. . . . The German Reich government and the German Volk are therefore unified in the decision to leave the disarmament conference and withdraw from the League of Nations until this actual equality of rights is no longer withheld from our Volk."[5]

The avowed unity of the "Reich government" and the "Volk" was supposed to find its widely visible expression in a Reichstag election and an accompanying plebiscite, which were likewise announced on October 14 and meant to demonstrate to the outside world that the government was in fact implementing the will of the people. As Hitler had explained in the previous day's cabinet meeting, by "calling on the German Volk to identify with the peace policy of the government through a plebiscite," one removes from "the world the opportunity of accusing Germany of an aggressive policy" and can "arrest . . . the attention of the world completely differently than before."[6] In conjunction with the votes carried out on November 12, each yielding actual results of over 90 percent approval, the withdrawal from the League of Nations became the Nazi regime's "first foreign policy coup." As the first "really spectacular signal of the rigorous protection of self-interests," it marked the start of the abolishment of the international order created after the First World War, which in the following years was advanced with similarly sensational steps and which over the 1930s increasingly dominated political events.[7]

But at the same time, the withdrawal from the League of Nations also formed a key domestic policy event, above all within the regime's planned restructuring of the political relationships between the government and the populace. Deliberations about allowing Germans to vote in a "Volksentscheid"—plebiscite—on government policy in fall 1933 had already been taking place since summer that same year.[8] As effective as the voting events were for foreign policy, they were equally importantly meant to have a separate significance domestically as well. With the fundamental restructuring of the political system over the previous nine months, the government had left no doubt about severing the connections established during the Weimar Republic between the government and the population: parliaments were stripped of their monitoring and decision-making functions, parties banned, and political reporting by the media brought under state control. The voting events of November 1933 dovetailed with this series of actions as well. When in October 1933 the Reichstag was dissolved as required for the new election, this also dissolved the Landtage (state parliaments), which in April that same year had been linked to the legislation of the Reichstag by the Preliminary Law for the Coordination of the States with the Reich.[9] De facto this meant the end of state-level parliamentarianism, since Landtag elections were no longer scheduled; then on January 30, 1934, the Landtage were also formally "abolished" with the Law for the Reconstruction of the Reich.[10]

While the election and plebiscite in November thus formed part of the effort to eliminate as completely as possible the Weimar democracy and its forms of democratic participation, their scheduling and the appeals of the government and Reich chancellor at the same time clearly showed that the government did not intend to exclude the populace from politics. Instead, it sought to create new forms of political participation and vigorously urged individuals to take part in them. Even though the "Call of the Reich Government to the German Volk," for example, with its recurring phrase of "the German Reich government and the German Volk" already anticipated the result of the votes, the text nonetheless ended with a request: "The Reich government directs to the German Volk the question: Does the German

Volk approve of its Reich government's policy presented to it, and is it prepared to declare it as the expression of its own view and its own will and to formally commit itself to it?"[11] Given that the withdrawal from the League of Nations had already occurred, the difference between this plebiscite and a true democratic vote was no more possible to ignore than in the case of the Reichstag election, where one could only vote for the NSDAP. Yet at the same time, the scheduling of the vote made it clear that, even under the changed conditions of the Nazi dictatorship, Germans were still supposed to participate in the political system.

Born in 1871 and working as a school director in Gotha in Thuringia, on October 15, 1933, Georg Witzmann wrote down in his diary his thoughts in reaction to the withdrawal from the League of Nations and the announcement of the voting events. They too were dominated by the tension mentioned above. "I write today under the immediate impression of the news arriving yesterday that Germany has withdrawn from the League of Nations and left the disarmament conferences, that Reichstag elections have been set for November 12, thus four weeks from today. For the time being, elections for the state parliaments are no longer supposed to take place at all," Witzmann began his entry, emphasizing that he was "writing intentionally under the first impression," not yet knowing what had led to the breaking-off of negotiations and "also not yet knowing the speech that Hitler held last evening on the radio." Nonetheless, he wanted to write down what he thought "to be absolutely certain now already." Describing the extraordinary nature of the news, he noted that "not a soul" had believed that "Reichstag elections were to take place again anytime soon." "After all, the era of parliamentarianism is supposed to be definitively over," and for Witzmann it was clear that "genuine elections can obviously also not even take place." The parties were "shattered" and "*forbidden*," their "organizations have been dissolved, the leaders, insofar as they are not sitting in prisons or concentration camps, have secluded themselves." Also, there "is no free press, likewise no freedom of assembly." And even if all of this were restored, Witzmann asked, who "today could risk, for example, making a statement against the regime?"

For Witzmann, it was clear that the Reichstag election could only be "a plebiscite of Hitler supporters and all those standing close to them, or who join them out of personal concern." And by no means did he count himself among them. "For me it is absolutely certain today already," he noted in summary, "one should not in truth be talking about a free vote."[12] Yet despite these unequivocal statements, Witzmann also understood the election announcement as a personal challenge and in the very same entry began thinking about how he should conduct himself when voting. In fact, he noted, the "government has an election slogan that everyone with national feelings must support with an ardent heart: the struggle for the honor and freedom of the Volk and fatherland." In Witzmann's opinion too, the "ignoble role" of Germany, "particularly also in questions of military armament," needed to be redressed, and thus he vigorously underscored that *"everyone"* must "collaborate on this." However, he immediately added, "Does one absolutely need to be a National Socialist for this?" He thus openly raised the question of his own role in the new political system. "Are there not people with national feelings also outside this party? Are they unworthy of collaboration?"[13]

The third part of this book pursues the Nazi regime's aspiration to redefine the relationships between the government and population and the changed forms of political action and evaluation that emerged after 1933 as part of the new political system of National Socialism. It thereby adopts a narrow concept of politics that focuses chiefly on the interaction between the actors, processes, and structures that are involved in the determination of generally binding political decisions.[14] Such a traditional concept of politics has come under criticism from historians in recent years. With good arguments, scholars have made the case for a "new political history" that pursues "the political" beyond the boundaries of classical political institutions.[15] But even though the following deliberations are very much intended as a contribution to a "new political history of National Socialism,"[16] it seems to me that, with regard to the highly politicized context of the Nazi dictatorship, such an expanded concept of politics is insufficiently distinctive. If the concept of politics is supposed to refer to a discrete problem under National Socialism and not to the totality of social life, it makes more sense to keep it narrow. Accordingly, the following centers on the "political system of National Socialism" and the question of how the populace was tied into this system under the dictatorship.

In chapter 6, I look at the basic conditions of the relationship between the rulers and the ruled in the Nazi dictatorship. I will first deal with the morale reports of state institutions and political exile groups, which have been intensely used in research of the Nazi period (1); I show how, in its use of this source material, scholarship of Nazi social history has adopted a specific perspective on relationships between the regime and the people that exhibits crucial blind spots. The chapter advocates a realigned perspective, one that does not ask quantitatively about how many contemporaries agreed with the regime but which instead can qualitatively reveal what consensus and political participation actually meant under the specific conditions of the National Socialist dictatorship. Following from this, the chapter continues by looking into the transformative dynamics that gripped individual political behavior in the 1930s (2). I show how, in parallel with the dismantling of the Weimar democracy, existing forms of political evaluation and action became questionable for Germans. At the same time, I emphasize that the Nazi regime itself developed and disseminated ideas for individual political conduct to which the Germans were supposed to adapt. Emerging from the interplay of these developments in the 1930s was a new political culture that must be grasped as an important part of the political system of National Socialism and as crucial to the involvement of the populace.

The resulting forms of political evaluation and action are then analyzed more closely in chapter 7. In a first step, it centers on the reception of mass-media political reporting, asking how Germans, while knowing about the state control of the media, followed political developments (1). After that, I look at concrete encounters between the "leadership and Volk" during radio broadcasts or mass festivals and the forms of political behavior that this produced (2). Both subchapters make the argument that the political culture of National Socialism was never characterized by the political homogeneity sought by the Nazi regime; emerging instead was a specific spectrum of various forms of political evaluation and action, which are assessed in this chapter. Building on this, in a last step I ask about how the interplay of the various forms of political behavior turned into political integration (3) and formed the unanimous support that found expression, for example, in the extreme voting results of National Socialism.

Chapter 8 finally takes the opposite perspective, inquiring how changes to the relationship between the government and the governed worked themselves out not in the political system but rather in the lives of individuals. Instead of looking at the integration of Germans into the political system, here the investigation turns to the actions undertaken by political authorities in the dimensions of the private. In two steps, I analyze to what extent, even under National Socialism, boundaries remained set with regard to interventions in private spaces (1) and how it remained possible in the 1930s to live a self-determined private life (2). In the response to this question, different threads and results from the other parts of this book are brought together at the end of this chapter.

6

A NEW POLITICAL CULTURE IN A NEW POLITICAL SYSTEM

1. What Is the "Volk" Thinking? The Observation of the Political Mood by the Nazi Regime, Exile Groups, and Historians

On the evening of November 12, 1933, the radio announced the preliminary results of the Reichstag election and plebiscite, which heralded an overwhelming approval of the regime's policies: 96.3 percent of eligible voters had participated in the plebiscite, 95.1 percent of whom agreed with the withdrawal from the League of Nations. In the Reichstag election, voter participation (95.2 percent) and approval of the NSDAP ticket (92.2 percent) were slightly lower but nonetheless constituted a major success for the Reich government.

While the next morning newspapers in Germany rejoiced and reported on the great enthusiasm sparked by the voting results within the entire population,[1] a great disillusionment prevailed among leading politicians of the workers parties who had fled abroad. The various exile groups had to some extent tied "substantial hopes" to the votes,[2] which for the first time had promised a chance to give visible expression to the presumed political dissatisfaction in the German Reich. Calls to vote were issued by both the Social Democratic and Communist camps. Through illegal networks set up since the spring, large numbers of smuggled leaflets, newspapers, journals, and brochures made their way to resistance groups that had remained in Germany.[3] At the same time, it was beyond doubt that "both elections [were] ... of little political value, since the most important preconditions for the voters' free formation of opinion did not exist in Germany" and one could not reckon with a "defeat of the government." Accordingly, the Executive Committee in Exile of the SPD (Sopade), which had fled to Prague, agreed that "what mattered" was "not so much the momentary success" but rather "that the party emerges publicly as a center of resistance."[4] Hence the slogan on the leaflet designed by the Sopade for the election (like the voting campaign publications of other resistance groups)[5] stated: "Invalidate the ballot! Plebiscite: no!" The leaflet called on supporters: "If you are a friend of freedom and peace, then ensure the spreading of our slogan." But it also targeted the political opponent. It wanted to show "National Socialists" "that we are not dead" and confidently announced: "We will soon make them even more clearly aware of it."[6]

However, the voting results severely disappointed such hopes. "The voting result of November 12 has left behind an effect that was not readily predictable," a Sopade publication admitted retrospectively as late as summer 1934. Even if "all critical evaluators" agreed from the outset that "the number of naysayers could comprise only a few million, the fact of seeing this result before you in black and white was nonetheless a bitter disappointment for many opponents." In light of the overwhelming approval, it was questionable whether any prospects of success actually existed for the Sopade's own very costly efforts to get rid of the Nazi dictatorship, so, as stated in hindsight, the result "unleashed a deep wave of depression."[7]

Immediate reactions to the announcement of the results were accordingly despondent. Prior to the voting date, the Central Committee of the KPD, like the Sopade, had called out: "Hurl your 'no' against the fascist executioners and warmongers a million time over"; this loud protest was something that "no terror and no election fraud" could prevent.[8] In its declaration regarding the "result of the so-called Reichstag election and plebiscite on November 12," it emphasized first and foremost the massive restriction of voting freedom. In this "forced vote," there was "also no longer the slightest residue of any kind of voting freedom"; political opponents had been intimidated "for weeks previously through threats of murder and unprecedented agitation," and "secrecy of the ballot was effectively abolished" and the "result falsified to a degree unprecedented in history." In this respect, it was "a perfidious lie of the Nazi regime . . . when it claimed that 40 million voters had agreed with its criminal policies. In truth, the number of those who, in full awareness that with their vote they risked the life, freedom, and existence of their person and their family, bravely hurled their challenge into the face of the regime of incendiaries and executioners amounts to many times that of the officially conceded numbers."[9]

Similar reactions that expressed dismay about the results while despondently clinging to earlier hopes also existed outside the communist spectrum—this notwithstanding all of the differences between the wings of the workers movement, which persisted even in exile. After the votes, even *Neuer Vorwärts*, published by the Sopade, appeared with a demonstratively optimistic headline: "Four Million German Revolutionaries." And with regard to the reactions of foreign observers, *Neuer Vorwärts* emphasized that it was wrong to believe that "in Germany a plebiscite had taken place in which the majority had decided for the government." The article countered the corresponding assessment of international newspapers, for example, by stating that in Germany there "had been nothing of the sort of what one calls an election or plebiscite in democratic countries," and, like the Central Committee of the KPD, pointed to the "naked violence" that had determined the votes. Against this background, the opposing voices are to be understood "not in terms of normal conditions [as] 'opposition'" but rather as an "army hostile to the system, a *core troop of the coming socialist revolution*."[10]

However, the persistent hope that much of Germany's population remained antifascist but was just currently suppressed by the Nazi regime had itself come under criticism among political exiles as early as summer 1933.[11] Just a few days before the withdrawal from the League of Nations, the Sopade publishing house brought forth a programmatic polemic that was highly respected among representatives of the political groups in exile and basically called into question the interpretation of the situation in Germany and the related political strategies. According to the text's analysis of developments over the past months, in spring 1933 "the large, once so powerful looking organizations of the working class, set up only for public mass agitation under democratic-legal conditions," were not just unable to appropriately "adapt to the new conditions of illegal struggle under fascism." "Much more severe" in the long term was "that they were fully incapable of grasping the social processes of the fascist revolution which were playing out around them, that, wholly uncomprehending and bewildered, they grasp the victory of German fascism as just a short episode in a society that in principle could always only be democratic and thus after a shorter or longer fascist dictatorship also must on its own return to democratic conditions."[12] But what "if such a revolutionary spontaneity [exists] only in the heads of the socialist parties, but not in reality," the brochure asked provocatively.[13] Under the programmatic title "Start anew!" (Neu beginnen), the text called for a critical analysis of the starting situation in Germany, especially of the social backing that supported the Nazi regime. Only "if the socialist fighters understand the roots, essence, and prospects of the fascist development with scientific clarity, if as revolutionary Marxists they draw clear consequences for their practices from the scientific analysis of the society" could they start working effectively against National Socialist Germany and for socialism.[14]

Having started before the plebiscites, the debate about this interjection sharply intensified as a result of the votes in November.[15] In December, the group behind the programmatic text, which had since come to be known as "Neu Beginnen," took the figures of the plebiscite themselves as an occasion to once more underscore its thesis.[16] "The extraordinarily high number of votes cast for the regime in the vote of November 12 has also led critical observers from abroad to see this result as falsified or as something to be traced back to direct coercion and terror," summarized Neu Beginnen just over a month after the votes, stressing again that this was based on "a mistaken understanding about the actual incursion of fascist ideology into all classes of German society." "Of course," the voting results were "not the expression of the actual opinion of large parts of the population," but even so, "the number of actual supporters of the regime still [is being] underestimated abroad." Instead of lending oneself to "subjectivistic illusions," one had to recognize that "precise observations of this vote show that the voting results on the whole correspond to the real mood. Even if in the main matter many 'corrections' may have been undertaken in rural districts and small localities. The overall result indicates *a tremendously rapid and strong fascization process* of society," which, even if discontent still existed in certain areas, had wrought "in general an affirmation of the new system."[17]

The new publication, however, did not just repeat the assessments of the previous programmatic text and very clearly establish the differences between its own position and those of other resistance groups by comparing the various reactions to the voting results.[18] At the same time, it was also an attempt to put the prescribed realignment of antifascist work into action. Along with the remarks on the reception of the voting results by those in exile, published with the new text entitled the *Dezember Bericht über die Lage in Deutschland* (December report on the situation in Germany) was a collection of "factory reports" and other announcements that the group had received from Germany and that were supposed to provide insight into the real political attitudes within German society. Wholly in keeping with the injunction to "tell it like it is!" this was supposed to provide the basis "to look at the facts of our times clearly in the face, even if they displease us or reveal our old prophecies as mistakes."[19]

The "December Report" formed the first of an entire series of "Reports on the Situation in Germany," which appeared successively in one- or two-month intervals until spring 1936 and with which Neu Beginnen tried from abroad to obtain information about political attitudes within German society. As much as the group demanded that voter support for the Nazi regime not be seen solely as the product of terror and propaganda, it also very clearly understood that it could not rely on official German government accounts when assessing the political situation. Thus, the clear results of the November votes were precisely what prompted the construction of a surveillance system (which was then also substantially expanded over the following months), through which since late 1933 regular reports of the local political situation were being smuggled across the border by comrades in Germany, systemically evaluated, and published in consolidated form.[20] In December 1933, Neu Beginnen was the "first German organization" of political exiles to start "regular reporting in a foreign country" on the societal backing of the Nazi regime, but it did not remain the only one.[21] Neu Beginnen's programmatic text and reporting activity, together with the impact of the November votes, actually led to a reorientation of political work, especially within the Social Democratic spectrum. Its most visible expression occurred with the publication starting in spring 1934 of the *Deutschland-Berichte der Sozialdemokratischen Partei Deutschlands* (Germany reports of the Social Democratic Party of Germany), regularly issued by the party's Executive Committee in Exile until the start of the war.[22] These reports, too, had their origins in the voting results of the previous year; after the results were announced, in the second half of November local party functionaries on their own accord began sending the party Executive Committee descriptions of the political situation.[23] Since spring 1934, the illegal network of Social Democratic liaison officers, originally set up primarily to distribute the party's own literature in Germany, began increasingly being used in the opposite direction—namely, to transport information about the political attitudes of the Germans out of the country.[24]

Political opponents on both sides of the border, however, were not the only ones who, in light of the overwhelming voting results in November 1933, began taking an interest in how things stood with the political attitudes of the German people and the backing for the Nazi regime. In its official statements on the voting results, the government admittedly presented these results demonstratively as proof of the comprehensive support from the "Volk." But at the same time, its security agencies began that very same month to interest themselves not only in the "opponents" and "enemies" of National Socialism but also increasingly in the political opinions of the population as a whole. Just three days after polling day, for example, the Hanover Gestapo (secret state police) sent out a confidential letter informing its subordinated police authorities that "an information conveyance facility [should] be set up for the purpose of informing and keeping up to date the State Police Authority and through its mediation the Secret State Police Office and the minister of the interior and minister president about the mood and currents of thought among the Volk."[25]

The Prussian Interior Ministry had basically already established a system for regular reporting in February 1933 (thus even before the Gestapo had been detached from the general administration and established) through which incidents of subversion and the activities of political and other "opponents" were supposed to be reported in detail to the regime.[26] Yet the letter of November 15 now called for a more comprehensive and "most precise orientation on the mood among the Volk" as a whole, meant to enable the regime to formulate "its decisions . . . in accordance with this." Accordingly, in future local Gestapo offices were to report not only on "anti-state activities and statements" but also on "general expressions of opinion about which measures of the regime are viewed as wrong or how the population wants to see them changed . . . . The purpose of the whole matter is to be able to research the mood among the people and submit this to higher places."[27] The letter from the Hanover State Police Authority and the "situation report" for the month of November, which the authority compiled in early December from the reports it received in return, along with the reports prepared at the same time by other Gestapo offices, marked a fundamental transition within the system of security police reporting. From pure "opponent analysis," the reporting system was now expanded to the comprehensive observation of the general political mood.[28]

The reporting system changed several times over the following years, both because of rivalries between different actors of the security police apparatus and also because other authorities and institutions began setting up their own reporting systems, which were likewise supposed to provide information on the attitudes of the population.[29] In this respect, the series of corresponding institutions ranged from general state prosecutors to the labor offices. The reporting system developed by Reich Propaganda Minister Goebbels was cultivated with particular intensity, and he gave it much more attention than the reports of the security agencies. Likewise, taking shape since 1934 within the NSDAP and its organizations and associations was a "wide-ranging reporting system reaching all the way to the local level and working in a monthly rhythm" for recording the political mood in the population.[30] Taken as a whole, the totality of observation efforts and the sheer mass of prepared reports constituted a remarkable expression of the major significance the Nazi regime assigned to the mood of the "Volk." At the same time, they reveal the Nazi regime's aspiration to react to mood changes as directly as possible with its policies. Not only for exile groups, which hardly had any direct impressions of the political situation, but within the Nazi regime as well, starting in fall 1933 observation developed into the central mode of approaching the population.

Within the historical scholarship, the many reports of political exiles, on the one hand, and the security authorities and other institutions of the Nazi regime, on the other, have received great attention since the late 1970s. Whereas in the 1960s and 1970s research interests were still determined chiefly by questions about decision-making within the political system of National Socialism,[31] since then they have increasingly been guided by the understanding that every form of rule—even a dictatorship—needs legitimation and recognition, as well as the cooperation of the ruled.[32] Established since the early 1980s, social history of National Socialism accordingly dedicated itself primarily to the relationships between the Nazi regime and society, which also continue to substantially determine scholarly debates about the Nazi period.[33] The morale reports by the regime and exile groups became one of the most important sources for this research, used in virtually every pioneering study of the early social history and history of everyday life of National Socialism. The research project Bayern in der NS-Zeit (Bavaria in the Nazi Period), which began the trend of researching the social history of National Socialism, began publishing its results in 1977, with its first volume dealing with the "social situation and political conduct as reflected in confidential reports."[34] These sources were also appropriately important in follow-up studies that emerged in connection with the Bavaria project—they were especially prominent in the case of Ian Kershaw's study on "antisemitism and popular opinion," an initial extract from his later pioneering studies on the "Hitler myth" and "popular opinion and political dissent in the Third Reich."[35] Franz Dröge, Detlev Peukert, and Timothy

Mason likewise built on the monthly reports of exile groups and the regime, attributing to them, in the words of Peukert, "a relatively large credibility."[36]

Editions of the reports were published in large numbers in the 1970s and 1980s and have been readily available ever since, which has helped establish an abiding research interest in "a supposedly subcutaneously hidden, thus genuine and unfalsified 'Volksmeinung.'"[37] Down to the present day, their development and the degree of societal support of the Nazi regime contained within them stand at the core of social-historical research into National Socialism, which is generally governed by the question of how many Germans approved of the regime and its policies. In this respect, the morale reports of exile groups and the regime do not merely continue to form an oft-used source. Rather, the current fierce debate about the "assumption of [the regime's] considerable social powers of cohesion" (Norbert Frei) and the associated characterizations of the political system of National Socialism as a "consensual dictatorship" (Götz Aly, Fank Bajohr) or "participatory dictatorship" (Sven Reichardt) are grounded in the research perspective developed with these sources.[38]

Nonetheless, the intensive exploitation of the morale reports also came under criticism right from the start,[39] and in recent years that criticism has widened once more by way of certain crucial objections. In this context, others, most notably Peter Longerich, have not only pointed out that, in having to compile a representative portrayal of a mood from unsystematic individual observations, reporters from the opposition and the regime alike stood before insurmountable problems—and the explanatory power of their reports on the attitudes of the German people is therefore dubious. Above all, Longerich raised the basic question of whether the entire historiographical "attempt . . . to find out the 'Volksmeinung' does not amount to chasing after a phantom." In this respect, the constant underlying hypothesis of the existence of a "popular opinion independent of the state public policy" is full of assumptions.[40] The existence of a public opinion is necessarily tied to a certain form of the public sphere, which simply did not exist under National Socialism. Longerich has argued that state control of public space "not only largely excluded the emergence of oppositional voices" but also "intended from the outset substantially to hamper, if not totally prevent, any broadly based oppositional, alternative, or even just independent formation of opinion."[41]

In particular, Longerich points out that the regime had its own theoretical notions about the public sphere, public opinion, and the political relationship between society and the government, which in the 1930s and 1940s generated real effects. But these were being overlooked if the inquiry into the "real" attitudes of the Germans implicitly also involved transferring present ideas about the emergence of collective political opinions and operational modes of the political public sphere to National Socialism.[42] One must bear in mind the contemporary understanding of the relationship between the regime and the Volk and its significance for National Socialist policies. Only then can one understand not only the special quality of the reports as a source but also the changes in political behavior and evaluation in the 1930s that I am bringing to the fore.

The Presumed Unity of the Regime and the People

The Nazi regime did not just have its own ideas about the relationship between the government and the population and public communication's role in establishing it. From the start, it also attempted to popularize these ideas, which can be illustrated quite vividly with the case of the campaign related to the election and plebiscite of November 1933. Beginning one week after the announcement of Germany's withdrawal from the League of Nations, the campaigns mounted by the regime and NSDAP for these voting events were not limited, as in previous elections, to soliciting electoral approval—and to that end explaining the withdrawal decision and highlighting the regime's previous successes.[43] Rather, the many speeches, rallies, and materials of the voting campaign were also supposed to impart to the Germans a new, decidedly nondemocratic meaning of voting in the new political system of National Socialism. "I believe that none of you would have believed that . . . after our last vote we would so quickly need to gear up for a new battle for votes," said the Prussian minister president and Reich aviation minister Hermann Göring in his Kiel campaign speech on October 28, 1933, very directly with the reference to the questionable role of voting in the National Socialist dictatorship. Göring was accordingly anxious to explain why—despite promises that the last Reichstag election in March was to have made "the final decision"— voting was once again necessary. Thus he interpreted the pending polls as a necessary "enormous demonstration of our nation's will to resist" vis-à-vis other states. "The purpose of the coming decision" lay in "showing the outside world on November 12 that we have become one Volk": "If March 5 brought the victory and the decision domestically, then we hope to God that on November 12, too, the world realizes that a new Germany has arisen."[44]

For him, there was no question that the voting events would yield the necessary unequivocal results. "We are not, like bourgeois politicians, afraid of the vote," Göring stated, exhibiting the same assurance as other campaign speakers.[45] In his many campaign events, Adolf Hitler repeatedly emphasized that he needed "no vote of the Volk" but that it was important "that the German Volk now steps up itself as a witness for the truthfulness" of government's asserted claim of having acted for the purpose of the German people.[46] And Reich Propaganda Minister Goebbels, responsible for directing the campaign, also pointed out when campaigning began on October 21, 1933, that the "German Volk" should "commit" itself to the policies of the government "in order to prove that the government, with its will for freedom, its resolve to preserve the equality of rights, does not stand alone, *rather that the entire Volk is backing the government in this.*" He proclaimed, "*On November 12 the Volk will step up and prove it. We are polling the Volk in the feeling that we have done what we could do . . . and are of the proud conviction that the entire Volk backs us up.*"[47] Historians like Karl Dietrich Bracher have argued that the regime wanted to make sure that "the Volk did not catch its breath," and tried to keep it in an "incessant frenzy of approval" so it would "forget that the votes too had long been robbed of their actual function"—namely, the "formation of political representations and free formation of political will." However, it seems to me that the campaign rhetoric suggests instead that the representatives of the Nazi regime were vigorously trying to communicate a realigned significance of voting.[48]

In this respect, the certainty about the voting results, aggressively exhibited already in the announcement of the election and plebiscite in mid-October and then reiterated many times during the campaign, was not just supposed to spread confidence and demonstrate strength. Nor did it just refer to the regime's foreign policy calculations related to the votes. Rather, mirrored in this certainty was precisely the National Socialist understanding of the public and public opinion, according to which the "Volksmeinung" was not understood "as the sum of the opinions represented by the individual members of the Volk" but rather the "'Volk' was basically conceivable only as a cohesive unity."[49] With the words "*one Volk, one Reich, one will*," during the campaign Hitler openly identified his own ideal of the political relationship between the regime and the population, for which the vote was supposed to be a "symbol," a "monument of unity."[50] Accordingly self-confident, the regime's leading representatives presented the demonstrative function of voting as a counterproject to its function as a democratic means of collective decision-making.

In late October 1933, for example, the front page of the *Völkischer Beobachter* featured an interview with Reich Interior Minister Wilhelm Frick, who was responsible for implementing the voting process. The very first question concerned the "purpose ... of the Reichstag election and plebiscite": "The election campaign of the National Socialist movement is in full swing. ... Nonetheless, here and there one still runs into uncertainties in circles of the electorate that still have not come to terms with the changed situation compared to previous elections. One asks: previously the various parties fought for the most votes; today all parties are banned with the exception of the NSDAP. Therefore what purpose does voting have if, after all, only one party can be elected?" As an answer and an explanation of the new meaning of voting, Frick emphasized that "confidence" was supposed "to be declared" in the government and that the vote had to be understood as an "*act of will that the German Volk thereby performs before the entire world.*"[51]

Similarly, in two interviews—entitled "Dr. Goebbels on the Coming Plebiscite" and "Why the Reichstag Election?"—Joseph Goebbels underscored the specific character of National Socialist voting events. He too took the question as to "what purpose ... the vote" had if "there are no longer any parties apart from the National Socialists," and in his answer, he pointed out that the pending "Reichstag election is *something completely new* in German history. It is supposed to and will for the first time show the entire German Volk in an unprecedented *unity front.*"[52] This election "is not about the interests of individuals or groups." Accordingly, when challenged with respect to the election and plebiscite "to evaluate the *prospects*, I mean, percentagewise, of the regime," Goebbels's documented response was clearly irritated. "That, in my opinion, is a wrong expression," noted the minister. "*There can be no talk here about the prospects of the government, nor about the prospects of any party.* I am convinced that in [this] question ... there can only be one unified opinion in the first place."[53] "No government" is "as directly intergrown with the Volk as the government of the National Socialist state ... because it itself comes from the Volk," and hence this connection did not need to be produced first by voting.[54]

In the National Socialist understanding, "Volksmeinung" and the Nazi regime were not grasped as independent entities; rather, their unanimity was assumed per se.[55] Compared to its democratic function, voting took on virtually the opposite significance. The government did not need to prove itself before the judgment of the ruled, but rather the other way around: the "Volk" had to demonstrate its level of political maturity by means of voting events. Finally, in his second interview, published two days before the vote, Goebbels had the question put to him whether "the Reichstag election [is] *a test* for the healthy sense and inner discipline of the German voter," and he confirmed this with an *"Absolutely!"* that was also accentuated in print. Whereas "the plebiscite" was about "the approval of the foreign policy decisions of the regime," "the Reichstag election is about no more and no less than the *clear decision* on the total work of *Adolf Hitler.* . . . Particularly the Reichstag election gives every German Volk comrade the opportunity to profess personal confidence to the Führer and savior of the nation."[56]

Combined with this vision of a basically de facto political unity between the government and the population—which admittedly could be subject to "mood fluctuations" but in which adverse opinions remained "by definition always either a temporary errancy or . . . limited to 'alien' groups on the margins of the Volk"—was an aspiration to mold the population to properly express this unity between the "Volk" and the government.[57] Thus, despite the demonstrative display of certainty regarding the voting results, the campaign speeches addressing the individual voters were correspondingly urgent and vigorous. It was the major "duty of every individual German," declared Goebbels, for example, "in the plebiscite *and* in the Reichstag election to step behind Hitler with an outright German 'yes.'" And Reich Interior Minister Frick spoke in his interview of the "single greatest responsibility" being placed on "every German voter."[58] At the end of his campaign speech on October 24, 1933, in the Berlin Sports Palace, the Reich chancellor himself did not just call out to his listeners, "And so I beg you, this time—really, for the first time in my life—give us now your votes." He also supplemented his plea with this demand: "Bring every Volk comrade to the urn, so that he has a say in the future of his Volk."[59]

The regime leadership did not make do with urgent admonishments. On voting day, a "vigorous transport service" did its part to ensure the extremely high voter turnout.[60] And in other respects, too, voting campaign directors used the state instruments of power to deliberately shape the voting results. In their December report, for example, Neu Beginnen documented that "presumably . . . still on the eve of the election [in Berlin] at least 2000 protective custody arrests occurred . . . sometimes with the comment, these people would only vote with no anyway."[61] But above all, for the first time, voting campaign director Goebbels, to prepare for the vote, made systematic use of the new instruments created in late summer and fall for the state control of the media's political reporting. Just four days after the withdrawal decision was announced, the Reich Propaganda Ministry informed the German newspapers that in the following weeks "a unified voting campaign, also with regard to the press," would be ensured by the director of the ministry's press section, who had been "appointed in the Reichsleitung of the NSDAP to safeguard the interests of the press during the votes."[62] The next day, the ministry supplemented this announcement with precise statements explaining that as of "Saturday, October 21," the date of the official opening of the voting campaign, "every confidential communication or technical instruction" of the government to the press would be conveyed to the newspapers "consecutively numbered," and this would be noted in a "logbook . . . as proof" that the individual newspapers had received "knowledge of this." At the same time, somebody at the newspaper was to sign for receipt, "so that here in black and white we have the proof that the instructions reached the hands of the editorial offices."[63]

Moreover, there was no room to doubt that the conveyed "concrete instructions of the government and the entire line" had to be "adhered to under all circumstances." The ministry stressed that "the government's directives" were to "receive the strongest consideration, practically all the way into the smallest details." It openly threatened that "the government is resolved to hold all editors, especially the chief editors, personally responsible if any violations occur," and underscored its disposition by pointing to what had happened to the *Essener Allgemeine Zeitung* as an example. A few days earlier in this newspaper, the caption for a picture of a carnival event had slipped below the photo of an SA march. For that reason, as representatives of the press were informed in the same letter, the "responsible editor, chief editor, and publisher [had been] taken away to a concentration camp" and the newspaper banned for four days.[64] In the following weeks, the regime fought its campaign for the vote with this system of state control of political reporting and in doing so seemed thoroughly satisfied with how the system worked. In a declaration made to his campaign workers in the aftermath of the vote, Goebbels thanked the "entire German press," which had "made up for much of that" which "in past times of opposition" had elicited "bitter reproaches" from the National Socialist movement. In this respect, too, as Goebbels explained, the voting event was supposed to become the "start . . . of a new domestic policy development."[65] And in fact, although the regulations were instituted "at first only for the voting campaign," he left them in place.[66]

The idea that the "Volk" was an "objective independent manifestation," along with which "the 'will of the Volk' [was] also an objective fact" that needed "to be distinguished from the subjective 'conviction of the Volk,' that is, the opinions, ambitions, and anxieties of the respective living members of the Volk," was a guiding light for the Nazi regime. The regime made "bringing about and maintaining" a situation in which "the will of the Volk and conviction of the Volk coincide" a central "task" of its own policy.[67] At the same time, this notion of an objective "will of the Volk" as a stand-alone entity had decisive implications for the "opportunities and limits of opinion research in the Third Reich," which were "substantially determined by the attitude of representatives of the NSDAP to propaganda and to the relative importance of public opinion in the Führer state."[68] It fed persistent doubts about the morale reports of security agencies and other authorities, which in spring 1936, for example, resulted in the Gestapo having to shut down its general reporting on the social mood. In light of the "grandiose voting results" in the Reichstag election on March 29, 1936, related to the remilitarization of the Rhineland, which proved "that the German Volk has thoroughly grasped the fundamental ideas of the policy of the Führer and Reich chancellor, totally affirmed them, and is in no way inclined to allow itself to be shaken in its trust in the Führer," the Prussian minister president Hermann Göring was convinced that the reports were too pessimistic in their assessments of the public mood and prohibited the Gestapo from continuing their production.[69]

Above all, however, the postulate of the unity between the government and the "Volk" also decisively shaped the reports, because, as Peter Longerich pointed out, "from this perspective" reporters could not see "the various voices within the Volk as 'having equal value.'"[70] In the reports, derogatory statements were not awarded the "status of a more or less well-founded 'opposing opinion'" because the reporters, given their notions about the public and public opinion, always already assumed that the "positive mood . . . showed the true 'attitude' of the Volk," whereas by contrast a "negative mood" was "just a superficial phenomenon" that could and needed to be quickly remediated through state intervention.[71] According to Longerich, the reports "obviously . . . say more about the reporter than about the German population" and therefore should not be understood as sources with which historical researchers can peer behind the facade of National Socialist public policy to see the "real" attitudes of Germans. Rather, the reports themselves should be grasped as a "formative element of an artificially produced, official public opinion" that substantially contributed to the state's unification of the population. Under the conditions of the Nazi public sphere, "the formation of collective opinion, that is, the process in which various individual opinions were reduced to a common denominator, took place quite substantially within the framework of the official mood reporting."[72]

In his investigation of morale reports focused on the persecution of the Jews, Peter Longerich thus concentrated not on the political attitudes of the Germans but rather on the ways in which the Nazi regime used those reports to form a certain image of public opinion. Together with other studies that similarly inquired into the governmental functions of mood monitoring, the confrontation with the morale reports in recent years has given rise to a new interest in the functionality of the public under Nazi rule, yielding far-reaching insights.[73] Yet, while this shift in perspectives is convincing, it evades and leaves unanswered the initial questions that exiled and regime actors originally tried to resolve through the reporting and that also motivated historical researchers to turn to the reports in the 1970s: What opinions did Germans hold about the Nazi regime? How did they react to its political decisions? In what way was the population thus included in the design of National Socialist policy? And what social backing did this produce for the regime? In Longerich's investigations, the political attitudes of the Germans and their reactions to the antisemitic policies of the regime only show up as "inhibitors and oppositions" to state efforts to create an integrated picture of the National Socialist public and not as an independent matter.[74]

Even if the reports are not actually suitable sources for answering these questions, at least they provide crucial hints as to where to start an investigation of them, since even the reports of exile groups had already recognized the inadequacy of their method early on. A few days before the publication of the first *Deutschland-Bericht* of the Sopade, an article entitled "The Mood in Germany" appeared in *Neuer Vorwärts* in early June 1934, describing impressions from a trip that the unnamed author had undertaken from exile to Germany. Right at the beginning of the text, which was also widely cited in the *Deutschland-Bericht* of May/June 1934, the author explained that the most important impression of his old homeland was how difficult it was to draw "himself a picture" of the political mood. He could hardly "get [people] to speak." "Nobody opens himself." This was not just because of the fear of denunciation; rather, it was more basically the case that "in Germany not only is there no public opinion, there is also no group opinion anymore. The individual is isolated, thinks and judges for himself.

This even applies to members of the NSDAP. The forced consolidation into one organization means, in truth, an atomization of political evaluation and attitude."[75]

Neu Beginnen noted something quite similar when in August 1934, just nine months after the vote in November, the regime once again called Germans to the ballot boxes to affirm the merging of the offices of Reich chancellor and Reich president in the person of Adolf Hitler. Despite the extensive reporting of the previous months, even now the group was still hardly able to precisely assess the results of the vote, which again signaled broad approval. This time the "Report on the Situation in Germany" argued that "from the total results of the Hitler vote of August 19, 1934, one cannot draw any significant conclusions about the actual picture of the German present," pointing out that "the voting numbers are no doubt falsified."[76]

Given that when assessing the voting in November 1933 Neu Beginnen had so vigorously insisted that, despite falsifications, the results corresponded "by and large to the actual mood," this conclusion was not convincing.[77] The text did not openly explain why in this case the completely different assessment was justified but noted that "in general the so-called democratic addition of voting figures [is] no longer the expression of the degree of maturity of the voting masses."[78] Neu Beginnen also noted the extensive isolation of the formation of political opinion, which made drawing general conclusions from the voting figures fundamentally dubious. The "total result" signified "indeed no more than that the no-votes compared to November 12 [1933] have doubled to 4.3 million, and that, with the addition of the nonvoters, this time somewhat more than 7 million compared with 4.5 million in November 1933 did *not* vote with 'yes.'" But to conclude from this in a rather typical way that the "opposition voices against the regime [have] gotten stronger" and that the "opposition [feels] somewhat more free" seemed questionable to Neu Beginnen.[79] Even though since fall 1933 the group had tried to use its reporting to arrive at an accurate analysis of the societal situation, on the occasion of the next polling date it ultimately had to concede that, even with this instrument, it could not estimate the degree of approval and opposition in Germany any more precisely. For Neu Beginnen, too, it seemed fundamentally doubtful whether the collective opinions assumed by the question even still existed.[80]

The regime's own vision of a given unity per se between the "leadership and Volk" was not just an ideological and theoretical foundation for National Socialist policy. Rather, in the 1930s it had real implications. It formed the basis for a deliberately formative public policy, which through political monitoring of and state influence on the political opinion of the Volk—by means of propaganda and violence—was supposed to give visible expression to the postulated unity. With various governmental intervention methods and impositions vis-à-vis the population and its political attitudes, the current "mood of the Volk" was supposed to be modeled according to the objective "will of the Volk." The morale reports of state and party authorities also did not simply contain the results of the "opinion research institute[s] of the dictatorship";[81] rather, along with terror and media control, they formed part of the apparatus with which the regime worked on shaping the National Socialist public. Within a few months, these measures fundamentally changed the existing ensemble of the forms of political evaluation and behavior, as a result of which Sopade and New Beginnen started to doubt their own reporting early on.

The exile organizations nonetheless continued monitoring the collective mood in Germany. Yet if historical researchers want to avoid simply repeating the perspective of contemporaries and their blind spots, they should take contemporary doubts more seriously and try to gain a different perspective on the relationship between the government and the governed. This is especially important precisely for the question about the transformation of the forms of political evaluation and action. This process is overlooked when historical studies, based on the reports of the regime or exile groups as well as on other sources, consistently take interest primarily in the extent of approval and consensus under National Socialism. If questions are asked about the "real" attitudes of Germans, then the opinions of Germans are inevitably grasped as being independent of National Socialist rule and its public policy—and it is not taken into account that the emergence of collective opinions presupposes public structures for the formation of opinion. "That the Volk, without the presence of corresponding communication channels, could collectively, so to speak on its own, bring forth more or less unified moods and opinion," writes Peter Longerich, is a "myth that was advanced not least by the National Socialist Volksgemeinschaft ideology" and its postulate of the existence of a so-called "will of the Volk."[82]

Since in this book, against the background outlined above, my subject is not the collective opinions of the Germans but rather the forms of political behavior and their transformations in the 1930s, the following chapters investigate the emergence of new forms of political action and evaluation in the Nazi dictatorship, as well as their significance for the new political system and the everyday life of Germans. In so doing, they shift the focus to the place where exiled observers, when doubting their own activity, also localized political opinions in the Nazi dictatorship: the individual and his or her personal occupation with the policies of the regime.

This development is far better documented by diaries than by the morale reports, since they permit the investigation of precisely those processes of "opinion formation based on general and permanent propaganda" that, as Ian Kershaw emphasized in his study for the Bavaria project, cannot be effectively approached by using morale reports because they allow for "hardly any findings to be made."[83] To be sure, Kershaw also insisted with respect to diaries that "expressions of opinion in original form" are not contained "in the surviving sources to a degree that is sufficient for representative surveys," but that is not a shortcoming for this kind of project.[84] Instead, as individualized and subjective sources, diaries reflect the specific conditions of the formation of political opinion under the National Socialist dictatorship even just by virtue of their form.

2. "Why Can I Not Heedlessly Believe?" The Transformation of Political Action and Evaluation in the 1930s

The degree of approbation toward the Nazi regime that became visible in the voting results of November 12, 1933, did not just surprise observers in political exile. The Gotha school director Georg Witzmann had already commented extensively on the announcement of the voting events, speaking in this respect about a "plebiscite of Hitler supporters and all those standing close to them," and as late as voting day, he expected an "almost 100% 'commitment' to the German Reich of Adolf Hitler."[85] On the day after the results were released, he noted, "I must confess that I actually believed that in the Reichstag election the number of those who did not commit themselves to the National Socialist party would be larger." Thus "the 'victory' [is] even bigger than I myself have assumed," although Witzmann added a qualification: "But since one cannot, of course, talk about an election contest, one also cannot justifiably speak about a victory."[86] Nonetheless, the result made a deep impression on him as well. To be sure, "the National Socialists" had often already announced that the "revolution is complete because the decisive victory has been achieved," Witzmann noted almost one week later, but "never yet with the same authority" as this time.

"November 12, 1933, formed, in my opinion, such an important episode in German history that I might well consider whether it is not time to bring these writings to an end."[87]

With this thought, Witzmann referred to the original purpose of his diary, which he had started in May 1933 under the direct influence of the restructuring of the political institutional order of the Weimar Republic. In previous years, the teacher's life journey had been closely intertwined with the republic's political development. In 1919, he had been elected as a member of the national-liberal German People's Party (DVP) to the Gotha state assembly, and when in 1920 the Free State of Sachsen-Gotha merged into the newly founded state of Thuringia, he also represented the party as faction leader in the new state parliament. Hitler's appointment as Reich chancellor had a correspondingly drastic impact on Georg Witzmann. With the reorganization of the German state parliaments in accordance with the Reichstag election results of March 5, 1933, implemented as part of the "Gleichschaltung" of the German states, he too lost his parliamentary mandate and thus a field of activity that in recent years had very much defined his life. "Fourteen years I have stood in public life, almost always at the forefront.... Then came the National Socialist wave, which completed inundated us and tore me from my parliamentary activity (definitively in mid-April 1933)," he noted in the first entry of his diary on May 21, 1933. A new life chapter began. "The time of action is over for now," Witzmann acknowledged, recording his intention to "use the time [to] keep a diary."[88]

Thus it is hardly surprising that his notes concentrate on political affairs, and in this respect his extensive and critical commentary on the announcement of the votes scheduled for November is not alone in making it clear that, as a former parliamentarian, he took particular notice of the changes to the political system and the dismantling of democratic rights. Even in his first entry, he pointed out that there was "no press freedom"; instead, there was "mail censorship, telephones are tapped.... In one generation one will hardly still believe the conditions under which we live today."[89] In the following months, he repeatedly made similar declarations. Yet at the same time, the diary entries did not simply bemoan the end of the Weimar Republic. "It is an interesting time, a time of tremendous new changes," Witzmann added immediately after the preceding quote. For him, it was "not easy to stand aside," and he hoped that this new phase of life would be "just a kind of rest and recovery time, and perhaps... the day will come when I can contribute again." For now, however, he had no choice other than to play "the inactive observer" and, "in face of the great happening that surrounds us and that we experience daily," keep a diary to "depict the internal connections as they appear to me, the problems of our time."[90]

The diary of Georg Witzmann did not just describe the political transition from the Weimar democracy to the Nazi dictatorship. In a twofold way, it was part of this change: it owed its existence to this transition, and at same time, its regular, almost daily entries helped Witzmann understand the transformation of the political system in spring 1933. Witzmann did not write to clarify his position toward National Socialism—he had already done that two years earlier. In April 1931, under his leadership, the DVP faction in the Thuringian state parliament, along with the SPD and KPD, had supported the nonconfidence motion that brought down the first state government in Germany with NSDAP participation. To be sure, this government had come about in the first place only because the DVP had also agreed to a bourgeois–National Socialist coalition.[91] As Witzmann stated in the state parliament, the reason the DVP faction ultimately allowed the coalition to break up was due to the "rudest kind of insults" propounded by the Thuringian Gauleiter and NSDAP faction leader Fritz Sauckel "against the German People's Party."[92] As a result, Witzmann's position toward National Socialism was resolved. In the following months, he received letters "from all parts of Germany" attacking him "as a high traitor and traitor to his country in the most scurrilous manner," and Sauckel had even personally threatened him in the parliamentary session, stating, "Today you are drawing the line. And you can believe: this line, this clarification of the circumstances, this departure of your party now to the left, shall bear its fruit."[93] It is not surprising that in fall 1933, after Witzmann's dismissal from state parliament, the Thuringian Education Ministry attempted to have him removed from the school system.

While other diarists in 1933 wrote about the start of the Nazi dictatorship because they were searching for their own position on the matter, Georg Witzmann dealt with it so much because of his interest in the political changes themselves. Precisely because he was a former parliamentarian, he could not overlook the massive incursions into the institutional structure of the Weimar Republic. Even so, his assessment of this generally remained just as uncertain as his entries in May and November 1933. On the one hand, Witzmann frequently had strong words to say about the "method of violation" with which the new regime suppressed other political opinions and excluded them from political decision-making.[94] On the other hand, however, he also saw plenty of good in the changes. Because of the "disgust . . . that the Germans feel about the interminable voting" and what he sensed as the "repugnance toward democratic parliamentarianism," he felt that a fundamental renewal of the political system was both necessary and welcome.[95] "The Reich constitution of 1919 was unbearable for us in the long term, its abolishment or at least fundamental modification necessary in the interest of the Volk and probably also hardly deferrable anymore," Witzmann wrote in mid-July, for example, and he acknowledged that in this respect "the victory of the National Socialist movement actually cleared the way for new developments."[96]

This fundamental tension in his political verdict led repeatedly to detailed discussions in his diary of basic political questions, concerning, for example, the appropriate form of government for Germans, the relationship between dictatorship and democracy, and above all the methods of the National Socialist seizure of power and whether these would succeed in the "time of construction." However, Witzmann never managed to reach an unequivocal assessment: time and again, his deliberations stressed that democracy had undoubtedly reached its end, but they remained unclear about the new arrangement this had started. In late June 1933, as the last democratic parties were being dissolved, he explained, for example, that with the "now successful destruction of the multiparty state," "first, the status quo was dissolved and . . . new forms created," so that now "the far more difficult part of the task [begins]: these forms need to be filled with content and life."[97] How this would happen, however, was not clear to him, yet Witzmann attributed his vague understanding not just to a lack of information but particularly to himself. Perhaps the new system could "no longer be understood at all by someone who grew up in completely different and now archaic trains of thought."[98]

Georg Witzmann's difficulties in arriving at a confident and for him satisfying assessment of the fundamental change of the political system were not due to a lack of resolve. Nor were they tactics of watchful waiting until political developments became more readily apparent. Rather, they revealed a basic uncertainty about how the new political system could even be properly evaluated. As a former parliamentarian, Witzmann was actually very well practiced in the evaluation and contemplation of political events, yet since spring 1933 he deemed his previous standards for political evaluation hardly suitable anymore. Witzmann's regular discussions in his diary therefore involved more than simply following along with events; they also amounted to a search for a new basis for political judgment and action under the emerging Nazi dictatorship.

Other Germans also had to acknowledge in spring 1933 that their previous measures for political evaluation were no longer valid, a realization that often led them to reflect in writing on the character of the changing political system. Consider Karl Möhring, for example, a pastor's son born in Erfurt in 1908 who during the 1930s studied in Göttingen. In the course of 1933, after Hitler's appointment as Reich chancellor, he not only had to concede that he had been too sure of his personal attitude toward National Socialism, but also had to accept that he had reached the limit of his ability to interpret general political events. Möhring believed himself to be practiced in such interpretation through his many years of diary writing, and he observed the "introduction of a new form of state" just as attentively in 1933.[99] Such observation was important not merely for working out his personal stance toward the Nazi regime.[100] Like Georg Witzmann, he wanted to sound out the political changes for himself and took various political events as occasions to fundamentally reflect on the political system and make predictions. Yet time and again he was forced to determine that he had been "wrong in my prophesies" and assessments "without . . . being able to provide reasons for this." This drove him again and again to engage in further discussions on the proper "concept of the state for the Germany of the moment" and made him hold fast to "basic considerations" about governmental order and the usefulness of voting in the new political system, through which he searched for better understanding.[101]

Other diarists discussed the fundamental political changes without making any connection to concrete political observations. Born in 1899, Franz Göll, for example, worked in a print shop and did not have an academic education. But he too wrote down extensive deliberations in his diary on the "now ruling government system of National Socialism."[102] Much like Georg Witzmann, Göll felt that, upon an "objective evaluation and critique," it was "undeniable" that the democratic "system [had] played itself out in a state of battle" during the past few years and that the "abolishment of the same" had been "possible only through an annihilation of the system and strong-willed disengagement."[103] Thus Göll too noted the drastic changes to the political system, which for him remained impenetrable. As late as summer 1933, for example, he saw Hitler's government as "only the transition of an interregnum" that would not last very long.[104]

Born in 1883 and involved in the Lebensreform movement during the Weimar Republic, Wolfgang Scharenberg even came to speak about the new political system's mode of operation outside his general diary. In 1934, he started a separate notebook that dealt exclusively and even more abstractly with questions about the political order. Scharenberg had headed up a few communities in Mecklenburg as a district chief (Amtshauptmann) from 1921 to 1926, and in this notebook he briefly looked back at the kind of "representation the population of this district" had chosen for itself during his time in office. He contemplated the "type of will formation" this had produced, then disclosed its "defects," and after that raised the question regarding better forms of political participation. In basic agreement with the regime, Scharenberg recognized that "the decisive factor is not that the will of the Volk is determined as mathematically as possible—the Volk as a mass has no comprehensible will—but rather that leader-types get into the representative assemblies."[105]

Such abstract discussions were not directly linked to complaints about the difficulty of forming opinions under the new political circumstances. Yet they too are symptomatic of the widespread uncertainly regarding standards of political evaluation. On the one hand, this is shown by the large number of diaries in which such commentary appears after 1933. On the other hand, however, it also becomes evident in the many comparisons that diarists made. Georg Witzmann, for example, recorded his doubts about whether he could still understand the innovative developments in the context of the relative importance of the Nazi regime's many elaborately celebrated holidays, in which he identified parallels with the Christian liturgy. "One must consider," he noted, "that the National Socialist leaders, and especially those working for the propaganda, are Catholics." He pointed out that the National Socialist leadership operated with the "same [methods] as those used by the Catholic Church. The splendor of the attire, the uniforms, the power of the symbols, monstrance and swastika, canopy and flags, the splendor of the festivals, regularly recurring feast days—these are all likewise proven weapons, like those introduced and implemented by the Jesuit order in its strict domain of obedience and discipline, in its [religious] exercises, etc., and the Catholic Church likewise in its hierarchy, and both in the elevation of the leader principle [Führerprinzip]."[106] Similarly, in his diary entries the Hamburg schoolteacher Hans Maschmann repeatedly compared the Nazi movement to the Catholic Church, emphasizing that this "form of state is of a Catholic spirit." Maschmann saw important similarities in both their internal power structures and their concern about "faithful" followers.[107]

Franz Göll, on the other hand, primarily explored the new political system by way of a comparison with the Soviet Union. "Both government systems have various congruities to show," he stated in his diary in summer 1933. "Both systems strive for their totality; apart from the views they sanction, they tolerate no others. . . . It is the system of the deprivation of rights of the individual personality. Among us the latter submerges into race, in Russia into class (proletariat)." As Göll expressly noted, his reference to these shared features was not meant as "opposition, but rather to depict the things as they might appear to a sober, dispassionate observer."[108] Just how apt and informative he considered his comparison became evident four weeks later when he spoke again about the similarities between Nazi and Soviet rule. As he noted with satisfaction in his summation, Göll believed that he had "first gained full understanding of the government system of the Soviets through National Socialism," although probably in the end it was precisely the other way around.[109]

For other diarists, an important key to understanding the new political system was the analogy with Fascist Italy. As early as February 1933, the Hamburg druggist Otto Kirchmann based his expectations regarding further political developments on the assumption that "the matter [would play out] wholly according to the fascist model." This led him to the assessment that the "Social Democrats, who after all were also rendered leaderless in Italy by the murder of Matteotti and then choked off," had nothing with which to counter National Socialist violence.[110] Georg Witzmann, too, noted in his discussions of summer 1933 that it was becoming "more and strongly . . . apparent how much the German National Socialists took over from Italian fascism."[111]

When assessing the changed political system, Germans did not just find helpful comparative reference points in their present. Many events that promised a better understanding could be found in history. This applied to recent German history, when for example, Hitler was compared to Bismarck or Frederick the Great, or when analogies were made with the German campaign of 1873 or the end of the war in 1918.[112] However, diarists also picked up on much older historical connections: they saw similarities between Hitler and Napoleon or Caesar and identified commonalities with the crisis of Attic democracy.[113] We could extend the list of reference points that people used, but even as it stands, it gives a sense of how, in light of the uncertainty of their own standards of political evaluation, Germans struggled to organize their impressions into familiar categories. In so doing, in the 1930s they established the spectrum of comparisons that historians still use today when trying to make sense of National Socialism as a "political religion," as a version of "totalitarianism" or "fascism," or as a phenomenon between the poles of historical continuity and singularity.[114]

The Images of the "Führer and Volk" and the Change of Political Behavior Patterns

However, the Germans' search for new guidelines for political evaluation and action that can be identified in many diaries did not arise solely from the challenge to existing standards of evaluation experienced by many people at the start of National Socialist rule. Rather, it was also vigorously promoted by the Nazi regime itself. Even though "all forms of democratic collaboration [were] purposefully" abolished as early as 1933, the regime made it abundantly clear that its construction of the new political system was "by no means [guided] by the ideal of a politically abstinent society."[115] Ernst Rudolf Huber, for example, a leading expert in constitutional law in the 1930s, described the difference between Weimar democracy and the political system of National Socialism as based precisely on the fact that the latter wanted "not to patronize the Volk comrades" but "rather invite them to actively participate." The National Socialist state did not want to set up laws as "barriers . . . for private arbitrariness" and keep watch "over the lawful conduct of the citizens with general supervision and monitoring." Rather, it summoned "every Volk comrade for responsible collaboration on the collective tasks."[116]

Even if the regime did not refer to it as such, through changes of the public representation of politics and the assertion of new forms of political action and evaluation based on these changes, it strove to establish a new political culture—one that was supposed to create a close connection between government and the governed, despite the exclusion of the population from political decision-making. And because the Nazi regime had destroyed the Weimar democracy's formalized connections between the regime and the people, this political culture of National Socialism—the specific nexus arising from the public representation of National Socialist politics and the forms of individual political behavior related to this public representation—had elemental significance for integrating society into the political system.[117]

The efforts to establish a new political culture and changed forms of political evaluation and action constituted an overarching guideline for National Socialist policy design and thus was also a key subject of the regime's public self-portrayal. As early as spring 1933, the new regime began propagating images of a society giving it wholesale support, which left exiled political opponents deeply puzzled over their accuracy. But the requirement on the part of the regime to constantly enact its rule in the media did not result mostly from the need to justify itself to foreign observers. Instead, this necessity arose as a direct consequence of the transformation of the system of political decision-making itself. Whereas in the Weimar Republic, as in all democratic systems, the legitimacy of political rule was generated above all through the visibility of the decision-making processes—for example, in the form of general elections or public parliamentary meetings—the monopolization of political decision-making in the "Führer state" and its concealment from the population created the need for a different way to visualize political rule.[118]

Along with referring to the success of the regime's policies, images of wholesale social approval, which substantially defined how the regime represented itself and were constantly reproduced, were primarily supposed to demonstrate the regime's legitimacy to the population. Yet in fact these images themselves produced the legitimacy they displayed in the first place. Regardless of the question of the degree to which German society actually supported the regime, in the 1930s societal approval on a larger scale became visible only in the images and mass spectacles produced by the regime—and only as a result of this visibility did it also become a political fact. Without institutionalized forms of the translation of "will of the Volk" in the political decision-making process, the Nazi regime remained dependent on constantly asserting the people's acceptance and support of its rule through its own policy on mass media and public communication. Thus the public sphere during the Nazi dictatorship did not just consist of the areas in which the regime secured its claim to power through police surveillance and media control and demanded visible commitment from the Germans. Nor did it form merely a central forum for the far-reaching educational efforts of the regime, which by way of public appeals and the (aesthetic) configuration of the public sphere as an expansive "educational space" worked on the creation of the "new man."[119] As part of the political system, the public sphere also constituted the space in which, throughout the entire duration of National Socialist rule, the regime constantly needed to demonstrate the support of the "Volk" to itself and to the population and thereby create the very legitimacy of its own rule from which it incessantly claimed to proceed.

The central aim of these images of ostensibly wholesale societal support was to make visible, audible, and palpable that very unity between the "leadership and Volk" whose existence was postulated by leading representatives of the regime. Whether in the large mass assemblies on Nazi holidays, the staging of Hitler speeches on the radio—as an oration by the "Führer" to faithful followers throughout the Reich—or in visual representations of encounters between the "Führer" and "his Volk," the depictions always aimed at showing the support of the German people for Adolf Hitler and his politics. They were supposed to vividly demonstrate that translating the "will of the Volk" into political decisions did not require any formal mechanisms, that instead the only critical factor was the relationship of loyalty between the "Führer" and "Volk" expressed in the enactments. As during the Weimar democracy, in the 1930s the "Volk" formed the basis for political rule. But now even studies of constitutional law vigorously emphasized that "the true will of the Volk could not be found through parliamentary elections and plebiscites, but rather that the will of the Volk was only brought forth purely and unadulterated through the Führer."[120] This did not require any institutional connections between the "Führer" and the "Volk" that might have restricted the "Führer's" authority to exercise power. Rather, the "Führer principle" was supposed to be based on the principle of "mutual loyalty," through which the "Führer" was bound to the "Volk" and as a result could recognize its will. At the same time, however, this meant conversely that political rule had to be supported by the population through "loyalty," which "must find its expression in free integration."[121] Official representations were supposed to lend expression to this conception of the political legitimation of the regime's rule. And even if, in each case, they showed only "the image of a scenario limited in space and time," this was presented as being "at one with the ostensible political reality of the Third Reich" and declared as general "proof for the joining together of the entire Volk and its Führer."[122]

Given the vast extent to which representations of the tight relationship between the regime and the population determined the public look and feel of National Socialist rule, historical scholarship has devoted plenty of attention to how Hitler was staged in the media as the "Führer of the German Volk" and how this was socially received.[123] Even so, disputes still persist about the degree to which these images—which are without doubt the result of deliberate self-staging by the regime—point to real integration mechanisms by which German society was involved, admittedly not in political decision-making, but nonetheless in the political system of National Socialism. Those historians who interpret the Nazi dictatorship as a form of "charismatic rule" or, further yet, as a "political religion" have primarily been the ones advocating the position that after 1933 the regime succeeded with its public policy in spreading a strongly idealized image of the "Führer"— the Hitler myth—and thereby engendered the identification of large segments of society with Hitler.[124] As a result, the bonds between the Nazi regime and the population were more "psychological and emotional rather than material," such that the integration of Germans into the political system was "largely affective."[125] Through Hitler as the "charismatic vehicle of political cohesive force," the Nazi dictatorship developed a "previously unknown ability to integrate the masses" that went "far beyond the sphere of profane politics": "the Germans venerated, glorified, and loved Hitler."[126]

Other historians have reproached this thesis—the idea that the "Hitler myth" was the "central motor for the integration, mobilization, and legitimation" of political rule under National Socialism[127]—for its own "proximity to the propaganda image" that the Nazi regime continuously drew precisely with its illustrative self-portrayals.[128] In contrast, critics maintain that it is doubtful whether the enthusiasm for Hitler was really sufficiently all-encompassing and socially widespread for the regime to draw legitimacy and support mainly from this wellspring. In part as a direct objection and in part as a modification to this thesis of charismatic integration, numerous studies have pointed at other mechanisms of Nazi rule that contributed to the bonding of society—namely, the violence of the National Socialist terror apparatus, which forced Germans with divergent views into fearful silence,[129] and practices of everyday life and governance that did not require any ideological conformity on the part of individuals.[130] These undoubtedly contributed to the stabilization of Nazi rule, yet they identify governance techniques that were notably not intended to create political participation opportunities for Germans.

However, if one is interested in the population's deliberate involvement in National Socialist policy, which existed despite all of the violence, it seems to me that the primary problem with the thesis of a political integration via the "faith in the Führer" is that previous studies have strongly limited their focus to the reception of the idealized image of the Führer. While historians have intensely analyzed the media construction of Hitler, they have paid very little attention to the simultaneous staging of the population as a political actor. So far, historians have interpreted the spectators in the pictures of "Führer and Volk" almost entirely in terms of their function for the "image of the Führer." Various studies have repeatedly pointed out that staging the Führer "required [the population] as choral resonance and backdrop extras" and that the constant reports about the masses of people enchanted and enthused by the "Führer" had turned "jubilation . . . into Hitler's identifying feature," which thereby figured as one of "the essential components of the Führer image."[131] Hitler was "often represented photographically as a ruler embedded in a relational web of connections," whereby the particularly large number of pictures during the 1930s of Hitler with masses of people "visually buttressed the Führer cult."[132] This interpretation is concisely bundled in the oft-cited phrase "ornament of the masses."[133] Even though Siegfried Kracauer crafted this phrase in 1927 with regard to the entertainment industry of the Weimar Republic, many historical studies find it especially apt for grasping the visual function of depicted spectators.[134] Even pictorial representations that do not show the "Führer" himself but only his cheering audience at mass assemblies or marches are interpreted along these lines, such that "even when Hitler did not become directly visible . . . he was always present in the consciousness of the observer" insofar as the "collective direction of the gaze and body posture [of the spectators]" brought the "Führer" to mind.[135] These interpretations are credible, yet they leave unanswered the obvious question: How did the public self-representation of the regime also stage the population as a political actor?

Representations of unfailingly enthusiastic masses of spectators were not just supposed to contribute to the staging of the "Führer." They were also directed to individual Germans "with the demand for emulation" and thereby purposely spread an idea of political action and evaluation to which the regime wanted educate the German people.[136] This is where the reconfiguration of the political relationships between government and the governed met with the National Socialist education project: the creation of the "National Socialist," of the "political man," was supposed to align individual life management and self-contemplation according to political categories and thereby closely tie the German people into the political system.[137]

The images of the "Führer and Volk" were also meant as concrete guidance for their observers, who were supposed to orient their behavior according to what was shown. Individuals were thus presented very concretely with boundless jubilation as a form of public expression and simultaneously as a form of active behavior with which they were supposed to meet "leadership" during encounters. At the same time, the stereotypical unfounded enthusiasm also brought into the picture an overarching ideal of political action and evaluation that called for Germans to put aside their own criticism or political discussions; instead, they were supposed to unconditionally believe in the regime and on certain occasions also profess this faith. With its self-representation, the regime staged a seductive "beautiful illusion" around itself and the "Führer" that was meant to impress and captivate people.[138] But in doing so, it also communicated new models of political action and evaluation that aimed at having individuals integrate themselves with enthusiasm and heedless faith into a jubilant collective. Whether this goal was achieved was the broad standard that the regime applied to the individual conduct of Germans—even in situations where the regime and the Volk did not directly come into contact.

If one takes this dimension of the images of the "Führer and Volk" into account as well, this raises rather crucial questions for the empirical examination of the social reception of the Hitler myth and the thesis that Germans were integrated with the political system of National Socialism on the basis of "love" and "adoration." Regardless of how the degree of enthusiasm for the "Führer" can be grasped through the sources,[139] whether it is at all possible to reliably ascertain the existence of emotional bonds between the "Führer" and the "Volk" on the basis of observable jubilation is thus quite questionable indeed. If the official images of Germans enthralled by Hitler are understood in the same way as the idealized "images of the Führer"—namely, as the product of a deliberate enactment—then the observable jubilance can basically also be understood as the deliberate appropriation of the propagated behavioral ideal.

In his investigation of "Hitler's charisma," Ludolf Herbst has pointed out that within the NSDAP in the 1920s, "believing in Hitler was . . . a question of party discipline," and accordingly "even major party players—such as Georg Strasser—who were skeptical about Hitler right to the end" had propagated "the charismatic image of the Führer."[140] Thus statements by NSDAP members, especially from the leadership circle, do "not in the first instance [attest to] the pervasiveness of the charismatic faith in the Führer, but rather to the binding force of the propaganda concept that worked with charisma" within the National Socialist movement.[141] The Führer/followers model had dominated the NSDAP since the founding of the party, and insofar as this model expanded into the underlying constitutional principle of the Nazi state, this idea can also be transferred to the period of National Socialist rule. For this period too, it is questionable whether observable jubilance indicates adoration, enthusiasm, and love, and thereby engendered affective bonds, or points to compliance with a behavioral norm for thoroughly rational political reasons. In this respect, the question regarding integration and the significance of the Hitler myth for this integration in the 1930s can only be answered by inquiring into the reception of the propagated notions of individual political behavior with which the regime wanted to induce individuals to unconditionally cheer the Führer and his policies.

The Orientation of Political Behavior According to Images of the "Führer And Volk"

Like the challenge to existing standards for political evaluation resulting from the massive incursions into the system of political decision-making, the behavioral ideal popularized by the Nazi regime also helped change the modes of political action and evaluation. The diaries of the 1930s show this as well, albeit often only with a second glance. But then it is precisely many of the diary entries venerating Hitler that show just how much the regime's own ideas about political behavior and evaluation influenced contemporaries. One does not find in them merely an emotional enthusiasm for the "Führer." Instead, they often show an enthusiasm for the "Führer" that conforms to the very model of political behavior spread by the self-representation of the Nazi regime. Against the background of close readings of the images of the "Führer and Volk," what stands out in these diaries is not only how often they made reference to the person of the "Führer" but also how they emphasized the social approval that supported him and the "unity of leadership and the Volk."

This was particularly the case in the reception of the results of the plebiscites and elections. While in fall 1933 Georg Witzmann reacted soberly to the broad approval of the withdrawal from the League of Nations and to the Reichstag election, other diarists like the Berlin doctor Walter Lindemann, born in 1906, celebrated the results entirely in terms of the official account, both as an achievement by Hitler and as the expression of the consensus between the "Volk" and the regime. When the withdrawal from the League of Nations was announced, Lindemann had already seemed certain that "if the German Volk [should] decide whether it agrees with the policies of his government . . . we [shall] answer with a joyful 'yes,' for: *Germany has awakened!*" He illustrated this estimation with a hand-drawn swastika, something he did only for major political occasions.[142] When the approval reached more than 90 percent, Lindemann did not merely see this as the confirmation of his prediction but at the same time also extolled the "quite fabulous" results as Hitler's personal achievement. It was "actually something wonderful what our great Führer *Adolf Hitler* has managed to do. Germany has awakened" and was "*unified through Adolf Hitler.*"[143]

As in this example, in many diary entries by other authors who commented on Hitler, admiration for the "Führer" frequently coincided with descriptions of the unity of the "Volk" and its approval of state leadership. Born in 1921, the schoolgirl Marianne Köhl wrote in her diary in spring 1936 about a Hitler speech she had followed on the radio, commenting above all on the "hurricane-like jubilation" that "flared up all over where our Führer, the true Volk's chancellor, showed himself. The Volk could not cheer its beloved Führer enough. . . . The eyes of all listeners clung to his lips, which say everything that lies deep in the hearts of good German men and women." Even after the "end of the speech," Köhl noted, "the storm of applause did not want to end," and "from faithful hearts . . . everybody [sang] the German national anthem."[144] And Inge Thiele, the young gardener from Solingen, reported in her diary in spring 1936 about a conversation with "a young man." Although she did not view him as one of "the most enthusiastic supporters" of Hitler, the previous day he had nonetheless attended a "Führer visit" in Cologne. Noting his first impressions, she wrote, "He was still very excited about the tremendous crowd of people that cheered the Führer." Only afterward did she point out that her acquaintance "said that he could not shout at all when he saw [Hitler] up close, that his saliva stopped coming, the Führer made such an impression."[145]

Without question, the countless references we can find to the enthusiasm unleashed by Hitler also created opportunities for writers to lend expression to the "greatness of the Führer" and the extraordinary abilities ascribed to Hitler in their diaries. Yet at the same time, these descriptions presented a different picture than diary entries such as those recorded by Helmut Böhme, the NSDAP Kreisleiter of Freiberg in Saxony born in 1902. When Böhme personally encountered Hitler during an address to Kreisleiter in August 1934, he noted afterward that he had "once again [stood] eye to eye across from my Führer and . . . again [experienced] the exhilarating feeling of being allowed to serve this man. He spoke to us for almost an hour and gave us strength and faith with every word."[146] In contrast to the case of Helmut Böhme, the entries that emphasize a general enthusiasm for the Führer notably do not claim any personal connection between the individual and "their" Führer.[147] In these entries, the diarists instead document that they were not alone in their enthusiasm and openly identity their excitement as part of a collective approval.

In the context of the challenge to standards of political evaluation, this can be seen as an attempt to orient one's own political judgment according to the behavior of others. At least for regime supporters, the formation of political opinion by no means occurred in private isolation outside the public sphere. However, the display of general jubilation for Hitler can be read additionally as an indication that individuals did not just take over the propagated idealized image of their "Führer" but rather tried to do so in a way that conformed to the regime's ideas on political conduct in the new political system. With the reference to the enthusiasm unleashed by and supporting Hitler, the diary authors recorded even more than their "faith" in Hitler; they simultaneously presented themselves as part of the cheering "Volk," which made their private diaries often sound like the official reports of the regime. In this respect, the enthusiasm for the Führer that can be found in diaries need not necessarily refer to an emotional bond of the respective authors to Hitler but rather can also be understood as part of a larger restructuring of forms of individual political behavior.

At the same time, the efforts to appropriate the propagated ideals of political behavior and evaluation were also reflected in more explicit ways in the daily notes of individuals. In fall 1933, for example, Inge Thiele listened to the broadcast of a Hitler speech from the campaign related to the voting in November. Only a few days earlier, she had decided that she "now believe[d] in Adolf Hitler," even though she "first sympathized with his opponents."[148] The radio speech, which she heard together with her boss and his family, impressed Thiele very much. Hitler "spoke so plainly and open-heartedly, emphasized so vigorously his coming from workers' circles, hence his understanding for their hardships and desires, that I involuntarily joined in with the Heil Hitler and Sieg Heil. All who were gathered in our little room, old and young, were enthused," the young woman reported in her diary, but she seemed to be very dissatisfied with the extent of her own enthusiasm. "And I, as quickly as I am excited, cool off just as quickly. Why do I always just have doubts again? Why can't I heedlessly believe? Am I exposed to too many impressions? When will I finally find the right path?"[149] To be sure, Inge Thiele had been impressed when hearing Hitler's speech, but this was not enough for her. Rather, she measured her perception against the ideal of political behavior disseminated the next morning by jubilant commentators on the radio and the pictures of enthusiastic listeners in the newspapers—an ideal that also demanded unalloyed enthusiasm. In the following years as well, Thiele did not just repeatedly report about her political behavior in her diary; she also made her private writing an important instrument with which she endeavored to adhere to the regime's expectations of her behavior.

Far more critically minded than Thiele, Georg Witzmann, the former member of the Thuringian state parliament, was by far not the only contemporary in the 1930s who spoke primarily about politics in his diary. Even people less specifically affected by the fundamental changes to the political system made their confrontation with the regime's policies and their presentation to the public a central topic of daily commentary. Diaries thus constitute a good basis for inquiring into the changes of personal political action and evaluation. In the interplay between the massive incursions into the existing system of political decision-making, which threw earlier categories of political evaluation into doubt, and the propagation of new forms of political action and evaluation that directly called for individuals to adjust their own behavior patterns, for many diarists their own relationship to the political system became a problem that they dealt with in writing. Their notes show how the bonding of the individual to the political system and therefore the relationship between the regime and the population transformed, and they also illustrate how this influenced their private life. As part of the changes in political action and evaluation, the diary entries thus document the emergence of a new political culture in which the transformed conditions of political decision-making and the changed public representation of politics combined with new forms of individual conduct. This interplay ensured the integration of the German people into the political system of National Socialism.

Looking this way at the transformation of personal political conduct and reflections on that conduct by diarists can therefore provide fundamental insights into the relationship between the regime and population and lead to a "new political history of National Socialism," which has recently seen a growing demand.[150] The currently popular interpretation of the political system of National Socialism as a "participation" or "consensual" dictatorship supported by "social forces of cohesion" might be credible. But thus far, it only vaguely describes how the connections between the government and governed highlighted by these concepts took shape. How the dictatorial regime benefited from the support of the Germans and how people were bound into the National Socialist formation of policy remains largely unexplained. This issue has frequently been the subject of major criticism, which as opposed to emphasizing consensus and social support has pointed to the Nazi regime's instruments of violence. It has raised questions about the degree to which it "makes sense to talk about a consensus when those who oppose what is happening are locked up or coerced into silence," and these questions cannot be dismissed out of hand.[151]

The view of the emerging political culture of National Socialism and the associated forms of political evaluation and behavior can bring us further in this regard. Diaries make it possible to ask about the specific relationships between the population and the regime that crystallized within the web of propagandistic representations of politics and transformed decision-making structures and the behavior of Germans. Only by answering such questions can we fully realize the analytical quality inherent to the concepts of a "consensual" or "participation dictatorship" and achieve a more precise understanding of the societal support for the policies of the Nazi regime. Instead of extending the list of corresponding characterizations with another new term, I intend in the following to supplement this list with knowledge about what "approval" meant under the conditions of the Nazi dictatorship, how people kept track of political developments and the actions of the National Socialist regime, how they acted politically themselves, and how this bound them into the new political system.

7

THE GOVERNMENT AND ITS VOLK

1. Watching the Government: Political Reporting in the Media and the Formation of Political Opinion in the Nazi Dictatorship

With its spectacular images of the "Führer and Volk," the Nazi regime elevated the direct encounter between government and the governed very much into a symbol of political communication and the society's integration into the political system, yet within their everyday lives, Germans regularly encountered the actions of their government first and foremost through the mass media. As in past decades, individuals primarily accessed political events through political reporting in the media, which also provided occasions for continual engagement with the actions of state decision-making authorities. Since its emergence in the second half of the nineteenth century, the mass press had contributed substantially to the "transformation of forms of political communication" and in the years prior to the First World War fostered the "politicization of society."[1] Fundamental changes to forms of government and political rule and the rapid expansion of the media market had been closely related. Democratization processes had created new maneuvering room and consumer classes for the media. And conversely, mass media first made possible the permanent and intense involvement of the populace in the formation of policy; at the end of the First World War, the populace was elevated as the basis for the legitimation of political power across the entire political spectrum, and this laid "the necessary foundation for both the Weimar Republic and the Third Reich."[2]

Correspondingly, the reception of political reporting was a central element of individual political behavior in the 1930s as well. The significance that the Nazi regime still ascribed to the mass media for the population's political integration was evident not only in its efforts to control the content of news reporting³ but also particularly in its attempts to promote the dissemination and consumption of news in general. Even in the National Socialist dictatorship, Germans were supposed to be permanently involved in government politics as consumers of media, which meant assigning political reporting by the press and radio a central function within the new political system, as emphasized time and again by politicians and political theorists. Thus Hans Münster, for example, the leading newspaper scholar of the 1930s, argued that National Socialism could only achieve "the leadership of the Volk [Volksführung] native to us Germans if the Führer knows at every moment that his Volk is thinking along, approving his policy from a full free heart and with clear understanding." This required the participation of "political" men who "feel that they share responsibility for the greater whole, and who approve of the Führer's resolutions not just emotionally but on the basis of specific knowledge."⁴ And this knowledge, according to Münster, was best conveyed through mass media. Wholly in line with this argumentation, regime actors in the 1930s repeatedly mounted advertising campaigns promoting the reading of newspapers. With headlines such as "Without Newspapers One Lives on the Moon," these campaigns specifically emphasized the importance of news reporting and "pilloried the non–newspaper reader for weeks on end," as one diarist noted.⁵

Above all, however, the Nazi regime looked to radio in its endeavor to expand the mass-media availability of political reporting.⁶ Indeed, it was by radio that the start of National Socialist rule made itself especially noticeable in the media. In spring 1933, radio in Germany was not even ten years old, and its development had already been strongly defined during the Weimar Republic by the question of how to handle political news reporting. Anxieties about the possibility of the party-political instrumentalization of the new medium had led to organizational and legal structures that, in striving for political neutrality, had largely banished politics from radio. In radio programming of the 1920s, "expressly political content ... [was] only minimally represented," and even news broadcasts had only a very minor role compared to classical music and lecture broadcasts for the educated middle class.⁷

In spring 1933, the programming suddenly changed. With broadcasts of political speeches and addresses, radio was raised to an instrument of the ruling parties during the new government's first few weeks in office, and they used radio intensely for the Reichstag elections that were called immediately after Hitler's appointment as Reich chancellor. Even though stronger state interventions in radio programming and an increase in openly political broadcasting had already occurred in 1932, the many broadcasts related to the March 1933 election attest to the increased significance of political content in broadcasting, which reached an unprecedented intensity. Even after the electoral victory of the ruling parties in early March, the percentage of broadcasts dedicated to political reports did not recede to the starting level of previous years. Born in 1866, the Andernach teacher and city archivist Stephan Weidenbach noted in his diary four days after the election, "On the radio still speeches for Hitler."[8] Fueled by staff redeployments at the broadcasting stations, a multitude of political transmissions, reports, and broadcasts would dominate radio programming in the following months as well.[9]

This development stood very much in contradiction to the criticism leveled at radio by the NSDAP during previous years. The party had seen radio, with its educated middle-class programming, as elitist and "alien" to the listening audience because it did not align itself with the entertainment needs ascribed to the "Volk."[10] For fear of repelling listeners with strongly politicized programs, but also to secure its own position of power vis-à-vis competing authorities, the Reich Propaganda Ministry therefore ultimately prohibited basically all transmissions of political events immediately after the 1933 November elections. Excluded from the ban were only events of a "purely state-political character" that "presupposed a general public interest." But even these cases required a "special directive from the Reich Propaganda Ministry," which meant that in the following years political broadcasts occurred in far fewer numbers and only during specific events.[11] Instead, designing radio programming "from the Volk—for the Volk" led to the prioritization of mainly popular light music, whose share of programming increased sharply over the 1930s.[12] The highly popular time slot between 7:00 p.m. and 10:00 p.m. was increasingly (and by the mid-1930s exclusively) reserved for music entertainment programs that the Nazi regime thought were well-liked and could draw broad segments of the population to the radio.[13]

Historians have frequently highlighted this fact, using it to argue that radio contributed most importantly to social integration and the preservation of power not by propagating regime policies but by providing entertainment and distraction from political problems.[14] But while certainly plausible, the thesis does not give enough attention to the prominent role of radio for individuals' everyday consumption of news. Even if broadcasts of political events and speeches significantly declined as of fall 1933, the direct thematization of regime activity played an important role precisely within the context of the new entertainment programming. Key radio functionaries, like Eugen Hadamovsky, who was installed as the Reich radio production director by Goebbels and who as of late 1933 had a decisive part in the orientation of radio toward entertainment, repeatedly stressed that radio and "its total program [had to] build on the foundation of light music and current news."[15] "After the hard day's work," radio was to bring "joyfulness and levity into the house again" because "only from relaxation" could the radio listener find "the way to the day's events that demand his attention."[16] Accordingly, the configuration of "National Socialist radio broadcasting" that began in fall 1933 involved not only the increase of popular music but also specifically the intensification of up-to-date political reporting.

During the Weimar Republic, political news had only been broadcast in a few far-flung time slots. In the late 1920s, none of the broadcasting companies had "provided for more than three news slots per day" in their programming. Most importantly, the "evening, the general main listening time, was completely free of news," which meant that even the few transmitted political reports only reached a small segment of the listening audience.[17] In this respect, increasing the number of news broadcasts to four—and, respectively, to seven prior to the occupation of Austria in spring 1938—significantly improved and "substantially" enhanced radio news.[18] In addition, in fall 1933 the various broadcasting stations began assigning news "a very central time slot" at 8:00 p.m., during the broadcast period from 7:00 p.m. to 10:00 p.m. slated for popular entertainment music.[19] After the primacy of entertainment programming had been definitively established in the mid-1930s, this news segment was ultimately the only spoken-word program in an evening time slot otherwise filled with popular music. National Socialist radio programming thus established the "German broadcasting tradition of presenting the main news of the day at 8:00 p.m.," which persists to this day.[20] Importantly, however, designed in this way, the radio program certainly did not consist of entertainment devoid of political topics; rather, it formed an ensemble of entertainment and political information. There are good reasons to assume that this did not come about, as Peter Reichel has argued, for example, because "the Nazi directors had to deal with a public that—depending on taste and education—preferred to be entertained or edified rather than politicized or even indoctrinated."[21] Speaking against this assessment, for example, is the fact that the program structure corresponded directly to the regime's own ideal of political behavior; as part of the regular evening program, politics was presented in a format that was decidedly not geared toward discussion or independent criticism but rather toward the passive reception of news about the actions of the regime. The evening news was supposed to make the following of political developments part of the radio listeners' everyday routine.

The diaries of the 1930s show in various ways that the mass media actually played its central role as the regime intended with respect to the individual's engagement with the regime's policies. This is conspicuously documented in diaries whose authors kept them entirely or chiefly for the continuous contemplation of government policies. The confrontation with political reporting was central here. For example, born in Pomerania in 1895 and working as a teacher in Lauenburg in the 1930s, Oswald Krause* started a diary in summer 1933 meant exclusively for recording the political news situation. The first entries consisted of extracts from media reports that Krause wrote down with reference to the date and place of publication. In addition, the largest proportion of the many entries with which Krause filled more than twenty school notebooks between 1933 and 1942 consisted of summaries of political news stories or excerpts from speeches by various regime representatives, which he transcribed from the newspaper and radio into his diary.[22] Born in 1900 in Hamburg, the Jewish attorney Kurt Rosenberg started writing a diary on March 23, 1933, likewise in the aftermath of political events. To be sure, he wrote down far more of his own impressions than did Oswald Krause, who primarily took note of reports. But Rosenberg too paid plenty of attention to media reporting, as evinced by the many press articles he clipped from the newspaper and pasted into his diary.[23]

Heinz Werner Hundertmark, who was born in 1922 in Frankfurt am Main and who during the 1930s attended public school and then enlisted with the Wehrmacht, compiled an extensive folder in 1939 into which he pasted not entire articles but rather the photos used to illustrate them in newspapers and magazines. They chiefly depicted regime representatives, political developments, or military events, and he furnished every one of them with a heading identifying their political context. Moreover, the young soldier added explanations beneath the photos, his word choice tightly aligned with the reports he had cut out. In one entry on the "cession of the Memel region to Germany," he officiously annotated the photo of the foreign ministers of Germany and Lithuania: "Lithuania's return of the Memel region occurred by way of a voluntary agreement. This arrangement is in accordance with the clearly expressed desire of the Memel-German population and will be advantageous to the future relations of the two countries. Picture: the moment of the signing of the agreement by the two foreign ministers of the countries of Germany and Lithuania."[24] Proceeding in this manner, during the year Hundertmark compiled his own synopsis of political events based on reporting in the press. Walter Lindemann, the Berlin doctor born in 1906, created a similar survey. Alongside the personal diary he had been keeping since the 1920s, he started a second booklet entitled "Political Diary," in which he pasted numerous newspaper reports, usually without photos. Lindemann had already previously dealt with political topics in his personal diary. Nonetheless, he now apparently felt it made sense to have a separate notebook for these topics. Unlike Hundertmark, he did not use his "Political Diary" to recapitulate the press reports but instead recorded his own thoughts about the various articles.[25]

Such press reports were also carried over into many other diaries, which clearly illustrates the central role of media reception for the political behavior of contemporaries. In a more indirect way, however, diaries also frequently show how this news consumption bonded diarists to the political system of National Socialism. Franz Wallner, the Munich laborer born in 1892 who in the diary he had kept since 1910 chiefly jotted down the stations of his daily routine and his daily income and expenditures, mentioned political events only when they affected the events of his day. The start of National Socialist rule in spring 1933 was the first event to find notable expression in his entries.[26] After that, political comments largely disappeared again from his diary, and they then reemerged more frequently only in the late 1930s. After his notes on the start of Nazi rule, in the following years Wallner's diary recorded the elections in fall 1933 and summer 1934, the "National Holiday of the German Volk" on May 1 each year, and two additional political events: the death of Reich President Hindenburg and a "Führer speech" broadcast on the radio in May 1934.[27] Other than that, the entries, as per usual, paid no attention to political events. In 1937 and especially 1938, however, Wallner's occupation with the regime's policies was documented by six times as many entries as he had made since summer 1933, and this was directly related to changes to his media consumption and the economic upswing Wallner experienced in the course of the 1930s.

The laborer, who had worked at various jobs since youth, had become unemployed a few months before Hitler's appointment as Reich chancellor, which was clearly evident in the overall balance sheets he prepared at year's end from the daily record of his income and expenses. Even though Wallner had already found a job again in summer 1933 as a delivery driver for a confectionary, his annual balance showed very low earnings even in comparison to his past income, which was also rather low. Wallner was not able to register any real economic improvement until 1936, when he was hired as a template fitter in a BMW factory in Munich. Admittedly, he received a termination notice just one year later, but, along with a few colleagues who had also been laid off, he was taken on at the army ordinance depot, which stabilized his sharp increase in earnings. At 1,529 Marks, Wallner's annual balance for 1937 amounted to three times his income for 1933.[28]

Nonetheless, it would be too simplistic to view the increased number of notes regarding regime policy merely as the result of his being satisfied with an economic advancement that he (might have) attributed to the regime. We see instead that Wallner increasingly came into contact with political reporting. On the one hand, the jobs at BMW and the army ordinance depot meant that Franz Wallner now became a regular listener of political radio broadcasts as part of his occupational activities. His daily notes repeatedly mentioned "factory musters" on the occasion of political events, which he also identified in this context with a few key words: "On the occasion of the visit of the Fascist leader Benito Mussolini, mustering of the personnel of the army ordinance depot," he noted in September 1937, for example. And half a year later, he wrote, "Factory mustering on the occasion of the reinstatement of German military sovereignty."[29] At the same time, in his brief entries Wallner always referred to the speeches of Hitler or other leading Nazi functionaries that were broadcast by radio during the events—in one case, the personnel even attended a Hitler speech at the Munich fair.[30]

On the other hand, however, the improved earnings allowed Franz Wallner to acquire his own radio in summer 1937, as shown by expenses for the "radio newspaper" and "radio license fee" regularly recorded ever since that time.[31] He also began listening to the radio in private, which likewise contributed to more political entries. "Evening 8:00 o'clock, listened to Führer speech by radio. Subject matter Czechoslovakia (results of the Chamberlain-Hitler conference)," he noted, for example, on September 29, 1938. Other comments about political events now appearing in his entries show that, as a radio listener, Wallner was following the actions of the regime more attentively than before.[32] His comments in this respect did not just pertain to central events like the Sudeten crisis or the annexation of

Austria in spring 1938. In May that same year, his diary similarly noted Hitler's state visit to Italy—Wallner learned about his arrival and departure from the news and noted their precise times.[33] Regardless of whether Wallner's improved economic situation actually influenced his satisfaction with the Nazi regime, his diary clearly reveals radio's large contribution to the fact that Wallner now concerned himself with regime policies more intensely than before and that political events found their way into his diary. With its broadcasts of political speeches and events and its news programs, the radio brought politics into the daily routine of Franz Wallner's professional and private life, which was the primary focus of his diary. As a radio listener, Wallner was confronted more consistently than ever before with the actions of the regime and the voices of leading politicians, and only in this constellation did he start reporting on them in his diary.

Diaries of the 1930s repeatedly show that radio increased the degree to which people dealt with regime politics. References to and descriptions of political radio broadcasts or radio reports are found in many diaries, whereas reports on entertainment programs are much less frequent and more marginal or, as in the case Franz Wallner, wholly absent. Of course, this does not mean that these diarists rejected or did not listen to entertainment and music, which were far more prevalent. However, the many references to the radio in connection with politics clearly underscore that individuals attributed an important role to mass media specifically for their involvement in political events. While newspapers and radio in the 1930s undoubtedly also provided Germans with entertainment, diarists wrote first and foremost about the media's political significance.[34]

Political Assessment in Light of State Control of the Media

The media retained its central role in the political system during the Nazi dictatorship. The state's massive encroachments on the autonomy of media reporting, however, profoundly changed the nature of the political reception of media reporting and the resulting relationship between the population and the regime. Germans were often keenly aware of the state's new monitoring and control actions, which applied to newspapers and radio and their political reporting.[35] Time and again, authors spoke openly in their diaries about how "the state . . . [is] the biggest newspaper provider," which "naturally selects the form and content of reporting such that any unnecessary strain and unsettlement of the population is avoided."³⁶ In March 1936, when the Hamburg master tradesman Hermann Frielingsdorf began writing down extensive discussions of the political situation under the heading "Observations on the Times," he began his first entry by noting how quiet it was that evening. "From the entire wide block with the many apartments that I can overlook from my office window, there is not a sound. No radio, no gramophone. Is it the quietness of the graveyard that lies over Germany?" asked Frielingsdorf, who stressed that he could not recall "that it had ever been this quiet in these hundreds of apartments. Regardless of what time it was after the war, almost every day, evening, or night, somebody celebrated a birthday, anniversary, or something else. . . . It was not always pleasant, but in contrast the current stillness is oppressive. There is a radio in almost every apartment, but the people seem not to want to listen anymore."³⁷

By and large, Frielingsdorf suggested that the evening stillness resulted from the "Gleichschaltung" of the mass media and the fact that Germans had turned away from the controlled mass media. He blamed the lack of "joy and exuberance" among his neighbors primarily on the "printed papers described as newspapers, filled almost exclusively with party politics and kids' stuff." It was "unbelievable," he noted, but the "German Volk of 65 million has had no more newspapers, books, for three years already. . . . For three years, not a single letter, neither in the papers nor in books, has been printed but that it has gone through strict party censorship."³⁸ The doctor Walter Lindemann, who would start his alternative "Political Diary" in 1937, made a similar point in his personal in early 1935, noting that "the press lies gagged on the ground. Many papers have already gone under."³⁹ And one week later, he added that it is "all the same today, whether one reads the Deutsche Allgemeine Zeitung, the Völkischer Beobachter, or a local paper. *They all contain exactly the same thing, namely, that which has been commanded from above.*"⁴⁰

The Hamburg schoolteacher Hans Maschmann, who in his diary was particularly preoccupied with regime politics, also noted that, in light of the political reporting in the media, the "life of the 'Führer' and statesmen, and not just that but also the reality of the domestic and foreign policy situation, play out *behind* the entire Volk. The latter only gets to see and hear what the masses can digest: ham-fisted half-truths and falsehoods."⁴¹ Maschmann realized just as clearly that this was combined with new expectations as to how these press reports were to be received: "The leadership of the NSDAP forbids exercising criticism of the news that it puts in the press," he noted as early as summer 1933. "One is ordered to believe it."[42]

Time and again, many other diarists also clearly identified the regime's demanding expectations of their individual political behavior in consuming mass media. Wolfgang Scharenberg, the former district chief from Mecklenburg who in 1934 had started discussing the proper form of political will formation in a separate notebook, contemplated the new "system" in his personal. He noted that it demanded "not only complete obedience but *inner, joyful* enthusiasm!" This annoyed Scharenberg. It remained a "secret how one was supposed to force oneself to do this," he commented in his diary. "An abject hypocrisy is being bred here."[43] For him, that hypocrisy became especially obvious precisely with regard to political reporting. "Even though we read and listen to the speeches of the Führer daily, we are nevertheless not able to properly evaluate them, for [if] we presume to do that and perhaps ask lower leaders to act in keeping with the speeches . . . then we are arrogant know-it-alls."[44]

Aware of both the state's control of political news and the demand to believe the media reports unconditionally, many Germans faced questions. How was one supposed to consume reporting? What basically was the relative importance of political criticism in the new political system? And how did critical deliberations shift the individuals' relationship to the regime? Diarists of the 1930s answered these questions in very different ways. Some of them still did not want to forgo their own independent evaluation of regime policy, as was the case with Hans Maschmann, for example. Considering himself an intellectual, the teacher repeatedly emphasized in his diary that the regime appealed "to the lower instincts of the masses," who are "void of criticism and judgment. The propaganda bosses of this movement understand how to properly construct the judgment of the masses."[45] But from his perspective, Maschmann had nothing in common with the "masses." Rather, time and again he firmly distinguished in his diary between those people who had "lost the capacity for self-criticism and independent evaluation" and "persons with a capacity for judgment"—namely, people like him.[46] It was "not important *what*" someone thinks, Maschmann insisted in summer 1934 in a manner wholly typical for his diary. "My question to you is *how* you think. Whether as a free man or as a slave" who does not use his reason but is determined by his "emotions or compulsions," like the "masses" fascinated by Hitler. "The essential thing that makes the *human being*, on what it always comes down to, what makes him *free*," underscored

Maschmann, "is beyond any mere outlook" and is determined by one's capacity for independent judgment.[47] And along these lines, Maschmann explicitly stated that, given the state's control and censorship of political reporting, he simply did not want to believe. "A free and German man is he who does not fall for the slogans and propaganda methods of the press," he noted programmatically in his diary in early February 1934.[48]

In the 1930s, many other diarists shared Hans Maschmann's aspiration to maintain their own political judgment, as opposed to believing as demanded by the regime. In general, a large proportion of the written engagement with political reporting served precisely this purpose: to form one's own judgment regarding regime policies in a situation where the state controlled the media. This intention was especially clear, for example, in the "Political Diary" started by the young doctor Walter Lindemann in fall 1937 to contemplate the policies of the regime and their presentation in the media. Whereas the seventeen-year-old soldier Heinz Werner Hundertmark in his diary supplemented press photos with his own entries that recapitulated the official reports and thereby aligned his personal judgment with the media, Lindemann pursued the opposite objective. Since November 1937, he had been compiling articles into "political reports," each covering around a one-week period, which he arranged into his own picture of the political situation. In structured sections, he specified the political subjects being covered by the news at the moment, adding to them by pasting particularly striking newspaper articles into his diary and commenting mainly on their truth content. Under a newspaper clipping beneath the heading, "Germany in a Struggle against the Church," which spoke with rich embellishment about Catholic care facilities as "dens of iniquity," Lindemann noted sarcastically, "No, not a crime novel, but rather an article from the *National Socialist 'Westdeutsche Zeitung.'*"[49] And already in his first "political report," occasioned by an article about the war between China and Japan, he had likewise pointed out matter-of-factly, "Now what is actually true or untrue about the whole matter, one cannot decide, because, after all, there has been no freedom of the press in Germany since '33. But that our 'yellow press' cannot be trusted has already been proven a hundred times over."[50]

With his "Political Diary," which he started in fall 1937, Walter Lindemann was obviously trying hard to not simply believe but to form his own judgment. Yet at the same time, the diary also shows the difficulty of formulating political criticism in light of the regime's demand for faith and loyalty vis-à-vis the "leadership." In previous years, Lindemann had frequently seemed uncertain whether independent criticism still constituted appropriate behavior within the new political system. In March 1934, for example, he reported in his diary on a Hitler speech broadcast on the radio, which did not meet his approval. It did not say "much new," noted Lindemann, "we just heard again that we have come so tremendously far, and that the glorious National Socialist movement is well on the way to bringing us paradise on earth. Thus far, however, the same consists only of wheedling new salary cuts from us every day in the form of 'voluntary' donations."[51] Even by then, such mockery was not out of place in Lindemann's diary. More than once, he had found the regime's constant self-praise particularly difficult to stomach. But this time he returned to his statements again the following day. "Coming back to yesterday's report, one is actually a defeatist and should actually consider that, without National Socialism, Germany would be in chaos today," he admitted at the beginning of this entry. He distanced himself even more from the previous day's comments by augmenting the sentence with the drawing of a swastika flag, a large swastika, and a black-white-red flag.[52] Not only was this the first time he had illustrated his diary since the October 1933 announcement of Germany's withdrawal from the League of Nations and of the new election and plebiscite; it was also one of only three times he drew flags in his diary during the 1930s without referring to a major political event.[53] For the time being, the entries in the days that followed actually no longer expressed any political criticism.

This did not remain a permanent condition, which would have led to the disappearance of political criticism, doubt, and mockery from his diary. Quite the contrary: just a short time later he started recording his own assessments of the regime's policies again. But given the regime's ideals regarding political behavior and evaluations, these assessments repeatedly posed a problem for Lindemann, and he continued to struggle with the tension between his aspiration to make his own assessments and the official expectations of his political verdicts. In November 1934, he reported in his diary that he had been in the "'Kaufhaus' on the Königsallee" in Düsseldorf (where the young doctor now lived), which gave him reason to complain about what he felt was the incomplete Aryanization of the department stores. From there he ultimately arrived at his general state of political frustration. "Now there are only *Kaufhofs*, no more Tietzs and Wertheims. These firms are now Aryan; they probably have taken a few Aryans onto their supervisory board. *Aryans as modest as Goebbels*, as chaste as Röhm, as chivalrous as . . . oh, I did not actually want to engage in politics,"

Lindemann wrote, finally breaking off his frustrations and coming back to speak about the Kaufhaus again, which was "also well visited." "They all shopped there, said 'Heil Hitler,' and disappeared,"[54] he wrote, thus ending his report with an allusion to the NSDAP's long-standing struggle against department stores,[55] which is why it seemed inappropriate to him for National Socialists to shop in such places. "One can certainly become pensive," Lindemann commented accordingly, but then he added, "or also leave it alone. For it is better."[56] As had been the case eight months earlier, here too Lindemann tried hard to keep himself from making political criticisms, as per the ideal of unconditional faith; and just like in March, he came back to speak about these comments in the next day's entry. But this time, he did not directly distance himself from his statements. Instead, he wrote what for him was a very unusual entry. Usually he took his cue from the day's events; but here, without direct cause, he wrote some remarkably extensive comments regarding his basic political standpoint. It was for him "a joyful gratification and my true pride," Lindemann noted, to have taken "the *straight völkisch path* since 1922 . . . *strictly nationalist, völkisch, and antisemitic.*"[57]

For many diarists still basically interested in forming their own political judgments, criticism in the 1930s became similarly problematic. Even Hans Maschmann, who in his diary frequently distinguished between the undiscriminating "masses" and people capable of independent thought, and who often professed that he did not want to "allow clear judgment to be clouded," that he wanted to consider "things really . . . as what they are,"[58] noted in April 1936, for example, "Am I really so embittered by life of the last twenty years that now, even if I want to, I cannot believe Hitler's words, which express my sentiments of the time when he was still nameless? Am I really so disappointed by life that I cannot believe in Hitler's sincerity? I ask myself this over and over." But making this confession in his diary, Maschmann then referred to the "morass of lies and slander" that surrounded Hitler, which was why he "could not believe him, especially him." To confirm once more that he retained his right to his own judgment, Maschmann immediately followed up by reporting a conversation he had had with a nun inspired by the "Führer": "She spoke about the absolute effect of his [Hitler's] personality and then added: 'I want to believe in him, I want to trust his sincerity, even if one day I must admit that it was all just a lie. This lie was then at least beautiful.'" But Maschmann did not want to envelop himself in this "beautiful delusion": "My resignation is not that desperate after all."[59]

The central problem confronting Walter Lindemann, Hans Maschmann, and other Germans was that the regime firmly viewed the propagated form of political behavior as being equivalent to a definitive statement: anyone who did not unconditionally believe the regime could not, from its perspective, be a supporter. But being a supporter was precisely the claim put forth by many of these diarists who, in light of the control of the media, insisted on making their own judgment. In his diary, the former Thuringian parliamentarian Georg Witzmann repeatedly opposed the regime's "demand for exclusivity and totality," which needed to be "combated and rejected." Nonetheless, he emphasized that, despite his differences with the NSDAP, somebody like him "who is nationalist, and who promises and guarantees to loyally support the present regime, must be welcome by the regime, even if he does not belong to the ruling party and does not allow himself to be stripped of the right to criticize individual regime measures."[60]

For Walter Lindemann as well, the striking decision in favor of his own political judgment with his "Political Diary" did not mean that he had become hostile to the regime. Quite the contrary, the doctor had not only worked hard to join the SA in 1933 but, as late as spring 1938, for example, he also celebrated the annexation of Austria with these words: "Enthusiastically we bow in this great hour *before the statesman's genius of our chancellor* Adolf Hitler."[61] And Hans Maschmann, too, emphasized that "in every worldview" there are always "free men" who make use of their reason and "slaves" who are determined by their emotions and thus controllable, thereby underscoring that his differences with the regime pertained to the form of political behavior but not to the political standpoint being represented.[62] This is where the search for an appropriate form of political conduct and evaluation met with one's basic commitment to the Nazi regime, the latter involving a process in which many people in 1933–1934 had likewise balked at the demand for unconditional adherence and, with the help of criticism, combined their existing self-views with the demanded political commitment.[63] These Germans, in particular, did not see criticism and support as contradictory when they thought about regime policies. Even people who, in light of the changes to the political system, still insisted on making their own political judgments could be very willing to affirm the regime. They just did not want to do so blindly.

Possibilities and Limits of One's Own Political Judgments

Germans who, despite the official demand for faith and loyalty, wanted to continue making political judgments themselves could not simply rely on media news coverage. Faced with the state's control of the media, they had to systematically gather and assess information on political events and developments on their own and assemble it into their own picture.[64] To do so, they developed a broad range of techniques with which they tried to distinguish between news and propaganda—between truth and lies—in their reception of reporting.

Thus many diarists, for example, devoted their attention primarily to the speeches of leading representatives of the state, which were often printed in newspapers or broadcast by radio (often many times over). There was comparatively less interest in reports or commentaries about political events. Instead of relying on the judgment of journalists, these people used original texts to engage in their own deliberations, which they indeed turned directly against evaluations in the media.[65] They also bolstered this effort by reading various different newspapers to obtain as much detailed, unprocessed information as possible or to compare different accounts on the same topic. In the process, these diarists repeatedly and deliberately drew on foreign newspapers to make up for the lack of information in the German press—which Walter Lindemann combined with the indignant remark that it is *"unworthy of a free German man to learn about the political situation of his people and country from a Swiss, thus a foreign, newspaper."*[66] In the 1930s, foreign newspapers could still be rather easily obtained, and not just in the major cities of Berlin, Hamburg, or Munich. In Fürth, too, with fewer than eighty thousand residents in the 1930s, the gingerbread baker Daniel Lotter, born in 1873, was regularly able to include reports from the *Baseler Nachrichten* and the British *Weekly Times* in his political deliberations in his diary.[67] Even Werner Stock, living in Lüdersfeld near Hanover, a village with fewer than one thousand residents, noted in his diary that he read foreign newspapers.[68]

In addition, people also searched outside the mass media for further sources of information that they could compare with newspaper and radio reports to review their truth content and achieve a more complete picture. Above all, things they could observe in their own daily lives played an important role. "In the newspapers there is constant mention of an economic upswing. Savings bank deposits are increasing, the number of unemployed is declining, and yet in Fürth affairs are getting ever worse," Lotter noted in February 1934, for example, and he was not the only one who repeatedly made such comparisons.[69] Other diarists noted political statements that they picked up on the streets or information they received from official authorities.⁷⁰ Along with deploying such personal observations to counter official accounts in the media, they also used rumors, which became an important source for their own assessments. The notary and attorney Ferdinand Beier, born in 1878 and working in Coesfeld in Westphalia, was especially systematic when noting rumors in his diary, and as in the case of many others, this helped him precisely when he was contemplating political developments. "Pharmacist F. from Dortmund tells me," he noted quite typically in mid-January 1938, "that of eighteen secondary high school students, nine were kept back from exams because of the non-granting of a political clearance certificate. Another secondary high school student, who after losing two years could have done his A-levels, was kept back because one of the decision-makers wanted to get revenge due to the uncovering of irregularities by his father.—In Bochum the brigade leader and all of the leading people at the slaughterhouse are mixed up in the embezzlements, one only need listen to the workers sometime."⁷¹

By no means did such rumors necessarily pertain only to events in one's own region. In December 1936, the gingerbread baker Daniel Lotter learned in Fürth in Bavaria that far to the north in Oldenburg "a crowd of people, against which the SA and Nazi posse were powerless, forced the Gauleiter to retract a decree." Because of the distance and "since the newspapers are not allowed to report on this matter," he could "not review the truth of these claims," Lotter commented.⁷² He returned to this story in his diary two weeks later. In his opinion, the "events in Oldenburg" had since "proved true" and were "more momentous than the first rumors said." However, this was still not being officially confirmed. Lotter noted that, "characteristically, the incidents, like any other unpleasantness, are hushed up by the newspapers," thereby expressly affirming how much his own political judgment was based not on the press but rather on precisely these kinds of information sources.⁷³

Like Daniel Lotter, other diarists also worked hard to gather their own information about political happenings so they could identify the control of political reporting as precisely as possible and take this into account in their political judgments. "In Westphalia a newspaper is banned for five weeks because it described the reports about the successes in battling employment as what they are: namely, a distortion of the facts," the Hamburg teacher Hans Maschmann wrote knowingly in his diary in summer 1933, adding that it was an "open secret" that in other parts of the country "reports are made about successes in Hamburg and Harburg and the other way around." "Since the incident in Westphalia, the propaganda leadership seems to be more careful; last week, the reports about successes in the struggle for work were sparser and more low-key," Maschmann wrote in closing, conveying the impressions he had gained from attentively reading newspapers and thus documenting his assessment of the actual status of the struggle against unemployment. At the same time, he thereby emphasized his viewpoint that media reports were basically untrustworthy.[74]

With its laborious efforts to control political reporting, the Nazi regime worked at creating uniformity in the political views of the "Volk." Using the media, it tried to spread a prescribed interpretation of political events within the population. This required the censorship and control of political reporting, which found sharp disapproval among many of those Germans who strongly did not want to be served up any political judgments. But at the same time, the mechanisms of media control turned these people into very attentive and active media users. These very same Germans paid especially close attention to the political accounts disseminated by the regime in an effort to distinguish as precisely as possible between truth and lies, between information and its whitewashed presentation.

Historians writing about the National Socialist public sphere have done very little empirical research into the concrete efforts of Germans to decipher the state-controlled political reporting. Nonetheless, such headstrong reception of the media has been deemed very important in basic assessments of the Nazi regime's public policy. "Even in a very extensively coordinated mass communication system," Konrad Dussel has pointed out, for example, "it was not possible to monopolize the flow of information and interpretation."[75] In this respect, the regime's propaganda reached its limits and was far less effective than expected. This is notably confirmed by diaries, with their extensive skepticism and critical statements.

From these limits, however, it has also been reasoned that "direct communication and one's own experience" had formed "the actual basis for judgment in broad parts of the population." Judgments supported in this way could "then be changed only slightly by the mass media."[76] Having formed their alternative opinions in their own way instead of being influenced by the media, Germans are said to have been able to discover hidden messages "between the lines" and to understand "even just small allusions" in the media.[77] But the diaries of the 1930s cast doubt on this optimistic interpretation, which, on the basis of headstrong media reception tacitly concludes that the formation of individual opinions was successful. The diary entries do not just show that Germans struggled against simply accepting political opinions and assessments from the mass media. They also clearly reveal the obstacles that impeded the independent formation of opinion outside the mass media. In this respect, apart from showing that many Germans in the 1930s were anxious about wanting to form their own political judgment, these diaries allow us to ask about whether their independent assessments of political events could succeed.

Even with intense effort, access to information was always severely limited, but this was not the only obstacle that made the project of decoding official accounts a difficult undertaking with questionable prospects of success. Even just the project itself and the place from which people were forced to try to read between the lines limited the options for forming an independent judgment. This can be illustrated, for example, by the intensive discussions of various diarists regarding the so-called Röhm putsch, a coup supposedly planned by a group of putschists within the Nazi movement around SA Leader Ernst Röhm, who allegedly renounced his loyalty to Hitler and, together with allies such as Gregor Strasser and Kurt von Schleicher, tried to overthrow the regime.[78] The public presentation of the event was a "propaganda coup par excellence," with which the regime tried, after the fact, to publicly legitimate the murder of Röhm and other competitors within the party and state leadership around Hitler.[79] In actuality, plans for such an overthrow did not exist, and the ostensible "moral transgressions," which were highly embellished in the propaganda (SA leaders were said to have been apprehended while with a group of "boy toys"), never occurred. The claims constituted one of the most direct lies of the National Socialist propaganda apparatus.[80]

Correspondingly, in their diaries many Germans fiercely criticized the regime's public policy with regard to the Night of the Long Knives. The former Thuringian parliament member Georg Witzmann, for example, wrote in his entry of July 2, 1934, that it could be "assumed from the outset, and so it also happened, that the propaganda boss would conduct the propaganda such that he had the person of the Führer shining in an even higher and purer light." But Witzmann only had scorn for this. "There he stands, how brave and resolute, pure and faithful, how great and gracious, but also how merciless when necessary! The Volk is bound to him more firmly than ever; the Hitler state stands there more firmly than ever!"[81] At the same time, he clearly criticized the fact that the regime "consistently refuses to answer important individual questions," emphasizing this point repeatedly in his diary. "How many persons were shot dead and which ones? Did . . . they also include, as reported by foreign radio: Kahr, Lossow, Seisser, Captain Ehrhardt? . . . What was actually the goal of the conspirators?"[82] "Why is one satisfied with general expressions: 'reactionary rebellion' etc.? . . . Why is the official reporting satisfied here only with mysterious insinuations?" Summing up, Witzmann wrote, "These are all ambiguities that by no means serve to increase confidence in the regime, despite how much this is now also being emphasized and stated in all tonalities, what tremendous enthusiasm is now being shown for the Führer in all of Germany."[83]

Other diarists who adopted a critical approach to the media of the regime similarly faulted "the murkiness of the operations,"[84] pointed in their writings to contradictions in official accounts, and brought to light the deliberate staging of Hitler as the "resolute Führer," which was meant to help the regime legitimate the murders. Thus Hans Maschmann, too, pointed out that "all of the newspapers outdo each other . . . in exploiting the events of June 30 in order to glorify Hitler."[85] Reich Propaganda Minister Goebbels knew "that the system falls with Hitler. When will the Volk disarm his methods? When will it comprehend that the 'greatness' of this man is systematically contrived?"[86] In his diary, Maschmann specifically used the Night of the Long Knives with pointed sarcasm to outline the general system of media control. "From time to time, when the mood among the people sinks and becomes dangerous, Hitler sends out his bards," Maschmann commented on July 13, 1934, referring to Hitler's key speech to the Reichstag justifying the murders of Ernst Röhm and his alleged coconspirators. "Goebbels starts the roundelay as cantor, and the entire choir from concert singers to medicant singers enthusiastically joins in, until the mood of the listeners is perfect again. Then 'he' appears, the Führer, the 'hero' himself in person and stages the final scene. Then they say: 'The entire Volk is being connected by loudspeaker.' And the Volk is made to understand how unified it is."[87]

In dealing with the news about the Röhm purge, many diarists worked hard to peer through the official propaganda and form their own picture of the events, which were obviously not openly presented in the press. Yet as much as they criticized the public policy of the regime, they themselves were hardly in a position to recognize the "canard of the 'Röhm putsch.'"[88] Instead, precisely because of their efforts to see through the propagandistic accounts of the regime, they believed the story about the putsch and the homosexual escapades of the murder victims. Summing up the situation in his diary, Georg Witzmann, for example, wrote that the "accusations being made against the conspirators" included "insurrection attempts against the Führer and the state, secret association with a foreign power, but moreover also a dissolute lifestyle beyond compare, disgraceful and disgusting sexual abnormalities, swankiness and gluttony, squandering of funds of the party and thus of the state, etc., etc." Commenting on the list of accusations, he wrote, "Now, these are all things that have been common knowledge in Germany for months, but woe to those who would have dared say this within even the smallest group."[89] Having criticized the regime for months, Witzmann now saw his criticisms confirmed by the very accusations that were concocted to disavow the supposed putschists and were disseminated by the controlled media, taking them as evidence of the regime's public policy designed to suppress criticism. "The faith in the truth of that which, day in and day out, has been presented to us as truth has started to totter and will not be recoverable again so soon," Witzmann noted hopefully.[90]

Many diarists who had recorded their critical thoughts on the new political system and its monitoring of the public sphere in previous months felt similarly validated. Karl Möhring, for example, felt "assured by the Röhm case that my view, which I last wrote down in summary last March to early May, is the right one."[91] Möhring noted in his diary that "the affair clearly showed that the Volk has often been kept in the dark about things" in past months.[92] On the occasion of Hitler's justification speech in mid-July 1933, Möhring, who considered himself an "advocate of National Socialism" with his "own opinion and independent criticism," summed up his intensive confrontation with various media in a long entry. "Because Hitler hesitated too long," the "leadership of the NSDAP" had found itself "in a quandary with this complot." Because of Hitler's speech, the party had now been "driven by necessity to give an in-depth report with scandalous details about the revolution, even though the account was bound to make a shocking impression on the surprised masses of faithful National Socialists and strengthen the critics in their criticism. So Hitler's account will, by and large, correspond to the facts. One was unable to whitewash things for three reasons," Möhring continued, going on to explain why, in his opinion, the story about the thwarted putsch had to be true.[93] And quite similar was the assessment of Hans Maschmann, who was just as earnestly interested in making his own judgment. In his diary, he wrote it was "typical" of the "behavior of the commandeered press," that since the press could "not conceal the weaknesses of the system," it made a "glorified person out of Hitler instead."[94]

Two things are striking about these diary entries. First, they contradict the established thesis regarding the social reaction to the Night of the Long Knives in June 1934. They cast strong doubts on the assumption that there was an "almost total absence of any criticism of Hitler" within the population after the news of the prevented coup, that "support and sympathy for the Führer" was found "even among those who had previously shown reserve towards the regime, and even among former opponents of Nazism," and that the propagandistic exploitation of the murders, "instead of intensifying unease at the ruthlessness of a head of government... unquestionably strengthened confidence in Hitler," as Kershaw has argued on the basis of the Nazi regime's morale reports.[95]

In contrast to the thesis that the staging of the "Röhm putsch" enlarged the substantive consensus between the regime and the population, the deliberations found in diaries of the 1930s about the murder operation and its representation in the media suggest that the propagandistic tale about the "putsch" sustained and strengthened contemporary criticisms, including those directed specifically against Hitler himself. These diarists could "in no way [perceive] the attitude of a hero" in his actions; they not only sharply criticized his performance but also seemed convinced that, on the whole, the revelations would severely damage the regime leader's reputation.[96] Georg Witzmann, for example, felt certain that the "simple, hard-pressed Volk" would be outraged at what was going on "behind the scenes" of the Nazi regime and that "the Führer... did not detect all of these people... [had] no idea about their dissolute lifestyle, and only became vigilant and strong as the conspiracy turned against him personally. The prestige of the Führer, too, must therefore suffer."[97]

Similarly, another diarist voiced the expectation that "the discovery of the lesion (a pestilential bubo) hits the party hard," something that "even Hitler's resolute attitude and the approval from the entire Reich" could not change.[98] Meanwhile, Karl Möhring was certain that, "among the large masses, the pious childish faith is now destroyed. Loyalty to the Führer is precisely what was set up as something sublime beyond all doubt. Now old fighters who have sworn loyalty to the Führer a hundred times have broken the oath."[99] Germans interested in making their own political judgments did not simply abandon this effort in light of the Führer's supposed energetic action. Instead, they formulated harsh criticisms of Hitler and the regime's public policy in their diaries.

The fact that there was no simultaneous increase of public criticism, that the expectations recorded by Möhring and others went unfulfilled, and that indeed, as Kershaw has emphasized, there was no "wave of revulsion and outrage directed at Hitler and his accomplices"[100] should not simply be read as proof that these writers had inadequate powers of prediction or held marginalized positions. Instead, the contradiction between such expectations and what actually occurred points to the second striking aspect of these diary entries—namely, that they draw attention to the fundamental and insurmountable obstacle with which Nazi public policy hampered individual political evaluations and, as noted by proponents of the Hitler myth, made private conversations and personal experience a problematic and questionable basis for judgment. The expectations of contemporaries (and Kershaw) completely failed to take into account that, given National Socialist public policy, these reactions and interpretations related to the events had no chance of becoming known beyond the individual's private surroundings. Although showing up frequently in the diaries of the 1930s, the interpretation of the supposed Röhm putsch as evidence of abuses in the new system could not become collective political opinion because the mechanisms that might have transported the corresponding estimations into the public sphere and combined them into a collective attitude did not exist. As these diarists quite rightly observed, after the supposed thwarting of the coup was announced, the regime's public policy used various instruments to try to demonstrate broad social support for the "Führer's" actions, and instead of being an objective corrective to the media accounts, the morale reports provided yet another tool for this endeavor. This was also a major reason that the regime's claim to power was not publicly challenged in summer 1934. Yet this had crucial implications for people's individual formation of political opinion, making it impossible for them to integrate their own political assessments on a larger scale or to situate them in relation to the way others generally perceived and evaluated the regime's activities. To be sure, diarists spoke frequently with friends and acquaintances about their political assessments and recorded their opinions as part of their political discussions in their diaries.[101] But these conversations could not replace the general framework that the media had provided during the Weimar Republic for the orientation of personal political opinion.

Because of state media control, mass media no longer performed its central function for the formation of individual opinion. Admittedly, they could certainly still be a source of information for attentive and active recipients. But assessments made on this basis had no independent point of reference that could help organize the individual's own evaluations. In practice, the fundamental issues faced by Germans when developing their political opinions could simply not be resolved this way. Bits of information gleaned from personal observation, the comparison of media reports, and overheard rumors could not be inserted into a general picture conveyed by the media, which meant that, beyond the issue of whether this information was accurate, its relative importance inevitably remained doubtful. News about the economic upswing in the 1930s, for example, could be set against observations of one's own surroundings that cast doubt on the official account. But this did not make it possible to sketch an independent picture of the country's economic development.

This problem ultimately also affected the central question of how to assess the degree of societal support for the regime's policies. This interested many diarists in their political discussions just as strongly as it did political observers in exile. But even in Germany, individual observations of political comments or dissatisfactions could not be assembled into a picture of the general mood. Without question, the Nazi regime did not successfully monopolize the formation of political opinions by Germans and direct the "flow of information and interpretation" as desired. Instead of creating broad approval, the propaganda, control of political reporting, and political control of public space stimulated condemnation and anger among many Germans, which was repeatedly reformulated in the diaries of the 1930s. In later years as well, diarists would, for example, go on to use references to the Röhm purge as evidence of the regime's abuses and its mendacious media policy, which it had no longer been able to conceal in the context of the so-called putsch.[102] Yet Germans could succeed in little more than steadily pointing out the regime's shortcomings and its control of opinion, through which they constantly cast doubt on the media's representations of politics and criticized them as falsifying. But from this position it was plainly impossible to achieve an alternative picture of political events.

The resulting uncertainty in one's personal judgment strongly contributed to making extensive reflections on political events an important form of political behavior even well after the start of National Socialist rule. At the start of that rule, uncertainty caused by the rapid conversion of the political institutional structure threw existing standards of evaluation into doubt for many Germans, thus prompting them to conduct detailed and fundamental discussions about the political changes. The control of political reporting entrenched this kind of confrontation with politics. In light of the regime's formative media policy, people who wanted to make their own judgment could not simply furnish political developments with their own assessment. Instead, they still needed essentially to sound out the meaning of the official representation of political events. In the middle and end of the 1930s as well, independent and extensive discussion of National Socialist policy formation and political decision-making still remained an important mode by which individuals scrutinized the actions of the regime and (also) provided a reason for keeping a diary.

This applied to many of those Germans who, at the start of National Socialist rule, had organized their diaries for dealing with politics. Diarists like Hans Maschmann or Daniel Lotter maintained their constant preoccupation with political reporting beyond the start of the war.[103] But so too did the former Thuringian parliamentarian Georg Witzmann; after the results of the vote in November 1933, he had wondered in his diary "whether it is not time" to stop writing about his confrontation with political events, yet he did nothing of the sort. Instead, he too regularly wrote down his extensive discussions and commentary on political events, which he followed in the media until well into the war.[104]

Other Germans only started using a diary in the mid-1930s to find their bearings in the area of National Socialist policy and to make their own independent judgments in the face of an officially controlled media. Inga Lusebrink*, for example, a Hamburg lawyer born in 1901, first started her diary on August 30, 1935, with these words: "A diary? Yes indeed; it is necessary. To organize for once the many severely depressing thoughts that buzz through my head in this day and age. And if it is only two lines a day. After the many things of the day, the time after 8:30 must belong to me. Otherwise there is no composure at work."[105] Her first entry already revealed that these "many thoughts" pertained chiefly to political topics. Here Lusebrink started with extensive deliberations on why "the Jewish question is being brought to the fore like that again" in the media coverage, which to her mind indicated a "certain plan" that she wanted to figure out by writing down her thoughts.[106] Lusebrink continued her diary in this manner, using it to follow political events in the media and trying to sound them out by writing.

Like Inga Lusebrink, Josef Herlitz, an elementary school teacher in Neersen on the Lower Rhine born in 1897, started his diary on February 1, 1938, with the intention of writing down, "descriptively and reflectively, the events of the day . . . insofar as they affect and are mirrored by the small circle of a human existence," which for him also meant systematically dealing with the political news and events that he followed in the press, which was "filtered for reasons of state."[107] Herlitz clearly understood that, for the regime, this filtered press was "useful for achieving the moods that accommodate state desires." "The Church can sing a song about that," commented the former member of the Catholic Center Party, and thereby clearly identified his reason for monitoring the regime: he wanted to use his diary entries specifically to get to the bottom of the "reality" of the news reporting on National Socialist church policy.[108]

Even though Herlitz, like other diarists, could hardly succeed with this plan, his diary documents a certain form of political behavior. It emerged from the state control of the mass media's political reporting and the reception of this reporting by individuals who, despite the censored and controlled media, wanted to form their own judgment on regime policy. Almost paradoxically, the control of political reporting ensured that it received special attention from many people who firmly condemned the regime's controlled distribution of political sentiments in German society. Such people did not just take notice of interpretations conveyed by newspaper reports and radio news. Rather, they often made political news the subject of intensive discussion, which is precisely what made them extremely active media users. Knowing about censorship and control measures, many Germans made an effort not to just absorb information and interpretations from the mass media but to form their own picture of political events. In this process, the diary became an instrument for constant political discussion. The literature has repeatedly assumed, for example, that "given the fear of reprisals, open political statements in contemporary diaries, letters, and private papers were naturally very rare."[109] But quite contrary to this assumption, National Socialist public policy actually turned the skeptical and critical discussion of political reporting within limited private spaces like the diary into a widespread form of political behavior in the new political culture of National Socialism.

Wanting to Believe

Deliberate political behavior in the 1930s, however, was not limited solely to the attempt to make independent political judgments. Whereas Germans could try to assert their own ideas against the claims of the regime, they could also make an active effort to adopt the new forms of political conduct and evaluation propagated by the government. This too can be traced in the diaries of the 1930s, even though the corresponding entries document the confrontation with the demands of the regime less explicitly than we find with regard to the search for personal political judgments. Whereas the latter form of political conduct was reflected in lengthy discussions in the diaries of the 1930s, efforts related to the desire to believe the regime found expression primarily in the simple registration of political events. As I will show, however, even these entries can be understood as deliberate political behavior.

In this respect, two potential misunderstandings should be avoided: first, in the following I am interested in individuals who deliberately dealt with the policies of the regime. I am not thereby claiming that Germans could only believe the regime through conscious effort. Despite all of the mobilization attempts by the Nazi regime, "political apathy" existed in the 1930s as well, which was often combined with a nonspecific confidence that the regime would actually do the right thing.[110] As under any system of political rule, such carefree lack of interest helped stabilize the Nazi dictatorship. In its efforts to reconfigure the relationship between the government and the "Volk," however, the Nazi regime used the concept of "belief" to describe a form of deliberate political conduct in which Germans were supposed to be simultaneously attentive and uncritical with respect to political events. In the following, I am interested in the ways individuals tried to fulfill this demand.

Second, when I examine diaries for these forms of conduct, I am not claiming that efforts to derive independent political judgments and to believe ruled each other out in the 1930s. Even though these two basic forms of deliberate political conduct within the political culture of National Socialism were fundamentally different, individual Germans were quite able to combine various elements from both. Thus, these basic forms should be understood as ideal types that could apply to individuals to a greater or lesser degree. What we are investigating in the following, therefore, is not the companion piece to the previously described efforts related to the independent-minded reception of politics. Rather, it constitutes the second of two poles marking either end of the spectrum of deliberate political behavior in the 1930s.

Born in 1875, the Berlin sales agent Hermann Schleifenbaum kept a collection of newspaper clippings in addition to his personal, where he also saved press articles related to domestic and foreign political developments. But unlike Lindemann, he refrained from organizing them into his own "political reports" and from making his own commentaries. He simply collected the articles in a folder formally organized according to subject areas, which he entitled "Various—Incidents Lying outside the Diary and Articles with Content of General Interest—Newspaper Clippings."

The compilation hardly documents anything apart from the fact that Schleifenbaum, too, attentively followed media reporting. By contrast, the personal that he kept at the same time mentioned regime politics and its mass-media presentation only rarely and briefly. "The *Reichstag* meets and resolves *to abolish the state governments and subordinate them directly to the Reich*," he noted without further comment, for example, on January 30, 1934, on the passing of the Law on the Restructuring of the Reich.[111] The diary report in early March 1936 was similarly matter-of-fact: "The Reichstag was convened and dissolved, the Rhineland supplied with troops, since France is heavily rearming and has entered an alliance with Soviet Russia against Germany. New vote on 3/29."[112] Despite such sober entries, the diary left no doubt that Schleifenbaum was politically interested and actively supported the Nazi regime. Thus his notes reported regularly and in greater detail, for example, on his involvement in the Reich Air Protection Corps and the National Socialist Organization of Crafts, Trade, and Commerce. This is also where he recorded his observations regarding the political attitude of acquaintances and neighbors, repeatedly making disapproving comments about how they shopped in Jewish stores, for example.[113] In his personal diary, Schleifenbaum left no doubts as to his agreement with the actions of the regime, even if his associated comments were seldom and brief, conveying little more than that he was following the news situation.

That Hermann Schleifenbaum was interested in documenting his unadorned attentiveness to political developments is suggested by the nature of his discussion of the Night of the Long Knives, which was the only event of the 1930s for which he did more than simply register the news. This discussion can be read as indicating that the announcement of the supposed coup attempt from within the regime could also irritate Germans who did not try to peer behind the facade of the official propaganda. Yet Schleifenbaum's entries on this matter are clearly different from the markedly opinionated statements noted by Hans Maschmann, Georg Witzmann, and other diarists related to this event.

Already on June 30, 1934, Schleifenbaum noted, "One is talking about a *putsch* against the Führer. A few major SA figures arrested and shot dead. General Schleicher shot himself dead during the arrest. In Wiessee Hitler came across *Röhm and Heines* in an unbelievable situation, boy toys, etc. etc. Gruppenführer *Ernst* fled to Hamburg or Bremen, was arrested there, according to other statements supposedly had 160,000 marks with him with which he wanted to go abroad."¹¹⁴ This alone was already a far more detailed treatment than Schleifenbaum's general coverage of political events. In addition, two days later he spoke about the murders again. "The Baseler Zeitung supposedly provided the names of those shot to death (eighteen). Seven are being named here," he noted on July 2, going on to report that he had heard that supposedly "an assassination of Hitler had already been planned" for the funeral of Carin Göring, Hermann Göring first wife, who died in 1932. "They hit the wrong one, *Himmler*, who supposedly was shot in the hand and rear and so forth."¹¹⁵

Hermann Schleifenbaum, too, took note of the reporting on the murders in the foreign press (albeit as related by others), of its differences compared to the official accounts in Germany, and of the many circulating rumors. As opposed to diarists like Georg Witzmann, Hans Maschmann, or Karl Möhring, however, he notably did not want to speculate about it on his own. "I consider much of it empty talk." On the contrary, in his diary Schleifenbaum explicitly adopted the media's representation of the events, which drew a sharp line between the putschists, who violated their loyalty obligations, and the "Führer," with his great strength of character—the same sharp line that other Germans found so dubious.¹¹⁶ A month after the Röhm murders, when upon the death of Reich President Hindenburg the regime leadership scheduled a plebiscite on the unification of the offices of Reich president and Reich chancellor, Schleifenbaum commented with the words "Bravo! The sympathies for Hitler are increasing by the same degree as the antipathies toward some of his helpers," adding to this assessment a direct reference to his entry on the Röhm murders.¹¹⁷

The reports about the "putsch attempt" spelled irritation for Hermann Schleifenbaum too, but this was not combined with an attempt to probe the causes and the regime's murky actions with his own thoughts. Even in this situation, he instead made a firm effort to align his perceptions with the official account. And this effort also explains the short comments on other political events: in accordance with the ideal of political behavior propagated by the regime, with the brief notes in his diary Schleifenbaum confirmed that he indeed followed political events, but did not make this the departure point for his own thoughts; instead, he thereby gave written expression to his unshakable faith in the regime.

With the pictures of the "Führer" being cheered by the "Volk," the Nazi regime disseminated a behavioral requirement that was, admittedly, aimed first and foremost at how people were supposed to act in public. But it left no doubt that the ideal of an unconditional faith in the regime also had a corresponding "inner attitude" defined by an "unquestioning, devoted confidence in the matter of National Socialism and the ability of the Führer (and those he commissioned) to always do the right thing."[118] In this respect, the demands placed on Germans' political behavior and judgment also aimed at the private sphere, in that political events were supposed to be closely followed but not scrutinized. In his diary, Schleifenbaum tried to live up to this highly conflicting demand. Whereas Georg Witzmann or Hans Maschmann worked at forming their own judgments, people like Schleifenbaum tried hard to internalize the regime's ideal of political behavior and align their actions accordingly.

These people also included the former seafarer Christoph Ahrens, born in 1878, who in Hamburg in the 1930s tried his hand as a painter and writer. In his diary, Ahrens repeatedly reflected on his political conduct. In summer 1934, after "the newspaper reported Röhm's dismissal and the radio the shooting" of the "putschists," he examined his own perception of the events in his diary:[119] "I wonder about myself. I am not agitated in the slightest, have a certain fatalistic feeling and at the same time I am gripped by a certain curiosity about what will probably come. To me it is as if all of this does not concern me and yet with great interest [I] follow the events, which however cannot clearly be seen from the newspapers."[120]

These indecisive observations do little to help us understand how the political events affected Ahrens. Yet they clearly reflect the regime's call for active and yet simultaneously uncritical involvement, which the author repeatedly took as a challenge for his own political behavior in subsequent entries. Six weeks later, when a visiting acquaintance told him "much about the exciting time in Munich around June 30 as the Röhm putsch was attempted," these descriptions did not lead Ahrens to call the official reports into doubt. "According to his account, Röhm had very cleverly and ruthlessly contrived his dirty affair," he noted in his diary instead, and then he affirmed that he did not want to give the matter much more thought. "Just lucky that chance and prudence had thwarted his [Röhm's] attack."[121] With the sense of relief that the putsch had been averted by happy coincidence, questions about its causes and the precise course of the murders no longer arose.

For Germans like Hermann Schleifenbaum and Christoph Ahrens, the effort to internalize the behavioral ideal propagated by the regime was closely connected to political reporting. But this did not lead to the kind of lengthy discussions recorded by those diarists who, in light of the state control of political reporting, nonetheless wanted to form their own opinion. Quite the contrary, this effort was reflected in the admittedly regular but usually only brief commentary on regime policies. We can see how this emerged from the internal logic of this form of political conduct by looking at the diary of Inge Thiele, the young gardener who on the occasion of a Hitler speech at the end of the voting campaign in November 1933 had asked in her diary why she could "not heedlessly believe."[122]

Thiele frequently used her diary in following years to query her political conduct as to whether it conformed to the requirements of the Nazi regime. For her, the recent decision she had made to "believe" in Hitler now was not merely an act of political commitment. She also made this decision the basis for her personal political behavior. The diary played an important role here. Thiele worked intensely in her diary to show her conformity with political reporting and regime policies. In February 1938, she reported in her diary how she had learned about a meeting between the Austrian federal chancellor and Hitler from French radio. For Thiele, this "unofficial encounter," which occurred in the context of the so-called Anschluss of Austria to the German Reich a few weeks later, was "overwhelming," even though "the radio (German) only [provided] a brief mention of facts, likewise the newspapers, without commentary and on Monday.—The experienced person knows that the headlines are not always what is most important, but rather have often distracted attention from what is important," Thiele wrote. Her comments on the matter clearly indicate that she was aware of the state control of the media and could very well take it into account in her deliberations.[123]

But this entry is by no means typical of the way Thiele thematized regime politics and its representation in the media. Instead, in her diary she was primarily concerned with displaying her own faith. Four years prior to this entry, she reported in February 1934, for example, about "several splendid speeches" that Goebbels had held "against the Church and hypocrisy." She described at length how the "sterilization act . . . seems to have excited the moral minds of the Church" and that there had been "opposing speeches." "To which the response of the Führer in his last great radio speech: 'If the Church wants to assume the support of the offspring of the congenitally diseased, then I will forgo the law.' More from Dr. Goebbels: 'If fate had made me an authoritative ecclesiastical prince, then after the national uprising I would have gone to Adolf Hitler and said: you have enough to do with domestic and foreign policy, leave the social welfare to us, as it is in actual Christianity.' But the Church failed; nothing of the sort occurred," Thiele commented, appropriating his argument and seeming outraged. "And now this attitude? They [the churches] should actually be happy that the National Socialists stopped Communism, for otherwise their glory would have long since ended. And woe if they now still want to sow confessional strife," she concluded threateningly. "Those times are definitively over and it will not be long before there is a single community of faith."[124]

Here and elsewhere in her diary, Inge Thiele was repeatedly concerned about emphasizing her conformity with the views of the regime and the political reporting in the media, although in later years this required much less space. By and large, extensive notes and approving comments about the regime's individual arguments, such as those in the entry of February 1934, occurred only during the first months of the diary, which was started in October 1933—the same months when Thiele still searched for an appropriate diary-writing style and was determining her relationship to the regime. But demonstrating her agreement with regime policies and media reporting did not always require detailed descriptions. In October 1935, for example, Thiele reported that in her work at the garden center she had to be very sparing with moss because "the importation of Iceland moss" had been "strongly restricted." "It is worse with butter and fat and meat. There is a lot of murmuring about it," she added with respect to the current situation. However, she then commented, "But our government will know why it is doing that."[125] In much the same way, the next summer she commented briefly on how "Germany-Austria have come to an agreement and the silent hostility is now to be transformed into mutual cooperation. One German Volk but two different state orders; this is supposed to be accommodated by both sides." In this case too, Thiele followed up her brief description with a single statement that nonetheless left no doubt about her approval: "That is peace policy without the League of Nations."[126]

Even with such brief snippets, one could use the diary to consistently show one's uncritical involvement with regime policy, although Thiele also frequently described more directly how satisfied she was in her role as a well-disposed interested observer. "Our government still has to deal a hell of lot with internal enemies," Thiele noted, for example, in her diary in August 1935. "One is constantly reading about conspiracy, currency smuggling by clergymen, attacks by Catholic boys on Hitler Youth boys, but they are on guard, next follows the dissolution of the Stahlhelm, concentration camp, everything will be avenged. There are strong interventions against the Jews too, everywhere one now runs into the sign: Jews are not wanted here. The *Stürmer* always puts out the weirdest stuff about Jews, shady characters and whiners. Nobody pulls off such racial Jewish faces like it does." In her diary, Thiele went no further than this list. She did not add any more detailed discussions or even just her own thoughts on the stated matters. Instead, she finished the entry with the words "Oh, life is so interesting again," which both underscored her participation in political events and at the same time closed the door on substantive analysis.[127]

Diaries repeatedly show that the concise registration of political events reported in the mass media can be very much understood as an expression of the effort to believe the regime as demanded and not simply as reflecting a minimal interest in politics. Born in 1879, Otmar Krämer was a domain counselor living in Weimar who, as early as February 3, 1933, celebrated the debut of the Hitler regime in his diary as the "start of a new era."[128] In the years that followed, his diary entries consistently included a separate section dedicated to "politics," while the entries themselves always covered a period of several weeks. "And now finally high politics," he wrote, starting his relevant notes for his entry of mid-May 1933. Yet he only jotted down a list of key words: "January 30, Hitler Reich Chancellor, dissolution of the Reichstag, Reichstag election, Reichstag fire, Day of Potsdam, Hitler's birthday, May 1 as Day of National Labor, boycott of the Jews, German Christians, Gleichschaltung, extermination of Marxism, autocratic rule of National Socialism, those are a few of the words and concepts that describe the political period since the last report." Then he added, as a supplement to the list, "German revolution only in its early stages," thereby pointing out the unforeseeable nature of further political developments on his own accord, without trying to figure them out in his diary. Instead, he simply noted, "Who knows how everything will still develop in domestic and foreign policy," thus signaling his intention to wait and see how political events would continue to unfold.[129]

In the diaries of the 1930s, the effort to adapt to the propagated ideal of political conduct and evaluation and to simply believe the regime led to what at first looks like a very paradoxical result: for Germans who understood themselves as National Socialists and wanted to fulfill the Nazi regime's expectations to a particularly high degree, regime policy often took up much less space than for authors who, while not necessarily disclaiming the regime, rejected its ideas about individual political conduct. This also applied to full-time NSDAP functionaries, like Helmut Böhme, the Kreisleiter of Freiberg in Saxony born in 1902, and Wilhelm Bollmann, who was born in 1896 and worked as a Gau training leader. To be sure, as Nazi functionaries they described their own activities for the NSDAP and the state at length in their diaries. But the diary entries of these individuals who dealt with the realization of Nazi policy rarely looked at any regime policies that that could be followed on a daily basis in the mass media but were not directly associated with their daily routine.[130]

As in previous decades, in the 1930s Germans continued to encounter regime politics above all through reports in the mass media. Accordingly, the reception of political reporting was central to the individual's political behavior. The Nazi state had recognized this as well and worked both on increasing mass-media consumption by Germans and on establishing its own forms and rules for reporting on regime politics. In addition to the comprehensive control of the content of political reporting, this reconfiguration also notably involved the development of the new mass medium of radio, which, through an ensemble of entertainment and news broadcasts, facilitated the quite extensive realization of the regime's expectations regarding individual political behavior. The state's intrusions into media reporting were supposed to motivate Germans to follow the reporting attentively but without criticism. Individuals were often just as aware of this expectation as they were of the state's interventions in the mass media, to which they reacted in different ways.

Despite the patronizing media policy of the Nazi regime, some people still tried making their own political judgments, even if, in light of insufficient information and the lack of reference points, it was generally impossible to arrive at an accurate evaluation of the political situation by criticizing the state's control of the media. In contrast, other Germans endeavored to believe the official political reporting and fulfill the expectations of the Nazi regime. This established two fundamentally different forms of political behavior, which basically contradicted each other. But they were not simply subsumed under the distinction between regime opposition and support. People who wanted to make their own judgments could also very well support the regime, and it was thoroughly possible for individuals to combine elements of both forms of behavior, despite all of the differences. Moreover, they exhibited major structural commonalities: both emerged from the interplay between state media control, the propagation of the regime's ideas of political behavior, and individuals' reactions to this. In both, the formative public policy of the Nazi regime was linked with the political actions and evaluations of Germans by way of the mass media. The newly emerging political culture of National Socialism was characterized both by the effort at individual judgment and by unconditional faith.

2. Encountering the Regime: Regime Appeals, Mass Festivals, and Individual Efforts to Participate

With its continuous political reporting, the mass media also played a prominent role in political communication between the government and the governed in the Nazi dictatorship. Yet at the same time, this communication was not limited to constant reports on regime activities. The regime also intended for the flow of "normal" political reporting to function as a backdrop against which to set off special events. These nonroutine events were especially important for the political culture of National Socialism because they constituted the place where the government and the governed directly met. The staging of National Socialist rule used for these encounters led to special forms of political behavior, which are the focus of this section.

The occasions for an encounter were provided, on the one hand, by the annually recurring holidays of the Nazi regime, which in its first months of rule established its own festival calendar.[131] Along with official state holidays celebrating the First of May, Hero Commemoration Day, and the harvest festival, this calendar included a range of remembrance days that commemorated the central stages of the rise of the NSDAP, such as the Hitler putsch, the proclamation of the party program, and Hitler's appointment as Reich chancellor. Diary templates and calendars of the 1930s often included brief references to these and other occasions.[132] Also included were recurring (party) political events, such as the Reich party rally of the NSDAP held annually in September or the birthday of Adolf Hitler on April 20. All of these days began with festivities, and, besides the celebrations of local party organizations or festivals held in urban spaces, the regime used some of these occasions to arrange elaborately prepared centralized events with sometimes hundreds of thousands of participants.[133] This applied first and foremost to January 30, May 1, the Reich party rally, the harvest festival, and November 9. With Hitler leading the way, the regime's top politicians made public appearances at these mass festivals and directly addressed the population in speeches. These events produced most of the pictures of the "Führer and Volk" the regime used to legitimate its rule, but mass events also created actual opportunities for direct encounters between the government and the governed.

With the help of mass media, even those Germans who could not attend in person were supposed to be able to participate. Thus media remained important for this form of communication as well, but the relationship of press and radio to the political event was fundamentally changed in that the regime suspended the media's role as an observer—a role that it otherwise at least formally retained. The media presentation of the festive event was already a key concern at the planning stage in the propaganda ministry's preparations for central events, with its priorities determining local operations and forms of festival staging. The mass festivals were deliberately set up as media events whose perception by society was decisively determined by the especially extravagant media presentation.[134] At the same time, however, the mass media were only supposed to function as a technical communication vehicle: while the regime usually allowed newspapers and radio to report on its policies in journalistic texts, at key mass festivals the media were just supposed to serve as a mouthpiece so that "leadership" could directly reach its "Volk."

This kind of direct appeal to the governed by the government did not just determine the regularly recurring festive days; it also determined, on the other hand, a series of major political events that were critically important for the development of regime policy until the start of the war. They too interrupted the normal workings of media reporting. In this respect, Germany's withdrawal from the League of Nations in October 1933 was just the first of an entire series of spectacular political events whose public announcement was not left to regular news reporting. Instead, the importance of the respective events was to be signaled by special editions of newspapers, public notices, and above all direct addresses to the "Volk" by government declarations and speeches from Reich Chancellor Hitler or his Reich propaganda minister. Since fall 1933, the list of regime decisions that generated moments of especially intensive politicization included the so-called Röhm putsch; the death of Reich President Hindenburg, with the associated transfer of the office's competencies to Reich Chancellor Hitler in summer 1934;

the so-called return of the Saarland to the German Reich; the reintroduction of compulsory military service in spring 1935; the occupation in the following year of the Rhineland, which had been demilitarized by the Treaty of Versailles; and the annexation of Austria and the Sudetenland in spring and fall 1938. This also enumerates the range of political events that historians view as the key milestones of the Third Reich's domestic and foreign policy development.[135] However, regime representatives repeatedly also addressed their "Volk" directly via mass media on occasions such as the extension of the economic Four-Year Plan issued in 1933 or other domestic policy decisions.

For Germans, the mass-media conditions and the state's expectations with regard to their personal political behavior markedly changed during these mass festivals and addresses. Their behavior was no longer supposed to consist only of the attentive, noncritical observation of the regime's activities via media reporting. Rather, they were now supposed to take an active part in the political events. The Nazi regime expected that the direct appeal to the population and the encounter—facilitated by the media—between the "leadership and Volk" would have an especially lasting and impressive effect for the integration of the German people into its politics. The festivals of National Socialism and the regime's addresses during decisive events formed a (if not the) central "locus of the charismatic authority relation," where the commitment of loyalty was supposed to be demonstrated by the population and renewed or strengthened for the individual listeners and spectators.[136] In this respect, both at festivals, with their "liturgy aimed at an intoxicating community experience," and at major political events, the encounter of the Germans with their "leadership" was staged as an "extraordinary experience."[137] Even though Hitler, like other regime representatives, always spoke about regime policy, these situations were different from the usual reporting of politics precisely because they hardly aimed at conveying information. Rather, they were about the desire to "grasp and captivate" listeners at their radios and participants gathered on location and to form the speeches primarily "into an event" for them.[138] The elaborate choreographies that determined the enactments of encounters were not about making National Socialist politics understandable but rather about making it come alive. The events were supposed to overwhelm and enthrall the people, and to incorporate them at an emotional level.[139]

With their exultation for the regime, the spectators were themselves supposed to become part of the enactment and event. In official accounts, spectator enthusiasm was declared to be a "bestowal of honor" and an "acclamation" and thus a form of direct political participation and involvement. For spectators assembled on-site, the official pictures of the cheering "Volk" formulated very directly how they were supposed to behave. But on these occasions, there were also concrete expectations of the individual political conduct of Germans participating by means of the mass media, with practices of reception being developed in conjunction with the forms for staging mass festivals in the media. This pertained above all to radio, which on the whole was assigned a key role in the staging of encounters because at least it could transport the sound of events and particularly the appeals of regime representatives in real time throughout the Reich. Even after the reorientation of radio programming after fall 1933, the radio was still supposed to perform the functions that been intensely rehearsed during the first months of Nazi rule. On March 21, 1933, the newly created Reich Propaganda Ministry for the first time organized a major state festival—namely, the convening of the newly elected Reichstag, elaborately celebrated as the Day of Potsdam. In addition to the "torchlight processions through all the cities and villages of the Reich," the Germans would be given the chance to take an "active part" in the "great historical event that is taking place these weeks in Germany." Even those who "are hindered by age and frailty" could "witness the [celebrations] in Potsdam and Berlin through the radio."[140]

Reich Propaganda Minister Joseph Goebbels, who on March 21 had been in office just one week, appeared very satisfied after the event, particularly with the radio broadcast. In his inaugural speech before the intendants of the radio stations on March 25, 1933, he emphasized that "in future [there should be] no event of political-historical consequence in which the Volk is not involved. We have proven that this works with the Day of Potsdam," and "these working methods that we have applied for the first time for the Day of Potsdam" must be further expanded.[141] With this in mind, in the following months of extreme politicization, radio stakeholders experimented intensely with ways of creating new forms of political participation using radio, which were soon also being directed at people apart from those who could not take part in (local) assemblies "for health reasons." For the Day of National Labor on May 1, 1933, the radio stations did more than just design a daylong program for broadcasting the main festival in the capital with cuts to events in other major German cities to attest to the scope of the "National uprising."[142] The game changer proved to be the Reich Propaganda Ministry's success in coordinating the timetables of the

May festivities in cities and towns, with the main festival being broadcast by radio, and making Hitler's address, held at the Tempelhof Field in Berlin and reproduced by loudspeakers throughout Germany, the climax of the events in local celebrations as well.[143] Together with innovative broadcasting techniques, previously tried out primarily for sports events, and alongside previously unknown programming concepts for broadcasting political events, the regime also developed new forms of political radio listening.

These were fundamentally broadened even more in the context of the 1933 November elections. For the broadcast of Hitler's speeches at the end of the election campaign in the Berlin Siemens factory, the regime for the first time urged that work be suspended during the midday broadcast period so people could listen to the speech at their workplace with their colleagues. Those who were not working were supposed to follow it with neighbors and friends. In contrast to the May festivities, the regime created an "experiential form that did not search out the festive get-together but rather retained the everyday environment of the workplace." This was related to the principle of the "honor of work" and efforts to integrate the labor force into society.[144] It also corresponded with the effort to make National Socialist regime policy a common component of the everyday life of Germans. At the same time, this established a form of collective radio listening that allowed the regime to react much more flexibly to political events because it required only that the radio broadcast be announced and "communal reception" (Gemeinschaftsempfang) commanded, obviating the need to organize events throughout the Reich at short notice.[145]

In the following years, communal radio listening at festive gatherings or at prescribed "communal receptions" became an established practice during major political events or key holidays. It strongly contributed to making radio listening in certain constellations itself a political behavior and probably hence also a subject for discussion in diaries of the 1930s. For the votes held in November 1933, the National Socialist Radio Chamber had emphasized that "in these days, since the dignity, honor, and unity of the German Volk should be made known to the entire world in powerful avowals, there should not be a single German house without a radio, which at all times creates the direct connection of each Volk comrade with the Führer and his fellow fighters in the regime and party." Anyone who was "not yet a radio listener" should "no longer [be allowed to] seclude himself from the major events of the present that determine the fate of the nation." In the context of decisive events such as the withdrawal from the League of Nations, "radio listening was not a matter of personal entertainment, but rather a state-political duty and necessity."[146] In later years as well, regime representatives time and again demanded that "radio listening" must "for every individual Volk comrade" become "such a matter of course that he is on the alert when the voice of the radio conveys to him the political demand of the hour."[147] Thus, on the occasion of mass festivals, local spectators were not the only ones who faced very concrete expectations regarding their behavior. The rest of the Germans also found themselves confronted with demands to join the masses of spectators as radio listeners and thus participate in person as well.

Recording One's Personal Participation

By changing the conditions of communication between the regime and the population, major political events and the holidays of the Nazi regime also imposed their own expectations on individuals and their political behavior. People did not just participate, as demanded, in encounters with the regime; some of them also dedicated a remarkably large amount of attention to these encounters in their diaries. This was especially true for precisely those diarists who otherwise took a deliberately noncritical approach when registering the news situation. For them, apart from documenting their routine uncritical awareness of the news, dedicating their attention to their encounters with the regime formed the other side of their effort to meet the regime's expectations as to their political behavior. It was no coincidence that the young gardener Inge Thiele noted her lament of "not [being able to] simply believe" on the occasion of Hitler's November 1933 speech from the Siemens factory and just a few months later expressed her agreement with regime policy through a long account in her diary of speeches by the Reich chancellor and the Reich propaganda minister. Later as well, she spoke about her perceptions and political actions above all in connection with encounters—direct and conveyed by media—between the regime and the Volk. She reviewed her own fulfillment of the regime's behavioral expectations on precisely these occasions.

On March 11, 1936, Thiele reported in her diary on the German military's reoccupation of the Rhineland a few days earlier, which had been demilitarized since the end of the First World War. She recounted at length the media's reports about the event, noting namely that "the Führer did this simply because France also violated the Locarno pact by concluding an arms pact with the Soviets and the Czech Republic"; that "what we do with our land is actually our concern"; and that "the Führer is striving for friendship" with France. She even described the places where troops were stationed on the Rhine as "freedom garrisons," just as in the official accounts. By virtue of its similarity to the official reports, Thiele's portrayal of the event shows how much she tried to unconditionally believe the regime. Yet she went even further. She also emphasized having "listened to the Führer during his Reichstag speech." "His voice often shook with emotion and responsibility. One must simply believe him and approve of what he does," she commented, reaffirming her faith in Hitler in general terms. "We youth must stand loyally by him."[148]

With their clear behavioral expectations, encounters between the government and the governed raised for Inge Thiele the question of whether she fulfilled them. Other Germans, too, saw themselves challenged precisely on the occasion of political radio broadcasts or mass events to account for how they dealt with demands made of their political conduct. Born in 1895, the village schoolteacher Wilm Hosenfeld from Thalau in Hesse, who joined the SA and the Nazi Teachers' League in 1933 and the NSDAP in 1935, was utterly crestfallen in his 1937 report on Hitler's speech for that year's May festivities, which he had heard on the radio at the local tavern. "At the end, during the Sieg Heil, I remained seated at first. The men present made no move to stand up, so I remained seated at first too. Yet during the Germany song we all stood up and sang along." Hosenfeld recriminated himself for this. "I should actually have initiated it, because I was also still wearing the party badge," which, from his perspective, particularly obliged him to act as a role model. In his own eyes, Hosenfeld had failed and thus could only guiltily confess that "if one is not thrilled about something . . . [there is no] momentum to suddenly seize a situation."[149]

Explicit reflections on personal political behavior such as those recorded by Inge Thiele and Wilm Hosenfeld in their diaries clearly show how sharply the encounter with "leadership" challenged precisely those Germans who consciously oriented themselves according to the regime's ideal of political evaluation and action. Yet such self-critical statements were by no means typical. Far more often, Germans documented their successful efforts in their diaries. As with the attentive and noncritical observation of the regime, it was also necessary to find a written form that could show one's participation—better yet, active involvement—in the mass festivals and regime appeals during major political events. Figuring here above all were the reception practices developed in connection with staged encounters.

Born in 1863, the widow Marita Schlichting*, for example, was the daughter of an Augsburg baker, without any learned vocation, who was already seventy years old at the start of National Socialist rule. In her diary, which she had kept with brief comments since 1885, she also haphazardly noted political news: "Germany withdrew from the League of Nations, German turn of fate"; "Hindenburg dies"; "Bolsheviks fired at German battleship *Deutschland*."[150] As per the expectations propagated by the Nazi regime, in her diary Schlichting refrained from making any commentary of her own, but in her case this was not due to an effort to adapt to the regime's ideas about the political behavior of Germans. Even prior to 1933, her brief notes on political events did not include discussion. But in the 1930s, this was also how Schlichting noted addresses by Hitler, which she followed on the radio.[151] Having noted the day of Hindenburg's death, she added a comment on his burial: "Eulogy Hitler: Whoever *so* keeps faith with his Volk should himself not be forgotten in faith." And a few days after her note on Germany's withdrawal from the League of Nations, she added a brief entry: "Hitler is speaking."[152] Schlichting's diary contains many such entries, yet they rarely make it possible to identify the political context. "Major speech of Hitler in the Reichstag: disarmament!" was the most detailed content-related description contained in her references to speeches.[153] In most cases, there were no references to the content of the addresses or any supplementary remarks on the political situation that might have provided the context for notes such as notes such as "Major speech of the Führer" or "Hitler's great speech in the Reichstag."[154] In these cases, Schlichting was not supplementing notes about the political news with references to broadcast speeches by the Nazi leadership. Instead, the political news was the event of the speech itself.

Much the same can also be seen in other diaries. Almost sixty years younger than Schlichting, the schoolgirl Rita Thomer*, for example, born in 1922, listed the following in her diary on May 31, 1937: "On 05/27 Goebbels held a speech against Catholicism. On 05/30 we were in the airport. Today in Spain a German ship was bombarded by communist aircraft."[155] Consider also the Weimar resident Otmar Krämer, who regularly wrote retrospective reports in his diary that included summaries of political developments over the past weeks. In his case, comments on political lectures, speeches, and radio broadcasts were integrated directly into his general recording of the political situation.

"In the public sphere and political life [Staatsleben], again there are all sorts of things to report," he began in February 1935, for example. This time too, his corresponding notes amounted to an unannotated list of political events: "On December 27 there was a blackout practice in Weimar, which worked very well. Even Werner played a part. Speaking in early January were Prof. Dr. Grimm—Essen, the famous defender of the Ruhr Germans on the Saar question, Herr Prof. Dr. Hildebert Böhm about Germans living abroad, and the envoy Dr. Stiewe about the prehistory of the World War, Dr. Lasch about the labor service. All as part of a lecture series of the Office for Traditions in the Weimar Hall. Then on January 1 there was the overwhelming plebiscite result of the Saar. The colonial hero von Lettow-Vorbeck spoke about the war in German East Africa. . . . On January 30 was the two-year anniversary of the Nazi regime. The reform of the Reich is being driven a bit forward again. Then a raid took place against the people of §175."[156]

Krämer's seamless transitions between political events and references to political rallies in his report clearly shows that speeches themselves had indeed become political events for him. In its propaganda, the regime repeatedly emphasized that whoever "experiences the tremendous announcements of intent of our Volk chancellor Adolf Hitler" on the radio or as a local spectator is joining ranks "in the great unity of destiny of the National Socialist State."[157] Against this background, references to radio broadcasts or speeches by leading regime representatives were more than the simple notation of the political developments or events to which the broadcasts or speeches referred. They allowed individuals to show that they did not question the official account of the political event and to point out that they had "participated" as a listener in the "event of political-historical consequence," as Goebbels had put it in spring 1933.

Germans who reported at greater length in their diaries about radio broadcasts also explicitly noted in their accounts that they themselves were part of the event. "Thanks to the radio," Inge Thiele wrote, for example, as part of an entry on the 1934 NSDAP party congress. "Through it we could participate in the great march." The *we* evidently referred to radio listeners as a whole, among whom Thiele included herself, since she in fact listened to the broadcast on her own.[158] And in March 1938, on the occasion of the annexation of Austria, she stressed: "We are witnessing it hourly, how our troops are being cheered."[159] The Solingen teacher Ludwig Lindholm, born in 1884, similarly noted the plebiscite on the merging of the offices of the Reich president and Reich chancellor in August 1934 in his diary: "In the evening we naturally sat at the radio and cheered along as the victory of our Führer became ever clearer."[160] And Marianne Köhl, a schoolgirl born in

1921 who regularly reported in her diary on the speeches of leading regime representatives, which she followed on the radio in her small home village in Bavaria, pointed out in October 1936, on the occasion of a "great speech" by Hermann Göring, that "from Annaheim, only four girls listened to this speech." It was an example of how little "interest these girls have in all important political things and how [little] enthusiasm they have for the fatherland," in contrast to Köhl herself.[161]

Even when diarists deeply regretted their inability to be on location at an event,[162] diary entries of the 1930s staged radio listening as an immediate involvement in the broadcast events, just as described by the official propaganda. In their diaries, Germans time and again emphasized that they listened to the broadcast together with others in "communal reception" and described their own reactions with extraordinarily vivid accounts. For example, Rudolf Briske, born in 1915, wrote in his diary in March 1935, "Saturday evening on the radio: I almost fall from the chair: Announcement of general military duty. Finally! Finally, one has found the courage to confront the others with faits accomplis."[163] Others wrote about how they wanted to "shout with enthusiasm . . . when I hear and read," or how they "could have cried already at the calling of the shouts of Heil coming from deepest hearts" that were transmitted by radio from mass events and addresses by the regime.[164]

The sense of involvement is also found in the diary of Luise Solmitz, who was born in 1889 and lived in Hamburg together with her daughter and husband (who was deemed Jewish) and who, despite massive discrimination in their everyday lives, was still excited about Hitler in the late 1930s.[165] In her report on the broadcast of Hitler's visit to Austria on the day of the so-called Anschluss, she noted that, because of the "ever more indescribable" cheering of the masses as Hitler appeared on the town hall balcony in Linz, her daughter "fled" and she and her husband "covered both ears" because "the cheering . . . did not want to end."[166] This comment was part of her portrayal of the day's radio broadcast, which went on for pages, by and large strongly underscoring her personal participation in the political event. Solmitz reported in detail how, on the night leading to March 12, she and her husband sat next to the radio "still at 00:30 hours at night" and waited "for news," until they finally witnessed Vienna in the "frenzy of enthusiasm." At midday they heard the Führer's proclamation read by Joseph Goebbels, which Solmitz summarized in her diary. And above all, she described the live broadcast of Hitler's visit: the masses waiting for the

"Führer," the repeated eruptions of cheers, the delays until Hitler's arrival, the many different efforts to bridge the waiting period with speeches and "dialogue between announcers and the Volk," and finally the "boundless jubilation" that greeted Hitler in Linz and Vienna. "What a day of emotional exaltation," Solmitz declared at the end of the long entry. And in closing, she explicitly pointed out her active participation in the political events, which had already been strongly highlighted by her logging of the radio broadcast itself: "Taking notes was fun."[167]

In contrast to everyday observations of the regime through routine political reporting, when writing on the occasion of encounters between the "leadership" and the "Volk," people like Inge Thiele, Ludwig Lindholm, Rudolf Briske, and Luise Solmitz did not just note the event but also reported on its staging in the media. This was not just because the regime had designed political holidays and major happenings as media events and that this was being transposed unfiltered to the diaries. Rather, in these reports, radio was often an explicit subject of the portrayal and not merely a technical transport vehicle, for the reference to one's own radio listening both vouched for the individual's personal participation and at the same time also documented that one's personal political behavior had fulfilled the Nazi regime's concrete expectations. This could be reflected in the diary in various ways: from brief notes on radio speeches that took the place of underlying political events to the detailed logging of political radio broadcasts. These descriptions, aided by festive staging and the associated practices of reception, vigorously underscored that one had taken part in the encounter with the regime.

By way of explicit descriptions of enactments and reactions to them, individuals could also transpose their participation into their diaries in cases where they followed mass festivals not on the radio but rather as local spectators. To be sure, given the far smaller number of spectators compared to radio listeners, such accounts are found less frequently in the diaries of the 1930s. But they often turn out to be far more detailed, no doubt because of the extraordinary nature of these events. In September 1938, Marianne Köhl, for example, the schoolgirl from the Bavarian village who regularly reported in her diary on political radio broadcasts, wrote down her impressions of a Hitler speech that she had followed not on the radio but rather as a participant on the grounds of the NSDAP party rally in Nuremberg.

Whereas for the radio broadcasts Köhl usually closely described the backdrop of sound, in this particular account she focused on the importance of the event's optical design. "Immediately on the first evening I went to the muster of the political leaders. Gleaming white, decorated with red flags and golden laurels, the front section of the Zeppelin Meadow gleamed. Thousands of people filled the broad circle and waited with the Führer's parading helpers for Adolf Hitler. Then it goes like an electric shock through the crowd and an exclamation full of jubilant enthusiasm: Heil, Heil our Führer. Sounds of fanfare blare in a roaring rhythm through the city and an oh of admiring astonishment goes through the crowd as the dome of light formed by many, many spotlights begins to shine," Köhl wrote, describing in detail the elaborate staging of the event, which also entirely determined her description of Hitler's speech. "And then the Führer speaks. But I do not understand what he says. I only become aware of individual sentences. I feel only the greatness and reverence of this moment. And sense also that I cannot fully grasp it, that now, in the middle of this large community in this overwhelming setting, I hear and also can see the Führer, although only from afar. Then when the Germany song also resounds and I sing it with all of the many German people who are now all filled with the same great experience as I am, the tears fall from my eyes with excitement and happiness."[168] As with the entries dedicated to radio broadcasts, a lot of space in Marianne Köhl's description was devoted to the elaborate staging of the party rally and the Hitler speech she heard at this event; and these constituted the direct reference point for the description of her personal reactions and those of other spectators.

Politics and Emotion

Descriptions of political radio broadcasts and above all reports by participants about mass festivals like the one by Marianne Köhl have attracted much attention among historians. Usually they are taken as evidence for the overwhelming power of a direct encounter with Hitler. They are seen as confirming the assumption that, "for many people, the impact of a direct encounter with Hitler at a distance of only a few meters"—generated "thousands of times" at each mass festival—"probably created an experience of high emotional significance."[169] In contrast, I would argue that even those reports can be understood as part of the endeavor by individuals to align themselves with the regime's idea of the political conduct of Germans and that they reveal a more complex relationship between politics and emotion than is generally thought.

Ever since the 1970s, many studies, especially those inspired by social psychology or psychoanalysis, have drawn on diaries, letters, and above all after-the-fact autobiographical reports and interviews with contemporary witnesses to point out that many Germans, when reporting on speeches by leading Nazi politicians and particularly Hitler himself, considered it "unimportant to convey what the Führer said" and wrote instead about the impressive staging and their own emotions.[170] This observation, which also applies to Marianne Köhl's report, has provided the basis for the thesis that the Germans, in their perception of National Socialist politics, were dominated less by political convictions and arguments than by apolitical emotions. "Reports about the Hitler speeches," argues Gudrun Brockhaus, for example, showed "how people used Hitler as the spokesman for their own longings and anxieties. He expresses what was closed off within oneself—for example, feelings of humiliation and hidden superiority, desires for revenge."[171] According to this view, during mass events Germans projected their own needs onto National Socialist politics. Hitler's speeches, in particular, were thus a "striking example for the emotionalization of politics" because they showed that people were drawn "to nationalism and National Socialism" by "not the content but rather the aspiration for greatness and unconditionality."[172] In accordance with this interpretation, Brockhaus and others have postulated that the "fascination of the Nazi movement . . . cannot be explained solely with thought, with 'mentalities,' with cognitive concepts." Instead, more attention must be paid to the dimension of "emotionally determined experience"[173] because individual political conduct during the 1930s was determined by "the dominance of emotion prior to cognition."[174] "Debate and reason were replaced by acclamation, presentation, regimentation and above all sentiment," according to Michael Burleigh's description of the effect of the Nazi dictatorship on the style of political communication, which was geared toward presenting "politics as feeling."[175] In this way, the regime successfully managed to generate "mass emotionality," the "presumably most unappreciated asset that National Socialism [produced] apart from hatred and prejudices."[176]

The emotionalization of political conduct is therefore often also understood as an expression of the depoliticization of Germans, whose actions admittedly still had political consequences but were no longer determined by political and rational motives. Mass events such as the Nuremberg party rallies did not provide any room for "politics in the classical sense," so "belief and fascination" were not generated "directly from the ideology of National Socialism and its political principles . . . but rather from the convincing momentum of the staging." "Suggestive directing ensured superficial effects and this way generated enthusiasm for minutes. Politics for the heart, not the mind."[177] In their analysis of Allied logs of eavesdropping on German prisoners of war in the 1940s, Sönke Neitzel and Harald Welzer have in this sense beheld the "deepest formative effects of the National Socialist project" as a "lasting depoliticization." To be sure, the eavesdropped conversations of captured soldiers voiced "criticism and skepticism," but the soldiers "do *not* have a political opinion on the National Socialist state, on dictatorship, on the persecution and destruction of Jews." "Political confrontations like arguing about decisions and perspectives, various positions or opinions hardly occur," which showed how "politics is replaced by belief, especially among the higher ranks."[178]

Even if many diary entries on encounters with the regime can at first glance be reconciled with this interpretation, it seems to me that the diaries of the 1930s actually point in another direction. First, they cast doubt on the general validity of this thesis. Looking at diarists who, despite all efforts by the Nazi regime to educate them to an unconditional faith in the regime, still clung to the desire to make their own judgments, one can seriously doubt that emotionalization actually gripped the Germans as a whole. Especially those entries occasioned by festivals and major political events clearly show that the effort to make one's own judgment was very much understood in direct contrast to the aspirations of the regime. During the NSDAP Reich party congress in fall 1933, Georg Witzmann, for example, the former Thuringian state parliamentarian, demonstratively pointed out in his diary that he "participated in not a single celebration on the radio, listened to not a single speech."[179] Nonetheless, he evidently followed the event and its addresses in the newspaper, which he also marked in his diary not only by denouncing the "cultural speech" Hitler held at the party congress as "superficial" but also by deliberating at length on whether it changed anything about Germany's tense international situation.[180]

Other diarists, when dealing with encounters organized by the regime, similarly tried to evaluate the speeches held on these occasions, and they often found the pretentious staging disruptive. Born in 1899, Nikolaus Sieveking was a book dealer who in the 1930s organized and cataloged newspaper articles for the Hamburg World Economic Archive. When the new Reichstag convened in March 1933, an event elaborately celebrated as the Day of Potsdam, he spoke in his diary with disgust about how "all of the sluggards and enfeebled" were letting themselves be "deluded again by the old fairy songs." "For someone to whom assiduous, critical deliberation amounts to the prime intellectual duty, the spooky hullaballoo of such a day passes by so far away, so endlessly far away," he commented on the festive event. "I will never take part in these things, the way they unwind only for the sake of bluster."[181] The elementary school teacher Hans Maschmann, who during the 1936 Reichstag election campaign wrote in his diary about listening to a Hitler speech on the radio "on the self-built headphones of my boy," struck a similar tone. "I *wanted* to listen, I hoped to be able to say yes," Maschmann noted, but when Hitler "blasted out the phrase of the 'successful tremendous experiment of world history,' I became so disgusted . . . that I tore the phones from my ears." Never has "a great man embodied his genuine greatness with such gesticulations the way Hitler does," Maschmann wrote, venting his aversion to the political spectacle. "Real greatness does not prostitute itself and at such an age does not allow itself be cheered like that by the masses."[182]

The state's control of the mass media and the manipulative interventions in political reporting became especially obvious in the political media events of the 1930s; as a result, the stage productions, designed to be overpowering, by no means only produced faith. Instead of assuming that "the festival, as an emotional communalization of followers, . . . also [gripped] those [Germans] who did not share the faith in the charisma of the 'Führer'" because "social pressure and the lack of alternatives in a society controlled by propaganda" were too large, I find it more plausible that, in fact, the encounter with the Führer was unable to impress and integrate Germans as a whole.[183] For many diarists of the 1930s, faith certainly did not replace politics. Rather, faced with media control and media monitoring, they inevitably came to rely on the continuous discussion of political developments. And this was only intensified by the regime's mass festivals with their firm expectations regarding individual political behavior. In this respect, the influence of the festival staging was restricted to those parts of the population that did not consciously repudiate the ideal of individual political conduct propagated by the regime.

For these Germans, mass appeals and political festivals could in fact radically change their modes of political action and judgment, with political content and argument taking a back seat to the expression of loyalty in forms established by the regime. Yet whether this means that emotions actually replaced rational deliberations, that this conduct should thus be construed as an expression of political irrationality and deep-seated depoliticization, seems doubtful to me. This is the second place where I find that diaries and contemporary reports by participants point in a direction different from that suggested by existing theses. The problem with postulates such as those of Michael Burleigh, who notes that attempts to explain the political behavior of Germans "with rationalistic categories and concepts" always lack an "element which only reference to unfulfilled religious needs can reconstitute," is simply that it is wholly questionable whether descriptions like Marianne Köhl's can really be understood as expressions of the needs of their authors.[184] As we have seen, diaries repeatedly document that they should not be read as the direct textualization of their authors' emotions.[185] Through their writing, diarists often tried to appropriate certain types of behavior and perception—for example, to comply with the Nazi regime's expectations related to personal political behavior. And in the case of regime appeals and mass festivals, this effort did not just include the question of whether people personally participated via the radio or on-site as demanded but also how they perceived these events.

In the context of the regime's expectations related to the political conduct of Germans and individuals' efforts to fulfill them, their corresponding writings can very much be read on multiple levels. Above all, it is questionable whether the apparent congruence between the regime's intended effects and contemporaneously recorded private descriptions of political assemblies actually constitutes evidence of the diarists' purely emotional involvement. Even just the fact that such portrayals often present only a very specific segment of the impressions someone could experience at the mass events can be raised as an objection to such an interpretation. Historical research in recent years has in many cases worked out the fracture points in National Socialist festive staging, pointing out how they could counteract the manipulative intentions. In their design, the mass events of the 1930s were by no means as perfect, all-encompassing, and unambiguously clear as the regime intended.[186]

Taken as a whole, descriptions from the 1930s thus also document many impressions of encounters with the government that the regime actually wanted to avoid. Born in 1893 and working in the 1930s as a civil registry employee, Werner Kramp, for example, noted on May 1, 1934, that around noon "the prospect of enduring three hours on the brooding-hot square (Hitler's speech was supposed to be broadcast through speakers at five) demoralized the best mindset," and he found amusement in how "without marshals . . . the train promptly" fell apart. He soon saw "how individuals sidled to the grating where there were unmonitored gaps." Kramp did not stay on the festival grounds until the radio broadcast either, preferring instead to listen to Hitler's speech by radio in a private group and afterward commenting on its pronouncements with his own ideas in his diary.[187]

Likewise living in Hamburg, Hans Maschmann had to take part in one of Hitler's visits to the Hanseatic city in summer 1934 as an elementary school teacher with his pupils, who had been "ordered to form a cordon." He also reported in his diary that the atmosphere among the spectators did not materialize as planned. "Enthusiasm did not arise; even the ecstatic cries of individual women faded away."[188] Against the background of such impressions, the fact that many reports of mass events nonetheless unerringly grasped precisely those limited aspects that the dramaturgy wanted to convey from enactments characterized by a far greater diversity of impressions suggests an alternative interpretation: these portrayals need not be understood straightforwardly as descriptions of actual experiences. The fact that impressions undesired by the regime are often completely absent from participants' reports on mass events, and that these reports come across "almost as having been copied from the propaganda back then," should not be hastily seen as "nonetheless a clear indication" that the events "did not fall short in their effect" and that participants let themselves be "carried away by the hullaballoo."[189] Rather, this circumstance can be more plausibly interpreted as a sign that individuals knew what they were supposed to perceive and how they were meant to experience the encounters with the regime. This was conveyed to them by the omnipresent pictures of the "leadership and Volk," which not only spread ideas about how one should behave politically but at the same time constituted instructions on how encounters with the regime should be taken in.

Individual portrayals more explicitly show that in their reports on mass festivals, many Germans made an effort to align their perception and representation of events according to the regime's standards. In fall 1935, three years before Marianne Köhl attended a rally, the pastor Erich Scheuer* had taken part in the Reich party congress and in a similar way reported in a letter to his sister how "wonderfully beautiful" the "days in Nuremberg" had been. "The atmosphere in Nuremberg, which immediately seizes and captures a traveler to Nuremberg, has its own magic. That which is seen and experienced is gripping not only for political reasons, however much the political naturally stands in the foreground, rather the whole thing is also a really large Volk's festival, where, like a large family, the old and young are delighted and excited about everything on offer." Prevailing everywhere at the "large marches and rally" was "an atmosphere just as joyful and harmonious as at the fireworks and the popular merriments." Scheuer, who was himself an NSDAP member, went on: "It was as if all of Nuremberg, with its hundreds of thousands of visitors, was a single large family, as if the army, party, and Volk reached out their hands in a covenant for life."[190] Like others, Scheuer did not focus on the political content of the party congress, even though, given the enactment that year of the Nuremberg Laws, it was the context for the announcement of truly precipitous political decisions. Instead, he too concentrated on the comprehensive staging of the multiday event, portraying its elements in a manner wholly in keeping with their underlying intention as an expression of the unity of "leadership and Volk."

But just because Scheuer described the event by letter to his sister primarily as an uplifting experience as intended by the staging does not mean that he did not perceive any other impressions. Directly after his portrayal emphasizing harmony, he in fact conceded, "For the one who must march and run along with the others, who for hours on end must conquer and secure his place in order to be able to see something," for him, "of course, the exterior of the party congress comes to the foreground more than the internal, the speeches, the declarations of the people in authority. The radio listener who is listening to everything at home," he pointed out, "has more of this internal matter."[191] As the brief comment shows, Scheuer was quite aware that the picture he drew in his report of an all-encompassing harmonious and communal party congress atmosphere did not include all of the impressions he took with him from Nuremberg. Instead, he described only a segment—namely, the part that the regime wanted to convey and encouraged people to perceive. And this segment was also what Scheuer tried get across in his letter to his sister.

On the one hand, Eric Scheuer's report undermines the widely held idea that, with emerging conflicts, the elaborate propagandistic arrangement could no longer shape the perceptions of participants and spectators as desired.[192] Even though the staging, with its aspiration for perfection, undoubtedly quickly reached its limits—for example, despite prohibitions and sentries, "the business with venal love [flourished] during the party congresses," and a "plenitude of undesired scenes"[193] occurred in Nuremberg in other connections as well—people were obviously still able to perceive the festive arrangement in terms of its underlying intentions. They could do so because they were well aware of the organizers' creative aspiration and could deliberately ignore other impressions. Likewise, the letter opposes the assumption that the effect of the mass festivals was subject to a "local limitation," since "despite all efforts" the regime never managed "to bridge the chasm, which existed every year, between the real on-site experience of the party congress and the representation in the media."[194] Scheuer's comment regarding the radio suggests rather that when it came to his effort to perceive the party congress as intended by the Nazi regime, he saw the media staging's stronger guidance of his personal perception more as an advantage than a fault. The media presentation of the mass festivals could never possibly be complete, but it also excluded many impressions that on-site participants actually needed to ignore if they wanted their personal impressions to approximate the regime's ideal. And even the thesis that in the course of the 1930s the events could "only [produce] states of communal rapture and euphoria for shorter and shorter intervals" before "the gray everyday routine with all of its troubles and misery pervaded again" is wholly questionable when considered against the pastor's report.[195] The question of how long the event's effects persisted hardly lines up with the perspective of Scheuer, who was obviously trying to remember the party congress in a certain way that could reassure him in hindsight, even amid "the gray everyday routine" of the coming months, that he had taken part and shared a stake in the politics of the regime.[196]

On the other hand, portrayals like those of Erich Scheuer also confirm that the effects of the mass events did not follow directly from the staging itself but rather required the individual's cooperation. This has already been variously presumed on the basis of theoretical deliberations. And in fact, the collective "states of rapture" of the mass assemblies of National Socialism required "the decision of the individual" to "join" in with them and thus must be understood as a "mélange of acceptance, desire, inducement, and navigation."[197] Yet the reports from the 1930s hardly suggest that the audience's contribution consisted primarily of "the willingness of the masses to delude themselves."[198] Rather, Scheuer's example and other portrayals in diaries show that there was a close relationship between the emotionalized perception of mass political events and the endeavor to conform to the official ideal of political behavior. As if to reassure himself, Scheuer expressly presented this conception of the political behavior of Germans again at the end of the report to his sister. He had the hope, the pastor concluded, "that after the clear statements of the persons in authority, especially the Führer, naturally, about the essence, goals, and tasks of the movement, much of the talk and much of the grousing will fall silent, which until now has still not wanted to fall silent. We have again advanced a tremendous amount." He combined this with a threat that affirmed his own perception of the event— namely, that "all those who can still be taught" should "listen to reason, so that history doesn't definitively go back to business as usual."[199]

Even in his last paragraph, despite distinctly referencing the "clear statements of the persons in authority," Scheuer did not speak about the content of the speeches but avoided any personal political confrontation with them. In his account, faith did in fact replace politics, but this certainly did not mean a depoliticization of his perception or behavior. Rather, his particularly open portrayal of the Nuremberg party congress shows an active effort to perceive the event correctly, which must itself be understood as political conduct. His enthusiasm did not leave Erich Scheuer blind to impressions that disturbed the picture of a successful unification of "leadership" and "Volk." Contrary to the thesis of a "dominance of emotion over cognition," wanting to behave with unconditional jubilation in accordance with the model propagated by the regime was for him a political decision. And this also meant perceiving the party congress the way it was publicly presented by the regime.

Other diaries frequently show the same sort of thing. The gardener Inge Thiele repeatedly made the reception of mass events and speeches the touchstone for her effort to orient her conduct according to the propagated ideal. In summer 1934, for example, the young woman, who lived in Solingen, attended the "Schlageter conference of the Hitler Youth" in nearby Düsseldorf. She later reported in her diary that "everything would have been festive had it not been so cold. The boys froze, if one observed them individually, but," she admonished herself, "the overall impression was uplifting, and that is indeed what matters."[200] And one year later, she summarized in her diary a speech that she had heard on the radio by Robert Ley about the Strength through Joy recreational organization: "Do not whine, go without, and atone and make the world into a vale of tears, but rather live, obtain strength through joy, joyfully and consciously, a life-affirming program." She then went on to comment that the "old-school types [ewig Gestrigen] with their mopey expressions and penitent statures do not belong in the Third Reich."[201] The failure of the entry to clearly indicate whether the last sequence characterizing the model of political conduct was still part of the summary of the speech or already part of Thiele's commentary ultimately underscores all the more clearly just how much she and other Germans tried to produce and demonstrate conformity between their own perceptions and propagandistic political enactments, especially during direct and mediated encounters with the regime.

The idea that Germans supported the regime because of their profound enthusiasm for the Führer is firmly anchored in historiographical and public thought and cannot be refuted with descriptions such as those of Marianne Köhl, Inge Thiele, and Erich Scheuer. Nor can those diaries be used to counter the thesis of the massive projection of private needs onto the Führer. But that is not what I am trying to do. Rather, it seems important to me that contemporary reports by Germans clearly indicate a more complex relationship between emotion and politics than these theses assume. Without question, emotions were very important to the political conduct of contemporaries, if only because the Nazi regime deliberately created moments for direct encounters between the regime and "its Volk" that were meant to integrate Germans emotionally through their elaborate design. But this did not simply occur by virtue of their suggestive force. On the one hand, people who insisted on making their own judgments despite the official control of political representations in the media rejected and evaded the ostentatious staging of the mass festivals and regime appeals. On the other hand, however, there also were Germans who neither explicitly rejected the manipulative public policy nor were solely determined by their emotions in their encounter with the regime. Yet the diaries cited here cannot rule out that, as historians have often assumed, some Germans were actually so enthused by Hitler and so intoxicated by the political enactments that they thoughtlessly cheered the regime.

Contemporary portrayals themselves, however, show above all that those Germans who identified especially intensely with the regime and actively supported it were hardly driven by their emotions. Quite the contrary, these people were moved to appropriate certain feelings and perceptions by motives that were decidedly political. In this respect, their efforts formed part of an endeavor to conform to the ideals of individual political action and evaluation popularized by the regime. This could occur in various ways, such as by briefly registering political events in a way that was specifically not meant as a point of departure for one's own discussions. But it could also occur through the effort to perceive the encounters between "leadership" and "Volk"—experienced via media or as an event participant—in the way such encounters were reported by the media. These individuals, too, were quite aware of the deliberate nature of such staging of regime policy, as is shown by the repeated emphasis in the diaries of the 1930s on personal radio listening and the bombastic configuration of the encounters between the government and the governed. However, these individuals did not reject this staging but rather tried as best they could to play the roles assigned to them in these spectacles.

Given the state's interventions in the media, some Germans felt challenged to sound out the policies of the regime themselves. But for individuals who wanted to believe the regime, knowledge about the staging and the concrete expectations formulated in the practices of reception and acclamation in fact created an opportunity to also document their regime-compliant participation (active yet uncritical) and their stake in the policies of the regime in their diaries. These people were not necessarily led by "unsatisfied religious needs" to politics, which they then perceived as an emotional spectacle, as an "experience." Rather, at least for some of them, during mass festivals it was a political decision that first brought them to actively work on those emotions that the spectacles were meant to awaken in them.

3. Supporting the Government: Political Integration and Political Popularity in the Nazi Dictatorship

Taken as a whole, diaries of the 1930s depict a different and more complex picture of the individual political behavior of Germans during National Socialist rule than is implied by the regime's own representations of cheering masses. The fundamental restructuring of the system's political decision-making, together with efforts to transform the political behavior of Germans, did not lead to the intended standardization of political evaluation and action in the political culture of National Socialism. Even if we cannot use diaries to determine the prevalence of specific forms of conduct, the analysis of the political actions of concrete persons does little to confirm the vision of a population that approved of regime policy out of an all-embracing enthusiasm for Hitler and the regime's ostentatious political spectacles.

Conscious political conduct in the 1930s moved instead between two different poles: the endeavor to hold fast to one's own political judgment even under the dictatorship and the effort to align one's political evaluation and action according to the precepts of the Nazi regime. In this respect, it was wholly possible for individuals to combine contrary forms of behavior.

Living in Hamburg, Luise Solmitz, for example, tried in the 1930s to believe in Hitler primarily with regard to foreign policy issues, yet at the same she recorded critical statements, particularly about Jewish policy. And in her brief diary notes, the widow Marita Schlichting not only repeatedly documented her own participation in regime addresses but also attentively followed the state's operation against the Protestant Church and the arrest of Martin Niemöller in 1937.[202] Instead of uniform enthusiasm, the interplay between the altered conditions of the political system, the openly propagated ideas of the regime regarding the political behavior of the population, and the concrete reactions of Germans produced forms of behavior that only partially corresponded to the popularized ideal of a "Volk" cheering out of an inner enthusiasm. What did this mean for the mechanisms of political integration and for the support the regime demanded from the population?

The results thus far indicate two things. First, they show that the research thesis proposing political integration through a supposedly all-encompassing enthusiasm for Hitler insufficiently explains the political bonding of Germans in the 1930s. The "Führer" was centrally important in a decidedly overarching way for the conscious political behavior of Germans. People who tried to get to the bottom of the regime's politics by means of their own discussions gave special consideration to Hitler because of his prominence within the transformed system of political decision-making, such that they often very carefully studied and interpreted the "Führer speeches." And individuals who emulated the regime's ideal of conduct tried to educate themselves to a comprehensive "Führer faith" and fulfill the postulated duties of loyalty toward Hitler. But this role of Hitler hardly corresponds to the one ascribed to the "Führer" in the model of charismatic rule. To be sure, Hitler formed a superordinate reference point for assessing regime policy and for the associated actions of Germans, but by no means did he provide for a comprehensive identification with the regime or cause the widespread political support repeatedly referred to by the Nazi regime. In this respect, there are good reasons to continue to critically reconsider the assumption that the "Hitler myth" was the "strongest bonding element between the regime and population."[203]

Second, diaries enable us to see what it was that—instead of a comprehensive substantive consensus between "leadership and Volk"—integrated the various forms of deliberate political conduct into the political system of National Socialism: above all, the preeminent role played by the mass media in Germans' evaluations and actions was centrally important for the far-reaching integrative capacity of the Nazi dictatorship in the 1930s. In dealing with regime politics, people could turn their gaze to various dimensions of political reporting and in their reactions present themselves as being critical or affirmative. But this did nothing to change the essential fact that the individual's political conduct was basically bound to and dependent on this political reporting. Even if state control of newspapers and radio failed to unify the political attitudes of the Germans as much as desired, with the help of mass media National Socialist public policy nonetheless deeply shaped on a large scale how individuals dealt with regime policy. Through the media, the regime decisively determined what people thought about when they dealt with regime policy and what they took to be noteworthy political "problems."

Where Germans sought to believe official accounts, their activities aimed precisely at continually adopting the media's portrayal, which became clear in diaries above all in crisis situations. In August 1939, for example, when the regime concluded the so-called Hitler-Stalin Pact with the Soviet Union in preparation for its attack on Poland, Inge Thiele spoke in her diary about how the "Führer" had given "us and the entire world" a "surprise . . . with the news that we have concluded an economic treaty and a 10-year nonaggression pact with Soviet Russia. With the 'Soviets,' where for six years we have only heard talk about them as the worst enemy," Thiele commented, thereby clearly showing how difficult it was for her to go along with the abrupt change in official political accounts. "Admittedly, nobody trusts the thing yet and [one] fears a trap," Thiele wrote, maintaining her skepticism, which had been shaped by many years of anti-Communist propaganda. But then she banished this thought with her next sentence—"But the Führer will certainly not do anything without reason and deliberation"—and still tried to believe the media reports.[204] At the same time, however, even those Germans who wanted to peer behind the facade of controlled media reporting were directly oriented in their endeavor by the very newspaper articles and radio programs whose veracity they wanted to determine. Even though they mistrusted the content of the media reports, the press and radio defined for them too which dimensions of regime policy they dealt with and when.

Historians have already repeatedly emphasized the significance of National Socialist media policy for "agenda setting" and pointed out that the question as to which aspect of a propagandistic account "stuck and the degree to which it lastingly dictated human practices ... [should] in each case [be] investigated in specific contexts."[205] This is strongly affirmed by diaries of the 1930s—for example, by their very different assessments of the murders in June 1934.[206] Yet at the same time, by virtue of this disparity they also suggest that the integration of Germans into the political system of the Nazi dictatorship basically grew less from the dissemination of political views through radio and newspapers than from precisely the interaction between the controlled media and media consumers itself.[207] The Nazi regime could only imagine the connection between government and the governed in the form of a comprehensive, substantive consensus, which was supposed to combine "leadership and Volk" into a political community. Hence it urgently tried to realize its ideal of political behavior, which, by way of the demand for unconditional faith, aimed for the substantive conformity of the government and governed. Yet the diaries of the 1930s and the fundamental logics of political behavior they reveal show that it was above all the communication accruing from these efforts that created the connections between the government and the governed. As a permanent "communication network," this integrated the "Volk" into the political system.[208] Because personal political assessments and actions were tightly coupled with the mass media, it was the media that set the thematic focus of the thoughts articulated by individuals in their diaries, even if their thoughts were independent and willful.

This is a major reason that even the intense discussions of the policies of the National Socialist regime by diarists like the former Thuringian state parliamentarian Georg Witzmann or the schoolteacher Hans Maschmann hardly coincide with our perspective today on the Nazi dictatorship. Whereas our judgment of National Socialism is guided less by specific political measures than by the many different—and at that point unknown—forms and institutions of violence brought forth by this political system, these only played a secondary role in the deliberations of diarists, even those who emphatically insisted on forming their own opinion. To be sure, Hans Maschmann, for example, routinely spoke in his diary about how the "German soul is being violated."[209] Yet he was not referring to the massive physical violence against those Germans declared to be "enemies" and "opponents." Rather, this formulation arose in direct connection with the intensive confrontation with political reporting and the regime's control of the media, which Maschmann discerned in the reporting. It referred to the fact that Hitler was a "demagogue" whose "convulsive gesticulations" needed to be repudiated by the "intellectual person . . . as a violation" and "brutality."[210] The "violation" Maschmann talked about time and again did not consist of physical violence but instead referred to the euphemistic and lying propaganda.

And even in deliberations of other diarists who were trying to arrive at judgments from a distance, subjects such as the Gestapo, concentration camps, or openly violent operations, which were seldom presented in the media and never as a part government policy, only received attention in isolated entries. There too, the focus was on discussing those dimensions of National Socialist policy that regularly figured in the reporting of the mass media and which gave people cause to constantly criticize the regime's manipulative public policy, which was continuously brought to mind by the media reporting. As much as these diarists tried to develop their own judgment from a distance, they too nonetheless remained within the spectrum of subjects stipulated by the regime via the media. To be sure, this was not inevitably the case, and isolated diaries also show time and again how certain individuals could better emancipate themselves from topics preset by the mass media.[211] Yet even most of the people who worked intensely on reaching their own political judgments never broke away from the mass-media agenda but remained closely tied to the political system of National Socialism by their focused discussion of media reporting.

In the diaries of the 1930s, the ability of the political system of National Socialism to communicatively bind people and what this meant for political integration is shown especially clearly by the rhythm in which individual authors spoke about regime policy. Generally, the two basic forms of political conduct determined, as shown, wholly different economies of political attention: diarists dealt with regime policy either more strongly through the continuous criticism of routine media reporting or mainly on the occasion of special events that the regime set apart from routine reporting. In this respect, the comparison of diaries of the 1930s makes it possible to identify many temporal phases in which some diarists fastidiously tried to get to the bottom of political events while at the same time other authors registered regime policies with brief comments at most. But such a comparison also reveals those moments when the contrasting political conduct was largely synchronized because of the Nazi regime's public policy. This applied, on the one hand, to spectacular political events, such as the June murders of 1934 or the Sudeten crisis in 1938. On the other hand, the public policy of the Nazi regime synchronized the political conduct of Germans above all during the Reichstag elections and plebiscites of the 1930s. These events formed key moments of political integration in the National Socialist dictatorship that are especially well suited for demonstrating how the opposing tendencies of the political conduct of Germans gave rise to that unanimous support of the regime that was constantly being proclaimed by the official pictures of the "Führer and Volk."

Voting Events as Moments of Special Political Attentiveness

In the historical research into National Socialism, quite in contrast to the electoral successes of the NSDAP during the Weimar Republic, the elections and plebiscites held after 1933 have hardly drawn much interest, given their meaninglessness for political decision-making.[212] Nonetheless, their voting results are frequently used to illustrate the general societal popularity of the regime. Robert Gellately, for example, insists in his study *Backing Hitler: Consent and Coercion in Nazi Germany* that, despite all manipulations, the elections "tend to show that a pro-Nazi consensus formed and grew."[213] Along these lines, he interprets the results of the Reichstag elections of March 1936, for example, as evidence that by 1936 "the Nazis" had managed to win the "support" of the last undecided population groups, "because they received no less than 99.9 per cent of the vote. Certainly, by then elections were heavily tilted in favour of the government.... At times, entire communities were reported to have voted 100 per cent for Hitler, when that was clearly not the case. There is little doubt, however, that an overwhelming majority of the German people did vote 'yes.'"[214]

Elections have frequently been used in much the same way by other studies as a barometer for the regime's social popularity: the arguments consistently note that even though the official results cannot be trusted, "it is difficult to doubt" that they express a large degree of "unforced support."[215] Coincidentally, this argumentation is wholly in line with contemporary interpretations of the voting results: Neu Beginnen and other actors in political exile were not the only ones using the election results to make very similar arguments. The propaganda of the regime repeatedly drew on the voting figures to retrospectively illustrate Hitler's growing popularity with the increase of approving votes. Yet the Reichstag elections and plebiscites that continued to be held even after the elections of November 1933 did not just create powerful political symbols. By way of their voting campaigns, which were organized with great effort despite the absence of political competitors, they generated particularly dense phases of politicization during the political present of the 1930s, both in mass media and also in individual confrontations with regime policy. Despite having lost their functional significance, voting events continued to constitute exceptional moments of comprehensive engagement with regime politics even after 1933.

In their volumes of the 1930s, diarists often identified this explicitly. During the campaign for the voting events in November 1933, for example, the young gardener Inge Thiele did not just decide to "believe" in Adolf Hitler and, on the occasion of his speech at the end of the campaign, query her own political conduct in relation to the aspirations of the regime. A few days after the voting date, she also noted in her diary with obvious satisfaction that her life was running "so quietly, so harmoniously now. . . . The internal-political waves no longer crash into each other but rather go calmly the same way. The heatedness and unrest give way to a pleasant relaxation."[216] The doctor Walter Lindemann recorded something similar in his private entries in spring 1938. On March 19, 1938, for example, he noted the "*start of the voting campaign*" for the Reichstag election set for the Anschluß of Austria in a separate entry in his "Political Diary" and also pointed it out in his regular diary: "Politically it is high season now. The election for the new Reichstag takes place on 04/10, which is now being zealously promoted."[217] Just a few days later, he reaffirmed this assessment using almost the same words: "*Politically* it is a large-scale operation now. Everything is gearing up for the election on April 10." And less than two weeks after the election date, he noted in conclusion, like Inge Thiele, that "*politically* it has become somewhat calmer nowadays."[218]

Born in 1919, the schoolgirl Lore Walb had to write an essay for school in 1936 on the topic of "voting season," which likewise shows that, even back then, election campaign periods were clearly seen as distinct moments of politicization.[219] And after the election of 1936, Hans Maschmann, the Hamburg elementary school teacher whose discussions in his diary of political events were especially thorough, also broadly summarized that when "the negative mood in the country" increases, it is "time for the power holders to once again unfold the theater of power with the usual bombast of methods that have nothing in common with the German spirit and German soul," which Maschmann believed to represent. "Precisely in opposition to it [the German soul], the brutality of this power principle emerges most clearly in such times of voting propaganda."[220]

As Hans Maschmann correctly noted, in contrast to the Weimar Republic, the substantial intensification of general politicization during voting campaign periods was not related to the recruitment of political leaders or decision-making. But it was also not simply the consequence of regime propaganda, as Maschmann supposed. Rather, a central reason for the prominent role of elections and plebiscites under National Socialism was that they spoke to the various forms of political behavior during the Nazi dictatorship. This was closely related to the fact that the voting events of the 1930s were always coupled with important political events. In this sense, the November election and plebiscite of 1933 occasioned by the withdrawal from the League of Nations formed an effective model that guided subsequent voting events. As in fall 1933, those voting events were related to momentous regime decisions that had already been made and implemented: the merging of the offices of Reich president and Reich chancellor in 1934; the remilitarization of the Rhineland in March 1936; the annexation of Austria by the German Reich in April 1938. The "Volk" was supposed to approve these measures retroactively by voting. This similarly applied to the special election for the Sudetenland Germans held in December 1938. In this case, Reichstag representatives were chosen in a by-election by residents of the Sudetenland, which had just been annexed a few weeks earlier by Germany in the wake of the Munich Accord. The January 1935 plebiscite in the Saarland on its reunification with the German Reich formed a special case; since the end of the World War, the Saarland had been administered by the League of Nations, which also monitored the voting. But this plebiscite, too, very much fit into the list: it occurred in the context of a major political event—and even though in this case most Germans in the old Reich were not called on to cast a vote themselves,[221] the mass-media campaign affected them as well.[222] Together with the Reichstag election held in March 1933, a total of seven national voting events were held after Hitler's appointment as Reich chancellor.

The tight coupling of voting events with important political decisions reflected the function that Adolf Hitler basically assigned to voting. Given his contemptuous opinion of democratic decision-making, he repeatedly justified the scheduling of votes by saying that he "acted first" and then held a vote to show "the other world ... that the German Volk stands behind me."[223] In this constellation, the voting events held under National Socialism had nothing to decide, but they always involved a subject that was actually politically relevant. While the regular staging of regime policy on annual holidays annoyed many Germans precisely because of its political insignificance, the context of voting events involved real, far-reaching political decisions whose consequences, moreover, could not yet be accurately assessed. In the days after regime decisions were announced, diarists attentively observed, by means of mass media, "what foreign countries think about the German step and what they want to undertake against it,"[224] especially when it came to severe encroachments on the postwar order of the Treaty of Versailles but also with regard to the plebiscite of 1934, which actually related to a domestic policy issue.[225]

The announcement of the vote itself strongly intensified the political relevance of the particular issue that became the subject of the vote. As in fall 1933, by order of the state, the mass media was purposefully and very closely involved in campaigns during later voting events, and the campaigns were run at great expense. In March 1936, for example, Reich Propaganda Minister Goebbels had already started making corresponding plans even as German soldiers were marching into the Rhineland on March 7.[226] That very day, he had German newspapers informed that "the German press will be used for this voting campaign to a very special degree and scope" and that in the coming weeks "one page [must be] made available to the [campaign] propaganda every day."[227] Once the election campaign started on March 10, 1936, a daily "voting campaign press conference" then gave precise instructions regarding the reporting.[228]

The systematic involvement of the mass media in advertising for the vote substantially increased the density of political reporting in the weeks between the announcement and the vote itself. And above all, it decisively expanded the kinds of media articles. Numerous articles that directly advertised for the vote took their place alongside journalistic reports about reactions abroad and the background on the decision by the German regime. As per instructions to the press, these articles were not supposed to be collected on a single page but "rather distributed in the individual sections."[229] The boundaries between journalistic texts and vote-related advertising became correspondingly ambiguous. The advertising included, first and foremost, many reports from the campaign rallies, which in short succession created a multitude of opportunities for an encounter between the "leadership" and "Volk" during these weeks. In the 1936 voting campaign, which lasted less than three weeks, Hitler himself spoke at eleven major events throughout the Reich.[230] Two years later, a total of fourteen mass assemblies, likewise held in close succession, took him through Germany and Austria, which had been annexed just a few weeks earlier.[231] Involved with him in the voting campaign were almost all of the regime politicians and leading NSDAP representatives. As a result, the daily voting campaign press conferences in March 1936 served primarily to coordinate reporting on speeches so as to avoid having "every newspaper on every day filled with 8 or 10 speeches."[232] At the same time, however, the press was repeatedly urged to publish, if not always the texts of the speeches, then at least "extensive atmospheric portrayals" of the various campaign events and to assign "special reporters" for Hitler's campaign trip.[233] And during voting campaigns, even the radio programming, which after the elections of November 1933 was generally dominated by entertainment music, recalled the highly politicized first months of Nazi rule because of the many broadcasts of speeches.[234] In hindsight on the day after the 1936 Reichstag election, the schoolgirl Lore Walb, born in 1919, noted, "In these two weeks, almost no day went by on which one of our leading men did not speak to the German Volk about the election on the 29th."[235] Thus all told, political reporting during voting events was filled with both journalistic reports on important international developments and broadcasts of regime addresses and speeches of leading politicians—and it offered various points of reference for the political behavior of individuals. Voting events thus synchronized the political behavior of Germans, in that they spoke simultaneously to the various basic logics of political behavior under the Nazi dictatorship. Hence, diarists like Inge Thiele, Walter Lindemann, and Hans Maschmann, who were interested in the political reporting of the mass media in very different ways, could all equally describe the voting campaign as a phase of intensified politicization.

At the same time, another factor contributed to the perception of voting events as periods of intense politicization: the mass media was not the only place where Germans encountered regime politics as a dominant topic. They also came into contact with it in their immediate social environment by casting their vote and above all by way of a grassroots voting campaign that was every bit as intense the advertising campaign in the media.[236] While the Reich propaganda minister already had difficulties controlling reporting in a way that coped with the plethora of major events featuring celebrity politicians, the number of grassroots campaign events arranged by local NSDAP organizations and other associations exceeded the number of major events many times over. In Schleswig-Holstein alone, for example, over 1,000 campaign events took place in the towns and municipalities in

March 1936. Of these, 135 occurred between March 16 and March 26 in the administrative district of Rendsburg alone. And even in the administrative district of Husum, with "only" 30 events, this still amounted to an average of three per day.[237]

As suggested by the difference between the neighboring administrative districts, the intensity of the voting campaign depended heavily on the respective local conditions. Yet overall, in the days prior to the voting date, people throughout Germany found themselves exposed in their daily life to a multitude of advertising activities. "Meeting follows upon meeting, processions chase each other, the children are being harnessed in the schools," noted Hans Maschmann, for example, in August 1934, regarding his impressions from Hamburg.[238] And shortly before the 1936 plebiscite, Stephan Weidenbach, the Andernach city archivist and teacher who turned his diary into a town chronicle, noted that "every day this week" there were "propaganda marches through the town, of the Hitler Youth, officials, etc., often two or three, for the vote."[239] As suggested here, the voting campaign was indeed not conducted by the NSDAP alone.[240] Other groups also became involved. Born in 1922, Rita Thomer from Leipzig, for example, noted in her diary that in April 1938 "our holidays [were] . . . postponed for eight days because of the vote" so that the school students could be deployed in the voting campaign. "We are doing almost nothing in school anymore, since we had to decorate it for the vote. A picture of it was already shown in the newspaper," reported Thomer, who pasted the corresponding newspaper article in her entry.[241] And the Berlin sales representative Hermann Schleifenbaum also reported repeatedly in March 1936 about how he was conducting "voting propaganda" with the Reich Air Defense League.[242]

At the end of the voting campaign, the varied advertising activities carried out at the grassroots level in towns and villages were brought together and directly tied to the regime's national voting campaign in the mass media. The radio broadcasts of central campaign events and the communal receptions organized for these occasions played an important role here. They were first tried out in 1933 specifically for Hitler's closing speech of the campaign. The broadcast began in November 1933 with a so-called minute of silence—previously announced in the media and introduced by wailing sirens throughout the country—during which everyday life and traffic were supposed to come to a standstill. As Luise Solmitz reported from Hamburg in her diary, in fall 1933 as a new element of political communication, the collective pause still required practice. "Just [as] the sirens [began], but not very urgently," she happened to be with her husband at the Altona central train station, "in front of which the people were undecided whether to walk or stand. So we stood when the train station clock showed 13:00 hours. A conductor took charge, looked at his watch, and after one minute commanded: 'Go on!'" As the couple subsequently entered a nearby café to listen to Hitler's speech, people "looked at us with surprise that we were walking instead of standing, for in [the radio broadcast from] Berlin the sirens were still sounding; thus the thing with Central European time does not completely work," Solmitz commented in her diary.[243]

National minutes of silence were also repeatedly used in other voting events as a method for the collective integration of the population and the coordination of political behavior. In 1936, as Hitler launched into his key campaign speech in the Krupp plants in Essen, again it was "sirens [that introduced] the voting campaign" and the communal reception of his address, as Luise Solmitz noted.[244] On this day, even the white-collar employee Werner Stock, living in Lüdersfeld, a rural settlement near Hanover with almost one hundred farmsteads, could write in his diary that "suddenly, at 16:00 hours, sirens and train whistles for one minute" announced the broadcast of the speech.[245] The sirens and minutes of silence stood here as symbols for the overarching goal of the grassroots campaign: not only to synchronize the political perception of the German people through the mass media but also to deeply intervene in the everyday life of the population and coordinate concrete behavior, as in a collective standstill.

Thus voting campaigns were not just periods during which the mass media spoke more intensely and demandingly than usual about regime politics. They were also phases of intensified personal political activity and more direct involvement with regime politics on the part of individual Germans, whether on their own initiative or forcedly. Diaries attest to this in many different ways. Born in 1920, Anton Gloeckner noted in his diary in March 1935 that "we are now in the middle of a voting campaign. Placards admonish the Germans to do their national duty"; time and again, he reported that he was practicing election advertising chants with his Hitler Youth group and performing them in a "canvassing march."[246] One week before the polling date, "Interior Minister Frick held a propaganda speech in the civic center. We formed a cordon along the Neckar."[247] And on the day before the polling date on Sunday, the Hitler Youth group attended a theater event en bloc, "the 'Play of the Millennium,'" which "finished [with a] commitment to the Führer. A play that will succeed," Gloeckner commented with an eye on the impending vote. He added in conclusion, "This evening a number of volunteers are pasting up posters. I have registered as well."[248]

We see something similar in the diary of Wilhelm Bollmann, the NSDAP Gau training director born in 1896. "The avalanche of meetings is now rolling over Germany again," Bollmann noted during the 1936 voting campaign, which reminded the "old fighter" of his activities as an election campaign speaker during the Weimar Republic. "So now as a caller I move in the fray again through Western and Central Germany. Four meetings this week. The second push follows next week."[249] And two years later, on opening day of the campaign for the Reichstag election and plebiscite on the annexation of Austria, he noted in much the same way, "Now it starts again. Plebiscite in Germany and Austria. I will carry out fifteen meetings. I am glad that I can do this. The 11th and 12th of March 1938 [i.e., the German army's march into Austria and the country's annexation] shall receive their legal blessing."[250]

Other people were less enthusiastic about being involved in voting campaigns. In April 1938, for example, the Coesfeld notary Ferdinand Beier noted that "in the train ... officials ... told [him] that they now had to appear at some event every evening. They are longing for these days to end."[251] Elsewhere too, campaign organizers did not rely on people's voluntary willingness to help out but instead obliged individuals to decorate their houses, for example, with flags and placards.[252] Yet despite all of the displeasure clearly arising from such measures, voting campaigns constituted periods of pronounced political attentiveness and activity for these people as well. Not just in the media but also in everyday life, voting events generated dynamics that made the German people directly aware of regime policies, just as during the first months of Nazi rule. Voting events impacted everyone.

This was not only illustrated by the extremely high levels of voter participation, which according to official statements amounted to almost 100 percent for all votes held after November 1933. As at the start of the Nazi dictatorship in 1933 and 1934, during the years that followed, diaries with otherwise little to say about regime policy show that such policy made its way into their entries precisely during voting campaign periods. In summer 1935, for example, Anna Deiker*, the daughter of a professor at the University of Bonn, started a diary. Deiker began "to keep a diary again" after she had finished reading the "Russian diaries" of Galina Djuragin, which appeared in Germany in the early 1930s and was widely read as an anti-Bolshevik "documentary novel" about the horrors of the young Soviet Union. Yet even though the model for her diary notably dealt with the consequences of political developments in one's personal life, Anna Deiker did not write about political topics. Instead, she reported primarily about people she met who "deserved not to be forgotten."[253] Thus, in her diary she noted visits and encounters in her father's professorial home, theater events, and other everyday experiences. Regime politics first appeared when in March 1936 Deiker inserted a total of five advertising flyers for the Reichstag election on March 29, including a leaflet on the "Germany trip of LZ Graf Zeppelin and LZ Hindenburg," which was organized as part of the election campaign. In her entry for the Sunday of the election, Deiker also reported how "the two airships sublimely circled over Bonn in the morning sunshine." She evidently saw this as a worthwhile event and good omen for election day, for she immediate continued: "This evening we will know how many Germans have given their word yes to the Führer, and then we will wait for what the world says."[254] Although brief, this remark nonetheless was the first diary entry that dealt with regime policy and thus clearly stood out from the others—so clearly that after the war the author wrote "no" on every one of the inserted voting campaign leaflets and commented on the remark about the election with the words "Not with me!"[255] Voting campaign periods were informed by all-round heightened attentiveness toward regime politics. And by way of the systematically controlled media and a grassroots voting campaign involving hundreds of thousands of activists, the regime successfully moved even those who were otherwise hardly interested to confront the politics of the regime.

Even so, at the same time the political behavior of Germans was still determined by the fundamental logics that also otherwise dominated the political culture of National Socialism. Diarists like Anton Gloeckner and Wilhelm Bollmann were strongly involved in the voting campaigns, but not because they believed they needed do their part to convince any last non-voters and thereby ensure the success of the mobilization as repeatedly announced in watchwords, on placards, and in speeches. For them, success was never in doubt. Their diary entries expressed the certainty—also constantly declared by the regime—that the voting results would show overwhelming popularity. Shortly after hearing the radio announcement of the occupation of the Rhineland on March 7, 1936, the Hitler Youth member Gloeckner noted, "Through a vote, the German Volk will unanimously declare its confidence in the Führer," exhibiting the same certainty that had informed Reichstag President Hermann Göring's comments to the parliament on Hitler's announcement of the vote.[256] In his description of his voting campaign activities, Gloeckner also seemed certain that "all of Germany will stand as one man behind the Führer."[257] No differently, Wilhelm Bollmann was already convinced at the start of the voting campaign in 1936 that "the election and plebiscite will be successful, even though many a Volk comrade still does not know where he belongs." He too was certain that "we will succeed."[258] To be sure, in spite of their certainty, they both felt it made sense to get intensely involved in the voting campaign, but notwithstanding all the pressure they created for other Germans, their behavior was not just aimed at influencing others. They also got involved because campaign meetings and canvassing marches gave them the opportunity to take an active part in regime politics. The engagement in the voting campaign was personally meaningful to them and expressed their kind of political conduct, which, along with the appropriation of the regime's own ideal, also included its transformed understanding of voting. In concord with the regime, for them the voting events under National Socialism were not about political decision-making or expressing an individual political opinion; rather, for them as part of the "Volk," voting events were about displaying support for the regime to themselves and others.

Conversely, diaries of Germans who, despite National Socialist public policy, endeavored to reach their own political judgments allow us to see how they tried to peer behind the facade of official statements and media reports during voting events as well. The Hamburg elementary school teacher Hans Maschmann, for example, explicitly pointed out with regard to the 1936 Reichstag election that "if Hitler now calls upon the Volk for a decision," Maschmann "also has the right to asked what unspoken purpose is supposed to be achieved with this plebiscite."[259] For him it was clear that this and other voting events had to be seen as "propaganda vehicles," and he was intensely interested in deciphering their underlying rationale.[260] When Hitler ended his campaign in 1936 in Cologne and the radio broadcast faded out with the sound of the bells of the Cologne Cathedral, Maschmann wondered whether Hitler wanted to make "his peace with the Catholic Church" or believed he "could vanquish its power over the faithful souls? . . . What is going on?"[261] And in instances where he thought his observations could prove concrete lies in media reports, he identified them. From an acquaintance, he learned, for example, that "the candles with which the houses needed to be illuminated on the access roads Hitler drove along during his visit were distributed by the party. But in the report, the talk is about the voluntary actions of the population."[262]

Thus what held for the grassroots voting campaign also held for the voting campaign in the mass media: like the transformed political reporting in the context of voting events, the canvassing on the streets and squares synchronized the political behavior of Germans above all by provoking individuals to deal more intensely with regime politics. In this respect, the grassroots voting campaign well and truly forced the topic of the engagement and its temporal rhythm on the people. Yet here too, the various forms of political behavior of the political culture of National Socialism could not be unified to create the "Volk" that stood solidly behind the regime as simultaneously presented and called for by the campaign propaganda. Instead, voting events were critically important for the political integration of National Socialism because they created concentrated moments of political communication that stood out from its usual rhythm. During voting events, the communication between the "leadership and Volk" encompassed an especially large number of Germans and concentrated political attentiveness far more strongly than usual on a single subject: the vote. As a result, it coordinated the cycles of political attentiveness of people with different forms of political behavior. Those who, as a rule, rarely dealt with regime politics, but who did so during voting events, were just as involved as those who tried to adapt to the regime's ideal of conduct and those who wanted to form their own political judgment. Unlike almost any other events of the 1930s, voting events provoked peak activity for very different types of individuals in their dealing with regime politics, making their political conduct part of the political system of National Socialism by means of temporal synchronization, not substantive assimilation.

Political Approval in the Nazi Dictatorship

If the political behavior of the German people therefore remained dominated by downright contradictory logics of action and evaluation even during voting campaigns, what brought about the comprehensive approval of the regime as proclaimed by the exorbitant voting results? For the early research of the 1950s and 1960s into the Nazi period, the answer to this question was clear even without closer investigation: the state manipulation of voting results. "A chance discovery allows for the proving of factual elements about which one already had no doubt . . . in light of the National Socialist regime," Theodor Eschenburg wrote, introducing a collection of documents verifying cases of the violation of fundamental voting principles, published in 1955.[263] And Karl Dietrich Bracher, who concluded his study on the "stages of the seizure of power" with a separate chapter on the elections of fall 1933 and summer 1934, likewise pointed out that the Nazi regime's massive interference in voting freedoms "substantially influenced" the overall results, even "if a general falsification of the voting results from above cannot be demonstrated."[264] Accordingly, he concluded his analysis of the establishment of the National Socialist dictatorship by looking forward to the Reichstag election of 1936, which made it "finally obvious that, in the meantime, the period of the seizure of power had been completed, the solidification of power achieved, any free expression of contrary opinion had become illusory, and the era of the 99% votes had begun." Only now had "totalitarian rule become all-encompassing, the total state also apparently internally unassailably consolidated."[265]

The state's configuration of the voting process and vote counting did, in fact, contribute substantially to the overall voting results, which ultimately reached a level of 99.1 percent approval during the Reichstag election and plebiscite of 1938. Even just the layout of the ballot shows how voters were given less and less room to express disapproval. While the ballots for the plebiscites in fall 1933 and summer 1934 still featured two fields of equal size situated side by side for marking the vote, the ballot for the plebiscite of 1938 finally had two circles of different sizes: one large circle positioned in the middle of the ballot and labeled "yes" and a substantially smaller field marked "no" that had been shifted to the lower right corner. The ballots for the Reichstag election in November 1933 and 1936, in fact, had only one circle for casting a vote for the NSDAP ticket.[266] Much the same applied to the principles of vote counting. In the run-up to the voting in November 1933, Reich Interior Minister Frick, who was responsible for managing the voting process, still instructed state governments to define the validity of ballots in very generous terms when counting votes. Along with simply marking a cross, even if a voter "in any other way signifies his will, whether it is that he enters the word 'yes' ('no'), or that he strikes out or marks with a cross one of the two rectangles, respectively, the circle, or that he crosses out or ticks one of the preprinted words 'yes' ('no')," the "ballot [was supposed to be] valid" and included in the count.[267] The rule created a lot of room for interpretation but basically left matters at distinguishing between yes and no votes and invalid ballots, which included primarily empty ballots. Then for the Reichstag election of 1936, it was ordered that all ballots that do not "for example, signify a 'no' or contrary will by crossing out, etc." were to be deemed as affirmative.[268]

At the same time, however, the provisions for counting votes also show that the official voting results were not simply contrived.[269] Rather, they referred back to regulations of the Weimar Republic and were still guided by the idea of the voter's intention. Interior Minister Frick "fully exploited the legal opportunities for the benefit of his party," but he "did not incite the voting boards to commit vote falsification."[270] Overall, the state's manipulation of voting results remained "within narrow limits." Even in the plebiscite of 1938, "direct falsifications of results were more the exception" than the rule.[271] The voting results could not be explained as the product of state interference and were not as symbolically representative of the supposedly all-encompassing terror of the Nazi regime as Karl Dietrich Bracher had thought, for example.

Yet to me it seems just as dubious to view the "results of the voting in the Third Reich, admittedly not in its full extent but nonetheless in terms of its trend," as a "gauge" for the "real mood in the population," as occurs in most of the recent scholarship.[272] The question about the degree to which democratic voting principles were violated is not the key to breaking down the voting outcomes under National Socialism and explaining why the variegated behavior of Germans led to a uniform voting result; rather, for this we need to analyze the concrete voting behavior of Germans themselves. This behavior by no means followed the rationalities suggested by the specific voting conditions under the Nazi dictatorship, those which led Karl Dietrich Bracher, for example, to speak about a "merely mechanical casting of votes, which the citizen . . . was commanded to do."[273] Rather, even just the extent to which people wrote in their diaries about casting their ballots already testifies strongly to the personal significance and attention that they gave to voting, despite knowing about the undemocratic voting conditions and the regime's excessive mobilization operations.

An example of this comes from the travel diary of the Solingen teacher Ludwig Lindholm, who in early 1934, shortly after the death of Reich President Paul von Hindenburg, departed for his summer vacation. On the date of the plebiscite for the merging of the offices of Reich president and Reich chancellor, Lindholm was still traveling and found himself in the Austrian Alps. Nonetheless, the election was clearly reflected in his travel diary. "A memorable day. Voting day, whether or not one approves of the new regulation after Hindenburg's death," Lindholm began his report on the Sunday of the vote. He described at length how that morning "thirteen giant automobiles brought the guests and eligible German voters of the Walsertal to Obersdorf. Prevailing there was a tremendous hubbub. Flags everywhere." However, Ludwig Lindholm and his wife did not search out the border village's polling station. Instead, as Lindholm pointed out, to cast their vote, they had "this time chosen something quite special: Our voting station was the Edmund Probst House on the Nebelhorn." Since it was "a hot day," the couple ascended to the Allgäu alpine chalet in the cable car, which had gone into operation in 1930. "At the top, a busy bustle already prevailed. Today we cast our votes with particular pleasure," Lindholm noted, going on to describe how a "small girl . . . also wanted to go behind the Spanish wall. The SA men had understanding for the darling girl, allowed it, and even gave the child a voting certificate, like the one we received." After casting their votes, the couple climbed the extra three hundred meters from the chalet to the peak of the Nebelhorn and enjoyed the "brilliant" view: "Over there the tremendous Zugspitze Massif, the Hochvogel pretty near, the Mädelegabel a giant spike, and other vast numbers of peaks." In the evening, the Lindholms and other vacationers were then returned by the buses that had brought them from the Austrian Walsertal that morning.[274]

Ludwig Lindholm's portrayal of how he cast his ballot is symptomatic in two ways: First, the organization of his personal act of voting and even just the fact that Lindholm recorded the day's events in such detail in his diary indicate the personal significance he attributed to the casting of his vote. Naturally, the Lindholm couple was also aware, in light of the expected result, that their votes were not a deciding factor. That they nonetheless organized their vacation day around the event clearly illustrates that their ballots were important to them. Second, precisely because it does not conceal the regime's mobilization activities on voting day, his description draws a very different picture of voting in the National Socialist dictatorship than is suggested by looking at the manifold interferences in voting freedom. The thirteen buses so fondly mentioned by Lindholm, which brought the German vacationers to the polling station, were part of the immense effort by various Nazi organizations to ensure the full participation of the German people in the vote. On voting day, an extensive "vote transport service" was organized in many places, mainly by NSDAP Ortsgruppen. It was supposed to exert "pressure on every individual to cast his ballot and vote in support of the regime."²⁷⁵ To do so, people who had not yet voted were identified using voter lists and brought to the ballot boxes.

Born in 1894, the teacher Kurt Neusen*, who in 1938 was deployed as an election assistant for the Reichstag by-election after Germany's annexation of the Sudeten territories, reported in his diary how the National Socialist Motor Corps (Nationalsozialistische Kraftfahrkorps, NSKK) brought "a few older or frail people to the polling station. Also, the director of the vote, with a few members, went to a few bedridden persons to have them give him the ballots. An NSKK man brought a supporter of the SdP [Sudeten German Party] to vote from almost as far away as Dreschen." Already at "4 o'clock I could go home," Neusen wrote to conclude his report, because by then "the last [voters had] appeared."²⁷⁶ The buses that collected the Lindholm couple from their vacation were an unusual variation of the comprehensive transport service but were undoubtedly part of it. However, this only became apparent at the end of Lindholm's report: on the return trip to Austria, he noted in conclusion, "Just after Obersdorf... an SA man stopped every vehicle and asked whether there still was anyone inside who had not voted. Close nearby, namely, was the last opportunity to do so."²⁷⁷ But Lindholm did not object to the fact that the regime was even pressuring voters on vacation to cast their ballots and then monitoring them as well. Quite the contrary, his description shows that his private interest in voting dovetailed with the regime's intrusions.

This is further underscored by the diary entry's illustrations. Apart from photos of the impressive alpine landscape, Lindholm also pasted in the diary the two voting certificates that he and his wife received after casting their ballot and that he mentioned in his report. These documents, too, were part of the regime's comprehensive effort to mobilize voters. For all voting events, the "Reich Propaganda Directorate... had special election and plebiscite placards produced, which were handed out to voters at the polling station and were to be worn visibly in public."²⁷⁸ On voting day, they were supposed to help Nazi activists working the streets as "transporters" identify those who had already voted—and, above all, those who had not. Therefore, they provided a good basis for the "meticulous hunt for nonvoters."²⁷⁹ The reason for the lack of pin-on indicators in 1934, when they were replaced by paper "receipts" with a field for a name and the plain imprint "has voted," was the short preparation period for the voting campaign after Hindenburg's unexpected death.²⁸⁰

Yet these receipts, too, fulfilled the purpose of voter monitoring. When the SA sentry stopped the buses filled with vacationers just before the border crossing and asked about nonvoters, he undoubtedly looked at the individual voter receipts. Nonetheless, this element of the systematic influencing of voters did not bother Ludwig Lindholm either. Instead, he instilled the official certificate with his own meaning by inserting it into his diary as proof of his personal participation in the vote. By casting his ballot during his summer vacation in 1934, Lindholm was not just performing a necessary duty that the transport and vote monitoring operations made difficult to avoid. Quite the contrary, both when casting his ballot and describing the event in his diary, he endeavored to present his act of voting as an individual political act, and this precisely while referencing the mobilization activities of the Nazi regime.

The importance of voting as an individual political act, despite the severely restricted voting options, to Germans who viewed themselves as National Socialists and adhered to the regime's behavioral ideal is also reflected, in particular, by the many violations of ballot secrecy. In the run-up to the November 1933 Reichstag election and plebiscite on the withdrawal from the League of Nations, Reich Interior Minister Wilhelm Frick had basically urged for the principle of ballot secrecy to be upheld, even though he was fully aware that this could hardly be reconciled with the transformed significance of voting in the Nazi dictatorship. In an interview with the *Völkischer Beobachter* shortly before the vote, Frick was asked whether the "secret ballot" was not "obsolete, like so many other peculiarities of the democratic-parliamentary system," given that the "act of voting in the new Reich [now had] the character of a public affirmation by the Volk." In his response, Frick basically agreed. Indeed, the "further development of the previous democratic-parliamentary voting operation in the direction of a public affirmation by the Volk wholly corresponds to National Socialist principles," and "political-tactical considerations" were the only reason it was "not expedient to change the voting law already for the vote on November 12."[281] Yet an official revision of voting law and voting procedures, which actually would have been logical, never came about for any of the later voting events either. Instead, in 1934 the Reich Interior Ministry still publicly stated that voters should cast their ballots "in a *free* and *secret* vote."[282] This was because of the fear that abolishing voting freedom could substantially reduce the propaganda value of voting events with regard to foreign countries. Accordingly, in the 1930s voting still basically took place secretly in polling booths; Ludwig Lindholm and his wife had cast their ballots behind a "Spanish wall" as well.

Yet at the same time, this tactical consideration made so little sense to many of the Nazi activists mobilized in the voting campaigns that they took massive action against ballot secrecy.[283] Ballot secrecy was already an oft-disputed subject in the grassroots voting campaigns of local regime representatives. In Tuttlingen in Baden-Württemberg, for example, in April 1938 at a rally on the Friday before the Sunday vote, the NSDAP Kreisleiter openly called for dispensing with polling booths: "A German who means to be honest" required "no 'voting cage' when voting! He makes his cross in the circle before the voting official," the Kreisleiter said, according to the Sopade reporter who summarized his speech.[284] During balloting on voting Sundays, there were many violations of ballot secrecy that, just as the regime feared, were attentively registered by reporters from exile. The reports by Neu Beginnen and Sopade list numerous cases where voting boards—composed mainly by NSDAP activists—failed to set up voting booths or voters could "not use the voting booths, so that it was directly a public vote."[285] "Sometimes one was only allowed into a booth upon energetic request."[286] In other polling stations, "booths [were] set up," but their use was "made difficult in that the slogan was issued: The proper German votes openly."[287]

The degree to which voting remained secret depended heavily on the respective circumstances within the individual polling stations. Even the reports from exile, which specifically looked for violations of ballot secrecy, indicated that this was clearly not always the case, recording, for example, that voting was "secret in almost all polling stations in Dresden": "The voters were directly shown to the booth by the voting officials. When the reporter, for example, wanted to cast his ballot outside the booth at the monitoring table, the voting official called out to him: 'Just go into the booth, you have enough time for that.'"[288] Another example comes from the Hamburg archivist Nikolaus Sieveking, who in 1933 attentively followed the dismantling of democratic institutions in his diary. In the fall of that year, having guessed that his "political credit" was not particularly high, he seemed "surprised" that he was supposed to act "again as secretary in my voting district." On voting day, he reported at length about the heavy congestion but did not mention any changes to voting procedure.[289]

However, it was not just voting boards that modified specific voting procedures according to the changed meaning of voting. Voters themselves also tried to do so, in that they deliberately avoided using erected booths. Reporting on the Reichstag election of 1936, a Sopade reporter in Bavaria told about how in one polling station "various people [had] started to mark the ballots outside the polling booth."²⁹⁰ Similar reports from other towns stated that "in the polling station . . . [there was] admittedly a polling booth," but it "was not used by many."²⁹¹ And in 1938, a reporter stated that, even though there were "two booths" at the polling station, they had been located "so far away from the tables generally being used" that "no voter trusted himself to use them."²⁹²

The reports from exile presented these examples as evidence of the "terror, vote influencing," and the "thousandfold methods of coerced voting and intimidation" that accompanied voting events for people who simply did not want to acquiesce.²⁹³ Indeed, the open voting by many voters and the actions of local voting boards often made casting an unobserved ballot impossible. But this conduct should not be understood merely as an effort to influence the voting decisions of others. Rather, it was much more an expression of a political self-understanding aligned with the regime's behavioral ideal and thus an expression of the personal importance these individuals assigned to voting as part of their own political behavior. If they wanted to believe in the regime and show loyalty with their vote, the raison d'être of the secret ballot, which protected *how* they voted, fell away. What now mattered was being able to cast their vote in a way that showed themselves and others *that* they voted and did their part as demanded to support the regime.

For Germans who, despite massive influencing efforts by the regime, did not vote or voted no, the violation of ballot secrecy often had serious consequences, which starkly reveal the boundaries of the integrative capacity of the political system of National Socialism: it could not assimilate direct contradiction, only violently suppress it.²⁹⁴ At the end of his report about casting his own ballot in 1934, Ludwig Lindholm noted as the day's only "anguish" that the daughter of the German landlord of their holiday apartment had "just the evening before allowed her sweetheart to persuade her not to go to the plebiscite. It was generally held badly against her in the village." And Lindholm added, "Will also not remain without consequences in the long term."²⁹⁵ Just how accurate such a prognosis could be is shown, for example, by the diary of Erwin Oehl. Born in 1907, the Communist painter had started his diary in spring 1933 during his preventive detention in the Landsberg prison, but he would not resume writing until April 1936, after a three-year hiatus. "1933 in Landsberg prison, in the first days of April, is the last time entries were made in the form of diary-like notes," wrote Oehl, who started writing his diary again after having been in exile for a few days. This time he used the diary to describe the circumstances and difficulties of his emigration: "On March 29, 36, 'voting.' Mr. Spann had previously instructed the schoolchildren: 'Anyone who votes no this time, we will badger him for the rest of his life.'" Thus began Oehl's report, in which he described how on voting Sunday he drove "home specifically to vote" and "made his will known . . . mainly in memory of the friends murdered in Dachau." Two days after the vote, Oehl was ordered to the NSDAP Kreisleitung, where he was told to leave "Germany as quickly as possible." The Kreisleiter showed him "the ballot on which Adolf Hitler is hugely crossed out. I make no comment and declare that I cannot comment in consideration of the free and secret ballot. 'There is a person who is prepared to testify under oath that this is your ballot.'" Then Oehl had to endure the "worst abuse, about lack of character, etc. etc.," during which he was openly threatened with being banned from his profession and stripped of his citizenship. "Do not believe that we will tolerate pictures of yours hanging in a public building in Germany. Your pictures will never hang in the savings bank. We will publicly burn them in the marketplace with the appropriate framing. By all means, make use of what I am telling you. I will apply for your denaturalization and go all the way to the Reich Interior Ministry.'"

Even though Oehl insisted in his report that the performance of the NSDAP functionaries who threatened him was "very dubious" and "less than convincing," his portrayal nevertheless conveys the massive violence that confronted him in the conversation. It was "difficult for him not to physically chastise me," Oehl noted regarding the statement by one his two interlocutors; the other had "a pistol ready in his right jacket pocket, just in case." "I will give you time until May 1," the Kreisleiter said, bringing the conversation to a close. "If you have not left Germany by then, I will have you beaten out of Germany."[296] Less than two weeks later, Oehl had fled helter-skelter to Zurich.

While the threats against Erwin Oehl occurred behind closed doors, in many other cases the violence against nonvoters and no-voters took place deliberately in public. Evidence for the visibility of the humiliating pillory processions and demonstrations led and organized by local NSDAP units in the aftermath of voting events comes first and foremost from photographs.[297] Born in 1871, Johannes Friedrich, a pastor in Aurich in East Frisia, also vividly reported in his diary about the public violence he experienced as a nonvoter on the evening of the voting day for the 1938 Reichstag election and plebiscite. As a member of the Confessing Church, Friedrich had already repeatedly come into conflict with the regime. But none of the consequences of these confrontations were as severe as those that followed his refusal to cast a ballot during the vote of April 10, 1938. In the course of the day, "SA people" had shown up three times "to ask whether we wanted to vote." Friedrich and his wife, who likewise did not vote, were spending the day of the vote visiting with friends, and each time he sent the activist transporters away. In the evening, as the couple approached their residence on the way home, "we heard great noise from screaming or shouting people. Eventually we could also understand the shouts: '1. 2. 3. 4. Here lives a traitor to the Volk who did not vote. Boo, boo, boo. Servant to Jews, servant to Jews, Judas." "This noise" had already been going on for "three-quarters of an hour" in front of their house, which Johannes and his wife could only reach by going through the garden. "The cries became more and more ugly, there was shaking at the door, kids rang the bell, and we sat upstairs in the study and waited for what would come." The couple was finally taken into preventative custody, while the "raging . . . [lasted] until the car with a policeman [Schutzpolizist] arrived in the back at the wall. . . . As we climbed into the car, the rabble also came to the car, hit the window with fists and snarled with pale, hate-filled faces. . . . With a clamor, we were accompanied all the way to jail. It was a proper blessing for the ears," Friedrich commented in his diary, "when, in the jail office, one could no longer hear any of the noise."[298] While his wife was released after one night, the Gestapo detained Friedrich for twelve days and forbade him from returning to his parish. Instead of returning to Aurich, Johannes Friedrich had to move to Göttingen and enter retirement.[299]

The violations of basic voting freedoms, which became especially apparent in the violence against nonvoters and no-voters, were often attentively noted by individuals who also typically tried to decipher official political reporting outside the context of voting events. The Nuremberg gingerbread baker Daniel Lotter, for example, noted in summary after the Reichstag election of 1936 that there were many rumors "that all unmarked ballots were counted as yes votes; they also forced every last man to vote and went so far as to go around the buildings with the ballot box in order to collect the votes of the old and sick."[300] On voting day in March 1936, the Hamburg elementary school teacher Hans Maschmann likewise noted that the election had been carried out "under the supervision of only party members. If someone had written the small word 'no,' then his longer stay behind the wall would certainly have been noticed. Moreover, the counting of the votes lay solely in the hands of party comrades. Monitoring of the count by an opposing side was absent. The doors are open for all kinds of deception."[301]

Also voting in Hamburg and reporting on the 1938 plebiscite in her diary, Luise Solmitz wrote that "the vote in our polling station" was not secret. "I marked 'yes' with a cross, folded the paper, [wanted to] push it into the envelope, which takes no longer for me than for others—then one of the voting assistants is looking into [the] booth. [He said] I have to do that on the window board, next person please. And so he stood there right next to me and looked stubbornly at my paper once more," which Solmitz had folded in a way that still left her voting decision visible.[302] "Mrs. Steier told Fredy the same, independently from me,"[303] she added, indicating, like Daniel Lotter, that restrictions of voting freedom were clearly a topic of discussion.

That such discussions about voting irregularities took place is also shown by diary of the civil registry employee Werner Kramp, albeit from the opposite perspective. In January 1934—that is, weeks after the plebiscite on the withdrawal from the League of Nations had been held—Kramp noted that "our worldly-wise seamstress" had talked about how "recently after the vote, in the gymnasium that serves as a polling station, [she had] observed that flash photographs were taken during the opening and emptying of the ballot boxes." Kramp saw this as "evidence that control [i.e., electoral fraud] [was] not practiced." Yet the very fact that he asked himself "why the Volk" was not informed "previously about the legitimacy of the vote" indicates that he too had heard rumors about fraudulent voting, which many voters—in contrast to people such as Ludwig Lindholm— found quite problematic and considered an encroachment on their personal voting behavior.[304]

Germans were well aware of the circumstances of voting, the frequent failure to ensure ballot secrecy, and also the consequences that might follow if a no-vote was revealed. Yet this did not keep those among them who insisted on making their own judgments from attributing value to their personal vote under these circumstances. Despite often severely criticizing the voting conditions in their diaries, these Germans in particular did not want to let their voting decision be taken from them, and they clung to the idea that by voting they were making their own political statement. Thus, diaries document not only an increased preoccupation with regime politics during voting events but also their authors' sometimes intensive deliberations on how they should behave in the polling booth.

The Hamburg resident Werner Kramp, for example, admitted in his diary in late October 1933 that "all non-job-related thought" was currently dominated by the election and the question of how he should vote. To this end, Kramp attentively registered the election speeches, discussing their contents in his diary. He noted, in particular, "three statements worth considering" from acquaintances "who, under the moral-political pressure of this Reichstag election, committed themselves differently."[305] Kramp reported on the various conversations at length, and in his writing over the following days, he continued thinking about how he should cast his ballot on voting day. His concerns pertained specifically to the upcoming new election for the Reichstag. On voting Sunday, Kramp began his report on the scheduled plebiscite and Reichstag election occasioned by the withdrawal from the League of Nations by commenting that "the rejection of Geneva and the disarmament game over there has led to the appeal to the Volk," and it was "self-evident" that the Volk would "cover the 'Führer'" in this matter. "But at the same time, a new Reichstag is supposed to be elected," and Kramp was by no means certain about how he should cast his ballot for this particular vote. Given the widespread "fear of surveillance," he had considered over the past few days whether it made sense to "vote differently for the Reichstag," so as to "proclaim the independence of balloting" to foreign countries. Yet "after daily vacillation, also contributing to which was again the knowledge that the nonvoter, as a naysayer, supports the Communists," Kramp ultimately deciding on, as he put it, a "distancing from the circumstances of the vote and the realization that a vibrant, faith-filled movement cannot be met with 'no' and passivity." Thus he gave his approval with both votes.[306]

The Göttingen student Karl Möhring reflected on his November 1933 ballots in much the same way. Although scheduled for the same day, the votes were conducted with separate ballots. Whereas Kramp had considered casting different votes for strategic reasons, Möhring actually decided on approval for the plebiscite but refused to approve the Reichstag election because he "certainly [wanted to vote] for the foreign policy of the government . . . but not for the NSDAP."[307] The new election of the Reichstag made no sense to Möhring, who repeatedly pointed out in his diary that the Reichstag "has absolutely no significance anymore and a unity party already exists."[308] "A common SA man will play a bigger role than a Reichstag delegate," predicted Möhring, who therefore considered the Reichstag election "unnecessary."[309] "It would be better to create a few new constitutional principles."³¹⁰ Nonetheless, Möhring wanted to indicate his approval of the withdrawal from the League of Nations and did so with his differently decided ballot.

The voting results themselves document that in fall 1933 Karl Möhring and Werner Kramp were not alone in thinking about the difference between the Reichstag election and the plebiscite. Not only did the 95.1 percent approval of the withdrawal from the League of Nations turn out to be higher than the 92.1 percent approval for the NSDAP ticket in the Reichstag election, but in total, over four hundred thousand fewer ballots were cast for the Reichstag election than for the plebiscite.³¹¹ Thus, the deliberations by Germans on the importance of these separate votes are still legible in these voting results. These results, together with diaries such as those of Werner Kramp, who, despite thinking along the same lines as Karl Möhring, decided yes for both votes, indicate the major importance of the distinction between Germany and National Socialism in the considerations of many Germans when casting their votes; the importance of this distinction would still hold sway in the years that followed.

In an entry on the 1933 November votes, the former Thuringian state parliamentarian Georg Witzmann accurately captured the conflict simmering in many diaries between a nationalist commitment of support and the fact that this meant giving encouragement to the Nazi regime. "*Everyone* must work together here" to win "the honor and freedom of the Volk and fatherland," he wrote, and at the same asked, "does one necessarily need to be a National Socialist to do so?"³¹² And the maxim he established during the voting campaign as a guideline for his own political actions— namely, "to support the regime in all national questions, but to reject and combat its claim to totality"—also describes an aspiration at the heart of intensive discussions of other diarists as well.³¹³

The problem with later votes, however, was that after fall 1933 the regime dispensed with twofold ballots, scheduling only a plebiscite in 1934 and only a Reichstag election in 1936, while using a single shared ballot in 1938 when, as in fall 1933, a plebiscite and Reichstag election were held at the same time. As a result, the opportunity to cast separate ballots ceased to exist, which meant that the difference between Germany's national interests and the interests of the Nazi regime was now of little help when personally deciding how to vote. What took precedence when voting, supporting Germany's national interests or establishing distance from the Nazi regime? The modified voting procedure and the concomitant question did not essentially change the intensive discussions about one's personal voting decision. But they put even more pressure on people to decide. Hans Maschmann, for example, struggled with this problem in each of the voting events of the 1930s. "Yesterday evening I heard Hitler's speech on the radio; today I feel nauseous and [?] miserable; and tomorrow I am supposed to 'vote,'" noted the Hamburg elementary school teacher the day before the plebiscite on the merging of the offices of the Reich president and Reich chancellor in August 1934. "He added nothing new to what was said before," Maschmann complained in his diary. "Always the same general aspects, without setting a specific political goal." None of this helped him with his decision on how to vote. Once again, Maschmann reflected at length on the political situation, which he had already repeatedly summarized over the past few days. "At times something within me speaks that tells me: Hitler is nothing other than a puppet of certain circles that are using him for their purpose. . . . Faith is not sufficient on its own in light of the materialistic intersection of economic and social realities. And yet: in light of Germany's situation, essentially caused by Hitler's nationalist-egocentric politics, he who loves his fatherland can do nothing other than give Hitler his vote tomorrow."[314]

Maschmann faced almost the same situation again one and a half years later, when in March 1936 he bitterly complained about the "obfuscation of strongly personal thinking and feeling," called the "entire so-called voting campaign absurd," and admitted that he did not believe in the official guarantee of ballot secrecy. Nonetheless, before the vote he stressed that "whoever loves Germany" must "cast his vote in the affirmative. We are standing there again, where nothing else is possible apart from merging with the common fate." And on voting day, Maschmann announced in his diary: "I voted with yes, not because I need this Führer, but because I carry my Volk in my heart, and am bound to its fate with my blood, and integrated into its history with my soul."[315] For the 1938 plebiscite, Maschmann now just articulated this argument plainly as follows: he gave "a full yes to the Anschluß of Austria" but "retreats from the noise and bluster that is being made about it." However, during the weeks prior to the vote, he had written just as intensely about politics as in previous voting campaigns.[316]

Hans Maschmann was not alone with such deliberations. Time and again, diarists admitted in their writings to voting yes or in favor the NSDAP ticket, despite their broad criticism of the Nazi regime, which was often especially acute during voting campaigns. The Hamburg druggist Otto

Kirchmann, for example, who in spring 1933 started within his fraternity an extensive exchange of letters about the political situation in Germany in which he clearly criticized the regime, pointed out in a letter of January 1934 that he had "in good conscience voluntarily affirmed both 'yeses' of the last vote [on the withdrawal from the League of Nations and the new Reichstag election] because a German and student fraternity member, even if he is *not* a party comrade, cannot act differently."[317] The doctor Walter Lindemann always specifically highlighted the voting campaign periods in his diary, but as they unfolded, he would rant at length about how "we now have to listen to voting speech and voting speech" and endure being lied to.[318] Yet despite his many sharp words, he wrote down the voting results with obvious satisfaction each and every time. As of the mid-1930s the doctor was admittedly no longer able to vote, having been accepted into the Wehrmacht as a soldier in the wake of the reoccupation of the Rhineland in 1936.[319] But his diary reflects the extent to which he nonetheless welcomed the sweeping voter approval. For example, he not only recorded the results directly on voting day in 1936 but also pasted in his first portrait photo of himself in a Wehrmacht uniform. For him, the photo symbolized the fulfillment of a long-held dream, yet in the context of his entry about the vote, it also signaled his basic approval of the regime.[320] Such deliberations also informed the decision of Johannes Friedrich, the pastor from Aurich who was driven from his town after refusing to vote in 1938. He decided not to take part in the vote because, as a supporter of the "Anschluß of Austria," he did not want to say no, but he did not want give his approval either, because that would have meant having to say "yes to the action against Niemöller and to the fight against the Church in our Volk."[321]

A similar dichotomy also led the Fürth gingerbread baker Daniel Lotter to finally vote affirmatively in the voting events of the 1930s. As with Hans Maschmann, his diary too shows that he struggled with his decision on how to vote in the plebiscite on the merging of the offices of the Reich president and Reich chancellor. "Under these circumstances, it is difficult to make a decision for the plebiscite tomorrow," Lotter acknowledged. "It must be conceded that with our terrible foreign-political situation, the solid unity of the German Volk is necessary. Then again, 'yes' means approval of June 30 [1934, the Röhm putsch] and its atrocious events, approval of our foreign policy, which shows nothing other than failures, and of domestic policy methods that have lost us any last residue of sympathy abroad."[322] The entries do not reveal what might have finally tipped the balance for

Lotter in this vote. In March 1936, the gingerbread baker again vacillated between national duty and criticism of the Nazi regime, but after voting day he reported, "Even though I could only decide to do so at the last minute, I too drew my X in the circle."[323] The "pangs of conscience" that plagued Lotter while voting were "allayed" by the fact that "at least I crossed out Streicher's name from the list"—referring to the well-known Nuremberg Gauleiter the gingerbread baker frequently mentioned with disgust in his diary.[324] "I worked it out for myself as if I had thereby crossed out that which is unpleasant, repulsive, indefensible about National Socialism, while I recognized those good and noble things it has created and strives for. Admittedly, it isn't true," Lotter commented on his own explanation. "But I could make no other decision, especially since, of course, an option to express one's different opinion was not provided."[325] This was undoubtedly correct, yet this is precisely why Lotter's entry so symptomatically represents the voting behavior of many Germans who sought to make their own judgments, because while openly speaking about the pressure he faced, he did not simply bow to it but rather tried to reconcile his approval with his attitude toward the Nazi regime.

The affirmative vote may seem strange to today's reader, given the simultaneous expression of massive criticism. But this conduct should not simply be dismissed as absurd or schizophrenic. Rather, bundled precisely in such a vote are the paradoxes of individual political behavior in the Nazi dictatorship, where many Germans still wanted to render their own political judgments but could only do so in an environment designed to prevent this from happening. Instead of revealing deficiencies of the respective voters, the contradictory voting behavior of contemporaries like Hans Maschmann, Daniel Lotter, and Otto Kirchmann demonstrates instead that the far-reaching changes of the system of political decision-making and the manipulative media policy of the regime deeply shaped not just the political behavior of Germans but also the political rationalities they could use as the basis for political evaluation and action. *Yes* and *no* were simply no longer balanced alternatives when facing the question, as posed by voting situations, regarding an individual's basic stance toward the Nazi regime; *yes* covered a broader spectrum of political opinions than *no*. By way of the intensive voting campaigns that ultimately enveloped the entire German people, voting events helped reproduce the dynamics of the first months of the "national revolution" of 1933–1934. And at the same time, the voting behavior of Germans revealed how voting events, even though always dedicated to concrete political situations, became very much a question about the individual's relationship to the regime. It was not by chance that when thinking about how to vote, Hans Maschmann repeatedly asked himself "whether I need to reproach myself for seeing everything only from the question of my field of view and not on a large scale." Or that he took himself "to court . . . [to ask] whether I am acting patriotically [vaterländisch]." Or that he checked "time and again . . . whether petty carping is what is driving me into opposition."[326] Nor was it a coincidence that Hans Maschmann, during the Reichstag election of 1936, after explaining the reasons for his approval, felt himself challenged again to define his basic position toward the regime: "I am a national socialist according to type-appropriate, human character. That is why this form of state is not a necessity, and the men who are in leadership today appear to me to lack the nobility of soul that is the precondition for genuine German national socialism."[327] Even though these individuals asked concrete political questions, in the constellation of forced voter mobilization and extensive grassroots and mass-media voting campaigns, voting events ultimately provoked the same question about commitment that essentially dominated the first months of Nazi rule and contributed to its particular dynamics. On voting day for the 1933 November election, the civil registry employee Werner Kramp wrote, "Today is the last voting day and first commitment day," thereby aptly identifying how the constellation of voting had changed.[328] The new constellation meant that *no* became a much more definitive political statement than *yes* because it placed the voter within the spectrum of everyone the Nazi regime declared as "enemies" and "opponents."

The relationship between the act of voting and the question of political commitment is revealed especially strongly in diaries of Germans whose voting rights were taken away by the Nazi regime during the course of the 1930s. As early as 1933, there had been vociferous calls to deny "volksfremde" and "volksfeindliche" groups the right to vote. Yet in consideration of how matters might look from foreign countries, not even protective-custody prisoners, who were entitled to vote through an exception regulation dating from the Weimar Republic, were excluded from voting. This meant that in November 1933, voting also occurred in prisons and concentration camps.[329] By contrast, German Jews were stripped of their right to vote in fall 1935 as a result of the Nuremberg Laws and the new rules regarding state citizenship rights. In early March 1936, the regime's announcement of the scheduling of the Reichstag election while German troops marched into the

Rhineland made Luise Solmitz enthusiastic about the foreign policy victory, but at the same time it also brought to mind the social isolation that she, her husband, and their daughter had fallen into because Friedrich Solmitz, who as a young adult had converted from Judaism to Christianity, was considered "Jewish" by the Nazi regime. One must "not think about what it means, Reich citizenship, the right to belong again, to vote, to fly flags, to earn money, to find a place for Gisela and have her marry, to keep a maid, in short: to be an equally entitled, free human being. To regain that which one took for granted," Solmitz noted two days after the election was announced. She went on: "I am allowed to vote, am a Reich citizen: the 'married to a Jew [jüdisch versippt]' has fallen away due to the Nuremberg Laws." But her husband was excluded from voting. "That would be proper bravery, true civil courage, if I went calmly and naturally to vote, passing through all the neighbors," deliberated Luise Solmitz. But then she asked herself whether she would muster the "bravery" for this or whether "I [should] stay away, because Fredy [her husband] is not permitted to vote? What a situation: the husband is not allowed to vote; the wife is allowed to."[330]

The many entries recorded by Luise Solmitz during the voting campaigns for this and the next plebiscite in 1938 were deeply marked by the simultaneity of her personal approval of the regime's foreign policy and her social marginalization, which she felt especially strongly during voting events. Two days before the Sunday of the vote in 1936, she noted not only the sirens that preceded Hitler's key speech for the conclusion of the campaign but also, after Hitler's speech from the Krupp plants in Essen, the order issued for a general "flying of flags." "But not at our place," Solmitz remarked bitterly. In past years, raising her black-white-red flag had been very important to her. "Flag flying through Sunday. Painful and humiliating for us. One must learn to bear it."[331] "The voting Sunday I have feared," she began her report on March 29, 1936, which once again encapsulated the ambivalence of the past weeks. "Still at the house door, I thought: you cannot do it. And then I went anyway. . . . At the booth, the sign that Jews are not eligible." Despite everything, Solmitz voted for the NSDAP party ticket and recorded the overall result in her diary with obvious approval: "99 percent for the Führer. That must make an overwhelming impression abroad. The Germany formerly eternally discordant and torn apart by parties, confessions, and tribes."[332] And Solmitz was also enthusiastic about the political events after German troops marched into Austria, even as she repeatedly admonished herself, in light of the impending vote, to "remember that one is excluded from the Volksgemeinschaft, like a criminal, an unworthy person."[333]

The Reichstag election also made the Jewish teacher and historian Willy Cohn particularly aware of his exclusion. On the day before the election in 1936, he had still noted in his diary that perhaps it was good that "we Jews . . . now for the first time have no right to vote, that we stand outside. Now we also no longer bear any responsibility; we cannot be at fault for any outcome."[334] Yet on election day he noted that it was "a very strange feeling, the first election to not participate," which made him think "about the war and the sacrifices that one has made for Germany."[335] Two years later, the Jewish doctor Emil Kronenberg from Solingen was unwilling to accept his exclusion from voting, and in his private notes he started an essay entitled "My Vote," occasioned by the Reichstag election and plebiscite related to the annexation of Austria. Not to be allowed to vote was "insulting," Kronenberg admitted, even if "everyone knows that it is not a vote, that men and women are being forced." Nonetheless, he wanted "nothing of his dignity" to be lost because of the exclusion. "Who can take it from me? No one! All of the roaring sounds being made in the world and in world history are incapable of this. So I will vote anyway," Kronenberg decided. He then asked himself the polling question and reinterpreted it in his own terms as the question, "Do you dedicate yourself to humanity?" And, by writing, he cast his vote and explained it with a detailed rationale. Kronenberg answered the question with a "quiet yes," writing an impassioned plea and impressive text with which he claimed his right to participate.[336] Yet he changed nothing about his real isolation and exclusion. His vote had no place in the elections and plebiscites staged by the regime.

The elections and plebiscites of National Socialism were inseparable from the question of political commitment and social belonging; this question basically defined the significance of the mooted alternative between saying yes or no, because voting events compelled individuals to make a definitive choice. At the start of National Socialist rule, many Germans had found a position toward the Nazi regime that refused the demand for unqualified commitment and declared their basic support for the new regime only as a mixture of proximity and distance.[337] For many people, this enabled them to hold fast to their independent political judgment and to claim belonging at the same time. In voting events, however, this ambiguous commitment could not be maintained because casting a vote required choosing between approval and rejection. Given the violence against nonvoters and no-voters and the exclusion of German Jews from voting, it is not very surprising that many Germans chose approval. Before the Friedrichs—the Aurich pastor and his wife who refused to vote in 1938—encountered the "mob" assembled in front of their house, they ran into their "neighbor Überdiek, inebriated on the wall," who asked Friedrich why he did not vote. Friedrich's answer—that he did not vote "because of the Church," that he did not believe in Hitler but rather believed that "God had sent Hitler"— did not satisfy the neighbor. "But you should not have done that," he responded to Friedrich's explanation. "Herr pastor, you are placing yourself outside the Volksgemeinschaft."[338] This is precisely what diarists like Hans Maschmann, Otto Kirchmann, and Daniel Lotter wanted to avoid, in part because they feared the consequences of social isolation but also because it did not conform to their political attitude toward the Nazi regime. Thus the decision forced by the regime between yes and no, between approval and rejection, engendered a form of commitment that people decidedly understood as not being in support of the Nazi regime, even though they knew full well that the regime ultimately benefited from their *yes*. All the same, their conduct has important implications for today's interpretation of the voting results of the 1930s. Given such political behavior, the simple conclusion that the "overwhelming majority of the German people did vote 'yes'"[339] is plainly unsatisfying. And instead of verifying the assumption that the voting results would "presumably not have been much different" even "with free voting under the supervision of the League of Nations,"[340] the analysis of the voting behavior of the German people and their thoughts about their ballots shows the wide extent to which voting events manifested a form of political support in which individual conduct and the conditions of National Socialism's political system were closely interwoven.

Thus voting events of the 1930s do, in fact, point to the conditions and mechanisms of political integration under Nazi rule, but not in the way suggested by historians when routinely referring to voting results as indices of comprehensive societal consensus. The reason voting events are a very questionable "gauge" for "mood of the population"[341] is not primarily because of the utterly unquantifiable influence of manipulation, mobilization, and violence. If one not only looks at the voting results but takes an interest in the votes themselves and the voting behavior of the Germans, it becomes clear, first and foremost, that the voting figures were ultimately very much the result of a specific political situation. Voting events formed singular moments in the political communication between the "leadership and Volk" and for precisely this reason cannot be used to draw conclusions about the "general mood." Instead of demonstrating the existence of comprehensive societal support per se, the voting events reveal above all the regime's ability to produce special moments of political integration. With voting events tied to momentous government decisions, the regime succeeded in creating phases of intense politicization: through the controlled deployment of mass media and extensive grassroots voting campaigns, in voting events the regime could generate dynamics that drew the entire population's attention to its policies. This occurred not by unifying the political views of the German people but by synchronizing the fluctuating attentiveness of their political behavior. In the 1930s, the two basic polarized forms of political behavior that defined the political culture of National Socialism also governed the voting events. On one end of the spectrum, voters tried to publicly show, as demanded, their "faith" in the regime by becoming involved in voting campaigns and casting their vote such that all could see; on the other end, the voting events provoked intensive discussions about the purpose of voting, the accompanying voting propaganda, the political development of the regime, and ultimately the question of how one should personally vote. Between these poles lay quite a diverse set of concrete modes of behavior, and people could more or less deliberately tend toward one side or the other. That they nonetheless ultimately voted yes across the board was directly related to the transformation of the political rationalities that informed the political actions and evaluations of individuals. The choice between approval and rejection was no longer a balanced alternative, because approval under these conditions encompassed a much broader range of political opinions. It could include great enthusiasm, but also partial dissent and individual positions founded on ambivalence.

The voting results conceal a web of modes of individual political behavior, mass-media presentations of politics, and regime activities that was far more complex than the extremely high approval figures suggest. Even though the results proclaimed substantive consensus, the integration of the population into the political system of National Socialism was ensured primarily by the specific communicative relationships between the government and the governed. This configuration did not conform to the official idea of unity between "leadership and Volk," yet the regime nonetheless benefited from any type of approval, regardless of the thoughts underlying individual votes. In its public policy, the regime repeatedly referred to the extremely high approval figures as evidence for the popularity of its policies. And during the voting events themselves, the regime tried to stylize these events as memorable symbols. In the Reichstag election of 1936, voters received, along with buttons for having voted (Abstimmungsmarken), an elaborately designed "commemorative sheet" so that they could long recall that they had given "my vote to the Führer" on this day.[342] Just how successful the regime could be in this regard is shown by the diary of Anna Deiker, the daughter of a Bonn professor, who first spoke about regime politics during the 1936 election. In May 1937, she reported in her diary on the crash of the airship *Hindenburg*, which she had seen on election day in Bonn. "Because of unfavorable weather, one-hour landing maneuver; then exploded just before landing. Terrible! Tragic! Incomprehensible! . . . On March 29 last year this proud ship passed over us in the morning sunshine. And now it is destroyed with so many human lives."[343] The fact that Deiker could mention the date of the election in her report was not just the sign of an especially good memory. Rather, in many official accounts, the propaganda had turned the voting date into a code for the unity between the "leadership and Volk." Deiker's report about the accident cited a political symbol, one that even she, as a diarist who barely showed any interest in political events, could firmly recall. Herein lay the political value of the elections and plebiscites: the regime used them to successfully establish an effective symbol for the success of its own policies, one that suggested all-encompassing support, even though behind it stood a substantially more complicated system of political integration and diverse political behaviors and evaluations.

8

THE PRIVATE AND THE LIMITS OF THE NATIONAL SOCIALIST POLITICAL SYSTEM

EVEN THOUGH THE NAZI REGIME DESTROYED THE DEMOCRATIC mechanisms of political decision-making and thus the population's opportunities for codetermination within the first months of its rule, the political system of National Socialism was largely set up for the involvement of individual Germans. Its corresponding capacity to create opportunities for nondemocratic participation and to violently coerce political participation is shown particularly clearly by an analysis of voting events. Yet precisely because this places the focus on exceptional phases of politicization when the Nazi regime was able to force Germans to confront regime policies in a way that extended deeply into their personal living environment, the question about the general reach of the political system outside of these special moments remains largely unresolved. What was the significance of "politics" for normal life under the Nazi dictatorship? Where did the boundaries run between the private and the political system? These are the questions that I now pursue in this chapter, which, with this complementary perspective, broadens the previous analysis of the individual's involvement in the political system and examines the degree to which the political system permeated the private. The analysis of the boundaries of the political system will also bring together various lines of argument and results that have been developed thus far.

The relationship between the private and the political system constitutes a core problem in the analysis of the political system of National Socialism, but not only in hindsight. It also preoccupied people during the 1930s—for example, the Berlin resident Charlotte Beradt. Born in 1901 in Lower

Lusatia as Charlotte Aron into a Jewish family, the young woman grew up in the capital and during the Weimar Republic worked as a journalist, including for the *Weltbühne*, which was strongly involved in the struggle against National Socialism. In the 1920s, she joined the KPD, but she broke away from Communism in the mid-1930s. Given this biography, the start of National Socialist rule encroached sharply on the young woman's life. As early as February 1933, she was denounced by a neighbor and detained for one night, whereupon she hastily fled her own apartment to stay with the lawyer and writer Martin Beradt. She had already been working for him as a private secretary since 1920, but they also had a long-standing intimate relationship. In summer 1938 while still living in Berlin, the couple married. One year later, her husband, who was also Jewish, was finally banned from working as a lawyer, and the violence of the November pogrom made it impossible for them to ignore the threat not only to their occupational life but also to their existence. Thus a few weeks before the start of the war, the couple fled first to London and a few months later farther to New York.[1]

Charlotte Beradt experienced the encroachment of politics during the 1930s more intensely than most Germans, but unlike Sebastian Haffner and other émigrés, she did not reflect on it in autobiographical texts.[2] Even though there was no longer a chance of publishing anything after 1933, she continued her journalistic work precisely on the question of the nature of current politics: until she fled Germany, she collected dreams. A few weeks after Hitler's appointment as Reich chancellor, an acquaintance had told her about a dream in which he was raising his arm in a Hitler greeting, but could only do so with immense effort: "It took me half an hour to get my arm up, inch by inch." Joseph Goebbels, who was present, "showed neither approval nor disapproval as he watched my struggle, as if it were a play." When the man was done, Goebbels "said just five words—I don't want your greeting—" and left. The scene played out in a factory in the presence of the entire personnel, and the dreamer was the factory manager. "There I stood in my own factory, arm raised, pilloried right in the midst of my own people.... And so I stood until I woke up."[3] Charlotte Beradt was fascinated by such dreams. For her, they depicted the political system's general incursion into the private in an extraordinarily forceful manner. "When a person sits down to keep a diary," she later explained, "this is a deliberate act, and he remolds, clarifies, or obscures his reactions. But while seemingly to record seismographically the slightest effects of political events on the psyche, these dreams—these diaries of the night—were conceived independently of their authors' conscious will."[4]

Charlotte Beradt wrote down the dream of the factory manager and began asking friends and acquaintances about similar dreams. "I asked a dressmaker, neighbor, aunt, milkman, friend—generally without revealing my purpose, for I wanted the most candid and unaffected responses possible.... A number of friends who knew of the project helped me gather material. The most important single contribution was made by a doctor who had a large practice and could query his patients unobtrusively."[5] In this way, she found out about more than three hundred dreams that reflected the political impositions of Nazi rule. Beradt recorded them, hid them away at first, and finally sent them as encoded letters to various addresses abroad, "where they were kept until I myself had to leave Germany."[6]

Twenty years after the end of the war, Charlotte Beradt assembled a selection of around fifty dream protocols, which she first published in German and later also in English.[7] *The Third Reich of Dreams* met with great interest both in Germany and in the United States. It found many readers, was reprinted multiple times, and has continuously remained important until today. The book made quite a prominent splash in the research of Nazi social history. Many historians have drawn on it to incorporate individual dreams into their accounts.[8] Detlev Peukert used Beradt's dream descriptions to great effect at the end of his influential survey of early research into the history of everyday life under National Socialism.[9] And Reinhart Koselleck, who wrote the afterword to a new edition published by the Suhrkamp Verlag in 1981, recognized her collection as a "first-rate source" for the "niches of seemingly private everyday life" that were penetrated "by the waves of propaganda and terror." According to Koselleck, her book was of "unique historical value as a source"[10] because it gave historians access to "levels that even diary entries do not reach."[11]

What the many moments of recourse by historians to Charlotte Beradt's dream descriptions fail to consider, however, is that *The Third Reich in Dreams* was anything but a plain "documentation," as Koselleck called the book.[12] This was noticed more clearly from a different perspective. The very same year the book appeared in 1966, it was reviewed in the predominantly Marxist journal *Das Argument* by a psychologist, who read Beradt's book not as a particularly intimate testament of the times but with the eye of a scientific critic. According to the reviewer's summary, in her book Charlotte Beradt tried to "prove that fascism went all out and nobody, even at night, could live in a reservation."[13] For her the dreams "served as a 'practical case' for Hannah Arendt's totalitarianism theory," with the author attributing "so much meaning" to the dreams "that she uses them as a criterion of a specific distinction between 'totalitarianism' and 'democracy.'" The reviewer found this interpretation unconvincing. He did not believe Beradt's representation of National Socialism, which had never been "such a fully conditioned science-fiction state," "not even in the program." Above all, he reproached her for inappropriately withholding "private determining factors" of the dreams and their "unexpressed latent" dimensions of meaning and instead forcing them into the corset of a deliberately political interpretation. Indeed "all of these dreams," the reviewer pointed out, "can also be dreamed in other times and in other countries; over such a short time span, the story just changes the props."[14]

Clearly reflecting an analytical approach to dreams that went back to Sigmund Freud, the review showed no understanding for Charlotte Beradt's historicizing interpretive method.[15] Nonetheless, it drew a fairly accurate picture of the book. In actual fact, Beradt was not just intent on redacting her transcripts of dreams from the 1930s; rather, she used her dream protocols to formulate a specific interpretation. She wanted to use the dreams to reveal that "the dictatorship's incursion right from the start into the person's most private realm, night and sleep," was a feature of this political system and thereby warn against political extremism.[16] In so doing, she mixed her 1930s notes about dreams with knowledge about National Socialism, tutored first and foremost by Hannah Arendt. Beradt had come to know the theorist while exiled in New York; they became friends, and in the 1950s she translated various essays into German for Arendt. In the 1960s, when compiling *The Third Reich of Dreams* from her dream transcripts, she was decisively influenced by one of Arendt's basic theses: that a particular feature of totalitarianism is that it does not only control political and public life but also implements the complete monitoring of private life.[17] Against this background, Beradt felt that the dreams described "more precisely and with greater subtlety" than awake contemporaries "ever could [have done] ... a phenomenon which later political scientists, sociologists, and medical experts were to define as the nature and effects on man of totalitarian rule."[18] Yet her book did not just refer back to scholarly research. At a time when political science and historical scholarship still focused almost exclusively on the analysis of the political structures and decisions of the Nazi dictatorship, with *The Third Reich of Dreams* Charlotte Beradt published the first empirical investigation of the boundaries of the political system in National Socialism, revealing by way of dreams how the reach of the system extended all the way into people's sleep.

On the question about the private and the boundaries of the political system, Charlotte Beradt's book simultaneously indicates two things. First, her project of collecting dreams in the 1930s attests to the already contemporary experience of the blurring of the political system's boundaries. Second, the book she published in 1966 was not simply the textualization of this experience but also already part of her scholarly interpretation. Even though Beradt mostly lets her dreamers speak and limits herself to brief commentary, by way of selection and organization she formulated an interpretation of National Socialist rule. The dreams in her collection show the "direct effect of totalitarian rule on its subjects" through the destruction of a private sphere protected from state access, which occurs in light of the blurring of the political system's boundaries.[19]

This was documented in an almost exemplary manner by the dream of a "life without walls," which Beradt places at the beginning of her account and which for her formed the quintessence of "dreams dictated ... by dictatorship."[20] In 1934, a forty-five-year-old doctor had a dream in which, after finishing work, "I was just stretching out quietly on the couch to relax with a book on Matthias Grünewald, when suddenly the walls of my room and then my apartment disappeared. I looked around and discovered to my horror that as far as the eye could see no apartment had walls any more. Then I heard a loudspeaker boom, 'According to the decree of the 17th of this month on the Abolishment of Walls ...' [ellipses in the original]"[21] The "dream imagery," commented Beradt, "so well illustrates the predicament any individual who resists collectivization must face that 'Life Without Walls' would be an appropriate title not only for this chapter but also for a scholarly study or a novel about life under totalitarian rule."[22] Also at the end of her book, when she again underscored the "lesson contained in all these political fables that were dreamt during the Third Reich," she summarized her argument with the "warning that totalitarian tendencies must be recognized ... before we begin to actually live the 'Life Without Walls.'"[23]

Charlotte Beradt's dream analysis was not only the first but also remained one of the very few source-based investigations into the limits of the political system in National Socialism. "To date there is very little empirical work on the private sphere in non-liberal regimes," Paul Betts accurately noted in reviewing the current state of research, and he blamed this mainly on the persistent influence of theories of totalitarianism.[24] Closely tied into the Cold War confrontation between the Eastern and Western blocs, the discussion about the difference between democracy and totalitarianism decisively contributed to making "a free private life" "a very marker of liberal democracy."[25] Privacy appeared in this sense as "the natural and exclusive offspring of liberalism and a distant relationship between state and citizen."[26] Thus for most scholarly observers, the question about the bounded nature of the political system, whether for the Communist regime or for the Nazi dictatorship, never arose or rather was answered from the outset with the interpretation Charlotte Beradt put forward in her analysis.

Moreover, in historiography about the Nazi period, the specific constellation in which social-historical research into National Socialism began in the late 1970s ensured that the question about the contours of the private in the Nazi dictatorship received very little attention. First conducted under the category of everyday life, research into the society of National Socialism has already gone on for forty years, fundamentally expanding the understanding of the National Socialist system of rule. But its early stages were heavily disputed. Alltagsgeschichte—the history of everyday life—was subjected to heavy criticism, which held that its perspective ultimately "came down to opposing the small world against the world of politics and political rule, of ideology and national events." A "contemplation of the National Socialist period from the viewpoint of the experiences and behavioral forms of the little people" who are "hardly active in the historical process" would lead "to a minimization, a trivialization of the catastrophic event" of National Socialism.[27] In the colloquium "Alltagsgeschichte of the Nazi Period: New Perspectives or Trivialization?" Klaus Tenfelde warned, for example, "it could easily happen that the enthusiasm for the normal, banal, and plainly routine someday conjures Hitler out of the social history of the Nazi period," and he seemed skeptical whether "everydayness [constitutes] *the* segment" of the National Socialist past "that [leads] us to the heart of a historical knowledge that is meaningful to the present."[28] In reaction to this criticism, proponents of the history of everyday life vigorously emphasized that the "goal of Alltagsgeschichte of the Nazi period" was "to convey new and more precise knowledge of this rule and its mode of operation."[29] The "ordinary," according to Martin Broszat, was "not being considered in its own right, but being made visible precisely in its connection to the extraordinarily political."[30] Historians of everyday life such as Detlev Peukert or Alf Lüdtke stressed this repeatedly: that the point of research into everyday life was precisely to reveal National Socialist policies in the everyday life of the "little people."[31] Even if the scholarship of Alltagsgeschichte basically tended to see itself as a perspective opposite that of totalitarian theory, many of the findings it brought to light against this background dovetailed nicely with Charlotte Beradt's phrase of the "life without walls" and upheld her interpretation: the "atomization" of the individual in an everyday life dominated by violence and political monitoring,[32] as well as the far-reaching access of local regime actors into private residences and everyday contexts of life.

While in the past thirty years research into everyday life and social history has therefore often affirmed the thesis about the far-reaching politicization of the private sphere, at the same time, "the private" and the associated question about the boundaries of the political system were never prioritized as a central research subject.[33] Even the term *private* itself was hardly used and did not receive the kind of basic thoughtful attention that was awarded to the category of the everyday. If "the danger of trivialization" could only be avoided by ensuring that "the ordinary is not considered in its own right but is set in relation to politics as the extraordinary,"[34] then the concept of the private, which denotes the opposition between everyday life and politics, could hardly be appealing. Hence, in studies of everyday life and social history, it appeared primarily in connection with the analysis of behavioral modes that stabilized power. Reference was made repeatedly to how individuals reacted to the many political demands in the public sphere by "retreat[ing] to private protective areas."[35] This retreat relegated "'politics' to spaces outside one's own area of perception,"[36] whereby the studies always emphasize that the concentration on personal life and one's own four walls ultimately contributed decisively to the stabilization of the Nazi dictatorship. Even if Germans used the "retreat into the private sphere ... as a personal protective wall against the totalizing aspirations of National Socialism,"[37] this behavior also meant "nonresistant integration."[38] Likewise, the private has been interpreted as a resource for National Socialist policy. Regarding political denunciations, for example, it has been shown that they were often based on "private motives."[39] And in the same way, approval of the Nazi regime has been traced back to the regime having realized "what millions of Germans had long yearned for in their private life."[40]

These arguments too were part of the general emphasis on the thorough politicization of the private, but they drew a substantially different picture than Beradt's dream protocols. The dreams described the private sphere as a place where people experienced the political system's incursions as particularly obtrusive and irritating. Scholarship about everyday life, in contrast, characterized the private as something that drew its political importance precisely from the circumstance of having still remained apolitical and "normal." In the dichotomy between these two different pictures, the boundaries between the private and the political system remain diffuse. In this respect, I would like to attempt to draw more precise contours here, using diaries to ask about where the reach of the political system in National Socialism stopped. This is not to claim, in response to Charlotte Beradt and Reinhart Koselleck, that diaries actually document the experiences of contemporaries better than descriptions of dreams, nor is it to question the project of a historicizing (as opposed to a psychologizing) interpretation of dreams. Regardless of whether the dream protocols should be recognized as having the "character of a preliterate event even if they were written down after the fact" and to what extent they transport political or personal meanings,[41] diaries seem to me to be informative for the question about the boundaries of the political system above all because this textual form, by virtue of its history, is particularly closely linked to the private. Diaries allow for a more comprehensive look at the private in Nazi Germany than do dreams.

Dimensions of the Private in National Socialism

The close relationship between the diary and the private becomes comprehensible by looking back over the development of the difference between the "public" and "private." This look can also be used to develop a more precise terminological understanding of the private. The term *private* relates to the formation of modern statehood during the transition from the Middle Ages to the modern period, arising initially in the sixteenth century to describe persons who were not officials. *Private* meant "the exclusion from the sphere of the state apparatus."[42] At this time, *public* was still a synonym for *statist*, with the words *public person*, for example, denoting a state servant.[43] *Private people*, on the other hand, were the subjects, who stood opposite the authorities and were excluded from political participation. While the distinction between private and public therefore originally indicated whether persons or things were part of the political system, these terms acquired their current effective meaning during the transition to modernity.[44] The word *private* still referred without interruption to something not belonging to the political system. But as terminologically appropriated by the emerging bourgeoisie, it no longer signified deficiency but rather was used for the self-assured reclamation of a separate sphere meant to be inaccessible to the state. Private was henceforth considered in the positive sense to be an apolitical area governed by different behavioral logics than those in the public sphere—an area through which the bourgeoisie aspired to be politically involved: in the public sphere, private people came together as a public and discussed their own interests and via public opinion formulated claims vis-à-vis the political institutions, which were now made increasingly responsible for ensuring the possibility of an untroubled private life. To this end, the private was conceptualized as a complementary sphere, which was supposed to be characterized not by the rationality of politics or economic life but rather by individual freedom, romantic love, and personal self-realization. Here "private people [understood] themselves as independent" of those behavioral logics that applied in the political public or in occupational life: "simply as human beings who could enter into a 'purely human' relationship with each other."[45]

At the same time, the private was closely linked to the small bourgeois family and above all to the bourgeois household, which as a safe haven isolated from the outside world was supposed to form the basis "for finding oneself" and becoming aware of one's "true" feelings by confronting one's own interiority. In the "intimate small-family relationships," the bourgeoisie discovered their "subjectivity,"[46] which also was supposed to form the basis for economic and political activities but not be determined by their constraints. Even business partners or acquaintances with different political views were supposed to be able to engage with one another in the private sphere on a "purely human" level outside all differences. For the pursuit of self-awareness, a range of practices evolved within the bourgeoisie, with reading and writing techniques taking on an especially important role. This also included diary writing, which admittedly already looked back on an older tradition, yet which in the eighteenth and nineteenth centuries was informed by the distinction between public and private and thus rose to become the prototypical medium of the private. Here bourgeois individuals could commune with themselves in solitude, questioning and sounding out their own interiority. Protected from the gaze of others, they were supposed to be able to gain unclouded self-knowledge through daily examination. Thus the idea of the bourgeois diary, deemed a "*journal intime*," staged the model of the private on a small scale, something that the lock-and-key diary albums emerging in the late nineteenth century exhibited already by virtue of their external form.[47]

Naturally, this model of bourgeois privacy was an ideal type that in historical reality remained fractured in multiple ways. The notion of an apolitical private space free from domination has been revealed as an ideological construct, especially from a feminist perspective, with the gender order operating precisely within this construct to massively constrain the life options of men and women. Not least, diaries can be used to show that the private households of the bourgeoisie did not simply cultivate "purely human" togetherness but rather were governed by specific preexisting emotional regimes for the individual's emotional life, within which people had to fit their own experience.[48] And with the emergence of the modern social-welfare state in the late nineteenth century, governmentally institutionalized options for intervening in private spaces—which earlier arose primarily from the domain of policing—also spread to spheres in which persons did not violate valid laws. Ever since its creation, the private was and remained political. But as an ideal-typical model, the idea of a private that is separate from politics and that is supposed to enable people to know themselves and achieve a self-determined lifestyle on the basis of that knowledge, had a lasting effect: with this model, one could demand the delimitation of state power,[49] something that was also codified with the emergence of the legal system. This is how the ideal-typical model of bourgeois privacy shapes the general understanding of the private and the diary to this very day.

Even though diary writing had fundamentally changed since the late nineteenth century, emancipating itself from the constraints of bourgeois writing practices, the idea of the diary as a medium of privacy still remained influential. In the 1930s, too, diarists still often viewed their writings as expressions of their own inner being, as something intimate that had to be protected from the eyes of others. In the covers of diaries, one still finds words admonishing that this "book [is] to be read by *no one*."[50] And writers frequently appeared outraged if others read their diaries without their permission. "Ten times worse than breaking into a letter," the white-collar employee Werner Stock commented angrily when, after a fierce conflict, his wife confessed to having read from his diary.[51]

The continued acceptance under National Socialism, even by the state, of the interpretation of the diary as a private medium is illustrated, for example, by a March 1937 verdict of the Reich Court, which in a landmark decision had to determine whether political statements "in the closest family circle" should be interpreted as insults to the Reich government. In the case being tried, a mother had written disparagingly about the Nazi regime in letters to her son, which were discovered and confiscated during a police search. Because of these comments, the letter writer was subsequently convicted under the defamation paragraph of the Criminal Code, against which she filed an appeal with the Reich Court. The litigation basically turned on whether "insulting statements in very confidential letters of a mother to her politically like-minded son," with whom "strictest secrecy from other persons" had been agreed, could even be actionable under criminal law. This was affirmed by the Reich Court when it rejected the appeal, because it saw the "enunciation . . . to another" person, even in the case of "confidential communications in a circle of friends," as fulfilling the necessary factual elements of the insult. Even "if confidentiality is promised," extant within the conversation between family members is "an intentional enunciation to another." As emphasized by the court, the factual elements of an insult are not fulfilled only "if the committer is conducting a soliloquy that, according to his belief, no other person can or is supposed to hear, or if he confides his thoughts to a diary that is not intended for the information of other persons."[52] Naturally, this decision did not mean that politically critical diaries discovered during residential searches elicited no consequences on the part of the Nazi regime's security apparatus, especially given that the Gestapo certainly did not feel that its actions were constrained by court rulings. The young Socialist Wilhelm Scheidler, for example, was taken into protective custody in fall 1933 and imprisoned in the Osthofen concentration camp after his diary was found during a residential search.[53]

Nonetheless, by virtue of how the Reich Court placed the diary alongside the unobserved soliloquy as a matter of course, the court decision illustrates the widespread nature of the interpretation of the diary as a medium of the private, even in the 1930s. In fact, Wilhelm Scheidler was ultimately acquitted in the court proceedings brought against him for malicious statements against the government because the state prosecutor never managed to prove that he had made the diary accessible to others.[54] Against the background of this understanding, diaries, in particular, strongly raised the question about the relationship between politics and privacy for Germans, and even just the degree to which diaries of the 1930s spoke about politics can be read as an initial answer to the question about the boundaries of the political system.

A brief look at the terminological history of the private does not just explain why diaries promise to provide informative insights into the boundaries of the political system but also helps us more precisely grasp the dimensions of meaning of *privacy* as a term. The bourgeois concept remained dominant beyond the twentieth century for the understanding of privacy, but it established "two different semantic models," which today equally invoke the term *private*.⁵⁵ For one, the term refers to spatial arrangements in which individuals are protected from the view and access of others, such as in their own residences. For another, the attribute *private*, however, also designates certain individual actions and decisions that can be made in private spaces as well as outside these spaces. With this dimension of meaning, the term aims at "a protected sphere of action and responsibility" in which individuals may act independently from external—for example, political—influences.⁵⁶ Both dimensions of meaning equally refer back to the bourgeois model of the private as a certain place where individuals can become aware of their "true" feelings and needs, which enables them to have a self-determined life—here the two dimensions of meaning are still causally connected in that spatial privacy is considered the precondition for private life. Yet this connection is no longer necessary in today's understanding of the term.

Nonetheless, previous theses about the private in National Socialism usually address both dimensions of meaning. The dream of the "life without walls" in Charlotte Beradt's interpretation did not just describe in a heavily symbolic way the aforementioned abolishment of private safe havens, which it also underscored in that she could trace the dream back to a tangible event—namely, the incursion of the block warden into the dreamer's apartment.⁵⁷ At the same time, for Beradt the dream also "relates to an abstraction" and together with the other dreams forms "images of the mental and moral effects in the dreamer's inner being."⁵⁸ The dreams about the Third Reich revealed to her not just the overreach into previously protected private spaces but also "the psychological extremes to which one can be driven by outside encroachments on one's innermost sphere, and how man can react in his very depths when the powers that be make it too difficult for him to love his neighbor, even the one dearest to him."⁵⁹ Indicative of the destruction of private spaces, the dreams thus opened for Beradt a perspective on the "psychology of totalitarianism"⁶⁰ and documented the "remaking [of] man" into persons "soon to be totally subjected."⁶¹ Extending across spatial boundaries, politicization "alienated [the individual] not only from all that is real in his life but also from his own character," ultimately stripping him of his subjectivity and self-determined life.⁶²

In a similar way, historical studies of everyday life repeatedly concluded from the destruction of a protected spatial privacy that self-determined decisions and intact self-images were impossible, even though these studies lacked sources that might have documented the inner reactions of contemporaries. Detlev Peukert, for example, emphasized that the frequent retreat into the private sphere too remained an illusion and that, "as a result, even in the last safe havens of private life, there was still the pressure to monitor oneself, to be wary of the surroundings."[63] This made it impossible for the person to "still [remain] oneself." Even if individuals opposed the encroachment of politics into their own life, "all elementary everyday relationships had lost the dimension of self-evident trust," as a result of which the person ultimately became an "individual divested of social relationships" in a totally "atomized" society.[64] Hans Dietrich Schäfer formulated this thesis in an especially pointed way, drawing on psychological models to make the case that Germans of the 1930s and 1940s had a "divided consciousness," which arose from boundless politicization.[65] He too stressed that this did not just apply to those Germans who got involved in the "simulated order of the Third Reich."[66] Even in places where "the Self ... disappointed in the state, withdrew and tried to bring reality into a bearable form through an extremely restricted focus on its inner world, being cut off from relationships triggered feelings of fear and helplessness; the consequence was apathy, paralysis, and letting oneself drift uncontrollably."[67] In the following, I argue that this falls short and that an understanding of the private and the boundaries of the political system in National Socialism can be developed first and foremost against the background of a separate consideration of the two dimensions of the private. In my view, diaries indicate above all that the private as a space separate from the system and the private as a lifestyle based on self-knowledge changed in different ways. I thus first turn to spatial privacy and ask about how far the access of the Nazi regime reached into private living areas. In so doing, I focus chiefly on the individual's personal residence as the classical location of privacy. After that I look at the private as a self-determined lifestyle. Although private spaces remain an important point of reference here as well, I no longer approach it from the side of the state but ask instead to what extent individuals could still control their premises and the political system's access to their own private sphere.

1. Private Spaces

If one queries diaries of the 1930s about the private in the sense of spatial arrangements, even just an initial glance can already provide abundant evidence for the thesis of an unlimited politicization during the Nazi period.

Diaries frequently document political institutions accessing and encroaching on the everyday life of Germans and their private safe havens. The way people intensely dealt with political subjects in their diaries is itself an expression of this: the Nazi dictatorship penetrated all the way into the entries of the diary, which writers viewed in the classical sense as a miniature of the bourgeois model of privacy and dedicated to reflections on their own inner being.[68] The breadth of insight into the modes of operation of National Socialist rule that this type of source can provide today is a direct consequence of the altered boundaries of the political system of National Socialism. This finding does not just confirm previous research theses. It also coincides with what leading regime politicians and experts in constitutional law highlighted in the 1930s as a central characteristic of the new political system and as its crucial difference from the Weimar Republic. As emphasized in a lecture in 1935 by the Prussian minister president and Reich aviation minister Hermann Göring, for example, National Socialism is, unlike the "bygone era," not determined by "the idea of the night-watchman state, according to which the state has nothing more important to do than to ensure that no harm comes to the individual in his strictly demarcated private sphere."[69] Instead, National Socialism proceeds "from a completely different, more natural conception of life and the state," in which the "primary element" is "not the individual but rather the community of all Volk comrades." [70] Thus a space for the individual that was basically protected from the access of the state could not exist. Constitutional legal experts of the Nazi regime also disputed, along these lines, the existence of private space withdrawn from the access of state institutions and protected by the constitutional state. Authors like Ernst Rudolf Huber and Otto Koellreutter lauded the "internal pervasion of the personal sphere of life and law with public ties" and stressed that the new political system, "with its decidedly anti-liberal attitude," was striving for "a markedly strong expansion of the 'political' sphere of life" at the expense of the private.[71]

Theoretically, this aspiration for the political system's boundless access was all encompassing, but it impacted the Germans in varying degrees. Göring's reference to the "community" as the overarching "conception of life and state" in National Socialism already indicates that the Nazi regime was not just intent on shifting the boundaries of the political system but rather made the state's access to private spaces itself dependent on political categories. The diaries of the 1930s forcefully illustrate the implications this had for various Germans, and thus they also provide for a second, more precise look at the private in National Socialism, allowing us to draw more precisely the contours of private spaces and the logics of their politicization.

Destroyed Privacy—Politicized Private Spaces

Because the private, too, was construed in relation to the category of the "community," the political encroachment into private safe havens was felt most forcefully by people deemed "enemies" and "opponents" by the Nazi regime. Jan Petersen, the Berlin Communist who reworked his diary notes from the first months of National Socialist rule into a novel, did not organize his experiential accounts of the terror of the SA and police with precise descriptions of the transformation of his surroundings merely by happenstance. The state's massively violent incursion into the residential neighborhoods of workers during the first weeks after Hitler's appointment as Reich chancellor strongly exemplified that boundless politicization which also would not halt at spaces hitherto distanced from the state—not even at the home, the classical locus of privacy.

While Petersen used the spatial order of his street as a leitmotif in his novel to work out the far-reaching and rapid social changes of the Nazi seizure of power, the brutality of this process found expression particularly in the incursion by the new power holders into the apartments of the protagonist (Jan) and his comrades. Time and again, the young comrades reassure one another that their apartments are "clean" of incriminating materials, and soon Jan stops keeping his writings at home because his own apartment no longer seems sufficiently secure. One of the most striking episodes from *Our Street* is a nighttime residential search during which Jan's friend and comrade Franz almost gets arrested. Only because Franz's mother is a light sleeper and hears the SA men and police in time as they clatter up the stairs at night does her son manage to escape through the window, while "behind him" there is already "thundering at the door of the flat." Remaining in the apartment are his mother and sister Käthe, who opens the door. "Her mother stood behind her. They had slipped on their coats. They both jumped back from the blinding glare of the electric torches. Pistol barrels flashed. The first man pushed the door wide open with his foot; it flew against Käthe's arm. They came into the kitchen: four special police [i.e., SA men] and two Schupos [i.e., regular police]."[72] Petersen described in detail how the intruders did not so much search but lay waste to the apartment. How they "threw the bedclothes to the floor, lifted the mattresses high and let them drop with a thud. Two S.A. men went into the kitchen. The women heard crockery clattering. They were moving the kitchen dresser. An S.A. man stood at the bookcase. He examined every book carefully; threw some to the floor. . . . The broad-shouldered man had flung the wardrobe open. He rummaged in all the suit pockets, even felt the hems of the dresses. He threw all the things already examined on to Käthe's bed. Then he took the pictures down and tapped the walls. He smashed a Lenin portrait on the edge of the table."[73] In the process, the SA man leading the troop threatened the women and asked about Franz. In Petersen's novel, he "shouted" and held "a pistol at the old woman's breast." They turned "their lamps on Käthe," and the SA man "suddenly went right up to the mother."[74] Petersen found powerful images for the intrusive violence of the nighttime incursion into the apartment, which he contrasted with the reactions of the two women: as Käthe opened the door, "her mother's hands, that were holding her coat together, suddenly stopped trembling." The sister, too, "pulled her coat closer, turned up the collar in front." In their responses to the SA man's threatening questions, the women speak "firmly," and Petersen has them speak assertively with exclamation marks.[75]

The contrast between rampaging SA sadists and imperturbable, stalwart Communists is well-known from the postwar antifascist literature geared to the ideal of "Socialist Realism."[76] However, in Petersen's novel, which was already written in 1934, this cannot be interpreted as resorting to a canonized constellation of figures that, by idealizing the Communist resistance, was meant to help politically legitimate so-called real socialism. To be sure, here too it is undoubtedly a stylized literary representation that cannot be read directly as a true-to-reality description of a historical event. Yet this stylization is precisely what gave expression to the experience of personal helplessness in the face of a political violence that advanced all the way into one's own private space, which Jan Petersen and other political opponents of the Nazi regime experienced as early as spring 1933. Given the unrestricted access of the political system, how better could the author have safeguarded the dignity of his protagonists than by equipping them with dauntlessness and fortitude?

The helplessness against political actors who were no longer bound to previously existing limits and who advanced all the way into personal private spaces is also found in accounts by German Jews about the massive violence of the pogrom in November 1938, even in cases where individual persons were fortunate enough mostly to escape the excesses. In late December 1938, a German Jewish refugee, who had arrived in New York just a few days earlier, wrote a long letter to relatives still living in Germany. Originally from the Palatinate, Siegfried Bernhardt* reported extensively on his experiences over the previous weeks: about the Sudeten crisis in September, during which he and his mother resolved to emigrate, moving from their small hometown to Mannheim to prepare; about the violent excesses they witnessed there on November 10; and about the arduous effort to organize their escape to the United States in the following weeks. The author pointed out that he could report everything "naturally only in very broad strokes because otherwise I would have had to write an entire novel."[77]

Nonetheless, his letter forcefully documented how deeply he had been disturbed by the violence of the anti-Jewish pogrom, particularly because of the infringement of private space. On the morning of November 10, Bernhardt had been out and about by car in Mannheim to sort out emigration matters, and along the way he saw the damage to Jewish stores and a synagogue. The first thing that came to mind was a "break-in . . . since one had not yet heard anything at home," but then he encountered "troops of approx. 15 to 25 men with axes and picks" who were smashing the installations in Jewish businesses. "So this was my initial experience in the morning on the way into the city," Bernhardt summarized in his letter, emphasizing that he was "initially of the opinion that the synagogues and businesses are being destroyed and with that everything is done."[78] Attacks on Jewish businesses and facilities had occurred time and again in the 1930s and had increased over 1938 with the radicalization of anti-Jewish policy. The actions taken against shops and synagogues occurred within an already familiar context, even though the boycott operations of the previous years had usually transpired without such widespread devastation.[79]

Yet what made Siegfried Bernhardt panic on November 10, and what he also powerfully described in his letter from exile, was that this time the violence reached the homes of German Jews. At midday, he learned "that these troops now also went into private apartments and there were smashing everything to pieces and the men were being arrested." Bernhardt drove "immediately home to Mother and prepared her and our house people," with whom they were staying in Mannheim, "for a possible visit by this company. As I stood on watch behind the curtains, such a troop also came through our street, but went past our building and around the corner. Three buildings down from our apartment, we then saw the books, pillows, clothes, household goods, etc. flying through the windows onto the street."[80] For fear of being arrested, Bernhardt left the apartment and drove back and forth through the city with the car. While doing so, he saw "that this destruction in the apartments was now in full swing." When driving around seemed too conspicuous to him, he went through the streets on foot and joined the spectators who gathered during the rampages. He did not return to the apartment where he was staying until the evening. "You heard that in the afternoon everything had blown over, yet you did not trust whether somebody might not come anyway who would get you because you had been forgotten." He was so afraid that he could not sleep or eat.[81]

Compared to others, Siegfried Bernhardt could still count himself lucky on November 10, 1938. He avoided arrest, abuse (which was often fatal), and the destruction of his private property. Yet nonetheless, the November pogrom had a drastic impact on him. The pogrom marked a profound break for Jewish life in Germany, and not just because of the concrete violence experienced by hundreds of thousands of German Jews in November 1938.[82] The marauding SA troops abused and killed many people. They smashed windows, business facilities, and home furnishings. And they destroyed those private safe havens that, although having been severely restricted by antisemitic regulations over the past few years, had basically been preserved because the latter also established legal limits. Because their private safe havens had initially seemed safe, many German Jews had believed that they could somehow ultimately come to terms with the anti-Jewish laws.[83] But the intrusions into homes and the violence that often spared not a single piece of furniture or equipment made it unavoidably clear that any chance for this was gone.

The housing shortage in the wake of the devastation strongly amplified this experience. The pogrom left many homes uninhabitable, forcing many Jewish families to seek accommodation with acquaintances, a situation that lasted weeks and months. Erna Becker-Kohen, who came from a Jewish family, converted to Christianity, and was married to a non-Jewish German, reported in her diary as late as April 1939 on a visit to Frankfurt am Main to see her mother, who had been "driven out of her house" during the pogrom. Becker-Kohen was deeply alarmed by her mother's state and the conditions in which she now had to live. "Her fear peers out of her eyes so sad and dear, how that distresses me. Where is she supposed to go? Is there not a single good soul in the big city anymore? Who will take pity on the Jewess, the woman of an alien race?"

Her mother was temporarily given "a small, squalid chamber for a few days," but she could not stay there permanently. Becker-Kohen tried to find her a better abode and "after much searching found a small place" in a convent where the "Vincentian Sisters, with much love, have accepted those with a different faith." But the new living situation did little to change the old woman's unfortunate situation. "Poor Mother! She is full of fear and completely intimidated," Becker-Kohen wrote in her diary, concluding her report about the search for an apartment, in the course of which the worried daughter, "apart from so much grief... [could] no longer bear the smug shelteredness in the house of my [non-Jewish] mother-in-law."[84] With the Law on Tenancies with Jews in April 1939, which made it possible to evict Jewish tenants and concentrate them in certain buildings, the Nazi regime ensured that residents rendered homeless because of the destruction during the pogrom continued to move closer together. The cramped living conditions of German Jews in so-called Jewish houses made them aware of their lack of private safe havens on a daily basis.[85]

Apart from the violent residential break-ins and the effects of the devastation of homes, another major factor in the destruction of private space in the pogrom was that state institutions no longer protected the spaces of German Jews. The boycott operations of previous years had always existed in tension with the state's monopoly on violence, which was disrupted by local SA and NSDAP activists[86] in violent operations against Jews and then at least superficially restored by the police when the actions ended. But this changed in the November pogrom. In many cases, assaulted Jews or neighbors called the police, but they did not intervene. And the raiders who came in the wake of the organized groups of thugs demonstrated just how defenseless this left Jewish spaces.

In the Rhineland on the night of November 9, 1938, a woman locked herself and her son in the bathroom as SA troops approached, and from there she first heard the "terrible smashing and screams" from the neighboring apartments. She then witnessed how the intruders finally broke down her apartment door as well and "with hatchets and pickaxes immediately broke my entire apartment to bits. The windows were smashed in, the furniture flattened, everything smashed to pieces, the pictures were cut up, the rests and seats of the furniture were hacked apart, and finally all of the furniture pieces were thrown on top of each other."[87] She found it especially shocking that, shortly after the uniformed intruders moved on, "private people came who started to plunder and steal in the apartment. They pulled out the genuine carpets. They took the men's clothing, women's clothing, linens, silver, in short everything they could take was carried out of the apartment. . . . Anything that was still whole was smashed to pieces by these people, and above all they searched for things that they themselves could use."[88] These people included many neighbors and the building custodian, who that very same night tried to evict the family from the apartment. Plundering was explicitly prohibited in the instructions to local Nazi activists, but it frequently occurred and made the loss of spatial privacy in the pogrom especially obvious.[89] In places where state authorities still protected Jewish property or went after plunderers, these measures aimed at Aryanizing the objects in an orderly and controlled manner but not at restoring private safe havens.

The assaults on individual persons also continued after the rampages came to an end. As late as January 1939, during her visit to Hamburg, Erna Becker-Kohen heard "daily . . . about new assaults on Jews. Who inquires into that?"[90] The wild plundering was often superseded by formal methods of expropriation, which for their part further advanced the destruction of Jewish privacy. Also in January 1939, the Berlin resident Thea Baumgarten, for example, reported in love letters to her husband on how she was combing the streets in search of Jewish residences that would soon be available. At one residential property company, she received a tip from a broker that "in the Konstanzer Straße, for example, fifteen Jews are still living in his buildings, whose terminations they are gradually expecting. . . . An apartment in the Konstanzer Straße: three rooms with a closet, hot water, heat, elevator RM 125. Grand buildings where I could endure for eternity. I left my address there and asked that they think of me in case of a 3½-, 4-, or 4½-room apartment. Then I properly scoured all of the cross-streets of the Konstanzer Straße. For one, namely, Jews galore are still living there today. Second, a bus travels through the Konstanzer Straße to Zehlendorf, and, for another, on these streets one building is always more magnificent than the next; the Jews certainly knew where it is beautiful. A very nice concierge woman in one of these buildings promised to write me immediately should Jews give notice."[91] In another letter the next day, Thea Baumgarten added that "in the upscale Jewish quarters long lists of things for sale are posted now at every second building" and described the offerings to her husband. "Among other things, one often reads Meyer's Conversation Lexicon. I believe I could buy it dirt cheap." The woman painstakingly listed the other items and asked her husband how much he was willing to pay for them. "Or are you actually against this?? Just write me your opinion. For orientation a few prices: dining room 100, men's study 80."[92]

Behind the massive sale of Jewish private property after the pogrom was, for one, the "atonement payment of Jews of German citizenship" in the amount of one billion Reich Marks, which was ordered immediately after the rampages and meant to force German Jews to pay for the damages collectively; separately from this, specific cases of destruction were to be remediated by the owners of residences and businesses. Second, the widespread "Aryanization" of Jewish private property was part of the massive and headlong exodus triggered by the violence. Charlotte Beradt and Siegfried Bernhardt were not the only ones who emigrated. After the violence of the pogrom, "there were very few Jews left who were not on the lookout for a place of refuge abroad," and even though only a fraction of them "still managed the leap across the border," this nonetheless meant that tens of thousands left their country over the next nine months before the war began.[93] In many cases, because of the restrictive emigration rules and high costs of fleeing, the spatial privacy of German Jews materially disintegrated almost completely. Erna Becker-Kohen visited her mother in Frankfurt the next and last time in August 1939 to help arrange her exit to Brussels. From there, the elderly woman was supposed to emigrate further to Chile, where Becker-Kohen's sister Ruth had already fled a few weeks earlier. The diary entry reported at length on the difficult goodbye. Becker-Kohen was under no illusions: it was goodbye forever. "I will never see you again." Embittered, she ended the entry recounting the emigration of her relatives, after which, "apart from a few photos of my loved ones, no mementos of the parental home [were left]. What was not stolen had to be sold to be able to pay for the expensive ship passage for Ruth."[94]

The pogrom of November 1938 and the ensuing exodus show particularly clearly where the connection of the private to the category of "community" led: while Germans declared as "enemies" and "opponents" lost the right to private spaces outside the access of political institutions, other Germans endeavored to profit in their private lives from the destruction and dissolution of the privacy of people who were "alien to the community" (gemeinschaftsfremd). The political system tightly bound the existence of private spaces to social belonging and the individual's commitment to the Nazi regime, which fundamentally politicized the private in the 1930s. Belonging based on individual commitment to the Nazi regime formed the decisive precondition for private spaces to be recognized as such by the political system, which meant that an apolitical private sphere could basically no longer exist under the Nazi dictatorship. Private spaces were not destroyed everywhere, but they were only respected by political institutions when their residents were recognized as belonging to the Nazi regime. Against this background, even the verdict of the Reich Court concerning the punishability of political conversations between family members, which affirmed the political system's very far-reaching access into private space, was sharply criticized in the *Juristische Wochenschrift*, the specialized journal for lawyers in the National Socialist Association of German Legal Professionals. According to the critique, by focusing on the question of whether an "enunciation to others" obtains, the verdict ultimately followed an obsolete "*individualistic* line of thought that is no longer admissible today." The court had thereby "wholly [neglected] the essence of the insult," which must be determined not formalistically according to the question of whether the statement was directed to others—and thus was public—but substantively.[95]

In terms of spatial arrangements that are out of bounds to access by political authorities, privacy was not supposed to exist; rather, privacy was to exist only as part of the political system. The intrusion of political actors into the homes of Germans declared as "enemies" and "opponents" and the lack of state protection of their spatial privacy formed in this sense a forceful expression of the fundamental politicization of the private, which rendered inconceivable the existence of safe havens that were detached and separate from the political system, and which ultimately turned the life of these people into a "life without walls." However, as emphasized already by Richard Grunberger in 1971, "most Germans never knew the constant fear of the early-morning knock on the door." Rather, "up to the outbreak of war most people retained the impression that within their own four walls life remained appreciably unchanged."[96]

However, the coupling of social belonging and privacy also had an ongoing impact on the private spaces of mainstream society by creating the constant need to verify that these spaces were political and associated with the Nazi regime. The less obvious counterpart to the violent intrusions into the homes of "opponents" and "enemies" (and also not comparable in terms of its consequences for residents) was the regular decoration of private homes with flags and the symbols of the regime on holidays and for political events. The regime vigorously pushed to achieve its ideal of a comprehensive political configuration of public space by also including private spaces, which led to repeated demands that people make their own homes part of the Nazi regime's political enactments. Particularly at the start of National

Socialist rule, many Germans struggled with the appeals to fly flags and show other standardized forms of commitment because they wanted to express their ambiguous personal standpoint even when using the strictly unambiguous symbols of National Socialism. Within the context of mutual observation among friends and acquaintances, neighbors and relatives, this produced a social dynamic that transformed the everyday social fabric and contributed to the isolation of all those Germans who were not allowed or did not want to commit to the regime.[97] Public commitments with the symbols of the Nazi regime, however, did not just communicate individual belonging and thus contribute to the exclusion of others; it also blurred the separation between private and public space. By way of such public commitments, private spaces were firmly identified as part of the political system while indicating that the system's principles and norms applied there as well. Even without the violent intrusion of political actors into personal residences, in the 1930s an apolitical spatial private sphere unaffected by the political system no longer existed.

Opportunities and Limits of Political Access to Private Spaces

The Nazi regime did not obtain categorical access to all private spaces but rather only where it doubted the commitment of their residents. However, this did not mean that it refrained from influencing the private spaces of Germans viewed as "Volk comrades." Quite the contrary, it simply used other access opportunities. Above all, the Nazi regime tried to use the NSDAP to create new instruments that would allow the political system to influence the immediate living environment of the Germans.

The structural reorganization of the party had become a necessity because of the flood of new members in spring 1933. At the same time, however, the extensive reconfiguration of NSDAP structures in the 1930s was also specifically meant to create opportunities for influencing spaces that were previously largely beyond the political system's reach.[98] First, the organizational changes included the differentiated articulation of the Nazi movement into a far-flung organizational network that was supposed to cover the entire life of the German people with its manifold formations and associations. Among the new Nazi organizations emerging in the early 1930s, the German Labor Front and National Socialist People's Welfare were especially important. They included many more people than the actual party, which was now called "the political organization," and they could actively help determine the lives of the Germans in a serious way through their influence on the economic and social policy of the Nazi regime.[99]

Second, the party structures themselves were also geared toward expanding the political system into the private spaces of individuals. After 1933, local party organizations were set up as central contact points that "were competent for practically all questions from the population at any time and with their presence were also to indicate to people that they could turn to the Hitler party in their part of the city or their village with their problems at any time."[100] In spring 1934, Ortsgruppenleiter (local chapter leaders) were obliged to hold regular consulting hours for the population.[101] Moreover, it was recommended that local chapters set up their own "Nazi advice centers," which were "widely spread" throughout Germany "in the lower domains of the NSDAP."[102] This was deliberately meant to enable local party structures—together with contact points for the Labor Front, People's Welfare, and other Nazi associations created at the local level—to act in private spaces as well.

In the mid-1930s, not only was the mission of local NSDAP groups redesigned, but so were the party structures themselves, in that the determination of territorial divisions was no longer based on the number of party members. Rather, the territorial responsibility of local NSDAP structures was now guided by the number of "households" and thus by the total size of the population that needed to be "cared for" (betreuen), as it was called in internal party jargon. In 1936, this was established first for the lowest party level, according to which the so-called blocks (Block) were now each to consist of no more than forty to sixty households.[103] Then in 1938, the local party chapters (Ortsgruppe) were also delineated according to an area's population density.[104]

The regime assigned crucial importance to the development of new political structures that reached into private spaces for realizing its plans of societal-political transformation. As shown, National Socialist policy was not limited to the violent suppression or destruction of repudiated lifestyles; instead, with its educational focus, it was always seeking to realize social transformation by motivating individuals to change the ways they lived and thought. The "very comprehensive mentoring assignment" associated with the rearrangement of party structures was supposed to help with this objective, setting for low-level Nazi functionaries the goal of "nothing less than the ideal picture of a harmonious 'Volksgemeinschaft.'"[105] A training text on the Blockleiter's responsibilities, created within the context of the reconfiguration of the blocks, accordingly instructed that he had to "take care that, in the area of his block, disputes are settled, that members of various occupations learn to understand each other and find themselves in a companionable life, the Volk comrades of his block area help each other, in short, that the Volksgemeinschaft called for by the National Socialist movement is brought about in the region entrusted to him."[106] This did more than just bear massively on the private; indeed, the basic educational orientation of National Socialist policy turned private spaces into an important political arena. This is where society was supposed to be reconfigured—namely, through the transformation of individual lifestyles and self-perspectives according to new political models and under the influence of political institutions. This is also what the Reich organization leader of the NSDAP and German Labor Front leader Robert Ley was aiming at in 1937 when he declared in a speech (often quoted in the literature, but usually abridged): "Private people no longer exist in National Socialist Germany. One is now only a private man when one sleeps. As soon as you step into day-to-day life, you are a soldier of Adolf Hitler."[107]

In contrast to the way that Charlotte Beradt and many historians have interpreted this quote, Ley was not issuing a threat related to the state's incursion into the private and the complete dissolution of private spaces.[108] Ley's postulate stood in the context of a call for individuals to practice daily "physical exercises" and in doing so help preserve and intensify the "vigor" of the "Volk." "Every individual must take part there," Ley had emphasized prior to the quoted passage.[109] His presentation was not trying to achieve state access but rather to mobilize the individual, who even in his private life was supposed to advance the Nazi regime's societal-political goals. And local party agencies were supposed to support the German people in this effort.

Nonetheless, in reality the conceptions of totality that guided the elaboration of the party structures clearly fell far short of the plan. Even the ultimately stipulated standard block size of forty to sixty households was already a compromise due to insufficient party resources. Plans had actually envisaged only twenty-five to thirty-five households,[110] but this goal seemed unreachable. In its internal survey in preparation for the reforms, the NSDAP was forced to realize that the average for the Reich in 1935 stood at 82.5 households per block, although there were large regional differences. In the Düsseldorf Gau, the average was 127.4 households; in

Württemberg-Hohenzollern, 48.[111] The central problem lay in finding suitable personnel for the many functionary positions at the lowest level. Only the growth of the party after 1933 allowed it to at least begin meeting its self-imposed objectives. Yet to do so, the Nazi leadership had to assign important mentoring work mainly to party members who had not joined until spring 1933 and who, from the perspective of party leaders, actually needed training themselves. In 1935, this cohort made up over 70 percent of Nazi functionaries at the lowest level.[112] Even at the Ortsgruppe level, expansion remained behind the party's aspirations. In 1935, for example, less than half of the Ortsgruppen had an official office, and the nationwide elaboration of basic party structures at the grassroots level did not achieve the envisaged coverage. To be sure, the number of Ortsgruppen exploded after 1933. Two years after the seizure of power, there were slightly more than 21,000 NSDAP Ortsgruppen, almost twice as many as in 1932.[113] By 1939 this number had increased again to almost 28,400 local chapters. But the party's expansion remained far below the number of approximately 50,000 municipalities registered at that time in the German Reich.[114] This too was a reason local party structures never managed to achieve the targeted level of postulated comprehensive politicization with the elimination of the political system's boundaries. The influence of Nazi functionaries remained heavily dependent on local conditions.

All the same, the party's activity itself called for a different kind of access to the private than the one forcibly experienced by Germans declared as "opponents" and "enemies." Of course, local party structures were closely involved in the violent intrusions into private safe havens and the destruction of the privacy of those considered "alien to the Volk." Not only did SA members collaborate as auxiliary police in 1933 in house searches and raids against Communists, Social Democrats, and other political opponents, as described by Petersen, but at the same time, NSDAP functionaries locally monitored the degree to which individual persons complied with the regime's demands for commitment, decorated their homes with flags, or made their "sacrifice" by contributing to the donation collections. Not least, by making regular reports, they contributed to the party's internal mood reporting system.[115]

Local NSDAP agencies often immediately sanctioned any violations they ascertained without regard to private safe havens. In summer 1935, during the wave of antisemitic boycott campaigns in preparation for the Nuremberg Laws, Otto Kirchmann—the Hamburg lawyer who had become a druggist because of his war injury—refused to contribute during a street collection by the Nazi People's Welfare. He explained that, because of the "Stürmer posters" currently being displayed, he could not support "collections for the benefit of any sort of party formation."[116] The activist collecting for the People's Welfare reported the incident, which led to Kirchmann being summoned three days later because of "a complaint matter"; at the duty station, he was then questioned about his motives and rebuked.[117] In the interview, Kirchmann asserted that he wanted to make another statement on the matter in a detailed letter, but this did not occur until almost two weeks after the incident. When, after another request from the People's Welfare, Kirchmann finally sent his letter, he first apologized for the delay, stating that "on the day after my visit to your office" he had experienced "the visit of the Kreisleiter of the party in my private residence, from which I first had to gain temporal and mental distance before I commented."[118]

Kirchmann voiced his indignation over the intrusion of a Nazi functionary (whom he mistakenly took to be the NSDAP Kreisleiter; the man actually represented the People's Welfare) not only in this introductory remark but throughout the entire letter. Once inside Kirchmann's private premises, the functionary repeated the allegations that had already been made against Kirchmann at the office and raised additional accusations: that Kirchmann commented "disparagingly about the party" in his store, refused to make the "German greeting," and was "not willing to make the sacrifice that every German Volk comrade must provide." In his letter, Kirchmann responded to the accusations at length, but above all complained about the behavior and demeanor of the Nazi functionary in his home. This outraged him so much that he backed away from his offer to donate a month's payment of his war victim's pension to the People's Welfare if they would remove the antisemitic sign. Instead, Kirchmann emphasized in his letter that he "draws from this the conclusion that I shall increase my contribution—already given monthly for many years—to the Evangelical Church Aid of the Bugenhagen Congregation, where at least it is not acknowledged with crudeness." At the end of the letter, Kirchmann made it clear that he could "prove an Aryan family tree that could withstand any kinship research," that he had "never been a member of a Freemason lodge, nor a pacifist society, nor any kind of denominational association," and "due to considerations of principle [had] never belonged to a political party." "Even today," this was something he did "not [want to] depart from." "I also content myself with being nothing more than a good German for the rest of my life. And I believe that as a war victim I have the right to see this wish respected."[119]

However heavily Otto Kirchmann complained about the demeanor of the functionary in his private premises, he also claimed his right to privacy vis-à-vis the regime by highlighting his social belonging. But the local regime representatives did not grant him this. A few weeks later, Kirchmann received a response to his letter from the Kreisleiter of the NSDAP, who with a few lines dismissed the "equally arrogant and cantankerous statements," cleared up the confusion with the People's Welfare functionary, and pointed out that he was "not in a position" "to waste my time on such hopeless cases like you. But I am glad to be able to gather from your letter that the Subdivisional Leader of the NSV, who called upon you back then, knew to answer you properly."[120] Kirchmann did not get the respect he demanded, and a few months later while the plebiscite for the remilitarization of the Rhineland was pending, Nazi activists covered the display window of his store with campaign advertising over and over again. Instead of being able to show his belonging by flying his own flags during the plebiscite, Otto Kirchmann was marked for all to see as a "deviant" who was not entitled to private protected spaces.

The political monitoring of their respective "sovereign territory" formed only part of the activity of local Nazi functionaries. The necessary "mentoring" work was a more laborious and also far more dominant part of their day-to-day activities, as shown, for example, by the "daily notebooks" of Karl Nieper, the Herne Ortsgruppenleiter and Kreisleiter, who in the 1930s regularly kept a record of the public consulting hours he held two mornings a week, during which individuals could turn to him in his capacity as Kreisleiter.[121] This work was far more banal than the rebuking of "grumblers," often barely touched on political issues (at least at first glance), and occurred not in the residences of supplicants but in the offices of the Nazi agencies. But the boundaries of the private were redefined even by way of these consulting sessions: the local leaders of the NSDAP too were aware that the goal of changing how people lived and thought could not be realized by threats, public shaming, and violent intrusions into their privacy but depended instead on their cooperation. The outline of the Blockleiter's tasks accordingly noted that his activities presupposed a "large measure of tact, careful handling of people, and the ability to empathize." The Nazi functionaries were not "commanders" of their respective "sovereign territory" but rather "spiritual advisers." The Blockleiter must "guard against gaining the reputation that he is monitoring the Volk comrades and will only cause them difficulties if they in some way do not feel at one with the worldview that we advocate."[122] Instead, such people had to be won over and persuaded.

The political system's ambition of determining and arranging the private led to the establishment of new political structures, which purposefully opened up spaces that had previously been remote from the state but in which access opportunities were also restricted by the regime's own political aspiration. With instruments of power no longer bound by the strictures of the constitutional state, it was always possible for the Nazi regime to occupy and dominate private spaces, especially by using local party structures. Yet the very societal-political plans of National Socialist policy itself opposed such an approach. These plans remained dependent on activating those Germans who were not excluded because of political or "racial" differences. Accordingly, the training material directed at the party's own functionaries repeatedly and clearly warned that "meddlesome behavior of the Blockleiter in his efforts to come into contact with a family can only have a harmful effect. There are simply people who do not like to allow third parties to look into their household circumstances, without them therefore necessarily being politically askew, or not conforming to the community."[123]

The fact that "broad parts of the population" in the 1930s "placed great value on their private sphere and did not cheerfully open the door to party functionaries" did not, as Kerstin Thieler has recently pointed out, reduce "the incentive of party leadership to want to penetrate into this area as well."[124] At the same time, however, the fundamental reliance of National Socialist social policy on "education" and the active cooperation of the German people meant that, if individuals insisted and their basic political commitment was not in doubt, then the political system's access to private spaces was revoked. Hence identifying one's own private premises with the symbols of the regime was intrinsically paradoxical: on the one hand, it declared one's residence to be part of the political system and affirmed the system's aspiration for its political categories and models to achieve validity there as well; on the other hand, however, it was precisely this commitment that deeply constrained the political system's access, because it forbade political authorities from violently intruding into private spaces, at least in places where Germans claimed their right to retreat and seclusion.

Therefore, despite the comprehensive politicization of the private, the options for action and influence in these spaces on the part of political actors remained confined to submitting offers of support and especially to appealing repeatedly to individuals that they align their lifestyles and self-perspectives according to the new political models within private space as well. This impotence helps explain the large number of educational aspirations spread by many educational actors and their fundamental importance for National Socialist policy. Because the political system only had restricted access to the private (despite the latter's basic politicization), regime actors strove all the more to bring their ideas on the realignment of individual lifestyles and self-contemplation into private spaces, above all through mass media and also in a very material way; even today, this is captured by the Volksempfänger (people's radio receiver) set up in the living room, an iconic image that is clearly ensconced in the memory of National Socialism.[125] Even those activities of Nazi functionaries that did not rely on media dissemination—recruitment efforts, dispute settlement work, the provision of practical advice during counseling hours, or personal appeals to individuals—could not function directly in the private.

As with the Nazi education project, whose actors could hardly control what would be retained in the private life of participants after their Nazi training camp experience had come to an end or what effects ideological demands would have in everyday life, local Nazi functionaries also remained strongly dependent on the cooperation of the Germans. Not until individuals picked up on what was being offered and made use of the party's "mentoring" could the political structures gain influence within the private. For Germans, this created a wide range of opportunities to codetermine how much the political system could look into and access their personal private spaces. Even though the Nazi regime established new political structures that reached deeply into what was previously private space, it nonetheless remained dependent on individual Germans to politicize the private themselves.

2. Private Life

As the look at the political system's access to private spaces has shown, in the 1930s spatial privacy was not just determined by an all-encompassing politicization. Rather, it was characterized by a dynamic in which the boundless politicization of private spaces and the expansion of the political system's access opportunities did not go hand in hand: the politicization of private spaces did not automatically entail increased maneuvering room for political authorities but rather restricted the latter in light of the regime's mobilization and educational efforts—at least in places where contemporaries could credibly claim social belonging.

This has serious implications for the oft-asserted historical thesis that the Nazi state's unbounded access to the private led to the "destruction of personality," for the equation taken from the bourgeois model of privacy does not work. Because private spaces did not become "without walls" as envisaged by Charlotte Beradt on the basis of her collected dreams, one also cannot derive the automatic process according to which "man ... [became] isolated, and so as not to fall apart because of this, [he bowed to] a pressure to conform," which ultimately only let him "survive at the expense of his inner freedom."[126] In expanding the opportunities for political influencing, the access of the Nazi regime to the private simultaneously relied on the mobilization of individuals and precisely for this reason restricted the regime's authority to exert power. Hence, for people whose commitment seemed certain to the regime, this access to the private did not move them into that inescapable situation where only self-destructive integration remained. Instead, it forced on them the need to constantly codetermine the boundary between the political system and the private in their own particular case.

This necessity applied to the entire spectrum of private life: whether and how Germans reacted to the political demands made of them by the regime in many different respects always also meant participating in the decision of how much and what influence "politics" and political institutions should be awarded in their own life. In this respect, the question about the private in the sense of a self-determined lifestyle under the conditions of the dictatorship has already been in the air in all three parts of this book. I here raise it again explicitly as a final point with regard to the deliberate political behavior of Germans, since in this context the question that directly follows from this—namely, about the boundary between the political system and personal privacy—was also very obvious to them. This topic found its way into the diaries of the 1930s with corresponding clarity, making it possible for us to understand the private in National Socialism not only from its spatial dynamics but also from the individual's own continual drawing of boundaries and from the behavioral logics that constituted this social space.

Hans Maschmann counted among the Germans who explicitly spoke in their diaries on the question about the relationship between their own privacy and the Nazi regime. In fall 1939, he described in hindsight the personal life plan that guided the way he had tried to lead his life over the last six and a half years. As he put it: "I live in a reclusion that is a voluntary banishment. But only this can preserve inner freedom for me. I would go into the disgraceful state of political and intellectual debasement were I to voluntarily join this party." The "one material attachment to this state," admitted Maschmann, who worked as a teacher in the civil service, is "the duty to my family," whose livelihood he needed to ensure.[127] This retrospective summary was not alone in being permeated by the ideas of a "classical" bourgeois privacy, according to which a "genuine" undisguised life was only possible in the seclusion of private spaces. The regular entries that Maschmann had recorded in his diary since 1933 were filled with the buzzwords of bourgeois privacy: "interiority,"[128] "seclusion,"[129] "retreat,"[130] "stillness."[131]

However, the central place of privacy in Hans Maschmann's diary is not so obvious from the many individual references. Its significance becomes clearer in the second topic to which Maschmann gave space in his diary, apart from his constant discussion of politics. The schoolteacher had started writing regularly in spring 1933 because of political events and throughout the entire 1930s wrote almost exclusively about politics, which mostly overshadowed all other areas of life. From his extensive writings, one learns little about his job, the growing up of his children, or his intimate relationships during this period. The only topic that regularly interrupted his continual political discussions was his garden. Maschmann repeatedly reported on how he had "worked in the garden," and described its "extravagant efflorescence" in detail.[132] "It will be spring. A warm rain fell today. I worked all day in the garden and was happy in heartfelt love for the earth, crops, flowers, and trees. A fruit tree radiates such joyful energy when it flourishes healthily!"[133]

In his diary, Maschmann staged his garden with literally florid descriptions as a place where he was free from the political worries that otherwise dominated his entries, where he could be himself. Yet even though the idyllic garden images interrupted his constant discussion of political events, they are also simultaneously part of them. They formed the deliberately created counterpart to his gloomy depiction of political events. "In the background of this spring is an unspeakable darkness, murkiness," he noted with regard to the political changes of the first months of 1933. "In front of this, the cherry trees stand in the fabulous field, in dormant simplicity."[134] Even the entry that spoke about "warm rain" and his "heartfelt love" of flowers and nature stood in direct connection with political discussions. Maschmann wrote it one day after the 1936 Reichstag election in a note that questioned the voting results by referring to manipulations he had personally observed, and in the same note, he wondered "whether it makes any sense for me to deal with all of these political things in this diary." He answered this affirmatively with the thought that his writings might "be of significance to my children . . . or be useful to a later objective writing of history, in which I together with my friends still believe, and which will come again. I live [in] the quiet hope that, apart from me, there still are some who record their national sorrows and burdens in this form."[135]

Maschmann thereby reaffirmed what he repeatedly stated in his diary: that in light of the political conditions of the Nazi dictatorship, it was necessary "to rescue the holiest elements of the German soul in the stillness of private life, at the hearth of the family," and to thereby preserve them for the future.[136] The reclamation of personal private spaces where he could be himself and for himself, something so obvious in Hans Maschmann's diary, was by no means an avoidance of politics. Rather, it formed part of his political behavior and evaluation, which occupied him at length by way of his constant discussion of political developments. Hence, his method of dealing exemplifies the extent to which the forms of deliberate political conduct—created by the interplay between the state's behavioral expectations, media representations of politics, and individual reactions—always contained something more: a concern about the relationship between the political system and private life in one's own case.

Accordingly, one can pursue the determination of the relationship between one's own life and politics in many diaries of the 1930s, although this determination did not always require the same kind of explicit, idealizing entries. We see it too, for example, in the way writers—especially those interested in making their own political judgments—applied an extremely narrow concept of politics to their political observations. Diarists like Daniel Lotter, Georg Witzmann, or Karl Möhring, who were just as clearly aware as Hans Maschmann of the restructuring of the political system and the growing dissolution of its boundaries, often restricted their discussion of political events to classical political institutions: governments, elections, parties. This limited focus should not simply be seen as evidence for the thesis that during National Socialism politics was "banned [by people] to spaces outside their own field of perception."[137] In their personal diaries, withdrawn from the access of the regime, these diarists deeply confronted the fundamental political questions and issues of the day, using their writing to debate political reporting. Moreover, they repeatedly discussed these things with friends and acquaintances and privately made their own political observations, which they compared to media reports.[138]

Making observations about the regime with the aim of forming one's own judgment and discussing political reporting actually brought "politics" into the private sphere; it did not push it out. This perspective did not keep politics out of one's life, but it kept out political institutions. From this point of observation, attributed to such institutions were only those fields of activity that the political system had traditionally claimed. This approach deliberately avoided reproducing National Socialist policy's dissolution of boundaries, and thus individuals continued to claim a distance from political events and their right to formulate their own political evaluations without personal consequences. The fact that so many diarists restricted their political discussions to the traditional institutions of the political system, even though clearly registering that the Nazi regime was reaching well beyond this scope, formed part of the attempt to preserve, at least for themselves, the classical separation between the private and the political even under the conditions of the Nazi dictatorship.

Looking at other diarists, we can see that this effort to delineate and safeguard personal spaces meant to be inaccessible to the Nazi regime was not a "natural" reaction on the part of the individual to the impositions of the regime. Germans who did not insist on their own political judgment often tried hard to live their private life not opposed to but with the political system, its actors, and its aspirations. This applied, for example, to all those who took up the new models of the Nazi education project and used them to align their own lifestyles or self-perspectives—namely, by trying to make themselves communal, reconceptualize their bodies, or integrate themselves into the ranks of their ancestors by researching their own lineage. Responsible for this were often not political motives but rather private interests in self-reflection and self-formation. But this notwithstanding, not only was the Nazi regime's influence on one's personal private life not supposed to be impeded; it was to be utilized to lead one's life.[139]

This also applied to many Germans who turned to the new local mentoring authorities, which were meant to make the Nazi regime appear not as a threat to individual privacy but as its guarantor.[140] In searching for support or advocacy in private affairs, Germans turned to local party agencies "for every conceivable sort of aid": "from having a window fixed, to drumming up business for a canteen, to having a child delivered."[141] Even Nazi functionaries not working in direct contact with the population saw themselves exposed to many expectations of support. Wilhelm Bollmann, the locksmith born in 1896 who in the 1930s worked as a Gau training director in Westphalia, repeatedly reported in his diary about how acquaintances, in particular, turned to him with their personal concerns and private problems and asked for support.

In October 1935, an acquaintance told him that "he had closed his business. I am supposed to help him, somehow." Bollmann felt that his opportunities to influence this case were widely overestimated, "but I encouraged him and also want to do what I can."[142] A few weeks later, it was a female employee who one evening visited him "suddenly at my stall," sat "herself in a chair and . . . started to cry. She said she had such great trust in me." The woman told him about a child living in a children's home in Kassel because her fiancé back then had left her in the lurch. "Now he [i.e., the former fiancé] wants to have the child for 2000 Marks and to take it into another marriage. . . . I am supposed to help her find foster parents."[143] Such inquiries hardly occurred because politically conscious Germans no longer wanted to resolve their problems privately but wanted to involve official agencies instead. Rather, behind such concerns, too, was the desire to benefit in private life from the far-reaching influence of the Nazi state. Yet even here, recourse to the regime's offers of mentoring was predicated on the tight connection between private life and political institutions, for the NSDAP agencies only granted support to those they deemed "politically reliable."[144] Thus individuals' private appeals for help also always opened up their private areas of life to the political authorities they addressed, granting those authorities access to their private sphere, which was precisely what mentoring work was supposed to secure for the political system.

Structured through a mutual interest in the private, the interaction between party authorities and the population often contained a very close connection between political behavior and private life. The diaries of the 1930s demonstrate this as well. Born in 1911, Franz Buesgen was an employee at the savings bank in Herne. On March 30, 1936, one day after the Reichstag vote on the remilitarization of the Rhineland, he applied to join the SA. He made the decision in direct connection with the overwhelming result of the vote. Just a few weeks earlier, on the third anniversary of Hitler's appointment as Reich chancellor, he had noted in his diary that he would "not be a bad SA man" and bemoaned that he was "not politically mature at the exact time" when "Germany's future was decided" and therefore "now [belonged to] the onlooking outsiders."[145] In light of the broad societal approval demonstrated by the vote, Buesgen had had enough with this situation and reported to the SA. "I cannot and do not want to stand apart."[146] While politically motivated, the decision to join also changed Buesgen's private life. One week after registering, Buesgen attended the "troop mustering of the SA for the first time," finished off a few related registration formalities, and looked forward to the prospect of going to work "for the first time as an SA man . . . on the birthday of the Führer," which happened to be the day scheduled for his swearing-in as an SA man. At the same time, he reported in the entry that he had received "a notification" "that my promotion letter (salary grade 15) will be handed over to me on this day. Finally an advancement," he noted happily.[147] Then on April 20, Buesgen described his swearing-in with an oath to Hitler, explaining that all new members touched the "Sturm flag" and then, after a festive ceremony, set off on their first "propaganda march." "After this, promotion. SA man Buesgen is a Sturmmann." The report closed with a sense of satisfaction that applied to both his acceptance by the SA and his professional betterment.[148]

Immediately upon joining the SA, Buesgen's political conduct and private life became closely linked, and his further entries show how greatly the presence of political actors shaped his life once he became a member. In April 1936, he regularly reported on his political activities: "Sturm evenings," cross-country marches that sometimes lasted several days, and his mandatory sports, all of which he very much enjoyed. Especially on Sundays, his diary now regularly noted, "After church attendance SA service."[149] A large portion of the time he had left after work at the bank was now filled by obligations arising from his SA membership, which also affected his diary writing. "My entries have become quite irregular," Buesgen admitted around half a year after joining. The "work at the bank" and the "SA service" made him "dog-tired" and left less room for his diary than before.[150]

The influence of political actors on his private life, however, was not just limited to the demand for time. In a lengthy entry in July 1936, he first reported on how, as part of an "ideological training session," superiors had spoken out against the Catholic Church, which clearly bothered him as a faithful Catholic. "In order not to disturb the whole group, I held myself back," he noted in his report, emphasizing that he had "sworn loyalty to two, the Lord God and the Führer, and I must keep these oaths." But this became more and more of a problem.[151] In his diary, he repeatedly spoke about the harangues against Catholicism within the SA, which climaxed in an unusually long entry about a Sturm evening in late August 1937. At this meeting, his SA Sturm had received a new Sturmführer, who in his inaugural speech announced that, in the foreseeable future, "the decision would come" to officially require all SA members to have their registered Catholic or Protestant confession "replaced by Gottgläubigkeit [i.e., nondenominational theism]." "The revisions will be carried out by the civil registries," Buesgen wrote, summarizing the statements of the new Sturmführer, who had filled them in "so that the order does not come as a surprise to you. You will need to decide. We [i.e., SA leaders] have already carried out the changeover in Berlin, etc."

The announcement left Buesgen in a serious bind. He discussed this "a little tentatively" at first with other SA men and then reached directly for his diary. "Ten minutes ago, as I put this down," he had still been "standing together with two old fighters who took a detailed stance on the entire question," Buesgen noted in his entry. He wrote at length, reproducing snippets of conversation and combining them with his own assessments, which all boiled down to the question of why there could not be a "free decision, National Socialist with or without a confession." "Have we not put our lives at the Führer's disposal, and he also wants to demand our soul? I cannot understand why the highest SA leadership is going to issue this order," another SA member had noted, and Buesgen blew the same tune: "This announcement by the Sturmführer will be going through how many heads: How do I react to this?" Buesgen pondered this problem deeply, emphasizing that he could "not say with a clear conscience . . . that the Church is nothing to me," as demanded by the announced directive, and could not see "why . . . the affiliation [should] not [be] possible," provided "the Church and its supporters honored the Third Reich and the accomplishments."[152]

Ultimately, Franz Buesgen did not need to decide, since the anticipated order never came. But the announcement led him to record in his diary, more clearly than usual, just how much he had opened his private life to the gaze and influence of the Nazi regime by turning to its political authorities. To be sure, this became especially obvious in the conflict between the threat to prohibit Christian commitments and his own religious views, but Buesgen never wrestled with the principle of SA's influence on his private life. In his diary, he only discussed the issue substantively, asking, namely, whether it was really necessary to enforce an official belief in God within the SA by way of an order. Buesgen never disputed that the SA leadership could intervene so deeply in his personal life and that he was subject to its directives even outside the specific circumstances of his service. Whereas Hans Maschmann and other diarists firmly reclaimed their own spaces, Franz Buesgen clearly understood that he lived his private life together with the Nazi regime, not in opposition to it.

The diaries of the 1930s repeatedly illustrate the contemporary awareness of the question of the relationship between the private and the political and the extent to which individuals actively tried to determine this relationship for themselves—which forcefully shows that Germans in the 1930s had not categorically lost their capacity for action and decision-making because of the destruction of private spaces. Instead, the diaries show very active and self-confident individuals whose actions actually codetermined the relationship between the private and the political and who worked very much on the determination of various relationships. They either wanted to uphold the classical distance between their own private life and politics or were willing, for the sake of personal betterment, to let political actors peer into their personal life and give them opportunities for influence. How individual Germans made their tangible decisions closely depended on how they reacted to the policies of the National Socialist regime and to the regime's demands for concrete political support. As with the political culture of National Socialism in general, here too we can conclude that the two alternatives establish a spectrum of behavior and not a clear opposition. Reclaiming personal private space to enable distanced political evaluation and practicing a private way of living that opened itself to the authorities of the political system were options that could be mutually combined. In any individual case, the relationship between the political system and the private did not need to correspond to either of these two poles, and the most widespread approach was probably to reclaim private safe havens while simultaneously drawing on specific options provided by the regime.[153]

Political Complaints and the Privacy of Others

Pointing in different directions, the active efforts of Germans concerning their own relationship between privacy and the political system were quite consequential. Through such efforts, some people tried to make the new political categories propagated by the Nazi regime apply within their private lives as well, while others upheld traditional ideas of privacy aimed precisely at ensuring that persons could still encounter one another in private without regard to having different political views. This led to a twofold situation: On the one hand, even under the Nazi dictatorship, an area remained that was different from the public sphere, in that it at least potentially accepted the validity of certain modes of behavior that were different from those found in public space, which was more strongly monitored. On the other hand, however, which behavioral logic applied in private largely remained unclear, which in turn led to many different insecurities.

For showing how strongly this uncertainty dominated the options and limits of a self-determined life in the 1930s, the diaries from this period are like a magnifying glass, especially in the context of denunciations. In the Nazi dictatorship, the direct result of the basic politicization of private spaces was not just the ability to request support from party agencies and state authorities for one's own affairs but also the opportunity to cast aspersions on other people. This ensured that individuals, notwithstanding their own efforts, could not simply determine their privacy autonomously. In conjunction with the demand for commitment and support for the Nazi regime, raised most forcefully during key political events like elections and plebiscites, Germans were constantly being asked to report to the political authorities those who violated the "duties of loyalty" arising from the Führer/followership relationship. In this respect, the basic politicization of the private not only allowed Germans to open up their personal private spaces to the regime to receive state support but also enabled them to break into the privacy of neighbors, acquaintances, colleagues, or relatives. Reports and complaints also created opportunities for political institutions to intervene in places where the affected persons themselves rejected state involvement. Despite all efforts to keep political actors out of one's own private spaces, individuals no longer held their private life completely in their own hands.

As has been worked out by the intensive research into the denunciation practices of Germans and their role in the political surveillance of German society, the motives underlying the reports made to local party offices or state authorities were usually not those political ones actually envisaged by the regime in its call for complaints.[154] Denunciations developed into a mass phenomenon above all because they could be deployed as a means of private conflict resolution. Instead of showing how people assumed political responsibility for the state, "the political denunciations of the Nazi period document all of the negative human characteristics, starting with feelings of envy, revenge, and hatred, through pure malice, nastiness, malevolence, and schadenfreude, to the blind lust for power and embittered rivalries."[155] And time and again, Germans did not just seize on actual political statements in private conflicts but deliberately tried to politicize disputes so that they could prevail with the help of political institutions.

Thus, in the 1930s it was not just at the expense of German Jews that individuals could attempt to better situate themselves in their own private life. Having already started in 1933 to map their personal environment according to people's respective positions toward the Nazi regime, Germans could profitably exploit this cartography too.[156] The Nazi regime attentively registered the private instrumentalization of political complaints and recognized that this fully contradicted its own societal-political goals. From the regime's perspective, privately motivated denunciations led to the "undermining of the trusting coexistence of Volk comrades amongst themselves" and to the "broad unsettling of family life."[157] However much official agencies called for reports, they also repeatedly castigated false accusations and attempts "'to put a political veneer' on private disputes."[158] Yet these conflicting appeals did nothing to change the fact that political reports to the political system's authorities remained "an option woven into the everyday routines of communication" of the 1930s and thus were always available to use for private purposes.[159]

But because of the various behavioral logics that claimed validity in the 1930s, denunciations did not constitute a universal tool for the pursuit of private interests, which is how they sometimes appear in the historical literature. During the 1930s, denunciations were not just inhibited by very real uncertainty about their prospects for success or by the residue of earlier social-milieu structures and the solidarities they supported—and thus by political dissent with the regime.[160] Rather, diaries of the 1930s repeatedly show how much the potential for reporting the private statements or actions of Germans confronted the tension between fending off and involving political authorities in the private. This becomes especially clear in the case of diarists who understood themselves as National Socialists and also tried to comport themselves in private in accordance with the political principles of the regime.

Born in 1913, Erich Kirk*, in his diary in April 1937, reported on a political discussion he got himself into during a chamber music rehearsal. Kirk was a student at the Stuttgart Music Academy and, given the student body's obligation to serve in the SA, had become an SA member. The duties this inevitably entailed very much bothered Kirk, who repeatedly complained about "SA coercion" and noted that he needed "first to get used to letting himself be coerced like a schoolboy again."[161] Even so, Kirk considered himself a "National Socialist."[162] This found expression in a diary report about a particular discussion during a rehearsal in April 1937, in which he bitterly complained about the "fanatical hatred" shown toward "the state of Adolf Hitler, our great Führer," which extended "even to the person of the Führer and his leading men." "How is it possible," Kirk wrote indignantly, "that a person who, by virtue of his position and his life, claims to be intelligent can lend full credence to the laughable atrocity fables from foreign countries about the supposedly medieval conditions in Germany? I cannot grasp such a thing. To suspect a man like Hitler in any sort of way amounts to a treason so egregious that it extinguishes the claim to be a German."[163]

Despite clear words in the diary that almost prototypically reflected the official demand for political loyalty, Kirk did not denounce the person involved in the discussion to the party, the police, or even just the management of the concert house. "I am in a conflict here as an SA man and at the same time as a musician who consorts in the highly musical house," Kirk wrote in his diary, reflecting openly on his own position and thinking at length about whether he had done the right thing. He had listened to the "baseless incriminations against great and meritorious men, half amused, half outraged," and now he asked himself whether his "silence [had been] a repudiation of or tacit agreement with the blasphemer." He rationalized his failure to speak up by pointing out that, "as a significantly younger man," he could not have influenced the opinions of his interlocutors. At the same time, however, he also noted, "I do not like to denounce in a political respect people whom I know and value as musical practitioners." Instead of reporting his interlocutor, the young music student thought instead about whether, "under these circumstances," he should step back from the group of musicians. But he rejected this idea, because making music together was very educational for him. "So it is simply necessary, when still playing together, to conceal my uneasy feelings in a political respect. Yet working there in this way is not a pleasure!" How many "employed persons," Kirk asked himself, probably have "to listen to such things in silence in order not to endanger their relationships and earnings opportunities?"[164]

Kirk's statements are not devoid of bitter irony, since generally in the 1930s far more Germans who were critical of the regime had to silently endure the political discussions of Nazi-minded colleagues to avoid endangering their jobs. Particularly given the many different opportunities to make denunciations and the long reach of the political institutions, constellations as described by Erich Kirck in his diary were far less typical than the opposite scenario. Yet this also makes his account informative, for the inversion of the actual power relationships clearly shows how the question of a denunciation directly confronted Germans with the contradictory behavioral logics of the private in the 1930s. On the one hand, Kirk felt it was wrong to express criticism of the Nazi regime even in private conversations. On the other hand, however, he also did not want to destroy the private situation by making a report to the political system's authorities because he "personally" knew the people involved in the discussion, valued them as musicians, and feared that a denunciation would make him so unpopular that further joint rehearsals would be impossible. Precisely the fact that Kirk made this kind of distinction between political statements and his personal relationship with his musician colleagues shows that he took classical ideas of privacy into account in his deliberations; ultimately, they also tipped the scales. To avoid endangering or even destroying the private relationship—even if perhaps for self-seeking reasons—Kirk was prepared to put aside his own political views.

The surviving materials from NSDAP agencies, police authorities, and other state agencies contain a multitude of examples of situations in which people, when weighing between the politicizing aspirations of the regime and traditional ideas of privacy, decided differently and also accepted personal conflicts within their milieu as part of the deal for making a report.[165] To the letters of denunciation that have already been evaluated by many studies and to the picture drawn with them, diaries can meaningfully add those cases in which people like Erich Kirk refrained from making reports. Scholarship focused on denunciations has generally been criticized because "the intensive study of the quantity and quality of the denunciations that are to be found in the judicial and Gestapo files" results in a skewed "overemphasis of this phenomenon," since these sources do not show the "presumably extremely large dark field of punishable actions [that] were not reported."[166] Diaries cannot help clarify any questions this raises about the scale of denunciations, but they show time and again that persistent traditional ideas of privacy could keep Germans from making accusations to the political authorities.

This can actually also be observed in the diaries of NSDAP functionaries. In October 1935, Wilhelm Bollmann, the Gau training leader in

Westphalia, noted in his diary that he had heard a conversation in a store in which a customer complained about the general shortage of butter. "When the whining became too absurd for me, I chimed in: 'Well, we won't starve!' Response: 'During the war, nobody starved either.' With that he went out, typical fat philistine. I almost kicked him in the rear." The episode only found its way into the diary because Bollmann was later annoyed that he had "let him go like that," thereby framing the event within the context of a potential denunciation.[167] Yet in this situation, even the NSDAP functionary did not react to the violation of fealty to the Führer and his policy by making a report to the party or even issuing a corresponding threat. He contented himself with merely confronting the "philistine" with his own opinion. In this case too, the conflict unfolded not according to the new possibilities created by the politicization of the private but rather within the channels of traditional privacy, which was supposed to ensure that citizens with different political opinions met on an equal footing. Even in places where people were very closely tied to the Nazi regime and understood themselves as "National Socialists," given the competing logic of politicization and the assertion of classical privacy, they too were unclear about how to behave in private encounters. Denunciations offered the persistent opportunity to make "the private public."[168] But this is also why, conversely, classical ideas of privacy stood in the way of making political reports. Despite the Nazi regime's extensive authority to exercise power, bringing political institutions into the private sphere did not simply rule out the option of rebuffing them; rather, in concrete situations, people always had to decide anew whether conflicts should remain in the private or be brought to the political-administrative level.

However, this decision was not just determined by the potential denunciator. In February 1939, Franz Buesgen, the employee at the savings bank in Herne, reported in his diary on a conversation at the home of acquaintances, during which he did not unexpectedly encounter reportable statements but rather deliberately provoked them. "We came to talk about politics, and since I know his bullheaded attitude, I coaxed him to make further admissions that could bring him into a concentration camp," Buesgen commented in his report on the visit. The conversation turned on the "megalomania" of Mussolini, fraud in the Reichstag election of the previous year, and the instigators of the violence of the November pogrom. "I cannot reproduce it word for word, but he was so foolhardy as to assert that what was happening here was just as bad as in Moscow," Buesgen wrote, summarizing the conversation, which ended when the interlocutor's daughter came along and asked that "the political speeches—the dispute—be stopped before dinner. I said that we were just expressing ourselves. Yes, she opined, politics is ghastly." Buesgen commented on this in the diary with this statement: "The way her father carries on with it, indeed!" But without further ado, he then went on with his report on the evening's conversations, which he conducted mostly with the daughter, who was quite interested in his job, his visits to the movie theater, and his book recommendations.[169]

Franz Buesgen did not report the politically precarious statements to anyone either. His response, that they were just "expressing" themselves, indicates that he too saw the situation as a private conversation. At the same time, however, on this evening he was playing a wicked game with the superiority that gave him the opportunity to make a denunciation. Yet his interlocutor's daughter, too, by ending the political conversation and shifting the discussion to other topics, had been actively concerned with what she evidently grasped as a threatening situation. The determination of the relationship between the private and the political system did not depend solely on the potential denouncers, even if they found themselves in a much stronger position of power. Their conversation partners also influenced the course of political discussions by aggressively asserting the application of private behavioral norms or, in critical situations, trying to avoid providing any reasons for a denunciation. The mapping of the social environment according to the proximity of individuals to the Nazi regime could be used in this sense too.

Even if the involvement of party and police agencies was not imperative, the tension between the politicization as intended by the regime and the ideas of privacy that still claimed validity profoundly marked everyday communications and private life, even without the direct presence of political institutions. Just how much this conflict could determine an individual's life is forcefully shown—yet again—by the diary of Hans Maschmann. His efforts to uphold the division between the political system and the private in his own life were not restricted to the idyllic stylization of his garden. They deeply shaped his everyday behavior. This did not mean that Maschmann no longer conducted political conversations; quite the contrary, he still regularly reported on them. However, he often combined them with political assessments of his discussion partners and as much as possible took care to formulate his political positions such that they did not cause offense—notably, by clearly underscoring his commitment to the regime and nonetheless insisting on being allowed to form his own opinion in private reclusion.¹⁷⁰ Yet despite his caution, he could not avoid becoming the victim of a denunciation attempt, which created a situation in which he could no longer maintain his private distancing from the political system.

In May 1939, he received a letter from Toronto thanking him for "[his] letter of February 12," which had pleased the sender very much. "And you can guess why. As an old Social Democrat and Freemason, you could no longer keep still, and so you are simply writing. When old [concentration] camp friends told me about your political stance, I right away thought: he is doing that only because he is either confused or worried. Our old Hans will never be a real Nazi." The letter praised Maschmann's political steadfastness under the conditions of the dictatorship, which he deftly knew how to conceal. "You say naturally quite rightly, when you write in your letter, that you believe in the imminent fall of this regime and are doing your best. I will send you some literature later. Your Marxist analysis was excellent.... Nonetheless, I would be somewhat more careful. You cannot afford such things." The letter was signed "your old Fritz," creating the impression of longtime friendship. But Maschmann did not know the letter writer. Instead, the letter was deliberately feigned and sent to him at his school in the hope that it would be opened there and passed on to the police. The letter was followed by two additional dispatches: "a journal from Toronto" and finally another letter, meant like the first to create the impression that it was written by a socialist émigré to a comrade who had stayed in Germany.¹⁷¹

Hans Maschmann was very frightened by the dispatches. Even weeks after the incident, when he first wrote in his diary about what had happened, he emphasized that he was now adding "the event that in the days of May not only extremely agitated me and my family but also deeply shook us and everyone I spoke to about it." In this connection, he stressed in his diary that he only wanted to live a private life in "reclusion" and to "preserve [his] inner freedom." However, the denunciation attempt had made this impossible. Maschmann was certain that the author of the letters "pursued the intention of delivering me to the Gestapo." Had they "been opened by the post office, then I would not have avoided investigative custody and a residential search, and I would only have been able to defend myself by protesting my innocence." He suspected that the instigators of the operation were other teachers from his school "who are pursuing me with hatred and where they mean to try to compromise me." For the letters, they had probably used a former colleague, with whom Maschmann had likewise quarreled and who had emigrated to North America a few years earlier. At any rate, as Maschmann learned from his personal inquiries, the relevant persons were still in contact by mail, and he had no "other acquaintances" on the other side of the Atlantic.[172]

In light of the danger arising from the dispatches, Maschmann decided to "hand over [the letters] to my administration and through them to the Gestapo," which a lawyer friend also advised him to do. Maschmann turned to his school inspector, explained the situation to him, and handed over the letters. The latter "decided to give the letters to the Gestapo and enjoined me to keep full confidentiality. He described the method by which one attempted to denounce me as a high traitor to the Gestapo as diabolical. He was determined to uncover the connections" and wanted to call the instigators of the operation, whom he too "suspected among the colleagues hostile to me, to account." For Maschmann, this was quite uncomfortable, because even though he wanted to protect himself with the official report, he personally did not want to denounce anyone. Even before he spoke to the school inspector, his wife, who was suffering under the situation, had made "the comment to our neighbor Herold that something dark bears down on us."[173] This bothered Maschmann, because even though the neighbors could "draw no conclusions [from the comment] and were not aware of the matter," "had something been undertaken against certain colleagues," they might have linked this to the comment. Accordingly, in his discussion with the school inspector, Maschmann had also emphasized that he needed to avoid doing anything, "so as not to become compromised in Volksdorf [the district where Maschmann lived]." "He replied, 'In this case you could not have acted differently; offense is always the best defense.' I could only respond that my only endeavor is, and has been for years, to live in peace and quiet, and that attacking someone is not commensurate with my character."[174]

Even in his reaction to the attempt to use the political institutions of the Nazi regime to severely harm him, Hans Maschmann found himself confronted by the tense relationship between politicization and the private sphere that he himself upheld; and while contact with the political authorities had become necessary, he wanted to keep it as narrowly confined as possible. His example clearly shows just how often Germans in the 1930s were repeatedly forced to decide on the relationship between their personal privacy and the political system, as well as how often, given their limited power of control, they were forced to make decisions they actually found objectionable. Yet at the same time, this again shows that individuals were well aware of this constellation and nonetheless still tried very hard to continue shaping their private life as they themselves determined. The specific dynamics of the politicization of the private compelled Germans to establish the boundaries of the political system in their private lives, but this situation also left spaces open for decision-making, which individuals tried to use for themselves in various ways. They were not simply victims of the politicization of the private, with its totalizing claim, but rather perforce its actors.

Hans Maschmann tried to minimize the influence of the political authorities and still uphold his lifestyle in accordance with the classical ideal of privacy, not only in his discussion with the school inspector but wherever possible. He also had made a concrete effort to maintain personal control over his privacy, despite the unavoidable involvement of political authorities. After having recently made daily entries in his diary again, he had last written two days before receiving the first letter from Toronto. With his next entry, which did not follow until one week later, Maschmann started a new notebook, in which he did not report on the incident, instead limiting himself to an allusion: "In a small place like ours, times of general upheaval give rise to hundreds of vulgarities, which although eluding the reach of the judge weigh all the more gravely before the eternal judge."[175] Not until September did Maschmann report on the events at length, recording them at the end of the diary notebook he had interrupted during the denunciation attempt. Looking back in his report, Maschmann also explained the unusual change in notebooks, which had occurred neither at year's end as usual nor because its pages were full.

Since "in the course of the event described in the following" he had been "forced to make use of the protection of the Secret State Police, I also had to expect that a residential search would also be carried out at my place."[176] This led him to bring "these my writings into safety" and to start a new notebook, where for the time being he was more ambiguous when recording his estimations of the political situation. Since spring 1933, when after a hiatus of many years Maschmann began his diary with the words "I am withdrawing to my diary again,"[177] he had filled hundreds of pages with his commentary on political developments and in the reclusion of privacy tried to find his own opinion on them. In the process, he had often sharply criticized the actions of the regime, even while at the same time repeatedly underscoring his basic support and commitment. Nonetheless, hiding his political writings from a possible seizure by the Gestapo was most certainly a prudent precaution. This action, however, was more than an effort to avoid arrest and torture. By hiding his diary, Hans Maschmann was also trying to maintain control over his private sphere, despite living in a thoroughly politicized environment that allowed political authorities to access private spaces that had previously been protected.

Private Life and National Socialist Policy

The different efforts of Germans to keep political institutions out of their personal private life or to use them specifically for their private benefit vividly illustrate one the basic features of life in Nazi Germany during the 1930s. In light of the Nazi ambition to comprehensively restructure society, private life could no longer be kept at a categorical distance from National Socialist politics and the authorities of the political system of National Socialism. Political actors often intruded on the lives of Germans, coerced political participation and support, and formulated wide-ranging aspirations with regard to their private lifestyles. Even where authorities of the Nazi regime were not directly present, private life in the 1930s always stood in the shadow of National Socialist politics.[178]

The challenges to the individual formulated by the regime in this respect differed in their intensity, which depended not just on the content of the demands but also on which individuals they affected. First and foremost, those particular demands tied most directly to the Nazi dictatorship's claim to power hardly left people any room to evade them entirely. The demands to commit to the Nazi regime and to distance "enemies" and "opponents," as well as to support the regime politically in elections and plebiscites, for example, were correspondingly comprehensive. By comparison, political aspirations with respect to people's everyday lifestyles and self-perspectives, propagated by various actors after 1933 for the education of the "new man," were less definitive because of the many different and often competing demands; hence they also did not develop the sort of inescapable pressure that ultimately confronted all Germans. Yet they too helped ensure that a private life categorically separate from politics ceased to exist in the 1930s.

For Germans, this had various implications, which depended heavily on whether individual life paths and former political views could be harmonized with the regime after 1933. Private life in the 1930s was decisively influenced above all by the question of how well a person could fulfill the demand for individual commitment. Those unwilling to make this commitment or prohibited from doing so by the regime from the outset soon found themselves socially isolated as "opponents" or "enemies," and, without safe havens, they constantly had to fear the political system's violent encroachment on their personal life. In contrast, those who met the demand for commitment usually had greater latitude either to closely align themselves with the models and precepts or to search for ways to combine their own biographical and political conceptions with the aspirations of the regime. But in these cases, too, the great extent to which National Socialist policies permeated the private life of Germans was unmistakable.

Contemporaries clearly registered the incursion of politics into their private life. Like Sebastian Haffner, they too were aware of the special "degree of intensity" of the historical happenings resulting from the abolishment of the "old distinction between politics and private life."[179] Being "aware of the remodeling of his own psychological make-up" made the émigré journalist no different "from most of his contemporaries."[180] Indeed, the political happenings of the 1930s repeatedly forced this realization on many Germans in their own life. Like Charlotte Beradt, they too described the general sense of National Socialist policy's extensive elimination of the boundaries with frequent references to the effects of the Nazi regime not only on their tangible awake experiences but also on their sleep. "Heard Hitler's election speech at the warrior monument. If his manner catches on, then we will only sleep lightly," the white-collar employee Werner Stock noted as early as March 1933 in his first entry on the start of National Socialist rule.[181]

The impossibility of peaceful sleep appears in many diaries of the 1930s as an image for the Nazi regime's incursion into personal life—as a prophecy or as an actual experience. In spring 1933, the young Social Democrat Wilhelm Scheidler barred "my bedroom door [at night], for I was afraid of the acts of violence of the local Nazis," as he recorded in his diary.[182] His fear was also reflected in many dreams about the violence of the new power holders Scheidler recorded during these weeks, which also dealt with the incursion of National Socialism into the private sphere. "I dreamed that my father was shot dead by National Socialists. I saw a horribly mutilated corpse on our sofa and upon waking up was still horrified by this image."[183] The appearance of many such dreams in his diary was also related to Scheidler's method of organizing the entry for each day under the rubrics of "morning," "midday," "evening," and "night." The degree to which his dreams, too, exemplified for him the political system's encroachment on the private sphere is shown by the way Scheidler, under this rubric of night, first defiantly announced that "I did not want to allow the Hitlers to rob me of my rest"[184] and then a few days later had to concede under the same rubric that "I never envisaged, however, the development of the political situation in this way. One is hardly physically safe and must be careful not to say too much."[185]

In later years as well, dreams with political content vividly revealed how deeply the Nazi regime penetrated into individuals' private areas of life. Born in 1896, the lawyer Fritz Koch, after having dreamed about the annexation of Austria in 1938, wrote in his diary, "Before falling asleep . . . [I] repeatedly recited the verse by Heine: 'Thinking of Germany at night, puts all thought of sleep to flight.' In this, I admitted to myself that the political situation deprives me much more of the peace of my waking life than of my sleep." But after the dream, which deeply frightened him, he corrected himself in the diary, noting that the "dream shows that the political things break into my sleep after all."[186] Whereas Koch dealt intensely with political questions in his diary at times, the textile factory worker Wolf Hofkotte*, born in 1919, was one of those Germans who, at least in their diaries, tried to maintain the fiction of a private life remote from politics. Having started keeping his diary in 1935, the young religious Christian used it first and foremost as a place to reflect upon devotions, Bible passages, and the lyrics of Christian songs and to record important events of his private life. Yet he too was unable to keep his diary free of politics.

In February 1937, Hofkotte noted "a dream that gave me much to think about," which he therefore wanted to write down. He dreamed that one morning he noticed that "the stars were [running] their course weirdly fast." He carefully observed the heavens and finally saw "the sun [rising] very leisurely in the *West*." "Suddenly a bolt of lightning from the *East* drove into the middle of the sun. In the moment this occurred, the sun rises up with a sudden lurch . . . and the *swastika* emerged clearly and distinctly in the middle of the sun." The writing "Sacred swastika!" appeared beneath the sun. "I stand there and in astonishment can neither move nor speak. Quickly the writing has already disappeared and, as I look closer, the sovereign eagle sits on the sun. Waving in the sun itself, however, is the National Socialist flag, not as the entire flag, but rather only the middle part is visible in the circle of the sun. And beneath it stands a text that says: 'Believe in the banner!' When I have read the text, I wake up horror-stricken."[187]

The political dreams of the 1930s made the new political system's deep incursions into personal life unmistakable to contemporaries as well, clearly showing them that the politicization of the private could only be evaded in part, not completely. Yet this did not mean that a private life and self-determined life decisions were no longer possible. As opposed to the conclusions drawn by Charlotte Beradt from her dream protocols in the 1960s, the dreams did not simply reveal the "people's deepest feelings and reactions as they became part of the mechanism of totalitarianism."[188] With regard to his dreams, Fritz Koch was deeply anxious to understand their "dark meaning," and to this end he obtained psychoanalytical advice literature.[189] In this respect, he saw his dream about the annexation of Austria, for example, "as the simple creative processing of a factual matter whose emotional impact in the dream essentially corresponds to the understanding in waking life," although he puzzled intensely over the meaning of specific details. And the textile factory worker Wolf Hofkotte followed up on his dream protocol by commenting that he had told his mother and a friend about the dream and that "both were dumbfounded. I myself can only (thus far) read from this that it is supposed to be a warning to me, which I want to take seriously."[190] Hofkotte did not draw on psychoanalytical interpretations to deal with his dream. But he too thought about it after waking up, told others about it, and otherwise continued keeping his diary, with its focus on religious questions and especially private events. Even if National Socialist politics pursued people into their very dreams, the dreamers were not simply at their mercy; rather, they tried to interpret their dreams and assign them a place in their conscious confrontation with the Nazi regime.

Instead of revealing the powerlessness of the individual in the Nazi dictatorship, diaries show another, highly differentiated picture of the connection between private life and National Socialist politics. They challenge today's ideas about the National Socialist dictatorship by revealing a privacy and an associated private life that do not conform to the bourgeois liberal model of the private and yet also do not simply document that "private lives [were] remodeled" to form "totally subjected" individuals.[191] They do not display that "duel" between an overwhelming and ruthless state and the "small, anonymous, unknown private man," as Sebastian Haffner described his life in his autobiography using the style of a generalized claim.[192]

Instead, diaries of the 1930s mostly show a form of private life that, to be sure, basically was not freely chosen but imposed by the regime, yet one in which people in fact made "politics" the foundation of a self-determined life. Integrating this into our picture of National Socialist rule poses a strong challenge, because the classical model of privacy is deeply inscribed in the way we have confronted the Nazi past. Moritz Föllmer and Hanne Leßau have recently shown that establishing a distance from National Socialism after 1945 relied notably on envisioning a sharp opposition between private life and the Nazi regime. This interpretation emerged only toward the end of the war and became successful over the following years because it conformed to the Western Allies' picture of the Nazi dictatorship as a collectivist regime of terror.[193] Especially through the denazification program, this interpretation found widespread use in Germany. As Hanne Leßau has pointed out, the life stories that Germans told in their defense after 1945 were often based on experiences they had had in the 1930s when positioning themselves toward the Nazi regime. However, partial differences with Nazi rule and private lifestyles, which in the 1930s had made it possible for many Germans to align themselves with the regime, were now presented as evidence of opposition and resistance.[194] This separation between private life and National Socialist politics did not just shape how individuals confronted their personal past but also how historians researched this past. This too explains the narrow focus of early research into Nazism on the political system and the highest leadership elite of the Nazi regime.[195] It formed the basis for the development in the 1980s of the concept of "Resistenz," which declared private life per se as a preliminary stage of political resistance.[196] And to this very day it informs the discussions of whether certain forms of behavior in the 1930s and 1940s must be viewed as "National Socialist" and whether or not certain persons were "Nazis."[197]

But precisely because their entries so often collide with the presumed separation of private life and National Socialist politics, diaries of the 1930s provide for riveting reading and new kinds of insights. They do not simply show how individuals tried to defend themselves against overwhelming structures. In these diaries, one can instead follow how respective authors, under political conditions purposefully laid out to change their ways and views of life, often vigorously struggled to live their own life with these structures. Even if the Nazi regime based its demand for commitment on a model that definitively distinguished between "supporters" and "opponents," many diarists worked hard at finding a way of establishing a commitment without the unqualified acceptance demanded by the regime so that they could combine their own political opinions and individual self-perspectives with the required political statement. Even where the Nazi regime forcefully established concrete symbolic forms of commitment and compelled Germans to use them, diarists thought intensely about how they could use the prescribed format to express their own specific stance toward the regime.

The political models of individual lifestyles and attitudes toward life through which the Nazi regime wanted to create "new men" influenced actual individual self-images and lifestyles primarily in situations where people could relate them to their own life: Where diarists tried to make themselves communal, this did not lead them to overcome their own interests. New body images could be adopted primarily in situations where people explored their own bodily experiences. And even the scientific categories and methods of racial studies were not straightforwardly applied with regard to one's personal origin but rather were influenced by existing self-images. The same applied to demands for political approval, in which case Germans either consciously attempted to make the ideal of unconditional faith propagated by the Nazi regime their own or tried to make their own political judgments despite the regime's obvious control of the mass media.

The diaries frequently document how Germans of the 1930s led their own private life within the conditions of Nazi rule, and this frequently set limits for National Socialist policy. The massive commitment to the regime in 1933–1934 was not based on the unqualified support actually demanded by the new regime. Consistently presented as something completely different, the "new National Socialist man" remained far less new in the private lives of Germans than the Nazi education project would have liked to see. And the broad approval visible during voting events was not founded on the unshakeable bond between the "Führer and Volk" used by the regime to legitimate its rule and policies. The realization of the Nazi regime's societal-political goals remained far behind their underlying ideas.

At the same time, the diaries of the 1930s make for readings that are not only captivating but also always disquieting. However much the process of realizing the regime's demands in private life imposed limits on National Socialist policies, this process made the policies possible in the first place. Even if commitments were not absolutely clear-cut, when mainstream Germans determined their personal relationship to the Nazi regime, they contributed decisively to the exclusion of Germans declared as "enemies" and "opponents." Although the National Socialist education project did not create the "new National Socialist man" depicted by its propaganda, it nonetheless led to a broad absorption of political categories into private lifestyles and self-contemplations. And regardless of how contemporaries reacted to calls for political support and despite whatever critical and independent thoughts they had about regime politics, this did nothing to change the fact that in elections and plebiscites, for example, most of them ultimately consented and thus contributed to the comprehensive political approval that shored up the regime.

Only in the rarest cases did the private life of Germans in the 1930s conform to the aspirations formulated by the Nazi regime, and its efforts at a new political society never made real the propagated models of the unified "Volksgemeinschaft," the "new man," or the solid unity of "Führer and Volk." But only with the massive transposition of these models into concrete lifestyles—which, given the regime's authority to exercise power, the individual often could not avoid and yet nonetheless also implemented—did the central components of National Socialist policy become realized. However much Germans searched for ways to live their own lives in the context of the politicization of the private, however much they strove for "a Third Reich, as I see it,"[198] precisely by doing so they also contributed in equal measure to the realization of the National Socialist societal project. In his thoughts on the concept of the "consensual dictatorship," Frank Bajohr has pointed out in an aside that through the "specific mixture of force and approval" that defined National Socialist rule, society itself became a "direct component of Nazi rule."[199] Diaries make it possible to understand in concrete terms what this comment means: an interpenetration of rule and private life, set in motion by the Nazi regime with its encroaching challenges to individual lifestyles, which proceeded through conflict and bore on individual behaviors, self-conceptualizations, and personal convictions—an interpenetration that remained characterized by diverse intentions and interests and required the active contribution of political institutions and individuals alike. It was only from this process that the dynamics emerged that made National Socialist rule what it was in the 1930s.

CONCLUSION

In the early morning of September 1, 1939, German soldiers crossed the Polish border with tanks, warplanes, and other modern weapons. The attack on the neighboring country that began World War II sealed the deliberate destruction of the postwar order created twenty years earlier after the First World War, which the German government had begun dismantling by withdrawing from the League of Nations and the disarmament conference in fall 1933. Officially, it always declared it wanted nothing other than to strive for a peaceful settlement in Europe. But since the annexation of Austria in the spring of 1938 at the latest, the leadership of the German Reich was systematically heading for war. In the fall of 1938, a military conflict had been imminent in the dispute with Czechoslovakia over the "return" of the Sudeten German minority and its territories to the German Reich. It was averted only because Czechoslovakia's allies, Britain and France, forced a negotiated solution by agreeing to Germany's demands just before the Germans planned to march into the country.

Since spring 1939, the German regime deliberately pursued the escalation of the already long-simmering German-Polish conflict to create a cause for war, which according to plans laid down in the spring was supposed to start no later than September 1, 1939. Nonetheless, even during these months the regime still took care to publicly announce its desire to maintain peace and to represent the attack on the neighboring country as a necessary reaction to Polish aggression. With ever more unreasonable demands and a propaganda campaign centered on the alleged terrorization of the German minority in Poland, the regime tried in August to provoke its neighbor into taking steps that would offer a justification for a German military intervention. Finally, with SD and SS members disguised as Polish soldiers and the forced involvement of concentration camp inmates, the regime staged multiple "border incidents," including the false flag attack on the German radio broadcasting facility in Gleiwitz near the Polish border on August 31, 1939, which was ultimately passed off as the reason for Germany's attack on the neighboring country.[1]

The fighting on September 1 began early in the morning around 4:30 a.m. Approximately one hour later, radio broadcasts spread the news in Germany about the start of combat operations with the reading of a "proclamation of the Führer." In this statement, Hitler emphasized that the "Polish state" had "refused the peaceful regulation of neighborly relations sought for by me," referred again to the "terror" that had been suffered by the German minority in Poland, and announced that he now had "no other means apart from henceforth countering violence with violence."[2] Then at 9:00 a.m. a special meeting of the Reichstag was announced, along with a speech by the "Führer" that took place one hour later, broadcast live by all of the radio stations. In his speech, Hitler emphasized that, "as always, here too I have tried by way of peaceful revision proposals to bring about a change of the unendurable state of affairs," by which he meant the fact that the "German city" of Danzig and the so-called Corridor did not belong to the German Reich. In so doing, he took a long look back over the ostensible peace efforts of the Nazi regime since the seizure of power in spring 1933, which had now all proved "futile." For the "Polish question" had to be solved. The German government's "love for peace," Hitler emphasized, should "not be confused with weakness or even cowardice." "I have therefore resolved to speak with Poland in the same language that Poland has used with us for months. . . . This night for the first time Polish regular soldiers fired on our own territory. Since 5:45 a.m. we have been returning the fire, and from now on bombs will be met with bombs!"[3]

On the morning of September 1, 1939, the situation many people had repeatedly speculated about during previous years became reality. Various opponents of National Socialism had already shared the slogan "Hitler means war" during the Weimar Republic, and after 1933, despite frequently expressing the desire for peace, the Nazi regime never managed to fully banish the slogan from the public sphere and German minds.[4] Time and again, foreign policy actions taken by the German government—the withdrawal from the League of Nations, the reintroduction of military conscription, the remilitarization of the Rhineland, the annexation of Austria—provoked for Germans the question of how other countries would react to Germany's unilateral actions and whether this would result in war.[5] In addition, other international developments, such as the Italian attack on Abyssinia in East Africa and above all the international proxy war emerging from the civil war in Spain, ensured that many diarists in the 1930s reflected on a possible new war.[6] Other diarists attentively registered German rearmament efforts, which grew more intense particularly starting in 1936; and ever since the previous year's reintroduction of compulsory military service, many young men and their relatives found themselves very directly confronted with the new preparations for war.[7] By no later the Sudeten crisis in fall 1938 and its dramatic international negotiations during the last days of September, the possibility of war loomed large for the Germans.[8]

When the war then started—unlike August 1914, but also unlike January 1933—there were no public outbreaks of enthusiasm or demonstrations of support in the streets and squares, neither in the capital nor in other cities. There were none of the mass marches or rallies that in previous years had so deeply shaped the public manifestation of National Socialism. This confused many contemporaries. Regime representatives and political observers at home and abroad drew attention to the difference between August 1914 and September 1939.[9] In their morale reports from the first days of the war, the security agencies of the Nazi regime repeatedly noted the lack of "war enthusiasm as in 1914."[10] In their assessments of the situation in Germany, exiled observers all noted that there was "no enthusiasm for war at all," and if one recalled "the outbreaks in the year 1914," then one must "automatically come to the conclusion" that "the mood looks very stagnant."[11]

In their entries about the start of the war, many diarists also used August 1914 as a point of comparison, among them Eduard Schulte, born in 1886, who did so with extraordinary detail. Previously, as the archivist of the city of Münster, Schulte had taken daily notes of the war-related events in the town between 1914 and 1918. In the 1920s, in accordance with a city council resolution dating back to the period of the war, Schulte had reworked his notes into a *Kriegschronik der Stadt Münster* (War Chronicle of the City of Münster), which was finally published in 1930.[12] In the final days of August 1939, as the Polish conflict intensified and military vehicles in the streets, a series of new ordinances, and the mobilization of soldiers signaled the imminent start of war, Schulte once again reached for his pen to keep a daily record. Even if the city archivist was thinking about making another official war chronicle, the entries themselves were not meant for publication. "The content of this folder 'Chronicle 1939ff' is secret," Schulte emphasized in a cover letter accompanying the diary. It was just "material" for a later chronicle of the new war.[13]

In keeping with the opening note, Schulte also did not adopt an official style but rather contemplated the start of the war in light of his own personal experiences at the beginning of the First World War. Already in his first entry, he recalled how "a quarter century ago, as I started my 'War

Chronicle of the City of Münster 1914–18,'" he had wandered through the streets to take in and document the atmosphere. Now in late summer 1939, he could only do so to a limited degree. "I'm not doing so well health-wise that I can constantly loiter around on the streets and study everything." Yet at the start of the war, Schulte recognized that the difference was not just that he had gotten older but that the manifestation of war itself differed profoundly from 1914. "No wall placards, no pamphlets, no flags, no marching music in front of troops marching out," he noted, describing the public picture of the war preparations, which had evidently been set in gear. According to his estimation, the "military machine" was already working "feverishly" in late August, even though mobilization had not yet been officially announced. It remained "almost unnoticeable from the outside; everything plays out 'underground.' . . . None of what there was 25 years ago: marching music, flower garlands, shouts of hurrah, and relatives, singing regiments, hortatory farewell banners."[14] Instead, the rumor circulated around town that in the barracks "soldiers cried! Everything is indeed altogether completely different than in 1914."[15]

Even historians have highlighted the difference between the beginnings of the two wars, pointing out that, "unlike at the start of the First World War, in September 1939 there was little war enthusiasm to be sensed in the German population. The atmosphere was wholly different, characterized by dismay, fear, apathy, passivity, anxiety, disquiet."[16] From the contemplation of the "two different war beginnings" of 1914 and 1939, many historians have also concluded that Germans felt a "profound dejection" at the start of the Second World War: instead of celebration, there prevailed a "touch of unwillingness for war."[17] Although the population did not oppose the war in September 1939, it did not go into the new war enthusiastically, but only reluctantly and with dismay.

What does this "reluctant loyalty" on the part of Germans, so often discerned by historical researchers, mean for the sweeping societal project that the Nazi regime started in 1933?[18] Between 1933 and 1939, the Nazi regime tried hard in many ways to change German society in accordance with its ideas. It did a lot to motivate those Germans that it did not consider "enemies" and "opponents" to commit themselves to National Socialism, shape their self-images and worldviews with new political models, and mobilize them to provide unconditional political support for the regime. All of these efforts were meant to bring about a solid unity of "leadership and Volk"—and also help Germany to thereby recover and preserve the solidarity it had possessed in summer 1914, the loss of which was seen by the extreme right during the Weimar Republic as the reason Germany lost the war in fall 1918.

In the more than six and a half years that lay between Hitler's appointment as Reich chancellor in January 1933 and the start of the war, the many societal-political endeavors of the Nazi regime had also in fact generated a dynamic in which many Germans began transforming their ways of thinking and behaving according to new political principles. But when the Nazi regime started the war in the seventh year of its rule, it did not look as if the "Volk" was standing behind its "leadership" or a unified Germany was going to war. As has been argued by various historians, the goal that "the Nazi regime worked toward by all available means, namely, to ignite an enthusiasm comparable to that of August 1914, was not achieved"; and accordingly, measured against its "self-set goal," one had to speak "straightaway about a failure" of the regime.[19] Did the social changes set in motion by the Nazi regime in the course of the 1930s therefore ultimately prove ineffective at the start of the war? Does the behavior of Germans in September 1939 show that, despite all of the deliberation and effort undertaken by Germans during the 1930s, the transformation they started remained nothing more than superficial?

I find that such an interpretation overlooks crucial elements, in part because a look at diaries and letters of the 1930s definitely raises doubt about arguments that confidently advance the idea of the "reluctant loyalty" of Germans in fall 1939. Moreover, with regard to the start of the First World War, precisely by using these kinds of sources, historians in recent years have drawn a far more complex picture of the social reactions in August 1914 than is asserted by the comparison of the two different war beginnings. In summer 1914, the Germans were by no means broadly enthusiastic about the war. The news of the general mobilization was received very differently in various regions and by different population groups.

In rural regions, the start of the First World War triggered mainly an "anxious-worried" reaction, which created a "decidedly dejected mood situation tinged with pessimism."[20] Farmers worried about the problems that would arise for operating their own estates because of the war-related absence of agricultural workers, and they feared the "sacrifices and devastation" that the war might bring.[21] Likewise, for cities one can "hardly estimate" how "comprehensively the 'roaring noise' [actually gripped] the population of the inner cities," not to mention the suburbs.[22] To be sure, "loud patriotic rallies" pushed their way to the foreground, but even so, "much still suggests that the basic mood remained relatively grave."[23] Moreover, in more distant city districts, it often looked completely different. Even in the capital, where observers witnessed the greatest jubilation, "the excitement of Berlin's inner city, shot through with chauvinism, had little in common with the serious mood in the working-class neighborhoods."[24] The "social-democratically oriented workers in early August still [confronted] the war more standoffishly to disapprovingly than approvingly or even enthusiastically."[25] The patriotic demonstrations and rallies at the start of the war were borne above all by the urban bourgeoisie. In particular, "students were the main carriers of that euphoric mood of anticipation, that public enthusiasm for the war which for a long time was seen as a general phenomenon of August 1914."[26] Yet the "enthusiasm that characterized the bourgeois public" gripped other social groups "only to a rather small degree."[27]

Instead of finding unified enthusiasm for the war in summer 1914, with the help of self-testimonials various studies have rendered "visible an entire spectrum of behavioral modes between the poles of fear and enthusiasm."[28] This is not much different from the range of reactions found in diaries from September 1939. Entries from various records written at this time also indicate that the start of war in 1939 was evaluated in many different ways. In fact, the notes of many diarists from the final days of August and early days of September 1939 report on the alarm and fear triggered by the onset of the war. Living in Hamburg with her daughter and husband, who was considered a Jew, Luise Solmitz attentively followed in her diary the escalating crisis with Poland and the "dark clouds of war, fear, and distress of separation" that settled on the minds of the German people.[29] With the start of combat operations, Solmitz saw Germany entering a "dreadfully feared" period "compared to which the Thirty Years War was a Whitsuntide excursion. . . . Why is it specifically us? Always us? Was 1914/18 not enough, more than enough!"[30] The elementary school teacher Hans Maschmann also hoped in the last days of August that "the nations become aware that concluding peace is more responsible than starting war," and on September 1, he had to note with resignation that "the unbelievable . . . [seems to be] happening."[31] In much the same way, the Fürth gingerbread baker Daniel Lotter prayed at the end of August that "the madness of war" could still be avoided, and after war broke out, he also held out hope that after the collapse of Poland things would "come to a reasonable agreement and rapid conclusion of peace."[32]

But diaries from the fall of 1939 also document entirely different reactions to the news of German soldiers marching into Poland. In her entry on the start of the war, Inge Thiele, the gardener born in 1914 who in her diary frequently affirmed her commitment to the Nazi regime, not only made a detailed record of Hitler's speech to the Reichstag and adopted his interpretation of an unavoidable armed encounter as her own but also reaffirmed her loyalty to Hitler, as she had already done repeatedly during earlier events: "If the Führer speaks, one simply believes him."[33] Born in 1919, Lore Walb, who in 1939 completed her schooling with a secondary high school degree, saw the start of the war as a reason to reintensify her diary writing, which had become quite sporadic in the last few months. She too did this not to record newly emerging fears and concerns but rather to take part in the historical events. "In historical days, I am taking up my writing again," she explained, opening her diary entry for September 3, 1939, in which she looked back in detail on the developments of recent weeks and finally concluded with an account of the start of the war that left no doubt about the necessity and legitimacy of the "war with Poland."[34] In the following days, Walb kept her diary again on an almost daily basis, with detailed notes pursuing the war's events and Germany's "overwhelming" successes, and she seemed "proud" of the accomplishments of the German soldiers, who conducted a "campaign" the likes of which "world history has indeed never witnessed before. It is just wonderful to be German."[35]

Not even the memory of the First World War, which contemporaries and historians alike repeatedly cited as an explanation for the supposedly worse atmosphere in 1939,[36] necessarily kept diarists from welcoming the new war. Ewald Hoffmann*, a bookkeeper born in 1910 who had lost his brother in the First World War and now in fall 1939 waited as a soldier for his first frontline deployment, recorded in his diary at the start of the war how much he loved "my field-gray comrades" and "Germany" and saw the war as new evidence for the "unified Volk," for which he was prepared to make "every kind of sacrifice."[37] Even though the mortal danger entailed by the war deployment was especially real to him in light of his fallen brother, this did not prevent him from simmering with excitement for his own deployment at the front. Rather, he considered his brother's death as an obligation for himself. "My brother, may I join you?" he asked in his diary a few weeks later. He himself had not yet been able to fight, "but brother, to take over from you, I am ready. Wilhelm, how close you are to me—I am the same as you."[38]

Many German Jews who had not successfully fled abroad by the start of the war also drew a completely different picture of the reactions of mainstream society from that of a nation reluctantly going to war. Erna Becker-Kohen, a Jewish woman from Berlin living in a so-called mixed marriage, who after the 1938 pogrom first helped her mother find new accommodations in Frankfurt and finally helped her emigrate, reported in her diary that after the start of the war she was "no longer safe in my home." "Already at the end of August, one had reckoned with an outbreak of war," so her husband brought "me with the child to a women's convent in Schlachtensee. He believed that in the enthusiasm for war they might beat me and the boy to death."[39] In his entry on the beginning of the war in 1939, the Jewish Romance language scholar Victor Klemperer did not write about a fearful population unwilling to go to war. As he did for other political events, he noted in detail in his diary what neighbors and acquaintances in Dresden were saying. His report fluctuated in this case between his own panic brought about by the news of the start of the war and the certainty of victory he detected among his discussion partners. While Klemperer and his wife thought about obtaining a "morphine syringe or something similar" so they could end their lives in light of a situation that now seemed hopeless, his discussion partners—"butter salesman, magazine salesman, cash messenger of the gas company, etc. etc."—were convinced that Germany would soon win the war against Poland and that other European countries would not intervene. "All in all: news and actions serious, popular mood absolutely certain of victory." Summarizing his observations of the "vox populi," Klemperer noted: "ten thousand times more arrogant than [19]14."[40]

Thus, the Germans did not react uniformly to the news of the start of the war in September 1939 either, and the spectrum of reactions found in diaries and other self-testimonies from the end of the 1930s is no different than from a quarter century earlier. What was different was the public manifestation of the start of the war. Yet just as one cannot simply conclude from the dominant jubilation in the press and public squares in August 1914 that most Germans actually went enthusiastically to war, the fact that the "scenery [was] completely changed" in 1939 does not mean that a "depressed mood" prevailed within the German population.[41] There is no question that "the atmosphere in summer 1939 differed fundamentally from that of 25 years earlier," but this does not demonstrate, as historians have argued, the "Germans' unwillingness for war."[42]

Rather, it is important to notice that the public manifestation of the social reactions to the start of the war dovetailed relatively smoothly with the picture that the Nazi regime tried to draw of its attack on Poland. Unlike what various historians have assumed, the propagandistic staging of the start of the war in 1939 was by no means designed to "generate an enthusiasm for war comparable to August 1914."[43] To be sure, since spring 1938 the Nazi regime had repeatedly spread the idea that Germany was being encircled by enemies, thus suggesting to Germans that "they found themselves in the same situation as in 1914, surrounded by jealous neighbors and warmongering competitors who were waiting for just the right moment for an attack on the peace-loving German Reich."[44] Yet when the war began in September, its presentation to the public did not aim at arousing memories of the cheering masses of summer 1914. Quite the contrary, the Nazi regime made every effort to avoid corresponding analogies, and to this end it even deviated from representational formats it had developed since 1933 for its public self-representation.

In mid-August 1939, as the march into Poland—first planned for August 25, then actually taking place one week later—drew closer, efforts at media control significantly intensified as well. In just the last week before the start of the war, "instructions [to the German newspapers] followed in rapid succession."[45] Almost 120 press directives were issued during regular and special supplemental evening and nighttime press conferences, several times by Reich Propaganda Minister Joseph Goebbels himself.[46] Yet unlike during voting events of previous years, the increased media control was not being used to generate mass support and collective enthusiasm. One year earlier when looking back at the Sudeten crisis, Hitler had noted "how *tremendous* the power of a press" could be against foreign countries when used and consistently controlled "as an *instrument* of leadership."[47] And this was the purpose that the mass media were now supposed to serve.

In previous years, the regime's actions during foreign-policy operations had always been accompanied by the direct appeal to the Volk, but in late summer 1939 it dispensed with this completely. From the "start of the Poland crisis," the Nazi regime "avoided looking the Volk in its face." No mass assemblies were organized; neither the Führer nor the Reich propaganda minister held any "Volk speeches" meant to stoke the mood of the population.[48] Instead of addresses, in the last days of August the radio mainly broadcast music.[49] The Reich party congress in Nuremberg was canceled at short notice, as was a celebration of the twenty-fifth anniversary of the Battle of Tannenberg planned for the end of August, both of which would have offered excellent opportunities to create images of the "Volk" cheering its "leadership" and readying for war.[50] In addition, the churches, which would have been majorly important for staging a widespread readiness for war, were informed on August 30, 1939, that "assemblies in which a position is taken on the present situation will [be] . . . undesirable in every regard."[51] In August and September, even the NSDAP refrained "deliberately . . . from the organization of demonstrations and rallies . . . whose task would have been to simulate a nationalistic frenzy of enthusiasm comparable to August 1914 among the Germany population."[52]

One year earlier, this had still been very different. At the climax of the Sudeten crisis, four days before the German ultimatum for ceding the Sudeten regions expired, Hitler had "in the decisive hour once more turned to the Volk and the world" with a speech in the Berlin Sports Palace, which was supposed to form the prelude to war.[53] The assembly was elaborately prepared by Reich Propaganda Minister Goebbels, the attending audience specially selected, the radio broadcast announced with advance notice, and the start of the assembly scheduled for the best evening broadcast time. As part of this arrangement, the jubilation triggered by the speech, which openly threatened Czechoslovakia with war, was purposely meant to recall the supposed enthusiasm for war of 1914. In order to "stage an enthusiasm à la 1914," as Hitler left the Sports Palace at the end of the assembly, the audience sang the "Fatherland Song" by Ernst Moritz Arndt, which had accompanied soldiers when they went to war at the beginning of the First World War.[54] Chanted loudly by the crowd after Hitler's speech as orchestrated by Goebbels, even the slogan "Führer commanded, we follow!" was geared toward unleashing an enthusiasm for war among the Germans and sending the nation to war as an inseparable unity of "leadership and Volk."[55]

But similar efforts were absent in 1939. The address held by Hitler on September 1 did not take place before masses of spectators symbolizing the "Volk." Staged instead in a special session of the Reichstag, the announcement of the war with Poland was far statelier, and rather than focusing on the euphoric all-encompassing support of the "Volk," it concentrated on the seriousness of the situation, which left no option apart from reaching for arms. It thus underscored the message of a nation forced to take up arms as proclaimed in Hitler's speech, which to this end even dispensed with the term *war* (a word that newspapers in summer 1914 had spread like wildfire) in favor of more nebulous phrases about "returning fire" and "retaliating." In the first Reich press conference after the invasion of Poland, the Propaganda Ministry now very expressly banned headlines "in which the word war is contained! According to the speech of the Führer, we are only striking back."[56] Instead of seeking to demonstrate general enthusiasm for the war, the public staging of the start of the war sought to convey the sense of a nation defending itself against a danger from abroad.[57] Pictures of cheering masses—which the Nazi regime had previously always used to reassure itself, the Germans, and the outside world that it had comprehensive societal support—would have contradicted this image of a nation forced to take defensive military measures.

Accordingly, unlike what had happened again and again for important political events during previous years, the Nazi regime refrained from mobilizing the German people to help stage the start of the war. On September 1, 1939, there were no calls to decorate houses with flags, which made it difficult for Victor Klemperer to believe his neighbor when he told Klemperer that morning about the start of combat operations. "We told ourselves, flags would already have to be appearing if the report was even halfway accurate."[58] The SA and SS admittedly ensured that the streets were blocked off for Hitler's drive from the Reich Chancellery to the Kroll Opera House, where the Reichstag session took place, but spectators were not specially mobilized to line the streets as when they had been recruited for voting campaigns, for example, with the help of school classes and factories.[59] And without any appeals to the "Volk," in the final days of August, the Germans had none of those occasions that in past years had created opportunities to personally participate in regime politics and that individual diarists often expected.

At midday on August 26, 1939, the Hamburg resident Luise Solmitz sat at her radio with her diary because she had heard that a "proclamation of the Führer" was to be broadcast at noon. Solmitz expected the "declaration of war" and wanted to follow this "fateful day of the first, very first order" on the radio and document it in her diary, as she had done before and as she would in fact do a few days later on September 1.[60] But on August 26, the radio broadcast nothing except "marching music." The announcement of Hitler's proclamation had only been a rumor, which had circulated in the city and reached Luise Solmitz by various routes.[61] In a similar way, the Coesfeld lawyer Ferdinand Beier complained in his diary that, when he read in the newspaper in late August that the "Führer and Reich chancellor" had met with Reichstag members, nothing was reported about what he had said. "Thus he is not talking to the German Volk at the moment," he commented on the report and thereby fixed on the precise difference compared to the public staging of major political events in past years.[62] Then when, on September 1, low-level Nazi functionaries wanted to report to the Wehrmacht and asked the Deputy Führer Rudolf Heß for leave, he announced that very evening that he had to deny "all these requests." As understandable as "the desire expressed in the requests" may be, the "decisive factor is not the desire of the individual" but rather the "interest of the whole."

"Every party comrade fulfills his duty at the place he is assigned until a new order determines him for a new assignment."[63]

The contrast of the start of the war in 1939 compared to the "August Experience" of summer 1914 was addressed openly and repeatedly in official statements during the first days of the war. The portrayal of Hitler's Reichstag speech published in the *Völkischer Beobachter* on September 2, 1939, highlighted the "quiet" mood of the Germans, stylizing it as the expression of a general dauntlessness. The article characterized the society's reaction to the "historical hour" of the start of the war by commenting, "All those things we would have liked to call out to the Führer in this hour—along with us, the millions in the expansive country—and yet we remained quiet in this moment." In this reaction, it recognized "the contemplation, the deep reflection on our devout strength and determination" of the Germans rallying around their "Führer."[64] Although the contrast to the start of the war in 1914 is only implicit here, it can hardly be overlooked, and in the following days and weeks, press articles and statements by leading politicians repeated these ideas again and again while making the contrast explicit.

In one of the first speeches by a leading Nazi politician after the start of the war, the leader of the German Labor Front, Robert Ley, expressly extolled the fact that "in Germany of today" there was "no cheap hurrah-patriotism to be found," but rather that everyone was "dignifiedly, composedly, and resolutely doing his duty to the last."[65] And still in September, a journal jointly published by the Propaganda Ministry and the Wehrmacht, which was supposed to anchor "within the entire German Volk . . . the memory of Germany's struggle for freedom," emphasized in the foreword of its first issue that "the struggle that was now forced upon Germany bears a very different character than earlier wars." "Missing are the blusterous enthusiastic rallies during the departure of the troops. . . . Every German, down to the last cottage, senses this magnitude all the more."[66] A similar point was emphasized in the summary of events that had occurred since the start of the war, which appeared in the same issue. "In contrast to the enthusiasm that was expressed with rousing rallies at the outbreak of the First World War in the first days of August 1914, the German Volk assimilated the start of the long-desired defense against Polish provocations and the declarations of war by England and France with calm and ironclad resolve." In the "serious" mood, this text too discerned "a Volk that, through National Socialist education, for a number of years has found its *inner solidarity* and does not first need to document it at a critical hour."[67]

Most notably, Joseph Goebbels insisted time and again during the first weeks of the war, even before the "Polish campaign" had been won, that the mood of September 1939 was far more promising for the further course of the war than that of summer 1914.[68] In January 1940, the minister gave an interview to the American journalist Lothrop Stoddard, who confronted him right at the beginning of the discussion with the "great difference between the popular mood now and in the last war." "There are no hurrahs, parades, bands and flowers as there were back in 1914." Goebbels confirmed the impression but pointed out that this was only because a quarter century earlier "the German people did not know what it was all about." Back then, the military and political leadership did not know how to convey to the Germans anything more than hollow phrases. But today the German Volk knew what the fighting was about, and accordingly it went to war with a firm attitude and clear understanding. "Listen, if I wanted to get the German people emotionally steamed up, I could do it in 24 hours," Goebbels underscored his assessment. "But they don't need it—they don't want it."[69] A few days earlier, in an internal lecture at the Reich Propaganda Ministry, he had already similarly pointed out that "the German Volk today finds itself in the position where he [i.e., Goebbels] wants it to be." According to the transcript, Goebbels emphasized that "if one wanted to, he could produce the enthusiasm of 1914 in three days. But he does not want that." The present "mood situation" is a "solider one, a better one for the ongoing war than 25 years ago."[70]

The thesis of a "better" mood at the start of the Second World War proved very popular among contemporaries. Karl Friedrich Kolbow, an NSDAP member since 1921 and state governor of the Province of Westphalia after 1933, noted in his diary in September 1939 that there was "no [noticeable] repetition . . . of the war enthusiasm of 1914"; "instead . . . the political understanding [is] much deeper and more serious." "The Germans have probably never before reached for weapons to defend their existence and future with such grim determination as nowadays."[71] And even the Münster city archivist Eduard Schulte, while repeatedly pointing out the difference between the beginning of the wars in 1914 and 1939, at the same time stressed that he could "discern very substantial progress compared to 1914. For blind chauvinism has given way to clear political understanding." That is "only thanks to National Socialism, which [is creating] a new worldview of the most worthwhile nature."[72]

Among leading employees in the propaganda apparatus, however, Goebbels's statements met with significant skepticism, as they have among historians, who saw them merely as an attempt to "cover up" the "failure" of the "psychological mobilization of the German population for a war."[73] Commenting on the minister's statement, the notetaker of the speech at the Reich Propaganda Ministry wrote that none of the listeners believed "that this is the real opinion of Dr. Goebbels." If so, it was a "serious error." "Such a disparagement of the intellectual and spiritual dedication of the German Volk of 1914" was not justified, and for the Reich propaganda minister to say that he "could manage in three days, or, as he commented to Stoddard, in 24 hours to generate the enthusiasm of 1914"[74] was illusory.

Naturally, Goebbels's statements were completely arrogant, if understood as suggesting that the propaganda apparatus could suddenly unleash among all Germans a genuine enthusiasm for the war—and there are good reasons to assume that this is what Goebbels meant. But at the same time, they contain a kernel of truth: The difference between the public images of the starts of the two wars did not arise because Germans were less willing to go to war in 1939 than a quarter century before. Of course it would also have been possible at the beginning of the Second World War to generate pictures of a jubilant public like those that had dominated the start of the war in 1914 and like those the regime had constantly brought forth in the past years. When Hermann Göring held a speech in the Rheinmetall-Borsig factories on September 9, 1939—the first time in weeks that a leading regime representative "spoke" to the Volk—the enthusiasm of the spectators, despite the "calm" and "serious" mood, did not differ from that of addresses in previous years.[75] In this respect, the impression of the "two different war beginnings" should indeed be attributed to the fact that this was not what Goebbels wanted: that the staging of the beginning of the war in 1939 was not meant to imitate but rather maintain a distance from the war enthusiasm of the First World War.

The differences between the war beginnings of 1914 and 1939 therefore do not prove the failure of the efforts to transform political society that largely defined the Nazi regime during the 1930s. They show instead how much German society and its members had changed between 1933 and 1939. August 1914 had marked an extraordinary moment in the transformation and democratization of the political public in Germany. To be sure, the jubilant demonstrations and gatherings on the streets and squares had only involved part of German society, but they had "profoundly changed the relationship between society and state."[76] This substantially contributed to the fact that Germans increasingly viewed themselves no longer as objects but as subjects of politics and started articulating their own demands and claims vis-à-vis the state. Notably, the street, as the public space previously used above all for imperial parades, processions, and homage ceremonies, now turned into a forum in which the "Volk" directed demands at its politicians. The particular structures of the public sphere and modes of political behavior of Germans that formed the basis for the Weimar democracy and the rise of National Socialism emerged in the First World War.[77]

This form of the political public and its associated modes of behavior also still dominated the processions and demonstrations of January 30, 1933, which emanated from the initiative of local NSDAP groups and their repertoire of public performances that were tried and tested during the Weimar Republic. Appearing in September 1939, however, was a completely different public sphere: the uniform reporting of newspapers and radio clearly showed the abilities of the Nazi regime to control the media in the area of political news. The absence of anti-war protests—of which there indeed were many in the summer of 1914, alongside the cheering processions[78]— demonstrated the level of political control that the regime had achieved over public space by means of police violence and political surveillance. Yet new controlling institutions and monitoring mechanisms were not the only things that characterized the transformed arrangement of the public sphere in 1939. Above all, the beginning of the war revealed that the behavior of Germans had become something different as well. In 1939, it was not just opponents of the war who, in light of the Gestapo and the danger of denunciation, refrained from taking their views on the new war into public space. Those contemporaries who supported the Nazi regime's decision to attack Poland or were happy about the initiated war did not venture forth in public either. To be sure, they might have complained in their diaries, for example, that by not addressing the "Volk" or not calling for the flying of flags the regime denied them the opportunity to actively participate in this event. But they never arrived at the idea of taking to the streets themselves or hanging swastika flags on their houses on their own accord. Overjoyed with Hitler's appointment as Reich chancellor, Max Dingler, the zoologist who had already joined the NSDAP in 1922, had wandered through the streets on January 30, 1933, and "watched for [an] SA procession";[79] on September 1, 1939, he was also intent on documenting his personal involvement in what was again a historical event. As at the beginning of Nazi rule, when he decorated the date of January 30 in the pocket calendar he was using as a diary with a red frame and a swastika, Dingler specially highlighted the start of the new war as well, drawing an iron cross in the date field of September 1, 1939. His entry for this day did not just directly note the start of the "war with Poland"; it also pointed out that he had dealt with "air defense preparations" at the office, blacked out his apartment in the evening, and "listened three times" to repeated broadcasts of the morning's "Führer speech" on the radio.[80] In 1933 and 1939, Max Dingler endeavored to document his participation in the day's historical event. But whereas at the start of the Nazi dictatorship this had drawn him out of the house and into the streets, the latter no longer served as the venue for demonstrations of commitment and support.

In 1914, streets and squares had become the space where Germans had so self-confidently elevated themselves as subjects of political power. After 1933, this principle had been inverted—only through the state's public relations work could the Germans now be summoned for political activities in public space to demonstrate comprehensive and unconditional support for the regime. This transformation found its true expression in the nonoccurrence of demonstrations in September 1939, as the Münster city archivist openly described in his notes on the start of the war with a look back at the war volunteers of the First World War, who in 1914 had been the "heroes of the day." Independent volunteering for war service had in fact been an important part of the public demonstration of support for the war and self-determined participation in the political events of summer 1914. Schulte traced the lack of similar numbers of war volunteers in 1939 back to the fact that, in light of the changed circumstances, volunteering for the Wehrmacht had become "irrational." "For the most finely prepared operation of the military machine, every volunteer would virtually mean a disruption of the apparatus. Everything is registered, every individual is temporally earmarked. The individual, too, must wait until his turn according to plan."[81] In the course of the 1930s, the Germans did not simply become apolitical or apathetic. They dealt intensely with politics, aspired to take part personally in political developments, and aligned their own ways of thinking and lifestyles according to new political categories. But they had developed new forms of political behavior that referred to the public relations work of the regime in a way that no longer included the independent articulation of political convictions in public space, won in 1914. Unless organized by the Nazi regime itself, even those Germans who backed its decisions no longer demonstrated their support on the streets.

The dynamics of social change that set in with the start of the Nazi dictatorship and whose reach could be seen at the start of the war did not end in fall

1939. They continued into the 1940s. But the war signified a decisive break that led to renewed changes, if only because the shared experiential context of German society that existed during the 1930s increasingly dissolved. A large part of at least the male German population consisted of occupying or frontline soldiers spread throughout the entire continent of Europe in wartime deployment. On the "home front," the bombings, which affected various parts of the Reich quite differently, and the growing differences between urban and rural regions due to food rationing and evacuations increasingly destroyed previous experiential contexts.[82] This deeply changed the underpinnings of individual and collective communication and put an end to many institutions that had decisively shaped the 1930s. Mass festivals like the Reich party congresses or the harvest festivals on the Bückeberg no longer took place during the war, nor did elections and plebiscites.[83] Even the number of speeches made by Hitler to the "German Volk" declined substantially during the war.[84] New forms had to be found for staging the unity of "leadership and Volk." As part of the self-staging of the Nazi regime, other themes gained importance, such as ceremonies to honor the fallen, which had to give meaning to previously unfamiliar experiences. Not least, the arrangement of the public sphere established in the 1930s, which was especially closely intertwined with forms of behavior developed by Germans during these years, changed massively in the 1940s, in large part because of the devastation of German cities and its effects on public topography.[85]

The challenges to the individual formulated by the Nazi regime at the start of its rule did not disappear. But under the conditions of the war, many of the ways of thought and lifestyles adopted by Germans in reaction to the new challenges in the 1930s could no longer be maintained, had to be modified, or took on previously unknown meanings. In addition, the war itself posed new challenges to the individual, which took their place alongside demands for basic commitment, the change of individual lifestyles and self-perspectives, and political support of the regime, combining with them or forcing them into the background. The encounter with "enemies" and "opponents" in occupied territories, as well as with the millions of prisoners of war and civilians brought from these areas to Germany, changed the nature of the question about social belonging and exclusion from what it been when applied to Jewish or politically discredited neighbors in the 1930s. With its destruction and suffering, the war created new challenges for individual self-conceptions and everyday ways of life and at the same time opened up previously unknown opportunities for (political) self-realization.[86] Both during the successes of the 1940s and also after the turning point of the war in 1943, the question about political approval of the regime was closely tied to expectations about the outcome of the war. In the struggle of competing nations, the significance of nationalism as the basis for individual commitment thus retained its credibility.[87] But above all, the war demanded that Germans interpret and cope with a violence of unprecedented scope and quality, which in the massive scale of dying and killing raised questions about who they were, the times in which they lived, and how they stood in relation to these times.[88] The challenges of the 1940s were different from those that had determined the previous years, and although the ways in which individuals dealt with them were also based on their experiences from the 1930s, they demanded new behaviors and interpretations.

Sebastian Haffner recognized this as well. Having fled into English exile one and a half years earlier, at the start of the war the journalist was still working on writing his autobiography. Using himself as an example, he wanted to report on the behavior of the individual under the Nazi dictatorship and the destruction of the private sphere. In the meantime, he had finished four large chapters, and with 270 manuscript pages had made it as far as fall 1933, but his story was far from complete. His outline also envisaged additional chapters that would actually have extended the book to his successful immigration to Great Britain.[89] Nonetheless, Haffner abandoned his work on the manuscript three weeks after the start of the war. Instead of his autobiography, he now wanted to "write something directly political in order to take the current situation into account."[90] Even before the end of the German campaign against Poland, he started on a new book, whose objective and writing style differed markedly from his previous writings. Whereas in his autobiography Haffner had "primarily investigated how regular Germans were turned into National Socialists, in fall 1939 he planned an updated situation analysis of the 'Third Reich.'" Meant as a "small manual for English propagandists," it was supposed to make a direct contribution to the impending military confrontation with National Socialist Germany.[91] He felt that the autobiography he had started was not suitable for this task. The war, Sebastian Haffner was convinced, required a new and different book.

NOTES

Introduction

1. Schmied, *Haffner*, 60.
2. On Sebastian Haffner's biography and his experiences in exile, see the details he provides in Haffner, *Als Engländer maskiert*; Schmied, *Haffner*, esp. 57–67; Soukup, *Ich bin nun mal Deutscher*, esp. 62–80.
3. Haffner, *Defying Hitler*, 6, 94.
4. Haffner, 7.
5. Haffner, 6.
6. Haffner, 7.
7. Haffner, 183.
8. Haffner, 7.
9. Soukup, *Ich bin nun mal Deutscher*, 74.
10. Harald Welzer even described Haffner's book as the "most systematic documentation to date of the rapid structural change of public space in the year of the so-called seizure of power." Welzer, *Täter*, 58.
11. W. Süß, "Zeitgeschichte als Demokratiewissenschaft."
12. Frei, "Epochenjahr 1933," 92–93.
13. Frei, 92.
14. This research began in the mid-1960s with a study by Allen, *The Nazi Seizure of Power*, which remains formative. Regarding the studies of the 1980s, see, for example, Buchloh, *Duisburg*; Schmiechen-Ackermann, "Nationalsozialistische Herrschaft," 530–532.
15. Wirsching, "'Mehrheitsgesellschaft,'" 10. Much the same has been pointed out recently by Bajohr, Meyer, and Szodrzynski, "Einleitung," 8.
16. Haffner, *Defying Hitler*, 181, 4.
17. Haffner, 5.
18. For example, Welzer, *Täter*, 58–63; Rüthers, *Verräter*, 5.
19. Haffner, *Defying Hitler*, 219.
20. Graf, *Zukunft der Weimarer Republik*, 326.
21. Graf, 326.
22. Speech by Adolf Hitler at the Berlin Sports Palace on February 10, 1933, quoted in Domarus, *Hitler*, 1/1:204.
23. See Hitler's speeches from spring 1933, Domarus, 1/1:191–384.
24. For detail on the recent discussion of the term *Volksgemeinschaft*, see Steuwer, "Was meint und nützt das Sprechen von der 'Volksgemeinschaft.'"
25. Wildt, "Politische Ordnung der Volksgemeinschaft."
26. On the history of the concept, see above all Götz, *Ungleiche Geschwister*; Jegelka, "'Volksgemeinschaft'"; the summary in Steuwer, "Was meint und nützt das Sprechen von der 'Volksgemeinschaft,'" 494–503.
27. Fritzsche, *Germans into Nazis*, 60–62; Verhey, *Spirit of 1914*.

28. Wildt, "'Volksgemeinschaft' als politischer Topos," 29–34; Mai, "'Verteidigungskrieg,'" 591–594; summarized in Steuwer, "Was meint und nützt das Sprechen von der 'Volksgemeinschaft,'" 497–498.

29. Bajohr and Wildt, "Einleitung"; Fritzsche, *Life and Death in the Third Reich*.

30. Adolf Hitler, "Aufruf der Reichsregierung an das deutsche Volk," quoted in Domarus, *Hitler*, 1/1:194.

31. Speech by Adolf Hitler at the Berlin Sports Palace on February 10, 1933, quoted in Domarus, *Hitler*, 1/1:205.

32. Haffner, *Defying Hitler*, 219.

33. Haffner, 3.

34. Nolte, *Ordnung der deutschen Gesellschaft*, 189.

35. Nolte, 192.

36. Graf, *Zukunft der Weimarer Republik*, 176.

37. Bruendel, *Volksgemeinschaft*, 102. See also Verhey, *Spirit of 1914*, 156–185.

38. Verhey, *Spirit of 1914*, 116. In detail, Fritzsche, *Germans into Nazis*, 79–82.

39. Wildt, "Führererwartung in der Weimarer Republik," 186.

40. While the various interpretations of the diary entries are dispersed throughout the different sections, readers interested in greater detail about specific diary authors can find them by using the index.

41. Klemperer, *I Shall Bear Witness*; Frank, *Diary of a Young Girl*. On the interest of scholars of the Nazi period in diaries, see Bajohr, "Das 'Zeitalter des Tagebuchs.'"

42. This is also criticized by Günther, "Something Completely Different," 59.

43. This is also shown by the fact, for example, that autobiographies like those by Sebastian Haffner are repeatedly referred to or treated as diaries—as in the case of Frede-Wenger, *Glauben und Denken*, 188, and Wildt, *Volksgemeinschaft als Selbstermächtigung*, 101.

44. From recent literature, see, for example, Fulbrook, *Dissonant Lives*; Maubach, *Die Stellung halten*; Rosenbaum, *Kinderalltag*. These and other studies usually refer back to the concept of "ego document" coined by Winfried Schulze, which covers a broad range of source types. In contrast, I use the concept "personal testimony." On this, see Krusenstjern, "Was sind Selbstzeugnisse?"

45. Thus, for example, Reuband, "Akzeptanz und Ablehnung," 316.

46. Lejeune, *On Diary*. For scholarly considerations on diaries as historical sources, see the articles in Steuwer and Graf, *Selbstreflexionen und Weltdeutungen*; Hämmerle, "Diaries"; Hüttenberger, "Tagebücher"; Henning, "Selbstzeugnisse."

47. Lejeune, "Diary as 'Antifiction,'" 202.

48. I am thus adopting a broad understanding of the diary that concentrates on the dating of entries as a defining characteristic. On this, see Lejeune, "Datierte Spuren."

49. A similar point is made by the literary scholar Angelika Linke, who views diary writing as a "pragmatic speech act." Linke, "Sich das Leben erschreiben."

50. Rak, "Dialogue with the Future," 19

51. Lejeune, "Continuous and Discontinuous," 179.

52. Lejeune, 179.

53. See the examples in Günther, "Something Completely Different," 27.

54. Sieg, "Kriegserfahrungen jüdischer Intellektueller," 154, 153.

55. Preßler, "Tagebücher aus der Zeit des Nationalsozialismus," 40.

56. Abrath, *Subjekt und Milieu*, 17.

57. Peter Fritzsche makes a similar point using the example of the white-collar employee Franz Göll in Fritzsche, *Turbulent World*, 32–77.
58. Lejeune, "Diary as 'Antifiction,'" 202, 203.
59. Lutz Niethammer coined a very pithy term for this circumstance, "Enttypisierungsschock" (detypification shock), in Niethammer, "Fragen—Antworten—Fragen," 410.
60. Föllmer, "Wie kollektivistisch war der Nationalsozialismus?," 39. Likewise in Büttner, "Alltag der Judenverfolgung," 89; Kershaw, "Alltägliches und Außeralltägliches," 274.
61. Moreover, this number of documents already creates a problem for representation: if the methodological issues I've outlined are taken seriously, then diary entries cannot be reduced to brief quoted snippets. Rather, their interpretation requires more detailed representations. The fact that ultimately only around 100 of the 140 evaluated diaries have found their way into the study is not because the others show no evidence for the presented interpretations but because there is a practical limit on what can be shown.
62. Stephen Kern formulates a similar idea, with the concept of "conceptual distance," in his study on philosophical and artistic discourses around the turn of the century. Kern, *Culture of Time and Space*, 7. With regard to diaries, see also Linke, *Sprachkultur und Bürgertum*, 41.
63. On the development of diary writing in the twentieth century, see the articles in Steuwer and Graf, *Selbstreflexionen und Weltdeutungen*, esp. Steuwer and Graf, "Selbstkonstitution und Welterzeugung," 10–27.
64. Linke, *Sprachkultur und Bürgertum*; Budde, *Bürgerleben*; R. Habermas, *Frauen und Männer des Bürgertums*, 269–278.
65. Reckwitz, *Das hybride Subjekt*, 155–171; Linke, *Sprachkultur und Bürgertum*, 292.
66. On the development of private German writing culture in the twentieth century, see Warneken, *Populare Autobiographik*, 10–26; Hämmerle, "Nebenpfade?"; Schikorsky, *Private Schriftlichkeit*.
67. Lejeune, "'Journal de Jeune fille,'" 141.
68. On this, see Lüdtke, "Writing Time, Using Space."
69. Hämmerle, "Nebenpfade?," 158.
70. Hartl, "Einführung zur Neuauflage," 7.
71. Görner, *Tagebuch*, 23. See also C. Vogelsang, "Tagebuch," 197; Breloer, *Geheime Welten*. On the historical origins of this interpretation, see page 76.
72. "Counter-discourses": Kämper, "Telling the Truth," 241; "extremely dangerous": Papp, *Deutschland von innen und von außen*, 24. Gudrun Brockhaus too assumes that "diaries . . . [were not] a matter for Nazi supporters, who were mostly disinclined toward the word and self-reflection" and that, additionally, they would "rarely [address] the current social and political situation, which the writers took for granted." Brockhaus, "Einführung," 25.
73. For a detailed discussion of the relationship between National Socialism and the diary, see pages 212–223. On the significance of individuality in National Socialism, see Föllmer, *Individuality and Modernity in Berlin*, 105–184.
74. Diary texts that remain illegible are indicated by [?]. Highlighting in the original is represented by italics. Some diarist names have been replaced with pseudonyms to protect personal rights. An overview of this is provided in the index. Where diarists are anonymized, any names mentioned in their texts have been tacitly changed as well. Where such changes occur for entries whose authors are cited under their real names, this is noted in the respective citation.
75. Lejeune, "Tagebuchforschung international," 292–293.

76. Fulbrook, *Dissonant Lives*, 155. The quoted diary is Akademie der Künste, Kempowski-Biografien-Archiv (AdK, Kempowski-Bio), 2918, II.

77. AdK, Kempowski-Bio, 2918, II, November 4, 1936.

78. Coined by the anthropologist Clifford Geertz, the term "thick description" is repeatedly applied to diaries; see, for example, Ehalt, "Vorwort," ii.

79. Fröhlich, *Herausforderung des Einzelnen*.

80. Broszat, "Vorwort," *Bayern in der NS-Zeit*, 1:12.

81. This and previous quote, Broszat, "Vorwort," *Bayern in der NS-Zeit*, 6:9.

82. Under the catchphrase of a "history from within," Mary Fulbrook has recently outlined a similar approach whose aspirations and premises I largely agree with. See Fulbrook, *Dissonant Lives*.

83. For a detailed discussion of the scholarly debate about the "Volksgemeinschaft" and its place in earlier research trends, see Steuwer, "Was meint und nützt das Sprechen von der 'Volksgemeinschaft.'" For an overview in English, see Steber and Gotto, *Visions of Community in Nazi Germany*.

84. Fundamental to the social history of National Socialism: Schoenbaum, *Hitler's Social Revolution*; Dahrendorf, *Gesellschaft und Demokratie*. The results of the research tradition that emerged from these works are summarized in Bavaj, *Ambivalenz der Moderne*.

85. This is also emphasized by Steber and Gotto, "Volksgemeinschaft."

86. This aspiration for change on the part of the Nazi regime with the concept of the "Volksgemeinschaft" was first prominently emphasized in Wildt, *Volksgemeinschaft als Selbstermächtigung*, esp. 9–25, 63–69, 352–374; and also in Bajohr and Wildt, *Volksgemeinschaft*. For the focus on social practice, see the succinct treatment in Bajohr, "Community of Action." With this focus, recent scholarship returned to approaches from the history of everyday life of the 1980s; see above all Lüdtke, "Einleitung"; Peukert, *Volksgenossen und Gemeinschaftsfremde*. For more detail and the reconciliation of additional literature, see Steuwer, "Was meint und nützt das Sprechen von der 'Volksgemeinschaft,'" esp. 516–519.

87. See above all Schmiechen-Ackermann, *"Volksgemeinschaft"*; Nolzen, "Nationalsozialismus und Volksgemeinschaft."

88. See the summary in Steuwer, "Jenseits von 'Mein Kampf.'"

89. Nolzen, "Nationalsozialismus und Volksgemeinschaft," 62.

90. Föllmer, "Subjective Dimension of Nazism," 1110.

91. Föllmer, 1129.

92. Föllmer, 1132.

93. Föllmer, 1110.

94. Haug, *Faschisierung des bürgerlichen Subjekts*, 7.

95. Föllmer, *Individuality and Modernity in Berlin*, 245.

96. Föllmer, 115–116.

97. Föllmer, 11.

98. Hellbeck, *Revolution on My Mind*.

99. Hellbeck, "Working, Struggling, Becoming," 341.

100. Hellbeck, *Revolution on My Mind*, 5.

101. On the discussion of Soviet subjectivity, see *Russian Review* 60, no. 3 (2001); *Kritika* 1, no. 1 (2000); Aris, *Metro als Schriftwerk*; Studer and Haumann, *Stalinistische Subjekte*; Herzberg, *Gegenarchive*.

102. On field post letters, see, for example, Didczuneit, Ebert, and Jander, *Schreiben im Krieg*; Latzel, *Deutsche Soldaten*; S. O. Müller, *Deutsche Soldaten*. On oral history, see, for

example, Niethammer and von Plato, *Lebensgeschichte und Sozialkultur im Ruhrgebiet*; Dörr, *Wer die Zeit nicht miterlebt hat*.

103. Nieden, *Alltag im Ausnahmezustand*; Garbarini, *Numbered Days*; Möckel, *Erfahrungsbruch und Generationsbehauptung*; Stargardt, *Witnesses of War*. See also the articles in Bajohr and Steinbacher, *Zeugnis ablegen*.

104. Bajohr, Meyer, and Szodrzynski, *Bedrohung, Hoffnung, Skepsis*; Wildt, "Self-Reassurance in Troubled Times." Diaries of the 1930s are also examined in the literary study by Bluhm, *Tagebuch zum Dritten Reich*, which is solely interested in the diaries of professional writers.

105. On the scholarly discussion about the use of situation reports and their value as sources, see pages 340–345 and 350–354.

106. See, for example, Lesko, *In Sachen Deutschtum*; Abrath, *Subjekt und Milieu*.

107. Laqueur, *Schreiben im KZ*, 31. On this, see also Schröder, *"Niemand ist fähig das alles in Worten auszudrücken."*

108. Fritzsche, "Nazi Modern," 7.

109. This and previous quotes, Fritzsche, *Life and Death in the Third Reich*, 9.

110. Fritzsche, *Turbulent World*, 6.

Part One

1. On the victory celebrations in Berlin and other cities on January 30, 1933, see Fritzsche, *Germans into Nazis*, 139–144. On the number of participants, see Evans, *Coming of the Third Reich*, 311.

2. On the concept of the propaganda march during the Weimar Republic, see Reichardt, *Faschistische Kampfbünde*, 114–119; Paul, *Aufstand der Bilder*, 133–142.

3. Interior Ministry's justification for the Law on the Introduction of a Holiday of National Work, April 21, 1933, quoted in Heuel, *Der umworbene Stand*, 127.

4. Heuel, *Der umworbene Stand*, 45–53, 61–66; Ruck, "1. Mai im Dritten Reich"; M. Schneider, *Unterm Hakenkreuz*, 91–100.

5. "An das ganze deutsche Volk," appeal of the Reich minister for public enlightenment and propaganda on May 1, 1933, quoted in Heuel, *Der umworbene Stand*, 581.

6. This and the previous quote, Dyck and Joost-Krüger, "Unsrer Zukunft eine Gasse," 226.

7. Heuel, *Der umworbene Stand*, 127.

8. Heuel, 114.

9. Heuel, 96.

10. Speech by Adolf Hitler, May 1, 1933 (critically annotated version), quoted in Heuel, 621–622.

11. Obenaus and Obenaus, *Aufzeichnungen Karl Dürkefäldens*, 42 (April 24, 1933).

12. This and the previous quote, Obenaus and Obenaus, 46–47 (May 2, 1933).

1. The Social Dynamics of the "Seizure of Power"

1. On the biography of Hans Schwalm/Jan Petersen, see Umlauf, *Exil, Terror, Illegalität*, 95–106. On the League of Proletarian-Revolutionary Authors, see Hein, *Bund proletarisch-revolutionärer Schriftsteller*.

2. On the fate of the members of the League of Proletarian-Revolutionary Authors after 1933, see the brief biographies in Hein, *Bund proletarisch-revolutionärer Schriftsteller*, 283–315.

On the resistance activity of the Berlin league after 1933 and the role of Hans Schwalm/Jan Petersen, see Hein, 171–206.

3. Umlauf, *Exil, Terror, Illegalität*, 17.

4. Petersen, *Our Street* [1938]. For a general discussion about the narrative structure, see Umlauf, *Exil, Terror, Illegalität*, 17–24; Trapp, "Kommunistischer Autor," 206–217; S. Bock, "Arbeiterkorrespondenten," 63–81. On the history of the book's formation, see Umlauf, *Exil, Terror, Illegalität*, 98–102; and on Petersen's autobiography, Petersen, *Bewährung*.

5. On the history of the early concentration camp in the Volkshaus Berlin Charlottenburg, see Mayer, "Berlin-Charlottenburg."

6. On the death of Hans Maikowski and his propagandistic stylization, see Reichardt, "Faschistische Kampfbünde, 494–496; Longerich, *Geschichte der SA*, 138–139.

7. This and previous quote, Trapp, "Kommunistischer Autor," 211.

8. Petersen, *Our Street*.

9. "From a 'Red' Street in Berlin: Heroes of Civil Strife," *Times* (London), January 19, 1938. Regarding the reviews, see the compilation in Petersen, *Unsere Straße*, 313–328.

10. On the Left Book Club, see Samuels, "'Left Book Club.'" An advance publication appeared in 1936 in the *Berliner Tagwacht* and in the *Komsomolskaja Prawda*, a journal of the state youth organization of the Soviet Union. The first Russian edition appeared that same year, *Moia ulitsa*. Moscow, 1936.

11. The first German edition appeared in 1947, published by the Dietz Verlag in Berlin. Post-1945 translations appeared in Poland (1949), Czechoslovakia (1951), Hungary (1955), Yugoslavia (1957), China (1959), Japan (1964), Romania (1966), and the Federal Republic of Germany (1978). For the publication history, see Berglund, "Deutsche Opposition gegen Hitler," 179–180.

12. On *The Seventh Cross*, see Wagner, *Kurs auf die Realität*, 119; on *Fear and Misèry of the Third Reich*, see White and White, *Furcht und Elend des Dritten Reichs*, 19; on *Professor Mamlock*, see Petersen, *Unsere Straße*, 322.

13. It is telling that new additions of *Our Street* have recently appeared in both German (Verlag am Park, 2013) and English (Faber and Faber, 2012).

14. Schumann, "Gewalt als Methode."

15. On the public nature of violence in 1933, see Hesse and Springer, *Vor aller Augen*; Wildt, *Volksgemeinschaft als Selbstermächtigung*.

16. Longerich, *Geschichte der SA*, 54–58; Reichardt, *Faschistische Kampfbünde*.

17. On the role of violence in 1933, see Bessel, *Political Violence*; Schumann, "Gewalt als Methode"; Longerich, *Geschichte der SA*, 165–179; Wachsmann and Steinbacher, *Linke im Visier*; Hördler, *SA-Terror*; Y. Müller and Zilkenat, *Bürgerkriegsarmee*.

18. Tuchel, "Organisationsgeschichte," 44.

19. Tuchel, 44.

20. On the early history of the concentration camps, see Drobisch and Wieland, *System der NS-Konzentrationslager*, 11–75; Benz and Distel, *Ort des Terrors*, vol. 2; Baganz, *Erziehung zur "Volksgemeinschaft."*

21. Benz and Distel, *Ort des Terrors*.

22. Longerich, *Geschichte der SA*, 74.

23. Schmiechen-Ackermann, *Arbeitermilieus*, 411.

24. This and previous quote, AdK, Kempowski Biographies, 5584, April 26,1933.

25. Röder, "Politische Emigration," columns 16–22; Benz, "Jüdische Emigration," columns 5–9.

26. Sauer, *Die Mobilmachung der Gewalt*, 245. On the evaluation of Sauer's estimate, see Longerich, *Geschichte der SA*, 172.
27. On other groups victimized by the violence, see H. Beck, *Fateful Alliance*, 236–243; Hörath, "Terrorinstrumente."
28. Peukert, *KPD im Widerstand*, 95.
29. On the role of forms of residence in the destruction of the workers' movement in 1933, see Schmiechen-Ackermann, *Arbeitermilieus*, 108–435.
30. Schmiechen-Ackermann, 163.
31. Petersen, *Unsere Straße*, 213, 256.
32. Peukert, *KPD in Widerstand*
33. The diary of Wilhelm Scheidler survives in the court file in Staatsarchiv (StA) Darmstadt, G 27, 217. A transcript of the document, which was written in shorthand, is located in the Archiv der Gedenkstätte KZ-Osthofen, 2/27/2. I would like to thank Benjamin Möckel for the reference to this diary.
34. Gedenkstätte KZ-Osthofen, 2/27/2, March 10, 1933.
35. Gedenkstätte KZ-Osthofen, March 10, 1933.
36. On the court proceedings, see the files in StA Darmstadt, G 27, 217.
37. Petersen, *Our Street* [1938], 137.
38. Deutsches Tagebucharchiv (DTA), 808 I/1, inner cover.
39. This and the previous quote, DTA, 808 I/4, February 3, 1933.
40. Bayerisches Hauptstaatsarchiv (BayHstA) München, NL Buttmann, no. 103, January 30, 1933.
41. DTA, 370, 15, January 30, 1933.
42. Stadtarchiv (StdA) Meißen, rep. XXI, no. 34, February 8, 1933.
43. StdA Meißen, May 7, 1933.
44. Graf, *Die Zukunft der Weimarer Republik*, 326.
45. Graf, 176.
46. Graf, 176. For the origins of the slogan "Germany awaken!" see Hartung, "Nationalsozialistische Kampflieder," 165–181.
47. Archiv der sozialen Demokratie (AdsD), NL Theodor Thomas, no. 2, January 30, 1933.
48. Landeshauptarchiv (LHA), NL Stephan Weidenbach, no. 8, January 30, 1933.
49. AdK, Kempowski-Bio, 5584, January 30, 1933.
50. StA Hamburg, 622-I/140, 1/28, January 30, 1933. (Bajohr, Meyer, and Szodrzynski, *Bedrohung, Hoffnung, Skepsis*, 152–153.)
51. On the concept of "conservative taming" and its failure, see Bracher, *Stufen der Machtergreifung*, 78–79; Jasper, *Die gescheiterte Zähmung*. On the relationship of the coalition partners, see H. Beck, *Fateful Alliance*, 236–243.
52. StA Hamburg, 622-I/140, I/28, January 31, 1933.
53. StA Hamburg, February 9, 1933. (Bajohr, Meyer, and Szodrzynski, *Bedrohung, Hoffnung, Skepsis*, 184.)
54. StA Hamburg, February 28, 1933. (Quote is missing from Bajohr, Meyer, and Szodrzynski, *Bedrohung, Hoffnung, Skepsis*.)
55. StA Hamburg, March 5, 1933. (Bajohr, Meyer, and Szodrzynski, *Bedrohung, Hoffnung, Skepsis*, 167.)
56. StA Hamburg, March 5, 1933. (Bajohr, Meyer, and Szodrzynski, *Bedrohung, Hoffnung, Skepsis*, 168.)
57. AdK, Kempowski-Bio, 5584, February 20, 1933, March 5, 1933.

58. StA Hamburg, 622-1/189, 2/9, March 19, 1933.
59. DTA, 779, 5, March 22, 1933.
60. AdK, Kempowski-Bio, 5482/77, section "Die 'nationale Revolution.'"
61. Koselleck, "Volk, Nation, Nationalismus, Masse," 398.
62. This and previous quote, StA Hamburg, 622-1/140, 1/28, February 28, 1933. (Quotes are missing from Bajohr, Meyer, and Szodrzynski, *Bedrohung, Hoffnung, Skepsis.*)
63. "Aufruf der Reichsregierung an das deutsche Volk," February 1, 1933, quoted in Domarus, *Hitler*, 1/1:192, 193.
64. This and previous quote, StdA München, NL Wallner, vol. 1, no. 3, January 31, 1933. Names changed.
65. StdA München, February 24, 1933, March 5, 1933, March 21, 1933, April 20, 1933, April 9, 1933.
66. DTA, 1798, 7; DTA, 1724, 4.
67. A striking example of a parental diary is found in Bruhns, *Meines Vaters Land*, 261. On parental diaries, see the detailed discussion in Gebhardt, *Angst vor dem kindlichen Tyrannen*, esp. 100–112.
68. StdA Münster, HS 128: "Kriegstagebuch" (1914–1918) and "Nachkriegs-Hausbuch" (1918–1933), March 16, 1933 (afterword).
69. DTA, 1798, 7, summer holidays 1933.
70. StdA Münster, HS 128, March 16, 1933 (afterword).
71. This and previous quotes, Monacensia, Literaturarchiv, NL Luise Klempt, July 8, 1933.
72. Monacensia, July 9, 1933.
73. Monacensia, November 14, 1933.
74. Fritz-Hüser-Institut für Literatur und Kultur der Arbeitswelt (FHI) Str-140, January 1, 1930.
75. This and the previous quote, FHI, Str-150, January 1, 1935.
76. FHI, Str-150, October 7, 1934.
77. DTA, 808 I/4, February 3, 1933.
78. This and the previous quote, StA Hamburg, 622-1/174, 2, December 31, 1934.
79. AdK, Kempowski-Bio, 5482/84, "Meine Stellung zum Nationalsozialismus," June 17, 1932.
80. Nolzen, "In die Jahre gekommen."
81. The difference between the government as the representative of the nation and of National Socialism is dealt with in detail on pages 102–111.
82. AdK, Kempowski-Bio, 1174, July 12, 1933.
83. AdK, April 20, 1933.
84. This and previous quote, AdK, July 12, 1933.
85. This and previous quotes, AdK, January 4, 1934.
86. AdK, July 12, 1933.
87. The Sklarek scandal was a corruption trial that, during the final phase of the Weimar Republic, caused huge waves in Berlin and was used especially by the NSDAP for antisemitic propaganda. On this, see Weigel, "Sklarek-Skandal."
88. Here and previous quotes, AdK, Kempowski-Bio, 5584, November 15, 1934. The entries cited in the diary entry are from October 4, November 10, and November 28, 1931.
89. This and previous quote, StA Hamburg, 622-I/140, January 28, February 9,1933. (Bajohr, Meyer, and Szodrzynski, *Bedrohung, Hoffnung, Skepsis*, 158.)
90. StA Hamburg, March 18, 1933. (Quote is missing from Bajohr, Meyer, and Szodrzynski, *Bedrohung, Hoffnung, Skepsis.*)

91. StA Hamburg, March 11, 1933. (Quote is missing from Bajohr, Meyer, and Szodrzynski, *Bedrohung, Hoffnung, Skepsis*.)
92. This and previous quotes, StdA Münster, HS 128, March 16, 1933 (afterword).
93. StdA Münster, March 16, 1933 (afterword).
94. StA Hamburg, 622-I/140, January 28, March 18, 1933. (Quote is missing from Bajohr, Meyer, and Szodrzynski, *Bedrohung, Hoffnung, Skepsis*.)
95. StdA Münster, HS 128, March 16, 1933 (afterword).
96. This and previous quotes, DTA, 639, Christmas 1933.
97. This and previous quotes, DTA, 326 I, 2, June 24, 1932.
98. DTA, January 16, 1933.
99. DTA, February 12, 1933.
100. DTA, August 18, 1933.
101. On the "massive rush" on the NSDAP in spring 1933, see Falter, "Die 'Märzgefallenen' von 1933"; Weigel, "'Märzgefallene' und Aufnahmestopp im Frühjahr 1933."
102. Evans, *Coming of the Third Reich*, 382. Something similar has been emphasized above all in the scholarship on the elite of the Nazi dictatorship. This is summarized by Herbert, "NS-Eliten in der Bundesrepublik," 115.
103. "Pure opportunism": Weigel, "'Märzgefallene' und Aufnahmestopp im Frühjahr 1933," 604. Likewise, for example, Thiel, "Akademische 'Zinnsoldaten,'" 177.
104. DTA, 326 I, 2, March 22, 1933.
105. DTA, March 22, 1933.
106. DTA, 639, October 14, 1934.
107. This and previous quote, StdA Munich, Nachlass Oehl, vol. 25, April 2, 1933.
108. This and previous quote, StdA Munich, March 31, 1933.
109. This and previous quote, StdA Munich, April 3, 1933.
110. StdA Essen, Archiv Ernst Schmidt, 19–538, 1.1, Lebensbericht "Einiges aus meinem Leben." The quote comes from a cover letter dated November 15, 1936, that Schössel sent to his children with his "life sketch" after the latter was completed.
111. Zentrum für Antisemitismusforschung (ZfA), Lebengeschichtliche Sammlung, Henry Marx, Tagebuch, March 28, 1933.
112. ZfA, March 20, 1933.
113. ZfA, June 19, 1933.
114. This and previous quote, ZfA, January 10, 1934.
115. ZfA, May 9, 1933.
116. ZfA, January 10, 1934.
117. This and previous quote, ZfA, August 17, 1934.

2. The Search for a Personal Stance toward the Nazi Regime

1. AdK, Kempowski-Bio, 5965/1, April 15, 1938.
2. AdK, March 31, 1933.
3. AdK, April 1, 1933.
4. BayHstA, Munich, NL Fritz Koch, no. 31, May 1934. After the war, the lawyer Fritz Koch became the president of the Aschaffenburg Regional Court in 1946 and one year later also became a judge at the Bavarian Constitutional Court. He was the Bavarian justice minister from 1954 to 1957.

5. DTA, 1315.
6. Verordnung des Reichspräsidenten zur Abwehr heimtückischer Angriffe gegen die Regierung der nationalen Erhebung, in Reichsministerium des Innern, *Reichsgesetzblatt* 1933, 1: 35; Verordnung der Reichsregierung über die Bildung von Sondergerichten, in Reichsministerium des Innern, 136.
7. Dams and Stolle, *Gestapo*, 89–90.
8. On the political instrumentalization of the criminal offense of "gross mischief," see Schmitz, "Wider die 'Miesmacher.'" On the Treachery Act and its application, see Dörner, *"Heimtücke"*; Dams and Stolle, *Gestapo*, 89–94.
9. AdK, Kempowski-Bio, 5965/1, April 1, 1933.
10. Schiefer, *Tagebuch eines Wehrunwürdigen* [1947], 4.
11. Jünger, *Strahlungen* [1949], 9.
12. Nebel, *Bei den nördlichen Hesperiden* [1948], 5–6. For discussion about diaries after 1945, see Peitsch, *Deutschlands Gedächtnis*, 232–259.
13. This and the previous quote, Peitsch, *Deutschlands Gedächtnis*, 232.
14. "Chronicler courage": Nieden, "Vergessenen Alltag der Tyrannei," 114; "openly without restraint": Heer, "Editorial," 8.
15. AdK, Kempowski-Bio, 1174, esp. entries in the second half of 1933.
16. ZfA, Lebensgeschichtliche Sammlung, Henry Marx.
17. AdK, Kempowski-Bio, 5584, 9, entries from April to June 1933.
18. I address this with more detail on pages 132–148.
19. This and previous quotes, AdK, Kempowski-Bio, 5965/1, April 16, 1933.
20. AdK, March 31, 1933, April 1, 1933.
21. AdK, July 3, 1933.
22. DTA, 1708, 7, July 2, 1933.
23. DTA, 565, September 25, 1933.
24. ZfA, Lebensgeschichtliche Sammlung, Henry Marx, March 28, 1933.
25. DTA, 565, September 25, 1933.
26. "Thoughts on National Socialism": Mecklenburgisches Landeshauptarchiv Schwerin (MLHA Schwerin), 10.9—S/8, April 13, 1934. "The 'National' Revolution": AdK, Kempowski-Bio, 5482/77, section "Die 'nationale' Revolution."
27. See, for example, the diary of the white-collar employee Franz Göll. On his "scribomaniacal" preoccupation with scientific problems and historical events, see Fritzsche, *Turbulent World* esp. 1–31, 108–186.
28. AdK, Kempowski-Bio, 1174, September 14, 1933.
29. Speech by Adolf Hitler, May 1, 1933, quoted in Heuel, *Der umworbene Stand*, 621–622.
30. Carl Schmitt, "Das gute Recht der deutschen Revolution," *Westdeutscher Beobachter*, May 12, 1933, quoted in Koenen, *Fall Carl Schmitt*, 397.
31. Pyta, "Schmitts Begriffsbestimmung," 235.
32. Hilberg, *Perpetrators, Victims, Bystanders*. This tripartite division basically described social roles that can be assumed in relation to one another. But even Hilberg already used them in the figurative sense in which they are mostly used today. On the significance of this division for Sebastian Haffner, see Haffner, *Jekyll & Hyde*.
33. This and previous quotes, AdK, Kempowski-Bio, 1174, September 14, 1933.
34. This and the previous quote, AdK, August 7, 1933.
35. AdK, September 14, 1933.
36. This and previous quotes, DTA 565, September 25, 1933.

37. This and previous quotes, Institut für sächsische Geschichte und Volkskunde Dresden, Lebensgeschichtliches Archiv (ISGV, LgA), Projekt 028, Chronik der Bauernfamilie Eichler, entry for 1933. On the Sachsenburg concentration camp, see Baganz, "Sachsenburg."
38. This and previous quotes, ISGV, LgA, Projekt 028, Chronik der Bauernfamilie Eichler, entry for 1933.
39. DTA, 749/I, 13, January 31, 1933.
40. Respectively, the Forschungsinstitut für Geistesurgeschichte and the SS-Forschungsgemeinschaft DeutschesAhnenerbe. On Herman Wirth and his role in Forschungsgemeinschaft Deutsches Ahnenerbe, see Kater, *"Ahnenerbe" der SS*, 41–43; Wiwjorra, "Ein gescheiterter Ideologe zwischen 'Ahnenerbe.'"
41. This and previous quotes, DTA, 749/I, 13, May 15, 1933.
42. On the German Faith Movement, see Baumann, *Deutsche Glaubensbewegung*.
43. MLHA Schwerin, 10.9—S/8, no. 3, January 18, 1934, 55.
44. MLHA Schwerin, February 7, 1933, 87.
45. Lesko, *In Sachen Deutschtum*, 359.
46. AdK, Kempowski-Bio, 1174, September 14, 1933.
47. MLHA Schwerin, 10.9—S/8, no. 3, August 21, 1932.
48. MLHA Schwerin, January 18, 1934.
49. Kershaw, *Hitler Myth*, 103.
50. On the role of autobiographical self-assurance within the National Socialist movement, see Fritzsche, "Being the Subjects of History"; Wichert, "Tatmensch"; Luckey, *Personifizierte Ideologie*; T. Abel, *Why Hitler Came into Power* [1938].
51. AdK, Kempowski-Bio, 5965/1, April 1, 1933.
52. This and previous quotes, AdK, April 4, 1933.
53. This and previous quotes, AdK, April 6, 1933.
54. This and previous quotes, AdK, April 8, 1933.
55. This and previous quotes, AdK, April 15, 1933.
56. This and previous quotes, DTA, 1315, April 15, 1934.
57. The speech is reproduced in excerpts in Thürauf, *Schulthess' Europäischer Geschichtskalender* 50 (1934): 94.
58. Jamin, "Ende der 'Machtergreifung,'" 209.
59. On the regime crisis of spring 1934, see Frei, *Führerstaat*, 9–16; Morsch, *Arbeit und Brot*, 178–181.
60. On the campaign against complainers and its context, see Longerich, *Joseph Goebbels*, 257–262; Frei, *Führerstaat*, 14–16; Sauer, *Mobilmachung der Gewalt*, 288–290.
61. This and previous quotes, "Dr. Goebbels eröffnet den Kampf gegen die Staatsschädinge," *Völkischer Beobachter*, May 13, 1934.
62. Frei, *Führerstaat*, 16. Similarly in Kershaw, *Hitler Myth*, 117.
63. Frei, *Führerstaat*, 14, 16.
64. AdK, Kempowski-Bio, 5965/1, June 29, 1934.
65. This and previous quotes, AdK, July 1, 1934.
66. This and previous quotes, DTA, 1315, May 5, 1934.
67. This and previous quotes, AdK, Kempowski-Bio, 1174, May 28, 1934.
68. AdK, January 4, 1934.
69. This has been described often and well in the scholarship, for example in the studies by Stöver, *Volksgemeinschaft*; Morsch, *Arbeit und Brot*. Newer investigations have largely confirmed these findings; see, for example, Aly, *Volkes Stimme*; Römer, *Kameraden*, 60–110.

70. Stöver, *Volksgemeinschaft*, 426.
71. Neitzel and Welzer, *Soldaten*, 54.
72. Thus in recent literature, for example, Römer, *Kameraden* (quote on p. 86). This is especially clear in Hoerkens, *Unter Nazis?*
73. "Dr. Goebbels eröffnet den Kampf gegen die Staatsschädlinge," *Völkischer Beobachter*, May 13, 1934.
74. Kershaw, *Hitler Myth*, 66.
75. Kershaw, 84.
76. On the Night of the Long Knives and their reception, see pages 389–393 and 398–400.
77. Kershaw, *Hitler Myth*, 257, 66.
78. Reichel, *Der schöne Schein*, 151.
79. For greater detail on this, see pages 367–370.
80. Römer, *Kameraden*, 94.
81. AdK, Kempowski-Bio, 5584, 10, June 26, 1933.
82. AdK, August 30, 1933.
83. AdK, August 31, 1933.
84. AdK, October 23, 1933
85. AdK, October 12, 1933, January 4, 1933. The German Christians were a movement within German Protestantism committed to a National Socialist interpretation of Christianity.
86. AdK, October 12, 1933
87. This and previous quotes, AdK, January 4, 1934.
88. This and previous quotes, ISGV, LgA, Projekt 028, Chronik der Bauernfamilie Eichler, Jahresbericht 1933.
89. On the tension between SA membership and religious conviction with regard to Franz Buesgen, see pages 498–500.
90. DTA, 401, October 1, 1938.
91. Reichel, *Der schöne Schein*, 151.
92. DTA, 172, vacation 1933.
93. AdK, Kempowski-Bio, 1174, July 12, 1933.
94. This and previous quotes, StdA Münster, HS 128, March 16, 1933 (afterword).
95. This and previous quotes, DTA, 1798, summer holidays 1933.
96. This and previous quotes, AdK, Kempowski-Bio, 1174, July 12, 1933.
97. AdK, August 3, 1933, August 7, 1933, September 14, 1933.
98. DTA, 1315, February 25, 1934.
99. DTA, 1315, February 25, 1934.
100. On Julius Streicher and his antisemitic smear sheet, see Roos, *Julius Streicher*.
101. This and previous quotes, DTA, 1315, July 2, 1934.
102. DTA, October 20, 1934.
103. Abel, *Why Hitler Came into Power* [1938], 143–146. The importance of nationalism for supporting the Nazi regime is succinctly highlighted in Wehler, "Radikalnationalismus."
104. This and previous quotes, StA Hamburg, 622-1/163 Familie Ahlers-Hestermann, D 10, no date (1934).
105. This and previous quotes, StA Hamburg, D 10, no date (1934).
106. Manigold, *Friedrich Ahlers-Hestermann*, 30.
107. ZfA, Lebensgeschichtliche Sammlung, Henry Marx, January 10, 1934.
108. DTA, 1315, April 15, 1934.

109. This and previous quote, DTA, November 20, 1934.
110. This and previous quotes, Gedenkstätte KZ-Osthofen, 2/27/2, March 10, 1933, March 11, 1933, March 12, 1933.
111. Gedenkstätte KZ-Osthofen, "brown murderers," March 12, 1933; "fighter for socialism," March 15, 1933.
112. This and previous quotes, Gedenkstätte KZ-Osthofen, May 1, 1933.
113. Gedenkstätte KZ-Osthofen, March 11, 1933.
114. This and previous quotes, Gedenkstätte KZ-Osthofen, April 25, 1933.
115. Gedenkstätte KZ-Osthofen, May 10, 1933.
116. This and previous quotes, Gedenkstätte KZ-Osthofen, May 17, 1933.
117. Gedenkstätte KZ-Osthofen, May 28, 1933.
118. AdK, Kempowski-Bio, 5965/1, May 1, 1933.
119. This and previous quotes, AdK, May 1, 1933.
120. This and previous quotes, AdK, May 1, 1933.
121. AdK, April 27, 1933.
122. This and previous quote, DTA, 1315, April 15, 1934.
123. DTA, May 27, 1934.
124. This and previous quotes, DTA, December 26, 1934.
125. This and previous quote, ZfA, Lebensgeschichtliche Sammlung, Henry Marx, December 21, 1933.
126. Limberg and Rübsaat, *Jüdischer Alltag*, 12 (quote); Barkai, *Wehr Dich!*, esp. 284–299. On individual diarists, see Rieker, "Victor Klemperers Identitätskonstruktion"; Rosenberg, *Einer, der nicht mehr dazugehört*; Cohn, *Kein Recht, nirgends*.
127. Siegel, "Zweiweltenmensch," 42–43.
128. Gesetz über das Staatsoberhaupt des Deutschen Reichs, in Reichsministerium des Innern, *Reichsgesetzblatt* 1934, 1:747.
129. Erlaß des Reichskanzlers zum Vollzug des Gesetzes über das Staatsoberhaupt des Deutschen Reichs vom 1. August 1934, in Reichsministerium des Innern, *Reichsgesetzblatt* 1934, 1:751.
130. Kershaw, "Führer und Hitlerkult," 19.
131. Regarding these occasions and the fluctuations of political attention, see pages 426–441.
132. DTA, 565/I, 1, June 1, 1934.
133. DTA, December 31, 1937.
134. DTA, July 25–August 18, 1937.
135. DTA, July 25–August 18, 1937, December 31, 1937.
136. DTA, December 31, 1937.
137. DTA, December 31, 1937.
138. StA Hamburg, 622-1/174, 2, December 31, 1936
139. ISGV, LgA, Projekt 028, Chronik der Bauernfamilie Eichler, annual reports 1919–1925, 1929–1932.
140. ISGV, annual reports 1934–1937.
141. See pages 379–405.
142. DTA, 1315, November 13, 1935.
143. DTA, January 5, 1936.
144. DTA, November 14, 1937.
145. DTA, March 15, 1936 ("good German"), December 1, 1935 ("opponent").
146. AdK, Kempowski-Bio, 5584, 14, August 18, 1937.

147. This and previous quote, AdK, Kempowski-Bio, 5965/1, March 11, 1935.
148. AdK, May 8, 1936.
149. AdK, May 11, 1936.
150. See, for example, September 3, 1934, March 30, 1936.
151. AdK, Kempowski-Bio, 5584, 15, February 20, 1938.
152. AdK, 14/3 1, October 22–28, 1937. Here in an article clipped from a newspaper article entitled "Weltanschauung und Religion im nationalsozialistischen Staat" by Hanns Kerrl, Lindemann underlined the statement, "National Socialism is a religious movement," adding the comment "But in *Mein Kampf* it says something different."
153. AdK, March 14, 1938.
154. AdK, 12, September 7, 1935.
155. AdK, 14/3a, November 12, 1938.
156. AdK, Kempowski-Bio, 1174, November 30, 1935.
157. This and previous quotes, AdK, November 30, 1935.
158. This and previous quotes, DTA, 639, fall 1936.
159. DTA, fall 1936.
160. This and previous quotes, DTA, September 15, 1937.
161. DTA, January 16, 1938.
162. DTA, January 16, 1938. Carl Ludwig Schleich was a surgeon and author. His memoir *Besonnte Vergangenheit: Lebenserinnerungen eines Arztes*, published in 1920, reached an audience of millions and to date counts among the most widely read German biographies.
163. This and previous quotes, Sächsisches Hauptstaatsarchiv Dresden (SächsHStA Dresden), 12728 Nachlass Walter Lohs, no. 1, August 4, 1934.
164. SächsHStA Dresden, August 4, 1934.
165. This and previous quotes, SächsHStA Dresden, March 8, 1935.
166. SächsHStA Dresden, June 28, 1935.
167. SächsHStA Dresden, June 29, 1937.

3. Establishing a Personal Stance toward the Regime While under Social Observation

1. This and previous quotes, DTA, 4071, April 30, 1933.
2. AdK, Kempowski-Bio, 5965/1, April 1, 1933.
3. Forschungsstelle für Zeitgeschichte in Hamburg, Archiv (FZH), X11/K32, letter from Kirchmann, November 12, 1933.
4. This and previous quote, FZH, letter from Kirchmann, March 30, 1933.
5. FZH, Letter from Kirchmann, March 30, 1933.
6. FZH, X11/K33, letter to Kirchmann, February 14, 1933. Name of addresser has been changed.
7. This and previous quote, FZH, letter to Kirchmann, March 13, 1933.
8. This and previous quote, FZH, letter from Kirchmann, May 7, 1933.
9. "Dr. Goebbels eröffnet den Kampf gegen die Staatsschädlinge," *Völkischer Beobachter*, May 13, 1934.
10. On the symbol propaganda of the Nazi movement before 1933, see Paul, *Aufstand der Bilder*, 165–177.
11. This is how Cologne head mayor Konrad Adenauer, after consulting with the district president, translated the radio message, which spoke about "doing justice to the

understandable Volksstimmung [mood of the people] in the next few days." On this, see Morsey, "Vom Kommunalpolitiker zum Kanzler," 75.

12. Schmiechen-Ackermann and Tullner, "Stadtgeschichte und NS-Zeit," 24.
13. The heavily symbolic operation still resonates in the many town histories that appeared with the title "Swastika over . . ." or ". . . under the Swastika," especially in the 1980s.
14. Carl Schmitt, for example, fixed the abolishment of the Weimar democracy on the reintroduction of the black-white-red flag, which the 1919 Weimar Constitution had deliberately replaced with the black-red-gold flag of the democratic movement of 1848. See Schmitt, *Staat, Bewegung, Volk* [1933], 5.
15. "Die Hakenkreuzfahne auf dem Limburger Rathaus und Kreishaus," *Nassauer Bote*, March 8, 1933, quoted in Nieder, "Sturm aufs Rathaus," 476.
16. In diaries too, the hoisting of the flags on the town halls in early March 1933 drew a lot of attention from authors, many of whom actually saw this as a turning point. See, for example, the diary of Helga Ritter, who felt that her appraisal of a "great political upheaval" was confirmed by the flags marking the electoral victory in March 1933. DTA, 1495, March 9, 1933.
17. Erlaß des Reichspräsidenten über die vorläufige Regelung der Flaggenhissung, in Reichsministerium des Innern, *Reichsgesetzblatt* 1933, 1:103. On March 7, two days after the Reichstag elections, Hindenburg had ordered the flying of the black-white-red flag for the memorial day on March 13, 1933. On this, see Weißmann, *Schwarze Fahnen*, 183–185.
18. "An das ganze deutsche Volk," appeal by the Reich minister for public enlightenment and propaganda on May 1, 1933, quoted in Heuel, *Der umworbene Stand*, 581.
19. StA Hamburg, 622-1/140, 1/28, April 22, 1933. (Bajohr, Meyer, and Szodrzynski, *Bedrohung, Hoffnung, Skepsis*, 195.)
20. This and previous quote, StA Hamburg, March 30, 1933. (Bajohr, Meyer, and Szodrzynski, *Bedrohung, Hoffnung, Skepsis*, 184.)
21. This is according to the constitutional law expert E. R. Huber, *Verfassungsrecht des Großdeutschen Reiches* [1939], 188. On the swastika's transition to state symbolism, see Weißmann, *Schwarze Fahnen*, 190–193.
22. Allert, *Deutsche Gruß*, 48. On the transformative effect of the Hitler greeting, see Bergerson, *Ordinary Germans*, esp. 21–4; also Fritzsche, *Life and Death in the Third Reich*, 19–24.
23. Nolzen, "Die NSDAP, der Krieg und die deutsche Gesellschaft," 104.
24. Gerhard L. Binz, "Der Haß gegen die Uniform," *Völkischer Beobachter*, July 7, 1932.
25. On this, see Elfferding, "Opferritual."
26. On this, see also pages 485–492.
27. FZH, X 11/K 33, letter from Kirchmann, May 7, 1933.
28. FZH, letter from Kirchmann, July 3, 1933.
29. FZH, letter from Kirchmann, July 3, 1933. Names changed.
30. This and previous quote, FZH, letter from Kirchmann, April 2, 1934. Names changed.
31. FZH, letter from Kirchmann, April 25, 1933. Names changed.
32. AdK, 6030/6, letter from Wächter, May 8, 1933.
33. Landesarchiv Berlin (LA Berlin), E Rep. 061-19, 15, December 31, 1933.
34. Theodor Thomas: AdsD, NL Theodor Thomas, 2, March 10, 1933, April 13, 1933, May 1,1933 ("play of flags"), April 20, 1934, August 6, 1934. Luise Solmitz: StA Hamburg, 622-1/140, 1/28, January 31, 1933, March 5, 1933, May 20, 1933, July 15, 1933.
35. LHA Koblenz, 700, 023, 8, March 21, 1933, March 24, 1933.
36. This and previous quote, DTA, 808 I, 8, May 16, 1933.
37. This and previous quotes, DTA, 1798, summer holidays 1933. On the relationship between Germany and Austria in summer 1933, see R. Schmidt, *Außenpolitik des Dritten Reiches*, 162.

38. On this problem, see Steuwer and Leßau, "Wer ist ein Nazi? Woran erkennt man ihn?"; Steuwer, "'National Socialists' and Other People."
39. Steuwer, "Was meint und nützt das Sprechen von der 'Volksgemeinschaft,'" 515–518.
40. See above all the studies by Wildt, *Volksgemeinschaft als Selbstermächtigung*; Kramer, *Volksgenossinnen*; Borggräfe, *Schützenvereine*.
41. Bajohr, "'Community of Action,'" 199.
42. Bajohr, 198.
43. AdK, 6030/6, letter from Wächter, May 8, 1933.
44. This and previous quotes, LA Berlin, E Rep. 061-19, 15, December 31, 1933.
45. This and previous quotes, LA Berlin, E Rep. 061-19, 15, December 31, 1933.
46. See the detailed discussion regarding this on pages 500–510.
47. Fulbrook, *Dissonant Lives*, 163. A similar point in Schäfer, *Das gespaltene Bewußtsein*, 154–157. On this, see also pages 463–475 and 510–513.
48. On the novel *Die Katrin wird Soldat*, published in 1930, and its author, Adrienne Thomas, see Biener, "Literarische Verteidigung des kleinen Glücks."
49. DTA, 1512, 1, September 2, 1933.
50. This and previous quotes, DTA, October 25, 1933.
51. This and previous quotes, DTA, October 25, 1933.
52. DTA, November 12, 1933.
53. DTA, January 2, 1934.
54. DTA, 1047, 2, August 23, 1933.
55. DTA, 2197, 13, March 3, 1933, March 5, 1933, March 6, 1933, March 10, 1933.
56. DTA, March 21, 1933, April 20, 1933, May 26, 1933.
57. DTA, March 21, 1933. He likewise marked the days on which he was accepted by the NSDAP (April 24, 1933) and when he first drove in uniform to neighboring Freiburg (August 13, 1933).
58. AdK, Kempowski-Bio, 5584, 9, March 5, 1933; AdK, Kempowski-Bio, 5584, 10, October 14, 1933.
59. On the social practice of flag decorations in 1933, see also Wildt, "Self-Reassurance in Troubled Times," 64–68.
60. StA Hamburg, 622-1/140, 1/28, March 31, 1933, March 3, 1933, March 6, 1933.
61. This and previous quotes, StA Hamburg, March 10, 1933. (Quote is missing from Bajohr, Meyer, and Szodrzynski, *Bedrohung, Hoffnung, Skepsis*.)
62. StA Hamburg, January 31, 1933. (Quote is missing from Bajohr, Meyer, and Szodrzynski, *Bedrohung, Hoffnung, Skepsis*.)
63. StA Hamburg, March 5, 1933. (Bajohr, Meyer, and Szodrzynski, *Bedrohung, Hoffnung, Skepsis*, 168.)
64. StA Hamburg, 622-1/140, 1/29, March 1, 1935.
65. StA Hamburg, March 1, 1935.
66. Broszat, Fröhlich, and Wiesemann, *Bayern in der NS-Zeit*, 1:353. On this, see also Bergerson, *Ordinary Germans*, 133–146.
67. FZH, X 11/K 33, letter from Kirchmann, May 14, 1933.
68. FZH, letter from Kirchmann, June 3, 1934.
69. In the weeks after Hitler's appointment as Reich chancellor, for example, hundreds of thousands of new members joined the "Stahlhelm: Association of Frontline Soldiers." On this, see J. Diehl, *Paramilitary Politics*, 294.

70. AdK, Kempowski-Bio, 5965/1, April 1, 1933.
71. This and previous quotes, AdK, June 15, 1933.
72. Only in a few isolated entries created at a later date did Maschmann also adopt the category of National Socialist as a self-description in his diary. However, in so doing he always emphasized the difference between himself and the NSDAP. See, for example, AdK, Kempowski-Bio, 5965/1, March 29, 1936, January 24, 1937.
73. AdK, Kempowski-Bio, 5965/2, letter from Maschmann, July 3, 1933.
74. AdK, letter from Maschmann, March 28, 1934.
75. This and previous quotes, AdK, 5965/1, August 16, 1933.
76. Fulbrook, *Dissonant Lives*, 115.
77. AdK, Kempowski-Bio, 1174, September 14, 1933.
78. StA Hamburg, 622-1/189, 2/9, April 30, 1933.
79. AdK, Kempowski-Bio, 5584, 9, February 27, 1933.
80. This and previous quotes, LHA Koblenz, 700/250, no. 45, April 13–24, 1933.
81. LHA Koblenz, April 13–24, 1933.
82. LHA Koblenz, April 13–24, 1933.
83. LHA Koblenz, April 13–24, 1933.
84. LHA Koblenz, April 13–24, 1933.
85. LA Berlin, E Rep. 061-19, 15, May 10, 1933.
86. StA Hamburg, 622-1/174, 2, February 24, 1934.
87. LHA Koblenz, 700/250, no. 45, April 13–24, 1933.
88. This and previous quotes, LHA Koblenz, 700, 023, 8, February 15, 1933.
89. Thieler, *"Volksgemeinschaft" unter Vorbehalt*, 177–178; Weigel, "'Märzgefallene' und Aufnahmestopp im Frühjahr 1933."
90. AdK, Kempowski-Bio, 5965/1, August 16, 1933.
91. StA Hamburg, 622-1/189, 2/9, April 2, 1933.
92. This and previous quote, StA Hamburg, April 30, 1933.
93. For a survey of the development of societies and associations in 1933, see Borggräfe, "Ausblendung und Aufarbeitung."
94. On "Parteigenossenförderung" (party comrade support), see Bajohr, *Parvenüs und Profiteure*, 17–48.
95. This and previous quote, DTA, 565/I, 1, September 25, 1933.
96. DTA, June 1, 1934.
97. For detail, see the study by Bergerson, *Ordinary Germans*.
98. AdK, Kempowski-Bio, 5584, 9, April 24, 1933.
99. AdK, April 24, 1933.
100. This and the previous quote, StA Hamburg, 622-1/189, 2/9, March 21, 1933.
101. DTA, 1708, 7, April 27, 1933, May 30, 1933 (quote), September 13, 1933, September 16, 1933, October 9, 1933.
102. Here and previous quote, DTA, July 4, 1933.
103. DTA, July 5, 1933.
104. Letter of the leader of the Bega chapter to the Gauleiter in Münster, March 15, 1933, in Landesarchiv Nordrhein-Westfalen (LA NRW), Ostwestfalen-Lippe, L 113, 151, fol. 223.
105. This and previous quote, StdA Meißen, Rep. XXI, no. 34, November 25, 1934.
106. Letter from the Kreisleiter to the Kreis court, April 15, 1934, in LA NRW, OstwestfalenLippe, L 113/361, fol. 277.

107. Eleven-point program of the NSDAP on the boycott operation, quoted in Comité des Délégations Juives, *Die Lage der Juden in Deutschland 1933* [1934], 296–298, here 297. For detail on the April boycott, see Ahlheim, *Deutsche, kauft nicht bei Juden!*, 241–262.

108. Ahlheim, *Deutsche, kauft nicht bei Juden!*, 241.

109. On the significance of the April boycott for Jewish policy, see Longerich, *Politik der Vernichtung*, 30–41.

110. Erste Verordnung zur Durchführung des Gesetzes zur Wiederherstellung des Berufsbeamtentums, April 11, 1933, quoted in Reichsministerium des Innern, *Reichsgesetzblatt* 1933, 1:195.

111. Julius Streicher, "Schlagt den Weltfeind," *Völkischer Beobachter*, March 31, 1933.

112. This and previous quote, Eleven-point program of the NSDAP on the boycott operation, quoted in Comité desDélégations Juives, *Die Lage der Juden in Deutschland 1933* [1934], 297.

113. Call of the Nazi Women's League, quoted in Comité des Délégations Juives, *Die Lage der Juden in Deutschland 1933* [1934], 65–66, here 65.

114. LHA Koblenz, 700, 032, 8, March 5, 1933.

115. LHA Koblenz, March 26, 1933. The entry refers to the previous weeks.

116. LHA Koblenz, April 1, 1933.

117. LHA Koblenz, March 5, 1933.

118. LHA Koblenz, April 1, 1933, April 4, 1933.

119. This and previous quotes, LHA Koblenz, April 1, 1933.

120. LHA Koblenz, April 5, 1933.

121. Ahlheim, *Deutsche, kauft nicht bei Juden!*, 262. For a summary of the various scholarly assessments on reactions to the boycott operation, see Ahlheim, 254–262.

122. Ahlheim, 256.

123. Wildt, *Volksgemeinschaft als Selbstermächtigung*, 362.

124. Wildt, 361–374.

125. The reporters for the Central Association of German Citizens of Jewish Faith, who recorded the course of the operations and the reactions to them, emphasized the importance of the "intimidation" of shoppers. Wildt, 282–284.

126. LA Berlin, E Rep. 061-19, 15, March 31, 1933.

127. AdK, Kempowski-Bio, 5584, 11, November 14, 1934.

128. Werner Kramp, for example, pointed out with regard to the April boycott that it was imposed "by the National Socialist party, not by the regime." StA Hamburg, 622-1/189, 2/9, April 1, 1933.

129. LHA Koblenz, 700, 023, 8, April 3, 1933.

130. LHA Koblenz, April 5, 1933, similarly April 1, 1933.

131. AdK, Kempowski-Bio, 5584, 16/2, November 12, 1938.

132. AdK, 14/3a, November 10, 1938, November 12, 1938, November 13, 1938.

133. Here and previous quotes, ZfA, Lebensgeschichtliches Archiv, Gegen Vergessen, für Demokratie, November 10, 1938.

134. Barkai, *Der Centralverein*, 284–286.

135. A survey of this in Borggräfe, "Ausblendung und Aufarbeitung."

136. One impression is provided, for example, by the letter of a female student who enrolled at the University of Munich in spring 1933. In her report about the matriculation process, she also mentioned that "for an hour long [she] had to fill out a form, 'what do you want to become,' 'was your grandfather a Jew,' 'are you Aryan'? etc.," but paid no further attention to this process. DTA, 1834/I, letter to parents, April 30, 1933.

137. StA Hamburg, 622-1/140, 1/28, May 20, 1933. (Bajohr, Meyer, and Szodrzynski, *Bedrohung, Hoffnung, Skepsis*, 205, 206.)
138. StA Hamburg, 622-1/140, 1/28, May 20, 1933. (Bajohr, Meyer, and Szodrzynski, *Bedrohung, Hoffnung, Skepsis*, 205, 206.)
139. StA Hamburg, April 1, 1933. (Quote is missing in Bajohr, Meyer, and Szodrzynski, *Bedrohung, Hoffnung, Skepsis*.)
140. StA Hamburg, May 28, 1933. (Bajohr, Meyer, and Szodrzynski, *Bedrohung, Hoffnung, Skepsis*, 211.)
141. StA Hamburg, June 13, 1933. (Bajohr, Meyer, and Szodrzynski, *Bedrohung, Hoffnung, Skepsis*, 217.) "Luise" refers to the Bund Königin Luise, a nationalist and monarchist women's organization of the late Weimar Republic that supported the NSDAP early on.
142. StA Hamburg, September 14, 1933. (Bajohr, Meyer, and Szodrzynski, *Bedrohung, Hoffnung, Skepsis*, 239.)
143. StA Hamburg, October 18, 1933, October 19, 1933. (Bajohr, Meyer, Szodrzynski, *Bedrohung, Hoffnung, Skepsis*, 249–250.)
144. This and previous quotes, StA Hamburg, 622-1/140, 1/29, February 6, 1934.
145. StA Hamburg, June 21, 1934.
146. This and previous quote, StA Hamburg, 1/28, June 13, 1933. (Bajohr, Meyer, and Szodrzynski, *Bedrohung, Hoffnung, Skepsis*, 217.)
147. StA Hamburg, September 14, 1933. (Quote is missing in Bajohr, Meyer, and Szodrzynski, *Bedrohung, Hoffnung, Skepsis*.) StA Hamburg, 1/29, March 8, 1934.
148. StA Hamburg, 1/28, October 18, 1933, October 19, 1933. (Bajohr, Meyer, Szodrzynski, *Bedrohung, Hoffnung, Skepsis*, 250.)
149. StA Hamburg, 1/29, February 19, 1934. Names changed.
150. StA Hamburg, June 27, 1934, June 28, 1934. Name changed.
151. StA Hamburg, July 13, 1935.
152. StA Hamburg, July 13, 1935.
153. StA Hamburg, March 1, 1935, March 17, 1935, April 20, 1935, August 2, 1935.
154. StA Hamburg, March 1, 1935.
155. On the creation of the Nuremberg Laws, see above all Essner, *Nürnberger Gesetze*. On their significance for the persecution of Jews, see also Longerich, *Politik der Vernichtung*, 102–115; U. D. Adam, *Judenpolitik im Dritten Reich*, 83–103.
156. Reichsbürgergesetz, in Reichsministerium des Innern, *Reichsgesetzblatt* 1935, 1:1146.
157. Gesetz zum Schutze des deutschen Blutes und der deutschen Ehre, in Reichsministerium des Innern, *Reichsgesetzblatt* 1935, 1:1146–1147, here 1447.
158. Reichstag, *Verhandlungen des Reichstags, 9. Wahlperiode 1933–1936*, Stenografische Berichte 6. Sitzung [September 15, 1935]), 458:60.
159. Reichsflaggengesetz, in Reichsministerium des Innern, *Reichsgesetzblatt* 1935, 1:1145.
160. This and previous quotes, StA Hamburg, 622-1/140, 1/29, September 15, 1935.
161. This and previous quote, StA Hamburg, September 20, 1935.

Part Two

1. Dissolution resolution of Reich leadership of the Center Party, May 7, 1933, printed in Morsey, *Deutsche Zentrumspartei*, 439–440, here 439. On the background of the self-dissolution, see Morsey, 405–411.

2. Gesetz ge en die Neubildung von Parteien, in Reichsministerium des Innern, *Reichsgesetzblat* 933, 1:479,
3. This and evious quote, "Erziehung des deutschen Menschen," *Völkischer Beobachter*, July 4, 1933.
4. "Adolf Hi er über Staat und Wirtschaft," *Völkischer Beobachter*, July 8, 1933. The speech is also pr ited in Michaelis and Schraepler, *Ursachen und Folgen*, 9:233–235, here 234.
5. Speech of ice Chancellor von Papen before the League of Universities, Marburg, on July 17, 1934, quo d in Forschbach, *Edgar J. Jung*, 154–174, here 161.
6. Röhm, "S und deutsche Revolution [1933]," 254. On the background to the conflict, see Longerich, *C schichte der SA*, 179–188.
7. "Adolf H er über Staat und Wirtschaft," *Völkischer Beobachter*, July 8, 1933.
8. "Erziehun des deutschen Menschen," *Völkischer Beobachter*, July 4, 1933.
9. Bracher, *ufen der Machtergreifung*, 302.
10. On this s Bracher, 298–303, quote on 299.
11. Hitler, *M n Kampf*, 2:1087 [1925].
12. "Erziehur des deutschen Menschen," *Völkischer Beobachter*, July 4, 1933.
13. Reference to the speeches are found in many propaganda pamphlets and pedagogical texts; see, for exa nple, Kallsperger, *Nationalsozialistische Erziehung im Reichsarbeitsdienst für die weibliche Jug d* [1939], 5 (motto of the book); Ramlow, *Deutsche Jungens auf Fahrt* [1934], 73; Tiefenbach, *SS* [1 34], 48; Huber, *Bauerntum und Bauerbildung im Neuen Reich* [1934], vi, 133.
14. This and r evious quotes, StA Hamburg, 622–1/189, 2/9, July 2, 1933.
15. "Erziehur des deutschen Menschen," *Völkischer Beobachter*, July 4, 1933.
16. StA Ham rg, 622–1/189, 2/9, July 2, 1933.

4. The Nation Socialist Education Project

1. Ministers meeting of March 7, 1933, in Repgen and Booms, *Akten der Reichskanzlei*, part 1, 1:159–166, ere 159.
2. Ministers meeting of March 11, 1933, in Repgen and Booms, 1:193–197, here 193. On the founding of the inistry, see Mühlenfeld, "Vom Kommissariat zum Ministerium."
3. On the cr ition of a state information policy in the First World War, see Anne Schmidt, *Belehr ng, Propaganda, Vertrauensarbeit*.
4. Speech or March 14, 1933, before members of the press, quoted in Goebbels, *Revolution der D utschen* [1933], 135–151, here 135–136.
5. Goebbels 135, 140.
6. Goebbels 139. On the political relationship between the "Volk" and the "regime," see the detailed disc ssion in the third part of this book.
7. On the co ception of propaganda in National Socialism, see above all Bussemer, *Propaganda*, 153 224.
8. Speech or March 14, 1933, before members of the press, quoted in Goebbels, *Revolution der D utschen* [1933], 135–151, here 138, 141.
9. Goebbels 40.
10. Goebbels, 146. On the press in the Nazi dictatorship, see Frei and Schmitz, *Journalismus im Dritten Reich*. On the establishment of the control instruments, see Sösemann, "'Auf Bajonetten läßt sich schlecht sitzen'"; C. Zimmermann, *Medien im Nationalsozialis us*, esp. 85–98; Welch, *Third Reich*, esp. 28–57.

11. Address to the intendants and directors of the radio broadcasting corporation, in Heiber, *Goebbels-Reden*, 1:82–107.
12. On Nazi radio broadcasting, see Diller, *Rundfunkpolitik im Dritten Reich*; Dussel, *Hörfunk in Deutschland*, 55–69.
13. On this, see the survey by Sösemann, *Propaganda*, 1:xxxviii–lix; Zimmermann, *Medien im Nationalsozialismus*.
14. Speech on March 16, 1933, to members of the press, quoted in Goebbels, *Revolution der Deutschen* [1933], 135–151, here 148–149.
15. Welch, *Third Reich*, 60.
16. Joseph Goebbels at the advertising convention in Vienna, 1938, quoted in Kundler, "Schatten auf dem Bilde Emil Dovifat," 294.
17. This and previous quote, Van Linthout, *Das Buch in der nationalsozialistischen Propagandapolitik*, 68. The difference was already pointed out by Steinert, *Hitlers Krieg und die Deutschen*, 23–24.
18. On this, see the detailed discussion in the third section of this book.
19. "Persistent and uninterrupted education": Address to the Working Men, in Hitler, *Die Reden Hitlers am Parteitag der Freiheit 1935* [1935], 43–45, here 44; "degenerative phenomena": Address to the Hitler Youth, in Hitler, 57–59, here 57; "all Germans": Final Address, in Hitler, 71–86, here 80.
20. Address to the intendants and directors of the radio broadcasting corporation, in Heiber, *Goebbels-Reden*, 1:92.
21. The terms *lifestyle*, *life management*, and *ways of life*, which I use synonymously, are oriented according to the sociological concept of "alltäglicher Lebensführung" (everyday lifestyle), which describes the "totality of everyday activities of persons that make up the life of a human being." Thus "lifestyle" is "not grasped . . . as a construction of meaning . . . but rather primarily as praxis." G. Voß, "Entwicklung und Eckpunkte," 30. On the other hand, the terms *self-perspective*, *self-contemplation*, and *self-images* refer to the reflection on and interpretation of one's own life.
22. Krieck, *Philosophie der Erziehung* [1925], 17–18. On National Socialist education concepts and the significance of Krieck, see Lingelbach, *Erziehung und Erziehungstheorien*, 50–94; Ehrhardt, "Erziehungsdenken und Erziehungspraxis," 58–117.
23. On the connection between education and propaganda, see above all Ehrhardt, "Erziehungsdenken und Erziehungspraxis."
24. Speech to filmmakers, August 23, 1933, in G. Albrecht, *Der Film im 3. Reich*, 26–31, ("weaving loom of the time": 29).
25. Quote in Köppen and Schütz, "Kunst der Propaganda," 8. On the departmental organization of the Propaganda Ministry in 1933, see Mühlenfeld, "Vom Kommissariat zum Ministerium," 82.
26. Herrmann and Nassen, "Die ästhetische Inszenierung von Herrschaft," 10. On political education through the aestheticization of the public, see Reichel, *Der schöne Schein*; Bussemer, *Propaganda und Populärkultur*; Offermanns, *Die wußten, was uns gefällt*, 133–171.
27. "Collective and individual patterns of perception": P. Diehl, "Körperbilder und Körperpraxen," 12; "educational space": Tenorth, "Eugenik im pädagogischen Denken," 42.
28. On this, see the recent discussions related to the creation and dissemination of National Socialist morality: Reiter, *Nationalsozialismus und Moral*; Gross, *Anständig geblieben*; Bialas, *Moralische Ordnungen*.
29. Kershaw, "How Effective Was Nazi Propaganda?," 182.

30. For a review of the current state of research, see Mühlenfeld, "Was heißt und zu welchem Ende studiert man NS-Propaganda."
31. On resistance and social milieus, see Broszat, *Bayern in der NS-Zeit*; Schlögl and Thamer, *Zwischen Loyalität und Resistenz*. For a review of the state of research, see Bavaj, *Die Ambivalenz der Moderne im Nationalsozialismus*, 62–69, 73–77.
32. See, for example, Longerich, "Nationalsozialistische Propaganda," 294; Sösemann, "Nationalsozialismus," 309.
33. Frei and Schmitz, *Journalismus im Dritten Reich*, 29.
34. This was already pointed out in early studies such as K.-D. Abel, *Presselenkung im NS-Staat*.
35. Fröhlich, *Tagebücher von Joseph Goebbels*, part 1, 2/II:201 (January 23, 1932).
36. On this, see Nagel, *Hitlers Bildungsreformer*.
37. "Educational school": Hierl, "Der Arbeitsdienst, die Erziehungsschule zum deutschen Sozialismus (1933)," in Hierl, *Ausgewählte Schriften und Reden* [1943], 2:95–97, here 96. "By no other institution": Hierl, "Arbeitsdienst und Wehrpflicht (1935)", in Hierl, *Ausgewählte Schriften und Reden* [1943], 2:199–205, here 203. On the Labor Service and its educational activities, see Patel, *Soldaten der Arbeit*.
38. On this, see G. Bock, *Zwangssterilisation im Nationalsozialismus*; Czarnowski, *Das kontrollierte Paar*; survey of the current state of research in Eckart, *Medizin in der NS-Diktatur*.
39. Transcript of the first meeting of the expert advisory council, quoted in Ganssmüller, *Erbgesundheitspolitik des Dritten Reiches*, 40–41.
40. G. Bock, *Zwangssterilisation im Nationalsozialismus*, 91.
41. Schnurr and Steinacker, "Soziale Arbeit im Nationalsozialismus," 259. On other policy fields, see, for example, Pantelmann, *Erziehung zum nationalsozialistischen Arbeiter*; M. Schneider, *Unterm Hakenkreuz*, 347–411.
42. Bracher, *Stufen der Machtergreifung*, 304.
43. Final address, in Hitler, *Die Reden Hitlers am Parteitag der Freiheit 1935* [1935], 80–81.
44. On this, see Wegehaupt, "*Wir grüßen den Haß!*"
45. "Gestalt und Aufgabe des Ortsgruppenschulungsleiters in Partei und Gemeinde," quoted in Reibel, *Das Fundament der Diktatur*, 133.
46. Gerhard Wagner, "Gesundheitsdienst der Partei und des Staates," in Conti, *Reden und Aufrufe* [1943], 41–55, here 51–52.
47. Koonz, *Nazi Conscience*, 83–88
48. Zeck, *Das Schwarze Korps*, 314, 313.
49. On the NSDAP Order Castles, see Heinen, *NS-Ordensburgen*; Vogelsang IP, *Fackelträger der Nation*; Ciupke and Jelich, *Weltanschauliche Erziehung in Ordensburgen des Nationalsozialismus*. On the Adolf Hitler Schools and the National-Political Education Institutes, see Scholtz, *NS-Ausleseschulen*; Feller and Feller, *Die Adolf-Hitler-Schulen*.
50. Quote in Weingart, Kroll, and Bayertz, *Rasse, Blut und Gene*, 403. For a detailed discussion on the Race Policy Office, see Uhle, "Neues Volk und reine Rasse."
51. Address before the Hitler Youth, in Hitler, *Die Reden Hitlers am Parteitag der Freiheit 1935* [1935], 57–59, here 57.
52. See Bollmus, *Das Amt Rosenberg*.
53. Lingelbach, *Erziehung und Erziehungstheorien*, 149.
54. Gaus, "Nationalsozialistischer Erziehungsstaat," 118

55. Speech by Robert Ley on June 12, 1936, before the NSLB, in *Deutsche höhere Schule* 3 (1936): 576, quoted in Ehrhardt, "Erziehungsdenken und Erziehungspraxis," 59.

56. Instead of using the term *education state*, which was already being used by contemporaries at that time, I therefore use the term *education project* for the Nazi educational efforts as a whole, as suggested by Hans-Ulrich Thamer. See Thamer, "Der 'Neue Mensch' als nationalsozialistisches Erziehungsprojekt."

57. On the significance of the difference between *Volk* and *Rasse*, see Koonz, *Nazi Conscience*, 9–10.

58. On the significance of the figure of the "new man" in National Socialism, see Fritzsche and Hellbeck, "New Man in Stalinist Russia and Nazi Germany"; Thamer, "Der 'Neue Mensch' als nationalsozialistisches Erziehungsprojekt."

59. Fritzsche, "On Being the Subjects of History," 163.

60. Föllmer, "Subjective Dimension of Nazism," 1120–1121.

61. Otto and Sünker, "Vorwort," 8.

62. On the figure of the "new man" before 1933, see Küenzlen, *Der Neue Mensch*; Gerstner, Könczöl, and Nentwig, *Der Neue Mensch*; Herrmann, *Neue Erziehung*.

63. Kerbs and Reulecke, "Einleitung der Herausgeber," 11. See also the articles in Nitschke et al., *Jahrhundertwende*.

64. Krabbe, "Lebensreform/Selbstreform," 74.

65. For a survey on the spectrum of the reform movements, see Kerbs and Reulecke, *Handbuch der deutschen Reformbewegungen*.

66. Fritzen, *Gesünder leben*, 218. On the relationship between the Lebensreform movement and National Socialism, see Fritzen, 64–106, 218–231.

67. Fritzen, 64.

68. Tenorth, "Einfügung und Formierung." On the intensely discussed case of Peter Petersen, see the detailed treatment in Döpp, *Jenaplan-Pädagogik im Nationalsozialismus*.

69. See the examples in Westphal, *Werbung im Dritten Reich*, 48; Schäfer, *Das gespaltene Bewußtsein*, 117–118. On advertising and its relationship to the Nazi regime, see the survey by Berghoff, "Von der Reklame zur Verbrauchslenkung"; Rücker, *Wirtschaftswerbung unter dem Nationalsozialismus*; König, *Volkswagen, Volksempfänger, Volksgemeinschaft*, 220–231.

70. Schultze, *So lebst du deutsch!* [1937].

71. On this see pages ??? ???

72. A similar point is made in Raphael, "Pluralities of National Socialist Ideology"; Merziger, *Nationalsozialistische Satire und "Deutscher Humor."*

73. Föllmer, "Volksgemeinschaft zwischen Bedeutungsvielfalt und Homogenitätsanspruch," 457–458.

74. IfZ, ED 363, 5, introduction.

75. IfZ, 4, introduction to "Gedanken. 1933. August."

76. IfZ, 4, August 1933 (Form und Haltung).

77. IfZ, October 1933 (Die Auflösung des großdeutschen Bundes und Gestaltung der Jugendbewegung).

78. IfZ, September 1933 (Die Menschen).

79. IfZ, 6, December 10, 1933.

80. IfZ, preface, November 1933.

81. On this, see the first part of the book, especially pages ???

82. DTA, 1315, April 15, 1934, February 2, 1936.

83. DTA, 565/1, 1, June 1, 1934.
84. Föllmer, "Subjective Dimension of Nazism," 1120–1121.
85. Föllmer, "Volksgemeinschaft zwischen Bedeutungsvielfalt und Homogenitätsanspruch," 458.
86. On this, see, for example, the discussion of the diary of Luise Klempt on pages ???
87. StA Koblenz, 700, 153, no. 186, November 11, 1934.
88. StA Koblenz, "Mein Lebensziel."
89. IfZ, ED 32 2/11, letter from Wiebus, November 15, 1936.
90. IfZ, for example, letters from Wiebus, October 16, 1936, November 25, 1936, February 10, 1937.
91. DTA, 1512 2, October 6, 1934.
92. IfZ, ED 3. /1, April 21, 1936.
93. IfZ, January 11, 1937.
94. IfZ, 11, letter from Köhl, October 25, 1936.
95. StA Hamburg, 622-1/189, 2/9, August 17, 1933.
96. On this, see the discussion on Wolfgang Scharenberg on pages ???
97. MLHA Schwerin, 10.9—S/8, no. 3.
98. On the relationship between religion and National Socialism, see the overview in Gailus and Nolzen, Zerstrittene "Volksgemeinschaft."
99. On this, see the discussions on Walter Lindemann on pages ???
100. "German sons of heroes" and "blood, race, and soil": AdK, Kempowski-Bio, 5584, notebook 11, April 19, 1935; "socialism": AdK, September 14, 1934.
101. For a brief overview of Nazi education, see especially Gaus, "Nationalsozialistischer Erziehungsstaat. Still seminal are Ehrhardt, "Erziehungsdenken und Erziehungspraxis"; Keim, *Erziehung unter der Nazi-Diktatur*. For a survey of the current state of research, see Horn and Link, *Erziehungsverhältnisse im Nationalsozialismus*.
102. Stahlmann and Schiedeck, *Erziehung zur Gemeinschaft*, 5.
103. Ehrhardt, "Erziehungsdenken und Erziehungspraxis," 92–93.
104. On the simultaneity of politicization and privatization, see Lüdtke, "Wo blieb die rote Glut," 25.
105. Speech for the opening of the Greater German Book Week, quoted in Van Linthout, *Das Buch in der nationalsozialistischen Propagandapolitik*, 41.
106. Speech for the opening of the Week of the German Book, November 5, 1934, quoted in Heiber, *Goebbels Reden*, 1:168–173, here 168–169.
107. This and previous quotes, Van Linthout, *Das Buch in der nationalsozialistischen Propagandapolitik*, 73, 76.
108. "Die Heimbücherei," *Buch und Volk* 5 (1938): 6, quoted in Van Linthout, 116.
109. On the subvention of books under National Socialisms, see Van Linthout, 159–244.
110. Speech for the opening of the Week of the German Book, November 5, 1934, quoted in Heiber, *Goebbels Reden*, 1:168–173, here 169.
111. Van Linthout, *Das Buch in der nationalsozialistischen Propagandapolitik*, 92.
112. Van Linthout, 110.
113. Van Linthout, 111
114. Van Linthout, 115.
115. C. Adam, *Lesen unter Hitler*, 318
116. C. Adam, 09.
117. This and previous quotes, Gohdes, "Vorwort [1933]."

118. For example, see the advertising in *Der Schulungsbrief* 1, no. 6 (1934): 37. On the editorial training methods of the NSDAP, see Wegehaupt, *Wir grüßen den Haß!*, 36–48.
119. On Nazi literary policy, see Barbian, *Literaturpolitik im NS-Staat*.
120. C. Adam, *Lesen unter Hitler*, 104–109. For a more general discussion about advice literature, see Haug, *Die Faschisierung des bürgerlichen Subjekts*, 107–118. In particular, parental advice literature has received substantial scholarly attention. See Brockhaus, "Dann bist Du verloren, liebe Mutter!"; Gebhardt, *Die Angst vor dem kindlichen Tyrannen*, 74–99.
121. Benze, *Wegweiser ins Dritte Reich* [1933], 3. On other guides, see Van Linthout, *Das Buch in der nationalsozialistischen Propagandapolitik*, 81.
122. Bouhler, "Zur Einführung [1936]," i–ii.
123. MLHA Schwerin, 10.9—H/14, V 6/60/1, October 24–25, 1936.
124. DTA, 749/I, 13, July 11, 1933.
125. LA Berlin, E Rep 200–43, no. 50, July 22, 1934–October 4, 1939.
126. On Göll and his interest in scientific questions, see Fritzsche, *Turbulent World*, 108–131.
127. FZH, X 11/K 36, letter from Kroll, July 20, 1934.
128. Mehnert, *Jugend in Sowjetrussland* [1932].
129. On the actions of the NSDAP against the book, see the review by Maria Faber, "Die Katrin wird Soldat," *Völkischer Beobachter*, February 1–2, 1931; the dissertation by Biener, "Die literarische Verteidigung des kleinen Glücks."
130. DTA, 1512, 1, September 17, 1933.
131. StA Hamburg, 622-1/189, 2/9, June 25, 1933.
132. StA Hamburg, July 2, 1933.
133. Roß, *Sprecherziehung statt Rhetorik*, 93–94.
134. For a survey, see Guhr and Knape, "Rhetorische Praxis in Deutschland," 466–469, 477. On the reorganization of the speaker system after 1933, see Pabst-Weinschenk, *Die Konstruktion der Sprechkunde*, 409–422.
135. Olbrich, *Geschichte der Erwachsenenbildung*, 246.
136. StA Hamburg, 622-1/189, 2/9, May 6, 1933.
137. StA Hamburg, May 16, 1933.
138. Mertens, *Schulungslager und Lagererziehung* [1937], 3.
139. Kraas, "Das Lager als Erziehungsform," 297.
140. Mertens, *Schulungslager und Lagererziehung* [1937], 4.
141. On camp pedagogy, see above all Kraas, *Lehrerlager 1932–1945*, 113–147; Schiedeck and Stahlmann, "Die Inszenierung totalen Erlebens."
142. Schiedeck and Stahlmann, "Die Inszenierung 'totalen Erlebens,'" 167. An overview of the various types of camps can be found in Stahlmann and Schiedeck, *Erziehung zur Gemeinschaft*, 73–87.
143. Mertens, *Schulungslager und Lagererziehung* [1937], 73.
144. Hierl, "Gedanken über Erziehen und Führen. Ansprache bei der Tagung der Kreisleiter der NSDAP in Sonthofen, 17.11.1937," in Hierl, *Ausgewählte Schriften und Reden* [1943], 2:263–275, here 264–265.
145. Patel, "Gemeinsame Arbeit," 347.
146. For detail on this and on educational practice in the training camps, see pages ???
147. This and previous quotes, Patel, "Gemeinsame Arbeit," 347.
148. Patel, 340.
149. On this, see Hocke, *Das europäische Tagebuch*; Wuthenow, *Europäische Tagebücher*.

150. Hocke, "Über das Tagebuchschreiben [1938],".
151. Hebbel, Tagebücher und Briefe [1935]. On the continued "classical" interpretation of the 1930s, see Agnes Rosenbusch, Die Tagebücher Friedrich Hebbels [1935]; Lisbeth Wittig, Der junge Hebbel [1937].
152. Bernfeld, Trieb und Tradition im Jugendalter [1931], 76.
153. Bernfeld, 83.
154. Bernfeld, 6.
155. Hocke, "Über das Tagebuchschreiben [1938]," 130.
156. To date there is very little research on this question. See above all Nieden, Alltag im Ausnahmezustand, 59–69; Schäfer, Das gespaltene Bewußtsein, 82–84.
157. Longerich, Heinrich Himmler, 22–73; Weiß, "Die Aufzeichnungen Hermann Görings," 366; Kleßmann, "Hans Frank"; Matthäus and Bajohr, Alfred Rosenberg; Fröhlich, Tagebücher von Joseph Goebbels.
158. The diaries of Max Dingler are held in the DTA, 370. On Karl Friedrich Kolbow, see M. Dröge, Tagebücher Karl Friedrich Kolbows.
159. See, for example, the diaries of Wilhelm Bollmann (AdK, Kempowski-Bio, 4842) and Helmut Böhme (StdA Meißen, rep. XXI, no. 34).
160. The appeal was disseminated in spring 1935 through the party's formations and affiliated associations and is also found in the internal journals of these organizations. For example, see "Aufruf an Alle!," Deutsches Recht: Zentral-Organ des Bundes Nationalsozialistischer Deutscher Juristen 5, no. 9 (1935): 260. The next year it was also made accessible to a broader public via the press. On this, see Rupnow, Vernichten und Erinnern, 72.
161. Fröhlich, "Einleitung zur Gesamtedition," 12.
162. Matthäus and Bajohr, Alfred Rosenberg. On the motivation for documenting political events and the role he played in them, see the first entry of May 14, 1934 (p. 119).
163. Fröhlich, "Einleitung zur Gesamtedition," 37–47.
164. "Aus meinem Tagebuch," excerpt from Joseph Goebbels for Else Janke (1923), quoted in Fröhlich, 30.
165. "Father confessor": Fröhlich, Tagebücher von Joseph Goebbels, part I, 1/I:285 (March 23, 1925); "conscience doctor": Fröhlich, 228 (September 23, 1924).
166. Fröhlich, 55 (June 27, 1924).
167. On the diary of the young Heinrich Himmler and its educated-bourgeois character, see Longerich, Heinrich Himmler, 22–30, 34–73.
168. Fröhlich, Tagebücher von Joseph Goebbels, part I, 4:395 (motto of the diary volume of November 1937 to February 1938).
169. "Die künftigen Historiker," Die Tat: Deutsche Monatsschrift 25, no. 3 (1933): 269–270.
170. Föllmer, "Subjective Dimension of Nazism," 1120.
171. Föllmer, Individuality and Modernity in Berlin, 113. Reference to this also occurs in Schäfer, Das gespaltene Bewußtsein, 123, but he interprets this as a contradiction with National Socialist ideology.
172. "Aufruf an Alle!," Deutsches Recht: Zentral-Organ des Bundes Nationalsozialistischer Deutscher Juristen 5, no. 9 (1935): 260.
173. Jaensch, "Jugendentwicklung und Neuformung des deutschen Menschentums [1939]," 183.
174. Making a similar point with regard to the Soviet Union is Hellbeck, Revolution on My Mind, 48–52.
175. Goebbels, Vom Kaiserhof zur Reichskanzlei [1934], 10.
176. Goebbels, Michael [1929].

177. Göring, "Aus dem Tagebuch eines Jagdfliegers [1923],". In the 1930s, excerpts were reprinted in schoolbooks. See *Deutschland-Berichte der Sopade*, 200.

178. "In a certain sense the first": Piper, *Alfred Rosenberg*, 43; Drexler, *Mein politisches Erwachen* [1919]. On National Socialist diary texts during the Weimar Republic, see the partially utopian text by Peter Waldenhagen, *Das dritte Reich* [1931].

179. Fritzsche, "On Being the Subjects of History."

180. As per the foreword in Goebbels, *Vom Kaiserhof zur Reichskanzlei* [1934],13. See also Karlheinz Schulze, *Um Deutschland* [1934]; Littmann, *Herbert Norkus und die Hitlerjungen von Beusselkietz* [1934]; Gerhard Pantel, *Befehl Deutschland* [1936]; Voß, *Wi Dickköpp* [1937].

181. Article series Ein alter Kämpfer erzählt, *Essener Anzeiger*, July 7, 1935 ("1926: 5000 Nationalsozialisten geloben . . ."), July 14, 1935 ("Alter Kämpfer blättert zurück . . ."), July 21, 1935 ("Durch Kampf und Not zum 3. Reich"), July 28, 1935 ("Kämpft weiter für das 3. Reich"); "Aus dem Tagebuch eines unbekannten Hitlerredners," *Völkischer Beobachter*, May 20–21, 1934.

182. See, for example, Rittweger, *Der unbekannte Redner der Partei* [1939]. On this, see also Koonz, *Nazi Conscience*, 87–88.

183. Van Linthout, *Das Buch in der nationalsozialistischen Propagandapolitik*, 111.

184. "Vom Kaiserhof zur Reichskanzlei: Gedanken zum neuen Buch von Dr. Goebbels," *Völkischer Beobachter*, May 16, 1934.

185. Fridel Marie Kuhlmann, "Und wir? [1936]," 338.

186. On the publication of war diaries in the 1930s, see, for example, Goes, *Mein Kriegstagebuch* [1935]; Walter Kublank, *Kriegstagebuch aus Flandern* [1934]; Baron von Loewenstern, *Elard: Der Frontflieger* [1937]. On publications in the 1940s, see Schäfer, *Das gespaltene Bewußtsein*, 8.

187. Maria Kahle, "Vorwort zur zweiten Auflage," in Kahle, *Akkordarbeiterin* [1937], 5–6, here 6.

188. See, for example, Purschke, *Das Mottenhaus* [1934]; Albrecht, *Tagebuch des Gerhard Thiele* [1935]; Kuckelsberg, *Deutsche Nordlandreise* [1937].

189. DTA, 1512, 2, April 9, 1935.

190. On the Hitler Youth, Labor Service, and KdF tours, see the examples on pages ??? On Lebensborn, see the examples in Schmitz-Köster, *Deutsche Mutter, bist Du bereit*, for example, 208–209.

191. On the tradition of the travel diary, see Wuthenow, *Europäische Tagebücher*, 165–180.

192. Göbels, *Jörg schreibt sein Hitler-Tagebuch* [1935]. See also the book for adolescents, Eggers, *Tagebuch einer frohen Fahrt* [1935].

193. Deutsches Historisches Museum, Berlin (DHM Berlin), D02 2003/327, *Jung Deutschland Tagebuch*.

194. Various examples of such preprinted formats can be seen at *Jugend! Deutschland 1918–1945*, http://www.jugend1918-1945.de. On this, see also Umbach, "Selfhood, Place and Ideology."

195. StdA Bergisch Gladbach, S 7/130.

196. Schuwerack, "Zur Gestaltung nationalpolitischer Schülerlehrgänge [1936]," 327. See also *Nationalpolitische Lehrgänge für Schüler* [1935], 167–170.

197. "Dienstanweisung für das Landjahr," in Reichsjugendführung, *Vorschriftenhandbuch der Hitler-Jugend [1942]*, 3:1905–1906. On this, see also the standardized daily schedule in Niehuis, *Das Landjahr*, 146.

198. Kraas, *Lehrerlager 1932–1945*, 262; Link, *Reformpädagogik*, 286–288.

199. Fritzsche, *Life and Death in the Third Reich*, 101.

200. See above all Nieden, *Alltag im Ausnahmezustand*, 59

201. On debate about the diary as an instrument for political education in the Soviet Union, see Aris, *Die Metro als Schriftwerk*, 117–152.
202. Wilhelm Decker, "Nationalsozialistische Feiergestaltung," *Völkischer Beobachter*, March 4, 1937.
203. Schliebe, "Gemeinschaftstagebücher [1934]," 233.
204. The pedagogue Friedrich Schneider, who was forced into retirement in 1934, paid much closer attention to the diary, mainly in his thoughts on "self-education." But his thoughts never had any effect in the 1930s and 1940s. See Schneider, *Die Selbsterziehung* [1936]; Schneider, *Praxis der Selbsterziehung* [1940], 99–117.
205. Schuwerack, "Zur Gestaltung nationalpolitischer Schülerlehrgänge [1934]," 330.
206. Quite telling, for example, is the study by Anna Kallsperger about the women's labor service, which was also based on "two East Prussian camp diaries" (p. 107), but she used them solely as sources and did not inquire into their educational significance. Kallsperger, *Nationalsozialistische Erziehung im Reichsarbeitsdienst für die weibliche Jugend* [1939].
207. Tenorth, "Pädagogisches Denken," 139.
208. StA Hamburg, 622-1/189, 2/10, November 12, 1933.

5. Political Self-Formation in the Nazi Education Project

1. Groß, *Rassenpolitische Erziehung* [1934], 27.
2. "Ambivalent": Kraas, *Lehrerlager 1932–1945*, 273; similarly also Patel, "Gemeinsame Arbeit," 347; "not as seamlessly": Tenorth, "Grenzen der Indoktrination," 348; "stuck": C. Zimmermann, *Medien im Nationalsozialismus*, 259.
3. For a new study that revamps corresponding older theses, see Rohkrämer, *Die fatale Attraktion des Nationalsozialismus*.
4. Ehrhardt, "Erziehungsdenken und Erziehungspraxis," 93.
5. On this, see the first section of this book, especially pages ???
6. Beck, *Geistige Grundlagen der neuen Erziehung* [1933], 17.
7. Beck, 16.
8. Beck, 17.
9. Föllmer, "Wie kollektivistisch war der Nationalsozialismus," 39. For detail on the connection between communality and individuality, see Föllmer, *Modernity in Berlin*. On communality as an educational objective, but hardly taking this connection into account, see, for example, Stahlmann and Schiedeck, *Erziehung zur Gemeinschaft*; Kraas, *Lehrerlager 1932–1945*; Patel, *Soldaten der Arbeit*.
10. This and previous quotes, MLHA Schwerin, 10.9, S/8, no. 4, April 3, 1937.
11. Krapfenbauer, *Die sozialpolitische Bedeutung der NS-Gemeinschaft 'Kraft durch Freude'* [1938], 12.
12. Krapfenbauer, 23.
13. Weiß, "Die Aufgaben der NS-Gemeinschaft ›Kraft durch Freude‹," in Hans Biallas and Gerhard Starcke, *Leipzig. Das Nürnberg der Deutschen Arbeitsfront*. Munich, 1935, 154, quoted in Buchholz, "Die nationalsozialistische Gemeinschaft 'Kraft durch Freude,'" 185.
14. On Strength through Joy and the available trips, see Baranowski, *Strength through Joy*; Spode, "Arbeiterurlaub im Dritten Reich"; König, *Volkswagen, Volksempfänger, Volksgemeinschaft*, 192–219.
15. This and previous quotes, DTA, 1724, Reise Mai 1934, 2.

16. König, *Volkswagen, Volksempfänger, Volksgemeinschaft*, 196.
17. On this, see Koshar, *German Travel Cultures*, 115–149 (quote on 134).
18. Engelbrechten and Volz, *Wir wandern durch das nationalsozialistische Berlin* [1937]. A copy of the brochure *Potsdam: Die Geburtsstätte des Dritten Reiches* is found in the diary of Ludwig Lindholm, StdA Solingen, Na 040, 13, August 25, 1935. On the political diaries of the 1930s, see Koshar, *German Travel Cultures*, 135–149; Siemens, "Dem SA-Mann auf der Spur."
19. StdA Solingen, Na 040, 13, August 25, 1935.
20. StdA Solingen, August 26, 1935.
21. StdA Solingen, August 26, 1935.
22. Party buildings in Munich: IfZ, ED 363, 11, Bericht der Italienfahrt; NSDAP rally grounds in Nürnberg: DTA, 565/I, 1, May 21–24, 1937; Ministries and Gestapo office in Berlin: AdK, Kempowski-Bio, 6301/1, 1, July 10, 1939, July 25, 1939.
23. DTA, 1512, 1, July 26, 1934. See also DTA, 3, August 3, 1937.
24. DTA, 2, May 25, 1935.
25. DTA, 3, September 6, 1936.
26. DTA, 1, July 26, 1934.
27. On this, see the foundational work by Anderson, *Die Erfindung der Nation*, 14–17.
28. On this, see, for example, Knoch, "Gemeinschaften im Nationalsozialismus," 37–50.
29. On this, see, for example, the diary of the community of barroom regulars "Quiet Corner" (Ruhige Ecke), which had been founded as early as 1931 but after 1933 was presented as a miniaturized expression of the community of the entire nation. DTA, 3086, 1.
30. On this, see Patel, "'Sinnbild der nationalsozialistischen Weltanschauung,'" esp. 33–41.
31. This and previous quote, AdK, Kempowski-Bio, 1174, January 4, 1934.
32. The Voluntary Labor Service was not set up as the Reich Labor Service until 1935, whereupon it became a mandatory service that all men—and starting in 1939 all women—had to fulfill between the ages of eighteen and twenty-five years old.
33. AdK, Kempowski-Bio, 1174, September 11, 1933.
34. AdK, January 4, 1934.
35. On this, see the corresponding discussion on pages ???.
36. This and previous quotes, DTA, 1512, 1, February 4, 1934.
37. On the training and travel camps, see the summary by Kraas, "Lager als Erziehungsform"; Patel, *Soldaten der Arbeit*; Kraas, *Lehrerlager 1932–1945*; Dudek, "Nationalsozialistische Jugendpolitik"; Schiedeck and Stahlmann, "Die Inszenierung 'totalen Erlebens.'"
38. Schmerbach, *Gemeinschaftslager Hanns Kerrl*, 147.
39. On his biography, see the entry for Erwin Sylvanus in *Lexikon westfälischer Autorinnen und Autoren*, accessed August 5, 2022, https://www.lexikon-westfaelischer-autorinnen-und-autoren.de/autoren/sylvanus-erwin. /
40. Archivamt des Landschaftsverbandes Westfalen-Lippe, Westfälisches Literaturarchiv (LWL-Archiv, Literaturarchiv), Nachlass Sylvanus, 1035/35, "Ostland ruft."
41. LWL-Archiv, "Ostland ruft."
42. This and previous quotes, LWL-Archiv, "Ostland ruft."
43. DTA, 3077, 1.
44. DTA, 3207, 1.
45. DTA, 1941, foreword.
46. This and previous quote, StdA Bergisch Gladbach, R 4/32, first entry.
47. Teachers had collective diaries written not only at elite schools but also at regular schools. See, for example, Elz and Erbar, *Ihr seid das Deutschland der Zukunft*.

48. This and previous quotes, LWL-Archiv, Literaturarchiv, Nachlass Sylvanus, 1035/35, August 31, 1936.

49. The commemoration work of the camps and the many corresponding brochures, photo albums, and badges have not been researched in detail. On this, see above all the references to commemorative newspapers issued by participants at the end of camp in Kraas, *Lehrerlager 1932–1945*, 261–273; Schuster and Kraas, "'Das Wortfeld "Kamerad" wird sinnerfüllt.'"

50. LWL-Archiv, Literaturarchiv, Nachlass Sylvanus, 1035/35, August 31, 1936.

51. This and previous quotes, DTA, 1941, foreword.

52. On future orientation as a key textual feature of diaries, see the expositions in the introduction and also Lejeune, "Continuous and the Discontinuous"; Dusini, *Tagebuch*, esp. 83–108.

53. See, for example, the comment of Henry Marx on page ???

54. IfZ, ED 30, 6, Easter 1934.

55. IfZ, 7, October 5, 1934.

56. This and previous quotes, IfZ, October 5, 1934.

57. This and previous quotes, IfZ, October 5, 1934.

58. Karl Leisner was consecrated as a priest in the Dachau concentration camp in 1944. He was beatified in 1996. On his biography, see Schmiedl, *Mit letzter Konsequenz*. His diary from the Reich Labor Service is published in Seeger, "Tagebuchaufzeichnungen Karl Leisners im RAD."

59. Seeger, "Tagebuchaufzeichnungen Karl Leisners im RAD," 120 (November 3, 1937).

60. Seeger.

61. DTA, 237, "The camp house." FAD stands for Freiwilliger Arbeitsdienst (Voluntary Labor Service).

62. DHM, Do 2006/200, "Bemerkung" (last page).

63. DHM, "Bemerkung" (last page).

64. DHM, "Bemerkung" (last page).

65. AdK, Kernowski-Bio, 1936 I, 1, March 29, 1936.

66. This and previous quotes, AdK, undated notes (April 1936).

67. On this, see Erren, *"Selbstkritik" und Schuldbekenntnis*; Unfried, *Ich bekenne*.

68. DTA, 237, "Das Lagerhaus."

69. This and previous quotes, DTA, 237, "Der Fahnenappell."

70. On the key importance of the morning and evening flag ceremony, see, for example, Seifert, *Kulturarbeit im Reichsarbeitsdienst*, 122.

71. DTA, 237, "Die Meckerstunde."

72. DHM, Do 2006/200.

73. IfZ, ED 30, 7, May 12, 1934.

74. IfZ, 07/28/1934.

75. One exception consists of the entries that Briske wrote in his camp diary regarding the so-called Röhm putsch, which he extensively discussed. On this, see IfZ, entries between June 30, 1934, and July 4, 1934.

76. This and previous quotes, Patel, "'Sinnbild der nationalsozialistischen Weltanschauung'" 39. Incisive on this also Patel, "'Auslese' und 'Ausmerze.'"

77. See, for example, Kraas, *Lehrerlager 1932–1945*, 274–293; Schmerbach, *Gemeinschaftslager Hanns Kerrl*, 147–148.

78. DHM, Do 2006/200, "Ein Tagesablauf."

79. This and previous quotes, DHM, "Lagerleben."
80. LHA Koblenz, 700, 153, 285, November 22, 1934.
81. AdK, Kempowski-Bio, 303/2, August 22, 1935.
82. DTA, 1783, 1, January 25, 1938.
83. DTA, "Tagesordnung."
84. The diary of Emil Kuhn was created in a camp for advanced students in the Rhine Province, where diary writing was prescribed for participants. See pages ???
85. Andreas Kraas uses this distinction to justify the special value as sources of "camp newspapers," booklets collectively designed as mementos by participants at the end of camp. In his research, Kraas prioritizes these sources over "log-oriented participant reports." By comparison, the more expansive camp newspapers, according to Kraas, reflected on camp experiences. Kraas, *Lehrerlager*, 262-263.
86. Fritzsche observed something similar with respect to the travel diary of Franz Göll in his report of a Strength through Joy vacation in 1935. Fritzsche, *Turbulent World*, 72-73.
87. AdK, Kempowski-Bio, 303/2, August 19, 1935.
88. AdK, August 24, 1935
89. DTA, 1636, July 18, 1939.
90. DTA, July 19, 1939.
91. DTA, 1941, July 9, 1939.
92. LWL-Archiv, Literaturarchiv, Nachlass Sylvanus, 1035/35, August 31, 1936.
93. IfZ, ED 363, 7, October 5, 1934.
94. IfZ, May 14, 1934.
95. IfZ, May 16, 1934.
96. DTA, 237, "Der Brief vom Arbeitsmann Bruno R. aus dem männlichen Lager Mangelshorst an Eva."
97. DTA, "Die nächtliche Waschung der Eva Schmidt."
98. StdA Dortmund, 400/20.
99. Hosenfeld, *"Ich versuche jeden zu retten,"* 208 (January 19, 1936).
100. This and previous quotes, Hosenfeld, 215 (September 15, 1936).
101. Hosenfeld, 213 (July 15, 1936).
102. Hosenfeld, 213 (July 18, 1936).
103. Hosenfeld, 228 (January 1, 1938).
104. Hosenfeld, 229 (February 19, 1938).
105. IfZ, ED 363, 7, for example June 13, 1934, July 4, 1934, July 16, 1934, September 6,1934.
106. DHM, D02 2006/200, "Werkabiturienten in der Praxis."
107. This and previous quotes, DHM, "Werkabiturienten in der Praxis."
108. DHM, "Stube 5."
109. IfZ, ED 363, 7, May 16, 1934.
110. Seeger, *Tagebuchaufzeichnungen Karl Leisners im RAD*, 55 (letter of April 9, 1937). ND refers to the Bund Neudeutschland, a Catholic youth organization founded in 1919.
111. This and previous quotes, Seeger, 54 (April 7, 1937).
112. Seeger, 86 (June 10, 1937). Leisner's reference to an "evil man" is in English.
113. LWL-Archiv, Literaturarchiv, Nachlass Sylvanus, 1035/35, "Ostland ruft."
114. DTA, 1156, for example, July 19, 1935, July 21, 1935. The novel *Ferien vom Ich* by Paul Keller had already appeared in 1916 but gained new popularity through the film adaptation by Hans Deppe. The phrase was also used by educational actors to characterize camp stays. Kraas, *Lehrerlager 1932-1945*, 274.

115. See, for example, Spode, "Arbeiterurlaub im Dritten Reich," 311–312.
116. Spode, 315.
117. DHM, Do 2006/200, "Lagerleben."
118. DTA, 1512, 1, April 14, 1934.
119. DTA, 1, June 25, 1934.
120. DTA, 1, April 8, 1934.
121. DTA, 1, March 10, 1934
122. Seeger, Karl Leisner im RAD, 29.
123. This and previous quotes, Seeger, *Tagebuchaufzeichnungen Karl Leisners im RAD*, 120.
124. This and previous quotes, DTA, 1512, 1, April 15, 1934.
125. DTA, 3, March 18, 1936.
126. DTA, 1, December 3, 1936.
127. DTA, 1, February 8, 1937.
128. Fritzsche and Hellbeck, "New Man in Stalinist Russia and Nazi Germany," 311.
129. Alfred Baeumler, "Politische Leibeserziehung," in *Sport und Staat*, ed. Arno Breitmeyer and Paul Gerhard Hoffmann (Berlin, 1937), 2:135–161, here 139.
130. Baeumler, 140.
131. P. Diehl, "Körperbilder und Körperpraxen im Nationalsozialismus," 17. On physical exercise of the Nazi education project, see Siemens, "Von Marmorleibern und Maschinenmenschen"; Pfeiffer, *Sport im Nationalsozialismus*; Bahro, *Der SS-Sport*; Marschik, *Sportdiktatur*; Wedemeyer-Kolwe, *Der neue Mensch*, 389–422.
132. On Nazi representations of the body, see Siemens, "Von Marmorleibern und Maschinenmenschen"; P. Diehl, *Körper im Nationalsozialismus*; Reichel, *Der schöne Schein*; Alkemeyer, *Körper, Kult und Politik*; Schmidtke, *Körperformationen*; P. Diehl, *Macht, Mythos, Utopie*; Wildmann, *Begehrte Körper*.
133. Alkemeyer, "Images and Politics of the Body," 60.
134. Alkemeyer, 60, 78.
135. P. Diehl, "Körperbilder und Körperpraxen im Nationalsozialismus," 12.
136. Schmidtke, "Disziplin, Kontrolle, Grenzüberwindung," 98, 99.
137. Ehrhardt, Erziehungsdenken und Erziehungspraxis," 111. On this, see Hitler, *Mein Kampf*, 2:1041–1045.
138. von Tschammer und Osten, *Sport und Leibesübungen im nationalsozialistischen Staat* [1937], 8.
139. Alkemeyer, "Images and Politics of the Body," 67.
140. Wilhelm Hehlmann, *Pädagogisches Wörterbuch*, 2nd ed. (Stuttgart, 1941), 247, quoted in Bernett, *Nationalsozialistische Leibeserziehung*, 68.
141. Patel, *Soldaten der Arbeit*, 249.
142. Alkemeyer, "Images and Politics of the Body," 64.
143. On the current state of research, see Siemens, "Von Marmorleibern und Maschinenmenschen." A good overview is also offered in the anthology by P. Diehl, *Körper im Nationalsozialismus*.
144. On invigoration through labor service, see Patel, *Soldaten der Arbeit*, 237. An increased sportiness is detected, for example, by Marschik, *Sportdiktatur*, 72.
145. Marschik, *Sportdiktatur*, 539.
146. This and previous quotes, Keys, "Body as a Political Space," 411–412, 413.
147. Siemens, "Von Marmorleibern und Maschinenmenschen," 682, 681.
148. Siemens, 62. The difficulties of a history of an individualized physicality under National Socialism become clear, for example, in the reviews of the study by Cachay, Bahlke,

and Mehl, *"Echte Sportler."* Especially trenchant: Michael Krüger in *Sportwissenschaft* 32, no. 3 (2002): 339–344. A basic assessment on this also in Piller, *Private Körper,* esp. 7–13, 279.

149. MLHA Schwerin, 10.9—S/8, no. 3, February 12,1934.
150. On disease, see the study by Cocks, *State of Health.*
151. Duden, "Das 'System' unter der Haut," 262.
152. Duden, *Geschichte unter der Haut,* 7. My deliberations do not follow the division established in the history of the body between the research of "experiences of the body" and "body discourses." I share the insight that "most of what appears in ego documents as the 'experience' of the speaking subject simply [refers] back to the discursive conditions that formed this experience." Sarasin, "'Mapping the Body,'" 120. But I do not draw from this the conclusion that one should above all investigate discourses; rather, with respect to the Nazi education project, my deliberations are interested in individuals' deliberately implemented adoption of discursive notions of the body for their own physicality.
153. Alkemeyer, "Images and Politics of the Body," 63.
154. Gebhardt, *Die Angst vor dem kindlichen Tyrannen,* 117, 106, 105.
155. Cocks, *State of Health.*
156. This and previous quotes, DHM, D02 2006/200, "Sport."
157. This and previous quotes, DHM, "Ein Tagesablauf."
158. This was urged by circulars from the Reich Youth Leadership 25/III dated August 19, 1938, and 19/IV dated May 19, 1939. Quoted in Reichsjugendführung, *Vorschriftenhandbuch der Hitler-Jugend* [1942], 3:1777.
159. DHM, D02 88/487.432, *Sport-Tagebuch der deutschen Jugend.*
160. The pages with the explanations from the Diary are printed in Sösemann, *Propaganda,* 2:1270–1272.
161. In certain contexts—for example, marriage permits for SS members or students—the acquisition of achievement badges was mandatory. Luh, *75 Jahre deutsches Sportabzeichen,* 59–61.
162. On the sports and achievement badges, see Luh, *75 Jahre deutsches Sportabzeichen;* Bernett, *Nationalsozialistische Leibeserziehung,* 246–253.
163. This is how the *Deutschland-Berichte der Sopade* (1934, p. 815) summarized the purpose of the Hitler Youth achievement badge. With regard to the *Sport-Tagebuch,* the official instructions of the Reich Youth Leadership stated, "Every German boy and every German girl should possess the *Sport-Tagebuch,* should regularly make entries or their sports achievements, and thereby attain an overview of their sports development." Reichsjugendführung, *Vorschriftenhandbuch der Hitler-Jugend* [1942], 3:1777.
164. DHM, D02 88/487.432, *Sport-Tagebuch der deutschen Jugend,* foreword.
165. This and previous quotes, DHM, foreword.
166. DHM, foreword. On the orientation toward achievement in sports, see Marschik, *Sportdiktatur,* 596–612.
167. Reichel, *Der schöne Schein,* 257–258.
168. Malitz, *Die Leibesübungen in der nationalsozialistischen Idee* [1933], 9.
169. Reichel, *Der schöne Schein,* 258. For detail on this, see also Marschik, *Sportdiktatur,* 58–72.
170. Malitz, *Die Leibesübungen in der nationalsozialistischen Idee* [1933], 6. On the communal orientation of sports, see Marschik, *Sportdiktatur,* 541–556.
171. Baeumler, "Politische Leibeserziehung [1937]," 155.
172. Luh, *75 Jahre deutsches Sportabzeichen,* 61–62.
173. Here and previous quotes, DHM, D02 2006/200, "Sport."

174. DTA, 1783, 1, July 24, 1938.
175. DTA, 1512, 3, collection of quotes at the end of the diary.
176. This and previous quotes, DTA, October 13, 1935.
177. This and previous quotes, AdK, Kempowski-Bio, 303, 1, September 8, 1935.
178. AdK, November 25, 1935.
179. DTA, 1991, 1. The appeal and compatibility of striving for achievement for contemporaries also emphasized, for example, by Marschik, *Sportdiktatur*, 639. Names changed.
180. IfZ, ED 30, 7, July 4, 1934. ADW refers to Allgemeiner Deutscher Waffenring (General German Arms Ring), a conglomeration of student dueling associations.
181. This and previous quotes, IfZ, July 4, 1934.
182. On physical exercise in the labor service, see Patel, *Soldaten der Arbeit*, 226–249.
183. This and previous quotes, IfZ, ED 363, 7, September 25, 1934.
184. von Gönner, *Spaten und Ähre* [1938], 226.
185. This and previous quotes, FZH, X 11/K36, letter from Kroll, undated (1934).
186. FZH, letter from Kroll, undated (1934).
187. This and previous quotes, FZH, letter from Kroll, undated (1934).
188. This and previous quotes, FZH, letter from Kroll, October 5, 1934.
189. This and previous quotes, DHM, D02 2006/200, "Arbeit."
190. Seeger, *Tagebuchaufzeichnungen Karl Leisners im RAD*, 55 (April 9, 1937).
191. AdK, Kempowski-Bio, 303, 1, May 13, 1936.
192. AdK, May 2, 1936.
193. AdK, September 29, 1936.
194. This and previous quotes, DTA, 302, I, 1, Letter from Stelzer, April 7, 1936.
195. DTA, letter from Stelzer, August 25, 1936.
196. DTA, letter from Stelzer, April 12, 1936.
197. DTA, letter from Stelzer, May 7, 1936.
198. DTA, 1512, 3, October 13, 1935. She slightly misquotes Hitler's speech; he actually said "swift as greyhounds."
199. This and previous quotes, DTA, March 10, 1934.
200. DTA, 1, May 3, 1934.
201. DTA, April 14, 1934.
202. On this, s. esp. Cocks, *State of Health*.
203. StA Hamburg, 622-1/189, 10, January 3, 1934.
204. On this, see the corresponding discussion on pages ???
205. AdK, Kempowski-Bio, 303, 1, February 20, 1936.
206. FZH, X 11, K36, letter from Kroll, October 5, 1934.
207. DTA, 1512, 2, March 3, 1935 (wrongly dated as February 3, 1935).
208. This and previous quotes, DTA, 3, July 15, 1936.
209. On this, see the corresponding discussion on pages ???
210. DTA, 1512, 3, March 6, 1937.
211. DTA, September 22, 1937. Previous quotes, DTA, April 2, 1937.
212. DTA, October 17, 1937.
213. DTA, 4, January 24, 1939.
214. DTA, 3, October 28, 1937.
215. DTA, 4, November 23, 1938.
216. Marschik, *Sportdiktatur*, 539.

217. On the historical development of racism, see the summary in Geulen, *Geschichte des Rassismus*; Mosse, *Geschichte des Rassismus in Europa*.
218. P. Diehl, "Körperbilder und Körperpraxen im Nationalsozialismus," 25.
219. P. Diehl, *Macht, Mythos, Utopie*, 109.
220. On Hans. F. K. Günther and his "race portraits," see P. Diehl, *Macht, Mythos, Utopie*, 105–109; Regener, *Fotografische Erfassung*, 253–263. On Günther's key importance to the popularization of racial scientific categories in the Nazi education project, see Harten, Neirich, and Schwerendt, *Rassenhygiene als Erziehungsideologie*, 139–144, 92–96.
221. This and previous quotes, P. Diehl, *Macht, Mythos, Utopie*, 108.
222. Ludwig Ferdinand Clauß and Arthur Hoffmann, *Vorschule der Rassenkunde auf der Grundlage der praktischen Menschenbeobachtung* (Erfurt, 1934), 3.
223. Clauß and Hoffmann, 14.
224. Clauß and Hoffmann, 3.
225. Fink, *Judenfrage im Unterricht* [1937], 16. For detail on this, see Harten, Neirich, and Schwerendt, *Rassenhygiene als Erziehungsideologie*.
226. "Solid part of school education": P. Diehl, "Körperbilder und Körperpraxen im Nationalsozialismus," 28; "racially conscious self-education": Surén, *Gymnastik der Deutschen* [1938].
227. Gebhardt, *Die Angst vor dem kindlichen Tyrannen*, 105.
228. AdK, Kempowski-Bio, A 37, August 18, 1939.
229. AdK, Kempowski-Bio, 5584, 10, January 17, 1934, January 18, 1934.
230. Hosenfeld, *Ich versuche jeden zu retten*, 239 (late 1938, early 1939).
231. Hosenfeld, 216 (November 17, 1936).
232. DTA, 1512, 1, August 1, 1934.
233. LHA Koblenz, 700, 153, 186, October 27, 1934.
234. AdK, Kempowski-Bio, 4842, 1, "Prolog."
235. AdK, November 1, 1935.
236. AdK, "Prolog."
237. This and previous quotes, StdA Münster, Nachlass Beier, 5, "Fahrt mit KdF nach Tirol, Weihnachten 1938," 15. The phrase "Defregger pictures" refers to Franz Defregger, an Austrian-Bavarian history painter of the late nineteenth century. Beier does not specify an exact sum.
238. This and previous quotes, IfZ, ED 363, 7, July 29, 1934.
239. This and previous quotes, von Gönner, *Spaten und Ähre* [1938], 148.
240. P. Diehl, "Körperbilder und Körperpraxen im Nationalsozialismus," 10.
241. Herbert, "Traditionen des Rassismus," 474.
242. For detail on the modification of racial thought at the turn of the nineteenth to the twentieth century, see Geulen, *Wahlverwandte*.
243. On this, see Parnes, "Biologisches Erbe."
244. Schmuhl, "Rassismus unter den Bedingungen charismatischer Herrschaft," 186.
245. Schmuhl, 188.
246. On the emergence of racial hygiene, see above all Weingart, Kroll, and Bayertz, *Rasse, Blut und Gene*; Schmuhl, *Rassenhygiene, Nationalsozialismus, Euthanasie*; Schmuhl, *Grenzüberschreitungen*.
247. Herbert, "Traditionen des Rassismus," 475.
248. On this, see the fundamental work by Peukert, *Volksgenossen und Gemeinschaftsfremde*.
249. Franke, *Vererbung, eine weltanschauliche Grundfrage* [1937].

250. Groß, Rassenpolitische Erziehung [1934], 21.
251. Groß, 22.
252. Surén, Gymnastik der Deutschen. Rassenbewusste Selbsterziehung [1938], 13.
253. Michligk, Ahnenforschung leicht gemacht [1934], 13.
254. Fritzsche, Life and Death in the Third Reich, 80.
255. Peukert, Volksgenossen und Gemeinschaftsfremde; Bock, Zwangssterilisation im Nationalsozialismus; Schmuhl, Rassenhygiene, Nationalsozialismus, Euthanasie; Herbert, "Traditionen des Rassismus." For detail on the educational dimension of racial hygiene, see Harten, Neirich, and Schwerendt, Rassenhygiene als Erziehungsideologie. Thus far the most detail on the social consequences is in Fritzsche, Life and Death in the Third Reich, 76–142.
256. On this, see Rupnow, "Judenforschung" im "Dritten Reich," 285–296.
257. On the capabilities and limits of "blood research" in the early twentieth century, see Spörri, Reines und gemischtes Blut.
258. On the history of genealogy in the first half of the twentieth century, see Zwilling, "100 Jahre genealogische Forschung"; Zwilling, "Mutterstämme."
259. This and previous quote, Zwilling, "Mutterstämme," 29.
260. Zwilling, 1.
261. Essner, Die "Nürnberger Gesetze," 41. Eugen Fischer developed the theses about the heritability of "racial qualities" in 1913 through genealogical methods in his study on the "bastardization problem for humans" in German Southwest Africa. On this, see Lösch, Rasse als Konstrukt, 53–81, 123–159.
262. Gesetz zum Schutz des deutschen Blutes und der deutschen Ehre, in Reichsministerium des Innern, Reichsgesetzblatt (1935): 1:1146–1147, here 1146.
263. Spörri, Reines und gemischtes Blut, 314.
264. On the Reichssippenkartei projects, see Schulle, "Das Reichssippenamt," 134–142. On the storage and central documentation of church books for genealogical purposes, see Haas, "'Zur restlosen Erfassung des deutschen Volkes'"; Wurm, "Die Mecklenburgische Sippenkanzlei."
265. This and previous quotes, Franke, Vererbung und Rasse [1938], 132.
266. This and previous quotes, Franke, 132–133. Here Gustav Franke approvingly cites Scheid, Einführung in die naturwissenschaftliche Familienkunde [1923].
267. This and previous quotes, "Freude am Familienarchiv," Neues Volk 6, no. 8 (1938): 31–35, here 34–35.
268. This and previous quotes, "Freude am Familienarchiv," 35.
269. Gebhardt, Die Angst vor dem kindlichen Tyrannen, 72–73.
270. Irene Moro-Drasch, Babys Tagebuch: Merkblätter und die Grundzüge der Säuglingspflege, 6th ed. (Graz, 1933), quoted in Gebhardt, Die Angst vor dem kindlichen Tyrannen, 73. A similar recommendation was also made in Tippelmann, Kleinkindererziehung in der deutschen Familie [1938], 151–169.
271. Franke, Vererbung und Rasse [1938], 131.
272. This and previous quotes, DTA, 448/II, 1, January 27, 1936.
273. For detail on this, see Ehrenreich, Nazi Ancestral Proof.
274. Gesetz zur Wiederherstellung des Berufsbeamtentums, in Reichsministerium des Innern, Reichsgesetzblatt (1933): 1:175–177, here 175; Erste Verordnung zur Durchführung des Gesetzes zur Wiederherstellung des Berufsbeamtentums, in Reichsministerium des Innern, Reichsgesetzblatt (1933): 1:195.
275. Reichsbürgergesetz, in Reichsministerium des Innern, Reichsgesetzblatt (1935): 1:1146. On the status of hybrids, see B. Meyer, Jüdische Mischlinge.

276. Richau, "Familienforschung und Ariernachweis," 89.
277. On this, see the list in Richau, 94–97; also Ehrenreich, *Nazi Ancestral Proof*, 58–61.
278. Richau, 104.
279. Today the documents collected in this process are found in the Landesarchiv Berlin, E Rep. 200–90 Nachlass Familie Wiese, no. 1 and 2. My account is based on them and the description of the holdings.
280. Dürre, *Erbbiologischer und eugenischer Wegweiser für Jedermann* [1933]; Denckler, *Wie finde ich meine Ahnen?*[1936]. On this, see also Ehrenreich, *Nazi Ancestral Proof*, 70–71, which among other things shows the growth of genealogical book titles after 1933.
281. On advertising efforts in the Weimar Republic, see Zwilling, "100 Jahre genealogische Forschung," 48–58; Schmuhl, *Rassenhygiene, Nationalsozialismus, Euthanasie*, 115–124.
282. On the establishment of advice centers, see Wisotzky, "Die rheinischen und westfälischen Stadtarchive im Nationalsozialismus."
283. Michligk, *Ahnenforschung leicht gemacht* [1934].
284. Michligk, 20.
285. Jörns and Schwab, *Rassenhygienische Fibel* [1934], 74.
286. For one of the first preprinted forms, see Eydt, *Der Rasse- und Gesundheitspaß* [1933].
287. DHM, Do2 2008/1180, *Der Ahnenpaß* (Berlin: Verlag für Standesamtswesen, 1936), first published 1934. On the role of civil registrars in family studies in the 1930s, see Maruhn, *Staatsdiener im Unrechtsstaat*. However, it does not provide a detailed account of the formation of the *Ancestral Passport*.
288. DHM, Do 70/176, *Ahnenpaß* (Munich: Zentralverlag der NSDAP, Franz Eher Nachfolger, n.d., ca. 1935), 5.
289. Ehrenreich, *Nazi Ancestral Proof*, 73, also with respect to the various variants and their distribution, 70–77.
290. Nahnsen, "Denkschrift betr. Familien-, Sippen- und Rassenkunde," 33.
291. Ehrenreich, *Nazi Ancestral Proof*, 64, 63.
292. For detail on this, see Schulle, "Das Reichssippenamt"; Ehrenreich, *Nazi Ancestral Proof*, 94–120.
293. StdA Essen, NL 643 Paul Maik, Heft *Meine Ahnen*.
294. DHM, Do2 89/2169, *Ahnenpaß*, hardcover version in red linen (Munich: Zentralverlag der NSDAP, Franz Eher Nachfolger, n.d., after 1937), 3.
295. DHM, Do 70/452II, Reichsverband der Standesbeamten Deutschlands, ed., *Deutsches Einheits-Familienstammbuch, zugleich Familienpaß* (Berlin: Verlag für Standesamtswesen, n.d., ca. 1938), 3. On the significance of the family book introduced in 1938, see Maruhn, *Staatsdiener im Unrechtsstaat*, 113–118.
296. This and previous quotes, DTA, 808 I, December 16, 1934.
297. The sculptor Ernst Barlach, for example, spoke in a letter from December 1933 about how the sight of his ancestral chart gave him "sorrow in his already at times intrinsically sorrowful bosom," and he would "rather crush it in a berserker rage than safekeep it." Barlach, *Briefe II*, 425.
298. Fritzsche, *Life and Death in the Third Reich*, 79.
299. Thus, for example, the ancestral passport in DHM, Do 86/117 I.
300. Hoppmann-König, *Mehr Gerechtigkeit wagen*, 1.
301. StdA München, Familien 644.
302. StdA München, Familien 825/3, letter to Krumbholz, November 17, 1939.
303. StdA München, 825/1 and 2.

304. This and previous quotes, curriculum vita printed in Müller-Botsch, *Den richtigen Mann an die richtige Stelle*, 95–96. For more detail on the life path of Hans Drescher, see Müller-Botsch, 9–147.
305. On the various forms of the "Aryan certificate," see Ehrenreich, *Nazi Ancestral Proof*, 61–62.
306. "Dein Blut dein höchstes Gut": DHM, DO2 99/2104, *Ahnenpaß* (Dortmund: National-Verlag Westfalia" Hans August Rumpf, n.d., ca. 1939), 43; further quotes: Otto and Stachowitz, *Abriß der Vererbungslehre und Rassenkunde* [1934], 65, 64.
307. StdA München, Familien 644.
308. Tippelmann, *Kleinkinderziehung in der deutschen Familie* [1938], 155.
309. This and previous quotes, AdK, Kempowski-Bio, 4842, 1, January 3, 1936.
310. This and previous quotes, AdK, January 3, 1936.
311. On this, see Maruhn, *Staatsdiener im Unrechtsstaat*, esp. 42–57, 62–91.
312. StA Hamburg, 622-1/189, 2/10, November 15, 1933.
313. StA Hamburg, November 21, 1933.
314. StA Hamburg, December 21, 1933.
315. This and previous quotes, StA Hamburg, December 28, 1933. Name changed.
316. StA Hamburg, December 31, 1933.
317. StA Hamburg, December 21, 1933.
318. This and previous quotes, StA Hamburg, December 21, 1933.
319. LA Berlin, E Rep 200-43, 4, November 2, 1933. For detail on Franz Göll as an "amateur scientist," see Fritzsche, *Turbulent World*, 108–131, on the significance of nature for human beings esp. 115–1 .
320. LA Berlin, E Rep 200-43, 4, July 30, 1933.
321. LA Berlin, July 30, 1933.
322. LA Berlin, May 19, 1934.
323. LA Berlin, July 28, 1934.
324. LA Berlin, November 11, 1934.
325. LA Berlin, November 15, 1934.
326. LA Berlin, November 11, 1934, November 15, 1934.
327. This and the previous quotes, LA Berlin, November 15, 1934.
328. LA Berlin, November 15, 1934.
329. LA Berlin, November 15, 1934.
330. Something similar is also pointed out in Leo, *Wille zum Wesen*, esp. 537–561.
331. LA Berlin, November 15, 1934.
332. LA Berlin, July 28, 1934.
333. Thus Ehrenreich views the circumstance that racial hygiene "in fact built on a rationalization that could have been shown to be questionable" and "no one questioned it" as evidence for a wide social consensus for brutal anti-Jewish actions." Ehrenreich, *Nazi Ancestral Proof*, xi–xvii.
334. DTA, 1512, 3, May 21, 1935; DTA, 1512, 4, July 24, 1939.
335. StA Hamburg, 622-1/189, 2/10, January 16, 1934.
336. StA Hamburg, February 12, 1934.
337. DTA, 1512, 3, September 22, 1935.
338. This and previous quotes, DTA, September 27, 1935.
339. DTA, September 27, 1935.
340. DTA, May 5, 1934.

341. This and previous quotes, LA Berlin, E Rep 200-43, 4, June 12, 1933.
342. LA Berlin, 5, March 30, 1938.
343. Ehrenreich, *Nazi Ancestral Proof*, 76.
344. Richau, "Familienforschung und Ariernachweis im Dritten Reich," 103.
345. This and previous quotes, LA Berlin, E Rep 200-43, 4, November 15, 1934.
346. LA Berlin, May 19, 1934.
347. This and previous quotes, LA Berlin, November 15, 1934.
348. Pfahler, *Warum Erziehung trotz Vererbung?* [1935], vi.
349. Pfahler, 23.
350. Pfahler, 145, 7.
351. Alfred Baeumler, "Rasse als Grundbegriff der Erziehungswissenschaft," *Internationale Zeitschrift für Erziehung* (1939): 252255., quoted in Lingelbach, *Erziehung und Erziehungstheorien*, 193.
352. Pfahler, *Warum Erziehung trotz Vererbung?* [1935], 8.
353. This and previous quotes, Pfahler, 12.
354. During the 1930s, the Nazi regime pursued the racial-hygienic exclusion of "hereditarily harmful" persons above all by means of sterilization. G. Bock, *Zwangssterilisation im Nationalsozialismus*. They also used isolation through concentration camp imprisonment. Ayaß, *"Asoziale" im Nationalsozialismus*, 138–179. Directly after the war began, the regime then switched to systematic murder with euthanasia. Schmuhl, *Rassenhygiene, Nationalsozialismus, Euthanasie*.
355. This and previous quotes, StdA Werl, Sammlung Wendelin Leidinger, 795, December 17, 1935.
356. StdA Werl, April 10, 1935.
357. StdA Duisburg, 41/624, 1, "Einleitung" and "Meine Erinnerungen."
358. StdA Duisburg, entries with headings "6. April 1935" to "15. Oktober 1937" (quote).
359. StdA Duisburg, "Meine Erinnerungen."
360. StdA Duisburg, "1. Mai 1935."
361. StdA Duisburg, "September 1935."
362. StdA Duisburg, "September 1935."
363. This and previous quotes, StdA Duisburg, "6. April 1935."
364. StA Hamburg, 622-1/189, 2/10, December 21, 1933.
365. StA Hamburg, December 21, 1933.
366. On this, see the corresponding discussions on page ???
367. StA Hamburg, 622-1/189, 2/10, January 3, 1934.
368. StA Hamburg, November 18, 1934.
369. StA Hamburg, November 18, 1934.
370. IfZ, ED 363, 6, October 30, 1934.
371. IfZ, October 30, 1934.
372. IfZ, November 5, 1933.
373. IfZ, October 30, 1933.
374. IfZ, January 30–31, 1934, November 29, 1933, November 11, 1933.
375. IfZ, November 11, 1933.
376. This and previous quotes, IfZ, November 11, 1933.
377. This and previous quotes, IfZ, November 29, 1933.
378. IfZ, March 1, 1934.
379. IfZ, December 31, 1933.

380. IfZ, October 30, 1933.
381. This and previous quotes, IfZ, January 30–31, 1934.
382. IfZ, December 10, 1933.
383. On this, see the first section of this book, particularly pages ???
384. IfZ, ED 30, 6, "Gründonnerstag 1934."
385. On this, see pages ???
386. IfZ, ED 303, 6, October 30, 1933.
387. Wichert, "Albert Leo Schlageter," 67.
388. Luckey, *Personifizierte Ideologie*, 59. The assessment of Heiko Luckey refers to the various publications about Horst Wessel but applies to National Socialist biographical literature in general. On this, see also Fritzsche, *On Being the Subjects of History*.
389. AdK, Kempowski-Bio, 303/1, September 2, 1935.
390. AdK, September 2, 1935.
391. This and previous quotes, AdK, September 2, 1935.
392. AdK, September 2, 1935.
393. AdK, September 2, 1935.
394. On this, see T. Abel, *Why Hitler Came into Power* [1938]; Schmid, "Zu den Motiven 'alter Kämpfer.'" An example of this is the diary of Wilhelm Bollmann, which likewise includes a prologue about his political involvement in the Weimar Republic. AdK, Kempowski-Bio, 4842, 1.
395. LA Berlin E Rep 200-43, 5, May 21, 1938. Also similar: "I constitute the capstone of a family. The more I have learned about this family, the more I am thereby strengthened in my view." LA Berlin, E Rep 200-43, 4, October 31, 1937.
396. AdK, Kempowski-Bio, 4842, 1, "Prolog."
397. Kershaw, "How Effective Was Nazi propaganda?"

Part Three

1. Statement made by Reich Chancellor Adolf Hitler to the commanders of the army and navy on February 3, 1933. Handwritten notes of General Lieutenant Liebmann, quoted in T. Vogelsang, "Neue Dokumente zur Geschichte der Reichswehr," 434–435.
2. Speech of Adolf Hitler to the Reichstag on May 17, 1933, quoted in Domarus, *Hitler*, 1/1:270–279, here 277, 278.
3. On the formation of the decision to withdraw, see the detailed discussion in Dengg, *Deutschlands Austritt aus dem Völkerbund*, esp. 278–308.
4. The various appeals and declarations are printed in Domarus, *Hitler*, 1/1:306–314.
5. This and previous quotes, Domarus, 1/1:307, 308.
6. Minister meeting of October 13–14, 1933, in Repgen and Booms, *Akten der Reichskanzlei*, part 1, 2:903–907, here 904, 905.
7. On prewar foreign policy, see the summary in R. Schmidt, *Außenpolitik des Dritten Reiches*. This and previous quote, Schmidt, 153.
8. Longerich, *Joseph Goebbels*, 247. In mid-July, the Nazi regime had also created the basis for such a vote with the Plebiscite Act. On this, see Jung, *Plebiszit und Diktatur*, 20–34.
9. Vorläufiges Gesetz zur Gleichschaltung der Länder mit dem Reich, in Reichsministerium des Innern, *Reichsgesetzblatt* (1933): I, 153–154.
10. Gesetz über den Neuaufbau des Reichs, in Reichsministerium des Innern, *Reichsgesetzblatt* (1934): I, 75.

11. Aufruf der Reichsregierung an das deutsche Volk vom 14.10.1933, quoted in Domarus, *Hitler*, 1/1:307–308, here 308.
12. This and previous quotes, IfZ, ED 22, 1, October 15, 1933.
13. This and previous quotes, IfZ, October 15, 1933.
14. On the concept of the political system, see Massing, "Politisches System."
15. On this, see the introductory discussions in Mergel, "Kulturgeschichte der Politik"; Frevert and Haupt, *Neue Politikgeschichte*; also Steinmetz, Gilcher-Holtey, and Haupt, *Writing Political History*.
16. Wildt, *Geschichte des Nationalsozialismus*, 90.

6. A New Political Culture in a New Political System

1. See, for example, "Der Novembertag der deutschen Ehre," *Völkischer Beobachter*, November 14, 1933; "Das Siegel," *Vossische Zeitung*, November 14, 1933; "Alles für Deutschland, alles für Hitler," *Schwedter Tageblatt*, November 13, 1933.
2. Kliem, "Der sozialistische Widerstand gegen das Dritte Reich," 74.
3. For the KPD, see the "Directive of the KPD regarding November 12, 1933," which was illegally distributed in Germany, quoted in *Dokumente des ZK der KPD 1933–1945*, 90–91.
4. This and previous from the Minutes of the Party Leadership Meeting on October 18, 1933, quoted in "Protokoll der Parteivorstandssitzung am 18. Oktober 1933," in Buchholz and Rother, *Der Parteivorstand der SPD im Exil*, 20–24, here 20–21.
5. On the KPD, see "The Antifascists of Germany Vote with an Unshakeable 'No'!," printed in *Dokumente des ZK der KPD 1933–1945*, 86–87; "Only Communism Will Bring Salvation! Down with the Regime of Hunger, War, and Terror! Appeal of the Central Committee of the Communist Party of Germany," printed in *Dokumente des ZK der KPD 1933–1945*, 88–90.
6. This and previous quotes, see the facsimile of the leaflet in Mehringer, "Die bayerische Sozialdemokratie bis zum Ende des NS-Regimes," 355. KPD leaflets also used graphic depictions to show how the ballot was supposed to be marked. See the facsimile in Omland, *Du wählst mi nich Hitler!*, 56.
7. This and previous quote, *Deutschland-Berichte der Sopade*, 1934, 287.
8. "Nur der Kommunismus bringt die Rettung! Nieder mit der Regierung des Hungers, des Krieges und des Terrors! Aufruf des Zentralkomitees der Kommunistischen Partei Deutschlands," printed in *Dokumente des ZK der KPD 1933–1945*, 88–90, here 88.
9. This and previous quotes, "Erklärung des ZK der KPD zum Ergebnis der sogenannten Reichstagswahl und Volksabstimmung am 12. November," quoted in *Dokumente des ZK der KPD 1933–1945*, 95.
10. This and previous quotes, "Vier Millionen deutsche Revolutionäre," *Neuer Vorwärts*, November 19, 1933.
11. On discussion in political exile, see the summary in M. Schneider, *Unterm Hakenkreuz*, 887–901.
12. This and previous quotes, Miles, "Neu beginnen," 5–6. The text appeared in fall 1933 in the publishing house of the Sopade, whose newspaper published a preprint extract in early October. See "Neu beginnen!," *Neuer Vorwärts*, October 1, 1933.
13. Miles, "Neu beginnen," 7.
14. Miles, 7.

15. On the reception of the text in fall 1933, see Vlator, "Wege zur Klarheit," *Neuer Vorwärts* supplement, October 22, 1933; Klaus Kautsky, "Eine Diskussionsgrundlage," *Zeitschrift für Sozialismus* 1, no. 2 (1933): 50–58; Ernst Anders, *Neu beginnen—zu welchem Ziel? Zeitschrift für Sozialismus* 1, no. 3 (1933): 98–101.

16. On the history of the group, already constituted since 1929 as a "Leninist organization," see Kliem, "Der sozialistische Widerstand gegen das Dritte Reich"; Stöver, *Volksgemeinschaft*, 77–87.

17. Here and previous quotes, Stöver, *Berichte über die Lage in Deutschland*, 2, 3.

18. Stöver, 4–.

19. This and previous quotes, Miles, "Neu beginnen," 8

20. On the messaging system of Neu Beginnen, see Stöver, *Volksgemeinschaft*, 95–101.

21. This according to the proud self-characterization in the brochure "Die illegale Organisation 'Neubeginnen,'" n.d., after 1945, quoted in Stöver, *Volksgemeinschaft*, 81.

22. *Deutschland-Berichte der Sopade*.

23. Stöver, *Volksgemeinschaft*, 67–68.

24. On the formation and development of the Deutschland-Berichte, see Stöver, *Volksgemeinschaft*, 55–76; Mehringer, "Die bayerische Sozialdemokratie bis zum Ende des NS-Regimes," 35–361; W. Plum, *Die "grünen Berichte" der Sopade*; Friedrich-Ebert-Stiftung, *Widerstand und Exil*, 596–608.

25. Confidential letter of the State Police Center in Hanover to the district administrators (Landräte) of November 15, 1933, quoted in Michaelis and Schraepler, *Ursachen und Folgen*, 9:354–356, 354–35.

26. On this, see the administrative order of State Secretary Gauert in the Prussian Ministry of the Interior, February 24, 1933, printed in Thévoz, Branig, and Lowenthal-Hensel, *Pommern 1934/35* 199–200.

27. Confidential letter of the State Police Authority in Hanover to the district administrators (Landräte) of November 15, 1933, quoted in Michaelis and Schraepler, *Ursachen und Folgen*, 9:354–356, 354–355.

28. The origin of the opinion-reporting operation in the November election and plebiscite was also still evident in the first edition of the "Mitteilungen des Geheimen Staatspolizeiamts" in Berlin, which appeared in mid-January 1934 and described the developments within the Reich since November 1933. Morsch, *Arbeit und Brot*, 20.

29. On the development of the reporting system in the security apparatus, see Morsch, *Arbeit und Brot*, 13–33; Eckert, "Gestapo-Berichte"; T. Müller, *Recht und Volksgemeinschaft*, 114–135.

30. See the summary in Longerich, *Davon haben wir nichts gewusst!*, 32–38 (quote on 38). On the judiciary, see Stadtarchiv Mannheim, *Verfolgung und Widerstand*. On the reporting system of the propaganda ministry, see Stahr, *Volksgemeinschaft*, 49–52. On the labor administration, see the reports quoted in Mason, *Arbeiterklasse und Volksgemeinschaft*.

31. For summarizing accounts of the debate that focused above all on the importance of Hitler for the formation of Nazi policy, see Kershaw, *Der NS-Staat*, 80–147; Hirschfeld and Kettenacker, *Der "Führerstaat."*

32. This is especially emphasized in Lüdtke, *Herrschaft als soziale Praxis*.

33. For detail on the current state of the research, see Steuwer, "Was meint und nützt das Sprechen von der 'Volksgemeinschaft'?," esp. 525–532.

34. Broszat, Fröhlich, and Wiesemann, *Bayern in der NS-Zeit*, vol. 1. Editions of the reports had already appeared since the 1960s. But the publication of reports increased

significantly after the Bavaria project. For an overview, see Longerich, *Davon haben wir nichts gewusst!*, 337–338.

35. Kershaw, "Antisemitismus und Volksmeinung"; Kershaw, *Hitler Myth*; Kershaw, *Popular Opinion and Political Dissent*.
36. F. Dröge, *Der zerredete Widerstand*; Peukert, *Die KPD im Widerstand* (quote on 205); Mason, *Arbeiterklasse und Volksgemeinschaft*.
37. Mühlenfeld, "Was heißt und zu welchem Ende studiert man NS-Propaganda?," 534.
38. Frei, "'Volksgemeinschaft,'" 110; Aly, *Hitlers Volksstaat*, 36; Bajohr, "Zustimmungsdiktatur"; Reichardt, "Faschistische Beteiligungsdiktaturen." Martin Broszat spoke in the 1980s about a "plebiscitarian dictator." Broszat, *Die Machtergreifung*, 176. In doing so, he took up a concept that political observers had already formed in the 1930s. See "Deutschlands neue Staatsform: Die plebiszitäre Diktatur—die totale Despotie," *Neuer Vorwärts*, August 19, 1934.
39. For a summary, Eckert, "Gestapo-Berichte."
40. Longerich, *Davon haben wir nichts gewusst!*, 27
41. This and previous quote, Longerich, 26.
42. This and previous quote, Longerich, 38–53, 316–319.
43. On the voting campaigns in fall 1933, see Omland, *Du wählst mi nich Hitler!*, 42–61; Stepanek, *Wahlkampf im Zeichen der Diktatur*, 29–76.
44. This and previous quotes, "Am 12. November müssen wir der Welt beweisen, daß wir ein Volk geworden sind," *Völkischer Beobachter*, October 29–30, 1933.
45. *Völkischer Beobachter*.
46. Speech of Adolf Hitler in Elbing on November 5, 1933, quoted in Domarus, *Hitler*, 1/1:325.
47. This and previous quotes, "Der Kampf um Friede und Gleichberechtigung," *Völkischer Beobachter*, October 22–23, 1933.
48. Bracher, *Stufen der Machtergreifung*, 475.
49. Longerich, *Davon haben wir nichts gewusst!*, 46, 47.
50. Domarus, *Hitler*, 1/1:323.
51. This and previous quotes, "Reichsinnenminister Dr. Frick zur Reichstagswahl," *Völkischer Beobachter*, October 29–30, 1933.
52. This and previous quotes, "Warum Reichstagswahl," *Völkischer Beobachter*, November 10, 1933. The interview is also printed in Michaelis and Schraepler, *Ursachen und Folgen*, 10:51–53.
53. This and previous quotes, "Dr. Goebbels über die kommende Volksbefragung," *Völkischer Beobachter*, October 19, 1933.
54. "Warum Reichstagswahl," *Völkischer Beobachter*, November 10, 1933.
55. Reich Chief Press Officer Otto Dietrich formulated this particularly concisely when he emphasized in a 1935 speech that "in Germany a public opinion in the true sense of the word only [existed] at all since the National Socialist worldview took hold of the Volk.... The public opinion of the German Volk is National Socialism!" Quoted in Longerich, *Davon haben wir nichts gewusst!*, 50.
56. This and previous quotes, "Warum Reichstagswahl," *Völkischer Beobachter*, November 10, 1933.
57. Longerich, *Davon haben wir nichts gewusst!*, 47. A similar point is made in Stahr, *Volksgemeinschaft*, 16–21, 39–41; T. Müller, *Recht und Volksgemeinschaft*, 131–132.

58. "Warum Reichstagswahl," *Völkischer Beobachter*, November 10, 1933; "Reichsinnenminister Dr. Frick zur Reichstagswahl," *Völkischer Beobachter*, October 29–30, 1933.
59. This and previous quote, Adolf Hitler's speech at the Berlin Sports Palace on October 24, 1933, quoted in Domarus, *Hitler*, 1/1:323–324, here 324.
60. Stöver, *Berichte über die Lage in Deutschland*, 3. For more detail about influencing the casting of votes in the 1930s, see pages ???
61. Stöver, 3.
62. Bohrmann, *NS-Presseanweisungen der Vorkriegszeit*, 1:162.
63. This and previous quotes, Bohrmann, 170.
64. This and previous quotes, Bohrmann, 170.
65. "Dr. Goebbels' Dank," *Vossische Zeitung*, November 14, 1933.
66. Bohrmann, *NS-Presseanweisungen der Vorkriegszeit*, 1:163.
67. This and previous quotes, Huber, *Verfassungsrecht des Großdeutschen Reiches* [1939], 195.
68. Stahr, *Volksgemeinschaft*, 20, 21.
69. Letter of the Prussian minister president of April 2, 1933, printed in G. Plum, "Staatspolizei und innere Verwaltung," 222–223. In the late 1930s, the SD took over the task of producing general morale reports. On this, see Boberach, *Meldungen aus dem Reich*.
70. Longerich, *Davon haben wir nichts gewusst!*, 47.
71. Longerich, 48.
72. This and previous quotes, Longerich, 318.
73. On this, see the summary in Steuwer, "Was meint und nützt das Sprechen von der 'Volksgemeinschaft'?"; Mühlenfeld, "Was heißt und zu welchem Ende studiert man NS-Propaganda?"; T. Müller, *Recht und Volksgemeinschaft*; Merziger, *Nationalsozialistische Satire und 'Deutscher Humor.'*
74. Longerich, *Davon haben wir nichts gewusst!*, 53.
75. This and previous quotes, "Die Stimmung in Deutschland: Bericht von einer Reise," *Neuer Vorwärts*, June 10, 1934. The quoted extract is also printed in *Deutschland-Berichte der Sopade*, 1934, 120.
76. Stöver, *Berichte über die Lage in Deutschland*, 232.
77. Stöver, 2.
78. Stöver, 23.
79. This and previous quotes, Stöver, 232.
80. The British ambassador in Germany pointed out something similar in his report on the voting of November 1933, printed in Michaelis and Schraepler, *Ursachen und Folgen*, 10:56–60, here 58.
81. As per Heinz Boberach on the SD, Boberach, *Meldungen aus dem Reich*, 1:11.
82. Longerich, *Davon haben wir nichts gewusst!*, 319.
83. Kershaw, "Antisemitismus und Volksmeinung," 291.
84. Kershaw, 291.
85. IfZ, ED 21, October 15, 1933, November 12, 1933.
86. This and previous quotes, IfZ, November 13, 1933.
87. This and previous quotes, IfZ, November 18, 1933.
88. This and previous quotes, IfZ, May 21, 1933.
89. IfZ, May 21, 1933.
90. This and previous quotes, IfZ, May 21, 1933.
91. On the Braun-Frick regime in Thuringia, see Neliba, "Wilhelm Frick."

92. "Georg Witzmann in der 79. Landtagssitzung vom 1. April 1931," *Verhandlungen des V. Landtages von Thüringen, 4. Abteilung: Stenographische Berichte*, vol. 2, Weimar: 1930–1932, 1822.
93. Briefe: Witzmann, *Thüringen von 1918–1933*, 177; "Fritz Sauckel in der 79. Landtagssitzung vom 1. April 1931," in *Verhandlungen des V. Landtages von Thüringen, 4. Abteilung: Stenographische Berichte*, Weimar: 1930–1932, 2:1827.
94. IfZ, ED 22, 1, May 22, 1933.
95. IfZ, May 22, 1933.
96. IfZ, June 11, 1933.
97. IfZ, June 30, 1933.
98. IfZ, August 21, 1933.
99. AdK, October 26, 1933.
100. On this, see the discussion on pages ???
101. AdK, Kempowski-Bio, 1174, November 14, 1933, September 11, 1933, October 26, 1933.
102. LA Berlin, E Rep 200-43, 4, August 22, 1933.
103. LA Berlin, July 23, 1933.
104. LA Berlin, July 23, 1933.
105. MLHA Schwerin, 10.9.-S/8, 10, 1–8.
106. IfZ, ED 22, 1, August 21, 1933.
107. AdK, Kempowski-Bio, 5965/1, 1, July 3, 1934. Also similar, for example, February 16, 1935.
108. This and previous quotes, LA Berlin, E Rep 200-43, 4, August 23, 1933.
109. LA Berlin, September 23, 1933.
110. FZH, 11/K 33, Letter from Kirchmann, February 5, 1933. The murder of Giacomo Matteotti is considered the start of the fascist dictatorship in Italy.
111. IfZ, ED 22, 1, March 7, 1933.
112. Bismarck: AdK, Kempowski-Bio, 5965/1, 6, April 12, 1938; Frederick the Great: AdK, Kempowski-Bio, 5584, 11, February 8, 1935; Befreiungskriege: AdK, Kempowski-Bio, 5965/1, 2, August 11, 1934; end of war, 1918: AdK, 1, June 15, 1933.
113. Napoleon: StdA Münster, Nachlass Beier, 5, July 21, 1939; Cäsar: AdK, Kempowski-Bio, 5965/1, 6, March 16, 1938; attische Demokratie: IfZ, ED 22, 1, June 9, 1933.
114. For an introduction, Schmiechen-Ackermann, *Diktaturen im Vergleich*.
115. Bajohr, "Zustimmungsdiktatur," 78.
116. This and previous quotes, Huber, *Verfassungsrecht des Großdeutschen Reiches* [1939], 197.
117. I am adopting the classical understanding of "political culture" as a "midlevel and mediating instance between the political institutions and the individuals." Pesch, *Handlungstheorie und Politische Kultur*, 11. In taking this perspective, I share the interest in the connection between the political system and society, which has moved to the margins in discussions about a "cultural history of politics." But as opposed to the political sciences, I do not see the condition of a political culture as being documented in the results of opinion surveys but rather in the interaction between individuals and political authorities as mediated through the public representation of political rule.
118. On the connection between the organization of power and the visualization of rule, see the groundbreaking work by Münkler, "Visibilität der Macht," esp. 214–217.
119. See the discussions in the second part of the book, especially pages ???
120. Huber, *Verfassungsrecht des Großdeutschen Reiches* [1939], 194.
121. This and previous quotes, Huber, 197.
122. Herz, *Hoffmann & Hitler*, 217.
123. See here the influential surveys by Reichel, *Der schöne Schein*; Thamer, *Verführung und Gewalt*, esp. 342–350, 417–434. Also the studies by Kershaw, *Hitler Myth*; Wehler,

Deutsche Gesellschaftsgeschichte, vol. 4; Herz, *Hoffmann & Hitler*; Nitz, *Führer und Duce*; Loiperdinger, Herz, and Pohlmann, *Führerbilder*; Kopperschmidt, *Hitler der Redner*; Thamer and Erpel, *Hitler und die Deutschen*.

124. On the interpretation of National Socialism as a "political religion," see especially Bärsch, *Die politische Religion des Nationalsozialismus*.
125. Kershaw, *Hitler Myth*, 257.
126. This and previous quotes, Frei, *Führerstaat*, 165–166.
127. Kershaw, *Hitler Myth*, 257.
128. Herbst, *Hitlers Charisma*, 12–13.
129. Prominently, for example, Mommsen, "Der Mythos der Volksgemeinschaft."
130. Prominently, for example, Bajohr, "'Community of Action.'"
131. "Choral resonance": Reichel, *Der schöne Schein*, 115; "Jubilation" as an "essential component of the image of the Führer": Herz, *Hoffmann & Hitler*, 217.
132. Nitz, *Führer und Duce*, 154, 225.
133. See, for example, Offermanns, *Ästhetische Manipulation und Verführung im Nationalsozialismus*, 22.
134. Kracauer, Das Ornament der Masse."
135. Herz, *Hoffmann & Hitler*, 217.
136. Herz, 219.
137. In this sense, in the 1930s the constitutional experts, as well, did not restrict themselves to the description of political structures but rather for their part promoted the education of Germans to "new men." See, for example, Koellreutter, *Der Deutsche Führerstaat* [1934], 10.
138. Reichel, *Der schöne Schein*.
139. On this, see Herbst, *Hitlers Charisma*, 12–13, 271–273.
140. Herbst, 200.
141. Herbst, 271.
142. AdK, Kempowski-Bio, 5584, 10, October 14, 1933.
143. AdK, November 12, 1933, November 14, 1933.
144. This and previous quotes, IfZ, ED 322/1, March 27, 1937.
145. This and previous quotes, DTA, 1512, 3, March 29, 1936.
146. StdA Meißen, Rep XXI, 34, August 11, 1934.
147. Many examples of a personal relationship between the individual and Hitler are also found in Eberle, *Briefe an Hitler*.
148. DTA, 1512, October 25, 1933. On this, see pages ???
149. This and previous quotes, DTA, November 12, 1933.
150. Wildt, *Geschichte des Nationalsozialismus*, 90.
151. Kershaw, "Volksgemeinschaft," 36. On this, see also Mommsen, "Amoklauf der 'Volksgemeinschaft'?"

7. The Government and Its Volk

1. Bösch, *Öffentliche Geheimnisse*, 471, 748.
2. Fritzsche, *Germans into Nazis*, 82. On changes to the relationship between the mass media and politics around 1900, see Bösch, *Mediengeschichte*, 109–12; also Bösch, "Katalysator der Demokratisierung?"
3. See the discussions on pages ???

4. This and previous quotes, Münster, *Die drei Aufgaben der Zeitungswissenschaft* [1934], 5.
5. StA Hamburg, 622-1/189, 2/12, October 29, 1936. On the Nazi regime's newspaper advertising, see Frei and Schmitz, *Journalismus im Dritten Reich*, 36–37 ("on the moon": 37). For a survey of the press under National Socialism, see, apart from the above, mainly C. Zimmermann, *Medien im Nationalsozialismus*, 85–128; Stöber, "Presse im Nationalsozialismus."
6. On radio under National Socialism and the development of radio programming, see above all the study by Dussel, *Hörfunk in Deutschland*, as well as the articles in the anthology of Marszolek and Saldern, *Zuhören und Gehörtwerden*.
7. Dussel, *Hörfunk in Deutschland*, 171.
8. LHA Koblenz, 700, 23, 8, March 9, 1933. Similar perceptions are also documented by letters from listeners that reached radio stations in spring 1933 and complained about the many political broadcasts. Rimmele, *Der Rundfunk in Norddeutschland*, 151.
9. On staff changes at radio stations, see Diller, *Rundfunkpolitik*, 108–128.
10. On the Nazi movement's criticism of radio during the Weimar Republic, see Rimmele, *Der Rundfunk in Norddeutschland*, 149–150.
11. This and previous quotes, directive of the Reich Propaganda Ministry of November 1933, quoted in Pohle, *Der Rundfunk als Instrument der Politik*, 278.
12. Eugen Hadamovsky, *Dein Rundfunk: Das Rundfunkbuch für alle Volksgenossen* (Munich, 1934), 45.
13. On programming development in the 1930s, see Dussel, *Hörfunk in Deutschland*, 181–198. On the distribution of radios, see König, *Volkswagen, Volksempfänger, Volksgemeinschaft*, 25–99.
14. See, for example, Saldern et al., "Zur politischen und kulturellen Polyvalenz des Radios," 363; C. Zimmermann, *Medien im Nationalsozialismus*, 257.
15. Hadamovsky, *Dein Rundfunk*, 51.
16. Hadamovsky, 73.
17. This and previous quotes, Dussel, *Deutsche Rundfunkgeschichte*, 59.
18. Dussel, 232.
19. This and previous quotes, Dussel, 232. Initial attempts with news scheduled at 8:00 p.m. had already occurred in 1932, "but only in fall 1933 did this model become more widely spread." Dussel, 232.
20. Dussel, 232.
21. Reichel, *Der schöne Schein*, 372.
22. StA Hamburg, 622-1/129, vol. 2.
23. Rosenberg, *Einer, der nicht mehr dazugehört*, 55.
24. This and previous quote, "Jahresheft" 1939 of Heinz Werner Hundertmark, "Abtretung des Memelgebietes an Deutschland," private holdings.
25. AdK, Kempowski-Bio, 5584, 14/3a.
26. On this, see the related discussions on pages ???
27. StdA Munich, NL Wallner, 1, 3, August 2, 1934, May 21, 1935.
28. StdA Munich, 3, Inventur 1933, and 2, 4, Inventur 1937.
29. StdA Munich, 2, 4, September 26, 1937, March 16, 1938.
30. StdA Munich, May 1, 1938.
31. StdA Munich, Inventur 1937.
32. StdA Munich, September 29, 1938.
33. StdA Munich, March 12, 1938, April 9, 1938, April 10, 1938, May 10, 1938, September 26, 1938, September 29, 1938, September 20, 1938, October 1, 1938.

34. Something similar is shown by the compilation of quotes regarding radio consumption in the 1930s from contemporary and retrospective self-testimonies and from literary works in Falkenberg, *Radiohören*, 58–69.
35. For more detail on control of the media, see pages ???
36. StdA Will ch, NL Herlitz, Tagebuch, May 26, 1938.
37. This and previous quotes, FZH, X 11/F3, 1, March 3, 1936.
38. This and previous quotes, FZH, March 3, 1936.
39. AdK, Kempowski-Bio, 5584, 11, January 1, 1935.
40. AdK, January 7, 1935.
41. AdK, Kempowski-Bio, 5965/1, 1, August 27, 1933.
42. This and previous quotes, AdK, August 4, 1933.
43. This and previous quotes, MLHA Schwerin, 10.9.-S/8, 8, "Gedanken über den Nationalsozialismus," p. 22.
44. MLHA Schwerin, "Gedanken über den Nationalsozialismus," p. 22.
45. "Lower instincts": AdK, Kempowski-Bio, 5965/1, 1, October 27, 1933; "void of criticism and judgment": AdK, July 14, 1933.
46. "Capacity for self-criticism": AdK, August 15, 1934; "capacity for judgment": for example, AdK, October 17, 1934.
47. This and previous quotes, AdK, July 15, 1934.
48. AdK, February 9, 1934.
49. This and previous quotes, AdK, Kempowski-Bio, 5584, 14/3a, November 18, 1937. The article focused on the Catholic Alexian Brothers.
50. AdK, November 18, 1937.
51. AdK, March 22, 1934.
52. AdK, March 23, 1934.
53. On the significance of flying flags for showing commitment to the Nazi regime, see pages ??? The other two times Lindemann drew flags without reference to major political events were when he was sworn in with the Reichswehr (March 16, 1936) and when his former student fraternity was dissolved (October 16, 1935).
54. This and previous quotes, AdK, Kempowski-Bio, 5584, 11, November 14, 1934.
55. On the actions of the Nazi movement against department stores in the Weimar Republic, see Ahlheim, *Deutsche, kauft nicht bei Juden!*, 90–105.
56. AdK, Kempowski-Bio, 5584, 11, November 14, 1934.
57. AdK, November 15, 1934. On the context for this entry, see the corresponding discussion on page ???
58. AdK, Kempowski-Bio, 5965/1, April 4, 1936.
59. This and previous quotes, AdK, April 4, 1936.
60. IfZ, ED 2 1, August 22, 1933.
61. AdK, Kempowski-Bio, 5584, 14/3a, March 14, 1938.
62. AdK, Kempowski-Bio, 5965/1, 2, July 15, 1934.
63. For detail on this, see the first part of the book, especially pages ???
64. See also the remarks in Stöber, "Presse im Nationalsozialismus," 290–293, which are based on the *Deutschland-Berichte der Sopade*.
65. See, for example, the reception of political speeches by Werner Kramp on pages ???
66. AdK, Kempowski-Bio, 5584, 11, January 7, 1935.
67. DTA, 1315, May 27, 1934 (*Weekly Times*), December 26, 1934 (*Basler Nachrichten*), May 8, 1935, November 13, 1935, November 5, 1936 (*Times*, *Basler Nachrichten*).
68. DTA, 1705, 8, May 16, 1934 (*Daily Mail*).

69. DTA, February 9, 1934.
70. For example, AdK, Kempowski-Bio, 5584, 12, November 26, 1935.
71. This and previous quotes, DTA, 1315, December 13, 1936.
72. This and previous quotes, DTA, 1315, December 13, 1936.
73. This and previous quotes, DTA, January 1, 1937. Lotter is speaking here about the so-called Battle of the Cross (Kreuzkampf) in the Münster region near Oldenburg in fall 1936. On this, see Zumholz, *Katholisches Milieu und Widerstand*.
74. This and previous quote, AdK, Kempowski-Bio, 5965/1, 1, August 27, 1933.
75. Dussel, *Deutsche Rundfunkgeschichte*, 118.
76. Dussel, 119. Similarly also Clemens, *Medien im Nationalsozialismus*, 98–101.
77. "Small allusions": Dussel, *Hörfunk in Deutschland*, 364. On "reading between the lines," see Stöber, "Presse im Nationalsozialismus," 292.
78. For a more detailed analysis of society's perception of the Röhm purge, see also Steuwer, "Reading Fake News."
79. Kershaw, *Hitler Myth*, 95. Here also detail on the public staging of the so-called Röhm putsch. On the background and the historical chain of events, see Longerich, *Geschichte der SA*, 206–219.
80. On the official account of the June murders, see above all Hitler's speech to the Reichstag in Domarus, *Hitler*, 1/1:410–424.
81. This and previous quote, IfZ, ED 22, 1, July 2, 1934.
82. This and previous quote, IfZ, July 9, 1934.
83. This and previous quote, IfZ, July 2, 1934.
84. StA Hamburg, 622-1/189, 11, July 4, 1934.
85. AdK, Kempowski-Bio, 5965/1, 1, July 1, 1934.
86. AdK, July 4, 1934.
87. This and previous quote, AdK, July 13, 1934.
88. Nieden and Reichardt, "Skandale als Instrument des Machtkampfes," 56.
89. This and previous quotes, IfZ, ED 22, 1, July 2, 1934.
90. IfZ, July 2, 1934.
91. AdK, Kempowski-Bio, 1174, June 30, 1934
92. AdK, June 30, 1934.
93. This and previous quotes, AdK, July 14, 1934.
94. AdK, July 4, 1934.
95. Kershaw, *Hitler Myth*, 85, 86, 89.
96. AdK, Kempowski-Bio, 5965/1, 1, July 11, 1934.
97. IfZ, ED 22, 1, July 2, 1934.
98. StA Hamburg, 622-1/189, 11, July 1, 1934. The formulation picks up on a phrase in the justification speech by Hitler, who had spoken about "burning out down to raw flesh the ulcers of our inner well-poisoning and the poisoning from abroad." Domarus, *Hitler*, 1/1:421.
99. This and previous quote, AdK, Kempowski-Bio, 1174, June 30, 1934.
100. Kershaw, *Hitler Myth*, 85.
101. See the discussions in the first part of the book, especially pages ???
102. See, for example, AdK, Kempowski-Bio, 5584, 12, June 30, 1935; 14, June 30, 1937; 14/3a, June 30, 1938.
103. On the focus of these diaries, see pages ???
104. IfZ, ED 22, 1, November 18, 1933. Witzmann initially continued his political discussions until 1938. He resumed them during the war in 1942 and wrote a second diary volume that went into 1944. However, even in the years between the diary volumes, he

continued monitoring political events, collecting newspaper clippings, and keeping notes in a looser format.

105. FZH, 11/L 2b, August 30, 1935.
106. This and previous quotes, FZH, August 30, 1935. What Lusebrink observed here was the propagandistic groundwork for the Nuremberg Laws, which were announced a few days later.
107. StdA Willich, NL Herlitz, 1, February 1, 1938 ("filtered for reasons of state": May 26, 1938).
108. This and previous quotes, StdA Willich, May 26, 1938.
109. Kershaw, "Alltägliches und Außeralltägliches," 274.
110. On the concept of "political apathy," see Huth, *Politische Verdrossenheit*, 84–94.
111. LA Berlin E Rep 061-19, 17, January 30, 1934.
112. LA Berlin March 8, 1936.
113. See the corresponding discussion on page ???
114. LA Berlin E Rep 061-19, 17, June 30, 1934.
115. LA Berlin July 2, 1934.
116. LA Berlin July 2, 1934.
117. LA Berlin August 2, 1934. The entry contains the addition "(see 06/20)," which is obviously incorrect. Meant is June 30, 1934.
118. Schmitz-Berning, "Glaube," 274.
119. StA Hamburg, 622-1/174, 2, June 30, 1934.
120. StA Hamburg, July 1, 1934.
121. This and previous quotes, StA Hamburg, August 18, 1934.
122. See the discussions on pages ???
123. This and previous quotes, DTA, 1512, 3, December 12, 1938.
124. This and previous quotes, DTA, 1, February 4, 1934.
125. This and previous quotes, DTA, 3, October 27, 1935.
126. DTA, July 8, 1936.
127. This and previous quotes, DTA, August 14, 1935. Peter Fritzsche notes a similar truncation of political discussions in diaries from the period of the war. Fritzsche, *Life and Death in the Third Reich*, 282.
128. See the discussions on page ???
129. This and previous quotes, DTA, 808 I, May 16, 1933.
130. StdA Meißen, Rep XXI, 34; AdK, Kempowski-Bio, 4842/1.
131. For details on the National Socialist holiday calendar, see above all Wilson, "Festivals and the Third Reich," esp. 47–57; also Reichel, *Der schöne Schein*, 209–212; Thamer, *Verführung und Gewalt*, 418–429.
132. See, for example, the *Tages-Notiz-Buch* of the J. C. König and Eberhardt publishing house, which in the 1930s contained many references to commemorative dates, predominantly related to the history of the NSDAP before and after 1933. StdA Bochum, NAP 2, 2.
133. On festivals in urban spaces, see above all Freitag, *Das Dritte Reich im Fest*; as well as Spona, *Städtische Ehrungen*; Plato, "Ein 'Fest der Volksgemeinschaft.'"
134. On the concept of the "media event," see Bösch, "Ereignisse, Performanz und Medien." On the significance of the media for festival planning, see, for example, Urban, *Konsensfabrik*; Marszolek, "Aus dem Volke für das Volk."
135. See, for example, Frei, *Führerstaat*; Thamer, *Verführung und Gewalt*; Broszat, *Der Staat Hitlers*.
136. Freitag, "Führermythos im Fest," 11.

137. Blaschke, "Reichserntedankfeste vor Ort," 126.
138. Rohkrämer, *Die fatale Attraktion des Nationalsozialismus*, 166, 167.
139. On the experiential focus of mass festivals and addresses, see Behrenbeck, *Der Kult um die toten Helden*, 210–343; Klimó and Rolf, *Rausch und Diktatur*; Reichel, *Der schöne Schein*, 114–138.
140. Appeal of the Reich Propaganda Minister of March 18, 1933, quoted in Wernicke, "Der Handschlag am 'Tag von Potsdam,'" 20.
141. Goebbels on March 25, 1933, before the intendants and directors of the radio corporations, quoted in Heiber, *Goebbels-Reden*, 1:82–107, here 96–97.
142. Marszolek, "Aus dem Volke, für das Volk."
143. Heuel, *Der umworbene Stand*, 126–133.
144. This and previous quote, Heuel, 359–360.
145. On "communal reception," see Pohle, *Der Rundfunk als Instrument der Politik*, 268–272.
146. This and previous quote, "Aufruf der Nationalsozialistischen Rundfunkkammer," *Völkischer Beobachter*, October 20, 1933.
147. Hans Hinkel, ed., *Handbuch der Reichskulturkammer* (Berlin, 1937), 301.
148. This and previous quotes, DTA, 1512, 3, March 11, 1936.
149. This and previous quotes, Hosenfeld, *Ich versuche jeden zu retten*, 220 (May 1, 1937).
150. DTA 877 I, 1, October 10, 1933, August 2, 1934, May 29, 1937.
151. That Marita Schlichting had her own radio is evident from the entry. DTA, March 8, 1934.
152. DTA, August 6, 1934 (Hindenburg's death), October 22, 1933 (withdrawal from League of Nations).
153. DTA, May 17, 1933.
154. DTA, January 30, 1937, February 20, 1938.
155. DTA, 1295 I, 1, May 31, 1937.
156. This and previous quote, DTA, 808 I, February 5, 1935. Existing since 1872, §175 of the Reich Criminal Code penalized sexual activity between men. The paragraph was intensified by the Nazi regime and formed an important instrument for the persecution of around one hundred thousand gay men under National Socialism.
157. "Aufruf der Nationalsozialistischen Rundfunkkammer," *Völkischer Beobachter*, October 20, 1933.
158. This and previous quotes, DTA, 1512, I, September 7, 1934.
159. DTA, 3, March 14, 1938.
160. StdA Solingen, Na 04, 12, August 19, 1934.
161. IfZ, ED 322/1, October 21, 1936.
162. DTA, 1495, II, 3, September 3, 1933.
163. This and previous quotes, IfZ, ED 363, 8, March 16, 1935.
164. "Shout with enthusiasm": DTA, 1512, 1, June 17, 1934; "could have cried": IfZ, ED 322/2, March 1938.
165. On this, see the discussion on pages ???
166. StA Hamburg, 622-1/140, 1/31, March 12, 1938.
167. This and previous quotes, StA Hamburg, March 12, 1938.
168. This and previous quote, IfZ, ED 322/2, September 1938.
169. Urban, *Konsensfabrik*, 30.
170. Theweleit, *Männerphantasien*, 2:121.
171. Brockhaus, *Schauder und Idylle*, 228. See also Brockhaus, *Attraktion der NS-Bewegung*; Marks, *Warum folgten sie Hitler?*; Rohkrämer, *Die fatale Attraktion des Nationalsozialismus*.

172. Brockhaus, *Schauder und Idylle*, 218.
173. This and previous quotes, Brockhaus, "Einführung," 15.
174. Brockhaus, 15.
175. Burleigh, *Third Reich*, 210, 211.
176. Burleigh, *Die Zeit des Nationalsozialismus*, 251–252. In this particular case, the German version of Burleigh's book deviates significantly from the English.
177. This and previous quotes, Zelnhefer, *Die Reichsparteitage der NSDAP*, 257, 258–259.
178. This and previous quotes, Neitzel and Welzer, *Soldaten*, 287–288.
179. IfZ, ED 22, 1, September 6, 1933.
180. IfZ, September 6, 1933.
181. This and previous quotes, diary of Nikolaus Sieveking, printed in Bajohr, Meyer, and Szodrzynski, *Bedrohung, Hoffnung, Skepsis*, 419 (March 21, 1933).
182. AdK, Kempowski-Bio, 5965/1, 3, March 20, 1936.
183. Freitag, "Führermythos im Fest," 16.
184. Burleigh, *Third Reich*, 210.
185. For detail on this question, see Linke, *Sprachkultur und Bürgertum*.
186. This is pointed out in studies as varied as Oswald, *Fußball-Volksgemeinschaft*; Urban, *Konsensfabrik*; and Blaschke, "Reichserntedankfeste vor Ort."
187. This and previous quotes, StA Hamburg, 622-1/189, 2/10, May 2, 1934.
188. This and previous quote, AdK, Kempowski-Bio, 5965/1, 2, August 18, 1934.
189. Alexander Schmidt, "In Marsch gesetzte Volksgemeinschaft," 11.
190. This and previous quotes, IfZ, ED 394/2, letter from Scheuer, September 24, 1935.
191. IfZ, letter from Scheuer, September 24, 1935.
192. For detail on this, see Steuwer, "Was meint und nützt das Sprechen von der 'Volksgemeinschaft'?," 514–515.
193. Zelnhefer, *Die Reichsparteitage der NSDAP*, 245, 247.
194. Urban, *Konsensfabrik*, 419.
195. Peukert, *Volksgenossen und Gemeinschaftsfremde*, 222.
196. On similar efforts in the Nazi training camps, see pages ????.
197. Klimó and Rolf, "Emotionen, Erfahrungen und Inszenierungen totalitärer Herrschaft," 22, ?–22.
198. Reichel, *Der schöne Schein*, 372.
199. This and previous quotes, IfZ, ED 394/2, September 24, 1935.
200. This and previous quote, DTA, 1512, 1, June 3, 1934.
201. This and previous quote, DTA, 2, July 12, 1935.
202. DTA, 877, 1. See, for example, the successive entries of January 30, 1937, and February 22, 1937: "Great speech of the Führer" and "Church conflict [Kirchenstreit], appalling, many resignations [i.e., from the Church]."
203. Ullrich, *Adolf Hitler*, 1:578.
204. This and previous quotes, DTA, 1512, 4, August 27, 1939.
205. C. Zimmermann, *Medien im Nationalsozialismus*, 259. Making a similar point in his summary is Mühlenfeld, "Was heißt und zu welchem Ende studiert man NS-Propaganda?," 538.
206. For more on this, see pages ??? and ???
207. Something similar is emphasized from a theoretical perspective in Bösch and Frei, "Die Ambivalenz der Medialisierung," 12.
208. On the concept of the "communication network" and its significance for social integration, see Luhmann, "Gesellschaftliche Komplexität und öffentliche Meinung," 172,

from which I received important suggestions regarding this point. See also Luhmann, "Öffentliche Meinung."
209. AdK, Kempowski-Bio, 5965/1, 1, July 9, 1934.
210. AdK, October 27, 1933.
211. See, for example, the diary of the Hamburg tradesman painter Hermann Frielingsdorf, who admittedly in his first entry presented the "radio" as the symbol for the Nazi dictatorship's comprehensive political control but hardly allowed the mass media to guide his critical discussions of Nazi politics. FZH, X 11/F3, 1.
212. On the elections of the Weimar Republic, see Falter, *Hitlers Wähler*. On their relative importance in the historical research, see Hohls, "Die NSDAP als erste deutsche Volks- und Protestpartei." On the elections under National Socialism, see above all the studies by Jung, *Plebiszit und Diktatur*; Hubert, *Uniformierter Reichstag*, 82–91, 235–286; Stepanek, *Wahlkampf im Zeichen der Diktatur*; Bracher, "Plebiszit und Machtergreifung." Also instructive is the local historical study by Omland, *Du wählst mi nich Hitler!* The paucity of research on elections under National Socialism compared to other dictatorial regimes is shown by Jessen and Richter, *Voting for Hitler and Stalin*.
213. Gellately, *Backing Hitler*, 15
214. Gellately, 15–16. This quote is particularly symptomatic for the purely illustrative use of the election results: first, the specified figure of the result is incorrect (it was actually 98.8 percent); and, second, the increase in yes votes compared to the previous plebiscite, alluded to by Gellately, was due primarily to a change in how votes were counted, not to a change in voting behavior. On vote counting in 1936, see Hubert, *Uniformierter Reichstag*, 270–271.
215. Kershaw, *Hitler Myth*, 63. Similar also Wehler, *Deutsche Gesellschaftsgeschichte*, 4:614, 621–622; Stöver, *Volksgemeinschaft*, 307–309.
216. DTA, 1512, 1, November 29, 1933.
217. This and previous quotes, AdK, Kempowski-Bio, 5584, 14/3a, March 19,1938; 15, April 4, 1938.
218. AdK, 15, April 8, 1938, April 22, 1938.
219. Walb, *Ich, die Alte—Ich, die Junge*, 74.
220. This and previous quotes, AdK, Kempowski-Bio, 5965/1, 3, April 3, 1936.
221. In the Saar plebiscite, entitled voters who lived in the territory of the Reich were brought to the Saarland. Paul, *Deutsche Mutter*, 356–364. In the special election for the Reichstag in 1938, in which only Sudeten Germans were entitled to vote, around 310,000 ballots were also cast in polling locations specially set up for this purpose in the old Reich and Austria. V. Zimmermann, *Die Sudetendeutschen im NS-Staat*, 113.
222. Jacoby, *Die nationalsozialistische Herrschaftsübernahme an der Saar*, 128. For detail on the campaign for the Saar plebiscite, see Paul, *Deutsche Mutter*.
223. Speech by Adolf Hitler on April 29, 1937, quoted in Zitelmann, *Selbstverständnis eines Revolutionärs*, 349.
224. DTA, 1315, March 8, 1936.
225. See, for example, DTA, 1708, 9, August 2, 1934.
226. Fröhlich, *Tagebücher von Joseph Goebbels*, part I, 3/II:31 (March 4, 1936).
227. Bohrmann, *NS-Presseanweisungen der Vorkriegszeit*, 4/1:253–254.
228. Bohrmann, 20.
229. Bohrmann, 253–254.
230. Overesch and Saal, *Das Dritte Reich*, 267.
231. Overesch and Saal, 434.

232. Bohrman, NS-Presseanweisungen der Vorkriegszeit, 4/I:275.
233. Bohrman, 274, 269. See here, for example, the thirteen-part article series "Mit dem Führer unterwegs. Kleine Stimmungsberichte einer großen Reise," Westdeutscher Beobachter, March 13–30, 193.
234. As yet there is no study on the voting campaign arrangements on the radio. The study by Stepanek, Wahlkampf im Zeichen der Diktatur, is mainly limited to the voting campaign material of the street campaign. On the press, see the discussion on Schleswig-Holstein in Omland, Du wählst mi nich Hitler!
235. Walb, Ich, die Alte—Ich, die Junge, 75 (March 30, 1936).
236. On the advertising material of street-level voting campaigns, see Stepanek, Wahlkampf im Zeichen der Diktatur.
237. The figures in Omland, Du wählst mi nich Hitler!, 135. For a look at other regions, see Stepanek, Wahlkampf im Zeichen der Diktatur, 136.
238. AdK, Kempowski-Bio, 5965/1, 2, August 13, 1934.
239. LHA Koblenz, 700, 023, 10, March 28, 1936.
240. On the nonetheless important voting campaign activities of the local NSDAP chapters, see Reibel, Das Fundament der Diktatur, 286–288.
241. This and previous quote, DTA, 1295 I, 1, April 5, 1938. On this, see also the instructions to the state education authority regarding vote propaganda, documented in Deutschland-Berichte der Sopade, 1936, 444–446.
242. LA Berlin, Rep 061-19, 17, March 20, 1936, March 25, 1936, March 28, 1936. See also Deutschland-Berichte der Sopade, 1936, 446–447.
243. This and previous quotes, StA Hamburg, 622-1/140, 1/28, November 10, 1933. (Quote is missing in Bajohr, Meyer, and Szodrzynski, Bedrohung, Hoffnung, Skepsis). She had already noted the announcement of "one minute of standstill" on November 6, 1933, for the coming Friday.
244. StA Hamburg, 1/30, March 27, 1936.
245. DTA, 1708 9, March 27, 1936.
246. AdK, Kempowski-Bio, 303/1, March 26, 1936, March 22, 1936, March 9, 1936.
247. AdK, March 26, 1936.
248. This and previous quotes, AdK, March 26, 1936.
249. This and previous quote, AdK, Kempowski-Bio, 4842/1, March 17, 1936.
250. AdK, March 23, 1938.
251. StdA Münster, NL Beier, 5, April 9, 1938.
252. On this, see Stepanek, Wahlkampf im Zeichen der Diktatur, esp. 142, 198–199.
253. This and previous quotes, StdA Bonn, SN 1/490, August 1, 1935.
254. This and previous quotes, StdA Bonn, March 29, 1936.
255. StdA Bonn, March 29, 1936. During the election of November 1933, the Munich resident Luise Kempt, too, confessed in her notes that she was "ashamed" because her diary rarely wrote about political events. See pages ??? in this book.
256. AdK, Kempowski-Bio, 303/1, March 7, 1936. Reichstag President Hermann Göring in Reichstag meeting of March 7, 1936, printed in Verhandlungen des Reichstages, vol. 458:9, Wahlperiode 193 (Berlin, 1936), 75–76.
257. AdK, Kempowski-Bio, 303/1, March 26, 1936.
258. AdK, Kempowski-Bio, 4842/1, March 17, 1936.
259. AdK, Kempowski-Bio, 5965/1, 3, March 21, 1936.
260. AdK, March 21, 1936.
261. AdK, March 29, 1936.

262. AdK, March 24, 1936.
263. Eschenburg, "Streiflichter zur Geschichte der Wahlen im Dritten Reich," 311.
264. Bracher, *Stufen der Machtergreifung*, 484–485.
265. This and previous quotes, Bracher, 498. Similar also Bracher, "Plebiszit und Machtergreifung."
266. The various ballots are printed in Jung, *Plebiszit und Diktatur*, 131–136.
267. Letter from Frick to the state governments, October 18, 1933, quoted in Hubert, *Uniformierter Reichstag*, 267–268. See here also for more detail on changes to the vote-counting process.
268. Letter of State Secretary Han Pfundtner, March 27, 1936, quoted in Hubert, 270.
269. This is also shown by the differences between various voting districts. On this, see, for example, Hubert, 273–274. With regard to Schleswig-Holstein, see Omland, *Du wählst mi nich Hitler!*; also Bracher, "Plebiszit und Machtergreifung."
270. Hubert, *Uniformierter* Reichstag, 269.
271. Hubert, 273, 274.
272. Stöver, *Volksgemeinschaft*, 308–309.
273. Bracher, *Stufen der Machtergreifung*, 477.
274. This and previous quotes, StdA Solingen, Na 040-13, August 19, 1934.
275. Reibel, *Das Fundament der Diktatur*, 288.
276. DTA, 1346, I, 3, part 2, December 4, 1938.
277. StdA Solingen, Na 040-13, August 19, 1934.
278. Hubert, *Uniformierter Reichstag*, 259.
279. Hubert, 259.
280. Omland, *Du wählst mi nich Hitler!*, 102.
281. "Reichsinnenminister Dr. Frick zur Reichstagswahl," *Völkischer Beobachter*, October 29–30, 1933.
282. Press notice of the Reich Interior Ministry of August 8, 1934, quoted in Omland, *Du wählst mi nich Hitler!*, 9.
283. Local NSDAP functionaries could also find affirmation from leading Nazi politicians who likewise criticized the secrecy of the ballot. On this, see, for example, the conflicts between Reich Interior Minister Wilhelm Frick and other Nazi leaders related to ensuring ballot secrecy, described by Hubert, *Uniformierter Reichstag*, 250–252.
284. *Deutschland-Berichte der Sopade*, 1938, 420.
285. *Deutschland-Berichte der Sopade*, 1936, 424. No voting booths present, for example, *Deutschland-Berichte der Sopade*, 1938, 420–421.
286. Stöver, *Berichte über die Lage in Deutschland*, 237 (report from Neu Beginnen of August/September 1934).
287. *Deutschland-Berichte der Sopade*, 1936, 433.
288. This and previous quote, *Deutschland-Berichte der Sopade*, 415.
289. Diary of Nikolaus Sieveking, in Bajohr, Meyer, and Szodrzynski, *Bedrohung, Hoffnung, Skepsis*, 453–454 (November 9, 1933, November 14, 1933).
290. *Deutschland-Berichte der Sopade*, 1936, 431.
291. *Deutschland-Berichte der Sopade*, 1936, 432.
292. *Deutschland-Berichte der Sopade*, 1938, 421.
293. *Deutschland-Berichte der Sopade*, 1936, 407.
294. The phrase "If Goebbels were entirely successful, Himmler would be unemployed," formulated already during the war by the sociologist Hans Speier, does not so much point to

a supposedly omnipresent threat of violence during National Socialism that determined the behavior of contemporaries, but aptly describes the basic limits of the integrative capacity of the political system of the 1930s. Speier, *Nazi Propaganda and Its Decline*, 376.

295. This and previous quotes, StdA Solingen, Na 040-13, August 19, 1934.
296. This and previous quotes, StdA München, Nachlass Oehl, 25, "Tagebuch 1936."
297. See the examples in Hesse, *Vor aller Augen*, 63, 65. On the importance of the visibility of violence under National Socialism, see Wildt, *Volksgemeinschaft als Selbstermächtigung*.
298. This and previous quotes, DTA, 1115, 23, April 10, 1938.
299. Delbanco, *Kirchenkampf in Ostfriesland*, 105–106.
300. DTA, 1315, April 18, 1936.
301. AdK, Kempowski-Bio, 5965/1, 3, March 29, 1936.
302. StA Hamburg, 622-1/140, 1/31, April 10, 1938.
303. StA Hamburg, April 10, 1938. Name changed.
304. This and previous quotes, StA Hamburg, 622-1/189, 2/10, January 8, 1934.
305. StA Hamburg, 2/9, October 27, 1933.
306. This and previous quotes, StA Hamburg, 2/10, November 12, 1933.
307. AdK, Kempowski-Bio, 1174, November 1, 1933.
308. AdK, October 17, 1933.
309. AdK, November 1, 1933, October 17, 1933.
310. AdK, October 17, 1933.
311. Statistisches Reichsamt, *Statistisches Jahrbuch* [1934], 53: 550. In total, just over 980,000 more votes were counted for the withdrawal from the League of Nations than for the NSDAP.
312. IfZ, ED 2, vol. 1, October 15, 1933.
313. IfZ, October 15, 1933.
314. This and previous quotes, AdK, Kempowski-Bio, 5965/1, 2, August 18, 1934.
315. "Obfuscation," "commonality of fate": AdK, 3, March 22, 1936; "I voted with yes": AdK, March 29, 1936.
316. AdK, 6, April 4, 1938.
317. FZH, 11/K 33, letter from Kirchmann, January 26, 1934.
318. AdK, Kempowski-Bio, 5584, 13, March 27, 1936.
319. By way of a regulation created during the Weimar Republic, the right to vote was suspended for members of the Reichswehr. See Förster, *Die Wehrmacht im NS-Staat*, 7.
320. AdK, Kempowski-Bio, 5584, 13, March 29, 1936.
321. DTA, 1115, 23, April 10, 1938.
322. This and previous quote, DTA, 1315, August 18, 1934.
323. DTA, March 29, 1936.
324. On this, see the comments on pages ???
325. DTA, 1315, March 29, 1936.
326. AdK, Kempowski-Bio, 5965/1, 3, March 21, 1936; 6, April 7, 1938.
327. AdK, 3, March 29, 1936.
328. StA Hamburg, 622-1/189, 2/10, November 12, 1933.
329. On the voting in November 1933 in the Dachau concentration camp, for example, see Steinbacher, *Dachau*, 114.
330. This and previous quotes, StA Hamburg, 622-1/140, 1/30, March 9, 1936.
331. StA Hamburg, March 27, 1936.
332. This and previous quotes, StA Hamburg, March 29, 1936.
333. StA Hamburg, 1/31, March 13, 1938.

334. Cohn, *Kein Recht, nirgends*, 316 (March 28, 1936).
335. Cohn, 316 (March 29, 1936).
336. This and previous quotes, StdA Solingen, Na 025-4, "Meine Abstimmung," n.d., March or April 1938.
337. On this, see the first part of the book, especially pages ????.
338. This and previous quotes, DTA, 1115, 23, April 10, 1938. Name changed.
339. Gellately, *Backing Hitler*, 15–16.
340. Wehler, *Gesellschaftsgeschichte*, vol. 4, 621.
341. Stöver, *Volksgemeinschaft*, 308–309.
342. DHM, Do 70/177.1II. A facsimile of the commemorative sheet is printed in *Deutschland-Bericht der Sopade*, 1936, 416.
343. StdA Bonn, SN1/490, Christi Himmelfahrt 1937.

8. The Private and the Limits of the National Socialist Political System

1. On the biography of Charlotte Beradt, see Steffen, *Haben sie mich gehasst?*, 309–316.
2. On Haffner, see the introduction to this book; on the significance of the concept of privacy for the autobiographical reflections of German emigrants, see C. Meyer, "'... nichts war mehr Privatangelegenheit'."
3. This and previous quotes, Beradt, *Third Reich of Dreams*, 4–5. Also in Beradt, "Dreams under Dictatorship [1943]," 333.
4. Beradt, *Third Reich of Dreams*, 9.
5. Beradt, 10–12.
6. Beradt, 12–13.
7. Beradt.
8. See, for example, P. Diehl, *Macht, Mythos, Utopie*, 128; Körte, "'Pyrotechniker der Macht,'" 430; Evans, *Third Reich in Power*, 107–108.
9. Peukert, *Volksgenossen und Gemeinschaftsfremde*, 280–282.
10. This and previous quotes, Koselleck, "Nachwort," 118, 132.
11. Koselleck, "Terror und Traum," 286.
12. For example, according to Koselleck, "Terror und Traum," 286. Similar, even though more precise, in Peukert, *Volksgenossen und Gemeinschaftsfremde*, 322, which refers to a "contemporary collection but retrospective commentary."
13. Werth, "Review," 514.
14. This and previous quotes, Werth, 515.
15. In her study, Charlotte Beradt clearly distinguished her methodology from psychological dream theories. Beradt, *Third Reich of Dreams*, 15–18.
16. Charlotte Beradt on her dream project in a letter to Karl Otten, March 7, 1962, quoted in Steffen, *Haben sie mich gehasst?*, 312.
17. On Hannah Arendt's theses regarding the private sphere, see the conclusive summary in Arendt, *Elemente und Ursprünge totaler Herrschaft*, 971–979, 720–724. On the significance of the distinction between public and private in Arendt's thought, see Thürmer-Rohr, "Öffentlichkeit/Privatheit." The influence of Arendt's theses on Beradt is also shown by the differences between the first—mainly descriptive—publication of her dream material during the war and the study she presented in the 1960s. See Beradt, "Dreams under Dictatorship"; Beradt, *Third Reich of Dreams*.

18. Beradt, *Third Reich of Dreams*, 5.
19. Beradt, 13.
20. Beradt, 9.
21. This and previous quotes, Beradt, 21.
22. Beradt, 22.
23. Beradt, 14–148.
24. Betts, *Within Walls*, 6.
25. Betts, 7. For detail on the persistent influence of the theory of totalitarianism on the scholarly understanding of privacy and subjectivity, see Krylova, "Tenacious Liberal Subject."
26. Betts, *Within Walls*, 5. On this, see the detailed but uncritical discussion in Raunig, *Herrschaft ohne Grenzen?*
27. With this and the previous quote, Martin Broszat summarized the criticism of the history of everyday life in the Nazi period. Broszat, "Referat," 12.
28. Tenfelde, "Referat," 33, 35.
29. Broszat, "Referat," 12–13.
30. Broszat, 14.
31. Peukert, "Referat"; Peukert, *Alltag unterm Nationalsozialismus*; Lüdtke, "Wo blieb die 'rote Glut'?"
32. On this, see the final chapter on the "atomization of everyday life" in Peukert, *Volksgenossen und Gemeinschaftsfremde*, 280–288.
33. A more detailed discussion of the private under National Socialism has emerged only recently, of which this book is a part. See in particular Harvey et al., *Private Life and Privacy in Nazi Germany*; Christians, *Das Private vor Gericht*; C. Meyer, *(K)eine Grenze*.
34. Winkler, "Referat," 29.
35. Zollitsch, *Arbeiter zwischen*, 242. See also the everyday-historical theses on the private sphere summarized in Bavaj, *Die Ambivalenz der Moderne im Nationalsozialismus*, 78–81.
36. Herbert, "'Die guten und die schlechten Zeiten,'" 91.
37. Zollitsch, *Arbeiter zwischen*, 225.
38. Schmiechen-Ackermann, *Arbeitermilieus*, 490.
39. Diewald-Kerkmann, *Politische Denunziation*, 136–149. For more detail on this, see pages ???
40. Wirsching, "Vom 'Lehrstück Weimar' zum Lehrstück Holocaust?," 12.
41. Koselleck, "Nachwort," 118.
42. J. Habermas, *Strukturwandel der Öffentlichkeit*, 24.
43. Habermas, 32, 24.
44. On this, see the discussions in Hölscher, "Öffentlichkeit."
45. J. Habermas, *Strukturwandel der Öffentlichkeit*, 66.
46. This and previous quotes, Habermas, 67. For detail on this, see also Reckwitz, *Das hybride Subjekt*, 42–274.
47. On this, see Gerhalter, "'Einmal ein ganz ordentliches Tagebuch,'" 66.
48. This is emphasized, for example, by Linke, *Sprachkultur und Bürgertum*.
49. Likewise, the privacy model could also be used to demand one's own space vis-à-vis neighbors, friends, or acquaintances and request to be treated in a "private" encounter without discrimination based on one's political views. For detail, see Bergerson, *Ordinary Germans*, 14–128.
50. DTA, 1295/I, 1.

51. DTA, 1708, 8, June 3, 1934.
52. This and previous quotes, "Dokumentation des Urteils des Reichsgerichts vom 18. März 1937 (5 D 760/36)," *Juristische Wochenschrift* 66, no. 37/38 (1937): 2389–2390, here 2389.
53. For detail on Wilhelm Scheidler, see pages ??? and ???
54. HStA Darmstadt, G 27, 217.
55. Rössler, *Der Wert des Privaten*, 19. Rössler also offers a good survey of the definitions of privacy in various scholarly disciplines. Rössler, 11–26.
56. Rössler, 18.
57. Beradt, *Third Reich of Dreams*, 22.
58. Beradt, *Dritte Reich des Traums*, 27. The passage in the German version differs significantly from the English.
59. Beradt, *Third Reich of Dreams*, 69.
60. Beradt, 16.
61. Beradt, 9, 18.
62. Beradt, 6.
63. Peukert, *Volksgenossen und Gemeinschaftsfremde*, 284.
64. Peukert, 284, 287.
65. Schäfer, *Das gespaltene Bewußtsein*.
66. Schäfer, 159.
67. Just how persistently this thesis dominates the historical treatment of National Socialism is shown by a side-by-side look at studies like Stippel, *Die Zerstörung der Person*, and Fulbrook, *Dissonant Lives*, which agree on this point despite being published fifty years apart.
68. See, for example, the discussion on Luise Klempt on pages ???
69. Göring, *Die Rechtssicherheit* [1935], 5.
70. Göring, 6.
71. "Internal pervasion": Huber, *Neue Grundbegriffe* [1935], 12; "anti-liberal attitude": Koellreutter, *Vom Sinn und Wesen* [1933], 33.
72. Petersen, *Our Street* [1938], 59–60.
73. Petersen, 60–61.
74. Petersen, 60–61.
75. Petersen, 60–61.
76. Barck, *Antifa-Geschichte(n)*, 123–193.
77. Letter dated December 29, 1938, printed in Barkow, Gross, and Lenarz, *Novemberpogrom*, 404–418, here 405.
78. This and previous quotes, Barkow, Gross, and Lenarz, 407.
79. On this, see Ahlheim, *Deutsche, kauft nicht bei Juden!*
80. This and previous quotes, Barkow, Gross, and Lenarz, *Novemberpogrom*, 408.
81. This and previous quotes, Barkow, Gross, and Lenarz, 410.
82. On the violence of the November pogrom, see the survey in Gross, *November 1938*.
83. On the deliberations of Jewish Germans about possibly emigrating, see Kwiet, "Gehen oder bleiben?"
84. This and previous quotes, Leo Baeck Institut (LBI), MM 6, Tagebuch von Erna Becker-Kohen, April 1939.
85. On the history of Jewish houses, see, using the example of Munich, Haerendel, *Kommunale Wohnungspolitik im Dritten Reich*, 395–405; H. Schneider, *Die "Entjudung" des Wohnraums*.
86. This is emphasized in Wildt, *Volksgemeinschaft als Selbstermächtigung*.

87. Report on the destructions in Düsseldorf, printed in Barkow, Gross, and Lenarz, *Novemberpogrom*, 338–342, here 339.
88. This and previous quote, Barkow, Gross, and Lenarz, 340.
89. On the plundering in the November pogrom, see Obst, *Reichskristallnacht*, 270–279.
90. LBI, MM, diary of Erna Becker-Kohen, April 1939.
91. AdK, Kerkowski-Bio, 1786, letter from Baumgarten, January 21, 1939.
92. This and previous quote, AdK, letter from Baumgarten, January 22, 1939.
93. Wetzel, "Auswanderung aus Deutschland," 419.
94. LBI, MM, diary of Erna Becker-Kohen, August 1939.
95. This and previous quotes, Mezger, "Beleidigung durch Äußerungen im engsten Familienkreis?," 332.
96. This and previous quotes, Grunberger, *Twelve-Year Reich*, 26.
97. On this, see the detailed discussion on pages ???
98. On the structure of local NSDAP structures, see especially Reibel, *Das Fundament der Diktatur*; Thieler, *"Volksgemeinschaft" unter Vorbehalt*, 85–194.
99. Thieler, *"Volksgemeinschaft" unter Vorbehalt*, 125–132.
100. Reibel, *Das Fundament der Diktatur*, 274.
101. Reibel, 27.
102. Reibel, 28; on the advice centers, 279–284.
103. Reibel, 51. On the blocks and the functionaries deployed there, see also Schmiechen-Ackermann, "Der 'Blockwart.'"
104. Reibel, *Das Fundament der Diktatur*, 57–64.
105. Thieler, *"Volksgemeinschaft" unter Vorbehalt*, 161.
106. "Aufgabe des Blockleiters sowie des Blockwartes" (unpublished manuscript, n.d., presumably 1937, quoted in Thieler, *"Volksgemeinschaft" unter Vorbehalt*, 161–162.
107. Robert Ley, "Unser Volk soll jung bleiben," in Ley, *Soldaten der Arbeit* [1939], 121–128, here 125.
108. Beradt, *Third Reich of Dreams*, 4, 18.
109. Robert Ley, "Unser Volk soll jung bleiben," in Ley, *Soldaten der Arbeit*, here 125.
110. Reibel, *Das Fundament der Diktatur*, 57.
111. Reichsorganisationsleiter der NSDAP, *Parteistatistik* [1935], 3:170.
112. Reichsorganisationsleiter der NSDAP, 2:60 (71.2 percent).
113. Reichsorganisationsleiter der NSDAP, 3:175. In 1932, there were 11,845 NSDAP Stützpunkte (bases) (up to 50 members) and Ortgruppen (local groups) (at least 51 members). The distinction between Stützpunkte and Ortgruppen was abolished in the reforms of 1938.
114. Reibel, *Das Fundament der Diktatur*, 395.
115. For details on this, see Thieler, *"Volksgemeinschaft" unter Vorbehalt*.
116. FZH, X 11 K 32, letter from Kirchmann to the NSV Hamburg-Winterhude, August 14, 1935.
117. FZH, letter of the Office for People's Welfare Hamburg-Winterhude to Kirchmann, August 2, 1935.
118. This and previous quotes, FZH, letter from Kirchmann to the NSV Hamburg-Winterhude, August 14, 1935.
119. This and previous quotes, FZH, letter from Kirchmann to the NSV Hamburg-Winterhude, August 14, 1935.
120. This and previous quotes, FZH, letter of the Kreisleiter to Kirchmann, September 23, 1935.

121. StdA Herne, o nsp, 61–69b (1934, 1937–1944). On the mentoring work of local Nazi agencies, see Reibel, *Das Fundament der Diktatur*, 274–306.
122. This and previous quotes, "Aufgabe des Blockleiters sowie des Blockwartes" (unpublished manuscript, n.d., presumably 1937), quoted in Thieler, *"Volksgemeinschaft" unter Vorbehalt*, 162.
123. "Aufgabe des Blockleiters sowie des Blockwartes," 163.
124. "Aufgabe des Blockleiters sowie des Blockwartes," 163.
125. On the radio and its impact on the separation between public and private, see Marszolek and Saldern, "Das Radio als historisches und historiographisches Medium," 23–25.
126. Koselleck, "Nachwort," 128.
127. AdK, Kempowski-Bio, 5965/1, 9, September 21, 1939.
128. AdK, 1, October 29, 1933; 3, April 3, 1936; 6, March 10, 1938.
129. AdK, 4, November 18, 1936; 10, August 26, 1939.
130. AdK, 1, April 30, 1933; 1, July 12, 1933; 3, April 3, 1936; 6, April 4, 1938.
131. AdK, 2, 12/31/1934; 3, February 22, 1936; 5, December 12, 1937.
132. AdK, 2, September 23, 1934; 1, May 5, 1933.
133. AdK, 3, March 30, 1936. On the garden as a private place, see the articles in the anthology Lamnek and Tinnefeld, *Privatheit, Garten und politische Kultur*, with regard to National Socialism above all the article by Wolschke-Bulmahn, "Freiheit in Grenzen," esp. 170–171.
134. AdK, 1, May 5, 1933.
135. AdK, 3, March 30, 1936.
136. AdK, 2, August 11, 1934.
137. This is according to the oft-cited thesis of Herbert, "'Die guten und die schlechten Zeiten,'" 9.
138. On this, see the discussion on pages ???
139. On this, see the discussions in the second part of this book.
140. For detail on this, see Föllmer, *Individuality and Modernity in Berlin*, 105–131.
141. Connelly, "Uses of Volksgemeinschaft," 902.
142. AdK, Kempowski-Bio, 4842/1, October 16, 1935.
143. AdK, November 5, 1935.
144. Detail on this in Thieler, *"Volksgemeinschaft" unter Vorbehalt*.
145. DTA, 4071, January 30, 1936.
146. DTA, April 2, 1936.
147. DTA, April 7, 1936.
148. DTA, April 20, 1936.
149. See, for example, DTA, April 19, 1936.
150. DTA, November 1, 1936.
151. DTA, July 19, 1936.
152. This and previous quotes, DTA, August 25, 1937.
153. These poles also cannot be equated with proximity or distance to the Nazi regime. Both presupposed a basic commitment to the regime, and among the many voices of the choir of National Socialist models for individual lifestyles and self-contemplation were also those that could grasp classical ideas of privacy, such as reclusiveness and independence, as part of a "National Socialist lifestyle." On this, see Föllmer, *Individuality and Modernity in Berlin*, 116; Schäfer, *Das gespaltene Bewußtsein*, 123.
154. On denunciation in National Socialism, see the summaries by Paul, "Private Konfliktregulierung, gesellschaftliche Selbstüberwachung, politische Teilhabe?"; Gellately,

"Denunciation as a Subject of Historical Research"; Böske, "Denunziationen in der Zeit des Nationalsozialismus," 12–130. Of the various studies on the subject, interesting for the context here is especially the work of Gisela Diewald-Kerkmann, which is based not on court or Gestapo files but on surviving materials from local party agencies. Diewald-Kerkmann, *Politische Denunziation*.

155. Diewald-Kerkmann, *Politische Denunziation*, 138.
156. Diewald-Kerkmann, 136–149.
157. Letter of the Reich Justice Minister to the Ministerial Councillor for Reich Defense, October 13, 1939, quoted in Diewald-Kerkmann, *Politische Denunziation*, 149.
158. "Das politische Mäntelchen: Polizei warnt Denunzianten," *Westfälische Neueste Nachrichten*, October 31, 1933, quoted in Diewald-Kerkmann, *Politische Denunziation*, 143.
159. Marszolek, "'Die Zeichen an der Wand,'" 209. On the contradictory attitude of the Nazi leadership toward denunciations, see the summary in Böske, "Denunziationen in der Zeit des Nationalsozialismus," 123–126.
160. Diewald-Kerkmann, *Politische Denunziation*, 126.
161. DTA, 779, 5, November 17, 1933.
162. DTA, 6, August 11, 1934.
163. This and previous quotes, DTA, 9, April 26, 1937.
164. This and previous quotes, DTA, April 26, 1937.
165. On the scope of denunciations, see the estimates of various historical studies brought together in Böske, *Denunziationen in der Zeit des Nationalsozialismus*, 89–167.
166. Dörner, "NS-Herrschaft und Denunziation," 61. Similarly Reuband, "Denunziation im Dritten Reich," 224–225.
167. This and previous quotes, AdK, Kempowski-Bio, 4842/1, October 16, 1935.
168. Jerouschek, Marßolek, and Röckelein, "Denunziation," 19.
169. DTA, 407, February 13, 1939.
170. On this, see the discussions on Hans Maschmann on pages ???
171. The letters are documented as a transcription in a report by Hans Maschmann on this incident in his diary entry of September 21, 1939. AdK, Kempowski-Bio, 5965/1, 9, September 21, 1939.
172. This and previous quotes, AdK, September 21, 1939.
173. This and previous quotes, AdK, September 21, 1939. Name changed.
174. This and previous quotes, AdK, September 21, 1939.
175. AdK, 10, May 14, 1939.
176. This and previous quotes, AdK, September 21, 1939.
177. AdK, 1, March 31, 1933.
178. Bajohr, "Zustimmungsdiktatur," 113–114.
179. Haffner, *Defying Hitler*, 6, 219.
180. Welzer, *Täter*, 58.
181. DTA, 1708, 7, March 4, 1933.
182. Gedenkstätte KZ Osthofen, 2/27/2, April 14, 1933.
183. Gedenkstätte KZ Osthofen, March 18, 1933. See also the entries for March 14, 1933, April 11, 1933, April 13, 1933.
184. Gedenkstätte KZ Osthofen, March 22, 1933.
185. Gedenkstätte KZ Osthofen, March 30, 1933.
186. BayHStA München, NL Fritz Koch, 31, April 29–30, 1938.
187. StdA Solingen, KL 228-1, February 15, 1937.

188. Beradt, *Third Reich of Dreams*, 9.
189. BayHstA München, NL Fritz Koch, 31, April 29–30, 1938, April 20, 1938.
190. StdA Solingen, KL 228-1, February 15, 1937.
191. Beradt, *Third Reich of Dreams*, 19, 18.
192. Haffner, *Defying Hitler*, 3.
193. Föllmer, *Individuality and Modernity in Berlin*, 189–194.
194. Leßau, *Entnazifizierungsgeschichten*, esp. 235–267.
195. On this, see Frei, *Epochenjahr 1933*, 90–95.
196. On the concept of resistance, see the critical deliberations in Fritzsche, "Where Did All the Nazis Go?"
197. For detail on this, Steuwer and Leßau, "Wer ist ein Nazi?"; Steuwer, "'National Socialists' and Other People."
198. AdK, Kempowski-Bio, 1174, January 4, 1934.
199. Bajohr, "Zustimmungsdiktatur," 111.

Conclusion

1. On the course of the start of the war, see Stargardt, *German War*, 24–28.
2. Proclamation by Adolf Hitler on September 1, 1939, quoted in Domarus, *Hitler*, 2/1:1307.
3. Domarus, 2/1:1312–1317, here 1312, 1313, 1314, 1315.
4. Above all, Social Democratic and Communist exile groups sought to convince Germany's neighboring states of the aggressiveness of National Socialism's expansion efforts with the "repeatedly disseminated slogan 'Hitler means war.'" Quoted in M. Schneider, *Unterm Hakenkreuz*, 938. By way of pamphlets—during voting campaigns, for example—the slogan also found its way to Germany. On this, for example, see the pamphlets reproduced in Mehringer, "Die KPD in Bayern," 127–128.
5. For example, DTA 1512, 3, March 11, 1936.
6. For example, AdK, Kempowski-Bio, 4913, September 17, 1936.
7. For example, LHA Schwerin, 10.9—H/14, December 2, 1936; DHM, Do2 2006/203.
8. For example, StdA Bonn, SN1/490, September 28, 1938.
9. See the examples in Steinert, *Hitlers Krieg*, 91–92.
10. Report of the Regime President of Lower Bavaria/Upper Palatinate of September 8, 1939, quoted in Kershaw, *Hitler Myth*, 144.
11. *Deutschland-Berichte der Sopade*, 1939, 980, 983.
12. Schulte, *Kriegschronik der Stadt Münster 1914/18* [1930].
13. StdA Münster, Stadt-Dok no. 42, introductory comment on the folder "Chronik Münster 1939," September 2, 1939.
14. StdA Münster, August 25, 1939.
15. StdA Münster, August 26, 1939.
16. This and previous quote, Wette, "Zur psychologischen Mobilmachung der deutschen Bevölkerung," 219.
17. Maier, "Zweierlei Kriegsanfänge." "Profound dejection," "touch of unwillingness for war": R. Schmidt, *Außenpolitik des Dritten Reiches*, 365.
18. The term *reluctant loyalty*, often used in the discussion about the start of the war in 1939, was already created in 1965 by Helmut Krausnick and Hermann Graml, albeit to

characterize the attitude of the German opposition. See Krausnick and Graml, "Der deutsche Widerstand und die Alliierten," 482.

19. Quote in Wette, "Ideologien," 141. This thesis is also often advocated today. See, for example, Bösch, Mediengeschichte, 187; R. Schmidt, Außenpolitik des Dritten Reiches, 367.

20. Ziemann, Front und Heimat, 44 (anxious-worried), 42 (mood situation).

21. Ziemann, 44.

22. Raithel, Das "Wunder" der inneren Einheit, 267.

23. Raithel, 275.

24. Kruse, Krieg und nationale Integration, 59.

25. Kruse, 60.

26. Levsen, Elite, Männlichkeit und Krieg, 172.

27. Kruse, Krieg und nationale Integration, 158.

28. Hoeres, Der Krieg der Philosophen, 152.

29. StA Hamburg, 622-1/140, 1/32, August 26, 1939.

30. StA Hamburg, September 1, 1939.

31. AdK, Kempowski-Bio, 5965/1, Heft 11: 1939, August 31, 1939, September 1, 1939.

32. DTA, 1315, August 26, 1939, September 14, 1939.

33. DTA, 1512.4, September 3, 1939.

34. Walb, Ich, die Alte—Ich, die Junge, 129–131, here 129, 131 (September 3, 1939).

35. "World history": Walb, 141 (September 27, 1939); "overwhelming": Walb, 139 (September 24, 1939).

36. See, for example, M. Schneider, In der Kriegsgesellschaft, 77; Stargardt, German War, 30.

37. Diary of Ewald Hoffmann, quoted in Breloer, Mein Tagebuch, 92 (September 3, 1939).

38. Breloer, 92 (November 26, 1939).

39. LBI, MM, diary of Erna Becker-Kohen, October 1939.

40. Klemperer, Die Tagebücher 1933–1945, September 3, 1939.

41. This is according to R. Schmidt, Die Außenpolitik des Dritten Reiches, 365.

42. Frei, Der Führerstaat, 133.

43. Wette, "Ideologien," 141. Likewise Wette, "Zur psychologischen Mobilmachung der deutschen Bevölkerung," 219.

44. Wette, "Ideologien," 135.

45. Topser-Ziegert, "Vorwort," 19.

46. On the control of the media at the start of the war, see Bonacker, Goebbels' Mann beim Radio, 55–57.

47. Treue, "Hitlers Rede vor der Presse," 185.

48. This and previous quotes, Domarus, Hitler, 2/1:1309.

49. Various diarists complained about this: for example, Luise Solmitz. StA Hamburg, 622-1/140, 1/32, August 26, 1939, August 31, 1939.

50. On the cancellation of the Reich party congress, see Urban, Konsensfabrik, 75–76. On the cancellation of the Tannenberg celebration, see the corresponding press directive in Bohrmann, NS-Presseanweisungen der Vorkriegszeit, 7/II:872.

51. Express letter of the Reich Minister for Church Affairs on August 30, 1939, quoted in Steinert, Hitlers Krieg, 95.

52. Pätzold and Weißbecker, Geschichte der NSDAP, 409. On the NSDAP's preparations for the start of war, see Weißbecker and Noack, "'Die Partei als Rückgrat der inneren Front.'"

53. This is how the purpose of the rally was characterized by Reich Propaganda Minister Goebbels, who organized the event. See Fröhlich, Tagebücher von Joseph Goebbels, part I, 6:111 (September 25, 1938).

54. Domarus, *Hitler*, I/2:933.
55. Domarus, I/2:932. In contrast to various claims in the literature, the slogan had already been created before this occasion. It is also found in photographs of Nazi assemblies that were made three years before. See the reference in Rother, *Reisen zu Dietrich Bonhoeffer*, 64.
56. Press directive of September 1, 1939, quoted in Sänger, *Politik der Täuschung*, 392.
57. The significance of this interpretation of a war forced on Germany from abroad is pointed out in Stargardt, *German War*, esp. 23–51.
58. Klemperer, *Die Tagebücher 1933–1945*, September 3, 1939.
59. The Berlin correspondent for the *Neue Züricher Zeitung* traced the fact that "only a thin row of spectators" had gathered "on the entry route of the Reich Chancellor in the area of the Brandenburger Gate" mainly to the situation that "the news of the convocation of the Reichstag was still hardly known." Quoted in Domarus, *Hitler*, II/1:1311. In contrast, in summer 1914, above all in Berlin, the population had besieged the newspaper editorial offices in the inner city to receive up-to-date news. The jubilant processions emerged from these masses of people. Fritzsche, *Germans into Nazis*, 13–18. As a result of the prevalence of radios in the 1930s, in September 1939 the Germans sat at home in front of their radios.
60. On this, see for example the description in Solmitz's entry on the annexation of Austria on pages ???
61. StA Hamburg, 622-1/140, 1/32, August 26, 1939.
62. StdA Münster, NL Beier, no. 5, August 29, 1939.
63. Decree by Rudolf Hess on September 1, 1939, quoted in *Deutschland im Kampf* 1, no. 1 (1939): 9.
64. Gunter d'Alquen, "Die geschichtliche Stunde," *Völkischer Beobachter*, September 2–3, 1939.
65. Speech by Robert Ley on September 5, 1939, in a factory in Berlin-Marienfelde, quoted in *Deutschland im Kampf* 1, no. 1 (1939): 42.
66. A.J. Brendt and H. von Wedel, "Geleitwort," *Deutschland im Kampf* 1, no. 1 (1939): 4, 3.
67. "Die Politik," *Deutschland im Kampf* 1, no. 1 (1939): 41–54, here 41.
68. See Goebbels's speech for the opening of the film festival session of the Hitler Youth and League of German Girls on November 5, 1939, in Goebbels, *Die Zeit ohne Beispiel* [1941], 212–217. Goebbels, "Die Zeit ohne Beispiel," *Das Reich*, May 26, 1940, and his speech at the Berlin Sports Palace on June 5, 1943, printed in Heiber, *Goebbels' Reden*, 2:218–239.
69. This and previous quotes, Lothrop Stoddard, "Goebbels Explains How England 'Forced War on German People,'" *Milwaukee Journal*, January 1, 1940.
70. Notes on the lecture by the Reich Propaganda Ministry on January 9, 1940, to the officers of the propaganda companies and officials of the Propaganda Ministry, dated January 17, 1940, Bundesarchiv-Militärarchiv (BArch-MA), RH 1/58 fol. 150–152, here fol. 150–151.
71. M. Dröge, *Die Tagebücher Karl Friedrich Kolbows*, 394 (September 14–17, 1939).
72. StdA Münster, Stadt-Dok no. 42, September 6, 1939.
73. Sywottek, *Mobilmachung für den totalen Krieg*, 236.
74. This and previous quotes, BArch-MA, RH 1/58 fol. 150–152, fol. 151.
75. The speech is printed in Mason, *Arbeiterklasse und Volksgemeinschaft*, 1044–1047.
76. Fritzsche, *Germans into Nazis*, 80.
77. Wildt, "Volksgemeinschaft und Führererwartung," 186; Fritzsche, *Germans into Nazis*, 81–82.
78. Kruse, *Krieg und nationale Integration*, 30–42.
79. DTA 370, 15, January 30, 1933.
80. DTA 370, 21, September 1, 1939.

81. StdA München, Stadt-Dok, no. 42, August 30, 1939.
82. See, for example, D. Süß, *Tod aus der Luft*; Kramer, *Volksgenossinnen an der Heimatfront*.
83. Even local festivities such as marksmen's festivals were considered inappropriate during the war. See Borggräfe, *Schützenvereine im Nationalsozialismus*, 70.
84. Marszolek, "Der Führer spricht," 211–212.
85. See, for example, Thamer, "Die Widersprüche der 'Volksgemeinschaft.'"
86. See, for example, Harvey, *Der Osten braucht Dich!*
87. This is emphasized, for example, in Stargardt, "Troubled Patriot"; Fritzsche, *Life and Death in the Third Reich*.
88. See, Fritzsche, *Life and Death in the Third Reich*; Fritzsche, *Iron Wind*; Stargardt, *German War*.
89. The surviving outline is reproduced in Haffner, *Geschichte eines Deutschen*, 296–297.
90. Schmied, *Haffner*, 65.
91. "Primarily investigated": Schmied, *Haffner*, 67; "small manual": letter from Sebastian Haffner, dated October 6, 1939, quoted in Schmied, 65.

BIBLIOGRAPHY

Note: The names marked with an asterisk are pseudonyms.

1. Archival sources

Akademie der Künste, Kempowski-Biografienarchiv (AdK, Kempowski-Bio), Berlin
A 37 (Henriette Weiss*)
303 (Anton Gloeckner*)
1174 (Karl Möhring*)
1786 (Thea Baumgarten*)
1936 I (Elli Wintgen*)
2918 (author anonymized)
4842 (Wilhelm Bollmann*)
5482 (Friedhelm Müller*)
5584 (Walter Lindemann*)
5965 (Hans Maschmann)
6030/6 (Annie Wächter*)
6301 (author anonymized)

Archivamt des Landschaftsverbandes Westfalen-Lippe (LWL), Westfälisches Literaturarchiv, Münster
Papers of Erwin Sylvanus

Archiv der sozialen Demokratie (AdsD), Bonn
Papers of Theodor Thomas

Bayrisches Hauptstaatsarchiv (BayHStA), Munich
Papers of Fritz Koch
Papers of Rudolf Buttmann

Bundesarchiv-Militärarchiv (BArch-MA), Freiburg i. Br.
RH 1/58 (general and personal affairs of the heads of the army command/supreme commander of the army, individual cases)

Deutsches Historisches Museum (DHM), Berlin
Do 70/176 ("Ahnenpass," circa 1935)
Do 70/452II ("Deutsches Einheits-Familienstammbuch," circa 1938)
Do 86/117 I (filled-out Ahnenpass with family photographs)
Do2 88/487.432 ("Sporttagebuch der deutschen Jugend")
Do2 89/2169 ("Ahnenpass," after 1937)
Do2 99/2104 ("Ahnenpass," 1939)
Do2 2003/327 ("Jung Deutschland Tagebuch")
Do2 2006 (Heinz Korsch*)
Do2 2008/1180 ("Der Ahnenpaß," 1936)

Deutsches Tagebucharchiv (DTA), Emmendingen
237 (Else Dietrich*)
302 (Hans Stelzer*)
326 (Gisela Brandt*)
370 (Max Dingle)
448 (Julia Bergerhoff*)
450 (Henning Zeng*)
565 (Wolfgang Söller*)
639 (Erich Rahmacher*)
749 (Charlotte Bücker*)
779 (Erich Kirk*)
808 I (Otmar Krämer*)
877 I (Marita Schlichting*)
1047 (author anonymized)
1115 (Johannes Friedrich)
1156 (Diary of a KdF voyage)
1295 I (Rita Thoner*)
1315 (Daniel Lotte)
3077 ("Tagebuch für Fahrten und Läger" of a HJ group from Herne)
1346 (Kurt Neuse*)
1495 (Helga Ritter*)
1512 (Inge Thiele)
1636 ("Bericht über eine KdF-Fahrt")
1708 (Werner Stock*)
1724 (Wolf Busse)
1783 (Doris Becker*)
1798 (Curt Weber*)
1834 (author anonymized)
1941 ("Tagebuch von der Großfahrt der Gefolgschaft 11/188")
1998 (author anonymized)
2197 (Claus Behr)
3086 (drinking club "Ruhige Ecke")
3207 ("Arbeitsmaidentagebuch")
4071 (Franz Buesgen*)

Forschungsstelle für Zeitgeschichte in Hamburg (FZH)
11—K 32–34 (Otto Kirchmann)
11—L 21–22 (Inga Lusebrink*)
S 11—F 3 (Hermann Frielingsdorf)
X 11—K 35–40 (Wolfram Kroll*)

Fritz-Hüser-Institut für Literatur und Kultur der Arbeitswelt (FHI), Dortmund
Papers of Artur Streiter

Gedenkstätte KZ Osthofen
2/27/2 (Wilhelm Scheidler)

Institut für sächsische Geschichte und Volkskunde Dresden (ISGV), Lebensgeschichtliches Archiv
Project 028, chronicle of Eichler farming family

Institut für Zeitgeschichte (IfZ), München
ED 22 (Georg Witzmann)
ED 322 (Marianne Köhl, Herbert Wiebus)
ED 363 (Rudolf Briske)
ED 394 (Herbert Müller-Werth, including Erich Scheuer*)

Landesarchiv Berlin
E Rep 061-19 Papers of Hermann Schleifenbaum*
E Rep 200-43 Papers of Franz Göll
E Rep 200-90 Papers of Alfred Wiese

Landesarchiv Nordrhein Westfalen, Abteilung Ostwestfalen-Lippe, Detmold
L 113 NSDAP and NS organizations in Lippe

Landeshauptarchiv Koblenz
700, 23 (Stephan Weidenbach)
700, 153, 186 (Kurt Frackmann*)
700, 153, 285 (Emil Kuhn*)
700, 250 (Walter Heckmann*)

Leo Baeck Institut (LBI), New York/Berlin
MM 6, Diary of Erna Becker-Kohen

Mecklenburgisches Landeshauptarchiv (MLHA) Schwerin
10.9—H-14 Papers of Clara Hacker
10.9—S/8 Papers of Wolfgang Scharenberg

Monacensia, Literaturarchiv und Bibliothek, Munich
Papers of Luise Klempt

Sächsisches Hauptstaatsarchiv (SächsHStA) Dresden
12728 Papers of Walter Lohs

Staatsarchiv Darmstadt
Abt. G 27, 217 (Court files of Wilhelm Scheidler)

Staatsarchiv Hamburg
622-1/129 Papers of Oswald Krause*
622-1/140 Papers of Luise Solmitz
622-1/163 Papers of Friedrich Ahlers-Hestermann
622-1/174 Papers of Christoph Ahrens*
662-1/189 Papers of Werner Kramp

Stadtarchiv Bergisch Gladbach
S 7/130 (material on the diary from the NAPOLA Bensburg)
R4/31 (diary from the NAPOLA Bensburg)

Stadtarchiv Bochum
NAP 2, 2 papers of Süther

Stadtarchiv Bonn
SN1/490 (Anna Deiker*)

Stadtarchiv Dortmund
400/20 ("Tagebuch vom Nordseelager")

Stadtarchiv Duisburg
41/624 (Fritz Funk*)

Stadtarchiv Essen
Ernst-Schmidt-Archiv, 19–538 (Fritz Schössel*)
Papers 643 (Frank Maik)

Stadtarchiv Herne
o nsp, 61–69b (Karl Nieper)

Stadtarchiv Meißen
Rep. XXI, 34 (Helmut Böhme)

Stadtarchiv München
Familien 644 (Klara Schötz)
Familien 825 (Paul Krumbholz)
Papers of Erwin Dehl
Papers of Franz Wallner

Stadtarchiv Münster
Hs 128 (Ludwig Fröcking*)
Papers of Ferdinand Beier
Stadt-Dok Nr. 42 ("Münstersche Kriegschronik 1939/40")

Stadtarchiv Solingen
Kl 228 (Wolf Hollotte*)
Na 025 (Emil Kronenberg)
Na 040 (Ludwig Lindholm*)

Stadtarchiv Werl
Collection Wendelin Leidinger (Thomas Vossen*)

Stadtarchiv Willich
Papers of Josef Herlitz

Zentrum für Antisemitismusforschung (ZfA), Technische Universität Berlin
Life history collection, Gegen Vergessen, für Demokratie (Paul Berger*)
Life history collection, Henry Marx

Private holdings
Yearbook of Heinz Werner Hundertmark

2. Printed sources

Printed sources are cited in the book with their year of publication in square brackets.

Articles in newspapers, anthologies, and journals
"Alles für Deutschland, alles für Hitler." *Schwedter Tageblatt*, November 13, 1933.

"Alter Kämpfer blättert zurück." Ein alter Kämpfer erzählt. *Essener Anzeiger*, July 14, 1926.
"Am 12. November müssen wir der Welt beweisen, daß wir ein Volk geworden sind." *Völkischer Beobachter*, October 29–30, 1933.
Anders, Ernst. "Neu beginnen—zu welchem Ziel?" *Zeitschrift für Sozialismus* 1, no. 3 (1933): 98–101.
"Aufruf an Alle!" *Deutsches Recht: Zentral-Organ des Bundes Nationalsozialistischer Deutscher Juristen* 5, no. 9 (1935): 260.
"Aufruf der Nationalsozialistischen Rundfunkkammer." *Völkischer Beobachter*, October 20, 1933.
"Aus dem Tagebuch eines unbekannten Hitlerredners." *Völkischer Beobachter*, May 20–21, 1934.
Baeumler, Alfred. "Politische Leibeserziehung." In *Sport und Staat*, edited by Arno Breitmeyer and Paul Gerhard Hoffmann, 2:135–161. Berlin: Hilfsfond für den deutschen Sport, 1937.
Beradt, Charlotte. "Dreams under Dictatorship." *Free World* 6, no. 4 (1943): 333–337.
Brendt, A. J., and H. von Wedel. "Geleitwort." *Deutschland im Kampf* 1, no. 1 (September 1939): 3–4.
Binz, Gerhard L. "Der Haß gegen die Uniform." *Völkischer Beobachter*, July 7, 1932.
Bouhler, Philipp. "Zur Einführung." *Nationalsozialistische Bibliographie: Monatshefte der Parteiamtlichen Prüfungskommission zum Schutze des NS.-Schrifttums* 1, no. 1 (1936/37): i–iv.
"Das Siegel." *Vossische Zeitung*, November 14, 1933.
Decker, Wilhelm. "Nationalsozialistische Feiergestaltung." *Völkischer Beobachter*, March 4, 1937.
"Der Kampf um Friede und Gleichberechtigung." *Völkischer Beobachter*, October 22–23, 1933.
"Der Novembertag der deutschen Ehre." *Völkischer Beobachter*, November 14, 1933.
"Deutschlands neue Staatsform: Die plebiszitäre Diktatur—die totale Despotie." *Neuer Vorwärts*, August 19, 1934.
"Die künftigen Historiker." *Die Tat: Deutsche Monatsschrift* 25, no. 3 (1933): 269–270.
"Die Stimmung in Deutschland: Bericht von einer Reise." *Neuer Vorwärts*, June 10, 1934.
"Dokumentation des Urteils des Reichsgerichts vom 18. März 1937 (5 D 760/36)." *Juristische Wochenschrift* 66, no. 37/38 (1937): 2389–2390.
"Dr. Goebbel' Dank." *Vossische Zeitung*, November 14, 1933.
"Dr. Goebbels eröffnet den Kampf gegen die Staatsschädlinge." *Völkischer Beobachter*, May 13, 1934.
"Dr. Goebbels über die kommende Volksbefragung." *Völkischer Beobachter*, October 19, 1933.
"Durch Kampf und Not zum 3. Reich." Ein alter Kämpfer erzählt. *Essener Anzeiger*, July 21, 1926.
Faber, Maria. Review of *Die Katrin wird Soldat*. *Völkischer Beobachter*, February 1–2, 1931.
"Freude am Familienarchiv." *Neues Volk* 6, no. 8 (1938): 31–35.
"From a 'Red' Street in Berlin: Heroes of Civil Strife." Review of *Our Street*. *Times* (London), January 19, 1938.
"5000 Nationalsozialisten geloben." Ein alter Kämpfer erzählt. *Essener Anzeiger*, July 7, 1926.
Goebbels, Joseph. "Die Zeit ohne Beispiel." *Das Reich*, May 26, 1940.
Gohdes, Otto. "Vorwort." *Schulungsbriefe des Reichsschulungsamtes der NSDAP und der Deutschen Arbeitsfront* 1, no. 1 (1933): 2.
Göring, Hermann. "Aus dem Tagebuch eines Jagdfliegers." In *In der Luft unbesiegt: Erlebnisse im Weltkrieg erzählt von Luftkämpfern Neumann*, edited by Paul Georg Paul, 209–214. Munich: J. F. Lehmanns Verlag, 1923.
"Hitler ist Deutschland." *Völkischer Beobachter*, November 14, 1933.
Hocke, Gustav René. "Über das Tagebuchschreiben." *Der Bücherwurm* 24, no. 6 (1938/39): 129–135.

Jaensch, Erich. "Jugendentwicklung und Neuformung des deutschen Menschentums." In *Charakter und Erziehung: Bericht über den XVI. Kongreß der Deutschen Gesellschaft für Psychologie in Bayreuth vom 2.-4. Juli 1938*, edited by Otto Klemm, 183–187. Leipzig: J. F. Lehmanns Verlag, 1939.
"Kämpft weiter für das 3. Reich." Ein alter Kämpfer erzählt. *Essener Anzeiger*, July 28, 1935.
Kautsky, Klaus. "Eine Diskussionsgrundlage." *Zeitschrift für Sozialismus* 1, no. 2 (1933): 50–58.
Kuhlmann, Friede Marie. "Und wir? Ein Nachwort." In *Frontschwestern: Ein deutsches Ehrenbuch*, edited by Elfriede Pflugk-Harttung, 337-338. Berlin: Verlag Bernard & Graefe, 1936.
Mezger, Edmund. "Beleidigung durch Äußerungen im engsten Familienkreis?" *Juristische Wochenschrift* 66, no. 37/38 (1937): 2329–2333.
"Mit dem Führer unterwegs: Kleine Stimmungsberichte einer großen Reise." *Westdeutscher Beobachter*, March 13-30, 1936.
Nahnsen, Georg. "Denkschrift betr. Familien-, Sippen- und Rassenkunde." *Zeitschrift für Niedersächsische Familienkunde* 17, no. 5/6 (1935): 33–35.
"Neu beginnen!" *Neuer Vorwärts*, October 1, 1933.
"Reichsinnenminister Dr. Frick zur Reichstagswahl." *Völkischer Beobachter*, October 29–30, 1933.
Röhm, Ernst. "SA und deutsche Revolution." *Nationalsozialistische Monatshefte* 4, no. 39 (1933): 251–254.
Schliebe, Georg. "Gemeinschaftstagebücher (Klassenbücher aus einem Internate)." In *Psychologie des Gemeinschaftslebens: Bericht über den XIV. Kongreß der deutschen Gesellschaft für Psychologie in Tübingen vom 22.-26. Mai 1934*, edited by Otto Klemm, 232–234. Jena: Fischer Verlag, 1935.
Schuwerack, Wilhelm. "Zur Gestaltung nationalpolitischer Schülerlehrgänge." *Zeitschrift für pädagogische Psychologie und Jugendkunde* 37, no. 8 (1936): 327–332.
Stoddard, Lothrop. "Goebbels Explains How England 'Forced War on German People.'" *Milwaukee Journal*, January 21, 1940.
Streicher, Julius. "Schlagt den Weltfeind." *Völkischer Beobachter*, March 31, 1933.
"Vier Millionen deutsche Revolutionäre." *Neuer Vorwärts*, November 19, 1933.
Vlator. "Wege zur Klarheit." *Neuer Vorwärts* supplement, October 22, 1933.
"Vom Kaiserhof zur Reichskanzlei: Gedanken zum neuen Buch von Dr. Goebbels." *Völkischer Beobachter*, May 16, 1934.
"Warum Reichstagswahl." *Völkischer Beobachter*, November 10, 1933.

Books and official texts

Abel, Theodore. *Why Hitler Came into Power*. Cambridge, MA: Harvard University Press, 1986. First published 1938.
Albrecht, Reinhard. *Das Tagebuch des Gerhard Thiele*. Plauen: Kurt Wolff Verlag, 1935.
Baron von Loewenstern, Elard. *Der Frontflieger: Aus Vorkriegs-, Kriegs- und Nachkriegsfliegertagen; Aufzeichnungen auf Grund eigener Tagebücher*. Berlin: Verlag Bernard & Graefe, 1937.
Beck, Friedrich Alfred. *Geistige Grundlagen der neuen Erziehung: Dargestellt aus der nationalsozialistischen Idee*. Osterwieck: A. W. Zickfeldt Verlag, 1933.
Benze, Rudolf. *Wegweiser ins Dritte Reich: Einführung in das völkische Schrifttum*. Braunschweig: Verlag E. Appelhans & Co, 1933.

Bernfeld, Siegfried. *Trieb und Tradition im Jugendalter: Kulturpsychologische Studien an Tagebüchern*. Beihefte zur Zeitschrift für angewandte Psychologie 54. Leipzig: Kommissionsverlag Johann Ambrosius Barth, 1931.

Clauß, Ludwig Ferdinand, and Arthur Hoffmann. *Vorschule der Rassenkunde auf der Grundlage der praktischen Menschenbeobachtung*. Erfurt: Verlag Kurt Stenger, 1934.

Conti, Leonardo, ed. *Reden und Aufrufe: Gerhard Wagner 1888–1939*. Berlin: Reichsgesundheitsverlag, 1943.

Denckler, Heinz-Eberhardt. *Wie finde ich meine Ahnen? Anleitung, wie man schnell seine arische Abstammung nachweist*. 2nd ed. Berlin: Heinz Denckler Verlag, 1936.

Drexler, Anton. *Mein politisches Erwachen: Aus dem Tagebuch eines deutschen sozialistischen Arbeiters*. Munich: Deutscher Volksverlag, 1919.

Dürre, Konrad. *Erbbiologischer und eugenischer Wegweiser für Jedermann*. 2nd ed. Berlin: Verlag Alfred Metzner, 1933.

Eggers, Kurt. *Tagebuch einer frohen Fahrt*. Leipzig: Gustav Weise Verlag, 1935.

Engelbrechten, Julius K. von, and Hans Volz. *Wir wandern durch das nationalsozialistische Berlin: Ein Führer durch die Gedenkstätten des Kampfes um die Reichshauptstadt*. Munich: Franz Eher Nachfolger Verlag, 1937.

Eydt, Alfred. *Der Rasse- und Gesundheitspaß als Nachweis erblicher Gesundheit und rassischer Vollwertigkeit*. Leipzig: Verlag Degener & Co., 1933.

Fink, Fritz. *Die Judenfrage im Unterricht*. Nuremberg: Verlag Der Stürmer, 1937.

Franke, Gustav. *Vererbung, eine weltanschauliche Grundfrage: Grundsätzliche Fragen der Erbund Rassenkunde, die alle angehen*. Munich, 1937.

———. *Vererbung und Rasse: Eine Einführung in Vererbungslehre, Familienkunde, Rassenhygiene und Rassenkunde*. 2nd ed. Munich: Franz Eher Nachfolger Verlag, 1938.

Göbels, Hubert. *Jörg schreibt sein Hitler-Tagebuch*. Schriften zu Deutschlands Erneuerung. Lese- und Arbeitsbögen für die deutsche Schule, no. 66. Breslau: Verlag Heinrich Handel, 1935.

Goebbels, Joseph. *Die Zeit ohne Beispiel: Reden und Aufsätze aus den Jahren 1939/40/41*. Munich: Franz Eher Nachfolger Verlag, 1941.

———. *Michael: Ein deutsches Schicksal in Tagebuchblättern*. Munich: Franz Eher Verlag, 1929.

———. *Revolution der Deutschen: 14 Jahre Nationalsozialismus*. Oldenburg: Gerhard Stalling Verlag, 1933.

———. *Vom Kaiserhof zur Reichskanzlei: Eine historische Darstellung in Tagebuchblättern (Vom 1. Januar 1932 bis zum 1. Mai 1933)*. Munich: Franz Eher Nachfolger Verlag, 1934.

Goes, Gustav. *Mein Kriegstagebuch*. Berlin: Verlag Dr. Hans Riegler, 1935.

Gönner, Rolf von, ed. *Spaten und Ähre: Das Handbuch der deutschen Jugend im Reichsarbeitsdienst*. Heidelberg: Kurt Vowinckel Verlag, 1938.

Göring, Hermann. *Die Rechtssicherheit als Grundlage der Volksgemeinschaft*. Hamburg: Hanseatische Verlagsanstalt, 1935.

Groß, Walter. *Rassenpolitische Erziehung*. Berlin: Verlag Junker & Dünnhaupt, 1934.

Hadamovsky, Eugen. *Dein Rundfunk: Das Rundfunkbuch für alle Volksgenossen*. Munich: Franz Eher Nachfolger Verlag, 1934.

Haffner, Sebastian. *Als Engländer maskiert: Ein Gespräch mit Jutta Krug über das Exil*. Munich: btb Verlag, 2008.

———. *Defying Hitler: A memoir*. New York, NY: Farrar, Straus and Giroux, 2002.

———. *Geschichte eines Deutschen: Die Erinnerungen 1914–1933*. Stuttgart: Deutsche Verlagsanstalt, 2000.
Hebbel, Friedrich. *Tagebücher und Briefe*. Edited by Heinz Amelung. Berlin: Deutsche Bibliothek, 1935.
Hierl, Konstantin. *Ausgewählte Schriften und Reden*. Vol. 2. 2nd ed. Munich: Franz Eher Nachfolger Verlag, 1943.
Hinkel, Hans, ed. *Handbuch der Reichskulturkammer*. Berlin: Deutscher Verlag für Politik und Wirtschaft, 1937.
Hitler, Adolf. *Die Reden Hitlers am Parteitag der Freiheit 1935*. Munich: Franz Eher Nachfolger Verlag, 1935.
Huber, Ernst Rudolf. *Neue Grundbegriffe des hoheitlichen Rechts*. Berlin: Verlag Junker & Dünnhaupt, 1935.
———. *Verfassungsrecht des Großdeutschen Reiches*. Grundzüge der Rechts- und Wirtschaftswissenschaft, Reihe A Rechtswissenschaft. Hamburg: Hanseatische Verlagsanstalt, 1939.
Huber, Franz. *Bauerntum und Bauernbildung im Neuen Reich: Grund- und Aufriß einer bauern- und volkhaften Landpädagogik*. Munich: Verlag R. Oldenbourg, 1934.
Jörns, Emil, and Julious Schwab. *Rassenhygienische Fibel: Der deutschen Jugend zuliebe geschrieben*. Berlin: Alfred Metzner Verlag, 1934.
Jünger, Ernst. *Strahlungen*. Tübingen: Heliopolis-Verlag, 1949.
Kallsperger, Anna. "Nationalsozialistische Erziehung im Reichsarbeitsdienst für die weibliche Jugend." PhD diss., University of Heidelberg, 1939.
Koellreutter, Otto. *Der Deutsche Führerstaat*. Tübingen: Verlag Mohr, 1934.
———. *Vom Sinn und Wesen der Nationalen Revolution*. Tübingen: Verlag Mohr, 1933.
Krapfenbauer, Hans. "Die sozialpolitische Bedeutung der NS-Gemeinschaft 'Kraft durch Freude.'" PhD diss., University of Nuremberg, 1937.
Krieck, Ernst. *Philosophie der Erziehung*. Jena: Eugen Diederichs Verlag, 1925.
Kublank, Walter. *Kriegstagebuch aus Flandern*. Reutlingen: Verlag Ensslin & Laiblin, 1934.
Kuckelsberg, Ernst. *Deutsche Nordlandreise: Ein Reisetagebuch*. Dresden: Limpert Verlag, 1937.
Ley, Robert. *Soldaten der Arbeit*. 2nd ed. Munich: Franz Eher Nachfolger Verlag, 1939.
Littmann, Arnold. *Herbert Norkus und die Hitlerjungen von Beusselkietz: Nach dem Tagebuch des Kameradschaftsführers Gerd Mondt und nach Mitteilungen der Familie*. Berlin: Steuben Verlag, 1934.
Malitz, Bruno. *Die Leibesübungen in der nationalsozialistischen Idee*. Munich: Franz Eher Nachfolger Verlag, 1933.
Mehnert, Klaus. *Die Jugend in Sowjetrussland*. Berlin: Fischer Verlag, 1932.
Mertens, Adolf. *Schulungslager und Lagererziehung*. Dortmund: Verlag W. Crüwell, 1937.
Michligk, Paul. *Ahnenforschung leicht gemacht: Wege zur Ahnentafel und Familienkunde*. Berlin: Industrieverlag Spaeth & Linde, 1934.
Münster, Hans Amandus. *Die drei Aufgaben der Zeitungswissenschaft*. Leipzig: Verlag Robert Noske, 1935.
Nationalpolitische Lehrgänge für Schüler: Denkschrift des Oberpräsidenten der Rheinprovinz (Abteilung für höheres Schulwesen). Frankfurt am Main: Verlag M. Diesterweg, 1935.
Nebel, Gerhard. *Bei den nördlichen Hesperiden: Tagebuch aus dem Jahr 1942*. Wuppertal: Marees Verlag, 1948.
Otto, Hermann, and Werner Stachowitz. *Abriß der Vererbungslehre und Rassenkunde einschließlich der Familienkunde, Rassenhygiene und Bevölkerungspolitik*. 2nd ed. Frankfurt am Main: Verlag M. Diesterweg, 1934.

Pantel, Gerhard. *Befehl Deutschland: Ein Tagebuch vom Kampf um Berlin.* Munich: Franz Eher Nachfolger Verlag, 1936.
Petersen, Jan. *Our Street: A Chronicle Written in the Heart of Fascist Germany.* London: Victor Gollancz Ltd, 1938.
Pfahler, Gerhard. *Warum Erziehung trotz Vererbung?* Leipzig: Teubner Verlag, 1935.
Purschke, Hilde. *Das Mottenhaus: Ein Tagebuch aus dem weiblichen Arbeitsdienst.* Leipzig: Armanen Verlag, 1934.
Ramlow, Gerhard, ed. *Deutsche Jungens auf Fahrt.* Berlin: Paul Franke Verlag, 1934.
Reichsjugendführung, ed. *Vorschriftenhandbuch der Hitler-Jugend.* Vol. 3. Berlin, 1942.
Reichsministerium des Innern, ed. *Reichsgesetzblatt: Jahrgang 1933–1935.* Berlin: Reichsverlagsamt, 1933–1935.
Reichsorganisationsleiter der NSDAP, ed. *Parteistatistik.* 4 vols. Munich, 1935.
Rittweger, Kurt. *Der unbekannte Redner der Partei: Tagebuchskizzen eines Redners.* Munich: Verlag J. B. Lindl, 1939.
Rosenbusch, Agnes. *Die Tagebücher Friedrich Hebbels: Ein Versuch ihrer Deutung.* Weimar: Dunker Verlag, 1935.
Scheidt, Walter. *Einführung in die naturwissenschaftliche Familienkunde/ Familienanthropologie.* Munich: J. F. Lehmann Verlag, 1923.
Schiefer, Jack. *Tagebuch eines Wehrunwürdigen.* Aachen: Grenzland Verlag, 1947.
Schmitt, Carl. *Staat, Bewegung, Volk: Die Dreigliederung der politischen Einheit.* Der deutsche Staat der Gegenwart 1. Hamburg: Hanseatische Verlagsanstalt, 1933.
Schneider, Friedrich. *Die Selbsterziehung: Wissenschaft und Übung.* Einsiedeln: Benziger Verlag, 1936.
———. *Praxis der Selbsterziehung in 48 erläuterten Beispielen.* Freiburg: Herder Verlag, 1940.
Schulte, Eduard. *Kriegschronik der Stadt Münster 1914/18.* Münster: Aschendorff Verlag, 1930.
Schultze, Friedbert. *So lebst du deutsch! Das Sittengesetz des deutschen Menschen.* Stuttgart: Georg Truckenmüller Verlag, 1937.
Schulze, Karlheinz. *Um Deutschland: Aus dem Tagebuch eines SA-Mannes.* Radolfzell: Heim Verlag, 1934.
Statistisches Reichsamt, ed. *Statistisches Jahrbuch für das Deutsche Reich.* Vol. 53. Berlin: Reimar Hobbing Verlag, 1934.
Surén, Hans. *Gymnastik der Deutschen: Rassenbewusste Selbsterziehung.* Part 1, *Unseres Körpers Schönheit und gymnastische Schulung.* 49th ed. Stuttgart: Franckh Verlag, 1938.
Thürauf, Ulrich, ed. *Schulthess' Europäischer Geschichtskalender.* Year 50: 1934. Munich: C. H. Beck Verlag, 1935.
Tiefenbach, A. [Herbert Blank, pseud.]. *SS: Ein Roman.* Oldenburg: Gerhard Stalling, 1934.
Tippelmann, Maria. *Kleinkinderziehung in der deutschen Familie.* Langensalza: Beltz Verlag, 1938.
Tschammer und Osten, Hans von. *Sport und Leibesübungen im nationalsozialistischen Staat, Grundlagen, Aufbau und Wirtschaftsordnung des nationalsozialistischen Staates.* Vol. 1, group 1, contribution 10a. Berlin: Industrieverlag Spaeth & Linde, 1937.
Verhandlungen des Reichstages. Vol. 458:9. Wahlperiode 1933. Berlin, 1936.
Verhandlungen des V. Landtages von Thüringen, 4. Abteilung: Stenographische Berichte. Vol. 2. Weimar, 1930–1932.
Voß, Bernhard. *Wi Dickköpp: Aus dem Tagebuch eines unbekannten SA-Mannes.* Rostock, 1937.
Waldenhagen, Peter. *Das dritte Reich: Unser zukünftiges Deutschland: Ein Tagebuch aus den Jahren 1926–1933 unter Darlegung und Erläuterung des Programms der NSDAP.* Leipzig: Vormarsch-Verlag A. Kaden, 1931.

Wittig, Lisbeth. "Der junge Hebbel als Gestalter seines Selbst." PhD, University of Berlin, 1937.
Witzmann, Georg. *Thüringen von 1918–1933: Erinnerungen eines Politikers*. Meisenheim am Glan: Anton Hain Verlag, 1958.

3. Edited sources

Bajohr, Frank, Beate Meyer, and Joachim Szodrzynski, eds. *Bedrohung, Hoffnung, Skepsis: Vier Tagebücher des Jahres 1933*. Göttingen, 2013.
Barlach, Ernst. *Die Briefe II: 1925–1938*. Edited by Friedrich Dross. Munich, 1969.
Boberach, Heinz, ed. *Meldungen aus dem Reich 1938–1945: Die geheimen Lageberichte des Sicherheitsdienstes der SS*. 17 vols. Herrsching, 1984.
Bohrmann, Hans, ed. *NS-Presseanweisungen der Vorkriegszeit: Edition und Dokumentation*. 19 vols. Munich, 1984–2001.
Breloer, Heinrich, ed. *Mein Tagebuch: Geschichten vom Überleben 1939–1947*. Cologne, 1984.
Buchholz, Marlis and Bernd Rother. *Der Parteivorstand der SPD im Exil: Protokolle der Sopade 1933–1940*. Archiv für Sozialgeschichte, Beiheft 15. Bonn, 1995.
Cohn, Willy. *Kein Recht, nirgends: Tagebuch vom Untergang des Breslauer Judentums 1933–1941*. Edited by Norbert Conrads. 2 vols. Cologne, 2006.
Comité des Délégations Juives, ed. *Die Lage der Juden in Deutschland 1933: Das Schwarzbuch; Tatsachen und Dokumente*. Frankfurt am Main, 1983. First published Paris, 1934.
Deutschland-Berichte der Sozialdemokratischen Partei Deutschlands (Sopade) 1934–1940. 7 vols. 4th ed. Frankfurt am Main, 1980.
Dokumente des ZK der KPD 1933–1945. Offenbach, 2002.
Domarus, Max. *Hitler: Reden und Proklamationen 1932–1945; Kommentiert von einem deutschen Zeitgenossen*. Vol. 1/1, *Triumph, 1932–1934*. Wiesbaden, 1973.
———. *Hitler: Reden und Proklamationen 1932–1945; Kommentiert von einem deutschen Zeitgenossen*. Vol. 2/1, *Untergang 1939–1940*. Wiesbaden, 1973.
Dröge, Martin, ed. *Die Tagebücher Karl Friedrich Kolbows (1899–1945): Nationalsozialist der ersten Stunde und Landeshauptmann der Provinz Westfalen*. Forschungen zur Regionalgeschichte 63. Paderborn, 2009.
Eberle, Henrik. *Briefe an Hitler: Ein Volk schreibt seinem Führer; Unbekannte Dokumente aus dem Moskauer Sonderarchiv—zum ersten Mal veröffentlicht*. Bergisch Gladbach, 2007.
Elz, Wolfgang, and Ralph Erbar. *"Ihr seid das Deutschland der Zukunft": Schule im frühen Nationalsozialismus (1934–1936) am Beispiel des Mainzer Gymnasiums; Edition eines Klassentagebuchs und Anregungen zur unterrichtspraktischen Umsetzung*. Bad Kreuznach, 2008.
Fröhlich, Elke, ed. *Die Tagebücher von Joseph Goebbels*. 32 vols. in three parts. Munich, 1993–2008.
Frank, Anne. *The Diary of a Young Girl*. New York, 1993.
———. *Die Tagebücher der Anne Frank*. Frankfurt am Main, 1988.
Heiber, Helmut, ed. *Goebbels-Reden*. 2 vols. Düsseldorf, 1971–1972.
Hitler, Adolf. *Mein Kampf: Eine kritische Edition*. Edited by Christian Hartmann, Thomas Vordermayer, Othmar Plöckinger, and Roman Töppel. 2 vols. Munich, 2016.
Hosenfeld, Wilm. *"Ich versuche jeden zu retten": Das Leben eines deutschen Offiziers in Briefen und Tagebüchern, im Auftrag des Militärgeschichtlichen Forschungsamtes*. Edited by Thomas Vogel. Munich, 2004.

Kellner, Friedrich. *"Vernebelt, verdunkelt sind alle Hirne": Tagebücher 1939–1945*. Edited by Sascha Feuchert, Robert Martin Scott Kellner, Erwin Leibfried, Jörg Riecke, and Markus Roth. 2 vols. Göttingen, 2011.
Klemperer, Victor. *Die Tagebücher 1933–1945: Kritische Gesamtausgabe*. Berlin, 2007. CD-ROM.
———. *I Shall Bear Witness: The Diaries of Victor Klemperer 1933–41*. London, 1998.
Matthäus, Jürgen, and Frank Bajohr, eds. *Alfred Rosenberg: Die Tagebücher von 1934 bis 1944*. Frankfurt am Main, 2015.
Michaelis, Herbert, and Ernst Schraepler, eds. *Ursachen und Folgen: Vom deutschen Zusammenbruch 1918 und 1945 bis zur staatlichen Neuordnung Deutschlands in der Gegenwart; Eine Urkunden- und Dokumentensammlung zur Zeitgeschichte*. Vol. 9, *Das Dritte Reich: Die Zertrümmerung des Parteienstaates und die Grundlegung der Diktatur*. Berlin, 1964.
———, eds. *Ursachen und Folgen: Vom deutschen Zusammenbruch 1918 und 1945 bis zur staatlichen Neuordnung Deutschlands in der Gegenwart; Eine Urkunden- und Dokumentensammlung zur Zeitgeschichte*. Vol. 10, *Das Dritte Reich: Die Errichtung des Führerstaates; Die Abwendung von dem System der kollektiven Sicherheit*. Berlin, 1965.
Miles. "Neu beginnen! Faschismus oder Sozialismus: Als Diskussionsgrundlage der Sozialisten Deutschlands." In *Drei Schriften aus dem Exil*, edited by Kurt Kotzbach, Internationale Bibliothek 76, 1–88. Berlin, 1974.
Obenaus, Herbert, and Sibylle Obenaus, eds. *"Schreiben, wie es wirklich war!" Aufzeichnungen Karl Dürkefäldens aus den Jahren 1933–1945*. Hannover, 1985.
Plum, Günter. "Dokumentation: Staatspolizei und innere Verwaltung 1934–1936." *Vierteljahrshefte für Zeitgeschichte* 13, no. 2 (1965): 191–224.
Repgen, Konrad, and Hans Booms, eds. *Akten der Reichskanzlei: Regierung Hitler 1933–1938*. Part I, *1933/34*. Vol. 1, *1. Januar 1933 bis 31. August 1933: Dokumente Nr. 1 bis 206*. Redacted by Karl-Heinz Minuth. Boppard, 1983.
———, eds. *Akten der Reichskanzlei: Regierung Hitler 1933–1938*. Part I, *1933/34*. Vol. 2, *12. September 1933 bis 27. August 1934: Dokumente Nr. 207 bis 384*. Redacted by Karl-Heinz Minuth. Boppard, 1983.
Rosenberg, Kurt F. *"Einer, der nicht mehr dazugehört": Tagebücher 1933–1937*. Edited by Beate Meyer and Björn Siegel. Göttingen, 2012.
Seeger, Karl-Heinz. "Tagebuchaufzeichnungen Karl Leisners im RAD." *Rundbrief des Internationalen Karl-Leisner-Kreises* 39 (1999): 41–127.
Seraphim, Hans-Günther, ed. *Das politische Tagebuch Alfred Rosenbergs: 1934/35 und 1939/40*. Munich, 1964.
Stadtarchiv Mannheim, ed. *Verfolgung und Widerstand unter dem Nationalsozialismus in Baden: Die Lageberichte der Gestapo und des Generalstaatsanwalts Karlsruhe 1933–1940*. Redacted by von Thomas Schadt. Veröffentlichungen des Stadtarchivs Mannheim 3. Stuttgart, 1976.
Stöver, Bernd. *Berichte über die Lage in Deutschland: Die Lagemeldungen der Gruppe Neu Beginnen aus dem Dritten Reich 1933–1936*. Archiv für Sozialgeschichte 17. Bonn, 1996.
Thévoz, Robert, Hans Branig, and Cécile Lowenthal-Hensel. *Pommern 1934/35 im Spiegel von Gestapo-Lageberichten und Sachakten*. Veröffentlichungen aus den Archiven preußischer Kulturbesitz 12. Cologne, 1974.
Treue, Wilhelm. "Hitlers Rede vor der Presse (10. November 1938)." *Vierteljahrshefte für Zeitgeschichte* 6, no. 2 (1958): 175–191.

Vogelsang, Thilo. "Neue Dokumente zur Geschichte der Reichswehr 1930–1933." *Vierteljahrshefte für Zeitgeschichte* 2, no. 4 (1954): 397–436.
Walb, Lore. *Ich, die Alte—Ich, die Junge: Konfrontation mit meinen Tagebüchern 1933–1945.* Berlin, 1997.

4. Literature

Abel, Karl-Dietrich. *Presselenkung im NS-Staat: Eine Studie zur Publizistik in der nationalsozialistischen Zeit.* Einzelveröffentlichungen der Historischen Kommission zu Berlin 2. Berlin, 1968.
Abrath, Gottfried. *Subjekt und Milieu im NS-Staat: Die Tagebücher des Pfarrers Hermann Klugkist Hesse 1936–1939.* Arbeiten zur kirchlichen Zeitgeschichte: Reihe B, Darstellungen 21. Göttingen, 1994.
Adam, Christian. *Lesen unter Hitler: Autoren, Bestseller, Leser im Dritten Reich.* Frankfurt am Main, 2013.
Adam, Uwe Dietrich. *Judenpolitik im Dritten Reich.* 1972. Reprint, Düsseldorf, 2003.
Ahlheim, Hannah. *"Deutsche, kauft nicht bei Juden!" Antisemitismus und politischer Boykott in Deutschland 1924 bis 1935.* Göttingen, 2011.
Albrecht, Gerd, ed. *Der Film im 3. Reich: Eine Dokumentation.* Karlsruhe, 1979.
Alkemeyer, Thomas. "Images and Politics of the Body in the National Socialist Era." *Sport Science Review* 4, no. 1 (1995): 60–90.
———. *Körper, Kult und Politik: Von der "Muskelreligion" Pierre de Coubertins zur Inszenierung von Macht in den Olympischen Spielen von 1936.* Frankfurt am Main, 1996.
Allen, William Sheridan. *The Nazi Seizure of Power: The Experience of a Single German Town, 1930–1935.* Chicago, 1965.
Allert, Tilman. *Der deutsche Gruß: Geschichte einer unheilvollen Geste.* Frankfurt am Main, 2005.
Aly, Götz. *Hitlers Volksstaat: Raub, Rassenkrieg und nationaler Sozialismus.* Frankfurt am Main, 2005.
———, ed. *Volkes Stimme: Skepsis und Führervertrauen im Nationalsozialismus.* Frankfurt am Main, 2006.
Anderson, Benedict. *Die Erfindung der Nation: Zur Karriere eines folgenreichen Konzepts.* Expanded ed. Frankfurt am Main, 1996.
Arendt, Hannah. *Elemente und Ursprünge totaler Herrschaft.* 10th ed. Munich, 2005.
Aris, Nancy. *Die Metro als Schriftwerk: Geschichtsproduktion und industrielles Schreiben im Stalinismus.* Berlin, 2005.
Ayaß, Wolfgang. *"Asoziale" im Nationalsozialismus.* Stuttgart, 1995.
Baganz, Carina. *Erziehung zur "Volksgemeinschaft"? Die frühen Konzentrationslager in Sachsen 1933–34/37.* Reihe Geschichte der Konzentrationslager, 1933–1945, 6. Berlin, 2005.
———. "Sachsenburg." In *Der Ort des Terrors, Geschichte der nationalsozialistischen Konzentrationslager,* vol. 2, *Frühe Lager: Dachau, Emslandlager,* edited by Wolfgang Benz and Barbara Distel, 194–200. Munich, 2005.
Bahro, Berno. *Der SS-Sport: Organisation, Funktion, Bedeutung.* Paderborn, 2013.
Bajohr, Frank. "'Community of Action' and Diversity of Attitudes: Reflections on Mechanisms of Social Integration in National Socialist Germany, 1933–45." In *Visions of Community in Nazi Germany: Social Engineering and Private Lives,* edited by Martina Steber and Bernhard Gotto, 187–199. Oxford, 2014.

———. "Das 'Zeitalter des Tagebuchs'? Subjektive Zeugnisse aus der NS-Zeit: Einleitung." In "... Zeugnis ablegen bis zum letzten...": Tagebücher und persönliche Zeugnisse aus der Zeit des Nationalsozialismus und des Holocaust, edited by Frank Bajohr and Sibylle Steinbacher, Dachauer Symposien zur Zeitgeschichte 15, 7–21. Göttingen, 2015.

———. "Die Zustimmungsdiktatur: Grundzüge nationalsozialistischer Herrschaft in Hamburg." In Hamburg im "Dritten Reich," edited by Forschungsstelle für Zeitgeschichte in Hamburg, 69–121. Göttingen, 2005.

———. Parvenüs und Profiteure: Korruption in der NS-Zeit. Frankfurt am Main, 2004.

Bajohr, Frank, Beate Meyer, and Joachim Szodrzynski. "Einleitung." In Bedrohung, Hoffnung, Skepsis: Vier Tagebücher des Jahres 1933, edited by Frank Bajohr, Beate Meyer, and Joachim Szodrzynski, 7–13. Göttingen, 2013.

Frank Bajohr and Sibylle Steinbacher, ed. "... Zeugnis ablegen bis zum letzten...": Tagebücher und persönliche Zeugnisse aus der Zeit des Nationalsozialismus und des Holocaust, Dachauer Symposien zur Zeitgeschichte 15. Göttingen, 2015.

Bajohr, Frank, and Michael Wildt. "Einleitung." In Volksgemeinschaft: Neue Forschungen zur Gesellschaft des Nationalsozialismus, edited by Frank Bajohr and Michael Wildt, 7–23. Frankfurt am Main, 2009.

———, eds. Volksgemeinschaft: Neue Forschungen zur Gesellschaftsgeschichte des Nationalsozialismus. Frankfurt am Main, 2009.

Baranowski, Shelley. Strength through Joy: Consumerism and Mass Tourism in the Third Reich. Cambridge, 2004.

Barbian, Jan-Pieter. Literaturpolitik im NS-Staat: von der "Gleichschaltung" bis zum Ruin. Frankfurt am Main, 2010.

Barck, Simone. Antifa-Geschichte(n): Eine literarische Spurensuche in der DDR der 1950er und 1960er Jahre. Cologne, 2003.

Barkai, Avraham. "Wehr Dich!": Der Centralverein deutscher Staatsbürger jüdischen Glaubens (C. V.) 1893–1938. Munich, 2002.

Barkow, Ben, Raphael Gross, and Michael Lenarz. Novemberpogrom 1938: Die Augenzeugenberichte der Wiener Library. Frankfurt am Main, 2008.

Bärsch, Claus-Ekkehard. Die politische Religion des Nationalsozialismus: Die religiöse Dimension der NS-Ideologie in den Schriften von Dietrich Eckart, Joseph Goebbels, Alfred Rosenberg und Adolf Hitler. 2nd rev. ed. Munich, 2002.

Baumann, Schaul. Die Deutsche Glaubensbewegung und ihr Gründer Jakob Wilhelm Hauer (1881–1962). Marburg, 2005.

Bavaj, Riccardo. Die Ambivalenz der Moderne im Nationalsozialismus: Eine Bilanz der Forschung. Munich, 2003.

Beck, Hermann. The Fateful Alliance: German Conservatives and Nazis in 1933; The Machtergreifung in a New Light. New York, 2008.

Behrenbeck, Sabine. Der Kult um die toten Helden: Nationalsozialistische Mythen, Riten und Symbole 1923–1945. Kölner Beiträge zur Nationsforschung 2. Vierow, 1996.

Benz, Wolfgang. "Die jüdische Emigration." In Handbuch der deutschsprachigen Emigration 1933–1945, edited by Claus-Dieter Krohn, Patrick von zur Mühlen, Gerhard Paul, and Lutz Winckler, 2nd ed., columns 5–16. Darmstadt, 2008.

Benz, Wolfgang, and Barbara Distel, ed. Der Ort des Terrors: Geschichte der nationalsozialistischen Konzentrationslager. 9 vols. Munich, 2005–2009.

Beradt, Charlotte. Das Dritte Reich des Traums. Frankfurt am Main, 1994. First published 1966.

———. *The Third Reich of Dreams*. Chicago, 1968.
Bergerson, Andrew Stuart. *Ordinary Germans in Extraordinary Times: The Nazi Revolution in Hildesheim*. Bloomington, IN, 2004.
Berghoff, Hartmut. "Von der 'Reklame' zur Verbrauchslenkung: Werbung im nationalsozialistischen Deutschland." In *Konsumpolitik: Die Regulierung des privaten Verbrauch im 20. Jahrhundert*, edited by Hartmut Berghoff, 77–112. Göttingen, 1999.
Berglund, Gisela. "Deutsche Opposition gegen Hitler in Presse und Roman des Exils: Eine Darstellung und ein Vergleich mit der historischen Wirklichkeit." PhD Diss., University of Stockholm, 1972.
Bernett, Hajo. *Nationalsozialistische Leibeserziehung: Eine Dokumentation ihrer Theorie und Organisation. Texte—Quellen—Dokumente zur Sportwissenschaft 1.* 2nd rev. ed. Schorndorf, 2008.
Bessel, Richard. *Political Violence and the Rise of Nazism: The Storm Troopers in Eastern Germany, 1925–1934*. New Haven, CT, 1984.
Betts, Paul. *Within Walls: Private Life in the German Democratic Republic*. Oxford, 2010.
Bialas, Wolfgang. *Moralische Ordnungen des Nationalsozialismus*. Schriften des Hannah Arendt-Instituts für Totalitarismusforschung 52. Göttingen, 2014.
Biener, Rebecca. "Die literarische Verteidigung des kleinen Glücks am Beispiel der Autorin Adrienne Thomas." PhD Diss., University of Siegen, 2005. http://dokumentix.ub.uni-siegen.de/opus/volltexte/2007/286/.
Blaschke, Anette. "Die Reichserntedankfeste vor Ort: Auf der 'Hinterbühne' einer nationalsozialistischen Masseninszenierung." In *'Volksgemeinschaft' als soziale Praxis: Neue Forschungen zur NS-Gesellschaft vor Ort*, edited by Dietmar von Reeken and Malte Thießen, Nationalsozialistische 'Volksgemeinschaft': Studien zu Konstruktion, gesellschaftlicher Wirkungsmacht und Erinnerung 4, 125–141. Paderborn, 2013.
Bluhm, Lothar. *Das Tagebuch zum Dritten Reich: Zeugnisse der Inneren Emigration von Jochen Klepper bis Ernst Jünger*. Bonn, 1991.
Bock, Gisela. *Zwangssterilisation im Nationalsozialismus: Studien zur Rassenpolitik und Frauenpolitik*. Schriften des Zentralinstituts für sozialwissenschaftliche Forschung der Freien Universität Berlin 48. Opladen, 1986.
Bock, Sigrid. "Arbeiterkorrespondenten und -schriftsteller bewähren sich: Jan Petersen: 'Unsere Straße.'" In *Erfahrung Nazideutschland. Romane in Deutschland 1933–1945: Analysen*, edited by Sigrid Bock and Manfred Hahn, Akademie der Wissenschaften der DDR, 44–98. Berlin, 1987.
Bollmus, Reinhard. *Das Amt Rosenberg und seine Gegner: Studien zum Machtkampf im nationalsozialistischen Herrschaftssystem*. Stuttgart, 1970.
Bonacker, Max. *Goebbels' Mann beim Radio: Der NS-Propagandist Hans Fritzsche (1900–1953)*. Munich, 2007.
Borggräfe, Henning. *Schützenvereine im Nationalsozialismus: Pflege der 'Volksgemeinschaft' und Vorbereitung auf den Krieg (1933–1945)*. Forum Regionalgeschichte 16. Münster, 2010.
———. "Zwischen Ausblendung und Aufarbeitung: Der Umgang mit der NS-Vergangenheit in Vereinen und Verbänden kollektiver Freizeitgestaltung." *Zeitgeschichte-online*, December, 2012. http://www.zeitgeschichte-online.de/thema/zwischen-ausblendung-und-aufarbeitung.
Bösch, Frank. "Ereignisse, Performanz und Medien in historischer Perspektive." In *Medialisierte Ereignisse: Performanz, Inszenierung und Medien seit dem 18. Jahrhundert*, edited by Frank Bösch and Patrick Schmidt, 7–29. Frankfurt am Main, 2010.

———. "Katalysator der Demokratisierung? Presse, Politik und Gesellschaft vor 1914." In *Medialisierung und Demokratie im 20. Jahrhundert*, edited by Frank Bösch and Norbert Frei, Beiträge zur Geschichte des 20. Jahrhunderts 5, 25–47. Göttingen, 2006.

———. *Mediengeschichte: Vom asiatischen Buchdruck zum Fernsehen*. Historische Einführungen 10. Frankfurt am Main, 2011.

———. *Öffentliche Geheimnisse: Skandale, Politik und Medien in Deutschland und Großbritannien 1880–1914*. Veröffentlichungen des Deutschen Historischen Instituts London 65. Munich, 2009.

Bösch, Frank, and Norbert Frei. "Die Ambivalenz der Medialisierung." In *Medialisierung und Demokratie im 20. Jahrhundert*, edited by Frank Bösch and Norbert Frei, Beiträge zur Geschichte des 20. Jahrhunderts 5, 7–23. Göttingen, 2006.

Böske, Stefan Christian. "Denunziationen in der Zeit des Nationalsozialismus und die zivilrechtliche Aufarbeitung in der Nachkriegszeit." PhD Diss., University of Bielefeld, 2008.

Bracher, Karl Dietrich. "Plebiszit und Machtergreifung: Eine kritische Analyse der nationalsozialistischen Wahlpolitik (1933–1934)." In *On the Track of Tyranny: Essays Presented by the Wiener Library to Leonard G. Montefiore, O.B.E., on the Occasion of His 70th Birthday*, edited by Max Beloff, 1–43. London, 1960.

———. *Stufen der Machtergreifung*. Cologne, 1974. First published as *Die nationalsozialistische Machtergreifung: Studien zur Errichtung des totalitären Herrschaftssystems in Deutschland 1933/34*, vol. 1, edited by Karl Dietrich Bracher, Wolfgang Sauer, and Gerhard Schulz. Cologne, 1960.

Breloer, Heinrich. *Geheime Welten: Deutsche Tagebücher aus den Jahren 1939 bis 1947*. Die andere Bibliothek 178. Frankfurt am Main, 1999.

Brockhaus, Gudrun. "'Dann bist Du verloren, liebe Mutter!': Angst und Rassismus in NS Elternratgebern." In *Körper im Nationalsozialismus: Bilder und Praxen*, edited by Paula Diehl, 33–49. Munich, 2006.

———. "Einführung: Attraktion der NS-Bewegung; Eine interdisziplinäre Perspektive." In *Attraktion der NS-Bewegung*, edited by Gudrun Brockhaus, 7–28. Essen, 2014.

———. *Schauder und Idylle: Faschismus als Erlebnisangebot*. Munich, 1997.

Broszat, Martin. *Der Staat Hitlers: Grundlegung und Entwicklung seiner inneren Verfassung*. 5th ed. Munich, 1975.

———. *Die Machtergreifung: Der Aufstieg der NSDAP und die Zerstörung der Weimarer Republik*. Munich, 1984.

———. "Referat." In *Alltagsgeschichte der NS-Zeit: Neue Perspektive oder Trivialisierung?*, edited by Martin Broszat, Kolloquien des Instituts für Zeitgeschichte, 11–20. Munich, 1984.

———. "Vorwort." In *Bayern in der NS-Zeit: Soziale Lage und politisches Verhalten der Bevölkerung im Spiegel vertraulicher Berichte*, vol. 1 of *Bayern in der NS-Zeit*, edited by Martin Broszat, Elke Fröhlich, and Falk Wiesemann, 11–19. Munich, 1977.

———. "Vorwort." In *Die Herausforderung des Einzelnen: Geschichten über Widerstand und Verfolgung*, by Elke Fröhlich, 7–11. Vol. 6 of *Bayern in der NS-Zeit*, edited by Martin Broszat and Elke Fröhlich. Munich, 1983.

Broszat, Martin, Elke Fröhlich, and Falk Wiesemann. *Bayern in der NS-Zeit: Soziale Lage und politisches Verhalten der Bevölkerung im Spiegel vertraulicher Berichte*. Vol. 1 of *Bayern in der NS-Zeit*. Munich, 1977.

Bruendel, Steffen. *Volksgemeinschaft oder Volksstaat: Die "Ideen von 1914" und die Neuordnung Deutschlands im Ersten Weltkrieg*. Berlin, 2003.

Bruhns, Wibke. *Meines Vaters Land: Geschichte einer deutschen Familie*. Munich, 2004.
Buchholz, Wolfhard. "Die nationalsozialistische Gemeinschaft 'Kraft durch Freude': Freizeitgestaltung und Arbeiterschaft im Dritten Reich." PhD Diss., University of Munich, 1976.
Buchloh, Ingrid: *Die nationalsozialistische Machtergreifung in Duisburg: Eine Fallstudie*. Duisburger Forschungen 29. Duisburg, 1980.
Budde, Gunilla-Friederike: *Auf dem Weg ins Bürgerleben: Kindheit und Erziehung in deutschen und englischen Bürgerfamilien 1840-1914*. Bürgertum: Beiträge zur europäischen Gesellschaftsgeschichte 6. Göttingen, 1994.
Burleigh, Michael: *Die Zeit des Nationalsozialismus: Eine Gesamtdarstellung*. Translated by Udo Rennert and Karl Heinz Siber. Frankfurt am Main, 2000.
———. *The Third Reich: A New History*. London, 2001.
Bussemer, Thymian. *Propaganda: Konzepte und Theorien*. 2nd rev. ed. Wiesbaden, 2008.
———. *Propaganda und Populärkultur: Konstruierte Erlebniswelten im Nationalsozialismus*. Wiesbaden, 2000.
Büttner, Ursula. "Der Alltag der Judenverfolgung und der Anteil der Bevölkerung." In *Die Deutschen und die Judenverfolgung im Dritten Reich*, edited by Ursula Büttner, 86–110. Frankfurt am Main, 2003. First published 1992.
Cachay, Klaus, Steffen Bahlke, and Helmut Mehl. *"Echte Sportler"—"Gute Soldaten": Die Sportsozialisation des Nationalsozialismus im Spiegel von Feldpostbriefen*. Materialien zur Historischen Jugendforschung. Weinheim, 2000.
Christians, Annemone. *Das Private vor Gericht: Verhandlungen des Eigenen in der nationalsozialistischen Rechtspraxis*. Göttingen, 2020.
Ciupke, Paul, and Franz-Josef Jelich, eds. *Weltanschauliche Erziehung in Ordensburgen des Nationalsozialismus: Zur Geschichte und Zukunft der Ordensburg Vogelsang*. Zur Geschichte und Erwachsenenbildung 20. Essen, 2006.
Cocks, Geoffrey Campbell. *The State of Health: Illness in Nazi Germany*. Oxford, 2012.
Connelly, John. "The Uses of Volksgemeinschaft: Letters to the NSDAP Kreisleitung Eisenach, 1939–1940." *Journal of Modern History* 68, no. 4 (1996): 899–930.
Czarnowski, Gabriele. *Das kontrollierte Paar: Ehe- und Sexualpolitik im Nationalsozialismus*. Ergebnisse der Frauenforschung 24. Weinheim, 1991.
Dahrendorf, Ralf. *Gesellschaft und Demokratie in Deutschland*. Munich, 1965.
Dams, Carsten, and Michael Stolle. *Die Gestapo: Herrschaft und Terror im Dritten Reich*. 3rd updated ed. Munich, 2012.
Delbanco, Hillari. *Kirchenkampf in Ostfriesland 1933-1945: Die evangelisch-lutherischen Kirchengemeinden in den Auseinandersetzungen mit den Deutschen Christen und dem Nationalsozialismus*. 2nd ed. Aurich, 1989.
Dengg, Sören. *Deutschlands Austritt aus dem Völkerbund und Schachts "Neuer Plan": Zum Verhältnis von Außen- und Außenwirtschaftspolitik in der Übergangsphase von der Weimarer Republik zum Dritten Reich (1929-1934)*. Europäische Hochschulschriften: Reihe III Geschichte und ihre Hilfswissenschaften 309. Frankfurt am Main, 1986.
Didczuneit, Veit, Jens Ebert, and Thomas Jander, eds. *Schreiben im Krieg, Schreiben vom Krieg: Feldpost im Zeitalter der Weltkriege*. Essen, 2011.
Diehl, James M. *Paramilitary Politics in Weimar Germany*. Bloomington, 1977.
Diehl, Paula. "Körperbilder und Körperpraxen im Nationalsozialismus." In *Körper im Nationalsozialismus: Bilder und Praxen*, edited by Paula Diehl, 9–30. Munich, 2006.
———, ed. *Körper im Nationalsozialismus: Bilder und Praxen*. Munich, 2006.

―――. *Macht, Mythos, Utopie: Die Körperbilder der SS-Männer*. Politische Ideen 17. Berlin, 2005.
Diewald-Kerkmann, Gisela. *Politische Denunziation im NS-Regime oder: Die kleine Macht der "Volksgenossen."* Bonn, 1995.
Diller, Ansgar. *Rundfunkpolitik im Dritten Reich*. Rundfunk in Deutschland 2. Munich, 1980.
Döpp, Robert. *Jenaplan-Pädagogik im Nationalsozialismus: Ein Beitrag zum Ende der Eindeutigkeit*. Pädagogik und Zeitgeschehen: Erziehungswissenschaftliche Beiträge 4. Münster, 2003.
Dörner, Bernward. *"Heimtücke": Das Gesetz als Waffe; Kontrolle, Abschreckung und Verfolgung in Deutschland 1933–1945*. Paderborn, 1998.
―――. "NS-Herrschaft und Denunziation: Anmerkungen zu Defiziten in der Denunziationsforschung." *Historical Social Research* 26, no. 2/3 (2001): 55–69.
Dörr, Magarete. *"Wer die Zeit nicht miterlebt hat. . . ."* 3 vols. Frankfurt am Main, 1998.
Drobisch, Klaus, and Günther Wieland. *System der NS-Konzentrationslager 1933–1939*. Berlin, 1993.
Dröge, Franz. *Der zerredete Widerstand: Zur Soziologie und Publizistik des Gerüchts im 2. Weltkrieg*. Düsseldorf, 1970.
Dudek, Peter. "Nationalsozialistische Jugendpolitik und Arbeitserziehung: Das Arbeitslager als Instrument sozialer Disziplinierung." In *Politische Formierung und soziale Erziehung im Nationalsozialismus*, edited by Hans-Uwe Otto and Heinz Sünker, 141–166. Frankfurt am Main, 1991.
Duden, Barbara. "Das 'System' unter der Haut: Anmerkungen zum körpergeschichtlichen Bruch der 1990er Jahre." *Österreichische Zeitschrift für Geschichtswissenschaften* 8, no. 2 (1997): 260–273.
―――. *Geschichte unter der Haut: Ein Eisenacher Arzt und seine Patientinnen um 1730*. Stuttgart, 1987.
Dusini, Arno. *Tagebuch: Möglichkeiten einer Gattung*. Munich, 2005.
Dussel, Konrad. *Deutsche Rundfunkgeschichte*. 2nd rev. ed. Konstanz, 2004.
―――. *Hörfunk in Deutschland: Politik, Programm, Publikum (1923–1960)*. Veröffentlichungen des Deutschen Rundfunkarchivs 33. Potsdam, 2002.
Dyck, Klaus, and Jens Joost-Krüger. "'Unsrer Zukunft eine Gasse': Eine Lokalgeschichte der Bremer Maifeiern." In *100 Jahre Zukunft: Zur Geschichte des 1. Mai*, edited by Inge Marßolek, 191–257. Frankfurt am Main, 1990.
Eckart, Wolfgang Uwe. *Medizin in der NS-Diktatur: Ideologie, Praxis, Folgen*. Vienna, 2012.
Eckert, Rainer. "Gestapo-Berichte: Abbildungen der Realität oder reine Spekulation?" In *Die Gestapo: Mythos und Realität*, edited by Gerhard Paul and Klaus-Michael Mallmann, 200–215. Darmstadt, 1995.
Ehalt, Hubert Christian. "Vorwort." In *"Sicherheit ist nirgends": Das Tagebuch von Arthur Schnitzler*, by Ulrich von Bülow, Marbacher Magazin 93/2001, i–iv. Marbach am Neckar, 2000.
Ehrenreich, Eric. *The Nazi Ancestral Proof: Genealogy, Racial Science, and the Final Solution*. Bloomington, IN, 2007.
Ehrhardt, Johannes. "Erziehungsdenken und Erziehungspraxis des Nationalsozialismus." PhD Diss., Free University of Berlin, 1968.
Elfferding, Wieland. "Opferritual und Volksgemeinschaftsdiskurs am Beispiel des Winterhilfswerks (WHW)." *Faschismus und Ideologie* 2 (Argument-Sonderband AS 62) (1980): 199–226.

Erren, Lorenz: "Selbstkritik" und Schuldbekenntnis: Kommunikation und Herrschaft unter Stalin (1917–1953). Ordnungssysteme: Studien zur Ideengeschichte der Neuzeit 19. Munich, 2008.
Eschenburg, Theodor. "Streiflichter zur Geschichte der Wahlen im Dritten Reich." Vierteljahrshefte für Zeitgeschichte 3, no. 3 (1955): 311–316.
Essner, Cornelia. Die "Nürnberger Gesetze" oder Die Verwaltung des Rassenwahns 1933–1945. Paderborn, 2002.
Evans, Richard J. The Coming of the Third Reich. New York, 2004.
———. The Third Reich in Power, 1933–1939. New York, 2005.
Falkenberg, Karin. Radiohören: Zu einer Bewußtseinsgeschichte 1933 bis 1950. Haßfurt, 2005.
Falter, Jürgen W. Die 'Märzgefallenen' von 1933. Neue Forschungsergebnisse zum sozialen Wandel innerhalb der NSDAP-Mitgliedschaft während der Machtergreifungsphase." Geschichte und Gesellschaft: Zeitschrift für Historische Sozialwissenschaft 24, no. 4 (1998): 595–616.
———. Hitlers Wähler. Munich, 1991.
Fauser, Peter, Jürgen John, and Rüdiger Stutz, eds. Peter Petersen und die Jenaplan-Pädagogik: Historische und aktuelle Perspektiven. Stuttgart, 2012.
Feller, Barbara, and Wolfgang Feller. Die Adolf-Hitler-Schulen: Pädagogische Provinz versus ideologische Zuchtanstalt. Weinheim, 2001.
Föllmer, Moritz. Individuality and Modernity in Berlin: Self and Society from Weimar to the Wall. New York, 2013.
———. "The Subjective Dimension of Nazism." Historical Journal 56, no. 4 (2013): 1107–1132.
———. "Volksgemeinschaft zwischen Bedeutungsvielfalt und Homogenitätsanspruch." Vierteljahrshefte für Zeitgeschichte 62, no. 3 (2014): 452–459.
———. "Wie kollektivistisch war der Nationalsozialismus? Zur Geschichte der Individualität zwischen Weimarer Republik und Nachkriegszeit." In Kontinuitäten und Diskontinuitäten: Der Nationalsozialismus in der Geschichte des 20. Jahrhunderts, edited by Birthe Kundrus and Sybille Steinbacher, Beiträge zur Geschichte des Nationalsozialismus 29, 30–52. Göttingen, 2013.
Forschbach, Edmund. Edgar J. Jung: Ein konservativer Revolutionär: 30. Juni 1934. Pfullingen, 1984.
Förster, Jürgen. Die Wehrmacht im NS-Staat: Eine strukturgeschichtliche Analyse. Beiträge zur Militärgeschichte 2. Munich, 2000.
Frede-Wenger, Britta. Glauben und Denken im Angesicht von Auschwitz: Eine Auseinandersetzung mit dem Werk von Emil L. Fackenheim. Mainz, 2005.
Frei, Norbert. Der Führerstaat: Nationalsozialistische Herrschaft 1933 bis 1945. Munich, 1987.
———. "Epochenjahr 1933: Der 30. Januar entschwindet dem historischen Bewußtsein." In 1945 und wir: Das Dritte Reich im Bewußtsein der Deutschen, edited by Norbert Frei, 83–96. Munich, 2005.
———. "'Volksgemeinschaft': Erfahrungsgeschichte und Lebenswirklichkeit der Hitler-Zeit." In 1945 und wir: Das Dritte Reich im Bewußtsein der Deutschen, edited by Norbert Frei, 107–128. Munich: 2005.
Frei, Norbert, and Johannes Schmitz. Journalismus im Dritten Reich. Munich, 1989.
Freitag, Werner, ed. Das Dritte Reich im Fest: Führermythos, Feierlaune und Verweigerung in Westfalen 1933–1945. Bielefeld, 1997.
———. "Der Führermythos im Fest: Feuerwerk, NS-Liturgie, Dissens und '100% KdF-Stimmung.'" In Das Dritte Reich im Fest: Führermythos, Feierlaune und Verweigerung in Westfalen 1933–1945, edited by Werner Freitag, 11–69. Bielefeld, 1997.

Frevert, Ute, and Heinz-Gerhard Haupt, eds. *Neue Politikgeschichte: Perspektiven einer historischen Politikforschung*. Historische Politikforschung 1. Frankfurt am Main, 2005.
Friedrich-Ebert-Stiftung, ed. *Widerstand und Exil der deutschen Arbeiterbewegung 1933–1945*. Bonn, 1981.
Fritzen, Florentine. *Gesünder leben: Die Lebensreformbewegung im 20. Jahrhundert*. Frankfurter Historische Abhandlungen 45. Stuttgart, 2006.
Fritzsche, Peter. *Germans into Nazis*. Cambridge, MA, 1998.
———. *An Iron Wind: Europe under Hitler*. New York, 2016.
———. *Life and Death in the Third Reich*. Cambridge, MA, 2008.
———. "Nazi Modern." *Modernism/modernity* 3, no. 1 (1996): 1–21.
———. "On Being the Subjects of History: Nazis as Twentieth-Century Revolutionaries." In *Language and Revolution: Making Modern Political Identities*, edited by Igal Halfin, 161–183. London, 2002.
———. *The Turbulent World of Franz Göll: An Ordinary Berliner Writes the Twentieth Century*. Cambridge, MA, 2011.
———. "Where Did All the Nazis Go? Reflections on Collaboration and Resistance." *Tel Aviver Jahrbuch für deutsche Geschichte* 23 (1994): 191–214.
Fritzsche, Peter, and Jochen Hellbeck. "The New Man in Stalinist Russia and Nazi Germany." In *Beyond Totalitarianism: Stalinism and Nazism Compared*, edited by Michael Geyer and Sheila Fitzpatrick, 302–341. Cambridge, 2009.
Fröhlich, Elke. *Die Herausforderung des Einzelnen: Geschichten über Widerstand und Verfolgung*. Vol. 6 of *Bayern in der NS-Zeit*, edited by Martin Broszat and Elke Fröhlich. Munich, 1983.
———. "Einleitung zur Gesamtedition." In *Die Tagebücher von Joseph Goebbels*, part III, *Register 1923–1945, Sachregister A–G*, edited by Elke Fröhlich, redacted by Florian Dierl, Ute Keck, Benjamin Obermüller, Annika Sommersberg and Ulla-Britta Vollhardt, 11–176. Munich, 2008.
Fulbrook, Mary. *Dissonant Lives: Generations and Violence through the German Dictatorships*. Oxford, 2011.
Gailus, Manfred, and Armin Nolzen, eds. *Zerstrittene "Volksgemeinschaft": Glaube, Konfession und Religion im Nationalsozialismus*. Göttingen, 2011.
Ganssmüller, Christian. *Die Erbgesundheitspolitik des Dritten Reiches: Planung, Durchführung und Durchsetzung*. Cologne, 1987.
Garbarini, Alexandra. *Numbered Days: Diaries and the Holocaust*. New Haven, CT, 2006.
Gaus, Detlef. "Nationalsozialistischer Erziehungsstaat: Ideologischer Anspruch und pädagogische Realität(en)." In *Die Kultur der 30er und 40er Jahre*, edited by Werner Faulstich, Kulturgeschichte des 20. Jahrhunderts, 111–128. Munich, 2009.
Gebhardt, Miriam. *Die Angst vor dem kindlichen Tyrannen: Eine Geschichte der Erziehung im 20. Jahrhundert*. Munich, 2009.
Gellately, Robert. *Backing Hitler: Consent and Coercion in Nazi Germany*. Oxford, 2001.
———. "Denunciation as a Subject of Historical Research." *Historical Social Research* 26, no. 2/3 (2001): 16–29.
Gerhalter, Li: "'Einmal ein ganz ordentliches Tagebuch'? Formen, Inhalte und Materialitäten diaristischer Aufzeichnungen in der ersten Hälfte des 20. Jahrhunderts." In *Selbstreflexionen und Weltdeutungen: Tagebücher in der Geschichte und der Geschichtsschreibung des 20. Jahrhunderts*, edited by Janosch Steuwer und Rüdiger Graf, 64–85. Göttingen, 2015.

Gerstner, Alexandra, Barbara Könczöl, and Janina Nentwig, eds. *Der Neue Mensch: Utopien, Leitbilder und Reformkonzepte zwischen den Weltkriegen*. Frankfurt am Main, 2006.
Geulen, Christian. *Geschichte des Rassismus*. Munich, 2007.
——. *Wahlverwandte: Rassendiskurs und Nationalismus im späten 19. Jahrhundert*. Hamburg, 2004.
Ginsborg, Paul. *Die geführte Familie: Das Private in Revolution und Diktatur 1900–1950*. Hamburg, 2014.
Görner, Rüdiger. *Das Tagebuch: Eine Einführung*. Artemis-Einführungen 26. Munich, 1986.
Götz, Norbert. *Ungleiche Geschwister: Die Konstruktion von nationalsozialistischer Volksgemeinschaft und schwedischem Volksheim. Die kulturelle Konstruktion von Gemeinschaften im Modernisierungsprozeß* 4. Baden-Baden, 2001.
Graf, Rüdiger. *Die Zukunft der Weimarer Republik: Krisen und Zukunftsaneignungen in Deutschland 1918–1933*. Ordnungssysteme: Studien zur Ideengeschichte der Neuzeit 24. Munich, 2008.
Gross, Raphael. *Anständig geblieben: Nationalsozialistische Moral*. Schriftenreihe des Fritz Bauer-Instituts 26. Frankfurt am Main, 2010.
——. *November 1938: Die Katastrophe vor der Katastrophe*. Munich, 2013.
Grunberger, Richard. *The Twelve-Year Reich: A Social History of Nazi Germany*. New York, 1971.
Guhr, Dagny, and Joachim Knape. "Rhetorische Praxis in Deutschland vom Beginn des 20. Jahrhunderts bis zur Gegenwart." In *Rhetorik und Stilistik: Ein internationales Handbuch historischer und systematischer Forschung*, edited by Ulla Fix, Andreas Gardt, and Joachim Knape, Handbücher zur Sprach- und Kommunikationswissenschaft 31, 463–487. Berlin, 2008.
Günther, Dagmar: "'And Now for Something Completely Different': Prolegomena zur Autobiographie als Quelle der Geschichtswissenschaft." *Historische Zeitschrift* 272 (2001): 25–61.
Haas, Reimund. "'Zur restlosen Erfassung des deutschen Volkes werden insbesondere Kirchenbücher unter Schriftdenkmalschutz gestellt': Kirchenarchivare im Spannungsfeld zwischen Kooperation und Enteignung 1933–1943." In *Das deutsche Archivwesen und der Nationalsozialismus: 75. Deutscher Archivtag 2005 in Stuttgart*, edited by Robert Kretzschmar, Astrid M. Eckert, Heiner Schmitt, Dieter Speck and Klaus Wisotzky, Tagungsdokumentationen zum Deutschen Archivtag 10, 139–152. Essen, 2007.
Habermas, Jürgen. *Strukturwandel der Öffentlichkeit: Untersuchungen zu einer Kategorie der bürgerlichen Gesellschaft*. 5th unabridged special ed. Neuwied, 1971.
Habermas, Rebekka. *Frauen und Männer des Bürgertums: Eine Familiengeschichte (1750–1850)*. 2nd ed. Bürgertum: Beiträge zur europäischen Gesellschaftsgeschichte 14. Göttingen, 2002.
Haerendel, Ulrike. *Kommunale Wohnungspolitik im Dritten Reich: Siedlungsideologie, Kleinhausbau und "Wohnraumarisierung" am Beispiel Münchens*. Studien zur Zeitgeschichte 57. Munich, 1999.
Haffner, Sebastian. *Germany: Jekyll & Hyde: 1939—Deutschland von innen betrachtet*. Berlin, 1998.
Hämmerle, Christa. "Diaries." In *Reading Primary Sources: The Interpretation of Texts from Nineteenth and Twentieth-Century History*, edited by Miriam Dobson and Benjamin Ziemann, 141–158. Abingdon, VA, 2009.
——. "Nebenpfade? Populäre Selbstzeugnisse des 19. und 20. Jahrhunderts in geschlechtervergleichender Perspektive." In *Vom Lebenslauf zur Biografie: Geschichte, Quellen und Probleme der historischen Biographik und Autobiographik*, edited by Thomas Winkelbauer, 135–167. Horn, 2000.

Harten, Hans-Christian, Uwe Neirich, and Matthias Schwerendt. *Rassenhygiene als Erziehungsideologie des Dritten Reiches: Bio-bibliographisches Handbuch*. Edition Bildung und Wissenschaft 10. Berlin, 2006.

Hartl, Peter. "Einführung zur Neuauflage." In *Berliner Aufzeichnungen 1942–1945: Unter Verwendung der Originaltagebücher neu herausgegeben und kommentiert von Peter Hartl*, by Ursula von Kardorff, 7–31. Munich, 1992.

Hartung, Günter. "Nationalsozialistische Kampflieder." In *Deutschfaschistische Literatur und Ästhetik: Gesammelte Studien*, edited by Günter Hartung, Gesammelte Aufsätze und Vorträge 1, 165–222. Leipzig, 2001.

Harvey, Elizabeth. *"Der Osten braucht Dich!": Frauen und nationalsozialistische Germanisierungspolitik*. Translated by Paula Bradish, Hamburg, 2010.

Harvey, Elizabeth, Johannes Hürter, Maiken Umbach, and Andreas Wirschung, eds. *Private Life and Privacy in Nazi Germany*. Cambridge, 2019.

Haug, Wolfgang Fritz. *Die Faschisierung des bürgerlichen Subjekts: Die Ideologie der gesunden Normalität und die Ausrottungspolitiken im deutschen Faschismus: Materialanalysen*. Das Argument: Argument-Sonderband 80. Berlin, 1986.

Heer, Hannes. "Editorial." In *Im Herzen der Finsternis: Victor Klemperer als Chronist der NS-Zeit*, 7–9. Berlin, 1997.

Hehl, Ulrich von. *Nationalsozialistische Herrschaft*. Enzyklopädie deutscher Geschichte 39. 2nd ed. Munich, 2001.

Hein, Christoph M. *Der "Bund proletarisch-revolutionärer Schriftsteller Deutschlands": Biographie eines kulturpolitischen Experiments in der Weimarer Republik*. Arbeiterkultur und Arbeiterbewegung 25. Münster, 1991.

Heinen, Franz Albert. *NS-Ordensburgen: Vogelsang, Sonthofen, Krössinsee*. Berlin, 2011.

Hellbeck, Jochen. *Revolution on My Mind: Writing a Diary under Stalin*. Cambridge, MA, 2006.

———. "Working, Struggling, Becoming: Stalin-Era Autobiographical Texts." *Russian Review* 60, no. 3 (2001): 340–359.

Henning, Eckart. "Selbstzeugnisse." In *Die archivalischen Quellen: Mit einer Einführung in die Historischen Hilfswissenschaften*, edited by Friedrich Beck and Eckart Henning, 5th expanded and updated ed., 135–144. Cologne, 2012.

Herbert, Ulrich: "'Die guten und die schlechten Zeiten.' Überlegungen zur diachronen Analyse lebensgeschichtlicher Interviews." In *"Die Jahre weiß man nicht, wo man die heute hinsetzen soll": Faschismuserfahrungen im Ruhrgebiet*, edited by Lutz Niethammer, vol. 1 of *Lebensgeschichte und Sozialkultur im Ruhrgebiet 1930 bis 1960*, 67–96. Berlin, 1983.

———. "NS-Eliten in der Bundesrepublik." In *Verwandlungspolitik: NS-Eliten in der westdeutschen Nachkriegsgesellschaft*, edited by Winfried Loth and Bernd-A. Rusinek, 93–115. Frankfurt am Main, 1998.

———. "Traditionen des Rassismus." In *Bürgerliche Gesellschaft in Deutschland: Historische Einblicke, Fragen, Perspektiven*, edited by Lutz Niethammer et al., 472–488. Frankfurt am Main, 1990.

Herbst, Ludolf. *Hitlers Charisma: Die Erfindung eines deutschen Messias*. Frankfurt am Main, 2010.

Herrmann, Ulrich, ed. *"Neue Erziehung," "Neue Menschen": Ansätze zur Erziehungs- und Bildungsreform in Deutschland zwischen Kaiserreich und Diktatur*. Geschichte des Erziehungs- und Bildungswesens in Deutschland 5. Weinheim, 1987.

Herrmann, Ulrich, and Ulrich Nassen. "Die ästhetische Inszenierung von Herrschaft und Beherrschung im nationalsozialistischen Deutschland: Über die ästhetischen und ästhetik-politischen Strategien nationalsozialistischer Herrschaftspraxis, deren mentalitäre Voraussetzungen und Konsequenzen." In *Formative Ästhetik im Nationalsozialismus: Intentionen, Medien und Praxisformen totalitärer ästhetischer Herrschaft und Beherrschung*, edited by Ulrich Herrmann and Ulrich Nassen, 9–12. Weinheim, 1994.

Herz, Rudolf. *Hoffmann & Hitler: Fotografie als Medium des Führer-Mythos*. Munich, 1994.

Herzberg, Julia. *Gegenarchive: Bäuerliche Autobiographik zwischen Zarenreich und Sowjetunion. 1800–2000 Kulturgeschichten der Moderne 11*. Bielefeld, 2013.

Hesse, Klaus, and Philipp Springer. *Vor aller Augen: Fotodokumente des nationalsozialistischen Terrors in der Provinz*. Essen, 2002.

Heuel, Eberhard. *Der umworbene Stand: Die ideologische Integration der Arbeiter im Nationalsozialismus 1933–1935*. Frankfurt am Main, 1989.

Hilberg, Raul. *Perpetrators, Victims, Bystanders: The Jewish Catastrophe, 1933–1945*. New York, 1992.

Hirschfeld, Gerhard, and Lothar Kettenacker, ed. *Der "Führerstaat": Mythos und Realität; Studien zur Struktur und Politik des Dritten Reiches*. Veröffentlichungen des Deutschen Historischen Instituts London 8. Stuttgart, 1981.

Hocke, Gustav René. *Das europäische Tagebuch*. Wiesbaden, 1963.

Hoeres, Peter. *Der Krieg der Philosophen: Die deutsche und britische Philosophie im Ersten Weltkrieg*. Paderborn, 2004.

Hoerkens, Alexander. *Unter Nazis? Die NS-Ideologie in den abgehörten Gesprächen deutscher Kriegsgefangener in England 1939–1945*. Berlin, 2014.

Hohls, Rüdiger. "Die NSDAP als erste deutsche Volks- und Protestpartei: Jürgen W. Falters Klassiker der historischen Wahlforschung." In *50 Klassiker der Zeitgeschichte*, edited by Jürgen Danyel, Jan-Holger Kirsch, and Martin Sabrow, 217–221. Göttingen, 2007.

Hölscher, Lucian. "Öffentlichkeit." In *Geschichtliche Grundbegriffe: Historisches Lexikon zur politisch-sozialen Sprache in Deutschland*, vol. 4, *Mi-Pre*, edited by Otto Brunner, Werner Conze, and Reinhart Koselleck, 413–467. Stuttgart, 1978.

Hoppmann-König, Klaus. *Mehr Gerechtigkeit wagen: Autobiographische Collage*. Bochumer Forum zur Geschichte des sozialen Protestantismus 7. Berlin, 2006.

Hörath, Julia. "Terrorinstrumente der 'Volksgemeinschaft'? KZ-Haft für 'Asoziale' und 'Berufsverbrecher' 1933 bis 1937/38." *Zeitschrift für Geschichtswissenschaft* 60, no. 6 (2012): 513–532.

Hördler, Stefan, ed. *SA-Terror als Herrschaftssicherung: "Köpenicker Blutwoche" und öffentliche Gewalt im Nationalsozialismus*. Berlin, 2013.

Horn, Klaus-Peter, and Jörg-W. Link, eds. *Erziehungsverhältnisse im Nationalsozialismus: Totaler Anspruch und Erziehungswirklichkeit*. Bad Heilbrunn, 2011.

Hubert, Peter. *Uniformierter Reichstag: Die Geschichte der Pseudo-Volksvertretung 1933–1945*. Beiträge zur Geschichte des Parlamentarismus und der politischen Parteien 97. Düsseldorf, 1992.

Huth, Iris. *Politische Verdrossenheit: Erscheinungsformen und Ursachen als Herausforderung für das politische System und die politische Kultur der Bundesrepublik Deutschland im 21. Jahrhundert*. Politik und Partizipation 3. Münster, 2004.

Hüttenberger, Peter. "Tagebücher." In *Einführung in die Interpretation historischer Quellen: Schwerpunkt: Neuzeit*, edited by Bernd-A. Rusinek, Volker Ackermann, and Jörg Engelbrecht, 27–43. Paderborn, 1992.

Jacoby, Fritz. *Die nationalsozialistische Herrschaftsübernahme an der Saar: Die innenpolitischen Probleme der Rückgliederung des Saargebietes bis 1935*.

Veröffentlichungen der Kommission für Saarländische Landesgeschichte und Volksforschung 6. Saarbrücken, 1973.

Jamin, Mathilde. "Das Ende der 'Machtergreifung': Der 30. Juni 1934 und seine Wahrnehmung in der Bevölkerung." In *Die nationalsozialistische Machtergreifung*, edited by Wolfgang Michalka, 207–219. Paderborn, 1984.

Janßen, Karl-Heinz, and Fritz Tobias. *Der Sturz der Generäle: Hitler und die Blomberg-Fritsch Krise*. Munich, 1994.

Jasper, Gotthard. *Die gescheiterte Zähmung: Wege zur Machtergreifung Hitlers 1930–1934*. Frankfurt am Main, 1986.

Jegelka, Norbert: "'Volksgemeinschaft': Begriffskonturen in 'Führer'ideologie, Recht und Erziehung (1933–1945)." In *Das Volk: Abbild, Konstruktion, Phantasma*, edited by Annette Graczyk, 115–128. Berlin, 1996.

Jerouschek, Günter, Inge Marßolek, and Hedwig Röckelein. "Denunziation: Ein interdisziplinäres Forschungsfeld." In *Denunziation: Historische, juristische und psychologische Aspekte*, edited by Günter Jerouschek, Inge Marßolek, and Hedwig Röckelein, 9–25. Forum Psychohistorie 7. Tübingen, 1997.

Jessen, Ralph, and Hedwig Richter, ed. *Voting for Hitler and Stalin: Elections under 20th Century Dictatorships*. Frankfurt am Main, 2011.

Jung, Otmar. *Plebiszit und Diktatur: die Volksabstimmungen der Nationalsozialisten; Die Fälle 'Austritt aus dem Völkerbund' (1933), 'Staatsoberhaupt' (1934) und 'Anschluß Österreichs' (1938)*. Beiträge zur Rechtsgeschichte des 20. Jahrhunderts 13. Tübingen, 1995.

Kämper, Heidrun. "Telling the Truth: Counter-Discourses in Diaries under Totalitarian Regimes (Nazi Germany and Early GDR)." In *Political Languages in the Age of Extremes*, edited by Willibald Steinmetz, 215–241. Oxford, 2011.

Kater, Michael Hans. *Das "Ahnenerbe" der SS 1935–1945: Ein Beitrag zur Kulturpolitik des Dritten Reiches*. Studien zur Zeitgeschichte 6. 4th ed. Munich, 2006.

Keim, Wolfgang. *Erziehung unter der Nazi-Diktatur*. 2 vols. Darmstadt, 1995, 1997.

Kerbs, Diethart, and Jürgen Reulecke. "Einleitung der Herausgeber." In *Handbuch der deutschen Reformbewegungen 1880–1933*, edited by Diethart Kerbs and Jürgen Reulecke, 10–18. Wuppertal, 1998.

Kern, Stephen. *The Culture of Time and Space, 1880–1918*. 2nd ed. Cambridge, MA, 2003.

Kershaw, Ian. "Alltägliches und Außeralltägliches: ihre Bedeutung für die Volksmeinung 1933–1939." In *Die Reihen fast geschlossen: Beiträge zur Geschichte des Alltags unterm Nationalsozialismus*, edited by Detlev Peukert and Jürgen Reulecke, 273–292. Wuppertal, 1981.

———. "Antisemitismus und Volksmeinung: Reaktionen auf die Judenverfolgung." In *Bayern in der NS-Zeit*, vol. 2, *Herrschaft und Gesellschaft im Konflikt, Teil A*, edited by Martin Broszat and Elke Fröhlich, 281–348. Vienna, 1979.

———. *Der NS-Staat: Geschichtsinterpretationen und Kontroversen im Überblick*. 4th ed. Reinbek bei Hamburg, 2006.

———. "Führer und Hitlerkult." In *Enzyklopädie des Nationalsozialismus*, edited by Wolfgang Benz, Hermann Graml, and Hermann Weiß, 5th expanded ed., 13–26. Munich, 2007.

———. *The "Hitler Myth": Image and Reality in the Third Reich*. Oxford, 2001.

———. "How Effective Was Nazi Propaganda?" In *Nazi Propaganda: The Power and the Limitations*, edited by David Welch, 180–205. London, 1983.

———. *Popular Opinion and Political Dissent in the Third Reich: Bavaria 1933–1945*. Oxford, 1983.

———. "Volksgemeinschaft: Potential and Limitations of the Concept." *Visions of Community in Nazi Germany: Social Engineering and Private Lives*, edited by Martina Steber and Bernhard Gotto, 29–42. Oxford, 2014.

Keys, Barbara. "The Body as a Political Space: Comparing Physical Education under Nazism and Stalinism." *German History* 27, no. 3 (2009): 395–413.

Kleßmann, Christoph. "Der Generalgouverneur Hans Frank." *Vierteljahrshefte für Zeitgeschichte* 19, no. 3 (1971): 245–260.

Kliem, Kurt. "Der sozialistische Widerstand gegen das Dritte Reich, dargestellt an der Gruppe 'Neu Beginnen.'" PhD Diss., University of Marburg, 1957.

Klimó, Árpád von, and Malte Rolf, ed. *Rausch und Diktatur: Inszenierung, Mobilisierung und Kontrolle in totalitären Systemen*. Frankfurt am Main, 2006.

———. "Rausch und Diktatur: Emotionen, Erfahrungen und Inszenierungen totalitärer Herrschaft." In *Rausch und Diktatur: Inszenierung, Mobilisierung und Kontrolle in totalitären Systemen*, edited by Árpád von Klimó and Malte Rolf, 11–43. Frankfurt am Main, 2006.

Knoch, Habbo. "Gemeinschaften im Nationalsozialismus vor Ort." In *"Volksgemeinschaft" als soziale Praxis: Neue Forschungen zur NS-Gesellschaft vor Ort*, edited by Dietmar von Reeken and Malte Thießen, Nationalsozialistische "Volksgemeinschaft": Studien zu Konstruktion, gesellschaftlicher Wirkungsmacht und Erinnerung 4, 37–50. Paderborn 2013.

Koenen, Andreas. *Der Fall Carl Schmitt: Sein Aufstieg zum "Konjuristen des Dritten Reiches."* Darmstadt 1995.

König, Wolfgang. *Volkswagen, Volksempfänger, Volksgemeinschaft: "Volksprodukte" im Dritten Reich: Vom Scheitern einer nationalsozialistischen Konsumgesellschaft*. Paderborn 2004.

Koonz, Claudia. *The Nazi Conscience*. Cambridge, MA, 2003.

Köppen, Manuel, and Erhard Schütz. "Kunst der Propaganda: Der Film im 'Dritten Reich': Einleitung." In *Kunst der Propaganda: Der Film im Dritten Reich*, edited Manuel Köppen and Erhard Schütz, 2nd rev. ed., 7–14. Bern, 2008.

Kopperschmidt, Josef, ed. *Hitler der Redner*. Munich, 2003.

Körte, Mona. "'Pyrotechniker der Macht': Bücherverbrennungen und ihre Wirkung in der Literatur." *Zeitschrift für Geschichtswissenschaft* 51, no. 5 (2003): 430–438.

Koselleck, Reinhart. "Nachwort." In *Das Dritte Reich des Traums*, by Charlotte Beradt, 115–132. Frankfurt am Main, 1994.

———. "Terror und Traum: Methodologische Anmerkungen zu Zeiterfahrungen im Dritten Reich." In *Vergangene Zukunft: Zur Semantik geschichtlicher Zeiten*, edited by Reinhart Koselleck, 278–299. Frankfurt am Main, 1989.

———. "Volk, Nation, Nationalismus, Masse." In *Geschichtliche Grundbegriffe: Historisches Lexikon zur politisch-sozialen Sprache in Deutschland*, vol. 7, Verw-Z, edited by Otto Brunner, Werner Conze, and Reinhart Koselleck, 141–431. Stuttgart, 1992.

Koshar, Rudy. *German Travel Cultures*. Oxford, 2000.

Kraas, Andreas: "'Den deutschen Menschen in seinen inneren Lebensbezirken ergreifen': Das Lager als Erziehungsform." In *Erziehungsverhältnisse im Nationalsozialismus: Totaler Anspruch und Erziehungswirklichkeit*, edited by Klaus-Peter Horn and Jörg-W. Link, 295–317. Bad Heilbrunn, 2011.

———. *Lehrerlager 1932–1945: Politische Funktion und pädagogische Gestaltung*. Bad Heilbrunn, 2004.

Krabbe, Wolfgang R. "Lebensreform/Selbstreform." In *Handbuch der deutschen Reformbewegungen 1880–1933*, edited by Diethart Kerbs and Jürgen Reulecke, 73–75. Wuppertal, 1998.

Kracauer, Siegfried. "Das Ornament der Masse." In *Das Ornament der Masse: Essays*, 50–63. Frankfurt am Main, 1977.

Kramer, Nicole. *Volksgenossinnen an der Heimatfront: Mobilisierung, Verhalten, Erinnerung.* Schriftenreihe der Historischen Kommission bei der Bayerischen Akademie der Wissenschaften 82. Göttingen, 2011.

Krausnick, Helmut, and Hermann Graml. "Der deutsche Widerstand und die Alliierten." In *Vollmacht des Gewissens*, edited by Europäische Publikation e. V., 475–521. Frankfurt am Main, 1965.

Krüger, Michael. Review of *"Echte Sportler"—"Gute Soldaten": Die Sportsozialisation des Nationalsozialismus im Spiegel von Feldpostbriefen*, by Klaus Cachay, Steffen Bahlke, and Helmut Mehl. *Sportwissenschaft* 32, no. 3 (2002): 339–344.

Kruse, Wolfgang. *Krieg und nationale Integration: Eine Neuinterpretation des sozialdemokratischen Burgfriedensschlusses 1914/15*. Essen, 1993.

Krusenstjern, Benigna von. "Was sind Selbstzeugnisse? Begriffskritische und quellenkundliche Überlegungen anhand von Beispielen aus dem 17. Jahrhundert." *Historische Anthropologie: Kultur; Gesellschaft; Alltag* 2, no. 3 (1994): 462–471.

Krylova, Anna. "The Tenacious Liberal Subject in Soviet Studies." *Kritika: Explorations in Russian and Eurasian History* 1, no. 1 (2000): 119–146.

Küenzlen, Gottfried. *Der Neue Mensch: Eine Untersuchung zur säkularen Religionsgeschichte der Moderne*. Munich, 1994.

Kühl, Stefan. *Die Internationale der Rassisten: Aufstieg und Niedergang der internationalen Bewegung für Eugenik und Rassenhygiene im 20. Jahrhundert*. Frankfurt am Main, 1997.

Kundler, Herbert. "Schatten auf dem Bilde Emil Dovifat." In *Emil Dovifat: Studien und Dokumente zu Leben und Werk*, edited by Bernd Sösemann, Beiträge zur Kommunikationsgeschichte 8, 289–305. Berlin, 1998.

Kwiet, Konrad. "Gehen oder bleiben? Die deutschen Juden am Wendepunkt." In *Der Judenpogrom 1938: Von der "Reichskristallnacht" zum Völkermord*, edited by Walter H. Pehle, 132–145. Frankfurt am Main, 1988.

Lamnek, Siegfried, and Marie-Theres Tinnefeld, eds. *Privatheit, Garten und politische Kultur: Von kommunikativen Zwischenräumen*. Opladen, 2003.

Laqueur, Renata. *Schreiben im KZ: Tagebücher 1940–1945*. Hanover, 1991.

Latzel, Klaus. *Deutsche Soldaten, nationalsozialistischer Krieg? Kriegserlebnis, Kriegserfahrung 1939–1945*. Krieg in der Geschichte 1. Paderborn, 1998.

Lejeune, Philippe. "The Continuous and the Discontinuous." In *On Diary*, edited by Jeremy D. Popkin and Julie Rak, translated by Kathy Durnin, 175–186. Honolulu, 2009.

———. "Datierte Spuren in Serie: Tagebücher und ihre Autoren." In *Selbstreflexionen und Weltdeutungen. Tagebücher in der Geschichte und Geschichtsschreibung des 20. Jahrhunderts*, edited by Janosch Steuwer and Rüdiger Graf, 37–46. Göttingen, 2015.

———. "The Diary as 'Antifiction.'" In *On Diary*, edited by Jeremy D. Popkin and Julie Rak, translated by Kathy Durnin, 201–210. Honolulu, 2009.

———. "The 'Journal de Jeune Fille' in Nineteenth-Century France." In *On Diary*, edited by Jeremy D. Popkin and Julie Rak, translated by Kathy Durnin, 129–144. Honolulu, 2009.

———. *"Liebes Tagebuch": Zur Theorie und Praxis des Journals*. Munich, 2014.

———. *On Diary*. Edited by Jeremy D. Popkin and Julie Rak. Translated by Kathy Durnin. Honolulu, 2009.

———. "Tagebuchforschung international: Zum Projekt einer Erhebung in Algerien." In *"Liebes Tagebuch": Zur Theorie und Praxis des Journals*, 289–309. Munich, 2014.

Leo, Per. *Der Wille zum Wesen: Weltanschauungskultur, charakterologisches Denken und Judenfeindschaft in Deutschland 1890–1940*. Berlin, 2013.

Lesko, Peter. *In Sachen Deutschtum: Biographie und Geschichte im Urteil über ein regimeloyales Tagebuch aus der NS-Zeit*. Dreieich bei Frankfurt am Main, 2012.

Leßau, Hanne. *Entnazifizierungsgeschichten: Die Auseinandersetzung mit der eigenen NS-Vergangenheit in der frühen Nachkriegszeit*. Göttingen, 2020.

Levsen, Soja. *Elite, Männlichkeit und Krieg: Tübinger und Cambridger Studenten 1900–1929*. Kritische Studien zur Geschichtswissenschaft 170. Göttingen, 2006.

Limberg, Margarete, and Hubert Rübsaat, ed. *Sie durften nicht mehr Deutsche sein: Jüdischer Alltag in Selbstzeugnissen 1933–1938*. Frankfurt am Main, 1990.

Lingelbach, Karl-Christoph. *Erziehung und Erziehungstheorien im nationalsozialistischen Deutschland: Ursprünge und Wandlungen der 1933–1945 in Deutschland vorherrschenden erziehungstheoretischen Strömungen, ihre politischen Funktionen und ihr Verhältnis zur außerschulischen Erziehungspraxis des "Dritten Reiches."* Sozialhistorische Untersuchungen zur Reformpädagogik und Erwachsenenbildung 6. 2nd rev. edition. Frankfurt am Main, 1987.

Link, Jörg-W. *Reformpädagogik zwischen Weimar, Weltkrieg und Wirtschaftswunder: Pädagogische Ambivalenzen des Landschulreformers Wilhelm Kircher (1898–1968)*. Untersuchungen zu Kultur und Bildung 2. Hildesheim, 1999.

Linke, Angelika. "Sich das Leben erschreiben: Zur sprachlichen Rolleninszenierung bürgerlicher Frauen des 19. Jahrhunderts im Medium des Tagebuchs." In *Autobiography by Women in Germany*, edited by Meredid Puw Davies, Beth Linklater, and Gisela Shaw, 105–129. Bern, 2000.

———. *Sprachkultur und Bürgertum: Zur Mentalitätsgeschichte des 19. Jahrhunderts*. Stuttgart, 1996.

Loiperdinger, Martin, Rudolf Herz, and Ulrich Pohlmann, eds. *Führerbilder: Hitler, Mussolini, Roosevelt, Stalin in Fotografie und Film*. Munich, 1995.

Longerich, Peter. *"Davon haben wir nichts gewusst!": Die Deutschen und die Judenverfolgung 1933–1945*. Munich, 2006.

———. *Geschichte der SA*. Munich, 2003. First published as *Die braunen Bataillone*. Augsburg, 1989.

———. *Heinrich Himmler: Biographie*. Munich, 2008.

———. *Joseph Goebbels: Biographie*. Munich, 2010.

———. "Nationalsozialistische Propaganda." In *Deutschland 1933–1945: Neue Studien zur nationalsozialistischen Herrschaft*, edited by Karl Dietrich Bracher, Manfred Funke, Hans-Adolf Jacobsen, 2nd ed., 291–314. Bonn, 1993.

———. *Politik der Vernichtung: Eine Gesamtdarstellung der nationalsozialistischen Judenverfolgung*. Munich, 1998.

———. *Stichwort 30. Januar 1933*. Munich, 1992.

Lösch, Niels C. *Rasse als Konstrukt: Leben und Werk Eugen Fischers*. Europäische Hochschulschriften: Reihe III Geschichte und ihre Hilfswissenschaften 737. Frankfurt am Main, 1997.

Luckey, Heiko. *Personifizierte Ideologie: Zur Konstruktion, Funktion und Rezeption von Identifikationsfiguren im Nationalsozialismus und im Stalinismus.* Internationale Beziehungen 7. Göttingen, 2008.

Lüdtke, Alf. *Eigen-Sinn: Fabrikalltag, Arbeitererfahrungen und Politik vom Kaiserreich bis in den Faschismus.* Hamburg, 1993.

———. "Einleitung: Herrschaft als soziale Praxis." In *Herrschaft als soziale Praxis: Historische und sozial-anthropologische Studien,* edited by Alf Lüdtke, Veröffentlichungen des Max-Planck-Instituts für Geschichte 91, 9–63. Göttingen, 1991.

———. "Macht der Emotionen—Gefühle als Produktionskraft: Bemerkungen zu einer schwierigen Geschichte." In *Rausch und Diktatur: Inszenierung, Mobilisierung und Kontrolle in totalitären Systemen,* edited by Árpád von Klimó and Malte Rolf, 44–55. Frankfurt am Main, 2006.

———. "Wo blieb die 'rote Glut'? Arbeitererfahrungen und deutscher Faschismus." In *Alltagsgeschichte: Zur Rekonstruktion historischer Erfahrungen und Lebensweisen,* edited by Alf Lüdtke, 224–282. Frankfurt am Main, 1989.

———. "Writing Time, Using Space: The Notebook of a Worker at Krupp's Steel Mill and Manufacturing; An Example from the 1920s." *Historical Social Research* 38, no. 3 (2013): 216–228.

Luh, Andreas. *75 Jahre deutsches Sportabzeichen: Sport und gesellschaftlicher Wandel.* Beiträge zur Deutschlandforschung 6. Bochum, 1989.

Luhmann, Niklas. "Gesellschaftliche Komplexität und öffentliche Meinung." In *Soziologische Aufklärung 5. Konstruktivistische Perspektiven,* 170–175. Opladen, 1990.

———. "Öffentliche Meinung." In *Politische Planung: Aufsätze zur Soziologie von Politik und Verwaltung,* 5th ed., 9–34. Wiesbaden, 2007.

Mai, Gunther. "'Verteidigungskrieg' und 'Volksgemeinschaft': Staatliche Selbstbehauptung, nationale Solidarität und soziale Befreiung in Deutschland in der Zeit des Ersten Weltkrieges, 1900–1925." In *Der Erste Weltkrieg. Wirkung, Wahrnehmung, Analyse,* edited by Wolfgang Michalka, 583–602. Munich, 1994.

Maier, Hans. "Ideen von 1914—Ideen von 1939? Zweierlei Kriegsanfänge." *Vierteljahrshefte für Zeitgeschichte* 38, no. 4 (1990): 525–542.

Manigold, Anke. *Der Hamburger Maler Friedrich Ahlers-Hestermann 1883–1973: Leben und Werk.* Beiträge zur Geschichte Hamburgs 29. Hamburg, 1986.

Marks, Stephan. *Warum folgten sie Hitler? Die Psychologie des Nationalsozialismus.* Düsseldorf, 2007.

Marschik, Matthias. *Sportdiktatur: Bewegungskulturen im nationalsozialistischen Österreich.* Vienna, 2008.

Marszolek, Inge. "'Aus dem Volke für das Volk': Die Inszenierung der 'Volksgemeinschaft' um und durch das Radio." In *Radiozeiten: Herrschaft, Alltag, Gesellschaft (1924–1960),* edited by Inge Marszolek and Adelheid von Saldern, Veröffentlichungen des Deutschen Rundfunkarchivs 25, 121–135. Potsdam, 1999.

———. "'Der Führer spricht...': Hitler und der Rundfunk." In *Hitler der Redner,* edited by Josef Kopperschmidt, 205–216. Munich, 2003.

———. "'Die Zeichen an der Wand': Denunziation aus der Perspektive des jüdischen Alltags im 'Dritten Reich.'" *Historical Social Research* 26, no. 2/3 (2001): 204–218.

Marszolek, Inge, and Adelheid von Saldern. "Das Radio als historisches und historiographisches Medium: Eine Einführung." In *Zuhören und Gehörtwerden*

I: Radio im Nationalsozialismus; Zwischen Lenkung und Ablenkung, 11–44. Tübingen, 1998.
———, eds. Zuhören und Gehörtwerden I: Radio im Nationalsozialismus; Zwischen Lenkung und Ablenkung. Tübingen, 1998.
Maruhn, Siegfried. Staatsdiener im Unrechtsstaat: Die deutschen Standesbeamten und ihr Verband unter dem Nationalsozialismus. Frankfurt am Main, 2002.
Mason, Timothy W. Arbeiterklasse und Volksgemeinschaft: Dokumente und Materialien zur deutschen Arbeiterpolitik 1936–1939. Schriften des Zentralinstituts für Sozialwissenschaftliche Forschung der Freien Universität Berlin 22. Opladen, 1975.
Massing, Peter. "Politisches System." In Handwörterbuch des politischen Systems der Bundesrepublik Deutschland, edited by Uwe Andersen, and Wichard Woyke, 5th updated ed., 528–532. Bonn, 2003.
Maubach, Franka. Die Stellung halten: Kriegserfahrungen und Lebensgeschichten von Wehrmachthelferinnen. Göttingen, 2009.
Mayer, Irene. "Berlin-Charlottenburg." In Der Ort des Terrors: Geschichte des nationalsozialistischen Konzentrationslagers, vol. 2, Frühe Lager, Dachau, Emslandlager, edited by Wolfgang Benz and Barbara Distel, 39–42. Munich, 2005.
Mehringer, Hartmut. "Die bayerische Sozialdemokratie bis zum Ende des NS-Regimes: Vorgeschichte, Verfolgung und Widerstand." In Bayern in der NS-Zeit, vol. 5, Die Parteien KPD, SPD, BVP in Verfolgung und Widerstand, edited by Martin Broszat and Hartmut Mehringer, 287–432. Munich, 1983.
———. "Die KPD in Bayern 1919–1945." In Bayern in der NS-Zeit, vol. 5, Die Parteien KPD, SPD, BVP in Verfolgung und Widerstand, edited by Martin Broszat and Hartmut Mehringer, 1–286. Munich, 1983.
Mergel, Thomas. Kulturgeschichte der Politik, Version: 2.0." Docupedia-Zeitgeschichte, October 22 2012. http://docupedia.de/zg/Kulturgeschichte_der_Politik_Version_2.0_Thomas_Mergel?oldid=97420.
Merziger, Patrick. Nationalsozialistische Satire und "Deutscher Humor": Politische Bedeutung und Öffentlichkeit populärer Unterhaltung 1931–1945. Beiträge zur Kommunikationsgeschichte 23. Stuttgart, 2010.
Meyer, Beate. "Jüdische Mischlinge": Rassenpolitik und Verfolgungserfahrung 1933–1945. Studien zur jüdischen Geschichte 6. Hamburg, 1999.
Meyer, Christian. (K)eine Grenze. Das Private und das Politische im Nationalsozialismus 1933–1940. Berlin, 2020.
———. "'... nichts war mehr Privatangelegenheit': Zur Semantik von Politisierungsprozessen in autobiographischen Berichten aus der Zeit des Nationalsozialismus." In "Politik": Situationen eines Wortgebrauchs im Europa der Neuzeit, edited by Willibald Stein, Historische Politikforschung 14, 395–416. Frankfurt am Main, 2007.
Möckel, Benjamin. Erfahrungsbruch und Generationsbehauptung: Die "Kriegsjugendgeneration" in den beiden deutschen Nachkriegsgesellschaften. Göttinger Studien zur Generationsforschung 16. Göttingen, 2014.
Mommsen, Hans. "Amoklauf der 'Volksgemeinschaft'? Kritische Anmerkungen zu Michael Wildts Grundkurs zur Geschichte des Nationalsozialismus." Neue Politische Literatur: Berichte über das internationale Schrifttum 53, no. 1 (2008): 15–20.
———. "Der Mythos der Volksgemeinschaft: Die Auflösung der bürgerlichen Nation." In Zur Geschichte Deutschlands im 20. Jahrhundert: Demokratie, Diktatur, Widerstand, 162–174. Munich, 2010.

Morsch, Günter. *Arbeit und Brot: Studien zu Lage, Stimmung, Einstellung und Verhalten der deutschen Arbeiterschaft 1933–1936/37.* Europäische Hochschulschriften, Reihe III Geschichte und ihre Hilfswissenschaften 546. Frankfurt am Main, 1993.
Morsey, Rudolf. "Die Deutsche Zentrumspartei." In *Das Ende der Parteien 1933*, edited by Erich Matthias and Rudolf Morsey, 279–453. Düsseldorf, 1960.
———. "Vom Kommunalpolitiker zum Kanzler." In *Konrad Adenauer: Ziele und Wege; Drei Beispiele*, edited by Konrad-Adenauer-Stiftung, 13–81. Mainz, 1972.
Mosse, George L. *Die Geschichte des Rassismus in Europa.* Frankfurt am Main, 1990.
Mühlenfeld, Daniel. "Vom Kommissariat zum Ministerium: Zur Gründungsgeschichte des Reichsministeriums für Volksaufklärung und Propaganda." In *Hitlers Kommissare: Sondergewalten in der nationalsozialistischen Diktatur*, edited by Rüdiger Hachtmann and Wienfried Süß, Beiträge zur Geschichte des Nationalsozialismus 22, 72–92. Göttingen, 2006.
———. "Was heißt und zu welchem Ende studiert man NS-Propaganda? Neuere Forschungen zur Geschichte von Medien, Kommunikation und Kultur während des 'Dritten Reiches.'" *Archiv für Sozialgeschichte* 49 (2009): 527–559.
Müller, Sven Oliver. *Deutsche Soldaten und ihre Feinde: Nationalismus an Front und Heimatfront im Zweiten Weltkrieg.* Frankfurt am Main, 2007.
Müller, Tobias. *Recht und Volksgemeinschaft: Zu den Interdependenzen zwischen Rechtspolitik und (instrumentalisierter) öffentlicher Meinung im Nationalsozialismus auf Grundlage der Lageberichte des Sicherheitsdienstes der SS.* Schriftenreihe rechtsgeschichtlicher Studien 1. Hamburg, 2001.
Müller, Yves, and Reiner Zilkenat, eds. *Bürgerkriegsarmee: Forschungen zur nationalsozialistischen Sturmabteilung (SA).* Frankfurt am Main, 2013.
Müller-Botsch, Christine. *"Den richtigen Mann an die richtige Stelle": Biographien und politisches Handeln von unteren NSDAP-Funktionären.* Frankfurt am Main, 2009.
Münkler, Herfried. "Die Visibilität der Macht und die Strategien der Machtvisualisierung." In *Macht der Öffentlichkeit—Öffentlichkeit der Macht*, edited by Gerhard Göhler, 213–230. Baden-Baden, 1995.
Nagel, Anne C. *Hitlers Bildungsreformer: Das Reichsministerium für Wissenschaft, Erziehung und Volksbildung 1934–1945.* Frankfurt am Main, 2012.
Neitzel, Sönke, and Harald Welzer. *Soldaten: Protokolle vom Kämpfen, Töten und Sterben.* 2nd ed. Frankfurt am Main, 2011.
Neliba, Günter. "Wilhelm Frick und Thüringen als Experimentierfeld für die nationalsozialistische Machtergreifung." In *Thüringen im Nationalsozialismus*, edited by Detlev Heiden and Gunther Mai, 75–94. Weimar, 1995.
Nieden, Susanne zur. *Alltag im Ausnahmezustand: Frauentagebücher im zerstörten Deutschland 1943 bis 1945.* Der andere Blick: Frauenstudien in Wissenschaft und Kunst. Berlin, 1993.
———. "Aus dem vergessenen Alltag der Tyrannei: Die Aufzeichnungen Victor Klemperers im Vergleich zur zeitgenössischen Tagebuchliteratur." In *Im Herzen der Finsternis: Victor Klemperer als Chronist der NS-Zeit*, edited by Hannes Heer, 110–121. Berlin, 1997.
Nieden, Susanne zur, and Sven Reichardt. "Skandale als Instrument des Machtkampfes in der NS-Führung: Zur Funktionalisierung der Homosexualität von Ernst Röhm." In *Skandal und Diktatur: Formen öffentlicher Empörung im NS-Staat und in der DDR*, edited by Martin Sabrow, 33–58. Göttingen, 2004.

Nieder, Franz-Karl. "Der Sturm aufs Rathaus 1933." In *Limburg im Fluss der Zeit*, vol. 1, *Schlaglichter aus 1100 Jahren Stadtgeschichte*, edited by Magistrat der Kreisstadt Limburg an Der Lahn, 473–485. Limburg an der Lahn, 2010.

Niehuis, Edith. *Das Landjahr: Eine Jugenderziehungseinrichtung in der Zeit des Nationalsozialismus*. Nörten-Hardenberg, 1984.

Niethammer, Lutz. "Fragen—Antworten—Fragen: Methodische Erfahrungen und Erwägungen zur Oral History." In *"Wir kriegen jetzt andere Zeiten": Auf der Suche nach der Erfahrung des Volkes in nachfaschistischen Ländern*, vol. 3 of *Lebensgeschichte und Sozialkultur im Ruhrgebiet 1930 bis 1960*, edited by Lutz Niethammer and Alexander von Plato, 392–445. Berlin, 1985.

Niethammer, Lutz, and Alexander von Plato, eds. *Lebensgeschichte und Sozialkultur im Ruhrgebiet 1930–1960*. 3 vols. Berlin, 1983–1985.

Nitschke, August, Gerhard A. Ritter, Detlev Peukert, and Rüdiger vom Bruch. "Einleitung zu 'Jahrhundertwende.'" In *Jahrhundertwende: Der Aufbruch in die Moderne 1880–1930*, edited by August Nitschke, Gerhard A. Ritter, Detlev Peukert, and Rüdiger vom Bruch, 1:9–12. Reinbek bei Hamburg, 1990.

Nitz, Wenke. *Führer und Duce: Politische Machtinszenierungen im nationalsozialistischen Deutschland und im faschistischen Italien*. Italien in der Moderne 3. Cologne, 2013.

Nolte, Paul. *Die Ordnung der deutschen Gesellschaft: Selbstentwurf und Selbstbeschreibung im 20. Jahrhundert*. Munich, 2000.

Nolzen, Armin. "Die NSDAP, der Krieg und die deutsche Gesellschaft." In *Die deutsche Kriegsgesellschaft 1939 bis 1945*, vol. 1, *Politisierung—Vernichtung—Überleben*, edited by Jörg Echternkamp, Das Dritte Reich und der Zweite Weltkrieg 9, 99–193. Munich, 2004.

———. *Die Ordnung der deutschen Gesellschaft: Selbstentwurf und Selbstbeschreibung im 20. Jahrhundert*. Munich, 2000.

———. "In die Jahre gekommen." Review of *Geschichte der NSDAP: 1920 bis 1945*, by Kurt Pätzold and Manfred Weißbecker. *Literaturkritik.de*. July 2009. http://www.literaturkritik.de/public/rezension.php?rez_id=13208&ausgabe=200907.

———. "Nationalsozialismus und 'Volksgemeinschaft': Plädoyer für eine operative Semantik." In *'Volksgemeinschaft' als soziale Praxis: Neue Forschungen zur NS-Gesellschaft vor Ort*, edited by Dietmar von Reeken and Malte Thießen, Nationalsozialistische 'Volksgemeinschaft': Studien zu Konstruktion, gesellschaftlicher Wirkungsmacht und Erinnerung 4, 51–63. Paderborn, 2013.

Obst, Dieter. *"Reichskristallnacht": Ursachen und Verlauf des antisemitischen Pogroms vom November 1938*. Europäische Hochschulschriften, Reihe III Geschichte und ihre Hilfswissenschaften 487. Frankfurt am Main, 1991.

Offermanns, Alexandra. *"Die wußten, was uns gefällt": Ästhetische Manipulation und Verführung im Nationalsozialismus, illustriert am BDM-Werk "Glaube und Schönheit"*. Texte zur Theorie und Geschichte der Bildung 22. Münster, 2004.

Olbrich, Josef. *Geschichte der Erwachsenenbildung in Deutschland*. Opladen, 2001.

Omland, Frank. *"Du wählst mi nich Hitler!": Reichstagswahlen und Volksabstimmungen in Schleswig-Holstein 1933–1938*. Hamburg, 2006.

Oswald, Rudolf. *"Fußball-Volksgemeinschaft": Ideologie, Politik und Fanatismus im deutschen Fußball 1919–1964*. Frankfurt am Main, 2008.

Otto, Hans-Uwe, and Heinz Sünker. "Vorwort." In *Politische Formierung und soziale Erziehung im Nationalsozialismus*, edited by Hans-Uwe Otto and Heinz Sünker, 7–8. Frankfurt am Main, 1991.

Overesch, Manfred, and Friedrich Wilhelm Saal. *Das Dritte Reich 1933–1939*. Droste Geschichtskalendarium: Chronik deutscher Zeitgeschichte; Politik, Wirtschaft, Kultur, vol. 2/1. Düsseldorf, 1982.
Pabst-Weinschenk, Marita. *Die Konstruktion der Sprechkunde und Sprechererziehung durch Erich Drach: Faktenfachgeschichte von 1900 bis 1935*. Magdeburg, 1993.
Pantelmann, Heike. *Erziehung zum nationalsozialistischen Arbeiter: Eine Diskursanalyse*. Munich, 2003.
Papp, Kornélia. *Deutschland von innen und von außen: Die Tagebücher von Victor Klemperer und Thomas Mann zwischen 1933 und 1955*. Berlin, 2006.
Parnes, Ohad. "Biologisches Erbe: Epigenetik und das Konzept der Vererbung im 20 und 21. Jahrhundert." In *Erbe: Übertragungskonzepte zwischen Natur und Kultur*, edited by Stefan Willer, Sigrid Weigel, and Bernhard Jussen, 202–242. Berlin, 2013.
Patel, Kiran Klaus. "'Auslese' und 'Ausmerze': Das Janusgesicht der nationalsozialistischen Lager." *Zeitschrift für Geschichtswissenschaft* 54, no. 4 (2006): 339–365.
———. "Gemeinsame Arbeit am 'Neuen Menschen.': Insassen und Personal in den Lagern des NS-Regimes." In *Personal und Insassen von "Totalen Institutionen": Zwischen Konfrontation und Verflechtung*, edited by Falk Bretschneider, Martin Scheutz, and Alfred Stefan Weiß, Historische Studien zu Institutionen und Orten der Separierung, Verwahrung und Bestrafung 3, 337–357. Leipzig, 2011.
———. "'Sinnbild der nationalsozialistischen Weltanschauung'? Die Gestaltung von Lagern und Ordensburgen im Nationalsozialismus." In *Weltanschauliche Erziehung in Ordensburgen des Nationalsozialismus: Zur Geschichte und Zukunft der Ordensburg Vogelsang*, edited by Paul Ciupke and Franz-Josef Jelich, Zur Geschichte und Erwachsenenbildung 20, 33–51. Essen, 2006.
———. "'Soldaten der Arbeit': Arbeitsdienste in Deutschland und den USA 1933–1945*. Kritische Studien zur Geschichtswissenschaft 157. Göttingen, 2003.
Pätzold, Kurt, and Manfred Weißbecker. *Geschichte der NSDAP 1920 bis 1945*. 3rd ed. Cologne, 2009.
Paul, Gerhard. *Aufstand der Bilder: Die NS-Propaganda vor 1933*. Bonn, 1990.
———. *"Deutsche Mutter—heim zu Dir!": Warum es mißlang, Hitler an der Saar zu schlagen; Der Saarkampf 1933–1935*. Cologne, 1984.
———. "Private Konfliktregulierung, gesellschaftliche Selbstüberwachung, politische Teilhabe? Neuere Forschungen zur Denunziation im Dritten Reich." *Archiv für Sozialgeschichte* 42 (2002): 380–402.
Paul, Gerhard, and Klaus-Michael Mallmann: *Milieus und Widerstand: Eine Verhaltensgeschichte der Gesellschaft im Nationalsozialismus*. Vol. 3 of *Widerstand und Verweigerung im Saarland 1935–1945*, edited by Hans-Walter Herrmann. Bonn, 1995.
Peitsch, Helmut: *"Deutschlands Gedächtnis an seine dunkelste Zeit": Zur Funktion der Autobiographik in den Westzonen Deutschlands und den Westsektoren von Berlin 1945–1949*. Berlin, 1990.
Pesch, Volker. *Handlungstheorie und Politische Kultur*. Wiesbaden, 2000.
Petersen, Jan. *Die Bewährung: Eine Chronik*. 2nd ed. Berlin, 1975.
———. *Unsere Straße: Eine Chronik; Geschrieben im Herzen des faschistischen Deutschlands 1933/34*. Cologne, 1983. First published 1947.
Peukert, Detlev. *Alltag unterm Nationalsozialismus*. Beiträge zum Thema Widerstand 17. Berlin, 1981.

———. *Die KPD im Widerstand: Verfolgung und Untergrundarbeit an Rhein und Ruhr 1933 bis 1945*. Düsseldorfer Schriften zur Neueren Landesgeschichte und zur Geschichte Nordrhein-Westfalens 2. Wuppertal, 1980.

———. "Referat." In *Alltagsgeschichte der NS-Zeit: Neue Perspektive oder Trivialisierung?*, edited by Martin Broszat, Kolloquien des Instituts für Zeitgeschichte, 39–42. Munich, 1984.

———. *Volksgenossen und Gemeinschaftsfremde: Anpassung, Ausmerze und Aufbegehren unter dem Nationalsozialismus*. Cologne, 1982.

Pfeiffer, Lorenz. *Sport im Nationalsozialismus: Zum aktuellen Stand der sporthistorischen Forschung. Eine kommentierte Bibliografie*. 2nd rev. ed. Göttingen, 2009.

Piller, Gudrun. *Private Körper: Spuren des Leibes in Selbstzeugnissen des 18. Jahrhunderts*. Selbstzeugnisse der Neuzeit 17. Cologne, 2007.

Piper, Ernst. *Alfred Rosenberg: Hitlers Chefideologe*. Munich, 2005.

Plato, Alice von. "Ein 'Fest der Volksgemeinschaft': Die 700-Jahr-Feier von Gera (1937)." In *Inszenierter Stolz: Stadtrepräsentationen in drei deutschen Gesellschaften (1935–1975)*, edited by Adelheid von Saldern, Beiträge zur Stadtgeschichte und Urbanisierungsforschung 2, 83–113. Stuttgart, 2005.

Plum, Werner, ed. *Die "grünen Berichte" der Sopade: Gedenkschrift für Erich Rinner (1902–1982)*. Bonn, 1984.

Pohle, Heinz. *Der Rundfunk als Instrument der Politik: Zur Geschichte des deutschen Rundfunks von 1923/38*. Wissenschaftliche Schriftenreihe für Rundfunk und Fernsehen 1. Hamburg, 1955.

Preßler, Christina. "Tagebücher aus der Zeit des Nationalsozialismus in der historisch-politischen Erwachsenenbildung: Ein Beispiel für zeitgeschichtliches Lernen." PhD Diss., Carl von Ossietzky University Oldenburg, 2004. http://oops.uni-oldenburg.de/146/1/prego4.pdf.

Pyta, Wolfram. "Schmitts Begriffsbestimmung im politischen Kontext." In *Carl Schmitt: Der Begriff des Politischen: Ein kooperativer Kommentar*, edited by Reinhard Mehring, 219–235. Berlin, 2003.

Raithel, Thomas. *Das "Wunder" der inneren Einheit: Studien zur deutschen und französischen Öffentlichkeit bei Beginn des Ersten Weltkrieges*. Bonn, 1996.

Rak, Julie. "Dialogue with the Future: Philippe Lejeune's Method and Theory of Diary." In *On Diary*, by Philippe Lejeune, 16–26, edited by Jeremy D. Popkin and Julie Rak. Honolulu, 2009.

Raphael, Lutz. "Pluralities of National Socialist Ideology: New Perspectives on the Production and Diffusion of National Socialist Weltanschauung." In *Visions of Community in Nazi Germany: Social Engineering and Private Lives*, edited by Martina Steber and Bernard Gotto, 73–86. Oxford, 2014.

Raunig, Florian. *Herrschaft ohne Grenzen? Der individuelle Freiraum als Parameter totalitärer Herrschaft*. Politikwissenschaft 41. Münster, 1996.

Reckwitz, Andreas. *Das hybride Subjekt: Eine Theorie der Subjektkulturen von der bürgerlichen Moderne zur Postmoderne*. Weilerswist, 2006.

Reeken, Dietmar von, and Malte Thießen, eds. *"Volksgemeinschaft" als soziale Praxis: Neue Forschungen zur NS-Gesellschaft vor Ort*. Nationalsozialistische "Volksgemeinschaft": Studien zu Konstruktion, gesellschaftlicher Wirkungsmacht und Erinnerung 4. Paderborn, 2013.

Regener, Susanne. *Fotografische Erfassung: Zur Geschichte medialer Konstruktionen des Kriminellen*. Munich, 1999.
Reibel, Carl-Wilhelm. *Das Fundament der Diktatur: Die NSDAP-Ortsgruppen 1932–1945*. Paderborn, 2002.
Reichardt, Sven. "Faschistische Beteiligungsdiktaturen: Anmerkungen zu einer Debatte." *Tel Aviver Jahrbuch für deutsche Geschichte* 42 (2014): 133–160.
———. *Faschistische Kampfbünde: Gewalt und Gemeinschaft im italienischen Squadrismus und in der deutschen SA*. Schriftenreihe des Arbeitskreises für Moderne Sozialgeschichte 63. Cologne, 2002.
Reichel, Peter. *Der schöne Schein des Dritten Reichs: Faszination und Gewalt des Faschismus*. Munich, 1991.
Reinicke, David, Kathrin Stern, Kerstin Thieler, and Gunnar Zamzow, eds. *Gemeinschaft als Erfahrung: Kulturelle Inszenierungen und soziale Praxis 1930–1960*. Nationalsozialistische "Volksgemeinschaft": Studien zu Konstruktion, gesellschaftlicher Wirkungsmacht und Erinnerung 5. Paderborn, 2014.
Reiter, Raimond. *Nationalsozialismus und Mora: Die "Pflichtenlehre" eines Verbrecherstaates*. Frankfurt am Main, 1996.
Reuband, Karl-Heinz. "Das NS-Regime zwischen Akzeptanz und Ablehnung: Eine retrospective Analyse von Bevölkerungseinstellungen im Dritten Reich auf der Basis von Umfragedaten." *Geschichte und Gesellschaft: Zeitschrift für Historische Sozialwissenschaft* 32, no. 3 (2006): 315–343.
———. "Denunziation im Dritten Reich: Die Bedeutung von Systemunterstützung und Gelegenheitsstrukturen." *Historical Social Research* 26, no. 2/3 (2001): 219–234.
Richau, Martin. "Familienforschung und Ariernachweis im Dritten Reich." *Herold-Jahrbuch* 17 (2012): 89–118.
Rieker, Yvonne. "'Sich alles assimilieren können und doch seine Eigenart bewahren': Victor Klemperers Identitätskonstruktion und die deutsch-jüdische Geschichte." In *Im Herzen der Finsternis: Victor Klemperer als Chronist der NS-Zeit*, edited by Hannes Heer, 21–34. Berlin, 1997.
Rimmele, Lilian-Dorette. *Der Rundfunk in Norddeutschland 1933–1945: Ein Beitrag zur nationalsozialistischen Organisations-, Personal- und Kulturpolitik*. Geistes- und sozialwissenschaftliche Dissertationen 41. Hamburg, 1977.
Röder, Werner. "Die politische Emigration." In *Handbuch der deutschsprachigen Emigration 1933–1945*, edited by Claus-Dieter Krohne, Patrik von zur Mühlen, Gerhard Paul, and Lutz Winckler, columns 16–30. Darmstadt, 1998.
Rohkrämer, Thomas. *Die fatale Attraktion des Nationalsozialismus: Über die Popularität eines Unrechtsregimes*. Paderborn, 2013.
Römer, Felix. *Kameraden: Die Wehrmacht von innen*. Munich, 2012.
Roos, Daniel. *Julius Streicher und Der Stürmer 1923–1945*. Paderborn, 2014.
Rosenbaum, Heidi. *"Und trotzdem war's ne schöne Zeit": Kinderalltag im Nationalsozialismus*. Frankfurt am Main, 2014.
Roß, Klaus. *Sprecherziehung statt Rhetorik: Der Weg zur rhetorischen Kommunikation*. Opladen, 1994.
Rössler, Beate. *Der Wert des Privaten*. Frankfurt am Main, 2001.
Rother, Hans-Jörg. *Reisen zu Dietrich Bonhoeffer: Tagebuchaufzeichnungen*. Frankfurt am Main, 1993.

Ruck, Michael. "Vom Demonstrations- und Festtag der Arbeiterbewegung zum nationalen Feiertag des deutschen Volkes: Der 1. Mai im Dritten Reich und die Arbeiter." In *100 Jahre Zukunft: Zur Geschichte des 1. Mai*, edited by Inge Marßolek, 171–188. Frankfurt am Main, 1990.

Rücker, Matthias. *Wirtschaftswerbung unter dem Nationalsozialismus: Rechtliche Ausgestaltung der Werbung und Tätigkeit des Werberats der deutschen Wirtschaft*. Rechtshistorische Reihe 229. Frankfurt am Main, 2000.

Rupnow, Dirk. *"Judenforschung" im "Dritten Reich": Wissenschaft zwischen Politik, Propaganda und Ideologie*. Historische Grundlagen der Moderne 4. Baden-Baden, 2011.

———. *Vernichten und Erinnern: Spuren nationalsozialistischer Gedächtnispolitik*. Göttingen, 2005.

Rüthers, Bernd. *Verräter, Zufallshelden oder Gewissen der Nation? Facetten des Widerstandes in Deutschland*. Tübingen, 2008.

Saldern, Adelheid von, Inge Marßolek, Uta C. Schmidt, Monika Pater, and Daniela Münkel. "Zur politischen und kulturellen Polyvalenz des Radios: Ergebnisse und Ausblicke." In *Zuhören und Gehörtwerden I: Radio im Nationalsozialismus: Zwischen Lenkung und Ablenkung*, edited by Inge Marszolek and Adelheid von Saldern, 361–376. Tübingen, 1998.

Samuels, Stuart. "Der 'Left Book Club.'" In *Linksintellektuelle zwischen den beiden Weltkriegen*, edited by Walter Laqueur and George L. Mosse, 96–126. Munich, 1969.

Sänger, Fritz. *Politik der Täuschung: Mißbrauch der Presse im Dritten Reich; Weisungen, Informationen, Notizen 1933–1939*. Vienna, 1975.

Sarasin, Philipp. "'Mapping the Body': Körpergeschichte zwischen Konstruktivismus, Politik und 'Erfahrung.'" In *Geschichtswissenschaft und Diskursanalyse*, 100–121. Frankfurt am Main, 2003.

Sauer, Wolfgang. *Die Mobilmachung der Gewalt*. Cologne, 1974. First published as *Die nationalsozialistische Machtergreifung: Studien zur Errichtung des totalitären Herrschaftsystems in Deutschland 1933/34*, vol. 3. Cologne, 1960.

Schäfer, Hans Dieter. *Das gespaltene Bewußtsein: Über deutsche Kultur und Lebenswirklichkeit 1933–1945*. Munich, 1981.

Schiedeck, Jürgen, and Martin Stahlmann. "Die Inszenierung 'totalen Erlebens': Lagererziehung im Nationalsozialismus." In *Politische Formierung und soziale Erziehung im Nationalsozialismus*, edited by Hans-Uwe Otto and Heinz Sünker, 167–202. Frankfurt am Main, 1991.

Schikorsky, Isa. *Private Schriftlichkeit im 19. Jahrhundert: Untersuchungen zur Geschichte des alltäglichen Sprachverhaltens "kleiner Leute."* Germanistische Linguistik 107. Tübingen, 1990.

Schlögl, Rudolf, and Hans-Ulrich Thamer. *Zwischen Loyalität und Resistenz: Soziale Konflikte und politische Repression während der NS-Herrschaft in Westfalen*. Geschichtliche Arbeiten zur westfälischen Landesforschung, A: Wirtschafts- und sozialgeschichtliche Gruppe 10. Münster, 1996.

Schmerbach, Folker. *Das "Gemeinschaftslager Hanns Kerrl" für Referendare in Jüterbog 1933–1939*. Beiträge zur Rechtsgeschichte des 20. Jahrhunderts. Tübingen, 2008.

Schmid, Christopher. "Zu den Motiven 'alter Kämpfer' in der NSDAP." In *Die Reihen fast geschlossen: Beiträge zur Geschichte des Alltags unterm Nationalsozialismus*, edited by Detlev Peukert and Jürgen Reulecke, 21–43. Wuppertal, 1981.

Schmidt, Alexander. "In Marsch gesetzte Volksgemeinschaft: Zur Intention und Wirkung der Nürnberger Reichsparteitage." In *Marschordnungen: Das Reichsparteitagsgelände in Nürnberg*, edited by Carolin Höfler and Matthias Karch, 10–21. Berlin, 2016.

Schmidt, Anne. *Belehrung, Propaganda, Vertrauensarbeit: Zum Wandel amtlicher Öffentlichkeitsarbeit in Deutschland 1914–1918*. Essen, 2006.
Schmidt, Rainer F. *Die Außenpolitik des Dritten Reiches 1933–1939*. Stuttgart, 2002.
Schmidtke, Adrian. "Disziplin, Kontrolle, Grenzüberwindung: Die Formierung des Jungenkörpers in der Erziehung des Nationalsozialismus." In *Die Bildung des Körpers*, edited by Johannes Bilstein and Micha Brumlik, Beiträge zur pädagogischen Grundlagenforschung, 90–101. Weinheim, 2013.
———. *Körperformationen: Fotoanalysen zur Formierung und Disziplinierung des Körpers in der Erziehung des Nationalsozialismus*. Internationale Hochschulschriften 483. Münster, 2007.
Schmiechen-Ackermann, Detlef. "Der 'Blockwart': Die unteren Parteifunktionäre im nationalsozialistischen Terror- und Überwachungsapparat." *Vierteljahrshefte für Zeitgeschichte* 48, no. 4 (2000): 575–602.
———. *Diktaturen im Vergleich*. 3rd ed. Darmstadt, 2010.
———. *Nationalsozialismus und Arbeitermilieus: Der nationalsozialistische Angriff auf die proletarischen Wohnquartiere und die Reaktion in den sozialistischen Vereinen*. Forschungsinstitut der Friedrich-Ebert-Stiftung, Reihe Politik- und Gesellschaftsgeschichte 47. Bonn, 1998.
———. "Nationalsozialistische Herrschaft und der Widerstand gegen das NS-Regime in deutschen Großstädten: Eine Bilanz der lokal- und regionalgeschichtlichen Literatur in vergleichender Perspektive." *Archiv für Sozialgeschichte* 38 (1998): 488–554.
———, ed. *"Volksgemeinschaft": Mythos, wirkungsmächtige soziale Verheißung oder soziale Realität im "Dritten Reich"? Zwischenbilanz einer kontroversen Debatte*. Nationalsozialistische "Volksgemeinschaft": Studien zu Konstruktion, gesellschaftlicher Wirkungsmacht und Erinnerung 1. Paderborn, 2012.
Schmiechen-Ackermann, Detlef, and Mathias Tullner. "Stadtgeschichte und NS-Zeit in Sachsen-Anhalt und im regionalen Vergleich. Forschungsstand, Fragen und Perspektiven." In *Stadtgeschichte in der NS-Zeit: Fallstudien aus Sachsen-Anhalt und vergleichende Perspektiven*, edited by Detlev Schmiechen-Ackermann and Steffi Kaltenborn, Geschichte, Forschung und Wissenschaft 13, 7–38. Münster, 2005.
Schmied, Jürgen Peter. *Sebastian Haffner: Eine Biographie*. Munich, 2010.
Schmiedl, Joachim. *Mit letzter Konsequenz: Karl Leisner 1915–1945*. Münster, 1999.
Schmitz, Gunther. "Wider die 'Miesmacher,' 'Nörgler' und 'Kritikaster': Zur strafrechtlichen Verfolgung politischer Äußerungen in Hamburg 1933 bis 1939; Mit einem Ausblick auf die Kriegszeit." In *"Für Führer, Volk und Vaterland . . .": Hamburger Justiz im Nationalsozialismus*, edited by Justizbehörde Hamburg, Beiträge zur neueren Hamburger Justizgeschichte 1, 290–331. Hamburg, 1992.
Schmitz-Berning, Cornelia. "Glaube." In *Vokabular des Nationalsozialismus*, edited by Cornelia Schmitz-Berning, 274–277. Berlin, 1998.
———. *Vokabular des Nationalsozialismus*. Berlin, 1998.
Schmitz-Köster, Dorothee. *"Deutsche Mutter, bist Du bereit": Alltag im Lebensborn*. 2nd ed. Berlin, 2003.
Schmuhl, Hans-Walter. *Grenzüberschreitungen: Das Kaiser-Wilhelm-Institut für Anthropologie, menschliche Erblehre und Eugenik 1927–1945*. Geschichte der Kaiser-Wilhelm-Gesellschaft im Nationalsozialismus 9. Göttingen, 2005.
———. *Rassenhygiene, Nationalsozialismus, Euthanasie: Von der Verhütung zur Vernichtung "lebensunwerten Lebens," 1890–1945*. Kritische Studien der Geschichtswissenschaften 75. Göttingen, 1987.

———. "Rassismus unter den Bedingungen charismatischer Herrschaft: Zum Übergang von der Verfolgung zur Vernichtung gesellschaftlicher Minderheiten im Dritten Reich." In *Deutschland 1933–1945: Neue Studien zur nationalsozialistischen Herrschaft*, edited by Karl Dietrich Bracher, Manfred Funke, and Hans-Adolf Jacobsen, Bonner Schriften zur Politik und Zeitgeschichte 23, 2nd expanded ed., 182–197. Düsseldorf, 1993.

Schneider, Hubert. *Die "Entjudung" des Wohnraums: "Judenhäuser" in Bochum; die Geschichte der Gebäude und ihrer Bewohner*. Schriften des Bochumer Zentrums für Stadtgeschichte 4. Berlin, 2010.

Schneider, Michael. *In der Kriegsgesellschaft: Arbeiter und Arbeiterbewegung 1939 bis 1945*. Geschichte der Arbeiter und Arbeiterbewegung in Deutschland seit dem Ende des 18. Jahrhunderts 13. Bonn, 2014.

———. *Unterm Hakenkreuz: Arbeiter und Arbeiterbewegung 1933 bis 1939*. Geschichte der Arbeiter und Arbeiterbewegung in Deutschland seit dem Ende des 18. Jahrhunderts 12. Bonn, 1999.

Schnurr, Stefan, and Sven Steinacker. "Soziale Arbeit im Nationalsozialismus: Auslese und Ausmerze im Dienste der Volkspflege." In *Erziehungsverhältnisse im Nationalsozialismus: Totaler Anspruch und Erziehungswirklichkeit*, edited by Klaus-Peter Horn and Jörg-W. Link, 253–273. Bad Heilbrunn, 2011.

Schoenbaum, David. *Hitler's Social Revolution: Class and Status in Nazi Germany, 1933–1939*. New York, 1966.

Scholtz, Harald. *NS-Auslesechulen: Internatsschulen als Herrschaftsmittel des Führerstaates*. Göttingen, 1973.

Schröder, Dominique. *"Niemand ist fähig das alles in Worten auszudrücken." Tagebuchschreiben in nationalsozialistischen Konzentrationslagern 1939–1945*. Göttingen, 2020.

Schulle, Diana. "Das Reichssippenamt: Eine Institution nationalsozialistischer Rassenpolitik." PhD Diss., University of Greifswald, 1999.

Schumann, Dirk. "Gewalt als Methode der nationalsozialistischen Machteroberung." In *Das Jahr 1933: Die nationalsozialistische Machteroberung und die deutsche Gesellschaft*, edited by Andreas Wirsching, Dachauer Symposien zur Zeitgeschichte 9, 135–155. Göttingen, 2009.

Schuster, Britt-Marie, and Andreas Kraas. "'Das Wortfeld "Kamerad" wird sinnerfüllt': Zum Sprachgebrauch von Lagerzeitungen aus nationalsozialistischen Schulungslagern." In *Kommunikationspraxis und ihre Reflexion in frühneuhochdeutscher und neuhochdeutscher Zeit: Festschrift für Monika Rössing-Hager zum 65. Geburtstag*, edited by Britt-Marie Schuster, Andreas Kraas, and Ute Schwarz, Germanistische Linguistik Monographien 2, 157–176. Hildesheim, 1998.

Seeger, Hans-Karl. "Karl Leisner im RAD." *Rundbrief des Internationalen Karl-Leisner-Kreises* 39 (1999): 20–40.

Seifert, Manfred. *Kulturarbeit im Reichsarbeitsdienst: Theorie und Praxis nationalsozialistischer Kulturpflege im Kontext historisch-politischer, organisatorischer und ideologischer Einflüsse*. Internationale Hochschulschriften 196. Münster, 1996.

Sieg, Ulrich. "Kriegserfahrungen jüdischer Intellektueller im Ersten Weltkrieg." In *Wissenschaften und Wissenschaftspolitik: Bestandsaufnahmen zu Formationen, Brüchen und Kontinuitäten im Deutschland des 20. Jahrhunderts*, edited by Rüdiger vom Bruch and Brigitte Kaderas, 142–161. Stuttgart, 2002.

Siegel, Björn: "'Ich glaube, ich bin ein Zweiweltenmensch': Kurt F. Rosenbergs Suche nach Kultur und Heimat (1933–1937)." In *"Einer, der nicht mehr dazugehört": Tagebücher*

1933–1937, by Kurt F. Rosenberg, 41–54, edited by Beate Meyer and Björn Siegel. Göttingen, 2012.

Siemens, Daniel. "Dem SA-Mann auf der Spur: Nationalsozialistische Erinnerungspolitik im Berlin der 1930er Jahre." In *SA-Terror als Herrschaftssicherung: "Köpenicker Blutwoche" und öffentliche Gewalt im Nationalsozialismus*, edited by Stefan Hördler, 147–163. Berlin, 2013.

———. "Von Marmorleibern und Maschinenmenschen: Neue Literatur zur Körpergeschichte in Deutschland zwischen 1900 und 1936." *Archiv für Sozialgeschichte* 47 (2007): 639–682.

Sösemann, Bernd. "'Auf Bajonetten läßt sich schlecht sitzen': Propaganda und Gesellschaft in der Anfangsphase der nationalsozialistischen Diktatur." In *Geschichtsbilder: Festschrift für Michael Salewski zum 65. Geburtstag*, edited by Thomas Stamm-Kuhlmann, Jürgen Elvert, Brigit Aschmann, and Jens Hohensee, Historische Mitteilungen im Auftrag der Ranke-Gesellschaft 47, 381–409. Stuttgart, 2003.

———. "Nationalsozialismus." In *Lexikon des gesamten Buchwesens*, edited by Severin Corsten, 2nd fully rev. ed., 5:307–319. Stuttgart, 1999.

———. *Propaganda: Medien und Öffentlichkeit in der NS-Diktatur*. 2 vols. Beiträge zur Kommunikationsgeschichte 25. Stuttgart, 2011.

Soukup, Uwe. *Ich bin nun mal Deutscher: Sebastian Haffner; Eine Biografie*. Frankfurt am Main, 2003.

Speier, Hans. "Nazi Propaganda and Its Decline." *Social Research* 10, no. 3 (1943): 358–377.

Spode, Hasso. "Arbeiterurlaub im Dritten Reich." In *Angst, Belohnung, Zucht und Ordnung: Herrschaftsmechanismen im Nationalsozialismus*, edited by Carola Sachse, Tilla Siegel, Hasso Spode, and Wolfgang Spohn, Schriftenreihe des Zentralinstituts für sozialwissenschaftliche Forschung der Freien Universität Berlin 41, 275–328. Opladen, 1982.

Spona, Petra. *Städtische Ehrungen zwischen Repräsentation und Partizipation: NS-Volksgemeinschaftspolitik in Hannover*. Beiträge zur Stadtgeschichte und Urbanisierungsforschung 10. Stuttgart, 2010.

Spörri, Myriam. *Reines und gemischtes Blut: Zur Kulturgeschichte der Blutgruppenforschung, 1900–1933*. Bielefeld, 2013.

Stahlmann, Martin, and Jürgen Schiedeck. "Erziehung zur Gemeinschaft, Auslese durch Gemeinschaft". Zur Zurichtung des Menschen im Nationalsozialismus*. Kritische Texte: Sozialarbeit/Sozialpädagogik, Sozialpolitik, Kriminalpolitik. Bielefeld, 1991.

Stahr, Gerhard. *Volksgemeinschaft vor der Leinwand? Der nationalsozialistische Film und sein Publikum*. Berlin, 2001.

Stargardt, Nicholas. *The German War: A Nation under Arms, 1939–1945*. London, 2015.

———. "The Troubled Patriot: German Innerlichkeit in World War II." *German History* 28, no. 3 (2010): 326–342.

———. *Witnesses of War: Children's Lives under the Nazis*. London, 2005.

Steber, Martina, and Bernhard Gotto, eds. *Visions of Community in Nazi Germany: Social Engineering and Private Lives*. Oxford, 2014.

———. "Volksgemeinschaft: Writing the Social History of the Nazi Regime." In *Visions of Community in Nazi Germany: Social Engineering and Private Lives*, edited by Martina Steber and Bernhard Gotto, 1–25. Oxford, 2014.

Steffen, Kirsten. *Haben sie mich gehasst? Antworten für Martin Beradt (1881–1949): Schriftsteller, Rechtsanwalt, Berliner jüdischen Glaubens*. Literatur- und Medienwissenschaft 70. Oldenburg, 1999.

Steinbacher, Sybille. *Dachau: Die Stadt und das Konzentrationslager in der NS-Zeit: Die Untersuchung einer Nachbarschaft*. Münchener Studien zur neueren und neuesten Geschichte 5. Frankfurt am Main, 1993.

Steinert, Marlis G. *Hitlers Krieg und die Deutschen: Stimmung und Haltung der deutschen Bevölkerung im Zweiten Weltkrieg*. Düsseldorf, 1970.

Steinmetz, Willibald, Ingrid Gilcher-Holtey, and Hans-Gerhard Haupt, eds. *Writing Political History*. Frankfurt am Main, 2013.

Stepanek, Marcel. *Wahlkampf im Zeichen der Diktatur: Die Inszenierung von Wahlen und Abstimmungen im nationalsozialistischen Deutschland*. Leipzig, 2014.

Steuwer, Janosch. "Jenseits von 'Mein Kampf': Zur Ideengeschichte des Nationalsozialismus." *Zeitschrift für Ideengeschichte* 10, no. 3 (2016): 97–106.

———. "'National Socialists' and Other People of the Twentieth Century." In *Unmastered Past? Modernism in Nazi Germany; Art, Art Trade, Curatorial Practice*, edited by Meike Hoffmann and Dieter Scholz, 62–75. Berlin, 2020.

———. "Reading Fake News: The 'Röhm Putsch,' the Hitler Myth, and the Consumption of Political News under the Nazis." In *Audiences of Nazism: Media Effects and Responses*, edited by Ulrike Weckel. Oxford, forthcoming.

———. "Was meint und nützt das Sprechen von der 'Volksgemeinschaft'? Neuere Literatur zur Gesellschaftsgeschichte des Nationalsozialismus." *Archiv für Sozialgeschichte* 53 (2013): 487–534.

Steuwer, Janosch, and Rüdiger Graf, eds. *Selbstreflexionen und Weltdeutungen: Tagebücher in der Geschichte und der Geschichtsschreibung des 20. Jahrhunderts*. Göttingen, 2015.

Steuwer, Janosch, and Hanne Leßau. "Wer ist ein Nazi? Woran erkennt man ihn?': Zur Unterscheidung von Nationalsozialisten und anderen Deutschen." *Mittelweg 36* 23, no. 1 (2014): 30–51.

Stippel, Fritz. *Die Zerstörung der Person: Kritische Studie zur nationalsozialistischen Pädagogik*. Donauwörth, 1957.

Stöber, Rudolf. "Presse im Nationalsozialismus." In *Medien im Nationalsozialismus*, edited by Bern Heidenreich and Sönke Neitzel, 275–294. Paderborn, 2010.

Stöver, Bernd. *Volksgemeinschaft im Dritten Reich: Die Konsensbereitschaft der Deutschen aus der Sicht sozialistischer Exilberichte*. Düsseldorf, 1993.

Studer, Brigitte, and Heiko Haumann, eds. *Stalinistische Subjekte: Individuum und System in der Sowjetunion und der Komintern, 1929–1953*. Zurich, 2006.

Süß, Dietmar. *Tod aus der Luft: Kriegsgesellschaft und Luftkrieg in Deutschland und England*. Munich, 2011.

Süß, Winfried. "Zeitgeschichte als Demokratiewissenschaft: Karl Dietrich Bracher und das Ende der Weimarer Republik." In *50 Klassiker der Zeitgeschichte*, edited by Jürgen Danyel, Jan-Holger Kirsch, and Martin Sabrow, 47–51. Göttingen, 2007.

Sywottek, Jutta. *Mobilmachung für den totalen Krieg: Die propagandistische Vorbereitung der deutschen Bevölkerung auf den Zweiten Weltkrieg*. Studien zur modernen Geschichte 18. Opladen, 1976.

Tenfelde, Klaus. "Referat." In *Alltagsgeschichte der NS-Zeit: Neue Perspektive oder Trivialisierung?*, edited by Martin Broszat, Kolloquien des Instituts für Zeitgeschichte, 33–38. Munich, 1984.

Tenorth, Heinz-Elmar. "Einfügung und Formierung, Bildung und Erziehung: Positionelle Differenzen in pädagogischen Argumentationen um 1933." In "Pädagogik und Nationalsozialismus," edited by Ulrich Herrmann and Jürgen Oelkers. *Zeitschrift für Pädagogik*, Beiheft 22 (1989): 259–279.

———. "Eugenik im pädagogischen Denken des nationalsozialistischen Deutschlands—oder: Rassismus als Grenzbegriff der Pädagogik." In *Pädagogik im Militarismus und im Nationalsozialismus: Japan und Deutschland im Vergleich*, edited by Klaus-Peter Horn, Michio Ogasawara, Masaki Sakakoshi, Heinz-Elmar Tenorth, Jun Yamana, and Hasko Zimmer, 33–44. Bad Heilbrunn, 2006.

———. "Grenzen der Indoktrination." In *Ambivalenzen der Pädagogik: Zur Bildungsgeschichte der Aufklärung und des 20. Jahrhunderts; Harald Scholtz zum 65. Geburtstag*, edited by Peter Drewek, Klaus-Peter Horn, Christa Kersting, and Heinz-Elmar Tenorth, 335–350. Weinheim, 1995.

———. "Pädagogisches Denken." In *Handbuch der deutschen Bildungsgeschichte*, vol. 5, *Die Weimarer Republik und die nationalsozialistische Diktatur*, edited by Dieter Langewiesche and Heinz-Elmar Tenorth, 111–153. Munich, 1989.

Thamer, Hans-Ulrich. "Der 'Neue Mensch' als nationalsozialistisches Erziehungsprojekt: Anspruch und Wirklichkeit in den Eliteeinrichtungen des NS-Bildungssystems." In *"Fackelträger der Nation": Elitebildung in den NS-Ordensburgen*, edited by Vogelsang IP, 81–94. Cologne, 2010.

———. "Die Widersprüche der 'Volksgemeinschaft' in den späten Kriegsjahren." In *"Volksgemeinschaft": Mythos, wirkungsmächtige soziale Verheißung odersoziale Realität im "Dritten Reich"? Zwischenbilanz einer kontroversen Debatte*, edited by Detlef Schmiechen-Ackermann, Studien zu Konstruktion, gesellschaftlicher Wirkungsmacht und Erinnerung 1, 289–300. Paderborn, 2012.

———. *Verführung und Gewalt: Deutschland 1933–1945*. Die Deutschen und ihre Nation 5. Berlin, 1994.

Thamer, Hans-Ulrich, and Simone Erpel, eds. *Hitler und die Deutschen: Volksgemeinschaft und Verbrechen; Eine Ausstellung der Stiftung Deutsches Historisches Museum Berlin*. Dresden, 2010.

Theweleit, Klaus. *Männerphantasien*. 2 vols. 2nd ed. Munich, 2002.

Thiel, Jens. "Akademische 'Zinnsoldaten'? Karrieren deutscher Geisteswissenschaftler zwischen Beruf und Berufung (1933/1945)." In *Kontinuitäten und Diskontinuitäten in der Wissenschaftsgeschichte des 20. Jahrhunderts*, edited by Rüdiger vom Bruch, Uta Gerhardt, and Aleksandra Pawliczek, Wissenschaft, Politik und Gesellschaft 1, 167–194. Stuttgart, 2006.

Thieler, Kerstin. *"Volksgemeinschaft" unter Vorbehalt: Gesinnungskontrolle und politische Mobilisierung in der Herrschaftspraxis der NSDAP-Kreisleitung Göttingen*. Veröffentlichungen des Zeitgeschichtlichen Arbeitskreises Niedersachsen 29. Göttingen, 2014.

Thürmer-Rohr, Christina. "Öffentlichkeit/Privatheit." In *Arendt-Handbuch: Leben, Werk, Wirkung*, edited by Wolfgang Heuer, Bernd Heiter, and Stefanie Rosenmüller, 302–304. Stuttgart, 2011.

Topser-Ziegert, Gabriele. "Vorwort." In *NS-Presseanweisungen der Vorkriegszeit: Edition und Dokumentation*, vol. 7/1, *1939*, edited by Hans Bohrmann and Gabriele Topser-Ziegert, 13–20. Munich, 2001.

Trapp, Frithjof. "Ein kommunistischer Autor beschreibt Widerstand und Verfolgung in Berlin 1933/34: Jan Petersen; Unsere Straße." In *Argonautenschiff: Jahrbuch der Anna-Seghers Gesellschaft Berlin und Mainz* 20 (2011): 206–217.

Tuchel, Johannes. "Organisationsgeschichte der 'frühen' Konzentrationslager." In *Der Ort des Terrors: Geschichte der nationalsozialistischen Konzentrationslager*, vol. 1, *Die Organisation des Terrors*, edited by Wolfgang Benz and Barbara Distel, 43–57. Munich, 2005.

Uhle, Roger. "Neues Volk und reine Rasse: Walter Gross und das Rassenpolitische Amt der NSDAP (RPA) 1934–1945." PhD Diss., University of Aachen, 1999.
Ullrich, Volker. *Adolf Hitler*. Vol. 1, *Die Jahre des Aufstiegs 1889–1939*. Frankfurt am Main, 2013.
Umbach, Maiken. "Selfhood, Place and Ideology in German Photo Albums, 1933–1945." *Central European History* 48, no. 3 (2015): 335–365.
Umlauf, Konrad. *Exil, Terror, Illegalität: Die ästhetische Verarbeitung politischer Erfahrungen in ausgewählten deutschsprachigen Romanen aus dem Exil 1933–1945*. Europäische Hochschulschriften, Reihe I Deutsche Sprache und Literatur 478. Frankfurt am Main, 1982.
Unfried, Berthold. *"Ich bekenne": Katholische Beichte und sowjetische Selbstkritik*. Studien zur historischen Sozialwissenschaft 31. Frankfurt am Main, 2006.
Urban, Markus. *Die Konsensfabrik: Funktion und Wahrnehmung der NS-Reichsparteitage, 1933–1941*. Göttingen, 2007.
Van Linthout, Ine. *Das Buch in der nationalsozialistischen Propagandapolitik*. Studien zur Sozialgeschichte der Literatur 131. Berlin, 2012.
Verhey, Jeffrey. *The Spirit of 1914: Militarism, Myth, and Mobilization in Germany*. Cambridge, 2004.
Vogelsang, Claus. "Das Tagebuch." In *Prosakunst ohne Erzählen: Die Gattungen der nichtfiktionalen Kunstprosa*, edited by Klaus Weissenberger, Konzepte der Sprach- und Literaturwissenschaft 34, 185–202. Tübingen, 1985.
Vogelsang IP, ed. *Fackelträger der Nation": Elitebildung in den NS-Ordensburgen*. Cologne, 2010.
Voß, Gerd-Günter. "Entwicklung und Eckpunkte des theoretischen Konzepts." In *Alltägliche Lebensführung: Arrangements zwischen Traditionalität und Modernisierung*, edited by Projektgruppe "Alltägliche Lebensführung," 23–43. Opladen, 1995.
Wachsmann, Nikolaus, and Sybille Steinbacher, eds. *Die Linke im Visier: Zur Errichtung der Konzentrationslager 1933*. Dachauer Symposien zur Zeitgeschichte 14. Göttingen, 2014.
Wagner, Frank. *Kurs auf die Realität: Das epische Werk von Anna Seghers (1935–1943)*. Berlin, 1975.
Warneken, Bernd Jürgen. *Populare Autobiographik: Empirische Studien zu einer Quellengattung der Alltagsgeschichtsforschung*. Untersuchungen des Ludwig-Uhland-Instituts der Universität Tübingen 61. Tübingen, 1985.
Wedemeyer-Kolwe, Bernd. *"Der neue Mensch": Körperkultur im Kaiserreich und in der Weimarer Republik*. Würzburg, 2004.
Wegehaupt, Philipp. *"Wir grüßen den Haß!": Die ideologische Schulung und Ausrichtung der NSDAP-Funktionäre im Dritten Reich*. ZfA, Dokumente, Texte, Materialien 82. Berlin, 2012.
Wehler, Hans-Ulrich. *Deutsche Gesellschaftsgeschichte*. Vol. 4, *Vom Beginn des Ersten Weltkrieges bis zur Gründung der beiden deutschen Staaten 1914–1949*. Munich, 2003.
———. "Radikalnationalismus und Nationalsozialismus." In *Die Politik der Nation: Deutscher Nationalismus in Krieg und Krisen 1760–1960*, edited by Jörg Echternkamp and Sven Oliver Müller, Beiträge zur Militärgeschichte 56, 203–217. Munich, 2002.
Weigel, Bjoern. "'Märzgefallene' und Aufnahmestopp im Frühjahr 1933: Eine Studie über Opportunismus." In *Wie wurde man Parteigenosse? Die NSDAP und ihre Mitglieder*, edited by Wolfgang Benz, 91–109. Frankfurt am Main, 2009.
———. "Sklarek-Skandal (1929)." In *Handbuch des Antisemitismus: Judenfeindschaft in Geschichte und Gegenwart*, vol. 4, *Ereignisse, Dekrete, Kontroversen*, edited by Wolfgang Benz, 339–342. Berlin, 2011.

Weingart, Peter, Jürgen Kroll, and Kurt Bayertz. *Rasse, Blut und Gene: Geschichte der Eugenik und Rassenhygiene in Deutschland*. Frankfurt am Main, 1988.
Weiß, Hermann. Notizen. "Die Aufzeichnungen Hermann Görings im Institut für Zeitgeschichte." *Vierteljahrshefte für Zeitgeschichte* 31, no. 2 (1983): 365–368.
Weißbecker, Manfred, and Gert Noack: "'Die Partei als Rückgrat der inneren Front': Mobilmachungspläne der NSDAP für den Krieg (1937 bis 1939)." In *Der Weg in den Krieg: Studien zur Geschichte der Vorkriegsjahre (1935/36 bis 1939)*, edited by Dietrich Eichholtz and Kurt Pätzold, 67–90. Cologne, 1989.
Weißmann, Karlheinz. *Schwarze Fahnen, Runenzeichen: Die Entwicklung der politischen Symbolik der deutschen Rechten zwischen 1890 und 1945*. Düsseldorf, 1991.
Welch, David. *The Third Reich: Politics and Propaganda*. 2nd ed. London, 2002.
Welzer, Harald. *Täter: Wie aus ganz normalen Menschen Massenmörder werden*. Frankfurt am Main, 2005.
Wernicke, Thomas. "Der Handschlag am 'Tag von Potsdam.'" In *Der Tag von Potsdam: Der 21. März 1933 und die Errichtung der nationalsozialistischen Diktatur*, edited by Christoph Kopke and Werner Treß, Europäisch-jüdische Studien, Beiträge 8, 8–46. Berlin, 2013.
Werth, Jürgen. Review of *Das Dritte Reich im Traum*, by Charlottle Beradt. *Das Argument* 8, no. 41 (1966): 514–515.
Westphal, Uwe. *Werbung im Dritten Reich*. Berlin, 1989.
Wette, Wolfram. "Ideologien, Propaganda und Innenpolitik als Voraussetzung der Kriegspolitik des Dritten Reiches." In *Ursachen und Voraussetzungen der deutschen Kriegspolitik*, edited by Wilhelm Deist, Manfred Messerschmidt, Hans-Erich Volkmann, and Wolfram Wette, Das Dritte Reich und der Zweite Weltkrieg 1, 25–173. Stuttgart, 1979.
———. "Zur psychologischen Mobilmachung der deutschen Bevölkerung 1933–1939." In *Der Zweite Weltkrieg: Analysen, Grundzüge, Forschungsbilanzen*, edited by Wolfgang Michalka, 205–223. Munich, 1989.
Wetzel, Juliane. "Auswanderung aus Deutschland." In *Die Juden in Deutschland 1933–1945: Leben unter nationalsozialistischer Herrschaft*, edited by Wolfgang Benz, 412–498. Munich, 1988.
White, John J., and Ann White. *Bertolt Brechts Furcht und Elend des Dritten Reichs: A German Exile Drama in the Struggle against Fascism*. Studies in German Literature, Linguistics, and Culture. New York, 2010.
Wichert, Lasse. "'Tatmensch aus dem Wiesental': Albert Leo Schlageter: Mythos und Narrativ." *Zeitschrift für Genozidforschung* 11, no. 2 (2010): 35–70.
Wildmann, Daniel. *Begehrte Körper: Konstruktion und Inszenierung des "arischen" Männerkörpers im "Dritten Reich."* Würzburg, 1998.
Wildt, Michael. "Die politische Ordnung der Volksgemeinschaft. Ernst Fraenkels 'Doppelstaat' neu betrachtet." *Mittelweg 36* 12, no. 2 (2003): 45–61.
———. *Geschichte des Nationalsozialismus*. Göttingen, 2008.
———. "Self-Reassurance in Troubled Times: German Diaries during the Upheavals of 1933." In *Everyday Life in Mass Dictatorship: Collusion and Evasion*, edited by Alf Lüdtke, Mass Dictatorship in 20th Century, 55–74. New York, 2016.
———. "'Volksgemeinschaft' als politischer Topos in der Weimarer Republik." In *NS-Gewaltherrschaft: Beiträge zur historischen Forschung und juristischen Aufarbeitung*, edited by Alfred Gottwaldt, Norbert Kampe, and Peter Klein, Publikationen der Gedenk- und Bildungsstätte Haus der Wannsee-Konferenz 11, 23–39. Berlin, 2005.

———. *Volksgemeinschaft als Selbstermächtigung: Gewalt gegen Juden in der deutschen Provinz 1919 bis 1939*. Hamburg, 2007.

———. "Volksgemeinschaft und Führererwartung in der Weimarer Republik." In *Politische Kultur und Medienwirklichkeiten in den 1920er Jahren*, edited by Ute Daniel, Inge Marszolek, Wolfram Pyta, and Thomas Welskopp, Schriftenreihe der Stiftung Reichspräsident-Friedrich-Ebert Gedenkstätte 14, 181–204. Munich, 2010.

Wilson, William John. "Festivals and the Third Reich." PhD Diss., Hamilton University, 1994.

Winkler, Heinrich-August. "Referat." In *Alltagsgeschichte der NS-Zeit: Neue Perspektive oder Trivialisierung?*, edited by Martin Broszat, Kolloquien des Instituts für Zeitgeschichte, 29–32. Munich, 1984.

Wirsching, Andreas. "Die deutsche 'Mehrheitsgesellschaft' und die Etablierung des NS-Regimes im Jahre 1933." In *Das Jahr 1933: Die nationalsozialistische Machteroberung und die deutsche Gesellschaft*, edited by Andreas Wirsching, Dachauer Symposien zur Zeitgeschichte 9, 9–29. Göttingen, 2009.

———. "Vom 'Lehrstück Weimar' zum Lehrstück Holocaust?" *Aus Politik und Zeitgeschichte* 62, nos. 1–2 (2012): 9–14.

Wisotzky, Klaus. "Die rheinischen und westfälischen Stadtarchive im Nationalsozialismus." In *Das deutsche Archivwesen und der Nationalsozialismus: 75. Deutscher Archivtag 2005 in Stuttgart*, edited by Robert Kretzschmar, Astrid M. Eckert, Heiner Schmitt, Dieter Speck and Klaus Wisotzky, Das deutsche Archivwesen und der Nationalsozialismus: Tagungsdokumentationen zum Deutschen Archivtag 10, 354–571. Essen, 2007.

Wiwjorra, Ingo Herman Wirth. "Ein gescheiterter Ideologe zwischen 'Ahnenerbe' und Atlantis." In *Historische Rassismusforschung: Ideologen, Täter, Opfer*, edited by Barbara Danckwort. Edition Philosophie und Sozialwissenschaften 30, 91–112. Hamburg, 1995.

Wolschke-Bulmahn, Joachim. "'Freiheit in Grenzen'? Zum Zusammenhang von Gärten, Privatheit und Politik in der Zeit des Nationalsozialismus." In *Privatheit, Garten und politische Kultur: Von kommunikativen Zwischenräumen*, edited by Siegfried Lamnek and Marie Theres Tinnefeld, 155–184. Opladen, 2003.

Wurm, Johann Peter. "Die Mecklenburgische Sippenkanzlei: Kirchenbücher im Dienst der Ausgrenzung der jüdischen Bevölkerung." In *Das deutsche Archivwesen und der Nationalsozialismus: 75. Deutscher Archivtag 2005 in Stuttgart*, edited by Robert Kretzschmar, Astrid M. Eckert, Heiner Schmitt, Dieter Speck and Klaus Wisotzky, Tagungsdokumentationen zum Deutschen Archivtag 10, 153–164. Essen, 2007.

Wuthenow, Ralph-Rainer. *Europäische Tagebücher: Eigenart, Formen, Entwicklung*. Darmstadt, 1990.

Zeck, Mario. *Das Schwarze Korps: Geschichte und Gestalt des Organs der Reichsführung SS*. Medien in Forschung und Unterricht, Serie A 51. Tübingen, 2002.

Zelnhefer, Siegfried. *Die Reichsparteitage der NSDAP in Nürnberg*. Schriftenreihe des Dokumentationszentrums Reichsparteitagsgelände 2. Nuremberg, 2002.

Ziemann, Benjamin. *Front und Heimat: Ländliche Kriegserfahrungen im südlichen Bayern 1914–1929*. Essen, 1997.

Zimmermann, Clemens. *Medien im Nationalsozialismus: Deutschland, Italien und Spanien in den 1930er und 1940er Jahren*. Vienna, 2007.

Zimmermann, Volker. *Die Sudetendeutschen im NS-Staat: Politik und Stimmung der Bevölkerung im Reichsgau Sudetenland (1938–1945)*. Veröffentlichungen des Instituts für Kultur und Geschichte der Deutschen im Östlichen Europa 16. Essen, 1999.

Zitelmann, Rainer. *Hitler: Selbstverständnis eines Revolutionärs*. Hamburg, 1987.

Zollitsch, Wolfgang. *Arbeiter zwischen: Weltwirtschaftskrise und Nationalsozialismus. Ein Beitrag zur Sozialgeschichte der Jahre 1928 bis 1936*. Kritische Studien zur Geschichtswissenschaft 88. Göttingen, 1990.

Zumholz, Maria Anna, ed. *Katholisches Milieu und Widerstand: Der Kreuzkampf im Oldenburger Land im Kontext des nationalsozialistischen Herrschaftsgefüges*. Berlin, 2012.

Zwilling, Martin. "100 Jahre genealogische Forschung zwischen Wissenschaft, Gesellschaft und Politik: Die Westdeutsche Gesellschaft für Familienkunde 1913–2013." In *100 Jahre Westdeutsche Gesellschaft für Familienkunde 1913–2013; Festschrift*, 15–128. Cologne, 2013.

———. "Mutterstämme: Die Biologisierung des genealogischen Denkens und die Stellung der Frau in Familie und Gesellschaft von 1900 bis zur NS-Zeit." *Tel Aviver Jahrbuch für deutsche Geschichte* 36 (2008): 29–47.

INDEX OF PERSONS

The index of persons lists the names of the authors of diaries, letters, and other self-testimonies. Historical figures are included only in their capacity as diarists. Anonymized names are marked with an asterisk.

Ahlers-Hestermann, Friedrich, 103–105
Ahrens, Christoph,* 58, 113, 159, 400–401

Baumgarten, Thea,* 482
Becker, Doris,* 245–246, 269–270
Becker-Kohn, Erna, 480–483, 523–524
Behr, Claus,* 19, 136–138
Beier, Ferdinand, 284–285, 387, 438, 527
Berger, Paul,* 157
Bergerhoff, Julia,* 293
Bernhard, Siegfried,* 479–480, 483
Böhme, Helmut, 21, 48–49, 151, 368–369, 404
Bollmann, Wilhelm,* 283–284, 301–302, 305–307, 326, 404, 438–440, 497, 504–505
Brandt, Gisela,* 64–67
Briske, Rudolf, 188–191, 192–193, 195, 197, 219, 237–238, 242–245, 248–249, 252–253, 271–273, 277, 285–286, 319–324, 326, 414–415
Bröcking, Ludwig,* 54–55, 63–64, 100
Bücker, Charlotte,* 84–86, 204
Buesgen, Franz,* 21, 98, 108, 122–124, 497–500, 505–506
Busse, Wolf,* 54, 99, 228, 258
Buttmann, Karoline, 48

Cohn, Willy, 62, 76, 459

Deiker, Anna,* 438–439, 462,
Dietrichs, Else,* 239, 241–242, 244–245, 249
Dingler, Max, 48, 214, 531–532
Drescher, Hans,* 300–302, 305–307
Dürkefälden, Karl, 35–36

Eichler, Karl Friedrich, 83–84, 86–87, 90, 98, 108, 133–114

Frackmann, Kurt,* 193, 197, 283–284
Frank, Hans, 213
Friedrich, Johannes, 449–450, 455
Frielingsdorf, Hermann, 380
Funk, Fritz,* 315–318, 321

Gloeckner, Anton,* 245–248, 270, 275, 277–278, 324–325, 437–440
Goebbels, Joseph, 213–216, 218
Göll, Franz, 204, 304–308, 311–313, 326, 358, 360
Göring, Hermann, 213

Hacker, Clara, 203
Haffner, Sebastian, 1–5, 7–11, 39–40, 81, 464, 511, 513, 534
Heckmann, Walter,* 143–146
Herlitz, Josef, 395–396
Himmler, Heinrich, 213
Hoffmann, Ewald,* 523
Hofkotte, Wolf,* 512 513
Hosenfeld, Wilm, 251–252, 282, 411
Hundertmark, Heinz Werner, 376–377, 382

Kirchmann, Otto, 123–126, 129–132, 139, 360, 455–456, 460, 488–490
Kirk, Erich,* 502–504
Klemperer, Victor, 12, 76, 524, 527
Klempt, Luise, 19, 55–56, 74
Koch, Fritz, 74–75, 512–513
Köhl, Marianne, 195, 197, 368, 413–417, 420, 425
Kolbow, Karl Friedrich, 213, 529
Korsch, Heinz,* 239–240, 242, 244–245, 252–253, 255, 265–266, 269, 274–275, 277–278

645

646 | Index of Persons

Kramp, Werner, 47, 150, 170–171, 196–197, 206–209, 211, 223, 277, 303–308, 309–311, 318–319, 420–421, 451–453, 457
Krämer, Otmar,* 47–49, 57, 131, 299, 403, 412–413
Krause, Oswald,* 376
Kroll, Wolfram,* 204–205, 273–274, 277–278
Kronenberg, Emil, 459
Krumbholz, Paul, 300
Kuhn, Emil,* 244–246

Leisner, Karl, 238–239, 253–254, 271
Lindemann, Walter,* 44, 50–52, 61–62, 67, 77, 96–99, 103, 108, 115, 117, 134, 137, 143, 149–150, 157, 193, 282, 367–368, 377, 380, 382–385, 386, 397–398, 432, 435, 455
Lindholm, Ludwig,* 288–229, 413, 415, 443–446, 448, 451
Lohs, Walter, 19, 120–121
Lotter, Daniel, 21, 75, 90, 93, 102–103, 105–106, 108–110, 115, 191, 386–387, 395, 450–451, 455–456, 460, 495, 522
Lusebrink, Inga,* 395

Maik, Franz, 298
Marx, Henry, 69–71, 77, 79–80, 102, 105, 110
Maschmann, Hans, 15, 19, 72–78, 80, 88–90, 93, 102, 105, 108–109, 115–116, 123, 140–142, 146, 359, 380–382, 384–385, 387–388, 390–391, 395, 398–400, 419, 421, 429–430, 432–433, 435–436, 440, 449, 454, 455, 456–457, 460, 493–495, 500, 506–510, 522
Möhring, Karl,* 60–61, 67, 70, 76–77, 80–82, 84, 86–87, 90, 93, 101–102, 118, 142, 230–245, 358, 391–392, 399, 452–453, 495
Müller, Friedhelm,* 58–59

Neusen, Kurt,* 44, 5
Nieper, Karl, 490

Oehl, Erwin, 21, 68–70, 448–449

Petersen, Jan, 39–41, 43–46, 81, 186, 477–478, 488
Pretzel, Raimund. *See* Sebastian Haffner

Rahmacher, Erich,* 64–67, 118–120
Rosenberg, Alfred, 213–214
Rosenberg, Kurt, 376

Scharenberg, Wolfgang, 85–87, 90, 198, 227, 263, 359, 381
Scheidler, Wilhelm, 45–46, 106–108, 473, 511–512
Scheuer, Erich,* 421–425
Schleifenbaum, Hermann,* 130–131, 134, 145, 156, 397–401, 436
Schlichting, Maria,* 412, 427
Schössel, Fritz,* 69
Schötz, Klara, 299–301, 305
Schulte, Eduard, 519–520, 529, 532.
Schwalm, Hans. *See* Jan Petersen
Sieveking, Nikolaus, 418–419, 447
Söller, Wolfgang,* 79–80, 82–84, 86, 112–114, 149, 191
Solmitz, Luise, 50–52, 62–64, 67, 128, 131, 137–139, 159–165, 414–415, 427, 436–437, 451, 458, 522, 527
Stelzer, Hans,* 276–277
Stock, Werner,* 79–80, 150, 386, 437, 472, 511
Streiter, Artur, 56–58, 74
Sylvanus, Erwin, 232–233, 235–236, 248

Thiele, Inge, 135–136, 194–195, 197, 205, 218–219, 229–231, 256, 258–260, 270, 276–279, 283, 309–311, 321, 368–370, 401–403, 410–411, 413, 415, 424–425, 428, 432, 435, 491, 522–523
Thomas, Theodor, 49, 131
Thomer, Rita,* 412, 436

Vossen, Thomas,* 315

Wächter, Annie,* 130–131, 134
Walb, Lore, 432, 435, 523
Wallner, Franz, 19, 53–54, 74, 377–379
Weber, Curt,* 54–55, 100, 132–133, 136
Weidenbach, Stephan, 19, 49, 131, 146, 154–156, 374, 436
Weiss, Henriette,* 282
Wiebus, Herbert, 194–195
Wiese, Alfred, 294–296
Wintgen, Elli,* 240–241, 246
Witzmann, Georg, 21, 332–333, 354–360, 367, 370, 385, 389–392, 395, 398–400, 418, 429, 453, 495

Zeng, Henning,* 325

INDEX OF SUBJECTS

Adult education centers (Volkshochschulen), 185, 207–208, 303
Ahnenpaß (Ancestral Passport), 296–301
Annexation of Austria (Anschluss) (1938), 375, 378–379, 385, 401–402, 407, 413–414, 432–433, 438, 454–455, 458–459, 512–513, 517–518
Anti-complainer campaign ("Meckerer-Kampagne"), 91–96
Anti-Semitism, 152–158, 395, 398, 403, 478, 488–489; April boycott (1933), 153–158, 403; Aryanization, 383, 482–483; November pogrom (1938), 117–118, 157, 464, 478–482, 505;
Aryan certificate, 160–162, 283, 293–300, 307

Body images, Nazi, 261, 263–265, 272, 277–278, 281, 287–288

Camps. *See* Training and education camps, concentration camps
Catholic Center Party (Deutsche Zentrumspartei), 63–64, 100, 143–144, 167–168, 396
Church. *See* Religion
Communality of the individual, 226–228, 231–235, 240–241, 245–260, 272–274, 277
Communists, 39–40, 43–47, 62–63, 68–69, 83–84, 100, 152, 154, 325, 337–339, 356, 360, 464, 477–478
Concentration camps, 43, 46, 54, 71, 83, 106, 157, 238, 257, 332, 348–349, 403, 429, 457, 473, 505

Day of National Labor, 33–35, 54, 106–109, 275, 377, 403, 405, 408, 411, 420
Day of Potsdam (March 21, 1933), 33, 66, 75, 229, 403, 408, 418

Day of the Seizure of Power (January 30, 1933), 33, 47–50, 53–54, 84–85
Denunciations, 45, 125, 134, 150, 163, 351, 469, 501–507, 509, 531
Der Stürmer, 102, 403, 489
Diaries: achievement books, 266–268, 270; history of, 18, 76–77, 212, 472–473; Nazi conceptions of, 213–223, 472–473; parental diaries, 54, 264–265, 292–293; travel diaries, 54, 100, 122, 132, 189, 228, 258, 443
Dreams, 241, 464–470, 493, 511–513

Education concept, Nazi, 177–178, 187–188, 191–192, 197–201, 209–210, 221–222, 243–244, 260–264, 274, 312–314, 327–328, 491
Educational instruments, 188–211; books/publications as, 200–205, 216–220, 291–292, 195–296, 312–314, 324; diaries as, 217–223; physical exercise as, 261–262, 271–272; political lectures as, 207–208. *See also* Ahnenpaß, Aryan certificate, genealogy, training and education camps
Emigration. *See* Exile
Emotion, 364, 366, 416–418, 422–426
Exile, 1, 42, 104, 337–342, 351–353, 447–449, 465–466, 479, 483, 534

Forward-looking orientation of Nazi policy, 11, 48–49, 99–100, 337
Fraternities, 124–125, 129, 310, 455

Genealogy, 290–308, 311–312, 318, 320–321. *See also* Ahnenpaß
"Germany has awakened," 48–49, 368
Gestapo (secret state police), 238, 342, 350, 430, 450, 473, 504, 507–510, 531

Health policy, 180–182, 264–265, 268, 276–279, 282, 309, 316–317
Hitler myth, 95–96, 99, 108, 343, 364, 366–367, 393, 427
Hitler Youth, 48, 64, 66–67, 119, 160, 182, 189, 194, 219–220, 232–236, 245, 247, 248, 266–268, 270, 275, 320, 322–325, 403, 424, 436–437, 439
Hitler, perception of, 96–99, 102–103, 106, 111, 117, 120, 367–370, 374, 389–392, 410–416, 419, 420–421, 427–428
Holiday calendar, 405–406, 410. See also Day of National Labor
Home search, 45, 472–473, 477–478, 509–512. See also Residence

Labor Service (Voluntary Labor Service, Reich Labor Service), 180, 219–221, 231, 233, 237–242, 244, 249, 252–253, 257–260, 265, 269, 271–276, 278–279, 285, 315, 319, 322, 413
League of German Girls (Bund deutscher Mädel, BdM), 194–195, 231, 247, 256, 258, 266, 267, 270, 277, 283. See also Hitler Youth
League of Nations, withdrawal from (1933), 90, 329–332, 345, 367, 383, 406, 409–410, 412, 433, 451–453, 517–518
Lebensreform (life reform movement), 85–87, 185–186, 198, 227, 263

Marriage loan, 294, 299, 316
Mass festivals/assemblies, 363, 405–407, 409–410, 415–425, 435, 525, 533. See also Nazi party rallies
Mass media: development and expansion of, 372–376, 401; news reporting, 372–376, 378–379, 380–382, 386, 396, 398, 410–411, 412–413, 524, 521; press, 175, 348–349, 372–373, 376, 379–380, 382, 389, 391, 396, 397–400, 406, 434–435, 525, 528; radio, 35, 136, 175, 368–370, 373–380, 383, 390, 400–401, 406–415, 418–419, 435–437, 492, 525–527, 532; state control of, 173–180, 348–349, 379–412, 393–395, 401, 428–430, 531
May day celebrations. See Day of National Labor

Mein Kampf, 97–99, 117, 120, 169–170, 183–184, 204, 261
Monitoring of public communication, 73–75, 77–78, 390–391, 488–491; Treachery Act, 75–76, 472–473
Moral reports, 340–345, 348–349, 351–354, 488, 519

"New Man," 168–171, 184–187, 190–193, 195, 199, 202, 211, 222, 224, 226–227, 260, 274, 286, 288, 293, 322, 327, 362, 510, 516
National Political Institutes of Education, 182, 220, 234
Nationalism, 51–52, 59, 70, 88, 103–111, 115, 117–118, 124, 156–158, 164, 333, 453–456, 458, 533
Nazi party: joining and membership in, 36, 59, 65–66, 81, 84, 120, 130, 133, 139, 144–147, 151–152, 202–203, 294, 301–302, 527–528 (see also "Old Fighters"); local structures and functionaries of, 84, 87–88, 95–96, 98, 126, 152–153, 213–214, 302–303, 404, 411, 436, 447, 449, 485–492, 501–502, 504–505; political "mentoring" by, 283–284, 485–492, 496–497
Nazi party rallies, 163, 183, 229, 251, 276, 290, 405–406, 413, 415–416, 421–423, 525, 533
Nazi People's Welfare, 128, 182, 263, 485, 489–490
Neu Beginnen, 339–341, 348, 352, 431, 447. See also Exile
Newspapers. See Mass media/press
Night of the Long Knives (Röhm purge) (1934), 95–96, 169, 389–394, 398–400, 429
Nuremberg Laws, 163–165, 245, 283, 294, 299, 310–311, 422, 457–458, 488

"Old Fighters," 87–88, 97, 217, 326, 438, 499
Opportunism, 65–66, 70, 104, 142–148, 150

Plebiscites. See Voting events
Political attention, rhythms of, 430, 434–435, 441, 463
Privacy model, bourgeois, 470–474, 476, 492–496, 508–510

Racial policy, 181–183, 280–282, 287–288, 308–311, 321; racial hygiene, 181, 185, 260, 287–291, 295–296, 298, 306–307, 311–313, 321; racial studies, 282–287, 291, 298, 306–308
Radio. *See* Mass media/radio
Reichstag elections. *See* Voting events
Religion, 83, 85, 97–98, 115, 198–199, 238–239, 254, 257, 315, 317, 360, 382, 387, 396, 401–403, 420–421, 426, 460, 449–450, 455, 460, 489, 498–499, 512, 525
Remilitarization of the Rhineland (1936), 350, 398, 407, 410–411, 433, 439, 455, 490, 497
Residences, 58, 97, 316, 380, 467, 469–485, 489–490
"Röhm purge". *See* Night of the Long Knives

SA, 41, 43–45, 91, 98, 117, 134, 153–154, 157, 161, 167–169, 182, 204, 217, 251–253, 267, 282, 349, 385, 387, 389, 444–445, 450, 477–478, 480–481, 497–500, 503, 531. *See also* Night of the Long Knives
Social Democrats, 45, 62, 69, 100, 106–108, 134, 167, 203, 339–341, 351–353, 356, 447–448, 507
Sopade. *See* Social Democrats, Exile
Sports, 64, 227, 243, 245–247, 253, 256, 262, 264–273, 275–278, 288, 309, 318, 498
Sports badges, 266–267, 269–270, 275. *See also* Diaries/achievement books
SS, 150, 230
Start of the war, 1939, 517–519; comparisons with 1914, 519–520, 522–524, 526, 528–532; perception of, 519–520, 522–524, 527, 531–532; staging of, 524–532
Sterilization, 181, 288, 314, 316–319, 401

Strength through Joy, 201, 218–219, 227–228, 254, 284, 424
Sudeten crisis (1938), 378, 407, 430, 433, 445, 519, 525
Symbols, Nazi 126–128, 130–131, 134–140, 146, 155–156, 158–159, 164, 187, 484–485, 491; flags, 34, 41, 46, 49, 51–52, 66, 126–129, 131, 134–135, 137–140, 156, 158–159, 163–165, 241–243, 245–246, 256, 232, 359, 383, 438, 444, 458, 484–485, 488, 490, 498, 512, 520, 527, 531; German greeting, 98–99, 128–129, 135, 139, 157, 159, 464, 489. *See also* NSDAP/joining and membership in

Training and education camps, 209–211, 218–221, 225, 230–260, 265–266, 271–272, 492
Travel, 189, 218–219, 227–231, 231–235, 250, 254, 443–444. *See also* Diaries/travel diaries

Violence in spring 1933, 43–47, 62–63, 75, 150, 477–478. *See also* Anti-Semitism/April boycott, Concentration camps
Visualization of rule, 361–367, 400, 405–406, 421, 431
Voting events: as political symbol, 431–432, 460–462; conception of voting, 330, 345–349, 433–434, 440, 476; electoral victory celebrations, March 1933, 126–127, 137; November election 1933, 330–332, 337–340, 345–348, 409; no-voters and non-voters, 445, 448–451, 456, 459–460, 490; voting campaigns, 154, 345–346, 348–349, 409, 432–441, 454, 490; voting procedure, 442–460

JANOSCH STEUWER is a historian of German and European History in the Twentieth Century at the Martin Luther University of Halle-Wittenberg. His book "*A Third Reich, as I See It,*" has won several awards in Germany, Austria, and Switzerland.